D1429264

LUX MUNDI

Hornet

OXFORD: HORACE HART
PRINTER TO THE UNIVERSITY

LUX MUNDI

A SERIES OF STUDIES IN THE RELIGION OF THE INCARNATION

EDITED

BY CHARLES GORE, D.D.

BISHOP OF WORCESTER

A quella Luce cotal si diventa,
Che volgersi da lei per altro aspetto
È impossibil che mai si consenta.

LONDON

JOHN MURRAY, ALBEMARLE STREET

1904

First Edition	November, 1889.
Second Edition	February, 1890.
Third Edition	February, 1890.
Fourth Edition	. March, 1890.
Fifth Edition	. May, 1890.
Sixth Edition	. May, 1890.
Seventh Edition	. May, 1890.
Eighth Edition	. June, 1890.
Ninth Edition	. July, 1890.
Tenth Edition	September, 1890.
Reprinted	. October, 1890.
Eleventh Edition . . .	January, 1891.
Twelfth (6s.) Edition . . .	. October, 1891.
Reprinted	. November, 1891.
Thirteenth Edition . . .	September, 1892.
Fourteenth Edition . . .	. May, 1895.
Reprinted	. December, 1898.
Reprinted	. March, 1902.
Fifteenth (2s. 6d.) Edition .	October, 1904.

ESSAYS

AND

CONTRIBUTORS.

—◦—

1. *Faith.*

Rev. H. S. HOLLAND, M.A., Canon of S. Paul's, sometime Senior Student of Christ Church.

2. *The Christian Doctrine of God.*

Rev. AUBREY MOORE, M.A., Hon. Canon of Christ Church, Tutor of Magdalen and Keble Colleges.

3. *The Problem of Pain: its bearing on faith in God.*

Rev. J. R. ILLINGWORTH, M.A., Rector of Longworth, sometime Fellow of Jesus and Tutor of Keble Colleges.

4. *The Preparation in History for Christ.*

Rev. E. S. TALBOT, D.D., Vicar of Leeds, sometime Warden of Keble College.

5. *The Incarnation in relation to Development.*

Rev. J. R. ILLINGWORTH.

6. *The Incarnation as the Basis of Dogma.*

Rev. R. C. MOBERLY, M.A., Vicar of Great Budworth, sometime Senior Student of Christ Church.

7. *The Atonement.*

Rev. and Hon. ARTHUR LYTTELTON, M.A., Master of Selwyn College, Cambridge, sometime Tutor of Keble College.

8. *The Holy Spirit and Inspiration.*

Rev. C. GORE, M.A., Principal of Pusey House, Fellow of Trinity College.

9. *The Church.*
> Rev. W. LOCK, M.A., Sub-Warden of Keble and Fellow of Magdalen Colleges.

10. *Sacraments.*
> Rev. F. PAGET, D.D., Canon of Christ Church, and Regius Professor of Pastoral Theology.

11. *Christianity and Politics.*
> Rev. W. J. H. CAMPION, M.A., Tutor of Keble College.

12. *Christian Ethics.*
> Rev. R. L. OTTLEY, M.A., Vice-Principal of Cuddesdon, late Senior Student of Christ Church.

PREFACE.

———

1. THIS volume is primarily due to a set of circumstances which exists no longer. The writers found themselves at Oxford together between the years 1875–1885, engaged in the common work of University education ; and compelled for their own sake, no less than that of others, to attempt to put the Catholic faith into its right relation to modern intellectual and moral problems. Such common necessity and effort led to not infrequent meetings, in which a common body of thought and sentiment, and a common method of commending the faith to the acceptance of others, tended to form itself. We, who once enjoyed this happy companionship, are now for the most part separated. But at least some result of our temporary association remains, which it is hoped may justify and explain the present volume.

2. For this collection of essays represents an attempt on behalf of the Christian Creed in the way of explanation. We are sure that Jesus Christ is still and will continue to be the 'Light of the world.' We are sure that if men can rid themselves of prejudices and mistakes (for which, it must be said, the Church is often as responsible as they), and will look afresh at what the Christian faith really means, they will find that it is as adequate as ever to interpret life and knowledge in its several departments, and to impart not less intellectual than moral freedom. But we are conscious also that if the true meaning of the faith is to be made sufficiently conspicuous it needs disencumbering, reinterpreting, explaining. We can but quote in this sense a distinguished French writer who has often acted as an inspiration to many of us. Père Gratry felt painfully that the dogmas of the Church were but as an 'unknown tongue' to many of the best of his compatriots. 'It is not enough,' he said, 'to utter the mysteries of the Spirit, the great mysteries of Christianity, in formulas, true before God, but not under stood of the people. The apostle and the prophet are precisely those who have the gift of interpreting these obscure and profound formulas for each man and each age. To translate into the common tongue the

mysterious and sacred language . . . . to speak the word of God afresh in each age, in accordance with both the novelty of the age and the eternal antiquity of the truth, this is what S. Paul means by interpreting the unknown tongue. But to do this, the first condition is that a man should appreciate the times he lives in. " Hoc autem tempus quare non probatis [1] ? " '

3. We have written then in this volume not as 'guessers at truth,' but as servants of the Catholic Creed and Church, aiming only at interpreting the faith we have received. On the other hand, we have written with the conviction that the epoch in which we live is one of profound transformation, intellectual and social, abounding in new needs, new points of view, new questions; and certain therefore to involve great changes in the outlying departments of theology, where it is linked on to other sciences, and to necessitate some general restatement of its claim and meaning.

This is to say that theology must take a new development. We grudge the name development, on the one hand, to anything which fails to preserve the type of the Christian Creed and the Christian Church ; for development is not innovation, it is not heresy : on the other hand, we cannot recognise as the true 'development of Christian doctrine,' a movement which means merely an intensification of a current tendency from within, a narrowing and hardening of theology by simply giving it greater definiteness or multiplying its dogmas.

The real development of theology is rather the process in which the Church, standing firm in her old truths, enters into the apprehension of the new social and intellectual movements of each age : and because 'the truth makes her free' is able to assimilate all new material, to welcome and give its place to all new knowledge, to throw herself into the sanctification of each new social order, bringing forth out of her treasures things new and old, and shewing again and again her power of witnessing under changed conditions to the catholic capacity of her faith and life.

4. To such a development these studies attempt to be a contribution. They will be seen to cover, more or less, the area of the Christian faith in its natural order and sequence of parts, but the intention is not to offer complete theological treatises, or controversial defences of religious truths : it is rather to present positively the central ideas and principles of religion, in the light of contemporary thought and current problems. The only one of the essays in fact which has any degree of formal completeness, is that on Christian Ethics, a subject on which the absence

---

[1] Gratry, *Henri Perreyve*, Paris 1880, p. 162.

of systematic books of a genuine English growth seems to justify a more detailed treatment.

5. The main omissions of which we are conscious are due to want of space. For instance, we should have been very glad to attempt a separate treatment of the subject of sin; though we hope the line that would be taken about it has been sufficiently indicated by more than one writer[1]. Again, we have left aside any detailed discussion of historical evidences; but it will be seen that our attempt has been so to present the principles of the Christian faith as to suggest the point of view from which evidences are intelligible, and from which they will, it is firmly believed, be found satisfactory. Once more, if we have not found room for a treatment of miracles, at least we hope that the Church's conception of God, as He manifests Himself in nature and in grace, which we have endeavoured to express, will at once acquit us of any belief in capricious 'violations of law;' and will also suggest a view of the world as disordered by sin and crying out for redemption, which will make it intelligible that 'miracles' should appear, not as violating law, but as a necessary element in its restoration as well as its completer exhibition; contrary, not to the fundamental order of the Divine working, but only to a superficial or mechanical view of it, or to a view which sin has distorted or preoccupation with physical science has unduly narrowed.

6. It only remains to explain that we have written not as mere individuals, but as ministers, under common conditions, of a common faith. This unity of conviction has enabled us freely to offer and accept mutual criticism and suggestion; so that without each of us professing such responsibility for work other than his own, as would have involved undue interference with individual method, we do desire this volume to be the expression of a common mind and a common hope.

C. G.

Pusey House,
Michaelmas, 1889.

PREFACE TO THE FIFTH EDITION.

The author of the Essay *The Holy Spirit and Inspiration* has endeavoured to obviate further misunderstanding of his meaning on one important point by rewriting some sentences on pp. 359-60 of the original edition (pp. 264-5 of this), in accordance with the *Corrigenda* inserted in the Fourth Edition.

[1] See pp. 153-4, 214-5, 232-4, 346-7.

PREFACE TO THE TENTH EDITION.

I.

THERE are two things which may fairly be regretted in regard to the criticisms—often the very kind and encouraging criticisms—which this book has received. There is, first, the disproportionate attention which has been given to some twenty pages on the subject of the inspiration of Holy Scripture, an attention so disproportionate as to defeat the object which the writers had in view in assigning to that subject its place in the general treatment of the work of the Holy Spirit—the object, namely, of giving it its proper context in the whole body of Christian truth : and there is, secondly, the fact that we have not generally succeeded in gaining the attention of our critics to the point of view from which these ' studies ' were written, and the purpose they were intended to serve.

Our purpose was ' to succour a distressed faith ' by endeavouring to bring the Christian Creed into its right relation to the modern growth of knowledge, scientific, historical, critical; and to the modern problems of politics and ethics [1]. We were writing as for Christians, but as for Christians perplexed by new knowledge which they are required to assimilate and new problems with which they are required to deal. What is needed to help men in such perplexity is not compromise, for compromise generally means tampering with principle, but readjustment, or fresh correlation, of the things of faith and the things of knowledge. In detail this will, no doubt, involve concessions, and that on both sides, because both sides have been liable to make mistakes [2]; but in the main what is to be looked for is a reconciliation which shall at once set the scientific and critical movement, so far as it is simply scientific and critical, free from the peril of irreligion, and the religious movement free from the imputation of hostility to new knowledge—as free as any movement can be, which is intensely concerned to nourish

---

[1] By the phrase ' to attempt to put the Catholic faith into its right relation to modern intellectual and moral problems ' (Preface to First Edition) it was not by any means intended to suggest that the modern problems or the modern sciences were the things of the first importance and the faith only secondary. What was intended was

that, as holding the Faith, we needed, as the Church has often needed, to bring that with which we are ourselves identified, into relation to the claims, intellectual and practical, made upon us from outside.

[2] Cf. Dr. Pusey, *University Sermons,* 1864–1879. ' Unscience, not science, contrary to faith,' pp. 18 ff.

and develop what is permanent and unchanging in human life. Such a reconciliation has more than once been effected in the past, though never without a preliminary period of antagonism[1] : our confidence that it will be effected anew in the future lies partly in the fact that we see it already taking place in some minds which seem to us to represent the best life and thought of our time both scientific and religious. One such at least [2] we knew and have lost, though only from present intercourse, in Aubrey Moore. Nobody could know him and think of him as 'compromising' either his faith or his science. He lived primarily and with deepest interest in his religious life and theological study, but he lived also with intense reality in the life of science. And the debt we owe to him, over and above the debt under which his personal character lays us for ever, is that of having let us see how the two lives of faith and of science can melt into one. He felt indeed and wrestled with the difficulties of adjustment. He had not, as it seemed to us, nearly finished his work in this respect. But he had done enough for our encouragement : enough to help us to believe that the best minds of the future are to be neither religious minds defying scientific advance, nor scientific minds denying religion, but minds in which religion interprets and is interpreted by science, in which faith and enquiry subsist together and reinforce one another. The reason why he should have been so soon taken from us and from the Church on earth—taken when 'our need was the sorest'—lies in the impenetrable mysteries of God. 'Si dolemus ablatum, non tamen obliviscimur quod datus fuit, et gratias agimus quod habere illum meruimus . . . Pusillus corde eram et confortabat me ; piger et negligens, et excitabat me [3].'

II.

It seems to us that a due regard to the point of view from which these studies were written would have obviated some of the criticisms upon them. For instance, it would have explained why we forbore to enter upon the questions which may be raised as to the seat and methods of Church authority. It was because these questions do not arise practically till the work has been done to which we were attempting to minister. When a man is once reassured that his faith in Christ is capable of rational justification, he begins naturally to enquire

---

[1] Cf. the history of the relations of the Church to Aristotelian philosophy : Milman, *Latin Christianity*, ed. 4, vol. ix. pp. 110 ff. ; and later the relations of Christianity to the Copernican astronomy : Salmon, *Infallibility of the Church*, p. 230.

[2] See the tribute to his memory by Mr. G. J. Romanes : *Guardian*, Jan. 29, 1890.

[3] From S. Bernard's most touching sermon (*in Cant.* 26) on the death of his brother Gerard.

what exactly the Christian religion involves in this or that detail, and how its manifestly authoritative character, as a Divine Revelation, is to find expression : but these enquiries hardly begin till the preliminary reassurance has been gained.

The *moral* authority of Christianity, of Christian lives and characters, does indeed exercise a determining influence on the promotion and recovery of faith ; but men do not often either win a hold on the creed for the first time, or recover it where it has been lost or impaired, because the theological authority of the Church enables them to take it on trust. The very grounds of that authority are for the moment too much in question to admit of the proper amount of deference being given to it. Thus it seemed to us better in this volume to be content with general statements as to the principle of Church authority[1], leaving out its detailed discussion as unsuitable to our present purpose.

Of course, however, we were conscious all the time that we were ourselves amenable to the bar of authority and were bound to feel sure that nothing we were saying was transgressing the laws which the Catholic Church has laid down. We should indeed be unanimous in disclaiming any desire to have ' license to say what we please' in our position as Church teachers. All meaning would be taken out of the effort and hope this book represents if we could not believe that we were speaking as the Church would have us speak. As the essay on Inspiration has been chiefly called in question on the ground of authority, the author of it must be allowed to plead that he did assure himself he was saying nothing which the Church in her past action had not left him free to say, while for the future he does earnestly desire in due course, and after due enquiry, an action of Church authority on the relation of modern critical methods to the doctrine of Inspiration ; and further he believes that the Anglican churches, holding as they do so conspicuous a place in traditional reverence for the Scriptures, while they are so free on the other hand from the obscurantist fear of historical enquiry, are more likely than any other part of the Church to arrive at determinations on the subject such as will be of material service to the whole of Christendom. But for the present there can be no doubt the subject is not ripe for any official or formal determinations.

III.

It seems to us also that some of the criticisms on the treatment of Inspiration in Essay VIII, which shall be presently dealt with, have

---

[1] See Essay VI. pp. 165-6, 183 ff.; Essay VIII. pp. 237-9 ; and Essay IX. pp. 281-6.

been due to the same forgetfulness of the writer's aim, and of the general aim of the whole book. Our traditional belief in the Bible is at the present time confronted with a body of critical literature which claims to overthrow a great many of the accepted opinions about the Old Testament Scriptures. The criticism is at least grave and important enough to claim attention, to necessitate that we should come to a more or less clear understanding of the relation in which our faith stands towards it. The writer of the essay did not write as a biblical critic but as a theological student and teacher, bound to give a candid consideration to a criticism which bears directly upon the sacred books of our religion. His object was not to discuss and determine questions of biblical criticism, but to explain, as it appears to him, the relation which theology is to take up towards them. And he wrote 'in the mind of those who have felt the trouble in the air : ' he wrote to succour a faith distressed by the problems criticism is raising. That faith is very widely distressed by them, and that not merely in academic circles, does not admit of question. Nor did it seem to him to admit of question that the best way to deal with this distress was not to attempt to solve problems, which, because of the immense area over which discussion ranges, do not admit of ready solutions; but to attempt to state the main conclusions criticism is claiming to have arrived at, as the critics themselves would have us state them ; to show that our Christian faith is not vitally affected by them ; and so to divert an anxious mind from problems which it cannot solve, at least at present, and fix it on the central truths of our religion, helping it to feel how, if it be once grounded on these central truths, the issue of the critical discussion can be awaited, with keen interest indeed, but without alarm. But this assurance of mind in face of the critical controversy is only possible if we see that the critical positions are in fact compatible with the real *inspiration* of Holy Scripture. Now the best way to give reassurance on this point seemed to be for the writer to make it plain that he himself felt the great force and appeal of the critical case, and that his conviction that the real Inspiration of the Old Testament was unaffected by it, did not depend upon its being underrated. Had the main purpose of the writer been to help to determine critical positions, he would have been bound to write both at greater length and also with more exactness and discrimination. But on the other hand, the purpose of reassurance would have had less chance of being successfully accomplished—as in some cases we have reason to believe with thankfulness that it has been accomplished or assisted—if the writer had been more reluctant to accept, at least hypothetically, what are claimed as critical results. We all know by experience that freedom and happiness in our attitude as Christians towards problems not easily solved, or even easily brought to crucial tests, are most readily secured if we can feel that our faith is, at the last resort, independent of the exact solution arrived at. Thus our object was to give to anxious enquirers, of whom there are surely an immense number most deserving of any help which can be given them, a freedom in regard to Old Testament problems as wide as the Catholic faith seemed to warrant.

IV.

We cannot but accept the very general suggestion of our critics that we ought to have attempted a separate treatment of the problem of sin. Some such treatment is now offered in the second appendix, and offered in the form of a republication of what has previously seen the light, so that it may be plain that the absence of it from earlier editions was not due to lack of conviction or unwillingness to deal with the subject. The appendix is not in fact more than a drawing out of what is involved in some passages of the essays taken together[1]. Thus the fifth essay takes up a very clear position as to the practical aspect which sin bears in human life. The fact is emphasized that sin, as our moral consciousness knows it and Christianity has successfully dealt with it, is a phenomenon unique in the world :—it is what nothing else is, violation of law. Now this is the essence of the Christian doctrine of sin, as S. John states it : ' Sin is lawlessness[2].' Sin and lawlessness are coincident terms. This view of sin is primarily *practical*; it may be represented in fact as a postulate required for successfully dealing with sin, a postulate justified and verified by its results. But because it is thus verified and justified, it passes like any other hypothesis which explains facts, in proportion to the range and thoroughness of the experience which tests it, out of the region of mere working hypotheses into that of accepted truths. Thus it is to the Christian consciousness an accepted truth, that sin, all down the long history of humanity, has been a violation of the divine order, a refusal of obedience, a corruption of man's true nature. Sin, as such, has always been a source of confusion, not of progress. We can indeed recognise how the movement and development in humanity has frequently[3] been in fact conditioned by sin ; but we should still contend that it has never been the sin in itself which has been the spring of

[1] See Preface, p. ix. note 1.
[2] Cf. Dr. Westcott's note on 1 S. John iii. 4, ἡ ἁμαρτία ἐστὶν ἡ ἀνομία.
[3] Cf. F. Lenormant, *Les Origines de l'histoire.* Paris, 1880, t. 1, p. 191.

' C'est dans la race de Qaîn que la Bible place l'invention des arts et des métiers. " Les fils du siècle sont plus habiles que les enfants de lumière."'

force and progress, but the faculties of will and intellect which sin was using. Always the will and intellect would have worked better and more fruitfully in the result if they had been free from the taint of selfishness and rebellion against God. Always sin, as such, has been a lowering and not a raising of human life : a fall and not a rise. Thus sin at the beginning of human life must have been not merely the awakening of moral consciousness, but the obscuring and tainting of it by lawlessness and disobedience. Sin, as all down its history, so in its origin, is a fall; a fall, moreover, entailing consequences on those who come after, in virtue of the inviolable solidarity of the human race. To this view of sin original and actual, Christianity appears to be bound ; and it is a view that, as we have now endeavoured to show [1], brings us into no conflict with scientific discovery. For science never attempts to prove that man might not have developed otherwise than as in fact he has, or that the actual development has been the best possible : nor has Christianity ever in its best representatives, certainly not in its patristic representatives, been identified with a denial that human history as a whole has been a development upwards from below [2]. The Old Testament is in fact among ancient literatures, the literature of development, of progress [3].

V.

The criticisms on our treatment of Inspiration have been so abundant, and have gone into such detail, that it will be obvious that any attempt to reply to them must be a more individual effort than the attempt to reply to the criticisms on the general aim and spirit of the book. For while the writers in this volume are at one as to the general attitude which they would wish the Church to assume towards the critical treatment of the Old Testament, as they are at one in the general line of treatment adopted throughout this volume, they cannot pretend to be at one on all the details of a complicated subject. The writer of the particular essay alone can be responsible for these : and with reference to them he must be understood to speak simply in his own person.

1. The passage about Inspiration was written under the conviction that recent criticism of the Old Testament represents a real advance in analytical method as applied to literature, and thus a most serious movement of thought. As such it has been estimated by the Bishop

[1] Cf. p. 393.
[2] Cf. p. 393, note 2.
[3] Cf. F. Lenormant, *Les Origines*, t. I, pp. 63-66. It is a pleasure to refer to this work by a distinguished Catholic and man of learning. The Preface is an admirable discussion of the relation of scientific enquiry to belief in Inspiration.

of Oxford in his recent Charge. He says, 'The Holy Scriptures of the Old Testament are now going through a process of analytical criticism which has, as we believe, had no parallel, for acuteness of investigation, carefulness of method, and completeness of apparatus, since the days in which they began to be regarded as a code of inspired literature, and certainly not since the days of our blessed Lord's life on earth; at which period we understand that to all intents and purposes the books which we receive, as the Canonical Old Testament Scriptures, had taken their existing form[1].' But like the scientific movement of our time, the critical movement has been accompanied by all the arbitrariness and tendency to push things to extremes which appears to be an almost inseparable attendant upon living and vigorous movements, ecclesiastical and secular. Further than this, its representatives have been—and here again the conditions of the scientific movement are reproduced—very frequently men personally opposed to the Christian faith, and even thoroughly rationalistic in temper and tone. But it does not follow in the case of criticism, any more than in the case of science, that we are not to learn a great deal from a movement characterized even predominantly by 'extremeness' and unbelief. And in fact, in the past fifty years there appears to have been a solid critical advance, underneath a great deal of controversial arbitrariness and irreligious insolence. Now I thought that I should best serve the purpose with which I was writing, if I went as far as I could in ungrudging recognition of the claims of criticism, and involved myself as little as possible in doubtful discussions; but I did also intend to express, and believed myself to have expressed with sufficient clearness[2], my own conviction that it was with the more conservative among the recent critics, and not with the more extreme, that the victory would lie. Thus when I said, in a sentence which has been specially criticized (partly because its wording was somewhat ambiguous), that criticism is reaching 'results as sure as scientific enquiry,' what I intended so to characterize was not the extreme conclusions of Wellhausen, but substantially the conclusions shared in common by Wellhausen and Dillmann, by critics theologically more conservative, like König and Riehm, by Delitzsch in his last position, by the French Catholic orientalist, F. Lenormant, as well as by an increasing body of English scholars[3]. Nor is there a single line of what I wrote which

---

[1] *Oxford Diocesan Gazette,* July, 1890 (Parker, Oxford), p. 91.

[2] The summary statements on pp. 258-9 as to the historical character of the Old Testament represent, I believe, a 'conservative' attitude, an attitude

towards the history very unlike that, for instance, of Wellhausen.

[3] See Ed. Riehm, *Einleitung in das A. T.* (Halle, 1889), §§ 15-18, 24, 27. F. E. König, *Offenbarungsbegriff des A. T.* (Leipzig, 1882), t. ii, pp. 321 ff.

would be affected, so far as I see, even if Professor Margoliouth were satisfactorily to make out his case for throwing back the period of the 'Middle Hebrew[1].' As to the grounds on which we have been asked to date the bulk of the Psalms below the Captivity, and even in the Maccabean period, they may appear indeed quite unconvincing; but it would have been utterly beside my purpose, as it would also have been out of my power, to give them adequate discussion[2], nor would it seem as if even so improbably late a date as that suggested would really affect their Messianic or spiritual character. Let us affirm then without any hesitation that there is a good deal of arbitrariness and extremeness in current criticism as applied to the Old Testament. But surely we should be the victims of a dangerous delusion if we were to imagine that because there is a good deal that is unsubstantial in recent criticism, therefore there is no substantial force in what really represents the successive labours of many generations of students. I do not think that we can conceal from ourselves that if we are to defend a purely conservative attitude in regard to Old Testament literature, we shall require quite different canons of evidence from those which we are able so successfully to use in vindicating the historical character of the New Testament: or again, in vindicating the claims of the apostolic ministry and the sacramental system to be part of the original fabric of the Christian Church. In other words, the critical principles of historical enquiry which *do* so amply justify us in retaining substantially the traditional position in regard as well to the New Testament documents as to our Church principles, *do not* carry

Cf. also *Hauptprobleme der Altisr.-Religionsgesch.* (Leipzig, 1884). F. Delitzsch, *Genesis*, Clark's trans. (Edinb., 1888), i. 19-38. F. Lenormant, *Les Origines*, Préface. I venture to think that those who want to study the modern criticism of the Old Testament would be less likely to be prejudiced against it if they were to begin their study with the assistance of Riehm and König, rather than of more rationalistic scholars. I ought to add that while the scholars mentioned above agree substantially as to the analysis of the Pentateuch, they differ as to the position assigned to the Priestly Code, which Dillmann and Riehm hold to be prior to Deuteronomy, Wellhausen, König and Delitzsch subsequent to it.

[1] *Essay on the place of Ecclesiasticus in Semitic Literature.* Oxford: Clarendon Press, 1890, pp. 20, 21. I allude to this essay because it has excited considerable interest, but it has not received favourable notice from critics either English or German. For a review by a very competent critic, see Prof. Nöldeke in the *Lit. Centralblatt*, July 12, 1890.

[2] I may say that the motive for what is said about Ps. cx on p. 264 was simply the conviction that our Lord in the passage there in question cannot fairly be taken as giving instruction on a critical question of authorship, not the difficulty of assigning the particular Psalm to the age of David. The solution which I propose, p. 264, as to our Lord's words is however only one of several which are possible even for those who agree with me in the conviction expressed above. See, for instance, Edersheim, *Life and Times of Jesus the Messiah* (London, 1884), ii. p. 406, and Bp. Thirlwall as quoted in Dean Perowne's *Commentary on the Psalms* (London, 1871), ii. pp. 302 ff.

us to the same point in the field of the Old Testament. No doubt there the vastness of the field is a permanent obstacle to uniformly certain results. A great deal must remain, and probably for ever, more or less an open question. But this necessary uncertainty, if it imposes on critics an obligation of caution, imposes also on us church-men an obligation of reserve in dogmatic requirement. We do not wish to run the risk of making a claim on men's minds for the accep-tance of positions for which we have only this to urge, that they cannot be absolutely disproved.

2. The changed view of the development of Old Testament litera-ture, such as can be truly said to be proposed for our acceptance by modern critics with a great deal of unanimity, *if it be granted for the moment that it is compatible with the real inspiration of the books*, involves no important change in our spiritual use of the Old Testa-ment ; in the use of it for the purposes of 'faith and morals.' This latter use of Scripture depends simply on our rightly interpreting the meaning of the books as they exist.

There is a great principle enunciated by S. Augustine in regard to the Old Testament which requires to be kept constantly in view. It is that as the Old Testament is manifested in the New, so the New Testament is latent in the Old[1]. In order to recognize this there is no discussion necessary of the method by which our 'Old Testament' received its present shape. The evidence of it lies in the Old Testament considered as a finished product. As such, we cannot study that 'divine library' without being struck both by its unity, so far greater than belongs to any other literature[2], and by the fact that like no other literature it looks forward to an end not yet attained, a divine event in which is to be its justification and its interpretation. The Old Testament demands the New to bring out its true meaning : the New appeals back to the Old to bear witness to the continuity of the divine purpose of which it is the outcome. It is from this point of view that we understand the appeal which, in the New Testament, is so constantly made to the older Scriptures. Whether they are appealed to, as in the Sermon on the Mount, as containing the record of a moral education, divine though imperfect, which the Christ was to

---

[1] S. Augustine, *Quæst. 73 in Exod.* : 'Quamquam et in vetere [Testamento] novum lateat, et in novo vetus pateat.' Quoted by Dr. Liddon, *The worth of the Old Testament*, p. 28.

[2] Cf. Didymus *in Psalm.* xxi. 19, where he interprets Christ's 'seamless robe,' of the Holy Scriptures which they 'part' who accept one and reject

another. 'This robe of Jesus is also indivisible, for it is seamless. Its unity is not enforced but natural [οὐ γὰρ βε-βιασμένην ἕνωσιν ἀλλὰ συμφυῆ ἔχει] : it is 'from above' [from the top, A. V.] because it is inspired ; it is 'woven throughout,' because in its whole force it is from above.'

complete[1]; or as by S. Paul, as the record of a preparatory and temporary discipline by means of external enactments of God, calculated to awaken the dull conscience of men to the reality and holiness of the divine will, and so to make men conscious of sin against God, and ready to welcome the dispensation of pardon and grace[2]; or, as in the Epistle to the Hebrews, as a system of ritual and ceremonial observances, in which were shadowed forth by the inspiring Spirit[3] the deep truths of the still-needed sacrifice, and the access to God not yet won for man; or finally, as by almost all the New Testament writers, as a prophetic dispensation in which the Messianic hope found gradual expression in fuller and exacter lineaments, and produced an anticipation which Christ only could satisfy[4]:—from any of these points of view, or from all taken together, we are concerned only with the Old Testament as it finally appears, not with the method by which it came into being. It cannot be too strongly emphasized that when we seek reassurance in regard to the inspiration of those books of the Old Testament, to which our Lord and His Church refer us, we find it primarily in the substance of the books as they are given to us, not in any considerations of the manner in which they came into existence[5].

And if this is so, it needs to be borne in mind that the responsibility for bringing it home to the consciences of men, the responsibility for thus preventing that breach in religious continuity which the change in critical and literary conceptions of the Old Testament might otherwise occasion, lies in a preeminent degree upon those of us who are most impressed with the valid elements of the recent criticism. It belongs to us to see to it that, so far as lies with us, the Bible shall not be less prized by the generations that are coming, as the divine, the inspired volume, than it has been by the generations that are

---

[1] S. Matt. v. 17-48, cf. xix. 8: 'Moses, because of the hardness of your hearts,' etc.

[2] After S. Paul, S. Augustine is the great exponent of this principle in early days; see esp. *de spiritu et littera*, xix. (34): Lex ergo data est ut gratia quaereretur; gratia data est ut lex impleretur.

[3] See esp. Heb. ix. 8, 'The Holy Spirit this signifying;' and cf. Dr. Westcott on this Epistle, pp. 233 ff.

[4] I would venture to recommend Riehm's *Messianic Prophecy* (Clark's trans.), as a summary account of prophecy both reverent and critical.

[5] Cf. Hooker's account of our grounds for believing that 'Scripture . . . is divine and sacred.' 'By experience,' he says, ' we all know, that the first outward motive leading men so to esteem of the Scripture is the authority of God's Church. . . . Afterwards the more we bestow our labour in reading or hearing the mysteries thereof, the more we find that the thing itself doth answer our received opinion concerning it.' Later again, as against 'infidels or atheists,' we must 'maintain the authority of the books of God . . . by such kind of proofs . . . that no man living shall be able to deny it, without denying some apparent principle such as all men acknowledge to be true.' *E. P.* III. viii. 14.

gone. It belongs to us to attend to the double admonition of the *De Imitatione*: 'Every scripture must be read in the same spirit in which it was written:' and 'Do not enquire who said this, but pay heed to what is said.'

3. There is one appeal which the New Testament makes to the Old which was not alluded to above, as it does not in fact fall naturally under S. Augustine's principle of the New Testament lying hid in the Old—namely the appeal to it as to a historical record of God's actual dealings with His people : a record of things which actually 'happened unto them for ensamples, and are written for our admonition.' But this appeal again would not be invalidated unless it were shown—not merely that there is an ideal element mixed with the history in the Old Testament record, but—that the element which is not mere narrative of events as they happened, the element of idealism, reaches to the point of obscuring the real significance of the facts and dis-torting their divine meaning. Whereas the truth is that the ideal element in the narrative comes from the real divine meaning in the facts being brought into emphatic prominence rather than overlooked; and we may depend upon it that no results of criticism have tended to weaken our belief that the chroniclers of Israel's history, whether prophetic or priestly, were inspired to see its true meaning and ten-dency, and from their different points of view to bring it out in its completeness. And it is important to remember in this connection that the Jewish idea of 'history' was never our modern critical idea of a mere record. They ranked their history from Joshua to the books of Kings under the head of 'prophecy,' and intimate to us by this very classification that they see in the historian one who not only records but interprets facts [1].

4. The changed view of the Old Testament books which modern criticism asks of us, concerns, then, not so much their contents, as the circumstances of their composition and the method by which they reached their present form. When we pass to this latter class of considerations we are prepared for any information which criticism or tradition can give us, while at the same time our indestructible

---

[1] The Chronicles and the later his-torical books, as is well known, were included in the third class of 'Hagio-grapha' with the Psalmists and Moralists.

The truth of this paragraph depends upon (1) the character, (2) the extent of the idealism of Old Testament facts. On this something more is said later on. Here I am only concerned to distinguish an idealism which truly interprets facts, even if it throws their spiritual meaning into high relief, from a merely imagina-tive treatment which perverts and dis-torts them. Thus if the Chronicler idealizes, it is by emphasizing, beyond the point of actual fact, the priestly element in the history which at the same time did both really exist and really represent the divine purpose.

conviction, fortified by the strongest internal testimony of the books, that here is the Holy Spirit's work, gives us an antecedent expectation that the mode of composition in the case of each book will be such as God in His condescension can have sanctioned and used. God, I say, in His condescension—because undoubtedly the whole Old Testament does represent a condescension of God to a low stage of human development. Here then we need the recognition of a second great principle which S. Augustine lays down, viz. that 'as wrong is done to the Old Testament if it be denied to come from the just and good God, so wrong is done to the New if it be put on a level with the Old [1].'

For all the reality of its inspiration the Old Testament is on a lower level than the New. Thus it is now almost universally recognised that God in the Old Testament is seen appealing to the human conscience at a low stage of its development, tolerating what was not according to His original will or His ultimate purpose [2], as in the case of divorce, and even, as in the case of Abraham's sacrifice, appealing to men to do things which in a more fully developed state of the conscience could not be even conceived of as commanded by God, in order that through their very obedience to the appeal they might be led higher into the knowledge of what God could, and could not, enjoin. How fully this principle in God's dealings was recognised and justified by the early Christian authorities has been already brought out in this volume [3].

Again, the same method of condescending to what was not in itself perfect, but was susceptible of a gradual education, appears in the institutions of the Old Testament law of worship. Modern enquirers are pressing upon us the fact that the ritual law of Israel is closely akin to the common ritual customs of Semite races. 'What I may call the natural basis of Israel's worship,' says Prof. Robertson Smith, 'was very closely akin to that of the neighbouring cults [4].' The peculiarity of Israel's religion lay in fact not in the ritual itself, but in the moral and theological turn given to the ritual. According to this view God in the law appears as diverting to good uses, by an act of condescension, ritual customs which it would have been premature to abolish. Such a view of the ritual is somewhat strange to the ears of modern Churchmen, but it was undoubtedly the prevalent view of the

---

[1] *De Gestis Pelag.* v. (15), 'Sicut veteri Testamento si esse ex Deo bono et summo negetur, ita et novo fit injuria si veteri aequetur.' S. Augustine does not perhaps carry out the recognition of this principle as fully as some other of the Fathers : for refs. see p. 241 f.

[2] S. Matt. xix. 8.

[3] See pp. 241 ff.

[4] *Religion of the Semites.* Edinburgh, 1889, p. 4.

law among the great writers of Christian antiquity. References to illustrate this have been given in the eighth essay[1].

But I may add to the passages there referred to another of very striking force. S. Chrysostom is explaining why God should have appealed to the astrological notions of the wise men and led them by no other leading than that of a star. It is because 'in exceeding condescension He calls them through what is familiar... In imitation of this Paul too reasons with the Greeks from an altar, and adduces testimony from the poets, while he harangues the Jews with circumcision, and makes from the sacrifices a beginning of instruction for those who are living under the law. For since to every one familiar things are dear, therefore both God Himself and the men who were sent from God, with a view to the salvation of the world, manage things on this principle. Think it not then unworthy of Him to have called them by a star; for by the same rule thou wilt find fault with all the Jewish rites also—both the sacrifices and the purifications and the new moons, and the ark, and the temple itself. For all these things had their origin from Gentile grossness. Yet God, on account of the salvation of those in error, endured to be worshipped by means of the very things through which those outside were worshipping demons, only giving them a slight alteration, that little by little he might draw them away from their customs and lead them up to the high philosophy.'

Now if we recognise that God in the Old Testament can condescend for the purposes of His revelation to a low stage of conscience, and a low stage of worship, what possible ground have we for denying that He can use for purposes of His inspiration literary methods also which belong to a rude and undeveloped state of intelligence? If He can 'inspire' with true teaching the native Semite customs of ritual, why can He not do the same with their traditions of old time? How can we reasonably deny that the earlier portions of Genesis *may* contain the simple record of primitive prehistoric tradition of the Semites[2], moulded and used by the Holy Spirit, as on all showing the record manifestly has been moulded and used, to convey the fundamental principles of all true religion? Or again, granted that, on the 'dramatic' hypothesis, Deuteronomy written not by

---

[1] p. 241, note 1. The passage here added is from S. Chrysost. *in Matt.* vi. 3. The same idea is discerned by Bp. Lightfoot in S. Paul; see on Gal. iv. 11.

[2] I use the word 'myth' for those primitive stories on p. 262. The legitimacy of this use may be disputed, see e.g. Riehm, *Einleitung*, p. 342. But I endeavour to explain exactly the sense in which the word is used. On Strauss's application of the myth theory to the Gospel narratives, I should quite assent to the remarks of Dr. Mill, *Mythical Interpretation of the Gospels* (Cambridge, 1861), pp. 97, 98.

Moses, but in Moses' name, to incorporate the Mosaic tradition, represents a literary method greatly inferior, in sense of exactitude, to the method of personal testimony as we have it in S. John[1], or of careful investigation and use of original testimony, as we have it in S. Luke[2]; granted this—how can we, in view of the manifest facts of God's condescension, find ourselves in a position to deny that He can have used such a method as a vehicle of His inspiration[3]? There is, it must be emphasized, no critical reason why we should assign the composition of any book of the Old Testament to the motive of fraud. No doubt hostile critics have sometimes suggested, for example, that the ' discovery' of the book of the law in the Temple in the days of Josiah was a 'got up' proceeding, the book having really been written and hidden at the very time in order to be ' discovered'; but there is no positive evidence at all to support such a view, while all the evidence is satisfied by the hypothesis that an earlier prophet, some hundred years previously[4], working upon an actual and possibly written tradition of Moses' last speech, had cast this tradition into the dramatic form and promulgated, as from Moses' lips, the law which he knew to represent ultimately Moses' authority or the authority of God in Moses. That such a method should have been adopted surprises us surely no more than that Hosea should have been led to use such extraordinary means, as he seems in fact to have been enjoined to use, of revealing God's mind of love towards His people. It involves no intention to deceive, and the discovery of this 'book of the law,' lost in the careless period which intervened, was a genuine discovery unattended by any element of fraud.

Once again, if the book of Chronicles contains not pure history but the priestly view of the history, granted that this priestly point of view was *morally* part of the divinely intended education of the chosen people, even though its intellectual method was as imperfect as ordinarily is the case with the treatment of traditions in ' schools' or religious orders, in nations or churches or families, is there any *à priori* reason why God, who used so much that was imperfect, should not have inspired the record of this tradition? Here again we must

---

[1] S. John i. 14, xix. 35, xxi. 24; 1 S. John i. 1-3.
[2] S. Luke i. 1-4.
[3] I would call attention in this connection to Dr. Salmon's remarks on S. Jude's use, even in the New Testament canon, of the traditions contained in the Assumption of Moses, and his quotation of the book of Enoch: see at the end of

his lecture on S. Jude's Epistle in the *Introduction to the New Testament.*
[4] Cf. Riehm, *Einleitung,* i. p. 246 : ' Das Gesetzbuch kann nicht erst unter Josia geschrieben sein, sondern es muss spätestens zur Zeit des Hiskia entstanden sein, und zwar bevor dieser König seine Reformation ganz durchgeführt hatte.'

emphasize that all that *criticism* requires of us is to recognise in the book of Chronicles the record of the history as it became coloured in the priestly schools; there is nothing here of a morally unworthy sort from the point of view of the contemporary conscience, but only the same features as are noticeable in the record of tradition all the world over[1]. Fraudulent dealing, forgery in literature, always involves the conscious and deliberate use of methods calculated to impose on others, *methods other than those sanctioned by the literary conscience of the time*[2].

No doubt a particular writer, like Wellhausen, may make a bias hostile to the supernatural apparent in his use of the critical method, and may give in consequence an antitheological turn to his reconstruction of history; just as many a scientific writer has done with scientific facts and scientific method. In view of this we must 'try the spirits' and not attribute too much force to the point of view of a particular individual. But this will not be at all the same thing as rejecting the modern method of criticism or repudiating those results which are certainly accepted by many critics who are as far as possible from rejecting the supernatural[3].

5. No serious attempt has, I think, been made to show that the view of the development of the Old Testament literature which the modern critical schools, with great unanimity, demand of us, is contrary to any determination of Church authority. By this it is not meant that the theology of the Church suggests this view: it is not the function of the Church to advance literary knowledge, except indirectly; and thus the Church has not had the power to anticipate the critical, any more than it had to anticipate the scientific movement. The advance of knowledge comes in all departments through the natural processes of intellectual enquiry. It is only now, in fact, that the critical problem is before the Church; but now that it is before the Church it does not

[1] A common feature in all traditions is what Wellhausen describes as the main characteristic of the Chronicler, 'the timeless manner of looking at things which is natural to him.' He 'figures the old Hebrew people as in exact conformity with the pattern of the later Jewish community.' *Proleg. to Hist. of Israel* (Edinburgh, 1885), pp. 190-193. In tradition what *is* authoritative tends to be represented as what *always has been* authoritative.

[2] Thus the Pseudo-Isidorian Decretals are properly called forgeries; and the evidence of this would lie in the fact that the author could not have afforded to disclose the method and circumstances of their production.

[3] Thus Riehm, whose position is described above on p. xix, has a noble section (*Einleit.* pp. 349 ff.) on the Pentateuch considered as the record of a Revelation. The conviction of the revelation of God is ascribed in part to 'the immediate impression which the Pentateuch makes. Anyone who reads it, so as to allow its contents to work upon his spirit, must receive the impression that a consciousness of God, such as is here expressed, cannot be derived from flesh and blood.'

seem that the Church ought to have any *more* difficulty in welcoming it and assimilating it, than it has had in welcoming and assimilating the legitimate claims of science.

With reference to the bearing of Church authority on the present discussion, there are three points which I should wish to urge. First, that the undivided Church never took action on the matter, in spite of an extravagant tendency to allegorism in Origen and those who were influenced by him.

Secondly, that as a result of this the patristic theology leaves a wide opening at least for what we may call the modern way of regarding the opening chapters of Genesis. Thus a Latin writer, of the fifth or sixth century, who gives an interesting summary of the Catholic faith, and is clearly nothing else but a recorder of accepted beliefs, after speaking of the origin and fall of man and woman, continues thus : ' These things are known through God's revelation to His servant Moses, whom He willed to be aware of the state and origin of man, as the books which he produced testify. For all the divine authority (i.e. the scriptural revelation) appears to exist under such a mode as is either the mode of history which narrates only what happened, or the mode of allegory in such sense that it cannot represent the course of history, or a mode made up of these two so as to remain both historical and allegorical [1].' A great deal more in the same sense as this might be produced.

Thirdly, it must be urged that since the division of Christendom no part of the Church appears really to have tightened the bond of dogmatic obligation. Our own formularies are of course markedly free from definition on the subject, and the refusal of the Roman Church to define the scope of inspiration, beyond the region of faith and morals, has been remarkable [2].

6. But does the authority of our Lord bind us to repudiate, in loyalty to Him, the modern views of the origin of the Old Testament books ? On this subject I wish to express my sincere regret that I should have written so briefly in my essay as to lay myself open to be misunderstood to suggest our Lord's fallibility as a teacher. I trust that the passage, as it has stood since the fourth edition [3], will be at least recognised as plain in its meaning and theologically innocent. I must ask leave to defer to another occasion the fuller discussion of this important subject in connection with the doctrine of the Person of Christ.

---

[1] *De fide Catholica.* The treatise is ascribed to Boethius : see Boetii, *Opuscula Sacra* (Teubner Series), p. 178. On the fresh evidence of the authorship of those treatises supplied by the *Anecdoton Holderi*, see Hodgkin's *Letters of*

Cassiodorus, London, 1886, pp. 80-1.

[2] See the account in Manning's *Temporal Mission of the Holy Ghost*, London, 1877, pp. 156-160, and p. 166. Cf. also Newman's words below, p. 257.

[3] pp. 264-5.

Meanwhile I would suggest that the longer one thinks of it the more apparent it will become that *any hypothesis as to the origin of any one book of the Old Testament, which is consistent with a belief in its inspiration, must be consistent also with our Lord having given it His authorisation.* If His Spirit could inspire it, He, in that Spirit, could give it His recognition—His recognition, that is to say, in regard to its spiritual function and character. Thus as we scan carefully our Lord's use of the Old Testament books, we are surely struck with the fact that nothing[1] in His use of them depends on questions of authorship or date; He appeals to them in that spiritual aspect which abides through all changes of literary theory—their testimony to the Christ : ' Search the Scriptures . . . they are they which testify of Me.' He would thus lead men to ask about each book of the Old Testament simply the question,—What is the element of teaching preparatory to the Incarnation, what is the testimony to Christ, which it supplies? I do not see how with due regard to the self-limitation which all use of human forms of thought and speech must on all showing have involved to the Eternal Son, it can be a difficulty in the way of accepting the modern hypothesis, that our Lord referred to the inspired books under the only name by which His reference would have been intelligible to His hearers. Unless He had violated the whole principle of the Incarnation, by anticipating the slow development of natural knowledge, He must have spoken of the Deuteronomist as ' Moses[2],' as naturally as He spoke of the sun ' rising.' Nor does there seem in fact any greater difficulty in His speaking of one who wrote ' in the spirit and power' of Moses as Moses, than in His speaking of one who, according to the prophecy, came ' in the spirit and power of Elias' as himself, Elias. ' If ye will receive it, this is Elias.' ' Elias is already come[3].'

Once more : if the Holy Spirit could use the tradition of the flood to teach men about divine judgments, then our Lord in the same Spirit can refer to the flood, for the same purpose. It has however been recently denied that this can be so, unless the tradition accurately represents history. ' I venture to ask,' Professor Huxley writes[4],

[1] Nothing—except, on the customary interpretation, His reference to Psalm cx. This does seem to lay stress on David's authorship, unless it be regarded, as it certainly seems to me fair to regard it, as a question, rather than as positive instruction at all—a question simply calculated to lead the Pharisees to examine their own principles. Unless it be so interpreted it does seem to depend, as an argument, on personal authorship, because unless it be by David, it seems very difficult to suppose it written in David's person. It would naturally be a Psalm in which *the King is addressed.*

[2] S. John v. 46-47.

[3] S. Luke i. 17; S. Matt. xi. 14; xvii. 12.

[4] *Nineteenth Century,* July, 1890, p. 20. The bulk of his argument is directed against a position different from mine. Here I am only concerned with a single point.

'what sort of value as an illustration of God's method of dealing with sin has an account of an event that never happened?' I should like to meet this question by asking another. Has the story of the rich man and Lazarus any value as an illustration of God's method of dealing with men? Undoubtedly it has. Now what sort of narrative is this? Not a narrative of events that actually happened, in the sense that there was a particular beggar to whom our Lord was referring. The narrative is a *representative* narrative [1], a narrative of what is constantly occurring under the form of a particular typical incident. Now the narrative of the flood belongs to a quite different class of literature, inasmuch as it is not due to any *deliberate* action of imagination; but it resembles our Lord's story *at least* in being representative. It is no doubt based on fact. The traditions of the flood in all races must run back to a real occurrence. But the actual occurrence cannot be exactly estimated. What we have in Genesis is a tradition used as a vehicle for spiritual teaching. As the story is told it becomes, like that of Dives and Lazarus, a typical narrative of what is again and again happening. Again and again, as in the destruction of Jerusalem, or in the French Revolution, God's judgments come on men for their sin: again and again teachers of righteousness are sent to warn of coming judgment and are ridiculed by a world which goes on buying and selling, marrying and giving in marriage, till the flood of God's judgment breaks out and overwhelms them. Again and again, through these great judgments there emerges a remnant, a faithful stock, to be the fountain head of a new and fresh development. The narrative of the flood is a representative narrative, and our Lord, who used the story of Dives and Lazarus, can use this too [2].

VI.

Professor Huxley's article alluded to just now is a somewhat melancholy example of a mode of reasoning which one had hoped had vanished from 'educated circles' for ever—that namely which regards Christianity as a 'religion of a book' in such sense that it is supposed to propose for men's acceptance a volume to be received in all its parts as on the same level, and in the same sense, Divine. On the contrary,

[1] The proper name 'Lazarus' is presumably used because of its meaning. It should be noticed that the story is not a *parable* proper like that of the Sower or the Prodigal Son.

[2] It may be remarked that to regard 'the flood' as a representative or typical expression of a whole class of divine judgments, helps us in interpreting S. Peter's use of it in 1 Peter iii. 19-20.

There is no reason for an exceptional treatment of those who perished in one particular flood, but there is every reason why 'the Gospel should have been preached to those who died' under God's physical judgments of old times, supposing these, as we must suppose them, not to represent God's final moral judgment on individuals: see 1 Peter iv. 6.

Christianity is a religion of a Person. It propounds for our acceptance Jesus Christ, as the revealer of the Father. The test question of the Church to her catechumens has never been : 'Dost thou believe the Bible ? ' but ' Dost thou believe that Jesus Christ is the Son of God ? ' If we do believe that, then we shall further believe in the Bible : in the Old Testament as recording how God prepared the way for Christ : in the New Testament as recording how Christ lived and taught, and containing the witness borne to Him by His earthly friends and ministers. The Bible thus ' ought to be viewed as not a revelation itself, but a record of the proclaiming and receiving of a revelation, by a body which is still existent, and which propounds the revelation to us, namely the body of Christians commonly called the Church [1].' The Bible is the record of the proclamation of the revelation, not the revelation itself. The revelation is in the Person of Christ, and the whole stress therefore of *evidential* enquiry should be laid upon the central question whether the Divine claim made for Jesus Christ by the Church is historically justified. The whole evidential battle of Christianity must thus be fought out on the field of the New Testament, not of the Old. If Christ be God, the Son of God, incarnate, as the Creeds assert, Christianity is true. No one in that case will find any permanent difficulty in seeing that in a most real sense the Bible, containing both Old and New Testaments, is an ' inspired volume.'

Now faith in the Godhead of our Lord is very far from being a mere matter of ' evidences.' On this enough is said by more than one writer in this volume [2]. But so far as ' historical evidences ' go, we have them in our generation in quite fresh force and power. For our New Testament documents have passed through a critical sifting and analysis of the most trenchant and thorough sort in the fifty years that lie behind us. From such sifting we are learning much about the process through which they took their present shape. But in all that is material we feel that this critical investigation has only reassured us in asserting the historical truth of the records on which our Christian faith rests. This reassurance has been both as to the substance, and as to the quality of the original apostolic testimony to Christ. As to its substance, because the critical investigation justifies us in the confident assertion—more confident as the investigation has been more thorough than ever before—that the Christ of our four Gospels, the Christ with His Divine claim and miraculous life-giving power, the Christ raised

---

[1] These words are Bishop Steere's : see the *Memoir* of him by R. M. Heanley, London, 1888, p. 404. He admirably characterizes the true function of the Bible in the Church. It is

(1) a criterion, not a teacher ; (2) a record of the proclamation of the revelation, not the revelation itself.

[2] See pp. 20 ff., 167 ff., 247 ff.

from the dead the third day and glorified at God's right hand, the Christ who is the Son of God incarnate, is the original Jesus of Nazareth, as they beheld Him and bore witness who had been educated in closest intercourse with Him. We are reassured also as to the quality of the apostolic testimony. In some ages testimony has been careless—so careless, so clouded with superstition and credulity, as to be practically valueless. But in the apostles we have men who knew thoroughly the value of testimony and what depended upon it, who bore witness to what they had seen, and in all cases, save in the exceptional case of S. Paul, to what they had seen over a prolonged period of years; whose conviction about Christ had been gradually formed in spite of much 'slowness of heart,' and even persistent 'unbelief'; formed also in the face of Sadducean scepticism and in the consciousness of what would be said against them; formed into such irresistible strength and unanimity by the solid impress of facts that nothing could shake it, either in the individual or in the body. Such testimony does all for us that testimony can do in such a case. It supports externally and justifies a traditional faith, which is commended to us at the same time internally by its self-evidencing power. And with that faith as the strength of our life we can await with confidence the issue of minor controversies.

It may be hoped that the discussion which this book has raised may do good in two ways.

It may enable people to put the Bible into its right place in the fabric of their Christian belief. It may help to make it plain that in the full sense the Christian's faith is faith only in a Person, and that Person Jesus Christ: that to justify this faith he needs from the Scriptures only the witness of some New Testament documents, considered as containing history: while his belief in the Bible as inspired is, speaking logically, subsequent to his belief in Christ, and even, when we include the New Testament, subsequent to his belief in the Church, as the Body of Christ, rather than prior to it [1].

There is also another good result to which we may hope to see the present controversy minister—the drawing of a clear line in regard to development between the Old Testament and the New. For all modern criticism goes to emphasize the gradualness of the process through which, under the Old Covenant, God prepared the way for Christ. Now all that can be brought to light in this sense, the Church

---

[1] Cp. pp. 248–250, where this is explained. The 'logical' order of belief is often no doubt not the order of experience. The Bible can draw men to itself, and through itself to Christ, before they take any heed of the Church. But to feel the power of inspiration is a different thing from having reasoned grounds for calling certain books inspired.

can await with indifference from a theological point of view, because it is of the essence of the Old Testament to be the record of a gradual self-disclosure of God continuous and progressive till the incarnation of Jesus Christ. It is, on the other hand, of the essence of the New Testament revelation that, as given in Christ and proclaimed by His apostles, it is, as far as this world is concerned, in its substance, final and adequate for all ages. It is this, because of its essential nature. If Christ is 'the Word made flesh,' the 'Son of God made Son of Man,' then finality essentially belongs to this disclosure of Godhead and this exhibition of manhood. 'He that hath seen Him hath seen the Father,' and he that hath seen Him hath seen perfect man, hath seen our manhood in its closest conceivable relation to God, at the goal of all possible spiritual and moral development. All our growth henceforth can only be a growth into 'the measure of the stature of His fulness '—a growth into the understanding and possession of Him who was once manifested. Finality is of the essence of the New Covenant, as gradual communication of truth was of the Old.

If these two results are obtained, we shall not be liable any more to be asked 'where we are going to stop' in admitting historical uncertainty. 'If you admit so much uncertainty in the Old Testament, why do you not admit the same in the New?' We shall not be liable to be asked this question, because it will be apparent that the starting-point as of enquiry, so of security, lies in the New Testament and then proceeds to extend itself to the Old. For us, at least, the Old Testament depends upon the New, not the New upon the Old.

Nor shall we be liable any more to be asked, ' Why, if you admit so much development in actual substance in the truth revealed under the Old Covenant, cannot you admit a similar augmentation under the New?' This question will be prevented, because it will be apparent that the essential conditions are different in the two cases. Progress in Christianity is always reversion to an original and perfect type, not addition to it : it is progress only in the understanding of the Christ. 'Regnum tuum, Domine, regnum omnium saeculorum; et dominatio tua in omni generatione et generationem.'

C. G.

PUSEY HOUSE,
        July, 1890.

The chief changes of any importance in this edition are (1) the addition of a note at the end of the first essay ; (2) the alteration of a few sentences on pp. 289, 296-7 (pp. 212, 217-8 of this edition) of Essay VII ; (3) the alteration of note 2 on p. 345 (p. 253 of this edition) and note 1 on p. 346 (p. 254 of this edition) in Essay VIII ; (4) the expansion on p. 357 (p. 262 of this edition), § 6 of the opening sentences ; (5) the addition of an appendix on *The Christian Doctrine of Sin.*

SYNOPSIS OF CONTENTS.

—•‡•—

I.

FAITH.

VII.

The Atonement.

VIII.

The Holy Spirit and Inspiration.

IX.

THE CHURCH.

X.

SACRAMENTS.

XI.

CHRISTIANITY AND POLITICS.

XII.

CHRISTIAN ETHICS.

I.

FAITH.

I. IN proposing to consider the origin and growth of faith, we have a practical, and not a merely theoretical, aim. We are thinking of the actual problems which are, at this moment, encompassing and hindering faith : and it is because of their urgency and their pressure, that we find it worth while to go back upon our earliest beginnings, in order to ask what Faith itself means. For only through an examination of its nature, its origin, and its structure, will it be possible for us to sift the questions which beset us, and to distinguish those to which Faith is bound to give an answer from those which it can afford to let alone.

We set out then on our quest, in the mind of those who have felt the trouble that is in the air. Even if we ourselves be not of their number, yet we all suffer from their hesitation : we all feel the imparted chill of their anxieties. For we are of one family : and the sickness, or depression of some, must affect the whole body. All of us, even the most confident, are interested in the case of those who are fearing for themselves, as they sadly search their own hearts, and ask, 'What is it to believe? Do I know what it is to believe? Have I, or have I not, that which can be called "faith"? How can I be sure? What can I say of myself?' Such questions as these are haunting and harassing many among us who find themselves facing the Catholic Creed, with its ring of undaunted assurance, with its unhesitating claim to unique and universal supremacy, and contrast with this their own faint and tentative apprehension of the strong truths, which are so confidently asserted. Such men and women are anxious and eager to number themselves among those that believe : but can they call this temper 'belief,' which is so far below the level of the genuine response which those Creeds obviously expect? Where is the blitheness of faith? Where is its unshaken conviction? Where is its invincible simplicity? Why is it that they only succeed in moving forward with such painful indecision?

B

Now, it is to this temper that this essay is addressed. It does not aim at convicting a hostile disbelief, but at succouring a distressed faith. And this it does under the conviction that, in so doing, it is responding to the peculiar character and needs of the situation.

For the urgency, the peril of the hour, lies, not so much in the novelty, or force, of the pressure that is brought to bear against faith, as in the behaviour of faith itself under the pressure. What has happened is, not that faith has been confounded, but that it has been challenged. It has been challenged by new social needs, by strange developments of civilisation, by hungers that it had not yet taken into account, by thirsts that it had not prepared itself to satisfy. It has been challenged by new scientific methods, wholly unlike its familiar intellectual equipment; by new worlds of facts opened to its astonishment through discoveries which have changed the entire look of the earth; by immense masses of novel material, which it has been suddenly and violently required to assimilate; by strange fashions of speech in science and history; by a babel of 'unknown tongues' in all departments of learning and literature.

Faith is under the pressure of this challenge: and the primary question is, how will it behave? What is it going to say, or do, in face of this exciting transformation which has passed over the entire surface of our intellectual scenery? How will it deal with the situation? Will it prove itself adequate to the crisis? To what extent can it afford to submit to the transforming process which has already operated upon the mind and the imagination? If it submit, can it survive? And in what condition? with what loss, or damage, or change? On every side these challenges reach it; they beat at its doors; they arrive in pelting haste; they clamour for immediate solutions.

Now faith, under these rapid and stormy challenges, is apt to fall into panic. For this, surely, is the very meaning of a panic—a fear that feeds upon itself. Men in a panic are frightened at finding themselves afraid. So now with faith; it is terrified at its own alarm. How is it (it asks itself) that it should find itself baffled and timorous? If faith were faith, would it ever lose its confidence? To be frightened is to confess itself false: for faith is confidence in God, Who can never fail. How can faith allow of doubt or hesitation? Surely for faith to hesitate, to be confused, is to deny its very nature. Thus many anxious and perplexed souls retreat before their own perplexities. Because their faith is troubled, they distrust and abandon their faith. The very fact that it is in distress becomes an argument against it.

It is at this point, and because of this particular peril that we are urgently required to consider very seriously the nature and conditions of faith. For our panic arises from our assumption that faith is of such a nature, that the perplexity, into which, now and again, we find ourselves thrown, must be impossible to it, must be incompatible with it. Now, is this so? Ought we to expect of faith that its confidence should never fail it—that its light should be always decisive? Is faith incriminated by the mere fact that it is in difficulties?

Let us, first, consider what has occurred. Perhaps the situation itself, if we quietly review it, will give a reason why it is that, just at the moment when we most need vigour and assurance, we should find ourselves stripped of all that tends to reassure.

For the peculiarity of the disturbance which we have got to en-counter lies in this, that it has removed from us the very weapons by which we might hope to encounter it. Faith's evidential material is all corroborative and accumulative; it draws it from out of an external world, which can never wholly justify, or account for the internal reality, yet which can so group itself, that from a hundred differing lines, it offers indirect and parenthetic and convergent witness of that which is, itself, beyond the reach of external proof. It is this gradual grouping of an outer life into that assorted perspective in which it offers the most effective corroboration of the inner truth, which faith slowly accomplishes upon the matter which human science presents to it. When once the grouping is achieved, so that the outer world, known under certain scientific principles, tallies harmoniously with its inner convictions, faith feels secure. The external life offers it pictures, analogies, metaphors—all echoing and repeating the internal world. Faith beholds itself mirrored: and, so echoed, so mirrored, it feels itself in possession of corroborating evidences. But the present scientific confusion seems to have shattered the mirror—to have broken up the perspective—to have dissolved the well-known groupings. It is true, as some of the essays which follow will try to show, that the convulsion of which we speak, lies, chiefly, in a change of position, or of level; so that great masses of the matter, now thrown into confusion, will be found to compose themselves afresh, under the newer conditions of review, and will appear again as part and parcel of the scientific scenery. It is a change of perspective more than anything else. But, no doubt, such a change is just of the character to upset us, to disturb us; for, during the change, while shifting from the old position to the new, we are in the very chaos of confusion; everything seems, for the moment, to be tumbling about around us: the entire scene grows unsteady; though, indeed, when once we have got our feet firmly placed at the new level of vantage, much, that once was familiar, is discovered to be back again in its place, looking much the same as of old. It is the *first* shock of this enforced transition which is so calculated to terrify: as when, for instance, men see their habitual reliance on the evidence for design in nature, which had been inherited from Paley, yield, and vanish, under the review of the facts with which the theory of evolution acquaints them. What they feel is, that their familiar mode of interpreting their faith, of justifying it, of picturing it, has abruptly been torn from them. That which once seemed to evidence it in the outer world, has ceased to be accepted or trusted. The habitual ways of argument, the accepted assumptions, which they had hitherto used as their supports and their instruments —have been withdrawn—have become obsolete. Faith is thrown back on itself, on its own inherent, naked vitality; it is robbed for the moment of that sense of solidity and security, which fortifies and re-freshes it, when the outer world of natural facts, and the inner world of intellect and fancy, all corroborate its confidence in itself, by harmonious attestations of its validity. The old world of things had been brought into this adaptation with the principles of belief. Faith was at home in it, and looked out over it with cheerfulness, and moved about it with freedom. But that old world is gone; and the new still lies untested, unsorted, unverified, unassimilated, unhandled. It looks foreign, odd, remote. Faith finds no obvious corroborations in it: there, where it used to feel buttressed and warm, it now feels chilly and exposed[1].

This is the first consequence, and it is serious enough in itself to provoke alarm. Faith cannot be at ease or confident, until the outer world responds to its own convictions; and yet ease and confidence are exactly what it is challenged to exhibit.

And then, when a man, under this sense of fear, deprived of ex-ternal testimonies, attempts to exhibit, to evoke, to examine, his inner conviction, in its inherent and vital character, as it is in itself, un-supported by adventitious aids, he is astonished at his own difficulty in discovering or disclosing it. Where is it all fled—that which he had called his faith? He had enjoyed it, had relied on it, had again and again asserted it in word and deed : and now, when he wants to look at it, when he is summoned to produce it, when he is challenged to declare its form and fashion ; he finds himself dazed, bewildered, searching helplessly for that which ever escapes him, grasping at a fleeting shadow, which baffles his efforts to endow it with fixity and substance. And, so finding, he grows yet more desperately alarmed : it seems to him that he has been self-deceived, betrayed, abandoned. He is bitterly sensitive to the sharp contrast between the triumphant solidity with which scientific facts bear down upon him, certified, undeniable, substantial, and the vague, shifty, indistinct phantom, into which his conviction vanishes as soon as he attempts to observe it in itself, or draw it out for public inspection.

Yet, if we consider what faith signifies, we shall see at once that

[1] Cf. on all this, an excellent statement in Mark Pattison's *Sermons,* Serm. 7.

this contrast ought to carry with it no alarm. It is a contrast which follows on the very nature of faith. If we had understood its nature, we could never have expected it to disclose itself under the same conditions as those which govern the observation of scientific facts. Faith is an elemental energy of the soul, and the surprise that we are undergoing at not being able to bring it under direct observation, is only an echo of the familiar shock with which we learn that science has ransacked the entire bodily fabric of man, and has nowhere come across his soul; or has searched the heavens through and through with its telescope, and has seen no God. We are upset for a moment when first we hear this ; and then, we recover ourselves as we recollect that, if God be what we believe Him to be, immaterial and spiritual, then He would cease to be Himself, if He were visible through a telescope : and that if the spirit of man be what we believe it to be, that is the very reason why no surgeon's knife can ever arrive at it.

And, as with the soul, so with all its inherent and essential acts. They are what it is : they can no more be visible than it can. How can any of the basal intuitions, on which our knowledge rests, present themselves to our inspection in the guise of external and phenomenal facts ? That which observes can never, strictly speaking, observe itself. It can never look on at itself from outside, or view itself as one among the multitude of things that come under its review. How can it ? It is itself the organ of vision : and the eye cannot see its own power of seeing. This is why natural science, which is an organised system of observation, finds that its own observing mind is absolutely and totally outside its ken. It can take stock of the physiological condition of thoughts or of feelings ; but they themselves, in their actual reality, are all rigidly shut out from the entire area of scientific research. Wherever they begin, it ends ; its methods abruptly fail. It possesses no instrument by which to make good its advance further. For the only instrument which it knows how to use, and by which alone it can search, and examine, is itself the object which it desires to submit to examination. But if *it* is to be examined, who, and what, is to conduct the examination ? The observing mind that turns round to explore itself, carries itself round as it turns. It can never say— ' Let me look at myself, as if I were a phenomenon, as a fact presented to my own consciousness,' for it itself would be engaged in the act of looking : it itself is the consciousness to which it proposes to present itself[1]. So again, the thought itself can never hope, by rigid analysing, to arrive at last at itself, as the final residue of the analysis, for it is itself, all along, employed as analyst. The process of analysis

[1] It is not intended to deny that the mind can ever know itself, but only that such knowledge can ever be won by methods of empirical observation.

is, itself, the real disclosure of what thought is : and this disclosure is made just as effectively even though the result of the analysis be to declare that it can discover nothing that corresponds to thought. It is, indeed, impossible that anything should so correspond, except the power to analyse ; but this power *is* thought : and every act of the analysis, which issues in the sceptical conclusion, has verified the real existence of thought. It is the same with all profound spiritual acts. None of them can ever be offered to public inspection : they can never be handed across to another, for him to look at. For they are living acts, and not external results. How can an act of will, or of love, be submitted to observation ? Its outward result is there to be examined ; but it, itself, is incapable of transportation. If anyone were to ask ' What is it you mean by thinking, or loving, or willing ? ' who could tell him ? It would be obviously impossible to explain, except to a being who could think, will, and love. You could give him illustrations of what you mean — signs—instances—evidences ; but they can only be intelligible, as evidences, to one who already possesses the faculties. No one can do a piece of thinking for another, and hand it over to him in a parcel. Only by thinking, can it be known what thought is : only by feeling can it be understood what is meant by a feeling : only by seeing, willing, loving, can we have the least conception of sight, or of will, or of love.

And faith stands with these primary intuitions. It is deeper and more elemental than them all : and, therefore, still less than they can it admit of translation into other conditions than its own ;—can still less submit itself to public observation. It can never be looked at from without. It can be known only from within itself. Belief is only intelligible by believing. Just as a man who is asked to say what love is, apart from all its outward manifestations and results, must be driven back on the iteration—' Love is—what love is : everyone who loves, knows ; no one who does not love, can ever know ; ' just as a man, who is challenged to describe and define his feelings or his desires, when stripped of all the outward evidences that they can possibly give of themselves, is thrown into inarticulate bewilderment, and can give no intelligible answer, and can fashion to himself no distinct feature or character, and can only assert, confusedly, that he feels what he feels, and that to desire is to desire ;—so with faith. The scientific convulsion has shaken and confused its normal modes of self-interpretation, its usual evidences, signs, illustrations : these outer aids at definition, by metaphor or by corroboration, are all brought under dim eclipse for the moment : their relative values have been thrown into uncertainty : they are undergoing temporary displacement, and no one is quite sure which is being shifted, and which can be trusted to stand firm. Faith, robbed of its habitual aids to expression, is summoned to show itself on the field, in its own inner character. And this is just what it never can or may do. It can only reiterate, in response to the demand for definition, 'Faith is faith.' 'Believing is—just believing.' Why, then, let ourselves be distressed, or bewildered, by finding ourselves reduced to this impotence of explanation? Far from it being an incrimination of our faith, to find ourselves caught in such a difficulty of utterance, it is just what must happen if faith be a profound and radical act of the inner soul. It is, essentially, an active principle, a source of energy, a spring of movement : and, as such, its verification can never take place through passive introspection. It verifies itself only in actions : its reality can only be made evident through experience of its living work.

II. We may, then, free ourselves from the sinister suspicions which belong to panic. It is not the superficiality of our faith, which is the secret of our bewilderment, but its depth. The deepest and most radical elements of our being are, necessarily, the hardest to unearth. They are, obviously, the most remote from the surface of our lives : they are the rarest to show themselves in the open daylight : they require the severest effort to disentangle their identity : they lie below all ordinary methods of utterance and expression ; they can only be discovered through careful recognition of the secret assumptions which are involved in the acts and words which they habitually produce. By these acts and words their existence and their force is suggested, but not exhausted—manifested, but not accounted for. These form our only positive interpretation and evidence : and such evidence must, therefore, always remain inadequate, imperfect ; we have always and inevitably to go behind it, and beyond it, in order to reach and touch the motive-energy which is disclosed to us through it. No wonder that we find this far from an easy matter. No wonder that, under the pressure of a hostile challenge, we often lose ourselves in a confused babble, as we struggle to make plain to others, or even to ourselves, these innermost convictions of our souls.

Indeed, such things can never be made plain : no one ought to expect that they should. For, if we think of it, the primary acts of spirit must be the *last* things that can ever be made plain ; for the entire life issuing from them is their only interpretation, so that only when that life is closed, can their interpretation be complete. And here, in faith, we are at the root of a life which, as we believe, it will take eternity to fulfil. And, if so, only in and through eternity can its full evidence for itself be produced, or its right interpretation be yielded.

Surely, this truth clears us from many clamorous demands, which ask of us an impossible verification. For if once we saw that we were employed in verifying the nature of that which, if it be real, can, confessedly, present us, on this side of the grave, only with the most fragmentary evidence of its character, we should put lightly aside the taunting challenge to produce such proof of our motive principle as will stand comparison with the adequate and precise evidences of a scientific fact, or which will submit to the rigid tests of a legal examination. If faith be faith, it could not, for that very reason, fulfil the conditions so proposed to it. These legal and scientific conditions are laboriously and artificially limited to testing the presence of a motive, or a force, which must be assumed to exist under fixed, precise, complete conditions, here and now. They pre-suppose that, for all practical purposes, its quantity cannot vary, or fluctuate. If it be present at all, it is present in a distinct and formal manner, open to definite measurement, expressing itself in unalterable characteristics. The entire consideration of its activity is strictly confined to the normal horizon of the actual world of present existence. These assumptions are the first necessity of all forms of science, without making which, it could not even begin. They are the conditions of all its success. But they are also its limitations : and as such, they most certainly exclude from their survey, anything that professes to exist after the manner of faith. For what is faith? It is no steady force, existing under certified and unvarying conditions which receive their final determination in the world about us. Faith is, while it is here on earth, only a tentative probation : it is a struggling and fluctuating effort in man to win for himself a valid hold upon things that exist under the conditions of eternity. In faith, we watch the early and rude beginnings, amid an environment that but faintly and doubtfully responds to it, of a power still in the womb—still unborn into its true sphere—still enveloped in dark wrappings which encumber and impede. We see here but its blind, uncertain pushings, its hesitating moves, now forward, now back, now strangely vigorous and assertive, and then again, as strangely weak and retreating. Its significance, its interpretation, its future possibilities, its secret of development—all these lie elsewhere, beyond death, beyond vision : we can but dimly guess, from its action here, what powers feed it, on what resources it can rely, what capacity of growth is open to it, what final issue determines the measure and value of its efforts and achievements here. Such a force as this is bound to upset all our ablest calculations. We can never lay down rules to govern and predict its capabilities. It will disappoint every conceivable test that we can devise for fixing its conditions. It will laugh at our attempts to circumscribe its action. Where we look for it to be weak, it will suddenly show itself strong : when we are convinced that we may expect a vigorous display of its capacities, it will mysteriously lapse. All this may terribly disconcert us. It may tempt us into angry declarations that such an incalculable existence is unworthy of scientific attention—is fanciful, is unreal. But the only lesson which we ought to learn is that methods adapted for one state of things are bound to prove themselves futile when applied to another. If we are employed in observing a life, which has its ground and its end in a world beyond the present, then all methods framed for the express and definite purpose of examining life as it exists here and now, will necessarily prove themselves ludicrously inapt. The futility, the barrenness, the ineptitude of our researches, lies, not with the faith against which we level our irritable complaints, but with the methods which, by their very terms of definition, proclaim themselves to be misplaced.

Where, then, must we dig to unearth the roots of faith? What are the conditions of its rise and exercise? Wherein lie its grounds, and the justification of its claim?

Faith grounds itself, solely and wholly, on an inner and vital relation of the soul to its source. This source is most certainly elsewhere; it is not within the compass of the soul's own activity. In some mode, inconceivable and mysterious, our life issues out of an impenetrable background: and as our life includes spiritual elements, that background has spiritual factors: and as our life is personal, within that background exists personality. This supply of life in which we begin, from out of which our being opens, can never cease, so long as we exist, to sustain us by one continuous act. Ever its resources flow in: ever its vital support is unwithdrawn. In some fashion or other, we all know that this must be so: and the Christian Creed only lifts into clear daylight, and endows with perfect expression, this elementary and universal verity, when it asserts that at the very core of each man's being lies, and lives, and moves, and works, the creative energy of the Divine Will—'the Will of our Father Which is in Heaven.'

We stand, by the necessities of our existence, in the relationship of sons to a Father, Who has poured out into us, and still pours, the vigour of His own life. This is the one basis of all faith. Unless this relationship actually exists, there could be no faith: if it exists, then faith is its essential corollary: it is bound to appear. Our faith is simply the witness to this inner bond of being. That bond, which is the secret of our entire existence, accounting for all that we are, or do, or feel, or think, or say, must become capable of recognition by a being that is, in any sense, free, intelligent, conscious: and this recognition by us of the source from whence we derive, is what we mean by faith. Faith is the sense in us that we are Another's creature, Another's making. Even as we not only feel, but feel that we feel; not only think, but know that we think; not only choose, but determine to choose: so, below and within all our willing, and thinking, and feeling, we are conscious of Another, whose mind and will alone make possible both the feeling that we feel, and also the capacity to feel it; both the thought that we think, and also the capacity to know it; both the will that we put forth, as well as the power to determine it. Every act, every desire, every motive of ours, is dependant on the source out of sight: we hang on Another's will; we are alive in Another's life. All our life is a discovery, a disclosure, of this secret. We find it out only by living. As we put out powers that seem to be our own, still even in and by the very act of putting them out, we reveal them to be not our own; we discover that we are always drawing on unseen resources. We are sons: that is the root-law of our entire self. And faith is the active instinct of that inner sonship: it is the point at which that essential sonship emerges into consciousness; it is the disclosure to the self of its own vital secret; it is the thrill of our inherent childhood, as it makes itself felt within the central recesses of the life; it is the flame that shoots into consciousness at the recognition of the touch of our divine fatherhood; it is the immediate response of the sonship in us to its discovered origin.

Faith, then, is an instinct of relationship based on an inner actual fact. And its entire office and use lies in realising the secret fact. For the bond is spiritual; and it can only realise itself in a spirit that has become aware of its own laws. No blind animal acceptance of the divine assistance can draw out the powers of this sonship. The reception of the assistance must itself be conscious, loving, intelligent, willing. The natural world can receive its full capacities from God without recognition of the source whence they flow in: but this absence of living recognition forbids it ever to surpass those fixed limits of development which we name 'natural.' But a creature of God that could not only receive but recognise that it received, would, by that very recognition, lay itself open to an entirely novel development; it would be susceptible of infinitely higher influences shed down upon it from God; it would admit far finer and richer inpourings of divine succours; it would be fed, not only from underground channels as it were, but by fresh inlets which its consciousness of its adherence in God would uncover and set in motion. The action of God upon His creatures would be raised to a new level of possibility: for a living and intelligent will has capacities of receptivity, which were altogether excluded so long as God merely gave, and the creature blindly and dumbly took. Faith, then, opens an entirely new career for creaturely existence; and the novelty of this career is expressed in the word 'supernatural.' The 'supernatural' world opens upon us as soon as faith is in being [1].

---

[1] The word 'super-natural' is obviously misleading, since it seems to imply that the higher spiritual levels of life are *not* 'natural.' Of course, the higher the life, the more intensely 'natural' it is; and the nature of God must be the supreme expression of the natural. But the word 'supernatural' is, in reality, only concerned with the partial and conventional use of 'nature,'

And this career, it will be seen, is markedly distinct from the natural in this—that it is capable of ever advancing expansion. All natural things, which blindly accept their life from God, must, perforce, have a decreed and certified development, limited by the conditions in which they are found existing. Their receptivity is a fixed quantity, determined by the character imposed upon them at creation, and bound to come to an abrupt arrest at some precise point [1]. But receptivity through conscious recognition is open to a development of which it is impossible for us to fix the limits. For this living recognition itself advances in its capacity to see and understand. Every act by which it recognises the Giver in the gifts, heightens and intensifies its power to recognise Him; and every increase of its power to recognise Him increases also its capacity to receive; and this increase will again react on the faculties of recognition. A vision opens out of spiritual growth, in which every step forward made through incoming grace, makes a new step possible, finds a fresh grace ever waiting to crown its latest gift with ever new endowment. The sonship that is at work underground in man, below the level of consciousness, at the hidden base of faith, is one that holds in it capacities which can only be evoked under the appeals of a living and voluntary faith. Faith is the discovery of an inherent sonship, which, though already sealed to it, already in action, nevertheless cannot but withhold its more rich and splendid energies until this discovery is made; and which discloses them only according to the progressive clearness and force with which the process of discovery advances. The history of faith is the history of this gradual disclosure, this growing capacity to recognise and receive, until the rudimentary omen of God's fatherhood in the rudest savage who draws, by clumsy fetich, or weird incantation, upon a power outside himself, closes its long story in the absolute recognition, the perfect and entire receptivity, of that Son of man, who can do nothing of Himself, ' but what He seeth the Father do,' and, for that very reason, can do everything : for whatsoever 'the Father doeth, the Son doeth also.'

Faith, then, is not only the recognition by man of the secret source of his being, but it is itself, also, the condition under which the powers, that issue from that source, make their arrival within him. The sonship, already germinal, completes itself, realises itself in man, through his faith. Not only is the unconscious human nature held by attachment to the Father who feeds it with hidden succours, but faith is, itself, the power by which the conscious life attaches itself to God ; it is an apprehensive motion of the living spirit, by which it intensifies its

---

as a term under which we sum up all that constitutes this present and visible system of things.

[1] It is this point of arrest which is reached and revealed by the process of Evolution, under the pressure of Natural Selection.

touch on God ; it is an instinct of surrender, by which it gives itself to the fuller handling of God : it is an affection of the will, by which it presses up against God, and drinks in divine vitality with quickened receptivity [1].

What then will be its characteristics ?   We have only to keep close to the conception of sonship, and we shall understand them well enough. Faith is the attitude, the temper, of a son towards a father.   That is a relationship that we all can understand for ourselves.   We know it, in spite of all the base and cruel corruptions under which, in the homes of man, its beauty lies disfigured.   Still, beneath disguises, we catch sight, in rare and happy conditions, of that beautiful intimacy which can spring up between a son and a father, where love is one with reverence, and duty fulfils itself in joy.   Such a sonship is like a spiritual instinct, which renders intelligible to the son every mood and gesture of the father.   His very blood moves in rhythm to the father's motives. His soul hangs, for guidance, on the father's eyes : to him, each motive of the father justifies itself as a satisfying inspiration.   The father's will is felt deliciously encompassing him about ; enclosed within it, his own will works, glad and free in its fortifying obedience.   Such a relationship as this needs no justifying sanction beyond itself : it is its own sanction, its own authority, its own justification.   ' He is my father ' : that is a sufficient reason for all this sympathetic response to another's desire.   'I am his son ' : that is the final premiss in which all argument comes to a close.   The willing surrender of the heart is the witness to a *fact* which is beyond argument, which accepts no denial, yet which is no tyrannous fate, but is a living and animating bond of blood, which it is a joy to recognise, and an inspiration to confess.

It is in such a spirit of sonship that faith reveals and realises itself. Faith is that temper of sympathetic and immediate response to Another's will which belongs to a recognised relationship of vital communion.   It is the spirit of confident surrender, which can only be justified by an inner identification of life.   Its primary note, therefore, will be *trust*—that trust of Another, which needs no ulterior grounds on which to base itself, beyond what is involved in the inherent law of this life.   Faith will ever discover, when its reason for action, or belief, are traced to their last source, that it arrives at a point where its only and all-sufficient plea will be ' God is my Father : I am His child.' That relationship is its root ; on the top of that relationship faith works ; as a witness to that relationship, it puts forth all the spiritual temper which, of necessity, follows on this intimacy of contact.

And, here, we find ourselves in the presence of the law by which faith claims to be *universal.*   Unless this inner relationship be a fact,

[1] Faith is spoken of, here and elsewhere, in its perfect and true form, as if unthwarted by the misdirection, and hurt of sin.

faith could not account for itself: but if it be a fact, it must constitute a fixed and necessary demand upon all men. All are, equally, 'children of God': and the answer to the question 'Why should I believe?' must be, for ever and for all, valid; 'because you are a child of God.' Faith is nothing but the spiritual temper and attitude, which belong, inherently, to such a fact. No one can escape from such a claim: for his existence constitutes the claim. If he be a child, it must be demanded of him, that he should display the characteristics of his childhood: the father must, of necessity, be concerned with the question of his own recognition by his son. Our manhood lies in this essential sonship: and, if so, then to be without faith, without the conscious realisation of the sonship, is to be without the fulness of a man's proper nature. It is to be inhuman: to be curtailed of the natural development: to be maimed and thwarted. It means that the vital outcome of the inner verity has been arrested; that the sensitive perceptions have been blunted and stunted; that the sonship in us has, somehow, lost touch with its true fatherhood.

We learn at once, as we consider this, the interpretation of that two-sided character, which surprises us in God's dealings with men:— i.e. the imperative rigour of His stated requirements, coupled with His wide and patient tolerance, in actual fact.

As a Father of all, He cannot, conceivably, be satisfied with anything short of complete recognition by His children. He must look for faith; He must require it of them all: He must leave no means untried by which to secure it: He must seek to win it at all costs: His love is inevitably and cruelly hindered, unless He can obtain it: and when He obtains it, He must passionately desire to establish, evoke, develop, perfect it: for each rise in faith is a rise in capacities of intercourse, of intimacy, between Father and son. We see how strenuous and zealous will be His efforts to build up faith in men: we understand how urgent, and pressing, and alarming will become His entreaties, His warnings, His menaces, His appeals, if faith is allowed to slide or fail. Loss of faith means a shattered home, a ruptured intimacy, a sundered love; it means that a Father must look on while the very nature He has made in His image shrivels and shrinks, and all hope of growth, of advancing familiarity, of increasing joy, of assured sympathy, is cut down and blighted. We all know the bitterness of a breach which scatters a family into fragments: and that is but a faint shadow of all which the great Father sees to be involved in the broken contact between Himself and His son. What standard have we by which to sound the abyss of divine disappointment, as God waits ready with gift upon gift of endless grace which He will pour out upon the child of His love, as the endless years open out new wonders of advancing intimacy; and lo! the channel by which alone the gifts can reach him, is choked and closed? Faith is the son's receptivity: it is that temper of trust, which makes the entry of succours possible: it is the medium of response: it is the attitude of adherence to the Father, by virtue of which communications can pass. If faith goes, all further action of God upon the soul, all fresh arrival of power, is made impossible. The channel of intercourse is blocked.

The demand, then, for faith by God is bound to be exacting, and urgent, and universal. But, then, this demand holds in reserve a ground of hope, of patience, of tolerance, of charity, which we can, in no single instance, venture to limit. For the faith, which it rigorously asks for, reposes, as we see, on an inner and essential relationship, already existent, which knits man to his God. Not even the Fall, with all its consequent accumulations of sin, can avail to wholly undo this primitive condition of existence. The fatherhood of God still sustains its erring children; the divine image is blurred, but not blotted out. Still, at the close of the long days, our Lord can speak to the wondering men who flock about Him, of One Who is even now their Father in Heaven. This objective and imperishable relationship, the underlying ground of all our being, is the pre-supposition of all faith, without which it would itself be impossible. And, this being so, God can afford to wait very long for faith to show itself. So long as its primary condition is there, there is always hope. The stringent demand is not inspired by the mind of a lawgiver, nor pressed home with the austerity of a judge; it expresses the hunger of a father's heart, to win the confidence and to evoke the capacities of the children of its love. Such a hunger is, indeed, more rigorous and exact than the letter of any law: it aspires after a more accurate correspondence; it is sensitive to more delicate distinctions: but, nevertheless, it holds, in its fatherliness, far wider capacities of toleration than lawgiver, or judge. That same heart of the father, which in its hunger of love is so exacting, will, out of the same hunger, never despair, and never forsake: it will never cease from the pursuit of that responsive trust which it desires; it will make allowances, it will permit delays, it will weave excuses, it will endure rebuffs, it will condescend to persuasion, it will forget all provocations, it will wait, it will plead, it will repeat its pleas, it will take no refusal, it will overleap all obstacles, it will run risks, it will endlessly and untiringly forgive, if only, at the last, the stubborn child-heart yield, and the tender response of faith be won.

Here, then, we seem to see why the nature of faith allows for two points which surprise us in God's dealings, as if with a contradiction. On the one hand, we hear Him, though prophet and priest, insisting, with severe precision, on the necessity of a right and accurate faith.

On the other, we cannot but recognise, in the open area of actual life, the evidences of a wide and almost boundless toleration. Again and again it must have seemed to us that the Church and the world gave thus, antithetical evidence of God's character. Yet, in truth, both speak the voice of one and the same God, Who, in His undivided love, both passionately seeks for the delicate and direct response of an accurate faith ; and, also, in order not to lose this final joy, ' suffereth long, and is kind, beareth all things, believeth all things, hopeth all things, endureth all things.' Yes !—has even to endure that men should pit His toleration against His love, and should argue that, because He will wait so long and quietly for the fruit that He desires to reap, therefore, He does not desire the fruit. In reality, the degree of the toleration, with which God will patiently wait for the fruits of faith, is the measure of the extremity of His desire for it. Just because he wants it so much, He waits so long.

III. If faith, then, be the witness and the exercise of our sonship in God, we can recognise at once the place it will hold among the other powers and capacities of our nature. We are so unfortunately apt to rank it as one among many faculties, and then to find ourselves engaged in agitating controversies concerning its limits and its claims. We have to secure for it, against the rest, a field for free dominion ; and that field is hard to define ; and rival powers beset it ; and there are raids and skirmishes on every frontier; and reason is ever making violent incursions on the one side, and feeling is actively besieging it on the other : and the scientific frontiers, which we are ever on the point of fixing, shift, and change, and vanish, as soon as we determine them ; and the whole force of Christian apologetics is spent in aimless and barren border-warfare.

But, if what we have been saying be true, the whole trouble turns on a mistake. Faith is not to be ranked by the side of the other faculties in a federation of rival powers, but is behind them all. It goes back to a deeper root ; it springs from a more primitive and radical act of the central self than they. It belongs to that original spot of our being, where it adheres in God, and draws on divine resources. Out from that spot our powers divide, radiating into separate gifts,—will, memory, feeling, reason, imagination, affection ; but all of them are but varying expressions of that essential sonship, which is their base. And all, therefore, run back into that home where faith abides, and works, and rises, and expands. At the root of all our capacities lies our sonship ; at the root of all our conscious life lies faith, the witness of our sonship. By adherence in God, we put out our gifts, we exercise our functions, we develop our faculties ; and faith, therefore, far from being their rival, whom they are interested in suspecting, and curbing, and confining within its limits, is the secret spring of their force, and the inspiration of their growth, and the assurance of their success. All our knowledge, for instance, relies upon our sonship; it starts with an act of faith[1]. We throw ourselves, with the confidence of children, upon an external world, which offers itself to our vision, to our touch, to our review, to our calculation, to our handling, to our use. Who can assure us of its reality, of its truth? We must measure it by those faculties under the manipulation of which it falls: but how can the faculties guarantee to us their own accuracy? How can we justify an extension of our own inner necessities to the world of outward things? How can we attribute to nature that rational and causative existence which we find ourselves forced to assume in it? Our justification, our confidence, all issue, in the last resort, from our sonship. Our powers have, in them, some likeness to those of God. If He be our Father, if we be made in His image, then, in our measure, we can rely upon it that we close with Nature in its reality; that our touch, our sight, our reason, have some hold on the actual life of things; that we see and know in some such manner, after our degree, as God Himself sees and knows. In unhesitating reliance upon our true sonship, we sally out and deal with the world; we act upon the sure conviction that we are not altogether outside the secret of objective existence. We refuse absolutely to doubt, or go behind the reports made to us by feeling, by memory, by thought. If once we are clear as to what the report is, we rest on it; we ask for no power to stand (as it were) outside our own experience, our own knowledge, so as to assure ourselves of their veracity. We are certain that our Father cannot have misguided us; that we are within His influence; that we are in modified possession of His truth; that our capacities reflect His mind. We could not have so confidently recognised, understood, and handled the world, if it had been wholly foreign to us. As it is, we lay instinctive hold upon it; we take spontaneous possession; we exert authority upon it; we feel our inherent right over it; we are at home in it; we move freely about it, as children in a father's house. Acting in this faith, all our capacities justify themselves to us; they respond to our reliance upon them; they develop into ever advancing strength under the motions of this trust; they form a continual and increasing witness to the verity of that sonship in which we have believed.

Faith, then, belongs to our entire body of activities. We live by faith. By faith, under the inspiration of faith, we put out our life, we set to work, we exercise faculties, we close with our opportunities, we have confidence in our environment, we respond to calls, we handle critical emergencies, we send out far abroad our experimental intelli-

[1] Cf. pp. 78, 79.

gence, we discover, we accumulate experiences, we build, and plant, and develop. An elemental act of faith lies at the root of all this advance; and every motion that we make, demands a renewal of that primitive venture. In all secular progress 'we walk by faith.' Every step revives the demand. Just as the earth, if it necessitates the idea of a primal creation, requires, by exactly the same necessity, an incessant renewal of that first creative act, so our life, if it required faith to start it, requires faith every moment to sustain it. Our faculties never arrive at a use which is self-dependent and self-originated, as if they could grow beyond the tentative conditions of their earliest assays. They originate in a venturous experiment; and, however long, and however complicated that experiment become, it retains its original character; it remains experimental to the end. The *results*, no doubt, justify the venture made; but, then, the first venture involved such immense assumptions, that no results reached can ever complete its justification, and so remove its tentative nature. For, by assuming a real correspondence between our faculties and the world with which they deal, it assumed that such a correspondence would never fail us; would be capable of infinite verification; would prove adequate to all possible experiences; would receive indefinite and progressive extension. No verifications ever reached can, then, exhaust the faith of that primitive venture; they can only serve to exhibit to it how far more was contained within that venture than it could ever have conceived. New knowledge, new experience, far from expunging the elements of faith, make ever fresh demands upon it; they constitute perpetual appeals to it to enlarge its trust, to expand its original audacity. And yet the very vastness of those demands serves to obscure and conceal their true character. This is the key to much of our present bewilderment. The worlds of knowledge and of action have assumed such huge proportions, have accumulated such immense and complicated resources, have gained such supreme confidence in their own stability, have pushed forward their successes with such startling power and rapidity, that we have lost count of their primal assumption. In amazement at their stupendous range, we are over-awed; we dare not challenge them with their hypothetical origin, or remind them that their entire and wonderful structure is but an empty and hollow dream, unless they are prepared to place their uttermost trust in an unverified act of faith. Given that trust, which relies on the reality of the bond which holds between our inner faculties and the outer world, then all this marvellous vision is rooted on a rock, has validity and substance. Withdraw that spiritual trust in our sonship, and all this fairy-world, won for us by science and experience,

> These cloud-capped towers, these gorgeous palaces,
> The solemn temples, the great globe itself,

C

> Yea, all which it inherit, shall dissolve,
> And, like an unsubstantial pageant faded,
> Leave not a rack behind.

Our secular and scientific life is an immense experiment in faith,—an experiment which verifies itself by success, but which justifies itself only if it remembers to attribute all its success to the reality of that hidden relationship to God, which is the key to all its capacities, the justification of all its confidence, and the security of all its advance.

Such a remembrance is not easy for it : for the exercise of the capacities is instinctive and spontaneous, and it requires an effort of reflection to question the validity of such exercise. And such an effort seems tiresome and impertinent in the heat of successful progress, in the thick of crowding conquests. The practical man is apt to give an irritated stamp on the ground, which to him feels so solid, and to deem this a sufficient answer to the importunate inquiry how he knows that he has any substantial world to know and to handle. For faith lies *behind* our secular life, secreted within it : and the secular life, therefore, can go on as if no faith was wanted ; it need not trouble its head with perplexing questions, whether its base be verifiable by the same standards and measures as its superstructure. Its own practical activity is complete and free, whether it discover its hidden principle or not : just as Mr. Jourdain's conversation was complete and free, long before he discovered that he was talking prose. We have to stand outside our secular life and reflect on it, to disclose its true spring. The appeal to faith here is indirect.

But, in religion, this hidden activity is evoked by a direct appeal : it is unearthed ; it is summoned to come forward on its own account. God demands of this secret and innermost vitality that it should no longer lie incased within the other capacities, but that it should throw off its sheltering covers, and should emerge into positive action, and should disclose its peculiar and native character. God, the Father, calls faith out of its dim background into the front of the scene. He does this under the pressure of invocations, which address their appeals through, and by means of, the secular and visible material, within and behind which He is ever at work. This had, indeed, always told of His invisible and eternal Godhead : but it did so indirectly, by requiring Him as its constant pre-supposition and base. Now, it is so used as to bring God into direct and positive evidence, by means of acts, which bring forward the energies of His immediate Fatherhood. All the growth of Eden had always testified to the existence and the name of God : but a new stage was reached when He was felt moving, in evening hours, amid the trees of the garden. And as the Father presses forward out of His silent background, so the secret sonship in man emerges out of its deep recesses in positive response, using its own secular faculties by which to carry itself forward into evidence and action. This definite and direct contact between the God Who is the hidden source of all life, and the faith which is the hidden spring of all human activity—this disclosure by the Father, met by this discovery by the son—this is Religion: and the history of Religion is the story of its slow and gradual advance in sanity and clearness, until it culminates in that special disclosure which we call Revelation; which, again, crowns itself in that Revelation of the Father through the Son, in which the disclosure of God to man and the discovery by man of God are made absolute in Him Who is one with the Father, knowing all that the Father does, making known all that the Father is.

Now here we have reached a parting of ways. For we have touched the point at which the distinctions start out between what is secular and what is sacred—between virtue and godliness—between the world and the Church. If 'Religion' means this coming forward into the foreground of that which is the universal background of all existence, then we cut ourselves free from the perplexity which benumbs us when we hear of the 'Gospel of the Secular Life;' of the 'Religion of Humanity;' of doctors and scientific professors being 'Ministers of Religion;' of the 'Natural Religion' which is contained within the borders of science with its sense of wonder, or of art with its vision of beauty. All this is so obviously true in one sense that it sinks to the level of an amiable commonplace; but if this be the sense intended, why is all this emphasis laid upon it? Yet if more than this is meant, we are caught in a juggling maze of words, and are losing hold on vital distinctions, and feel ourselves to be rapidly collapsing in to the condition of the unhappy Ninevites, who knew not their right hands from their left.

The word 'Religion,' after all, has a meaning: and we do not get forward by labouring to disguise from ourselves this awkward fact. This positive meaning allows everything that can be asked in the way of sanctity and worth, for nature and the natural life. All of it is God-given, God-inspired, God-directed; all of it is holy. But the *fact* of this being so is one thing: the *recognition* of it is another; and it is this recognition of God in things which is the core and essence of religion. Natural life is the life in God, which has not yet arrived at this recognition: it is not yet, as such, religious. The sacred and supernatural office of man is to press through his own natural environment, to force his spirit through the thick jungle of his manifold activities and capacities, to shake himself free from the encompassing complexities, to step out clear and loose from all entanglement, to find himself, through and beyond all his secular experiences, face to face with a God, Who, on His side, is for ever pushing aside the veil which suggests and conceals him, for ever disengaging Himself from the phenomena through which He arrives at man's consciousness, for ever brushing away the confusions, and coming out more and more into the open, until, through and past the 'thunder comes a human voice;' and His eyes burn their way through into man's soul; and He calls the man by his name, and takes him apart, and hides him in some high and separate cleft of the rock, far from all the glamour and tumult of crowded existence, and holds him close in the hollow of His hand as He passes by, and names to him, with clear and memorable voice, the 'Name of the Lord, the Lord God, merciful, gracious, long-suffering, abundant in goodness and truth, forgiving iniquity, and Who will by no means clear the guilty.' Here is Religion. It is the arrival at the secret; the discovery by the son of a Father, Who is in all His works, yet is distinct from them all,—to be recognised, known, spoken with, loved, imitated, worshipped, on His own account, and for Himself alone.

Religion, in this sense, is perfectly distinct from what is secular: yet, in making this distinction, it brings no reproach: it pronounces nothing common or unclean. It only asks us not to play with words: and it reminds us that, in blurring this radical distinction, we are undoing all the work which it has been the aim of the religious movement to achieve. For the history of this movement is the record of the gradual advance man has made in disentangling 'the Name of God' from all its manifestations. Religion is the effort to arrive at that Name, in its separable identity, in its personal and distinct significance. It is the fulfilment of the unceasing cry 'Tell me Thy name!' In religion we are engaged in the age-long task of lifting the Name, clear and high, above the clang and roar of its works, that through and by means of all that He is, we may pierce through to the very God of gods, and may close with Him in the blessed solitude of a love which knits heart to heart and spirit to spirit, without any withholding interval, with no veil to hinder or intervene.

The growth of faith, then, means the gradual increase of this personal contact, this spiritual intimacy between Father and son. To achieve this increasing apprehension of the Father's character and love, faith uses, as instruments and as channels, all its natural faculties, by which to bring itself forward into action, and through which to receive the communications, which arrive at it from the heart and will of Him, Who, on His side, uses all natural opportunities as the material of a speech, which is ever, as man's ear becomes sensitive and alert, growing more articulate, and positive, and personal.

The entire human nature,—imagination, reason, feeling, desire,— becomes to faith a vehicle of intercourse, a mediating aid in its friendship with God. But faith itself lies deeper than all the capacities of which it makes use : it is, itself, the primal act of the elemental self, there at the root of life, where the being is yet whole and entire, a single personal individuality, unbroken and undivided. Faith, which is the germinal act of our love for God, is an act of the whole self, there where it is one, before it has parted off into what we can roughly describe as separate and distinguishable faculties. It therefore uses, not one or other of the faculties, but all ; and in a sense it uses them all at once, just as any complete motion of will, or of love, acts with all the united force of many combined faculties. A perfect act of love would combine, into a single movement, the entire sum of faculties, just because it proceeds from that basal self, which is the substance and unity of them all. So with faith. Faith, the act of a willing adhesion to God the Father, proceeds from a source deeper than the point at which faculties divide.

And this has a most vital bearing on the question of faith's evidences. It is here we touch on the crucial characteristic which determines all our logical and argumentative position.

For, if a movement of faith springs from a source anterior to the distinct division of faculties, then no one faculty can adequately account for the resultant action. Each faculty, in its separate stage, can account for *one* element, for *one* factor, which contributed to the result : and that element, that factor, may be of greater or less importance, according to the rank of the faculty in the entire self. But, if the movement of faith has also included and involved many other elements which appear, when analysed out, in the domains of the other faculties ; then the account which each separate faculty can give of the whole act, can never be more than partial. Its evidence must be incomplete. If the central self has gathered its momentum from many channels, it is obvious that the amount contributed by any one channel will be unable to justify the force exerted, or to explain the event that fol-lowed. If we track home each faculty employed to this central spring of energy, we shall see that each points to the result, contributes to it, suggests it ; but the result will always be more than the evidence, so collected, can warrant.

This limitation, which we may allow about other faculties, is apt to become a stumbling-block when we apply it to the high gift of reason. Reason, somehow, seems to us to rise into some supreme and indepen-dent throne ; it reviews the other faculties ; and is, therefore, free from their limitations. We fear to hint that it has any lord over it. How can we assume such a lordship without dubbing ourselves irrational obscurantists, who in folly try to stamp out the light ?

But we are not, in reality, dreaming of limiting reason by any limitations except those which it makes for itself. We are not violently attempting to make reason stop short at any point, where it could go on. We are only asking, is there any point at which it stops of itself, and cannot go further? We propose to use reason right out, to press it to its utmost limit, to spur it to put forth all its powers; and we assert that, so doing, reason will, at last, reveal its inability to get right to the end, to carry clear home. And why? Because the self is not only rational but something more: it combines, with its unbroken, central individuality, other elements besides reason: and therefore, of sheer necessity, whenever that central self puts out an elemental act in which the integral spring of personal energy takes part,—such as an act of will, or love, or faith,—then, reason can be but one factor, but one element, however important, in that issuing act: and if so, then it can give but a partial account of it; its own contribution can not wholly explain, or justify the result. In Bishop Butler's language, the utmost that reason can do is to make it 'very probable.'

The real root-question in this time-worn controversy is just this: is, or is not, reason the most primal and elemental act of the integral personality? If it is, then, of course, it regulates and determines all subordinate acts. Everything must finally submit to its arbitration: for everything, if tracked back far enough, must terminate in an act of reason.

But if, as Christianity asserts, the ultimate and elemental self be a moral will, that can believe, and love, then, though this self contains in it reason, it also goes back behind reason. Reason is indeed one of its essential elements, but it is not its entire essence, for this includes within itself, that which appears as feeling, and desire, and imagination, and choice, and passion, as well as that which shows itself as reason. When, therefore, the self puts out its primitive power, it will do actions which satisfy reason, indeed, but which reason cannot exhaustively analyse, or interpret, since the entire force of reason, if it were all brought into action, would still be only a partial contribution to the effect.

As a fact, we all of us are perfectly familiar with this limitation, in affairs of affection and friendship. We never have here that paralysing awe of reason, which haunts us in matters of religion. We never allow ourselves to be bullied into submission to its supremacy. We should laugh at it, if it attempted to dictate to us; or to account for all our motives. Not that we are at war with it: or are shirking it: or are afraid of it. We can have affections and friendships, which have every possible justification which reason can offer. Every conceivable expediency can unite to authorise and approve them. Every interest may be served by them. They may stand every test which a cool common-sense, or a calm impartial judgment, or an acute calculation of consequences can apply to them. They may be the very embodiment of reason. And yet, by no amount of calculated expediencies, by no pressure of rational considerations, could we dream, for one moment, that our friendship was accounted for. If ever it could trace its origin to these motives, it would cease to be what we thought it. The discovery would destroy it. All possible considerations and calculations might have been present, and yet they would be utterly powerless to create in us the love. And the love, however gladly it may recognise the approving considerations, would repudiate, with amazement, and with laughter, any presumption on their part to say, 'this is why you love.'

It is the same with all primal acts of heroism. They may be absolutely rational: yet, they would cease to be heroic, they would never be done, if they did not call upon a force, which, indeed, may determine its direction by reason, but which uses quite other motives to induce itself to act. Utilitarianism, which attempts to account for such heroic momentum by purely rational considerations, finds itself reduced to shifts which all those can see through, who refuse to be juggled out of their own experiences. It is the same with all the higher forms of moral energy. All of them go beyond their evidences. They all lift the rational motives, which suggest and determine the direction of their activity, by an impulsive force, which has in it the power of initiative, of origination. Every high act of will is a new creation. As the gunpowder sleeps, until the spark alights upon it, so the directions of reason remain below the level of action, until the jet of a living will fuses its fire with their material. The act which results may, indeed, be capable of complete interpretation on reasonable grounds: it may be able to show reasons which account for every fragment of it: yet, still, the living force which drew together, and combined all those separate reasons into a single resultant act, has a creative and original character. The series of reasons, however complete, cannot account for the result, for they cannot possibly account for their own combination: and without this combination of their momentum the result would not be there.

It is well to recall briefly this character of the moral will, the affections, the love, of man. For these are faith's nearest and dearest allies. It is here, in these elemental motions, that faith finds its closest parallel. It is something very like an act of will, a movement of love, an heroic and chivalrous moral venture. And whenever we desire to understand its relations to reason, we must persistently recall the attitude towards reason taken by these fundamental forms of energy; only remembering that faith is yet more elemental, yet more completely the act of the central integral self, even than these. Where they leave reason behind, it will do so yet further. Where they call upon something deeper, and more primitive than reason, it will do the same, and yet more triumphantly. It is not that either it or they are without reason : or that they stand outside reason, consulting it so far as they choose, and then dropping it ; it is not that reason may not be found in every corner and fragment of their activity, pervading, colouring, restraining, limiting, directing, justifying it : but simply that what we call the rational self is not only rational, but also something more : that, if analysed out, the reason will not appear as the root and core of the man, but rather as an element inhering in a yet more central base : and that whenever the energy of vital action is put out, we are driven to look through and beyond reason, if we would unearth the source whence the act springs.

The relation, then, of reason to faith is not strange, or forced, or unfamiliar to us, if it is much the same as its relation to the affections, or to moral acts and intuitions. We know what to expect, what part it ought to play in such a case. As in a case of heroic moral daring, or high affection, so, in a matter of faith, we shall expect that reason, with its arguments and its evidences, will play all round and about it, will go before it, discussing the path to follow, will follow after it, unravelling the secret forces at work in it : will watch, and analyse, and learn, and warn ; will reconnoitre, and examine, and survey, and discover : will justify, interpret, defend, assist. But yet we shall expect, also, that the act of faith will do more than all the arguments can anticipate : that it will hold itself free from them all : that it will appeal, not to them, but to its own inherent force, for the final decision : that it will move by instinct, by spontaneity, by inspiration : that it will rush past all evidences, in some great stride ; that it will brush through scruples that cannot be gainsaid, and obstacles that cannot be got over; that it will surprise, that it will outdo, that it will create ; that it will bring novel forces into play, invisible, unaccountable, incalculable ; that it will fly, when reason walks ; that it will laugh, when reason trembles : that it will over-leap barriers which reason deems final. As with love, so with faith, it will take in all evidences, it will listen to all proofs ; but when they have done their utmost, it has yet got to begin ; it itself, after all its calculations, must make the actual spring, which is the decision. Out of itself, it draws its strength : out of itself it makes its effort; by being what it is, it sees what it sees, it does what it does. It uses the evidence ; but uses it to leap from, to go further. Its motives, advances, efforts, issue from within itself. Just as the lover's final answer to the question, 'why did you do that?' must be, 'because I loved'; so the final answer of the believer, in explanation of an act, can never be wrung out of the reasonable grounds for so acting; it must always be 'because I believed.' Just as man first acts, and speaks, and reason, following behind, can at last discover that his actions were all consecutive, and that his language has a perfect grammar ; so faith has always to make its venture, prompted and inspired from within, and only long afterwards can it expect to learn that if it has been true to itself, to its proper promptings, then its action can, by slow and plodding reason, be thoroughly interpreted and justified. Faith is, above all things, anticipatory. The sonship, within, anticipates what the Father has in store for it: by means of affection, by rapid instincts of love, it assumes what it cannot yet verify, it foretells the secrets that lie hidden within the Father's eyes. So anticipating, it makes its venture;—a venture which love alone can understand and justify, though the faithfulness of the eternal and supreme Father ensures that the anticipation shall receive its full verification.

If this be the relation of faith to reason, we see the explanation of what seems, at first sight, to the philosopher, to be the most irritating and hypocritical characteristic of faith. It is always shifting its intellectual defences. It adopts this or that fashion of philosophical apology; and then, when this is shattered by some novel scientific generalisation, faith, probably after a passionate struggle to retain the old position, suddenly and gaily abandons it, and takes up with the new formula, just as if nothing had happened: it discovers that the new formula is admirably adapted for its purposes, and is, in fact, just what it always meant, only it has unfortunately omitted to mention it. So it goes on, again and again; and no wonder that the philosophers growl at those humbugs, the clergy!

But they are criticising faith as if it were a theory, as if knowledge were its province, while, in truth, the seat of faith lies back behind the region of knowledge. Its radical acts and motives are independent of any particular condition of thought or science: they are deeper recessed; they exist in their own right, and under their own conditions. True, they may not be able to express themselves, to get their energies forward, to set themselves free, to manifest themselves, except through the mediation of knowledge,—through the instruments and channels which the science of the day provides them. But this does not confuse their inherent and distinct character. They never identify themselves with the tools they use. They sit quite loose to the particular state of thought, the formula, the terms, through which they make their way out into action. And, moreover, since the acts of faith are more radical than those of reason, and since they belong to the entire man acting in his integrity, they therefore of necessity anticipate, in their degree, all that the man, by slow development, by the patient industry of reasoning, will laboriously disclose. Lying deeper than all knowledge, they hold in them the condition under which all knowledge will be arrived at. They constitute the activity which ought to be at the background of all our reasoning. No particular or partial state of knowledge can exhaust their significance. Each step knowledge makes does but illustrate, in some new fashion, the relation of all knowledge to faith—does but elucidate the characteristics of that primal sonship. In each fresh discovery or generalisation, faith finds a new instrument for expressing its old convictions; it is taught to see the weak points, the imperfections of its former expressions; it understands where they hold good, and where they failed; it gets out more of itself than ever before, through the new channels opened to it; it discovers more of its own character by finding better modes in which to manifest it. It does but half know itself, so long as its expression is encumbered.

The advance of secular knowledge, then, is for faith, an acquired gain: for by it, it knows itself better; it sees more of what was involved in its vital convictions. It has a struggle, no doubt, in dropping off the expressions that have grown familiar to it, and in detecting the fresh insight into its own nature which it can win by the new terminology: but when once it has mastered the terms, new lights break out upon it, new suggestions flash, new capacities disclose themselves. It has won a new tool: when it has become familiarised with the use of it, it can do great and unexpected things with it.

But, for all that, it is but a new tool, worked by the old convictions; they have not changed, any more than love changes, though the slow development of married life may carry the lovers into unknown experiences, in foreign lands, under changed skies. The two, if they be faithful, learn far more of what the love they plighted means, as each sweeping revolution carries them hither and thither, than ever they understood on the wedding day; yet it is ever the old love then pledged, which they hold fast to the end. Its identity is emphasised by the changes. So with faith. It may absorb its energies in the joy of wielding the particular instrument with which, at any one moment, science supplies it. But it will never the least fear to drop it, so soon as the advancing skill and the pushing minds of men have elaborated for it some yet more delicate and subtle tool, wherewith to give free play to its native vitalities.

For faith is moved by but one solitary passion—the hope of cleaving, closer and ever closer, to the being of God. It is, itself, nothing but this act of personal adherence, of personal cohesion; and all else is, for it, material that can be subdued to this single service. Each bettering of knowledge intensifies the possibilities of this cohesion; and, for that, it is welcomed. It opens out fresh aspects of the good Father: it uncovers new treasures of His wisdom: therefore, for faith, it is an ever-mounting ladder, by which it draws nearer and nearer, spirit to spirit, heart to heart. No idle or indifferent matter this; and right knowledge, therefore, is for faith, a serious and pressing need. And, moreover, faith is pledged to use all possible guidance and direction in making its great act of self-surrender to God. And it is the peculiar office of reason, and of the rational conscience, to guard it from any distorted and unworthy venture. Faith has to make its leap; but to make it exactly in that direction, and in no other, where reason points the way. It is bound therefore to use all its intelligent resources: it may not fall below the level of its highest reason without the risk of sinking to a superstition. This is the radical difference between what we here claim, and that which a superstition demands of us. A superstition asks faith to shut its eyes. We ask it to open them as wide as it can. We demand this of it as a positive duty. It is bound, as an act of the whole man, to use every conceivable means and security which knowledge can bring it. For so alone can it secure itself against the hazards which encompass its adventure. It cannot afford to enter on that venturous committal of itself less equipped and instructed than it was open to it to be. It must put all to use that can better its offer of itself to God.

It is, in this seriousness, that faith is apt to embrace so fast the dominant scientific or philosophical creed. It has found, through this creed, a new and thrilling insight into God's mind, and it fastens on this precious gift; and dwells delightedly on it, and spends itself in absorbing the peculiar truths which this particular way of thinking brings to the front. So that, at last, when the smash comes, when the floods break in, when the accumulation of new facts outside the old lines necessitates a total reconstruction of the intellectual fabric, faith seems to have gone under with the ruined scheme to which it had attached itself so firmly.

Yet, if ever it has implicated its own fate with that of any particular form of knowledge, it has been false to itself. It has no more right to identify itself with any intellectual situation than it has to pin its fortunes to those of any political dynasty. Its eternal task lies in rapid readjustment to each fresh situation, which the motion of time may disclose to it. It has that in it which can apply to all, and learn from all. Its identity is not lost, because its expressions vary and shift: for its identity lies deep in personality; and personality is that which testifies to its own identity by the variety and the rapidity of its self-adaptation to the changes of circumstance. So with faith. Its older interpretations of itself are not false, because the newer situations have called for different manifestations. Each situation forces a new aspect to the front. But ever it is God and the soul, which recognise each other under every disguise. Now it is in one fashion and now in another: but it is always one unalterable wisdom which is justified, recognised, and loved, by those who are her children.

We will not, then, be the least afraid of the taunt, that we are all accepting and delivering from our pulpits that which once threw us into anger and dismay. Only let us learn our true lesson; and, in our zeal to appreciate the wonders of Evolution, let us hold ourselves prepared for the day which is bound to come, when again the gathering facts will clamour for a fresh generalisation : and the wheel will give one more turn ; and the new man will catch sight of the vision which is preparing; and the new book will startle ; and the new band of youthful professors will denounce and demolish our present heroes; and all the reviews and magazines will yelp in chorus at their heels, proclaiming loudly that now, at last and for ever, the faith, which has pledged itself so deeply to the obsolete and discredited theory of Evolution, is indeed dead and done with. Faith will survive that crisis, as it has survived so many before : but it will be something, if it does not drag behind it the evil record of passion, and blindness, with which it has too often disgraced its unwilling passage from truth to truth.

IV. But here our objections take, perhaps, a new turn altogether. 'Ah, yes!' it will be said ; 'faith, if it were a simple surrender of the soul to God, a childlike adhesion of the spiritual sonship in us to its Father, Who is in heaven, might sit loose to all formulæ, theories, discoveries, in the way described. Faith, if it limited itself to this mystical communion, might be beyond the scope and criticism of reason. But this is not the least what you really ask of us. The faith, for which you practically plead, the only form of faith actually open to us, has rashly left these safe confines : it has implicated itself with a vast body of facts recorded in a book. It has involved itself in intricate statements of dogma. How can you claim to be free from the control of logic and criticism, in things so directly open to logical treatment ? This spiritual faith of yours has mixed itself up with alien matter, with historical incidents, with intellectual definitions : here are things of evidence and proof. Here its locks are shorn; its mystic strength is gone. Delilah holds it fast ; it is a prisoner in the hands of the Philistines. If you will retreat again back into the region of simple spiritual intuitions, and abandon to reason this debatable land, how gladly would we follow you ! But that is just what you refuse to do.'

Now, here is the serious moment for us of to-day. It is quite true that all would be plain and easy, if we might be allowed to make this retreat—if we might limit our claims for the spirit to that simple childlike intuition which, instinctively, feels after, and surrenders to, the good Father in heaven. But what would that retreat mean ? It would mean an attempt, desperate and blind, to turn back the world's story, to ignore the facts, to over-leap the distinctions of time and place, to deny experience, to force ourselves back into primitive days, to imagine ourselves children again. Simple intuitions of God, simple communion with the Father, unquestioned, undistracted,—this is the privilege of primitive days, when minds are simple, when experience is simple, when society is simple. Plain, easy, and direct situations admit of plain, easy, and direct handling. But our situation is not plain, easy, or direct. Our minds are intricate and complicated; our story has been a long and a difficult one; our social condition is the perplexed deposit of age-long experiences. The faith, which is to be ours to-day, must be a faith of to-day. It cannot remain at the level of childhood, when nothing else in us or about us is the least childlike. It cannot babble out in pretty baby-language, when the situation with which it has to deal is terribly earnest, serious, perilous, and intense. It must be level with its work; and its work is complicated, hard, disciplined : how can it expect to accomplish it without effort, without pain, without training, without intricacy? The world is old; human life is old; and faith is old also. It has had many a strange and stormy experience; it has learned much on the way; it has about it the marks of old troubles; the care, the patience, the completeness of age, have left their stamp upon it. It has had a history, like everything else ; and it reaches us to-day, in a form which that history behind it can alone make intelligible. Four thousand years have gone to its making— since Abraham first laid hold, in a definite and consistent manner, of the faith which is ours to-day. All those centuries it has been putting itself together, growing, enriching itself, developing, as it faced and measured each new issue, each gathering complication, each pressing hazard. This long experience has built up faith's history : and, by study of that history, we can know why it was that faith could not stand still at that point where we should find it so convenient to rest. Faith appeals to its own story to justify its career ; it bears about that history with it as its explanation, why, and how it has arrived at its present condition. That history is its proof how far it has left its first childhood behind it, how impossible it is, at the end of the days, to return to the beginning. The history, which constitutes our difficulty, is its own answer. For there, in that Bible, lies the recorded story of the facts which pressed hard upon the earliest intuition of God, and drove it forward, and compelled it to fix itself, and to define itself, and to take a firmer root, and to make for itself a secure dwelling-place, and to shape for itself a career. The Bible is the apology which our faith carries with it, and offers as a proof of the necessity which has forced it to go beyond its primitive efforts, until it has reached the stage at which we now encounter it. It portrays there, before our eyes, how it all began ; how there came to this man and to that, the simple augury, the presage, the spasm of spiritual insight, the flash, the glimpse, the intimation ; until there came the man, Abraham, in whom it won the emphasis, the solidity, the power, of a call. 'Oh! that we might be content to feel, as he the presence of the Everlasting! Why not leave us in peace, we cry, with the simple faith of Abraham?' And the answer is plain : 'because it is the nineteenth century after Christ, instead of the nineteenth century before.' We are making a mistake of dates. Let us turn to our Bible and read. There we watch the reasons disclosing themselves why that simple faith could not abide in arrest at its first moment; why it must open a new career, with new duties, and new responsibilities, and new problems. The seed is sown, but it has to grow; to make good its footing amid the thick of human affairs; to root itself in the soil of human history; to spread itself out in institutions; to push its dominion; to widen its range; to become a tree that will fill the land. Before Abraham, it was but a flying seed, blown by the winds; now, it is a stable, continuous, masterful growth. It must be this, if it is ever to make effective its spiritual assertions over the increasing intricacy of human affairs.

What, let us ask, is that life of faith which historically began with Abraham? It is a friendship, an intimacy, between man and God, between a son and a father. Such an intimacy cannot be idle or stagnant; it cannot arrest its instinctive development. It holds in it infinite possibilities of growth : of increasing familiarity, of multiplied communion. And, thus, such a friendship creates a story of its own; it has its jars, its frictions, its entanglements; alas! on one side, its lapses, its quarrels, its blunders, its misunderstandings : and then, on the other, its corresponding indignations, and withdrawals, and rebukes; and yet again, its reconciliations, its reactions, its pardons, its victories. Ever it moves forward on its chequered path : ever God, the good Friend, spends Himself in recovering the intimacy, in renewing it, in purging it, in raising it. Its conditions expand : its demands intensify : its perils deepen : its glories gather : until it consummates its effort in the perfected communion of God and man—in Him, Who completes and closes the story of this ever-growing intimacy, by that act of supreme condescension which brings down God to inhabit and possess the heart of man : and by that act of supreme exaltation, which uplifts man into absolute union with the God Who made him.

This is the story : the Bible is its record. As a body of incidents and facts it must be subject to all the conditions of history and the laws of evidence ; as a written record it introduces a swarm of questions, which can be sifted and decided by rational criticism. This entails complications, it must be confessed ; but they are inevitable. The intimacy between man and God cannot advance, except through the pressure of connected and recorded experience. A human society which has no record of its past is robbed of its future. It is savage : it cannot go forward, because it cannot look back. So with this divine friendship. Its recorded experiences are the one condition of its growth. Without them it must always be beginning afresh : it must remain imprisoned at the starting-post. The length and complexity of its record is the measure of its progress ; even though they must present, at the same time, a larger surface to the handling of criticism, and may involve a deeper degree of obscurity in details.

And, after all, though details drawn out of a dead past permit obscurity, the nature and character of the main issue become ever more fixed and distinct, as the long roll of circumstances discloses its richer secrets. The very shift and confusion of the surface-material throws out, in emphatic contrast, the firm outlines of the gathering and growing mystery. Ever the advance proceeds, throwing off all that is accidental, immaterial, subservient : ever man becomes clearer in his recognition of the claims made on him by the hope which God keeps ever before Him, ' They shall be my people: I will be their God.' Ever the necessities of such an intimate affection point to the coming of the Christ. Christ is the end, the sum, the completion, of this historic friendship : and His advent is, therefore, absolutely unintelligible unless it is held in relation to the long experience, which He interprets, justifies, and fulfils. Faith in Christ is the last result, the ultimate and perfected condition of that faith of Abraham, which enabled him to become the first friend of God. And the immense experience that lay between Abraham and St. Paul, can alone bridge the interval, can alone exhibit the slow and laborious evolution, through which the primitive apprehension of God was transformed into the Christian Creed—that mighty transformation, spread out over two thousand years of varied history, which our Lord summed up in the lightning-flash, ' Your father Abraham rejoiced to see my day : and he saw it, and was glad.' The Book is the record of those tested and certified experiments, which justified our Lord in asserting that to believe in God was, necessarily, to believe in Him. No one can understand that assertion, unless by seeing it worked out, in detail, by the searching logic of experience.

Faith in Christ, then, includes faith in the Bible : and, in saying that, we have already cleared away much of the difficulty that beset us. For our faith in Christ becomes the measure and standard of our faith in the Bible. We believe in it as the record of our growing intimacy with God. Faith is, still, a spiritual cohesion of person with person,—of the living soul with a living God. No details that intervene confuse this primitive relation. Only, that cohesion was not reached at one leap. It is ancient : it has traversed many incidents and trials : it has learned much: it has undergone patient apprenticeship: it has been bonded by the memory of multitudinous vicissitudes. Like all else that is human, it has grown. The details of events are the media of that growth. In *that* character they are vitally essential to the formed intimacy : but in that character alone. They are not valued for their own sake ; but for the cause which they served. Belief in God never changes its character, and becomes belief in facts : it only developes into a deeper and deeper belief in God, as disciplined by facts. The facts must be real, if the discipline is to be real : but, apart from this necessity, we are indifferent to them. We can listen to anything which historical criticism has to tell us, of dates and authorship ; of time and place. It may supply all the gaps in our record, showing how the material there briefly gathered, had, itself, a story, and slowly came together, and had sources and associations elsewhere. All such research adds interest to the record, as it opens out to us the action of the Divine Intimacy, in laying hold of its material. We watch it, by the aid of such criticism, at its work of assimilation ; and, in uncovering its principles of selection, we apprehend its inner mind : we draw closer to our God. The more nearly we can ally the early conditions of Israel to those of Arabian nomads, the more delicate and rare becomes our apprehension of that divine relationship, which, by its perpetual pressure, lifted Israel to its marvellous supremacy, and which, by its absence, left the Arabian to be what he is to-day.

The point at which criticism must hold off its hands is, of course, a most subtle matter to decide. But we can, at least, be sure of this— that such a point will be no arbitrary one ; it will be there, where criticism attempts to trench on the reality and the uniqueness of the Divine Intimacy, which those incidents served to fashion, and those books detected and recorded, and Christ consummated. Our faith in Christ must determine what, in the Bible, is vital to its own veracity. There is no other measure or rule of what we mean by inspiration.

The preparation for Christ, then, necessitates such complications as these. And the character of His advent intensified and thickened them. For, while asking of us the purest form of spiritual adherence, He makes that demand in a shape which is imbedded throughout in concrete historical facts, which, as facts, must be subject to the thumb of critical discussion, and to all the external handling of evidence and argument.

And, then, on the top of this, He has, of necessity, raised the question of his own Personality to such a pitch of vital value, that the full force of man's intellectual activities is drawn towards its consideration, —is summoned to contemplate, and measure, and apprehend it,—is compelled to examine and face its tremendous issues. The supreme act of personal surrender, for which Christ unhesitatingly asks, cannot conceivably pass beyond its child-stage without forming a direct and urgent challenge to the intellect to say how, and why, such an act can be justified, or such a claim interpreted. No faith can reach to such an absolute condition without finding itself involved in anxieties, perils, problems, complications. Its very absoluteness is a provocation to the questioning and disputing mind,—to the hesitating and scrupulous will. And the result, the inevitable result, of such a faith—proposed, as it was, to a world no longer young and childlike, but matured, old, thoughtful, experienced—is the Dogmatic Creeds. We clamour against these intellectual complications : we cry out for the simple primitive faith. But, once again, it is a mistake of dates. We cannot ask to be as if eighteen centuries had dropped out, unnoticed— as if the mind had slumbered since the days of Christ, and had never asked a question. We cannot hope to be in the same condition after a question has been asked, as we were before it had ever occurred to us to ask it. The Creeds only record that certain questions have, as a fact, been asked. Could our world be what it is, and not have asked them ? These difficulties of a complicated faith are only the reflection of the difficulties of a complicated life. If, as a fact, we are engaged in living a life which is intricate, subtle, anxious, then any faith which hopes to cover and embrace that life, cannot escape the necessity of being intricate, subtle, and anxious also. No child's creed can satisfy a man's needs, hunger, hopes, anxieties. If we are asked to throw over the complications of our Creeds, we must beg those that ask us, to begin by throwing over the complications of this social and moral life.

But still, with the Creeds as with the Bible, it is the personal intimacy with God in Christ which alone is our concern. We do not, in the strict sense, believe *in* the Bible, or *in* the Creeds : we believe solely and absolutely in Christ Jesus. Faith is our living act of adherence in Him, of cohesion with God. But still, once more, we must recognise that this act of adhesion has a history : it has gradually been trained and perfected : and this has been accomplished through the long and perilous experiences recorded in the Old Testament ; and it has been consummated in the final sealing of the perfected intimacy attained in Him, in Whose person it was realised and made possible for us : and it has been guarded and secured to us in the face of the overwhelming pressure of eighteen strong, stormy, and distracted centuries. And therefore it is that we now must attain our cohesion with God, subject to all the necessities laid upon us by the fact that we enter on the world's stage at a late hour, when the drama has already developed its plot and complicated its situations. This is why we cannot now, in full view of the facts, believe in Christ, without finding that our belief includes the Bible and the Creeds.

V. Faith is, still and always, a spiritual intimacy, a living friendship with God. That is what we must be for ever asserting. That is the key to all our problems ; and once sure of this in all its bearings, we shall not be afraid of a taunt which is apt to sting especially those of us who are ordained. It is conveyed, in its noblest form, in a book of Mr. John Morley's, on Compromise. No one can read that book without being the better or the worse for it. The intense force of high moral convictions acts upon us like a judgment. It evokes the deepest conscience in us to come forward, and stand at that austere bar and justify itself, or, in failing to justify itself, sink condemned. And in that book he asks the old question, with unequalled power : how can it possibly be honest for men to sign away their reason at the age of twenty-three ?—to commit themselves to conclusions which they cannot have mastered—to anticipate beforehand all that experience may have to teach ? In committing themselves to positions which any new knowledge or discovery may reverse, they have forbidden themselves the free use of their critical faculties : they have resigned their intellectual conscience.

What do we answer to that severe arraignment ? Surely we now know well. Faith is an affair of personal intimacy, of friendship, of will, of love : and, in all such cases, we should know exactly what to do with language of this type. We should laugh it out of court. For it is language which does not belong to this region. It is the language, it expresses the temper, of the scientific student—a temper, an attitude specialised for a distinct purpose. That purpose is one of gradual advance into regions as yet untouched and unsuspected—an advance which is for ever changing the relations and classifications of those already partially known. The temper essential to such a purpose must be prepared for discovery, for development, for the unexpected ; it is bound to be tentative, experimental, hypothetical—to be cool, critical, corrective. It deals with impersonal matter ; and it must itself, therefore, be as far as possible impersonal, abstract, non-moral, without passion, without individuality, without a private intention, or will, or fixed opinion.

But such a temper, perfectly justified for scientific purposes, is absolutely impotent and barren in matters of moral feeling and practice.

The man who brings this temper into play in affairs of the will, or the heart, or the imagination, in cases of affection, friendship, passion, inspiration, generosity, in the things of home, of war, of patriotism, of love, is in the wrong world : he is a living blunder : he has no cue, no key, no interpretation. He is simply absurd.

And religion stands with these affairs. Just as we see well enough that if love were approached in this scientific spirit, it could not even begin, so it is quite as certain that, if faith were approached in this spirit, it could not even begin.

Mr. Morley has mixed up two different worlds. He is criticising that form of knowledge, which consists in spiritual apprehension of another's personality through the whole force of a man's inherent, and integral, and personal, will and desire, by the standard of another form of knowledge altogether, which consists in gradual and experimental assimilation of foreign and unknown matter through specialised organs of critical observation.

This latter knowledge is bound to be as far as possible emptied of personal elements. But our knowledge is nothing if not personal : it is the knowledge which issues, and issues only, out of the personal contact of life with life. And this is why it can afford to anticipate the future. For a person is a consistent and integral whole : if you know it at any one point, you know it in a sense at all points. The one character, the one will, disclose themselves through every partial expression, and passing gesture, and varying act. Therefore it is that, when two personalities draw towards one another in the touch of love, they can afford to plight their word. For love is the instinctive prophecy of a future adherence. It is the assurance, passing from soul to soul, that no new discovery of what is involved in their after-life together can ever deny, or defeat, or destroy their present mutual coherence in each other. That adhesion, that adaptability, which has been proved at a few points, will necessarily be justified throughout. The marriage-pledge expresses the absolute conviction that the present experience is irreversible, except by wilful sin. Whatever novelties the years bring with them, those two characters will abide what they are to-day. Growth cannot radically alter them.

Love, then, is this confident anticipation, which takes the future in pledge. And where this anticipation breaks down, it must be through human infirmity, wrong, misunderstanding.

And our knowledge of Christ is this knowledge of love ; wherever it exists, and so far as it exists, it issues out of personal contact, personal inter-action. This is why, in its tested and certified form, i. e. in the accumulated and historic experience of the Catholic community, it can rationally justify its anticipation of an unbroken adherence.

And it can do so with complete confidence, because, here, on the side of Christ, there is no infirmity which can endanger the plighted faith : there is no lapse, no decline possible. Christ must be loyal, for He is sinless. And more : being sinless, He is consistent. Every part of Him is in harmony with the whole : in Him there is no unsteadiness, no insecurity. Such a flawless character is identical with itself : wherever it is touched, it can be tested and approved.

What, then, can upset our trust in Him ? What can disturb our knowledge of Him ? What fear of change can the years bring on ? We may know but a tiny fragment, a fringe of this love of His to us, yet that is enough : to have felt it at all is to trust it for ever. We cannot hesitate to commit ourselves to One Who, if we know Him in any way, is known to be, by inward, personal, inherent necessity, the 'same yesterday, to-day, and for ever.'

Yes !—but still it may be pleaded, that this anticipatory adherence, which might justifiably be given to a person beloved, cannot be pledged to dogmatic definitions. These, at any rate, are matters not of love, but of reason : they must be liable to critical examination, to intellectual revision. It is the pledge given to believe these dogmas in the future, which is such an outrage on intellectual morality.

Now, this protest, forcible and obvious as it looks at first sight, is still guilty of confusing the criticism which belongs to one province of knowledge with that which belongs to another. These dogmas of faith do not the least correspond to the classifications and laws of physical science ; and for this reason, that the matter to which they relate is wholly different in kind. Dogmas represent reason in its application to a personal life : scientific generalisations represent reason as applied to matter, from which the conditions of personality have been rigorously and rightly excluded. The difference is vital ; and it affects the entire character of the working of reason.

The dogmatic definitions of Christian theology can never be divorced from their contact in the personality of Christ. They are statements concerning a living character. As such, and only as such, do they come within the lines of faith. We do not, in the strict sense, believe in them : for belief is never a purely intellectual act ; it is a movement of the living man drawn towards a living person. Belief can only be in Jesus Christ. To Him alone do we ever commit ourselves, surrender ourselves, for ever and aye. But a personality, though its roots lie deeper than reason, yet includes reason within its compass : a personality cannot but be rational, though it be more than merely rational ; it has in it a rational ground, a rational construction ; it could not be what it is without being of such and such a fixed and organic character. And a personality, therefore, is intelligible ; it lays itself open to rational treatment ; its characteristics can be stated in terms of thought. The Will of God is the Word of God ; the Life is also the Light. That which is loved can be apprehended ; that which is felt can be named. So the Personality of the Word admits of being rationally expressed in the sense that reason can name and distinguish those elements in it, which constitute its enduring and essential conditions. The dogmas now in question, are simply careful rehearsals of those inherent necessities which, inevitably, are involved in the rational construction of Christ's living character. They are statements of what He must be, if He is what our hearts assure us ; if He can do that for which our wills tender Him their lifelong self-surrender. Unless these rational conditions stand, then, no act of faith is justifiable; unless His personality correspond to these assertions, we can never be authorised in worshipping Him.

But, if so, then we can commit ourselves to these dogmas in the same way, and degree, as we commit ourselves to Him. We can do so, in the absolute assurance that He cannot but abide for ever, that which we know Him to be to-day. We know Him indeed, but 'in part:' but it is part of a fixed and integral character, which is whole in every part; and can never falsify, in the future, the revelation which it has already made of itself.

The real question, as to Christian dogma, lies in the prior question —Is Christianity justified in claiming to have reached a *final* position? If the position is rightly final, then the intellectual expression of its inherent elements is final also. Here is the deep contrast between it and science. The scientific man is forbidden, by the very nature of his studies, to assume finality for his propositions. For he is not yet in command of his material. Far, very far, from it. He is touching it on its very edge. He is engaged in slowly pushing tentative advances into an unknown world, looming, vast, dim, manifold, beyond his frontier of light. The coherence of his known matter with that huge mass beyond his ken, can be but faintly imaged and suspected. Wholly unreckoned forces are in operation. At any moment he may be called upon to throw over the classification which sums up his hitherto experience; he may have to adopt a new centre; to bring his facts into a novel focus; and this involves at once a novel principle of arrangement. In such conditions dogma is, of course, an absurdity. But, if we are in a position to have any faith in Jesus Christ, then we must suppose that we have arrived at the one centre to all possible experiences, the one focus, under which all sights must fall. To believe in Him at all is to believe that, by and in 'this Man, will God judge the world.' In His personality, in His character, we are in possession of the ultimate principle, under which the final estimate of all things will be taken. We have given us, in His sacrifice and mission, the absolute rule, standard, test, right to the very end. Nothing can fall outside it. In Him, God has summed up creation. We have touched, in Him, the 'last days,' the ultimate stage of all development. We cannot believe in Him at all, and not believe that His message is final.

And it is this finality which justifies dogma. If Christianity is final, it can afford to be dogmatic; and we, who give our adhesion to it, must, in so doing, profess our adhesion to the irreversible nature of its inherent principles: for, in so doing, we are but re-asserting our belief in the absolute and final sufficiency of His person.

Let us venture, now, to review the path that we have travelled, in order that we may see at what point we have arrived. Faith, then, is, from first to last, a spiritual act of the deepest personal will, proceeding out of that central core of the being, where the self is integral and whole, before it has sundered itself off into divided faculties. There, in that root-self, lie the germs of all that appears in the separate qualities and gifts—in feelings, in reason, in imagination, in desire; and faith, the central activity, has in it, therefore, the germs of all these several activities. It has in it that which becomes feeling, yet is not itself a feeling. It has in it that which becomes reason, yet is not itself the reason. It holds in it imaginative elements, yet is no exercise of the imagination. It is alive with that which desires, craves, loves; yet is not itself merely an appetite, a desire, a passion. In all these qualities it has its part: it shares their nature; it has kindred motions; it shows itself, sometimes through the one, and sometimes through the other, according to the varieties of human characters. In this man, it can make the feeling its main instrument and channel; in that man, it will find the intellect its chief minister; in another, it will make its presence known along the track of his innermost craving for a support in will and in love. But it will always remain something over, and beyond, any one of its distinctive media; and not one of these special-ities of gift will ever, therefore, be able to account wholly for the faith which puts it to use. That is why faith must always remain beyond its realised evidences. If it finds, in some cases, its chief evidences in the region of feeling, it is nevertheless open to deadly ruin, if ever it identifies itself with these evidences, as if it could rely on them to carry it through. It may come into being by their help; but it is never genuine faith, until it can abide in self-security at those dry hours, when the evidences of positive feeling have been totally withdrawn. And as with feeling; so with reason. Faith looks to reason for its proofs: it must count on finding them; it offers for itself intellectual justifications. It may arrive at a man by this road. But it is not itself reason; it can never confuse itself with a merely intellectual process. It cannot, therefore, find, in reason, the full grounds for its ultimate convictions. Ever it retains its own inherent character, by which it is constituted an act of personal trust—an act of willing and loving self-surrender to the dominant sway of another's personality. It is always this, whether it springs up instinctively, out of the roots of our being, anticipating all after-proof, or whether it is summoned out into vitality at the close of a long and late argumentative process. No argument, no array of arguments, however long, however massive, can succeed in excusing it from that momentous effort of the inner man, which is its very essence. Let reason do its perfect work: let it heap up witness upon witness, proof upon proof. Still there will come at last the moment when the call to believe will be just the same to the complete and reasonable man as it always is to the simplest child—the call to trust Another with a confidence which reason can justify but can never create. This act, which is faith, must have in it that spirit of venture, which closes with Another's invitation, which yields to Another's call. It must still have in it and about it the character of a vital motion,—of a leap upward, which dares to count on the prompting energies felt astir within it.

Faith cannot transfer its business into other hands to do its work for it. It cannot request reason to take its own place, or achieve its proper results. There is no possibility of devolution here; it cannot delegate its functions to this faculty or to that. It is by forgetting this that so many men are to be found, at the close of many arguments of which they fully acknowledge the convincing force, still hovering on the brink of faith, never quite reaching it, never passing beyond the misery of a prolonged and nerveless suspense. They hang back at the very crisis, because they have hoped that their reasoning powers would, by their own force, have made belief occur. They are like birds on a bough, who should refuse to fly until they have fully known that they can. Their suspense would break and pass, if once they remembered that, to enter the Kingdom of Heaven, they must always be as little children. They must call upon the child within them. At the end, as at the beginning, of all the argumentative work, it is still the temper of a child which they must bring into play. There must still be the energy of self-committal,—the movement of a brave surrender. Once let them turn, enforced by all the pressure of reasonable evidence, to this secret fount of life within the self, and back flows the strength which was theirs long ago, when the inspiration of their innate sonship moved sweetly in them, breeding confidence, secure of itself, undaunted, and unfatigued. That sonship abides in us all, cumbered and clouded though it be by our sin; it abides on and on, fed by the succours of a Father Who can never forget or forsake, and Who is working hitherto to recover and redeem. And while it abides, faith is still possible. For its native motions are the spontaneous outcome of that spiritual kinship which, if once alive and free, impels us towards Him by Whose love we have been begotten. Reason and feeling, proof and argument —these are means and instruments by which we can invoke this sonship into action, and release it from much which fetters and enslaves. But it is the actual upspringing force of the sonship itself, which alone can be the source of belief. And as it is given to all to be sons of God, through the eternal sonship of Christ, therefore it is open to all to count upon possessing the conditions of faith in God.

NOTE.—This essay has, for its sole aim, the reassurance of an existing faith in face of temporary perplexities. It therefore takes faith as a present and possible fact. It assumes man to be a creature who believes. And it tries to show why such belief, if it be there, should not be discouraged by difficulties which belong to the very nature of its original grounds.   For this it recalls the depth and security with which the roots of faith run back into the original constitution of man; which original constitution, however broken, thwarted, maimed, polluted by sin, remains still in us as the sole pledge and ground of our possible redemption in Christ, Who comes to restore the blurred image of God in us, and Who must find in us the radical elements of the supernatural nature which He enters to renew.   To its enduring existence in the heart of man Christ always appeals.   Men are still children of their Father Who is in heaven; and therefore He can demand, as the sole and primal condition of redemption, *Faith*, which is the witness of the unlost sonship.   That faith He still assumes to be possible, by the invitation to man to believe and so be healed.   He makes this invitation just as if it were in man's own power to respond to it without for the moment touching on the necessity which, through the very effort to believe, man will discover for himself—i. e. the necessity of God's gift of the Spirit to make such belief exist.   Such a gift belonged to the original condition of unfallen man, when his *nature* was itself supernaturally endowed with its adequate and sustaining grace.   Such a gift had to be renewed, after the ruin wrought by sin, both by the restoration of the broken sonship within the man through the beloved Son, as well as by the renewal of the evoking and sustaining Spirit that should lift up, from within the inner sonship, its living cry of Abba, Father.   The right to believe, and the power to believe, had both to be re-created.

But all that was so re-created has, for its preliminary ground, the original constitution of man's sinless nature; and, in all our treatment of redemption, we must begin by recalling what it was which Christ entered to restore.   That original condition was the pledge of the recovery which God would bring to pass; and, throughout the interval between fall and rescue, it could anticipate the coming Christ by the faith which rejoiced to see His Day, and saw His Glory, and spake of Him.   Therefore the faith which Christ raises to its new and higher power by concentrating it upon His own Personality, is still, at core, the old faith which was the prophetic witness given, under the conditions of the earlier covenant, by that great army of the Faithful which is marshalled before us by the author of the Epistle to the Hebrews, who most certainly considers it possible and justifiable to emphasise the continuity that holds between the faith of Abraham and the faith of the redeemed.

THE CHRISTIAN DOCTRINE OF GOD.

I. THE object of this essay is not to discuss the so-called 'proofs' of the existence of God, but to shew what the Christian doctrine of God is, and how it has grown to be what it is, out of the antagonisms of earlier days ; and then to ask—What fuller realization of God's revelation of Himself is He giving us through the contradictions and struggles of to-day? If it is true that 'the only ultimate test of reality is persistence, and the only measure of validity among our primitive beliefs the success with which they resist all efforts to change them[1],' it is of first importance to discover what it is which, through all the struggles of past history, the religious nature of man has persistently clung to. Much which was once dear to the religious consciousness, and which seemed at the time to be an integral part of the religious idea, has been given up. A former age abandoned it with regret, and looked forward with gloomy foreboding. A later age looks back with thankfulness, and recognises 'the good Hand of our God' leading us to truer knowledge of Himself.

It would be idle to deny, after all due allowance has been made for the natural tendency to believe that the present is the critical moment, not only for us, but for the world at large, that the crisis of the present day is a very real one, and that the religious view of God is feeling the effects of the change, which is modifying our views of the world and man. When such a fundamental idea is challenged, men are naturally tempted to adopt one of two equally onesided attitudes, to commit themselves either to a policy of unintelligent protest, or to a policy of unconditional surrender. And if the one is needlessly despairing, the other is unwarrantably sanguine. The one asks,—'How much must I give up, of what religion has always been to me, that a little of the old may survive amidst the new?' The other asks,—'How little of the old need I keep, so as not to interfere with the ready acceptance of the new?' The one view is pessimist, the other optimist. Both have their representatives in our day, and each

---

[1] Fiske, *Idea of God*, p. 139, quoting H. Spencer.

party is profoundly conscious of the danger to which the other is exposed. The advocates of the one view, finding themselves 'in a place where two seas meet,' think it safer to ' run the ship aground'; those of the other ' seeing they cannot bear up against the wind ' prefer to ' let her drive.' But if the spirit of the one is merely protestant, the spirit of the other is certainly not catholic.

In contrast with these one-sided views, we propose to approach the question in the full conviction that the revelation of God in Christ is both true and complete, and yet that every new truth which flows in from the side of science, or metaphysics, or the experience of social and political life, is designed in God's providence to make that revelation real, by bringing out its hidden truths. It is in this sense that the Christian revelation of God claims to be both final and progressive ; final, for Christians know but one Christ and do not ' look for another'; progressive, because Christianity claims each new truth as enriching our knowledge of God, and bringing out into greater clearness and distinctness some half-understood fragment of its own teaching. There are, no doubt, always to be found Christians, who are ready to treat new knowledge as the Caliph Omar treated the books in the library of Alexandria,—' they agree with the Koran and are unnecessary, or they disagree with it and must be destroyed.' But an intelligent Christian will not ask, ' Does this new truth agree with or contradict the letter of the Bible ? ' but ' How does it interpret and help us to understand the Bible ?' And so with regard to all truth, whether it comes from the side of science, or history, or criticism, he adopts neither the method of protest nor the method of surrender, but the method of assimilation. In the face of new discoveries, the only question he is anxious to answer is this,—' What old truth will they explain, or enlighten, or make real to us ? What is this new world of life and interest which is awaiting its consecration ? " Truth is an ever-flowing river, into which streams flow in from many sides[1]." What is this new stream which is about to empty itself, as all knowledge must, into the great flood of Divine truth, "that the earth may be filled with the glory of the Lord, as the waters cover the sea"?'

Such a hopeful attitude does not, indeed, imply that the assimilation of the new truths will go on as a matter of course. The Christian knows that the acceptance of truth is a moral, as well as an intellectual, matter, and in the moral world there is no place for *laisser faire*. He expects to be called upon to struggle ; he expects that the struggle will need his utmost effort, moral and intellectual. His work is both to keep and to claim ; to hold fast the faith ' once for all delivered to the saints,' and yet to see in every fragment of truth a real revelation of the mind and will of God. He has no cut and dried answer to

[1] S. Clem. Alex. *Strom.* I. v.

objections; he does not boast that he has no difficulties. But he does claim to look out upon the difficulties of his day, not only fearlessly, but with hope and trust. He knows that Christianity must triumph in the end, but he does not expect all difficulties to be removed in a moment. And he is strong enough, if need be, to wait.

II. Whether anyone is really guilty of what Hume calls the 'multiplied indiscretion and imprudence' of dogmatic atheism, whether positivism can rightly be so classed, whether agnosticism is not atheism to all intents and purposes, are questions which fortunately lie outside the scope of the present enquiry. As for polytheism it has ceased to exist in the civilised world. Every theist is, by a rational necessity, a monotheist. But we find ourselves, in the present day, face to face with two different views of God, which though they constantly, perhaps generally, overlap, and even sometimes coincide, yet imply different points of view, and by a process of abstraction can be held apart and contrasted with one another. Many devout Christians are philosophers and men of science; many men of science and philosophers are devout Christians. But the God of religion is not the God of science and philosophy. Ideally, everyone will allow that the religious idea of God, and the scientific and philosophical idea of God must be identical, but in actual fact it is not so, and in the earlier stages of the development of both, there is a real antagonism. To accept this antagonism as absolute is, by a necessary consequence, to compel one to give way to the other. We cannot long hold two contradictory truths. We find ourselves compelled to choose. We may have Religion or Philosophy, but not both.

Very few, however, are prepared to go this length. It is much more usual to get rid of the antagonism by adopting one of two alternative methods.

(1) Of these the first is a suggested division of territory, in which religion is allotted to faith, and philosophy and science to reason. Such an expedient, though not uncommonly, and perhaps even wisely, adopted by individuals, who refuse to give up either of two truths because they cannot harmonize them, becomes ridiculous when seriously proposed as a solution of the difficulty. Moreover the proposed division of territory is unfair to start with. 'Give us the Knowable, and you shall have the rest, which is far the larger half,' sounds like a liberal offer made by science to religion, till we remember that every advance in knowledge transfers something from the side of the unknown to the side of the known, in violation of the original agreement. Mr. Herbert Spencer calls this division of territory a 'reconciliation[1].' But if anything in the world

[1] Cf. Herbert Spencer, *First Principles*, Pt. I.

could make religion hate and fear science and oppose the advance of knowledge, it is to find itself compelled to sit still and watch the slow but sure filching away of its territory by an alien power. We say nothing here of the fact that Mr. Herbert Spencer's division ignores the truth that knowledge of correlatives must be of the same kind[1], and that if knowledge has to do with one and faith with the other, either faith must be a sort of knowledge, or knowledge a sort of faith. We merely notice the unfairness of a division which assumes rationality for science, and leaves irrationality to religion.

Curiously enough, however, there are many devout people, who would be horrified at the thought that they had borrowed from Agnosticism, and who have nevertheless made a similar division of territory. They are the people who stake all upon what reason cannot do. They have no interest in the progress of knowledge. The present gaps in science are their stronghold, and they naturally resist every forward step in knowledge as long as they can, because each new discovery limits the area in which alone, according to their imperfect view, faith can live. Every triumph of science on this theory, as on Mr. Herbert Spencer's, becomes a loss, not a gain, to religion. The very existence of God is bound up with that part of His work in nature which we cannot understand, and, as a consequence, we reach the paradox that the more we know of His working, the less proof we have that He exists. Modern apologetic literature abounds in this kind of argument. It is the devout form of the worship of the unknowable. Yet it is no wonder that people who take refuge in gaps find themselves awkwardly placed when the gaps begin to close.

(2) The other alternative is even more commonly adopted, for it fits in well with the vagueness and want of precision in language, which is at a premium in dealing with religious questions. This consists in frittering away the meaning of definite terms till they are available for anything, or adopting a neutral term which, by a little management and stretching, will include opposites. This is the method of indefinite inclusion. The strength of the former alternative lay in the appearance of sharp scientific delimitation of territory : the strength of the latter in its unlimited comprehensiveness. A term is gradually stripped of the associations which make it what it is, it is 'defecated to a pure transparency,' and then it is ready for use. The term 'God' is made merely 'a synonym for nature[2]'; religion becomes 'habitual and permanent admiration[3],' or 'devout submission of the heart and will to the laws of nature[4]'; enthusiasm does duty

[1] See this criticism excellently stated in Caird's *Phil. of Religion*, pp. 32, etc.
[2] *Natural Religion*, iii. p. 45, quoted by Martineau.
[3] Ibid., iv. p. 74.
[4] Frederic Harrison's *New Year's Address*, 1884.

for worship, and the antagonism between religion and anything else disappears.

Now so far as this represents, negatively, a reaction against intolerance and narrowness, and positively a desire for unity, there is not a word to be said against it. Its tone and temper may be both Christian and Catholic. But the method is a radically false one. It is not a real, but only an abstract, unity which can be reached by thinking away of differences. As Dr. Martineau says, in his excellent criticism of this method, 'You vainly propose an *eirenicon* by corruption of a word.' 'The disputes between science and faith can no more be closed by inventing "religions of culture" than the boundary quarrels of nations by setting up neutral provinces in the air[1].' 'A God that is merely nature, a Theism without God, a Religion forfeited only by the "nil admirari" can never reconcile the secular and the devout, the Pagan and the Christian mind[2].' As well might we attempt to reconcile the partizans of the gold and silver shields by assuring them that in reality the shields were silver gilt.

We are left, then, face to face with the opposition between the religious and the philosophic or scientific view of God. The counter-charges of superstition and anthropomorphism on the one side, and of pantheism and rationalism on the other, serve to bring out the antithesis of the two views. No division of territory is possible. There may be many sciences, each with its defined range of subject-matter; but there can be only one God. And both religion and philosophy demand that He shall fill the whole region of thought and feeling. Nor can any confusion or extension of terms help us to a reconciliation, or blind us long to the true issue. The conflict is too real and too keenly felt to admit of any patched-up peace. The idea of God, which is to claim alike the allegiance of religion and philosophy, must not be the result of compromise, but must really and fully satisfy the demands of both.

III. What then are these demands considered in abstraction from one another? We are at once met by the difficulty of defining religion. But if we cannot define religion, or trace it back to its hidden source, we can at least discover its characteristics, as we know it after it has emerged from the obscurity of prehistoric times, and before any conscious attempt has been made to reconcile religion and philosophy, or find a middle term between them.

Now traditional definitions of religion, given as it were from within, and constructed with no view of opposition to, or reconciliation with, philosophy, are agreed in representing religion as a relation between man and the object or objects of his worship, and this implies, not only the inferiority of the worshipper to that which he worships, but

---

[1] *A Study of Religion*, vol. i. pp. 11, 12.　　　　　[2] Ibid., p. 15.

also something of likeness between the related terms, since, as even Strauss allows, in our inmost nature we feel a kinship between ourselves and that on which we depend[1]. It is quite indifferent which of the rival etymologies of the word 'religion' we adopt[2]. S. Augustine[3], following Lactantius, speaks of religion as 'the bond which binds us to One Omnipotent God.' S. Thomas[4] adopts almost unchanged the definition given by Cicero : it is 'that virtue which has to do with the worship of a higher nature known as the Divine.' It is not too much to say that, for the modern religious world, religion implies at least the practical belief in a real and conscious relation between the inner life of man and an unseen Being. And whatever of mystery there may be about that unseen Being, it would seem as if a real relationship demands so much of likeness in the related terms, as is implied in personality.

It is here that we reach the point at which we are able to distinguish between the religious and the philosophical ideas of God. It is not that religion and philosophy necessarily contradict or exclude one another, but that they approach the problem with different interests. Religion demands a personal object, be that object one or many. It is committed to the belief in a moral relationship between God and man. Philosophy demands unity whether personal or impersonal. For philosophy is nothing if it does not completely unify knowledge. And it seems as if each finds lacking in the other that which it values most and thinks of first. The only hope, then, of reconciliation is in the idea of God as personal, and yet one. So long as religion retains a trace of polytheism or dualism, philosophy can have nothing to say to it. So long as philosophy has no room for a personal God, religion must exclude philosophy. The whole issue of the controversy lies here. If the belief in a personal God is to be called anthropomorphism, religion is hopelessly anthropomorphic. With the disappearance of anthropomorphism in this sense, as Professor Fiske rightly sees[5], religion disappears. But we cannot escape anthropomorphism, though our anthropomorphism may be crude or critical[6]. We do not read our full selves into the lower world, because we are higher than it ; we do not transfer to God all that belongs to our own self-consciousness, because we know that He is infinitely greater than we are. But we should be wrong not to interpret Him by the highest category within our reach, and think of Him as self-conscious life. Christianity

---

[1] *Old Faith and New,* § 41.

[2] 'Hoc vinculo pietatis obstricti Deo et religati sumus, unde ipsa religio nomen accepit, non ut Cicero interpretatus est, a relegendo,' Lact. *Inst.* iv. 28.

[3] *De verâ religione,* sub fin.

[4] *Sum. Theol.* 2. 2. 81. Art. 1.

[5] *Idea of God,* p. 117.

[6] See Seth's *Hegelianism and Personality,* pp. 223, 224, one or two sentences from which are, almost verbatim, transferred to the text.

refuses to call this anthropomorphism, though it stands or falls with the belief that, in his personality, man is in the image of God. An anthropomorphic view of God for a Christian means heathenism or heresy: a theomorphic view of man is of the essence of his faith [1].

The religious idea of God may, of course, become philosophical without ceasing to be religious. If there is to be a religion for man as a rational being it must become so. But there is a point beyond which, in its desire to include philosophy, religion cannot go. It cannot afford to give up its primary assumption of a moral relationship between God and man. When that point is surrendered or obscured the old religious terms become increasingly inapplicable, and we find ourselves falling back more and more on their supposed philosophical equivalents, the 'Infinite' or the 'Absolute,' or the Universal Substance, or the Eternal Consciousness, or the First Cause, or the Omnipresent Energy. But these terms, which metaphysicians rightly claim, have no meaning for the religious consciousness, while, in metaphysics proper 'God' is as much a borrowed term as 'sin' is in non-religious ethics. Moral evil is 'sin' only to those who believe in God; and the infinite is only 'God' to those in whom it suggests a superhuman personality with whom they are in conscious relation. Even when religion and philosophy both agree to speak of God as 'the Infinite,' for the one it is an adjective, for the other a substantive. The moment we abandon the idea of God as personal, religion becomes merged in philosophy, and all that properly constitutes religion disappears. God may exist for us still as the keystone in the arch of knowledge, but He is no longer, except as a metaphor, 'our Father, which is in heaven.'

IV. Religion then, properly and strictly, and apart from extensions of the term made in the interests of a reconciliation, assumes a moral relationship, the relationship of personal beings, as existing between man and the Object of his worship. When this ceases, religion ceases: when this begins, religion begins. But of the beginnings of religion we know nothing. Prehistoric history is the monopoly of those who have a theory to defend. But we may take it as proven that it is at least as true that man is a religious, as that he is a rational, animal. 'Look out for a people,' says Hume, 'entirely destitute of religion. If you find them at all, be assured that they are but few degrees removed from brutes [2].' Hume's statement is confirmed by the fact that those who would prove that there is no innate consciousness of Deity are driven to appeal to the case of deaf mutes

---

[1] Justin Martyr (*Exhort. ad Graec.*, ch. xxxiv) explains the anthropomorphisms of polytheism as an inversion of the truth that man is in the image of God.

[2] Hume, *Essays*, II. 425.

and degraded savages [1]. Whether monotheism was a discovery or a recovery, whether it rose on the ruins of polytheism, or whether polytheism is a corruption of a purer faith, is a question we need not attempt to settle. Nor need we decide the priority of claim to the title of religion as between nature-worship, or ancestor-worship, or ghost-worship. The farther we go back in history the more obviously true is the charge of anthropomorphism so commonly brought against religion. The natural tendency to treat the object of religion as personal exists long before any attempt is made to define the conditions or meaning of personality, and includes much which is afterwards abandoned. For religion in its earliest stages is instinctive, not reasoned. It is 'naively objective.' It is little careful to clear up its idea of the nature and character of its God. It is still less anxious to prove His existence. It is only when conscience grows strong, and dares to challenge the religion which had been instinctively accepted, that men learn to see that God not only is, but must be, the expression of the highest known morality. It is only when the light of conscious reason is turned back upon religious ideas, that polytheism becomes not merely untrue, but impossible and inconceivable. What religion starts with is not any theory of the world, but an unreasoned belief in a Being or beings, however conceived of, who shall be in a greater or less degree like the worshipper, but raised above him by the addition of power, if not omnipotence ; greatness, if not infinity ; wisdom, if not omniscience.

But, while implying from the first something of a moral relationship between man and the object of his worship, religion does not always conceive of that Object as necessarily holy or perfectly wise. There are religions which are both immoral and childish. They have in them no principle of growth, and therefore they are the opponents alike of moral and intellectual progress. *Tantum relligio potuit suadere malorum* is the reflexion of Christian apologists, as well as of the Roman poet, on the religions of heathenism. Hence, it is argued, 'Religion is the enemy of morals and of science. Away with it. It is a mere matter of feeling, which cannot and ought not to stand before the imperious challenge of conscience and reason.' Such a view has both truth and falsehood in it. The religious idea of God must be able to justify itself to our moral and to our rational nature, on pain of ceasing to exist. But religion cannot be thus shut up to one part of our nature, nor can one part of our nature be set against the rest. There is, as Herbert Spencer is fond of pointing out [2], a kind of idolatry of reason in the present day. Reason has exposed many superstitions only to become itself the final object of super-

---

[1] H. Spencer, *Eccl. Inst.*, p. 1.   [2] *Psych.* vol. ii. §§ 388–391.

stition. Men forget that, after all, reasoning is only 're-coordinating states of consciousness already coordinated in certain simpler ways,' and that that which is unreasoned is not always irrational. Rationality in man is not shut up in one air-tight compartment. 'There is no feeling or volition which does not contain in it an element of knowledge[1].' This is the truth which Hegel has seized when he speaks of religion as 'reason talking naively.' You can no more shut up faith to the compartment of feeling than reason to the compartment of the intellect. Religion claims the whole man, and true religion is that which can make good its claim.

The natural history of religion, then, is the history of the process by which that which has its secret birthplace behind all the distinctions of modern psychology, establishes its claim on man, absorbing into itself all that is best and truest in his moral and intellectual being, as conscience and reason successively emerge into conscious activity: while, from another point of view, it is the progressive purification of the religious idea of God till He is revealed as, what He is to a thinking Christian of to-day, the Object of reverent worship, the moral ideal, the truth of nature and of man.

Such an end is not attained in a moment. It is the result of a process with which we are familiar elsewhere, viz. evolution by antagonism. The true has to be separated from the false. Immoral and irrational conceptions of God have to be thrown aside. It is only after what looks like an internecine struggle between religion and morality that man learns the truth about the character of God, and only after a conflict with philosophy and science, which seems to threaten the very life of religion, that he learns what can be known of the Divine Nature. For among religions, too, there is a struggle for existence, in which the fittest survive. And the test of fitness is the power to assimilate and promote moral and intellectual truth, and so to satisfy the whole man. An ideally perfect religion is not 'morality touched by emotion,' but a worship which reflects itself in the highest known morality, and is interpreted and justified to itself by reason. It is this process, as we know it in history, that we proceed to examine.

V. The statement that religion, even in its most elementary forms, takes for granted some relationship of likeness between the worshipper and the Object or objects of his worship, by no means implies that all religion associates the highest morality with its idea of God. On the contrary, we know that not only are there immoral religions, but that immorality sometimes lingers on in religion long after it is condemned elsewhere, and that a people will permit as a religious duty what,

---

[1] Caird, *Philosophy of Religion*, p. 162.

E

according to their thinking, nothing but religion would justify. We cannot, then, at all accurately gauge the moral condition of a people by the received teaching about its gods, for morality is often far in advance of religion, and the character which in a god or goddess is protected by a religious halo is looked upon as hateful or impure in man or woman. The sense of dependence, which, though it does not constitute the whole, is yet an essential element in the religious consciousness, the awe which, in a low state of development, shews itself in a grovelling fear of the invisible beings, makes it impossible for the worshipper to judge his god by the standard he applies to his fellow man. The god may be lustful, but his lusts must be respected; he is strong and vengeful and must by all means be kept in a good temper, cajoled, or outwitted, or bribed, or humoured. His commands must be obeyed, without question or resistance. But by and bye the moral nature learns its strength, and begins to assert its independent right to speak. Morality outgrows religion. The relations between religion and morals become more strained. Some heretic dares to say that the Gods are immoral; that they are men 'writ large,' and bad men too. Their claim to reverence is challenged. There is a moral awakening. Soon the old religion is treated with scorn and contempt, and either a new religion takes its place, coming in as it were on the crest of the wave of moral reformation, or the old religion is purified and becomes the foster-mother of the new morality, giving to it a divine sanction, and receiving from it in turn new strength and vitality. Or failing these, men abandon religion in the supposed interest of morals. A religion with mysteries may be tolerated, but a religion once seen to be immoral is at an end. For a time ethics, with a background of metaphysics or politics, prevails, but gradually it tends to drift into a mere prudentialism, while a merely mystical philosophy tries in vain to satisfy those deeper instincts which reach out to the unseen.

In the history of Greek thought the collision came in the days of Xenophanes. Long before what is sometimes called the era of conscious morality, Greece had outgrown its traditional religion. Greek philosophy at its birth was mythology rationalized, and the beginning of independent morality in Greece shewed itself in a criticism of the religious teaching of Homer and Hesiod. The scathing satire of Xenophanes reminds us at times of the way in which Isaiah speaks of the idolatry of his day. It is not only wrong, it is capable of a *reductio ad absurdum.* Anthropomorphism, immorality, childish folly—these are the charges which Xenophanes brings against the worship of Magna Graecia. Anaxagoras had already been banished for suggesting that the god Helios was a mass of molten iron, but Xenophanes turns into open ridicule the religion of his day.

'Homer and Hesiod,' he says, 'ascribe to the gods all that among men is held shameful and blameworthy, theft, adultery, and deceit [1].'

'One God there is mightiest among gods and men, who neither in form nor thought is like to men. Yet mortals think the gods are born and have shape and voice and raiment like themselves. Surely if lions and cows had hands, and could grave with their hands and do as men do, they too would make gods like themselves, horses would have horse-like gods, and cows gods with horns and hoofs [2].'

When the age of moral philosophy begins, amidst the unsettlement of the sophistic period, the same protest is taken up by Plato. In Xenophanes the protest of the reason and the conscience went together. In Plato the criticism of the received theology is more distinctly a moral criticism. God cannot lie or deceive. He cannot be the cause of evil. He is good, and only the source of good. He is true in word and deed. If not, we cannot reverence Him. It cannot be true that the gods give way to violent emotions, still less to sensuality and envy and strife [3]. 'For God cannot be unrighteous, He must be perfectly righteous, and none is like Him save the most righteous among men [4].'

Here we have a collision between an immoral religious conception of God and a morality which is becoming conscious of its own strength. And what was the result ? Religion in Greece received its death blow. It had no real recuperative power. It could not absorb and claim the new morality. Homer and Hesiod, the 'Bible' of the Athenian, were too profoundly immoral. A Kephalus might go back in silent protest to his sacrifice, but the youth of Athens turned from religion to morality. When we pass from Plato to Aristotle, the last trace of religion in morals has disappeared. Theology has become Metaphysics, and has no place in the world of practical life. The religious element has disappeared from philosophy, and is only revived in the mysticism of Neo-Pythagoreanism and Neo-Platonism. In metaphysics and science we owe everything to the Greeks; in religion, as distinguished from theology, we owe nothing.

From the Greeks we turn to the Jews, to whom alone, among the nations of the pre-Christian age, we of the modern world trace back our religious lineage. We speak of the religion of the Old Testament as 'revealed' in contrast with all other pre-Christian religions. Is that distinction tenable ? If so, what does it mean, and what justifies us in making it ? It is clear that the answer must be sought in what the Old Testament revelation is, rather than in the process by which the Jews became the appointed depositaries of it. For whatever were

---

[1] Ritter and Preller, *Hist. Phil. Graec.*, 7th ed. § 82.
[2] Ibid., § 83.
[3] Plat. *Rep.* 377-385.
[4] *Theæt.* 176 C.

the prehistoric elements out of which the religion of Israel came, whether Assyrian or Accadian or Indo-German or Egyptian, and whatever were the steps by which Israel was led [1] to that doctrine of God which constituted its mission and its message to the world, as we look back from the point of view of Christianity we see that the religion of Israel stands to the teaching of Christ in a relation in which no Pagan religion stands [2]. The Law and the Prophets were for all the world 'a sacred school of the knowledge of God, and the ordering of the soul [3].' If it is true that the Bible only records the later and more important stages in a process which began in prehistoric times amidst the various forms of polytheistic worship, even if it could be shewn that the history, as we have it, has been subjected to successive revisions, that its laws have been codified, its ritual elaborated, its symbolism interpreted, it would still remain true that the religion of Israel, which begins where its history begins, and of which, indeed, its history is little more than the vehicle, is bound up with the assertion of Monotheism. The central fact of its revelation is this, 'Hear, O Israel, the Lord our God is One Lord.' The central utterance of its law is, 'Thou shalt have none other gods but Me.' The unity of God, that truth which other religions were feeling after and tending towards, stands out clearly and distinctly as the characteristic of the religion of Israel, and is fearlessly claimed as an inheritance from the patriarchal age.

And not less remarkable than the assertion of the unity of God is the assumption that this One God is a God of Righteousness. He is 'a God of truth and without iniquity; just and right is He.' Here, again, it was not that the religion of Israel asserted what other religions denied, but that Israel proclaimed clearly and with increasing certainty a truth which the highest contemporary religions were struggling to express. In the religion of Israel the pre-Christian world rose to articulate religious utterance. Its highest and truest intuitions found a voice. Israel had yet much to learn and much to unlearn as to what true morality is. It had anthropomorphisms of thought and language to get rid of. It had to rise in Psalmist and

---

[1] H. Spencer, of course, follows Kuenen in assuming a polytheistic origin of Hebrew monotheism. See Kuenen, *Religion of Israel*, i. 223.

[2] It is strange that Mr. Darwin should have failed to see that this was the answer to his difficulty. It appeared to him, he tells us (*Autobiography*, p. 308), 'utterly incredible that if God were now to make a revelation to the Hindoos, he would permit it to be connected with the belief in Vishnu, Siva, &c., as Christianity is connected

with the Old Testament.' Incredible, no doubt. But why? For the very reason which makes it 'incredible' that man should be evolved directly from a fish, as Anaximander is said to have taught, and not incredible that he should be evolved, as Darwin teaches, from one of the higher vertebrates. The very idea of development, whether in species, or religions, implies a law, and order in the development.

[3] S. Athan. *De Incarn.* c. xii.

Prophet to moral heights unknown to the patriarchal age. But the remarkable thing is that the claim is made. Morality is claimed for God : God is declared to be irrevocably on the side of what man knows as righteousness. And this truth is proclaimed not as a discovery but as a revelation from God Himself. It was this, not less than the proclamation of monotheism, which made the teaching of the Old Testament what it was. It consciously transformed the natural law of 'might is right' into the moral truth that ' right is might.'

And the consequences of this new departure in the religious history of man were far-reaching. It made the difference between the religion of Israel and all other religions a difference not merely of degree but of kind. The worship of the Lord and the worship of the heathen gods becomes not only a conflict between the true and the false in religion, but between the moral and the immoral in practice. More than this, it changes the mere emotional feeling of awe and dependence on invisible powers into trust and confidence. If God is irrevocably on the side of right, the nation or the individual, that is struggling for the right, is fighting on the side of God. It was this which made the great Hebrew leaders, and the Psalmists after them, take it for granted that their cause was the cause of God, and that the Lord of Hosts was with them. Even the wars of extermination were the expression in act of the utter antagonism between good and evil, the cause of God and that of His enemies. And when Saul spared Agag it was from no excess of charity, no glimpse of a higher morality ; it was an act of moral weakness. Finally, this claim of morality for God precluded the possibility of such a collision as took place in the history of the Greeks. The progressive development of morals in the Old Testament, and the gradual unfolding of a perfect character [1] was also for Israel a progressive revelation of the character of God. Step by step the religious idea advanced with moral progress. And, as they advance, the contrast with other religions becomes more marked. ' It was the final distinction between Polytheism and the religion of Israel that the former emphasized power, the latter the moral element to which it subordinated and conjoined power [2].' And this moral conception of God was constantly kept before the people. If they lapse into idolatry and adopt heathen practices and heathen ideas of God, the prophets are ready with the warning that God is the God of Israel, only because Israel is a chosen people to bear His name and His truth before the world ; and if they are false to their mission, they will be rejected. If, again, the sacrificial system loses its moral significance as the recognition of the holiness of God and the sinfulness of the sinner, and the forward-pointing look towards the great

---

[1] It is needless to say that this section is largely indebted to Dean Church's *Discipline of the Christian Character.* [2] *Edinb. Rev.*, Apr. 1888, p. 512.

moral fact of the Atonement, and becomes merely ritual, and per-functory, and formal, the prophets dare to denounce even the divinely ordered sacrifices as things which God hates.

Yet it was not that, in the religion of Israel, morality was made the essential thing, a nucleus of morals, as it were, with a halo of religious emotion round it. It was that the religious and the moral conscious-ness are brought together in a real unity. To love the Lord is to hate evil. God is One who gives His blessing to the righteous, while the ungodly and him that delighteth in wickedness doth His soul abhor. He, then, who would ascend into the hill of the Lord and stand in His holy place, must have clean hands, and a pure heart, and a lowly mind. The Lord God is holy. He has no pleasure in wickedness, neither shall any evil dwell with Him. Righteousness and judgment are the habitation of His seat. The sacrifice that He loves is the sacrifice of righteousness. He is to be worshipped in the beauty of holiness. What he requires of man is that he shall do justly, and love mercy, and walk humbly with his God.

All this, which comes out no doubt with increasing clearness in the Psalms and Prophets, is already implicit in that earlier claim made by the religion of Israel, that the true God is on the side of righteousness, and that to be false to righteousness is to be a traitor to God. In this union of religion and morality neither is sacrificed to the other. Each gains from its union with the other. The religious idea of God, and the religious emotions which gather round it, are progressively purified with the growth of moral ideas; and morality receives new life and strength when the moral law is seen to be the unfolding of the character of a Righteous God, and moral evil is known as 'sin' against a Personal Being. The earnest moral protest which in Greece was directed against the national religion, is found in the Old Testament making common cause with the national religion against the immoral beliefs of heathenism. Hence the Jew was not called upon, as the Greek was, to choose between his religion and his conscience. He never felt the strain which men feel in the present day, when a high and pure morality seems ranged against religious faith. For the Jew every advance in moral insight purified, while it justified, that idea of God, which he believed had come down to him from the 'Father of the Faithful.' His hope of immortality, his faith in the ultimate triumph of the God of Israel, were alike based upon the conviction that God is a God of justice and mercy, and that the Righteous One could not fail His people, or suffer His holy One to see corruption. Even though with the growth of morality, and the fuller unfolding of the character of God, there came, like a shadow cast by light, the deepening consciousness of sin as the barrier between man and God, the Jew refused to believe that the separation was for ever. Sin was a disease which needed healing, a bondage which called for a deliverer, a state of indebtedness from which man could not free himself. But Israel believed in and looked forward to, with confidence and hope, the Redeemer who should come to Zion and save His people from their sins.

The final revelation of Christianity came outwardly as a continuation and development of the religion of Israel, and claimed to be the fulfilment of Israel's hope. It was a 'republication' of the highest truth about God which had been realized hitherto. For it came 'not to destroy but to fulfil.' God is still the Eternally One, the Eternally Righteous. Not sacrifice but holiness, not external 'works' but inward 'faith,' not the deeds of the law, but the righteousness which is of God—this is what He requires. He is still the God of Israel. But Israel according to the flesh had ceased to be the Israel of God, and the children of faithful Abraham, in whom, according to the ancient promise, all the families of the earth should be blessed, are to be gathered from east and west and north and south, from circumcised and uncircumcised, barbarian, Scythian, bond or free, and recognised as one family under the one Father. If Christianity had been this and this only, Christ might have claimed to be a great prophet, breaking the silence of 400 years, restoring the ancient faith, and truly interpreting and carrying forward the spirit of the ancient revelation. But He claimed to be more than this. He claimed, as the Son of God, to be not only the true, but the only, Revealer of the Father. For 'no man knoweth the Father but the Son, and he to whom the Son shall reveal Him.' What fresh characteristics, then, has this new revelation to add to the Old Testament teaching about God? He is still One, the only God. He is perfect Righteousness, yet, as even the older religion knew, a God of loving-kindness and tender mercy, 'Who wills not the death of the sinner.' But more than all this, He is now revealed to man as Infinite Love, the One Father of humanity, Whose only begotten Son is Incarnate and 'made man that we may be made God.' Not one jot or tittle of the old revelation of God, as a God of Righteousness, is lost or cancelled. The moral teaching is stern and uncompromising as ever. God's love, which is Himself, is not the invertebrate amiability, or weak good-naturedness, to which some would reduce it. 'The highest righteousness of the Old Testament is raised to the completeness of the Sermon on the Mount[1].' 'The New Testament,' it has been said, 'with all its glad tidings of mercy, is a severe book[2].' For the goodness and the severity of God are, as it were, the convex and the concave in His moral nature. But what seized upon the imagination of mankind as the distinctive revelation of Christianity was the infinite love and

[1] *Discipline of the Christian Character*, p. 85.   [2] Ibid., p. 87.

tenderness and compassion of this Righteous God for sinful man. It was this which shone out in the character of Christ. He was Very God, with a Divine hatred of evil, yet living as man among men, revealing the true idea of God, and not only realizing in His human life the moral ideal of man, but by taking human nature into Himself setting loose a power of moral regeneration, of which the world had never dreamed.

The advance which the Gospel of Christ makes upon the Old Testament revelation consists then, not only in the new truth it teaches as to the character of God, but in the new relation which it establishes between God and man. So soon as men learn the Old Testament truth that God is eternally on the side of righteousness, the awe and cringing fear, which lies behind heathen religions, and justifies us in calling them superstitions, gives place to trustful confidence, which deepens into faith, and gathers round it those affections and desires for union with God which find expression in the book of Psalms. The saints of the Old Testament could 'rest in the Lord' and wait for the vindication of His Righteousness in human life ; they could yearn for His presence and hope for the day when they should 'see the King in His beauty.' But they were yet separated from Him by the unobliterated fact of sin. Enoch 'walked with God,' Abraham was called 'the friend of God,' Moses 'the Lord knew face to face,' David was 'a man after God's own heart,' Daniel 'a man greatly beloved.' But one and all of these fell short, and necessarily fell short, of the closeness of that union which is the Christian's birthright. In the Gospel, God is revealed as one with man. And this truth changed the whole attitude and atmosphere of worship. There was worship still, for humanity was not merged and lost in Godhead. There is no Christian ring about the statement [1] that 'in Christianity, in the consciousness that he is partaker of the Divine existence, man no longer sustains the relation of Dependence but of Love.' Rather the antithesis between dependence and freedom is destroyed. As perfect love casts out fear, yet leaves reverence, so the consciousness of union with God, as distinct from absorption in Him, while it destroys the last remnant of what is servile and degrading in religious emotion, and gives man freedom, yet gives the freedom of loving dependence upon God. And by this gift it sets free new affections and appeals to new motives. It was the assured consciousness of union with God which gave the first Christians their power in the great moral struggles of their day. Their moral ideal with its loftiness, its purity, its perfect truthfulness, would by its very perfectness have paralyzed effort, had they not believed that they were one with Him Who had not only proclaimed but realized it, that they could do all things

---

[1] Hegel, *Phil. of Hist.*, p. 247, Eng. Tr.

through Christ which strengthened them. And the horror of sin, which was a characteristic note of Christian ethics, was due to the same fact. Unrighteousness, not only as under the Old Testament, ranged a man on the side of the enemies of God, but according to its degree tended to break the supernatural bond which through the Incarnation united men with God. Impurity, which meant so little for the civilized world of the first Christian centuries, was for the Christian not defilement only, but sacrilege, for his body was God's temple. The love of the world was enmity against God, yet the neglect of social duties, and of all that is now summed up in the 'service of man,' was for the Christian *ipso facto* the declaring himself outside the love of God, just as, conversely, the love of the brethren was the proof that he had 'passed from death unto life.'

Thus in primitive Christianity the religious and the moral consciousness were at one, as in the Old Testament, but both are now raised to their highest level. Free scope is given for the development of both, and the satisfaction of the demands of both, in Christian life and Christian worship. Side by side they fought and triumphed over heathenism, taking up and assimilating all that was best and truest in non-Christian ethics. And though Christians were long in learning what manner of spirit they were of, it seemed as if a real conflict between religion and morals, within the area of Christianity, was impossible.

And yet again and again, in the history of Christianity, such a conflict has come about. Every moral reformation within the Church was a protest of the conscience against unworthy views of God ; every new Order that was founded was a nursery of moral reformation. Yet every protest against formalism and unreality in religion, every attack on ecclesiasticism and 'priestcraft' in the Church, or on worldliness and laxity in professing Christians, owed its strength to the reassertion of the truth, that in the Christian idea religion and morals are inseparably united. The moral reformer always claimed Christianity on his side, when attacking the Christianity of his day. This was conspicuously so in the great moral upheaval of the sixteenth century. In actual fact, religion and morality had separated. And the nearer one got to the centre of Western Christendom, the more open and unabashed the neglect of morality was. In Italy of the fifteenth century renaissance we see, in strange confusion, 'all that we love in art, and all that we loathe in man[1].' It seemed as if, as in the old riddle, a swarm of bees had settled in the dead lion's carcass, and there was sweetness instead of strength, corruption where once was life. When the new century opened, Borgia was the supreme Bishop of the West, and the strength of the protest of Christianity against immorality may

[1] *Cont. Rev.*, Oct. 1878, p. 645.

be gathered from the list of prices to be paid to the pardoner. The devout retired from the contest into the severer discipline of the monastic life, and hoped against hope for the days of a *Papa angelicus*, who never came. Yet when the strained relations of religion and morals resulted in a revolution, it never occurred to those, who had a moral reformation at heart, to say that religion was outgrown, and morality must henceforth take its place. They appealed from the Christianity of the sixteenth century to the Christianity of Christ. Even of those who, in their fear of popery, broke away farthest from the Christian idea of God, all, if we except the Anabaptists, claimed the Bible on their side. It was a genuine moral revolt against a religion which had come to tolerate immorality. The hatred of 'ecclesiasticism' and 'sacerdotalism' was not at first a rejection of the Church and the Priesthood, but a protest against anything which, under the sacred name of religion, becomes a cover for unreality, or makes sin a thing easy to be atoned for. The Reformation was a moral protest, and its results were seen within as well as outside the Roman communion. The Council of Trent was a reforming Council ; the Jesuits were the children of the Reformation ; and Roman Christianity in the strength of its own moral revival, even in the moment of defeat, became again 'a conquering power [1].'

On the other hand, those whose first impulse was a protest in favour of a moral religion and a belief in a God who hates iniquity, have bequeathed to the world a legacy of immorality, of which they never dreamt, and of which we, in the present day, are feeling the full effects. Lutheranism starts with the belief that God is love : Calvinism with the conception of God as power. With the former, the desire, at all costs, to guard the belief in the freedom of God's grace, led to a morbid fear of righteousness, as if it were somehow a rival to faith. With the latter, a one-sided view of the power of God gradually obscured the fact that righteousness and justice eternally condition its exercise. If the one was, as history shews us, in constant danger of Antinomian developments, the other struck at the root of morality by making God Himself unjust. Forensic fictions of substitution, immoral theories of the Atonement, 'the rending asunder of the Trinity' and the opposing of the Divine Persons, like parties in a lawsuit [2], were the natural corollaries of a theory which taught that God was above morality and man beneath it.

How deeply these false views of God have influenced English religious thought is shewn by the fact that every attack on the moral, as distinguished from the intellectual position of Christianity, is demonstrably an attack on that which is not Christianity, but a mediaeval

---

[1] Ranke, *Popes*, i. 395.
[2] Döllinger, *The Church and the Churches*, p. 239.

or modern perversion of it. J. S. Mill's well-known words[1], 'I will call no being good, who is not what I mean when I apply that epithet to my fellow creatures,' was a noble assertion of 'immutable morality' against a religion, which alas ! he mistook for Christianity. The conscience of to-day,—and it is a real gain that it should be so,— refuses to believe that the *imprimatur* of religion can be given to that which is not good, or that God would put us to moral confusion. It would rather give up religion altogether than accept one which will not endorse and advance our highest moral ideas.

But men do not always stop to make the necessary distinctions. On the one side they see a traditional view of religion which they cannot harmonise with the highest morality ; on the other, they see a morality, which, though it has grown up under the shadow and shelter of religion, seems strong enough to stand alone. And their first thought is 'Away with religion. We have outgrown it. Henceforward we will have morals unencumbered by religion.' What would be the effect on the morals of a nation of thus renouncing the religious sanction it is not safe to predict. In individuals certainly it sometimes has disastrous results. But there is one thing which those who talk about the 'secularization of morals[2]' seldom take into account, and that is the effect on what, in contrast to morals, they call religion. The religious consciousness always refuses to be treated as defunct, and the religious emotions, if they no longer find their object in a God of Righteousness, and are no longer controlled by morality, will not be satisfied with the worship of the Unknowable or of idealized humanity, but will avenge themselves, as they have done again and again, in superstition[3].

And the attempt to do without religion in morals is as unphilosophical as it is dangerous. It is parallel to what, in the region of morality proper, we all recognise as a false asceticism. It is the attempt to crush out, rather than to purify. When men realize the danger of giving the rein to the animal passions, there are always to be found moralists who will treat these passions as in themselves evil, and advocate the suppression of them. And only after an antinomian revolt against that false teaching do men realize that morality is not the destruction, but the purification and regulation of the passions. So with religion and the religious emotions. The function of morality is to purify the religious idea of God, and religion and morality are strong and true in proportion as each uses the help of the other. But

---

[1] *Examination of Sir W. Hamilton's Philosophy*, p. 103.
[2] H. Spencer, *Data of Ethics*, pref.
[3] See Ihne's remarks on the separation of morals and Religion in Rome at the time of the Punic wars. 'The religious cravings were not satisfied, and men were carried either to the schools of Greek Philosophy or to the grossest and meanest superstition.' *Hist. of Rome*, vol. ii. pp. 477, 478.

neither can treat the other as subordinate. God is more than what Kant makes Him, the ultimate justification of morality : morality is more than what some religious people would have it, obedience to the positive commands of even God Himself. In experience we find them separate and even opposed : ideally they are one, united not confused. Separated, religion tends to become superstitious, morality to degenerate into a mere prudentialism, or at least an expanded utilitarianism. United, religion gives to right that absolute character which makes it defiant of consequences ; morality safeguards the idea of God from aught that is unworthy of the worship of moral beings.

As the result of all the conflicts which have raged round the idea of God so far as morals are concerned, one truth has burned itself into the consciousness of both the apologists and opponents of religion, a truth as old indeed as the religion of Israel, but only slowly realized in the course of ages, the truth, namely, that the religious idea of God must claim and justify itself to the highest known morality, and no amount of authority, ecclesiastical or civil, will make men worship an immoral God. And already that truth has thrown back its light upon questions of Old Testament morality. We no longer say, ' It is in the Bible, approved or allowed by God, and therefore it must be right.' It was this view which, in every age, has given its protection to religious wars and intolerance and persecution. But we look back and see in the perspective of history how God in every age takes man as he is that He may make him what he is not. We see in the Old Testament not only the revelation of the Righteousness of God, but the record of the way in which, in spite of waywardness and disobedience, He raised His people to the knowledge of the truth.

VI. But the religious idea of God in our day, as in former ages, is challenged not only by conscience, but by the speculative reason. And there is a close parallelism between the two conflicts. When religion and morals are opposed, men naturally say, ' Give us morals ; away with religion.' And the answer is—True religion is moral ; that which is not moral is not true ; and morality without religion will not only leave the religious consciousness unsatisfied, but fall short of its own true perfection. So when religion and philosophy are opposed, men say once more, ' Give us reason ; away with religion.' And the answer again is—True religion is rational : if it excludes reason, it is self-condemned. And reason without religion fails of its object, since, if philosophy can find no place for religion, it cannot explain man.

But here again nothing is gained by confusing the issue, or denying the actual fact of the collision. We may say with Lacordaire, ' God is the proper name of truth, as truth is the abstract name of God.' But it is not a matter of indifference from which point we start, whether with religion we approach God first as a moral Being, or with philosophy seek for Him as the truth of man and nature. The motto of Oxford University, *Dominus Illuminatio mea*, altogether changes its meaning if we read it *Illuminatio Dominus meus*. As Réville says, 'A religion may become philosophical, but no philosophy has ever founded a religion possessing real historical power [1].' And it is a fact patent to the observation of all, that it is easier to make religion philosophical than to make philosophy in any real sense religious. The reason of this is obvious. Religion is not only first in the field, it covers the whole ground before either morals or science have attained their full development, or even emerged into conscious life. But when we speak of philosophy, we have reached a stage in which the reason has already separated itself from, and set itself over against, the religious consciousness, and must either absorb religion into itself, in which case religion ceases to be religion, or must leave religion outside, though it may borrow and appropriate religious terms. If, then, the idea of God is to appeal to both the religious consciousness and the speculative reason it must be by claiming philosophy for religion, not by claiming religion for philosophy. It is from within, not from without, that religion must be defended.

In Greece the traditional polytheism was challenged, as we have seen, at once on the side both of morals and metaphysics. To Xenophanes, indeed, the unity of God is even more essential than His morality, and the attack on anthropomorphism is as much an attack upon the number of the gods of Hesiod as upon the immoral character attributed to them. In the unity, however, which Xenophanes contends for, the religious idea of God is so attenuated, that we hardly know whether the One God is a person, or an abstraction. Indeed, it is hard to see how a champion of Eleaticism could consistently have held the personality of God, as we understand it, without falling under his own charge of anthropomorphism. In Plato the same difficulty appears, only complicated or relieved by the fact that while from the moral side he talks like a theist, from the metaphysical his teaching is pantheistic. Is the 'Idea of Good' personal? Is it a God we can love and worship, or only a God we can talk about? Is the vision of Er a concession to popular views, or the vehicle of moral and religious truth? The question is hardly more easy to decide with regard to Aristotle. The religious atmosphere, which lingers on in Plato, has disappeared. What of the religious belief? Did Aristotle in any intelligible sense hold the personality of God? Great names are ranged on both sides of the mediaeval controversy. Who shall decide? But whether or no anything of religion survived in philosophy, it was not strong enough to withstand the attack of the moral and the speculative reason, still less to claim these as its own. It is

[1] *History of Religions*, p. 22.

not on the side of religion, but of speculation, that we are debtors to the Greeks.

Among the Jews, on the other hand, speculation seems hardly to have existed. Religion was satisfied to make good her claim to the region of morals. God was One, and He was Righteous, but the mystery which enveloped His nature the Old Testament does not attempt to fathom. 'Clouds and darkness are round about Him, yet out of the thick darkness comes the clear unfaltering truth that 'Righteousness and judgment are the habitation of His seat.' Jewish religion and Greek speculation had little contact, and less kinship, till the best days of both were passed. But in the days of the dispersion we get the beginning of the mingling of those streams which were only united under the higher unity of Christianity. 'With the Jews of the East,' it has been said, 'rested the future of Judaism : with them of the West, in a sense, that of the world. The one represented old Israel, groping back into the darkness of the past ; the other young Israel, stretching forth its hands to where the dawn of a new day was about to break [1].' The Septuagint translation threw open to the Greek world the sacred books of Israel. The Apocrypha, with all its glorification of Judaism, was both an apology and an eirenicon [2]. It seemed as if in Wisdom personified might be found a middle term between the religion of Israel and the philosophy of Greece, and the life of righteousness might be identified with the life of true wisdom. The Jews of Alexandria were thus willing to find a strain of truth in Greek philosophy, and Alexandrian Greeks were found ready 'to spiritualize their sensuous divinities [3].' But the result was a compromise, in which the distinctive elements of each were not harmonized but lost. There was no fusion as yet of Jewish and Greek thought, only each was learning to understand the other, and unconsciously preparing for the higher synthesis of Christianity.

Whether we think of Christ as the 'Son of Man,' or as the Revealer of God, Christianity is bound to transcend national distinctions, and to claim not only the whole of humanity, but the whole of man, his reason, no less than his heart and will. And this Christ did in a special way. He not only speaks of Himself as 'the Truth,' and as having come 'to bear witness to the Truth,' but the very complement (if we may say so) of His revelation of the Father was the sending 'the Spirit of Truth,' who should teach His disciples all things. This possession of 'truth' is always spoken of by Christ as a future thing, implicit indeed in Himself, Who is the Truth, but only to be explicitly declared and brought to remembrance when the Spirit of Truth should

[1] Edersheim, *Life and Times*, i. p. 17.

[2] See Edersheim, i. pp. 31, etc.

[3] Hegel, *Philosophy of History*, p. 343, Eng. Tr.

come. He was to guide them 'into all truth.' 'Ye shall know the truth, and the truth shall make you free.' It was inevitable, then, that the question should arise,—Will this religion, which has broken through the narrowness of Judaism, and yet by its belief in a God of righteousness and love combated and triumphed over heathen immorality, have the power to assimilate and absorb the philosophy of Greece? The great crisis in the world's history, as we see it, looking back from the security of eighteen centuries, was this:—Will Christianity, with all its moral triumphs, become a tributary to Greek philosophy, as represented by the Schools of Alexandria, or will it claim and transform the rational, as it has transformed the moral, progress of humanity? The answer of Christianity is unhesitating. Christianity is truth, and there is only one truth. Christianity is wisdom, and there is only one wisdom; for the wisdom of the world is not wisdom but folly. And at once the rival claim is made. Why not a division of territory? Knowledge for the philosopher; faith for the Christian. The Gnostics taught, as a modern philosopher teaches, that religion is 'reason talking naively,' and that, good as it is for ordinary people, the Gnostic can afford to do without it. Every one knows the answer of the Apostles to the insidious suggestions of Gnosticism. To S. Peter it is 'a damnable heresy, even denying the Lord who bought us[1].' To S. Paul it is the 'science falsely so called[2];' the 'knowledge which puffs up[3];' the 'wisdom of this world[4].' To S. John, Cerinthus was 'the enemy of the truth[5].' To S. Polycarp, Marcion is 'the firstborn of Satan.' It never occurred to the Apostles, or the Apologists after them, to retreat into the fastnesses of a reasonless faith. For with them faith was implicit knowledge, and the only knowledge that was true.

It was the collision of Christianity with Greek thought which gave rise to Christian theology in the strict sense of the term. Its necessity was the claiming of Greek as well as Jew; its justification was the belief in the presence of the Spirit of truth; its impulse the desire 'to know the things which are freely given to us by God[6].' The first Christians were not theologians. They were 'unlearned and ignorant men.' When Christ preached, the common people heard Him gladly, the publicans and the harlots believed Him, the poor found in His teaching 'good news,' and a few fishermen devoted their lives to Him. But the Scribes and Pharisees stood aloof; and the rationalistic Sadducees asked Him captious questions; and the Herodians, the Erastians of the day, tried to involve Him with the secular power. It was only when challenged by an earnest, but non-religious philo-

---

[1] 2 S. Pet. ii. 1.
[2] 1 Tim. vi. 20.
[3] 1 Cor. viii. 6.
[4] 1 Cor. iii. 19.
[5] Euseb. iii. 28.
[6] 1 Cor. ii. 12.

sophy, that reason came forward, in the strength of the Spirit of truth, to interpret to itself and to the world the revelation of Christ. Religion and theology in different ways have to do with the knowledge of God and of spiritual truth. They have the same object, God, but their aims and their methods are different. Religion knows God; theology is concerned with the idea of God. Religion sees; theology thinks. Religion begins and ends in an almost instinctive attitude of worship; theology rationalizes and defines the characteristics of the Object of worship. As reason seeks to interpret feeling, so theology interprets religion. It makes explicit what is implicit in religion. 'As the intellect is cultivated and expanded, it cannot refrain from the attempt to analyse the vision which influences the heart, and the object in which it centres; nor does it stop till it has, in some sort, succeeded in expressing in words, what has all along been a principle both of the affections and of practical obedience[1].' It takes the facts which the religious consciousness has seized, seeks to bring them into distinctness before the mental vision, to connect them with one another in a coherent system, and find in them the explanation and unity of all that is. Christian theology grows naturally out of the Christian religion. But religion is a divine life; theology a divine science.

This explains the fact that though both religion and theology have to do with the knowledge of God, and ideally work in perfect harmony, yet they are often found opposed. Theology is always in danger of becoming unreal. What is an interpretation for one age becomes 'a tongue not understanded' in the next. Hence when a revival of religious life comes, it frequently shews itself in an attack on the received theology. Theology is no longer regarded as the scientific expression of the very truths which religion values; it is conceived of as the antithesis of religion, and reformers dream of a new theology which shall be for them, though they know it not, the old theology was to their predecessors, the handmaid and guardian of religious truth. When Martin Luther said that 'an old woman who reads her Bible in the chimney corner knows more about God than the great doctors of theology,' he was emphasising the severance which, in his day, had come to exist between a religious life and theological orthodoxy. And when in his *Table Talk* he says, 'A Jurist may be a rogue, but a theologian must be a man of piety,' he touches a real truth. A hundred years later, amid the confusions and unrealities of the seventeenth century, John Smith[2], the Cambridge Platonist, said the same: 'They are not always the best skilled in divinity,' he says, 'that are most studied in those pandects into which

[1] Newman's *Arians*, ch. ii. § 1.
[2] *Natural Truth of Christianity*, §§ 1, 2.

it is sometimes digested.' 'Were I to define divinity, I should rather call it *a divine life* than *a divine science.*' Technically, no doubt, he was wrong, for theology is a science and not a life, but, like Luther, he was vindicating the truth that it is possible for quite simple people to *know God*, though they have no knowledge of theology, and that theology, when it becomes speculative and abstract, ceases to be theology. A theologian, as Mazzini says of an artist, 'must be a high-priest or a charlatan.'

But the world dislikes a high-priest, and good people dislike a charlatan. And the consequence is that theology, ancient or modern, is attacked from two very different points of view, by those who look upon it as the antithesis of 'the simple Gospel,' and by those who approach it from the side of speculative thought. Theology claims to be a divine science. Religious people attack it because it is a science; philosophers because it claims to be divine. To the former, religion expressed in rational terms ceases to be religion; to the latter, that science is no science which claims for itself unique conditions. Yet S. Paul seems to recognise both the necessity and the uniqueness of theology when he says to the Greeks of Corinth, 'We received not the spirit of the world, but the spirit which is of God, that we might know the things that are freely given us by God.'

It is the relation of Christian theology to philosophy and science with which we are specially concerned. But it is impossible to pass by the objection to theology which comes as it were *ab intra* from the side of religion. For if it is valid, then Christianity may as well give up at once any idea of being the religion of man. Yet people say, 'Why have a theology? Human reason cannot search out "the deep things of God;" it will only put new difficulties in a brother's way; why not rest content with the words of Holy Scripture, with simple truths like "God is love," and simple duties like "Love one another," and leave theology alone?' Now without denying what George Eliot calls 'the right of the individual to general haziness,' or asserting that every Christian must be a theologian, we may surely say that Christianity is bound to have a theology. And even individual Christians, if they ever grow into the manhood of reason, must have a theology, or cease to be religious. The protest against theology from the side of religion looks modest and charitable enough till we remember that religious haziness is generally, if not always, the outcome of moral laziness; that it implies the neglect of a duty and the neglect of a gift;—the duty of realizing to the reason the revelation of Christ, and the gift of the Spirit of Truth to enable us to do it. More than this, the protest against theology in the interests of religion is irrational and suicidal. To tell a thinking man that he need not interpret to his reason what religion tells him of God, is like saying to him, 'Be

F

religious if you will, but you need not let your religion influence your conduct.' If Christianity had been content to be a moral religion, if it had abandoned its claim to rationality and had left Greek specu- lation alone, it must have accepted either the Gnostic division of territory, or recognised an internecine conflict between religion and philosophy. And it did neither; but, under the guidance of the Spirit of Truth, Christian theology arose and claimed the reason of the ancient world.

Thus as the religion of the Old Testament claims morality for God, so Christianity goes further and claims to hold the key to the in- tellectual problems of the world. So far as the nature of God is concerned, Christianity met the intellectual difficulties of the first centuries by the *Doctrine of the Trinity*.

From time to time people make the discovery that the doctrine of the Trinity is older than Christianity. If the discoverer is a Christian apologist, he usually explains that God has given anticipatory revela- tions to men of old, and points out how they fall short of the revelation of Christianity. If he is an opponent of Christianity, he triumphantly claims to have unmasked the doctrine and tracked it down to a purely natural origin. 'People think,' says Hegel, 'that by pronounc- ing a doctrine to be Neo-Platonic, they have *ipso facto* banished it from Christianity[1].' Men have found the doctrine, or something like it, not only in the Old Testament but in Plato and Neo-Platonism, and among the Ophite Gnostics, in the Chinese Tao-Té-Ching and the 'Three Holy Ones' of Bouddhism, in the Tri-mûrti of Hinduism and elsewhere. Why not? Revelation never advances for itself the claim which its apologists sometimes make for it, the claim to be something absolutely new. A truth revealed by God is never a truth out of relation with previous thought. He leads men to feel their moral and intellectual needs before He satisfies either. There was a preparation for Hebrew monotheism, as there was a preparation for the Gospel of Christ. There was an intellectual preparation for the doctrine of the Trinity, as there was a moral preparation for the doctrine of the Incarnation. If the Christian doctrine of the Incarna- tion is distinguished from the *avatars* of Hinduism, and the incarna- tions of Thibetan Lamaism, by its regenerative moral force, the Christian doctrine of the Trinity is no less distinguished from the pseudo-trinities of Neo-Platonism and its modern developments by the fact that for eighteen centuries it has been the safeguard of a pure Monotheism against everything which menaces the life of religion.

But Christian theology is not 'a philosophy without assumptions.' It does not attempt to prove *sola ratione* the doctrine of the Trinity,

[1] *Phil. of Hist.*, p. 343, Eng. Tr.

but to shew how that which reason demands is met and satisfied by the Christian doctrine of God. Starting with the inheritance of faith, the belief in the Divinity of Christ, and trusting in the guidance of the Spirit of Truth, it throws itself boldly into the rational problem, fights its way through every form of Unitarianism, and interprets its faith to itself and to the world at large in the doctrine of the Triune God. Its charter is the formula of Baptism, where the 'treasures of immediate faith are gathered up into a sentence, though not yet formulated into a doctrine [1].'

To the Greek mind two things had become clear before Christianity came into the world, and it would be easy to trace the steps by which the conclusions were reached. First, Reason, as relation-giving, seeks for unity in the manifoldness of which it is conscious, and will be satisfied with nothing less. But Eleaticism had convincingly proved that an abstract unity can explain nothing. Quite apart from questions of religion and morals, the Eleatic unity was metaphysically a failure. Plato had seen this, and yet the 'dead hand' of Eleaticism rested on Platonism, and the dialogue *Parmenides* shewed how powerless the Doctrine of Ideas was to evade the difficulty. Thus the Greeks more than 2000 years ago had realized, what is nowadays proclaimed, as if it were a new discovery, that an absolute unit is unthinkable, because, as Plato puts it in the *Philebus*, the union of the one and the many is 'an everlasting quality in thought itself which never grows old in us.' The Greeks, like the Jews, had thus had their 'schoolmaster to bring them to Christ.' They had not solved, but they had felt, the rational difficulty; as the Jews had felt, but had not overcome, except through the Messianic hope, the separation of man from God. But as the Trinitarian doctrine took shape, Christian teachers realized how the Christian, as opposed to the Jewish, idea of God, not only held the truth of the Divine Unity as against all polytheistic religions, but claimed reason on its side against all unitarian theories. They did not, however, argue that it was true because it satisfied reason, but that it satisfied reason because it was true.

They started, indeed, not with a metaphysical problem to be solved, but with a historical fact to proclaim, the fact of the Resurrection, and a doctrinal truth to maintain, the Divinity of Him who rose. And starting from that basis of fact revealed in Christ, they found themselves in possession of an answer to difficulties which at first they had not felt, and thus their belief was justified and verified in the speculative region.

The truth for which they contended, which was enshrined in their sacred writings, was that 'the Father is God, the Son is God, and the

[1] Dorner, *Hist. of Doct.* i. pp. 362, etc.

Holy Ghost is God. And yet they are not three Gods, but one God.'
But the Fathers do not treat this doctrine merely as a revealed
mystery, still less as something which complicates the simple teaching
of Monotheism, but as the condition of rationally holding the Unity of
God. 'The Unity which derives the Trinity out of its own self,' says
Tertullian, 'so far from being destroyed, is actually supported by it [1].'
'We cannot otherwise think of One God,' says Hippolytus, 'but by
truly believing in Father, and Son, and Holy Ghost [2].' 'The supreme
and only God,' says Lactantius, 'cannot be worshipped except through
the Son. He who thinks that he worships the Father only, in that he
does not worship the Son also, does not worship the Father [3].'
'Without the Son the Father is not,' says Clement of Alexandria,
'for in that He is a Father He is the Father of the Son, and the Son
is the true teacher about the Father [4].' So Origen argues,—If God
had ever existed alone in simple unity and solitary grandeur, apart
from some object upon which from all eternity to pour forth His love,
He could not have been always God. His love, His Fatherhood, His
very omnipotence would have been added in time, and there would
then have been a time when He was imperfect. 'The Fatherhood of
God must be coeval with His omnipotence; for it is through the Son
that the Father is Almighty [5].' This was the line of argument afterwards developed by S. Athanasius when he contended against the
Arians that the Son was the reality or truth [6] of the Father, without
whom the Father could not exist; and by S. Augustine, when he
argues that love implies one who loves and one who is loved, and love
to bind them together [7]. Even one so unphilosophically minded as
Irenaeus [8], cannot but see in the Christian doctrine of the relation of
the Father and the Son, the solution of the difficulty about the infinity
of God: 'Immensus Pater in Filio mensuratus; mensura Patris
Filius.' While philosophy with increasing hopelessness was asking,
How can we have a real unity which shall be not a barren and dead
unity, but shall include differences? Christianity, with its doctrine of
God, was arguing that that which was an unsolved contradiction for
non-Christian thought, was a necessary corollary of the Christian
Faith [9].

The other truth which Greek thought had realized was the immanence of reason in nature and in man. When Anaxagoras first declared
that the universe was the work of intelligence, we are told that he
seemed 'like a sober man amongst random talkers.' But both Plato
and Aristotle accuse him of losing the truth which he had gained

---

[1] *Adv. Prax.* ch. iii.
[2] *Cont. Noet.* § xiv.
[3] *Inst.* iv. c. 29.
[4] *Strom.* v. 1.
[5] *De Princ.* I. ii. § 10.

[6] *Adv. Arianos* i. § 20.
[7] *De Trin.* viii. 10 and ix. 2.
[8] Iren. *Adv. Haer.* IV. iv. 1. 2.
[9] Cf. pp. 333–336.

because he made intelligence appear only on occasions in the world, dragged in, like a stage-god, when naturalistic explanations failed[1]. The conception of creation out of nothing was of course unknown to Anaxagoras. Intelligence is only the arranger of materials already given in a chaotic condition. With Aristotle too it is reason which makes everything what it is. But the reason is in things, not outside them. Nature is rational from end to end. In spite of failures and mistakes, due to her materials, nature does the best she can and always aims at a good end[2]. She works like an artist with an ideal in view[3]. Only there is this marked difference,—Nature has the principle of growth within herself, while the artist is external to his materials[4]. Here we have a clear and consistent statement of the doctrine of immanent reason as against the Anaxagorean doctrine of a transcendent intelligence. If we translate both into the theological language of our own day, we should call the latter the deistic, the former the pantheistic, view ; or, adopting a distinction of supreme importance in the history of science, we might say that we have here, face to face, the mechanical and the organic view of nature. Both were teleological, but to the one, reason was an extra-mundane cause, to the other, an internal principle. It was the contrast between external and inner design, as we know it in Kant and Hegel; between the teleology of Paley and the 'wider teleology' of Darwin and Huxley and Fiske; between the transcendent and immanent views of God, when so held as to be mutually exclusive.

It is these two one-sided views which the Christian doctrine of God brings together. Religion demands as the very condition of its existence a God who transcends the universe ; philosophy as imperiously requires His immanence in nature. If either Religion denies God's immanence, or Philosophy denies that He transcends the universe, there is an absolute antagonism between the two, which can only be ended by the abandonment of one or the other. But what we find is that though Philosophy (meaning by that the exercise of the speculative reason in abstraction from morals and religion) the more fully it realizes the immanence of God, the more it tends to deny the transcendence, religion not only has no quarrel with the doctrine of immanence, but the higher the religion the more unreservedly it asserts this immanence as a truth dear to religion itself. The religious equivalent for 'immanence' is 'omnipresence,' and the omnipresence of God is a corollary of a true monotheism. As long as any remains of dualism exist, there is a region, however small, impervious to the Divine power. But the Old Testament doctrine of creation, by ex-

---

[1] Plat. *Phaed.* 98 B.   Arist. *Met.*
A. 4.
[2] p. 455[b]17.   The references are to   the Berlin edition.
[3] p. 199[a]8, 18 : 415[b]17 : 731[a]24.
[4] p. 1070[a]7, 1033[b]8, 753[a]3.

cluding dualism, implies from the first, if it does not teach, the omnipresence of God. For the omnipotence of God underlies the doctrine of creation, and omnipotence involves omnipresence. Hence we find the Psalmists and Prophets ascribing natural processes immediately to God. They know nothing of second causes. The main outlines of natural science, the facts of generation and growth, are familiar enough to them, yet every fact is ascribed immediately to the action of God. He makes the grass to grow upon the mountains; He fashions the child in the womb; He feeds the young ravens; He provides fodder for the cattle; He gives to all their meat in due season; when He lets His breath go forth they are made; when He takes away their breath they die and return to dust.

This doctrine of the omnipresence of God, as conceived by religion, had however yet to be fused with the philosophical doctrine of immanence. And here again the fusion was effected by the Christian doctrine of God, as Trinity in Unity. The earlier Apologists concern themselves first with the vindication of the Divine attributes, God's separateness from the world as against Greek Pantheism, His omnipresence in it as against a Judaising deism. But the union of God's transcendence with His immanence, and with it the fusion of the religious with the philosophic idea of God, is only consciously completed by the Doctrine of the Trinity[1]. The dying words of Plotinus, expressing as they did the problem of his life, are said to have been,— 'I am striving to bring the God which is within into harmony with the God which is in the universe.' And the unsolved problem of Neo-Platonism, which is also the unsolved problem of non-Christian philosophy in our day, is met by the Christian doctrine of God. All and more than all that philosophy and science can demand, as to the immanence of reason in the universe, and the rational coherence of all its parts, is included in the Christian teaching: nothing which religion requires as to God's separateness from the world, which He has made, is left unsatisfied. The old familiar Greek term ΛΟΓΟΣ which, from the days of Heracleitus, had meant to the Greek the rational unity and balance of the world, is taken up by S. John, by S. Clement, by S. Athanasius, and given a meaning which those who started from the Philonian position never reached. It is the personal Word, God of God, the Only Begotten of the Father, who is one in the Holy Spirit with the Father. 'The Word was God.' 'By Him all things were made.' 'He the All-powerful, All-holy Word of the Father spreads His power over all things everywhere, enlightening things seen and unseen, holding and binding all together in Himself. Nothing is left empty of His presence, but to all things and through all, severally and collectively, He is the giver and sustainer of life. . . . He, the

[1] Dorner, *Hist. of Doct.* i. p. 366.

Wisdom of God, holds the universe like a lute, and keeps all things in earth and air and heaven in tune together. He it is Who binding all with each, and ordering all things by His will and pleasure, produces the perfect unity of nature, and the harmonious reign of law. While He abides unmoved for ever with the Father, He yet moves all things by His own appointment according to the Father's will[1].' The unity of nature is, thus, no longer the abstract motionless simplicity of Being, which had been so powerless to explain the metaphysical problems of Greece. It is the living Omnipresent Word, coeternal and consubstantial with the Father, and the philosophical truth becomes an integral part of that Christian doctrine of God, which, while it safeguarded religion and satisfied reason, had won its first and greatest victories in the field of morals.

VII. The Christian doctrine of God triumphed over heathen morality and heathen speculation neither by unreasoning protest nor by unreal compromise, but by taking up into itself all that was highest and truest in both. Why then is this Christian idea of God challenged in our day? Have we outgrown the Christian idea of God, so that it cannot claim and absorb the new truths of our scientific age? If not, with the lessons of the past in our mind, we may confidently ask,— What fuller unfolding of the revelation of Himself has God in store for us, to be won, as in the past, through struggle and seeming antagonism?

The fact that the Christian Theology is now openly challenged by reason is obvious enough. It almost seems as if, in our intellectual life, we were passing through a transition analogous to that which, in the moral region, issued in the Reformation. Even amongst those who believe that Christian morality is true, there are to be found those who have convinced themselves that we have intellectually outgrown the Christian Faith. 'The only God,' we have been told lately[2], 'whom Western Europeans, with a Christian ancestry of a thousand years behind them, can worship, is the God of Abraham, Isaac, and Jacob; or rather, of S. Paul, S. Augustine and S. Bernard, and of the innumerable "blessed saints," canonized or not, who peopled the ages of Faith. No one wants, no one can care for, an abstract God, an Unknowable, an Absolute, with whom we stand in no human or intelligible relation.' 'God, as God,' says Feuerbach[3], 'the infinite, universal, non-anthropomorphic being of the understanding, has no more significance in religion than a fundamental general principle has for a special science; it is merely the ultimate point of support, as it were, the mathematical point of religion.' Yet it is assumed that this

[1] S. Athan. *Contra Gentes*, § 42.
[2] Morison's *Service of Man*, p. 48.
[3] Quoted by W. S. Lilly, *Nineteenth Century*, Aug. 1888, p. 292.

is all that remains to us, and we are left in the following dilemma,—
'An anthropomorphic God is the only God whom men can worship,
and also the God whom modern thought finds it increasingly difficult
to believe in[1].'

In such a state of things it is natural that men should turn to
pantheism as a sort of middle term between religion and philosophy,
and even claim, for the unity of the world, the venerable name and
associations of God. But the remarkable thing is that in the numberless attempts to attack, or defend, or find a substitute for Theism, the
Christian, or Trinitarian, teaching about God rarely appears upon the
scene. Devout Christians have come to think of the doctrine of the
Trinity, if not exactly as a distinct revelation, yet as a doctrine necessary
for holding the divinity of Christ, without sacrificing the unity of God.
Ordinary people take it for granted that Trinitarianism is a sort of extra
demand made on Christian faith, and that the battle must really be
fought out on the unitarian basis. If unitarian theism can be defended,
it will then be possible to go farther and accept the doctrine of the
Trinity. It is natural that when Christians take this ground, those
who have ceased to be Christian suppose that, though Christianity is
no longer tenable, they may still cling to 'Theism,' and even perhaps,
under cover of that nebulous term, make an alliance not only with
Jews and Mahommedans, but with at least the more religious representatives of pantheism. It is only our languid interest in speculation
or a philistine dislike of metaphysics, that makes such an unintelligent
view possible. Unitarianism said its last word in the pre-Christian
and early Christian period, and it failed, as it fails now, to save
religion except at the cost of reason. So far from the doctrine of the
Trinity being, in Mr. Gladstone's unfortunate phrase, 'the scaffolding
of a purer theism,' non-Christian monotheism was the 'scaffolding'
through which already the outlines of the future building might be
seen. For the modern world, the Christian doctrine of God remains
as the only safeguard in reason for a permanent theistic belief[2].

It is not difficult to see how it is that this truth is not more
generally recognised. The doctrine of the Trinity, by which the

---

[1] Morison, *Service of Man*, p. 49.

[2] It is far from our purpose to under-
value the work of Dr. Martineau. No
more earnest and vigorous, and so far
as it goes, no truer defence of religion
has been published in our day. But his
strength lies mainly in his protest
against what destroys religion, and in
his uncompromising assertion of what
religion, as a condition of its existence,
demands. He has done little to shew
us how these demands can be rationally
satisfied, how the personal God, which

religion demands, is even an intelligible
idea. He wavers between a view which
logically developed must result in pantheism, and a view implying a distinction in the Divine nature, which carries
him far in the Trinitarian direction.
More often he contents himself with
leaving the speculative question alone,
or storming the rational position by the
forces of religion and morals. See *A
Study of Religion*, vol. ii. p. 145 compared with p. 192.

Christian idea of God absorbed Greek speculation into itself, had but little *point d'appui* in the unmetaphysical western world. It bore the *imprimatur* of the Church; it was easily deducible from the words of Holy Scripture; it was seen to be essential to the holding of the divinity of Christ. But men forgot that the doctrine was 'addressed to the reason[1];' and so its metaphysical meaning and value were gradually lost sight of. In the days of the mediaeval Papacy, ecclesiastical were more effective than metaphysical weapons, and Scholasticism knew so much about the deepest mysteries of God, that it almost provoked an agnostic reaction, in the interests of reverence and intellectual modesty. With the Reformation came the appeal to the letter of Holy Scripture, and the age of biblical, as contrasted with scientific, theology. The only scientific theology of the Reformation period was the awful and immoral system of John Calvin, rigorously deduced from a one-sided truth.

Then came the age of physical science. The break up of the mediaeval system of thought and life resulted in an atomism, which, if it had been more perfectly consistent with itself, would have been fatal alike to knowledge and society. Translated into science it appeared as mechanism in the Baconian and Cartesian physics : translated into politics it appeared as rampant individualism, though combined by Hobbes with Stuart absolutism. Its theory of knowledge was a crude empiricism; its theology unrelieved deism. God was 'throned in magnificent inactivity in a remote corner of the universe,' and a machinery of 'second causes' had practically taken His place. It was even doubted, in the deistic age, whether God's delegation of His power was not so absolute as to make it impossible for Him to 'interfere' with the laws of nature. The question of miracles became the burning question of the day, and the very existence of God was staked on His power to interrupt or override the laws of the universe. Meanwhile His immanence in nature, the 'higher pantheism,' which is a truth essential to true religion, as it is to true philosophy, fell into the background.

Slowly but surely that theory of the world has been undermined. The one absolutely impossible conception of God, in the present day, is that which represents Him as an occasional Visitor. Science had pushed the deist's God farther and farther away, and at the moment when it seemed as if He would be thrust out altogether, Darwinism appeared, and, under the disguise of a foe, did the work of a friend. It has conferred upon philosophy and religion an inestimable benefit, by shewing us that we must choose between two alternatives. Either God is everywhere present in nature, or He is nowhere. He cannot be here and not there. He cannot delegate His power to demigods

[1] Newman's *Arians*, p. 84.

called 'second causes[1].' In nature everything must be His work or nothing. We must frankly return to the Christian view of direct Divine agency, the immanence of Divine power in nature from end to end, the belief in a God in Whom not only we, but all things have their being, or we must banish Him altogether. It seems as if, in the providence of God, the mission of modern science was to bring home to our unmetaphysical ways of thinking the great truth of the Divine immanence in creation, which is not less essential to the Christian idea of God than to a philosophical view of nature. And it comes to us almost like a new truth, which we cannot at once fit it in with the old.

Yet the conviction that the Divine immanence must be for our age, as for the Athanasian age, the meeting point of the religious and philosophic view of God is shewing itself in the most thoughtful minds on both sides. Our modes of thought are becoming increasingly Greek, and the flood, which in our day is surging up against the traditional Christian view of God, is prevailingly pantheistic in tone. The pantheism is not less pronounced because it comes as the last word of a science of nature, for the wall which once separated physics from metaphysics has given way, and positivism, when it is not the paralysis of reason, is but a temporary resting-place, preparatory to a new departure. We are not surprised then, that one who, like Professor Fiske, holds that 'the infinite and eternal Power that is manifested in every pulsation of the universe is none other than the living God,' and who vindicates the belief in a final cause because he cannot believe that 'the Sustainer of the universe will put us to permanent intellectual confusion,' should instinctively feel his kinship with Athanasianism, and vigorously contend against the view that any part of the universe is 'Godless[2].'

Unfortunately, however, the rediscovery of the truth of God's immanence in nature, coming, as it has done, from the side of a scientific theory, which was violently assailed by the official guardians of the Faith, has resulted for many in the throwing aside of the counter and conditioning truth, which saves religion from pantheism. It seemed as if traditional Christianity were bound up with the view that God is wholly separate from the world and not immanent in it. And Professor Fiske has been misled[3] into the belief that S. Augustine is responsible for that false view. It is almost incredible to anyone, who has read any of S. Augustine's writings, that, according to this view, he has to play the *rôle* of the unintelligent and unphilosophical

---

[1] Cf. Fiske, *Idea of God*, pp. 103, 104. Martineau, *A Study of Religion*, ii. 172, 173.

[2] *Idea of God*, cf. § v. and pp. 105–110.

[3] Apparently by Prof. Allen's *Continuity of Christian Thought*.

deist, who thinks of God as 'a crudely anthropomorphic Being, far removed from the universe and accessible only through the mediating offices of an organized church [1].' And not only is S. Augustine represented as a deist, but S. Athanasius is made a pantheist, and the supposed conflict between science and religion is, we are told, really the conflict between Athanasian and Augustinian ideas of God [2]. Yet, as a matter of fact, S. Athanasius and S. Augustine both alike held the truths which deism and pantheism exaggerate into the destruction of religion. If S. Athanasius says, 'The Word of God is not contained by anything, but Himself contains all things. ... He was in everything and was outside all beings, and was at rest in the Father alone [3]:' S. Augustine says, 'The same God is wholly everywhere, contained by no space, bound by no bonds, divisible into no parts, mutable in no part of His being, filling heaven and earth by the presence of His power. Though nothing can exist without Him, yet nothing is what He is [4].'

The Christian doctrine of God, in Athanasian days, triumphed where Greek philosophy failed. It accepted the challenge of Greek thought, it recognised the demands of the speculative reason, and found in itself the answer which, before the collision with Hellenism, it unconsciously possessed. It is challenged again by the metaphysics of our day. We may be wrong to speculate at all on the nature of God, but it is not less true now than in the first centuries of Christianity, that, for those who do speculate, a Unitarian, or Arian, or Sabellian theory is as impossible as polytheism. If God is to be Personal, as religion requires, metaphysics demands still a distinction in the Unity which unitarianism is compelled to deny. But, further, the Christian doctrine of God is challenged by the science of nature. Science, imperiously and with increasing confidence, demands a unity in nature which shall be not external but immanent, giving rationality and coherence to all that is, and justifying the belief in the universal reign of law. But this immanence of God in nature unitarian theism cannot give, save at the price of losing itself in pantheism. Deistic it might be, as it was in the last century; deistic it can be no longer, unless it defiantly rejects the truth which science is giving us, and the claims which the scientific reason makes.

It remains then for Christianity to claim the new truth and meet the new demands by a fearless reassertion of its doctrine of God. It has to bring forth out of its treasury things new and old,—the old almost forgotten truth of the immanence of the Word, the belief in God as 'creation's secret force,' illuminated and confirmed as that is

[1] Fiske, *Idea of God,* p. 94.
[2] Ibid., § vii.
[3] *De Incarn.* c. 17.

[4] *De Civ. Dei,* vii. c. xxx; cf. too *De Gen. ad lit.* iv. c. 12; *Enchir. ad Laur.* c. 27.

by the advance of science, till it comes to us with all the power of a new discovery. Slowly and under the shock of controversy Christianity is recovering its buried truths, and realizing the greatness of its rational heritage. It teaches still that God is the eternally existent One, the Being on Whom we depend, and in Whom we live, the source of all reality and the goal to which creation moves, the Object alike of religion and philosophy, the eternal Energy of the natural world, and the immanent reason of the universe. It teaches that He is the eternally Righteous One, and therefore the Judge of all, irrevocably on the side of right, leading the world by a progressive preparation for the revelation of Himself as Infinite Love in the Incarnation of the Word, stimulating those desires which He alone can satisfy, the yearning of the heart for love, of the moral nature for righteousness, of the speculative reason for truth. When men had wearied themselves in the search for a remedy for that which separates men from God, the revelation is given of Him Who 'shall save His people from their sins.' And when reason had wandered long, seeking for that which should be Real and yet One, a God Who should satisfy alike the demands of religion and reason, the doctrine of the Trinity is unfolded. It was the gradual revelation of God answering to the growing needs and capacity of man.

VIII. It follows from the point of view adopted in the foregoing essay that there can be no proofs, in the strict sense of the word, of the existence of God. Reason has for its subject-matter, the problem of essence, not of existence, the question, 'What is God?' not 'Is there a God?' Proof can only mean verification *à posteriori* of a truth already held. We approach the problem with an unreasoned consciousness of dependence on a Being or Beings who are to us invisible. This we interpret crudely, or leave uninterpreted. The belief may express itself in ancestor-worship, or nature-worship, or what not. But as our moral and intellectual nature develops, its light is turned back upon this primitive undefined belief. Conscience demands that God shall be moral, and with the belief that He is, there comes confidence and trust, deepening into faith and hope and love : the speculative reason demands that God shall be One, the immanent unity of all that is. And the doctrine of God, which is best able to satisfy each and all of these demands, persists as the permanent truth of religion. But neither conscience nor the speculative reason can demonstrate[1] God's existence. And it is always possible for men to carry their distrust of that which is instinctive so far as to assume that it is always false because they have found that

[1] S. Thos. Aq. *Sum. Theol.* I. i. Quaest. 2, says that the Existence of God is demonstrable, but he explains that he does not mean strict demonstration, *demonstratio apodeictica*, but *demonstratio ab effectibus*.

t is not always true. Reason cannot prove existence. The so-called proof, *a contingentia* (which underlies H. Spencer's argument for the existence of the Unknowable), is an appeal to that very consciousness of dependence which some people consider a weakness, and a thing to educate themselves out of. The appeal to the *consensus gentium* can establish only the generality, not the strict universality, of religion. It will always be possible to find exceptions, real or apparent, to the general rule; while as for what is known as the *ontological* argument, which on principles of reason would justify the instinctive belief, it requires a metaphysical training to understand it or at least to feel its force. There remain, however, the two great arguments from conscience and from nature, which are so frequently discussed in the present day.

With regard to the first, there is no doubt that the belief in God will in any age find its strongest corroboration in the conscience. Even in the mind of a Felix the ideas of 'righteousness, temperance, and judgment to come' had a strange and terrifying coherence. There is that much of truth in the statement that religion is founded in 'fear.' But the argument from conscience has been weakened by being overstated. Conscience, as we know it, has won, not indeed its existence, but the delicacy of its moral touch, and the strength of its categorical imperative,' from the assured belief in a real relationship between man and a holy and loving God. When that belief has ceased to exist, conscience still survives, and it is possible and justifiable to appeal to it as a fact which can be explained by religion, but without religion must be explained away. But it is a mistake to suppose that we can take the untrained and undeveloped conscience, and argue direct from it to a righteous God. The *lumen naturale*, in its lowest development, gives but a faint and flickering gleam. We cannot argue back from it to a God of love, or even a God of righteousness, unless we interpret it in the fuller light of the conscience which has been trained and perfected under the growing influence of the belief. The idea of 'duty,' which is so hard to explain on utilitarian grounds, is not to be found, as we know it, in Greek ethics. For it implies a fusion of morals with religion, as we can trace it in the history of Israel, and the teaching of Christian ethics. If it is impossible to explain duty as the result of association between the ideas of public and private advantage, it is no less impossible to make it an independent premiss for a conclusion which is presupposed in it.

The argument from nature is closely parallel. It is hard for those, whose lives have been moulded on the belief in God, the Maker of heaven and earth, to understand the inconclusiveness of the argument to those who have abandoned that belief, and start, as it were, from outside. Consequently it has been made to bear more than it can carry. No doubt the evolution which was at first supposed to have destroyed teleology is found to be more saturated with teleology than the view which it superseded. And Christianity can take up the new as it did the old, and find in it a confirmation of its own belief. But it is a confirmation not a proof, and taken by itself is incomplete. It is a great gain to have eliminated chance, to find science declaring that there must be a reason for everything, even when it cannot hazard a conjecture as to what the reason is. But apart from the belief of our moral nature, that in the long run everything must make for righteousness, that the world must be moral as well as rational, and that the dramatic tendency in the evolution of the whole would be irrational if it had not a moral goal, the science of nature is powerless to carry us on to a Personal God. But the strength of a rope is greater than the strength of its separate strands. The arguments for the existence of God are, it has been said, 'sufficient not resistless, convincing not compelling[1].' We can never demonstrate the existence of God either from conscience or from nature. But our belief in Him is attested and confirmed by both.

In this matter, the belief in God stands on the same level with the belief in objective reality. Both have been explained away by philosophers. Neither can be proved but by a circular argument. Both persist in the consciousness of mankind. Both have been purified and rationalized by the growth of knowledge. But the moment reason attempts to start without assumptions, and claims exclusive sovereignty over man, a paralysis of thought results. There have been, before now, philosophers who professed to begin at the beginning, and accept nothing till it was proved, and the result was a pure Pyrrhonism. They could not prove the existence of an external world. They believed it, even if they did not, like Hume, exult in the fact that belief triumphed over demonstration, but there was no sure ground for believing that the world was not a mere cerebral phenomenon, except the curiously rational coherence of its visions. Even Prof. Huxley, in his ultra-sceptical moods, admits this. He says[2] that 'for any demonstration that can be given to the contrary effect, the "collection of perceptions," which makes up our consciousness, may be an orderly phantasmagoria generated by the Ego, unfolding its successive scenes on the background of the abyss of nothingness.' But no one, least of all a man of science, believes this to be so. He takes reality for granted, and only tries to interpret it aright, i. e. in such a way as to make a rational unity of the facts perceived. Tell a

[1] *The Existence of God.* By Rev. R. F. Clarke, S.J., p. 6.
[2] Huxley's *Hume*, p. 81.

scientific specialist,—' I am not going to let you beg the question. You must first prove that nature exists, and then I will hear about the science of nature,' and he will say 'That is metaphysics,' which to him is probably a synonym for an intellectual waste of time. ' Look at nature,' he will say, 'what more do you want? If nature had been merely a phantasmagoria there would have been no science of nature. Of course you must make your "act of faith [1]." You must believe not only that nature exists, but that it is a cosmos which can be interpreted, if you can only find the key. The proof that nature is interpretable is that we have, at least in part, been able to interpret her. There were people in John Locke's day who professed to doubt their own existence, and he was content to answer them according to their folly. " If anyone," he says [2], "pretends to be so sceptical as to deny his own existence (for really to doubt of it is manifestly impossible) let him, for me, enjoy his beloved happiness of being nothing, until hunger, or some other pain, convince him to the contrary." ' We do not call a scientific man unreasonable if he answers thus, though he is justifying his premises by his conclusion. We know that he that would study nature must believe that it is, and that it is a rational whole which reason can interpret. And ' he that cometh to God must believe that He is, and that He is the rewarder of such as diligently seek Him.' We feel our kinship with both before our instinctive consciousness is justified by reason.

And there is a remarkable parallelism in the process of verification. The counterpart of the theological belief in the unity and omnipresence of God is the scientific belief in the unity of nature and the reign of law. But that belief, though implicit in the simplest operation of reason [3], is not consciously attained till late in the history of science. And even when it is reached, it is not at once grasped in all its wealth and fulness. It is thought of as mere uniformity, a dull mechanical repetition of events, which is powerless to explain or include the rich variety of nature and the phenomena of life and growth. It is to meet this difficulty that J. S. Mill naively assures us that 'the course of nature is not only uniform, it is also infinitely various [4].' But soon the truth is grasped, that the reign of law is a unity which is higher than mere uniformity, because it is living and not dead, and includes and transcends difference. It is the analogue

---

[1] ' The one act of faith in the convert to science, is the confession of the universality of order and of the absolute validity, in all times and under all circumstances, of the law of causation. This confession is an act of faith, because, by the nature of the case, the truth of such propositions is not susceptible of proof.' Huxley in *Darwin's Life and Letters*, vol. ii. p. 200.

[2] *Essay* IV. 10. § 2.

[3] Cf. Green's *Works*, vol. ii. p. 284.

[4] *Log*. Bk. III. ch. iii. § 2.

in science to that higher and fuller view of God in which He is revealed as Trinity in Unity.

But as these parallel processes of verification go on, the truth is forced upon the world that religion and philosophy must either be in internecine conflict, or recognise the oneness of their Object. 'We ⁓nd the philosophers,' says S. Clement, 'know the same God, but not in the same way[1].' Philosophy and religion have both been enriched by wider knowledge, and as their knowledge has become deeper and fuller, the adjustment of their claims has become more imperatively necessary. Few in our day would willingly abandon either, or deliberately sacrifice one to the other. Many would be ready to assent to the words of a Christian Father ; 'when philosophy and the worship of the gods are so widely separated, that the professors of wisdom cannot bring us near to the gods, and the priests of religion cannot give us wisdom ; it is manifest that the one is not true wisdom, and the other is not true religion. Therefore neither is philosophy able to conceive the truth, nor is religion able to justify itself. But where philosophy is joined by an inseparable connection with religion, both must necessarily be true, because in our religion we ought to be wise, that is, to know the true Object and mode of worship, and in our wisdom to worship, that is, to realize in action what we know[2].'

It is sometimes argued,—You have let in more than the thin end of the wedge. You admit that 'it is the province of reason to judge of the morality of the Scripture[3].' You profess no antagonism to historical and literary criticism. Under the criticism of reason, Fetichism has given way to Polytheism, Polytheism to Monotheism, even Monotheism has become progressively less anthropomorphic. Why object to the last step in the process, and cling to the belief in a Personal God ? Simply because it would make the difference between a religion purified and a religion destroyed. The difference between the 30,000 gods of Hesiod, and the One God of Christianity, is a measurable difference : the difference between a Personal God and an impersonal reason is, so far as religion is concerned, infinite. For the transition from Monotheism to Pantheism is made only by the surrender of religion, though the term 'theism' may be used to blur the line of separation, and make the transition easy.

Religion has, before all things, to guard the heritage of truth, the moral revelation of God in Christ, to 'contend earnestly for the faith once delivered to the saints,' and to trust to the promised guidance of the Spirit of Truth. And reason interprets religion to itself, and by interpreting verifies and confirms. Religion therefore claims as its

[1] *Strom.* vi. 5.
[2] Lact. *Instit.* IV. iii.
[3] Butler's *Analogy*, Pt. II. ch. iii. p. 183.

own the new light which metaphysics and science are in our day throwing upon the truth of the immanence of God : it protests only against those imperfect, because premature, syntheses, which in the interests of abstract speculation, would destroy religion. It dares to maintain that 'the Fountain of wisdom and religion alike is God: and if these two streams shall turn aside from Him, both must assuredly run dry.' For human nature craves to be both religious and rational. And the life which is not both is neither.

III.

THE PROBLEM OF PAIN.

THE problem of pain, always prominent in a sensitive age, has been exceptionally emphasized in the literature of modern pessimism as an objection to Theism in general, and Christianity in particular. The existence of pain is urged as incompatible with the belief in a God who is at once omnipotent and benevolent, that is with Theism in its ordinary form; while Christianity is further charged with being a religion of pain, a religion which has increased the sum of actual and the expectation of prospective pain, darkening the shadow that lies upon our race. Suffering is not a subject upon which anything new can be said. It has long ago been probed, to the utmost limit of our capacity, and remains a mystery still. But, in face of the adverse use now made of it, it may be well to bear in mind how much has been said and is to be said upon the other side.

To begin with, there are two classes of pain, animal and human, which however intimately they may be connected must, for clearness, be considered apart. The universality of pain throughout the range of the animal world, reaching back into the distant ages of geology, and involved in the very structure of the animal organism, is without doubt among the most serious problems which the Theist has to face. But it is a problem in dealing with which emotion is very often mistaken for logic. J. S. Mill's famous indictment of nature, for example, is one of the most emotional pieces of rhetoric of which a professed logician was ever guilty. When a certain class of facts is urged in objection to our Christian belief, we are entitled to ask how many of those facts are known, and how many are only imagined. There is of course a scientific use of the imagination, but it is only permissible within the bounds of possible, or at least conceivable verification. Imaginative conjectures which, from the nature of the case, will never admit either of verification or disproof are poetry and not science, and must be treated as such in argument. With all the changes that have passed over our knowledge, we may still do well to attend to the caution with which Butler begins his Analogy:—

'One cannot but be greatly sensible how difficult it is to silence imagination enough to make the voice of reason even distinctly heard ; as we are accustomed from our youth up to indulge that forward delusive faculty, ever obtruding beyond its sphere ; of some assistance indeed to apprehension, but the author of all error : as we plainly lose ourselves in gross and crude conceptions of things, taking for granted that we are acquainted with what indeed we are wholly ignorant of.'

This needs repeating, because much of the popular knowledge of the day consists in the acceptance of results without examination of the methods of their attainment; somewhat as, in the countryman's simple faith, a thing must needs be true because he has seen it in a book. While the case in point is further confused by the fact that imagination has an important bearing on all our conduct towards the lower animals, and cannot, for that purpose, be too emotionally developed. But it is one thing to err on the safe side in practice, and another to convert such possible error into argument.

What then do we really know about the suffering of animals ? No reasonable man doubts that they suffer. But the degree and intensity of their suffering is almost entirely a matter of conjecture. We speak of, and are affected by the mass of animal suffering ; but we must remember that it is felt distributively. No one animal suffers more because a million suffer likewise. And what we have to consider is the amount which an individual animal suffers. We have no knowledge, but we are entitled to meet conjecture by conjecture. We may fairly suppose that the animals do not 'look before and after,' and it is this that gives its sting to human pain. Again, they would seem like children to give strong indications of slight pain. Further, many muscular contortions which simulate extreme suffering are believed on scientific evidence to be due to quite other causes. And then there are the phenomena of fascination, which may well resemble the experience of Livingstone in the lion's mouth. While many pains are prophylactic and directly contribute to the avoidance of danger and maintenance of life. All these considerations may mitigate our view of animal suffering. But a stronger argument is to be drawn from our profound ignorance of the whole question. Animals can perceive colours invisible to us; they seem to have organs of sensation of whose nature we know nothing; their instincts are far more numerous and finer than our own; what compensations may they not have? Again, what are they? Had they a past? May they not have a future? What is the relation of their consciousness to the mighty life which pulses within the universe? May not Eastern speculation about these things be nearer the truth than Western science? All these questions are in the region of the unknown, and the unknowable; and in face of them the Theistic position is simply this. We believe, on complex and cumulative proof, in an omnipotent and benevolent Creator. That belief is a positive verdict of our reason, interpreting evidence which we consider irresistible. And against such a conclusion no presumption of the imagination, which from the nature of the case cannot possibly be verified, has any logical validity at all: not to mention that such presumptions admit of being met by as probable presumptions on the other side. We decline to arraign our Creator for a deed which we have not even the means of knowing that He has done.

' All difficulties as to how they (the animals) are to be disposed of are so apparently and wholly founded in our ignorance that it is wonderful they should be insisted upon by any but such as are weak enough to think they are acquainted with the whole system of things.' . . . . 'What men require is to have all difficulties cleared; and this is, or at least for anything we know to the contrary it may be, the same as requiring to comprehend the Divine nature, and the whole plan of providence from everlasting to everlasting [1].'

But with human suffering the case is different, for here we are in a measure behind the scenes. We watch the process no longer from the outside but from within; and though it still remains mysterious, its mystery is full of meaning. In saying this we make two assumptions; first, that moral evil is an ultimate fact for us, in our present state of being, in the sense that it can neither be explained nor explained away: and, secondly, that character and not pleasure, being, and not feeling, or to phrase it more generally, the greatest goodness of the greatest number, is the primary end of ethics. The first of these assumptions most men are willing to admit, while the few philosophical attempts to disprove it have conspicuously failed. The second has the assent of all moralists except the hedonists, and those who without being aware of it are hedonists in disguise; the pessimism, for example, which makes so much of pain, being simply disappointed hedonism. Starting then from these premises, the problem of practical ethics is the formation of character in the face of moral evil. And in the solution of this problem pain and sorrow have a place which no other known agency conceivably could fill.

To begin with its simplest if lowest aspect, pain is a punishment; and without importing any *a priori* notions into the question, we find punishment to be a necessary element in the evolution of character. Punishment is a complex thing, and the tendency of civilization is to lay stress upon its corrective rather than its vindictive aspect. But

[1] Butler, *Analogy.*

we must remember that with uncivilized races this cannot be the case; and that pains and penalties, considered simply as retrospective vengeance for the past, have been historically, and in some cases still are, essential to our social development. Indeed, it is a shallow view that regards vengeance as a survival of savagery. Vengeance is intimately bound up with our sense of justice, and the true difference between the savage and the sage is that what the one eagerly inflicts upon his neighbour, the other would far more willingly inflict upon himself. Plato expressed this once for all when he said that the sinner who is punished is happier than the sinner who escapes scot free. We rightly shrink, as far as possible, from sitting in judgment on our fellow-men; but we feel none the less that our own ill deeds demand a penalty, which may vary from bodily suffering to interior shame, but which in one form or another must be endured before we can recover our self-respect. And self-respect is a necessary factor in all moral progress. Punishment, then, considered as vengeance, is a necessity for the social development of barbarous races; and though less obviously, quite as really for the personal progress of the civilized man.

Now, without committing ourselves to the statement that suffering was introduced into the world by sin, which is not a Christian dogma, though it is often thought to be so, a vast amount of the suffering in the world is obviously punishment, and punishment of a very searching kind. For not only are obvious vices punished with remorse, and disease, and shame, but ignorance, impatience, carelessness, even mistakes of judgment are punished too, and that in a degree which we are apt to consider disproportionate; forgetful that consequences are God's commentaries, and this apparent disproportion may reflect light upon the real magnitude of what we often are too ready to consider trivial things.

But these punishments, it is urged, fall on the innocent as well as the guilty. And this leads us to another point of view. Pain is not only punitive. It is also corrective and purgatorial. And this again is a fact of ordinary experience, quite apart from the further consideration of why it should be so. Among primitive races the penalties of law, by the merely mechanical process of forcibly restraining certain actions, slowly elevate the social tone. And as men rise in the scale of development and begin to be a law to themselves, the same process is continued within the individual mind. The pains and penalties of evil doing, physical and mental, tend to correct and purify the character; and when we say that men learn wisdom by experience, we mostly mean by experience of something painful. Of course, the most obvious form of this correction is that in which the suffering can be recognised by the sufferer as merited, because due to his own misdeeds. But apart from such causal connection, what we call unmerited suffering exercises the same influence in an even greater measure. Its forces, not being exhausted in the work of neutralising past evil, are able to expand and expend themselves in a positive direction, elevating, refining, dignifying the character to an infinite degree. The men of sorrows are the men of influence in every walk of life. Martyrdom is the certain road to success in any cause. Even more than knowledge, pain is power. And all this because it develops the latent capacities of our being as no other influence can. It requires no mystic insight to see the truth of this. However unable we may be to account for it, it is a fact of everyday experience, visible to ordinary common sense. And this being so, there is nothing of necessity unjust in what we call unmerited suffering, not even in the sad inheritance by children of the results of parental sin. For while the sight of the miserable entail may, if rightly used, become the parent's punishment, its imposition may be the child's call to higher things. True, like all other useful agencies, it often fails of its end; but such failure is of the problem of evil, not of the problem of pain.

And, lastly, with men, as with animals, suffering is largely prophylactic. Bodily pain sounds the alarm bell of disease in time for its removal. Mental and moral pain arrest the issues of ignorant or evil courses before it is too late. While the desire to remove pain from ourselves, or better still from others, is among the strongest incentives of the scientific discoverer, the patriot, the philanthropist. And though it may seem a fallacy to credit pain with the virtues which spring from the desire for its removal, common sense rises above logic and recognises the real value of a spur without which many of our noblest activities would cease.

Now, though all these considerations naturally lead on into theology for their further treatment, yet it should be noticed that they are in no sense exclusively theological. The penal, the corrective, the preventive, and the stimulating uses of pain are all recognised in the average man's philosophy of life. Indeed, they are too obvious to need dwelling on at any length. But the point to be noticed is, that taken together, they cover a very great deal of ground. For it is hardly too much to say that in one or other of its various aspects, every human being has need of suffering for the due development of his character. And this is a fact which should go far to outweigh much brilliant declamation of the pessimists. Pessimism, in fact, stereotypes and gives a fictitious permanence to what is only one among our many moods of thought. It harps upon the fact that we naturally shrink from pain. It ignores the fact that we are conscious of being the better for it, and unable to conceive progress without it. And though these considerations afford no solution to the speculative mystery of pain, they make in the direction of a speculative solution. They do not explain why pain exists, but they shew us that its existence, in the only region in which we can really test it, is eminently useful, and therefore consistent with providential and beneficent design. Their precise logical relation to the Theistic argument might be put as follows : Arguments drawn from many departments of life and thought converge in favour of Theism, but one large and important department, that of human suffering, blocks the way. When, however, we isolate and examine that department, we find that even within its limits the evidence of provident purpose is prominent, if not preponderant. Its prominence is certainly enough to neutralize the negative bearing of the department upon the general argument. Its preponderance, which many if not most men would admit, carries us further and makes the net evidence of the whole department an affirmative contribution to Theism.

So far common sense carries us. But when we turn to the place of pain in the religions of the world, two further thoughts are suggested. In the first place, the belief in a future life, which is common to almost all religions, at once opens endless vistas of possibility before us. The pain which has failed to purify here, may yet purify hereafter ; the high-handed wrong-doing, which has seemed to go unpunished here, may there meet with its righteous due. The pains which we have thought excessive here, may there be found to have worked out for us a far more exceeding weight of glory. And so the particular difficulty which arises from the unequal incidence of earthly suffering may one day find its adequate solution. No doubt there is an element of truth in the familiar taunt that belief in a future life has been a curse as well as a blessing to the world. In some stages of culture, for example, the future life has been supposed only to emphasize the inequalities of the present : the slave living on in everlasting slavery, and the warrior in incessant war. But this has been a partial and a passing phase of thought, which rapidly gave way before more ethical conceptions. The ethical conceptions in their turn, which were based on future rewards and punishments, confessedly could not produce a very high type of morality. But they have filled their place, and that a large one in the history of human development, while even after ceasing to be the dominant motives, they still witness to the ineradicable expectation of our race, that holiness and happiness, sin and failure, shall one day coincide. More serious and sad is the fact that distorted dreams of future punishment have often reflected a lurid light upon the whole of life ; goading zealots into cruelty, sinners into madness, thinkers into unbelief ; and have lingered on, as savage survivals, even into Christian times, to the hopeless obscuration, in many minds, of the creed that God is Love.

But even here we must draw distinctions. Early races express intensity by an accumulation of material metaphors—fecundity by an hundred breasts, omnipotence and omniscience by an hundred arms or a thousand eyes. And so, when they saw the unrighteous man enjoy the fruits of his unrighteousness, and die in unrebuked defiance of laws human and divine, their sense of outraged justice could not but express itself in terms of material horror. We have grown to be more pitiful, more refined in our moral thinking, less dogmatic about unknown things : yet neither our moral experience nor our Christianity has availed to remove the dread of that unutterable 'pain of loss,' which the passing of a soul in obdurate impenitence has ever suggested to the mind of man. And however confidently therefore we may put aside the distortions, and debasements, and interested exaggerations which have darkened the thought of future punishment, we must remember that the thought itself was no alien introduction into history ; but due to the instinctive craving of the human heart for justice; man's own tremendous verdict on his sin[1]. But the universality, or at least extreme generality of the belief in a continued existence, is quite distinct from the particular pictures of it which the imagination has variously drawn ; much as the universality of conscience is distinct from its varying content among diverse races and in different ages. And the broad fact remains that from the dawn of history the majority of mankind have believed in and looked with confidence to a future life to rectify, and therefore justify, the inequalities of earthly suffering ; however much their views have varied as to what should constitute rectification.

Secondly, there is an instinctive tendency in all religions, from the savage upwards, to view pain, whether in the form of asceticism or sacrifice, as inseparably connected with an acceptable service of the gods or God. The asceticism of poor Caliban foregoing his little mess of whelks, and that of the Hindoo whose meritorious sufferings are expected to prevail, by intrinsic right with heaven ; the hideous holocausts of Mexico, and the paper substitutes for offerings of the parsimonious or hypocritical Chinee are widely different things. But they all spring from a common instinct, variously distorted, yet persistent through all distortions, and progressively refined, till it culminates in the Hebrew substitution of the broken heart for the blood of bulls and of goats. It is the custom of some modern writers to represent the higher forms of sacrifice as merely survivals of the savage desire to propitiate the gods by food. But this is not an adequate analysis even of the savage creed. Naturally enough the primitive hunter, to whom food is the chief good, may think food the worthiest offering to the gods. But it is not simply food, but his own food, that

[1] Cf. pp. 377–8.

he offers, the choicest morsel, that which it costs him something to forego. In other words, the root of sacrifice is self-sacrifice, however crudely it may be expressed. Of course, the primitive hypocrite would seek to evade personal suffering as naturally as the civilized hypocrite will give alms at another man's expense. But sincerity must come before hypocrisy, and the sacrificial instinct is in origin sincere. Its first account of itself may be irrational, and its earlier manifestations often blundering and repulsive; and if it were now only a survival, the same should be true of its later forms, for survivals are not commonly improved in the process of surviving. But so far from this being the case, it has been refined by successive developments and is as integral an element of later as of earlier religions, being in fact the symbolic statement that a more or less painful self-surrender is the necessary condition of all human approach to the divine. Natural religion then, in the widest use of the term, carries us on beyond common sense, in attributing a mysterious value to suffering here, and expecting an explanation of its anomalies hereafter. The first belief may be called mystical, the second hypothetical, and yet the two together have done more to reconcile man to his burden of sorrow than all the philosophic comments on the uses of adversity; for they have seemed to lift him, though blindfold, into a loftier region, where he felt himself inbreathing power from on high. And so here, as in other things, natural religion leads on into Christianity.

The relation of Christianity to the problem of pain, may be best seen by contrasting it with the empirical optimism of common sense. Enlightened common sense, as we have seen, is fully aware of the uses of sorrow; but it looks at the usefulness through the sorrowfulness, as a compensation which should make the wise man content to bear his pain. The change which Christianity has effected consists in the reversal of this view of the subject. Once for all, it has put the value before the painfulness in our thoughts. The Author and Finisher of our faith, 'for the joy that was set before Him, endured the Cross, despising the shame,' and 'our light affliction, which is but for a moment, worketh for us a far more exceeding weight of glory, while we look not at the things which are seen but at the things which are unseen.' It bids us not wait 'till the sorrow comes with years,' but take up our cross, from the first moment of our conscious discipleship. And accordingly the real Christian looks at sorrow not from without, but from within, and does not approach its speculative difficulty till he is aware by experience of its practical power. Consequently he cannot explain himself to the merely external critic. He may urge in argument such general considerations as have been touched upon above, and meet the pleas of pessimism with the counterpleas of philosophic optimism; but if pressed for the inner secret of his own serenity, he can only answer with the esoteric invitation, 'Come and see.' Enter the dim sanctuary of sorrow through the shadow of the Cross. Abide there, and as your eyes grow accustomed to the darkness, the strange lines upon its walls which seemed at first so meaningless, will group themselves into shapes and forms of purposeful design.

Once for all the sinless suffering of the Cross has parted sin from suffering with a clearness of distinction never before achieved. The intellectual Greek had tended to confuse the two as kindred forms of ignorance; the weary Oriental as kindred consequences of our imprisonment in the body, 'the too too solid flesh'; the self-righteous Jew viewed blindness, or death from a falling tower, as evidence of exceptional sin. Everywhere in the ancient world the outlines of the two were undefined, and their true relation of antagonism misunderstood. But the sight of perfect sinlessness, combined with perfect suffering, has cleared our view for ever. Sin indeed always brings suffering in its train, but the suffering we now see to be of the nature of its antidote; an antidote often applied indeed with inexorable sternness, but in its intention wholly merciful. Thus every sin has its appropriate suffering. Bodily indulgence brings bodily disease; cruelty ends in cowardice; pride and vanity in shame. And though the suffering of itself cannot convert the sinner, it can and does prevent both the gratification and contagion of the sin. Then comes the more terrible sorrow of remorse; and remorse is potential penitence, and penitence potential purification. But while sin thus involves suffering, suffering does not involve sin. It is not only an antidote, but one of those antidotes which taken in time is prophylactic. And this is not only true of the pains of self-denial and self-sacrifice, the voluntary bearing of the cross, but of many an involuntary sorrow also. Delicate health, Plato's bridle of Theages, inherited pain, privation, bereavement, may all refine the character and train the spiritual eye to that purity of heart that shall see God. Pain in fact, in its manifold methods, is like the angel of the Eastern story, changing its form incessantly to cope with the shifting shapes of sin, and passing by turns into a lion, a bird, a sword, a flood, a flame, in sleepless eagerness to follow and find, and slay and quench and burn away the least last lingering particle of evil. So far from being our enemy it is our safest ally in the battle of life, and we fail through shrinking from the stern alliance. We suffer because we sin; but we also sin because we decline to suffer.

Still, the very sharpness of the severance between sin and suffering on the Cross forces upon us the further question—Why should the sinless suffer? The vicarious suffering of Christ is said to conflict with our sense of justice. And it does so, as misrepresented in much popular theology. But rightly viewed, it is the climax and complete expression of the process to which we owe the entire evolution of our race. The pleasures of each generation evaporate in air ; it is their pains that increase the spiritual momentum of the world. We enter into life through the travail of another. We live upon the death of the animals beneath us. The necessities, the comforts, the luxuries of our existence are provided by the labour and sorrow of countless fellow-men. Our freedom, our laws, our literature, our spiritual sustenance have been won for us at the cost of broken hearts, and wearied brains, and noble lives laid down. And this is only the human analogue of that transference of energy by which all life and move-ment is for ever carried on. The sun is so much the cooler by the heat it daily gives to earth ; the plant and tree the weaker by the force that has matured their fruit ; the animal generations exhausted in continuing their kind. And how should their Creator draw all men unto Him, but through the instrumentality of His own great law of sacrifice ? If we shrink from our share in the conditions of the solemn legacy, it is easy to persuade ourselves that the system of things is wrong. But if we accept it, and resolve that we too in our turn will spend and be spent for others, we find beneath all the superficial suffering the deep truth of the benediction, ' It is more blessed to give than to receive.' And in the experience of that benediction we see further still into the mysterious significance of sorrow.

Further ; but not yet to the end. For the human heart desires more than merely to work for others. It desires to be one with those for whom it works. Love is the highest form of that unity ; but even short of actual love, we instinctively crave communion and sympathy with our kind. And it is no morbid view of life to say that sorrow brings about this union in a way that joy does not. There is some-thing, under our present conditions, in the very expansiveness of joy which dissociates, while sorrow seems to weld us, like hammer strokes on steel. It is the nationality whose members have together struggled for existence, the soldiers who have faced the shock of battle side by side, the persecuted party, the husband and wife who have known common suffering that are most intimately, indissolubly one. Nor is this union merely negative like the bond which fellow-prisoners feel, and yet would eagerly escape from if they could. It is due to a dis-tinct sense that the common crisis has aroused all that is highest and noblest and most spiritual, and therefore most sympathetic in the soul.

But again, it is only in the light from the Cross, that we can see why pain should possess this power. For in that light we understand how pain unites us to each other, because, as even natural religion dimly felt, it unites us to God, and therefore through Him to those who in Him live and move and have their being. It unites us to God because it purifies us, because it detaches us from earth, because it quickens our sense of dependence, because it opens our spiritual vision, and above all because He too, as man, has suffered. But the mystics who have seen furthest into heavenly things have felt that it unites us to God in still more vital wise, as being, at least in its form of sacrifice, the very beating of the heart of love. And so they have raised the question,—Has it not an antitype far in the illimitable depths of the unseen? For we are told that God is Love; and love, as we know it, must be shewn in sacrifice; though the sacrifice grows painless in proportion as the love is pure. And when we recall how in the days of our Lord's ministry on earth, Father, Son, and Holy Spirit bore their witness each to other, but no one of the Holy Persons ever to Himself, we are led on to wonder whether 'in the light that no man can approach unto,' where the Three are One, some higher analogue of what we call sacrifice does not for ever flame; whose radiant reflection on the universe only becomes shadow when it falls on a world of sin. But however these high things may be, the simplest Christian feels and knows that, in his present state, the unitive way, the way to union with both God and man, is the 'via dolorosa,' the way of the cross:—a serious and solemn belief, which is very far from leading to complacency, in presence of the awful spectacle of animal and human pain; but still is based on sufficient experience to justify the hope that all its mystery will be one day solved. More than this we do not expect, for the intellect, in our Christian view, is as much on its probation and as liable to error as the will; and inordinate curiosity not less misleading than inordinate desire.

IV.

PREPARATION IN HISTORY FOR CHRIST.

THE paradox of Divine mystery implied in the words 'The Word was made flesh,' is not exhausted by a right understanding of the Person of Christ. It extends to the relations between Christ and History. On the one hand, the Incarnation of the Son of God appears as supreme, solitary, unique, transcending all analogies of experience, all limitations of nationality or generation, determined before the world was, beyond the power of any antecedents to pro-duce, the entry of a new thing into the world. It appears, in short, as a miracle. But, on the other hand, it appears as an historical event, occurring at a particular date, appealing to the feelings and fulfilling the hopes of the time, a climax and a new point of departure in the historical order. It does this, necessarily, because this is involved in the act of taking flesh, of entering simply, literally, naturally into the conditions of human life. Such a thing occurs, and must occur, in the natural order. To say this is not to dictate what a Divine reve-lation must be, but only to shew what Christianity asserts of itself. In this way it was good in God's sight that His revelation should come.

It follows from this, in the first place, that there must be two ways, both valid and necessary, of approaching in thought and study Christ manifest in the flesh. We may treat the fact of His appearing with little or no reference to historical relations, for its own inherent un-changing truth and meaning. We may also treat it as clothed in historical event, to be understood in its relations with what went before and followed after and stood around. The two methods sup-plement one another. It may be true that the simple personal claim which the solitary figure of Jesus Christ makes upon us, by its un-alterable moral dignity and beauty, its typical humanity, its unearthly authority, is the strongest that can be made : none the less may that claim be confirmed and reinforced if we see the same figure as it were upon an historical throne; if it should become clear that what went before (and what followed after) does, in any way, pay homage to Him; if the *manner* of His appearing in place and time be calculated to heighten the impression which the *fact* of it makes.

And in the second place, it follows that to start in any historical treatment of the subject of this paper from the central twofold assertion as to Christ, made by S. John in the phrase 'The Word was made flesh,' is to obtain at once the right clue to the lines which it should follow.

(1) To do so is not to beg the question or to fetter the enquiry, but only to define what kind of evidence, if any, the study of Christ's relation to foregoing history can yield. We see that it must be such as works in us the conviction that He both does, and does not, occur 'naturally' at the time and place when He appeared; that history leads up to Him and prepares His way, and yet that no force of natural antecedents can account for Him or for His work. It is true that evidence for either side of this two-sided impression may have sufficient weight to determine faith especially with individual minds. The contrast between Christ and all else in history, arresting the attention and suggesting the thought of special Divine presence, may of itself be a spring of faith: or, upon the other hand, a clear discernment of His natural supremacy in history may lead a man on to higher truth. But the true evidence, as corresponding to the true and full claim, will be that which suggests the conclusion with simultaneous and equal force from either side.

(2) If the aim is not evidence but instruction, and we desire simply to understand better what is true of our Lord's relation to history, it will still advantage us greatly to start from the same point. We shall be able to recognise freely and without fear of contradiction or confusion, on the one side, the way in which the lines of history, of human experience, aspiration, achievement, character, need, lead up to Christ and issue in Him: and on the other, the unearthly and peculiar greatness of Him Who spake as never man spake, Who taught as one that had authority and not as the Scribes, Who was not convinced by any of sin: Whose daily intimacy with a disciple issued in that disciple's confession, 'Thou art the Christ, the Son of the Living God.' Such a method, starting from the Christian claim, and trying to trace out all that it involves, need not be only for the believer, any more than the quest for evidence or witness is for those only who do not believe. The Christian tests the foundations, and welcomes every corroboration, of his faith: while, in dwelling on the character of the work and of its relations to all else, the non-believer may come to find the conviction grow upon him that it was indeed 'wrought of God.'

(3) From the same point, we see at once to what double misunder-

standing or double attack the Gospel not only may but must be liable. On the one side, it may be refused a hearing as miraculous ; it may be understood as violating the natural order which it transcends ; it may be regarded and resented as an anomaly in history. On the other side, a consideration of the aptness of its occurrence when and where it did occur, and of its harmonious relations to many lines of tendency will suggest the suspicion that it may be after all only a result, though a supreme and surprising result, of historical forces. In a word, it may be accused at once from separate, possibly from the same, quarters as too supernatural and too natural to be what it claims to be. It is all-important to notice at the outset that liability to this double attack is an inevitable incident of its true character and of that which makes its glory, viz. the presence of true Godhead under truly human conditions.

But to return to the main point.

The importance and interest of the subject of this paper may be inferred, as we have seen, directly from what the Incarnation claims to be. But we are not left to infer it for ourselves. Nothing is clearer or more striking than the place which it occupied from the outset in the declaration of the Gospel. Jesus Himself spoke of the Scribes of the kingdom as 'bringing forth out of their treasure things new and old'; and laid it down as a first principle of His kingdom that He was 'not come to destroy, but to fulfil[1].' While with surprising and commanding clearness He centres men upon Himself, and distinguishes Himself from all who came before Him, from 'the prophets and the law which prophesied until John'; He yet with evident care draws the new out of the old, and fits it on to the old : He delineates His own mission as a climax in a long appeal of God to Israel[2], and the opposition to Him and His, as a chapter of *dénouement* in the history of an old conflict between God and the ungodly[3]. He sees a 'necessity' for the happening of things to fulfil what had been said of old[4]. The very pith of the disciples' ignorance is their failure to see how the features of His work and character had been traced beforehand, and the supreme teaching which they receive from Him is that which discloses His correspondence to the whole tenor of the Scriptures of the past[5]. The teaching of the Apostles, and of those who followed them, is faithful to these lines. Though they have to convince the world of an Event which works a revolution, which is to turn men from darkness to light : though their perfect confidence in their own truth makes them see the things that went before as elements, 'weak and beggarly elements[6],' and they have moreover battles to

---

[1] S. Matt. xiii. 52 ; v. 17.
[2] S. Matt. xxi. 33–38.
[3] S. Matt. v. 12 ; xxiii. 30–37.
[4] S. Mark xiv. 49 ; S. Luke xxii. 37.
[5] S. Luke xxiv. 25, 26, 44.
[6] Gal. iv. 9.

fight against these 'elements' set up again as antagonists: though their adherence to the Old Testament was an ever fruitful source of difficulty and attack (of which Judaizing and Gnostic controversies are the record), yet nevertheless they unswervingly maintained the inspiration of the Old Testament, and stood upon it; and we distinguish without hesitation as their normal, primary, characteristic method that of appeal to the correspondence between their Gospel and every hope and word of Israel's faith: the 'revelation of the mystery .. is .. by the scriptures of the prophets .. made known to all nations[1]. The Hebrews who wistfully look back to their temple, law, and ritual, are not taught a stern forgetfulness of what had been, nor led vaguely to spiritualize its meaning, but are led to recognise in each part of the ancient system a line which leads up to Christ. Finally, the disciple who sets the true being of his Master in monumental and awful splendour as the Word who 'was with God and was God' now made manifest in the flesh, in the same breath carries us to the very core and source of all that can be implied in preparation by declaring the same Word to have been 'in the world' before, to have been the author of all things, and the unseen light of men[2].

The relation of Christ to history, or the preparation for the Gospel, is then no afterthought of our own or any recent time. It was Augustine's saying that Christianity was as old as the world[3]: and Tertullian's (one of almost venturesome boldness) that in the previous history Christ was schooling Himself for incarnation[4]. But it is not difficult to see that our own time is one which is specially fitted to appreciate and handle this aspect of the Christian truth. Our cultivation of the historical method, our historical realism or sense of the relation of persons or events to historical setting, our recognition of the part played in forming structure, function, character, by gradual process, by heredity, by evolution, our developed understanding of the links by which the parts and successions in all nature, and not least in what is human, are bound together—all these go to form a habit of mind which in presence of such a Revelation as that of the Gospel will at once busy itself, whether for satisfaction, for edification, for controversy, or for interpretation, with the relation of the Truth to the world into which it came, to all from amongst which it sprung. In such a time it is natural that attack should try to shew that facts which historical criticism has done much to secure, and a Life which it has become impossible to treat as a myth, are simply explicable

[1] Rom. xvi. 26. So the pages of the early apologists are to our feeling almost cumbered by the profuseness of their appeal to these Scriptures.
[2] S. John i. 1, 14, 9, 10.
[3] *Ep.* cii. 12.

[4] *De Carne Christi* vi. Eum Christum qui jam tunc et adloqui . . . humanum genus ediscebat in carnis habitu: cp. *adv. Prax.* xvi. ediscebat Deus in terris cum hominibus conversari.

according to the natural laws of historical causation. It is natural that Christianity should be explained as the flower and bloom of Judaism, or as sprung from the fusion of Greek and Jewish influences in a Galilean medium. Such explanations may not be new, but they are urged with new resources and a more subtle ingenuity. They have the advantage of being the sort of explanations which are naturally most congenial to the time. But out of the very stress of such attacks may come a special corroboration of Christian truth. The experiment is crucial : it can hardly be expected that attack of this kind can ever command greater skill and resource than it does at present. If therefore it should be proved to fail : if we are able to look men in the face and ask whether when all allowance is made for the subtle 'chemistries' of history and for the paradoxical way in which historical results spring from what precedes them, it is possible to think that Jesus Christ and His religion were a mere growth from antecedents—then we have here the prospect of such a confirmation of faith as no age less historically scientific could, in that kind, give and receive.

But this negative result, great as its value may be, can only be part of what Christian science may yield in this sphere for the elucidation and support of faith. It should surely be able to display with greater breadth and delicacy than ever before that correspondence between the Revelation of Christ and what went before it, which was of old indicated by saying that Christ came in the 'fulness of the time.' It should be able to enhance, and not (as men fear) to impair, the evidence of a Divine presence and influence, preparing for that which was to come, moulding the plastic material of history for a 'far-off Divine event.' It may seem as if this was not so. It may seem, for example, as if the severity and activity of historical and linguistic criticism had dimmed the clearness of those correspondences between prophetic utterances spoken centuries before Christ and the points in Him or His work whereby they were fulfilled, which were once so clear. It may seem, it is evidently true, that stricter canons of interpretation forbid for us that unbounded use of the happy expedient of allegory which could make everything in the Old Testament speak of Christ. But even if this were so (and with regard to prophecies we only partially grant it), is there no countervailing gain to reckon? The hand of God may be seen in what is marvellous, startling, exceptional, unexplained. Can it not be seen as distinctly and as persuasively in what is orderly, steadfast, intelligible, and where our reason, made in God's likeness, can follow along in some degree with the how and the why of His working? It was Christ's will to give special signs, yet the curiosity which 'sought after a sign' was not honoured by Christ like that wisdom which 'discerned the signs of the

H

times,' and so could see the force of the special signs that were given,
because it saw them in their true moral and spiritual context [1]. Have
we any reason to hope that our time may be suffered to do (and even
be doing) something for the interpretation of the witness of history to
Christ which has not been done before, and which is even an advance
upon what has been done? Let us consider for a moment (in order
to answer this question) what it is which specially engrosses the
interest and admiration of all of us in the different branches of modern
study and enquiry. It is the beauty of *process*. The practical men
among us watch process in its mechanical forms as contrived by
invention. The naturalists and the men of science have to an extraordinary extent developed our perception of it in nature : they shew us
its range, and its incredible delicacy, flexibility, and intricacy ; they
shew us its enormous patience in the unceasing yet age-long movements which by microscopic or less than microscopic changes accumulate the coal, or lessen the mountain ; they shew us the wonderful
power of adaptation by which it accommodates itself to surroundings,
and appropriates and transforms them to its need. The embryologist
developes its wonders as it makes 'the bones to grow in the womb of
her that is with child.' And the historians in their sphere do the like :
it is for them, if not the beginning and end of their work, at least the
most powerful of their methods, to shew the processes by which
institutions, customs, opinions, rise and decline ; to arrange the facts
so as to display on their chart the steps of growth, the stages of
decay; to shew influences blending to form events, and parting again
to destroy or re-shape them.

There is beauty in all this, more than we can, perhaps, altogether
analyse or explain. As living beings we sympathise with the life and
movement of it all (or, as in the case of intricate machinery, with the
imitation of life) compared with what stands stark, solid, unchanging ;
as intelligent beings we revel and delight in its intricacy, and, further,
we are gratified by the way in which it subdues with explanation what
would be anomalous, abrupt, motiveless, in the way of change or
event. It gives us something like the pleasure which we take in the
beauty of the exquisite subtle curves and shaded surfaces of a Raphael
figure compared with the rough outline of a Dürer woodcut. But we
could not long rest in the admiration of mere process, whether
delicate or colossal. There is a rational element present in, or controlling, our sense of beauty, which asks whence and whither, which
demands unity in detail ; and this finds altogether new and delightful
gratification when it can see a relation, a meaning, a grouping, a
symmetry, of which processes are the ministers and instruments.

It is, then, this idea of beauty in process that we bring with us a

[1] S. Matt. xi. 4, 5 ; xii. 39 ; xvi. 3.

we approach to behold the facts and method of God's Redemptive Work. It is altogether too strong in us to be left behind as we cross the threshold of this region ; it is too much connected with all our thinking and experience. It is very possible that there may be exaggeration about it in us : and it is indispensable for us to recognise this, 'le défaut de notre qualité.' But all the same we cannot disown, though we must control, what is so specially our own. And if our love of process is prepared to be critical, it is also prepared to be gratified : and there is opened a prospect of fresh witness to the truth of the unchanging Gospel, if it should be found that its introduction into this world is ushered in by all the beauty of process, with all the grandeur of slow unhasting preparation, the surprises of gradual transformation, the delicacies of combination, which process allows.

Such a sight is much more than wonderful, and has in it, if our ideas of what is Divine are not very narrow, much more evidence of God's hand than any mere wonder can have. But it is as wonderful as anything can be. And if we still plead that our sense of wonder stipulates for exceptionalness, it has its own way of satisfying this— the way of uniqueness. For those features which we admire in process are capable, if combined with a certain degree of grandeur, complete- ness, and particularity, of conveying to us the impression of a unique thing. We may dismiss as a dialectical refinement the objection which has been made that, as is doubtless true, 'everything is unique.' None the less, there is a meaning in our ordinary language when it applies the epithet 'unique' to certain persons, classes, or things. A man of science may properly speak of a certain uniqueness in the way in which natural conditions are combined so as to make life possible : a historian will certainly miss truth if he does not recognise a special uniqueness in certain historical epoch-making moments. In pro- portion as we believe in Mind ordering the things of nature and history, such uniqueness will have speaking significance. And as uniqueness has its degrees, and rises according to the scale, quantity, character and completeness, of that which goes to make it up, so its significance will rise proportionately, until at last, arriving at unique- ness, which seems to us absolute, we gain evidence that there is before us a Supreme Thing, a true centre to the world. The evidence is not indeed demonstrative, but it is in a high degree corroborative, and it is the highest which history can offer. It is this evidence of unique- ness which, as it seems to me, we of the present day may with special fitness seek, and shall with special welcome find :

(1) in the shaping of world-history towards the Christian era,

(2) in the special preparation of the Jewish nation.

Within the compass of a paper like the present, it is impossible to do more than indicate the lines which, even without any high degree of special education, a Christian's thought may travel in tracing the Divine work of preparation and witness.

I. In the first part of our enquiry the distinction between an outward and an inward working suggests itself as convenient, though necessarily imperfect: the one consisting in a moulding of the material facts of history, such as the geographical distribution of peoples, and the political and social order; the other in a like use of the changes in thought, feeling, and the like.

(1) It can never be altogether too hackneyed to dwell on the strange value to the world's history of the two peninsulas which we know as Greece and Italy, thrust out into that Mediterranean Sea, which was itself so remarkable as a centre and 'medium' of the western world, binding its many nations together. They share with other lands of the temperate zone all its possibilities of hardy and vigorous life: but, besides this, their sky and sea, their conveniences and difficulties, had a special stimulus to give to their early inhabitants. They were extraordinarily well suited to be the seed-plots of civilization. And these seed-plots were aptly fertilized, first by the Phoenicians, those carrier-birds of antiquity dropping seed along the Mediterranean coasts: and then by the happy contact between Greece and the other Greece opposite, to which the island bridges of the Aegean linked it, where, on the narrow strip of coast plain and rich river valley between the sea and the high plateaus of Asia Minor, the Ionians enjoyed, as Herodotus says[1], the fairest climate in the world. Upon this debouched, with the rivers from the interior, the highways along which travelled westward the civilization or the power of the dimly known but highly important early Phrygian monarchy, or from yet farther east, of the mighty Assyria. The recent discoveries of Prof. Ramsay and others re-interpret and emphasize to us this early connection between the Asian lands and Greece in Europe, of which the Lion Gate of Mycenae is a monument. What Greece thus took with her left hand she could pass across with her right to yet another Greece, 'Great Greece,' in Sicily and Southern Italy. But we may easily fail to recognise how much all this delicate and tender growth depended on favourable circumstance, and we cannot too carefully mark how space was made awhile for it to spring. The 'hills stood about' both peninsulas on the North to shelter them from intrusion: but this barrier, sufficient for ordinary times, would hardly have resisted the heavy thrust of the later pressure of population from the East and North-East, which, when it did begin, so nearly crushed Rome, and which, if it had come earlier, might have easily stifled Greek and Roman civilization in the cradle. The reader of the Persian Wars will watch almost with awe within how little Greece came of what appeared alike

[1] Hdt. i. 142.

to Asiatic and Greek a certain subjection to the Persian. A difference of twenty years earlier, the chance of a different temper in the little Athenian people, the use by Darius of the methods of Xerxes, would, humanly speaking, have decided the other way the fate of western civilization. It is easier again to admire than to explain the happy fortune which brought the mountain kingdom of Macedon to its moment of aggression just too late to hurt the flowering and fruitage of Greece, just in time to carry its seed broadcast over Eastern, Syrian, and Egyptian lands. From all the sequence of the Graeco-Roman history which follows, and in which nothing is more important to all the purposes of Providence than the simple fact of the order of these two, Greek first, Roman second, we can here select only one feature of capital importance, viz. the transformation of a world intensely localized and sub-divided into one as singularly united and homogeneous. Follow S. Paul and see his circuits, watch him claiming the safeguard of the same Roman citizenship in the Macedonian town and in the capital of Palestine, laying hold at Caesarea on the horns of a central tribunal of justice at Rome, borne thither by the sails of the carrying trade in the 'ship of Alexandria,' meditating a journey into Spain, numbering among his Roman converts, as seems probable, one who had a direct connection with Roman Britain, writing in the same Greek to Rome and to the highlanders of Galatia, never crossed in his journeys by any track of war, never stopped by any challenge of frontier or custom-house: these are so many object-lessons to shew what the 'Pax Romana' and the Roman unity of power and organization imported for the growth of a world-religion. This was the time when it could be complained that it was impossible to flee from the Caesar's wrath because the Caesar owned the world. And to make the impression more distinct, let the eye travel backward a little, or forward a little: backward into the second or even the first century B.C., when this same Mediterranean world was still in greater part an unconsolidated chaos of political débris; when the tumult of the Macedonian and Syrian wars of Rome and then of her desolating civil strife filled the world with noise and occupied its thought and destroyed its peace; when the sea was impassable because of pirates, and when the West was still in great part unsubdued and formidable barbarism: or forward, across the space during which the Gospel had spread its influence and struck its roots and won its power, to the time so soon following, when the lands that had known no war were again traversed by the armies of rival emperors, and the barbarians began to dismember the West, and the gloom of a great fear preoccupied men's hearts. To say nothing of the middle ages, what unity of the Mediterranean world and the lands affiliated to it has the whole of later history got to shew, that can compare for a moment with the unity of the early Empire, focussed in its cosmopolitan capital Rome?

And in this there is much more than a mechanical provision for the progress of a world-religion. It is not merely that its heralds find a complete facility of communication, peaceful conditions, and a ' lingua franca ' ready for their use. We must realize how the unity had been obtained. It had been by pulverizing separate nationalities, separate patriotisms, separate religions; by destroying or leaving only in a municipal form the centres round which human energy and loyalty had been wont to gather. Thus the world had been turned into that ' cold and icy plain ' of which M. Renan speaks. And it is not too much to say that this process had destroyed just so many barriers to the entrance of Christianity. We have only to realize what had been previously the universal character of the worships of the western world, viz. that they had been local, the common and exclusive possession of the citizens of one place or state, and inextricably bound up with the being and welfare of that particular community. Such religions, and people bred under them, would have met Christianity, not so much with criticism of its doctrines, or with rival doctrines of their own, as with ideas and a frame of mind so alien to a spiritual and universal religion like the Gospel that it would have found no foothold in attacking them. Conceive the force with which what even in the second century after Christ the heathen objector urged, ' it is not creditable to alter the customs handed down to us from our fathers [1],' would have come from the Roman of the earlier Republic, or the Greek of the times of freedom. Nay, we may without rashness hazard the conjecture that had it been possible for the Gospel to overcome these conditions it would have done so prematurely and with loss: that they were in their time and place ministers of good: that they were bound up with that vigorous energy of development within one small limited horizon, by which, as we shall see, the preparation of the heathen world was carried out.

It was the negative aid of the Empire to Christianity that it destroyed these. But it lent more positive help. It created a demand, or at least a need, for a universal religion. Of this there are several proofs. The religious phenomena of the time other than Christianity supply the first. There is an attempt, or more than one attempt, to provide such a religion. There is the attempt by way of comprehension, of making all the gods live together as joint inhabitants of a common Pantheon. There is the attempt by way of construction, in the worship of the one Power about which there was no doubt, the Goddess Rome, and of the Emperor her deified representative. There is also, we may perhaps add, the attempt by way of philosophic

[1] Clem. Alex. *Protrept.* cx. init.

thought. For philosophy at this time had a religious bent which increased not improbably as the circulation of Christian thought stole unknown through the veins of society : and it felt after the One Being whose Personal existence and Fatherhood it waveringly discerned, but whom yet it could not steadily distinguish from a personified order of nature. Such a religious idea, needed to complete Cicero's commonwealth of the Universe comprehending Gods and men, may be seen with increasing clearness in Seneca, Epictetus, and Aurelius. The need of a universal religion is thus directly shewn. But other proofs, as clear though less direct, are to be drawn from the other departments of human thought. For literature was already a unity, into which whatever the genius of provincials like Lucan, or Seneca, or Pliny contributed was gathered up. And it is a commonplace that the greatest constructive result of the imperial period was the creation or development of a universal code of law.

(2) In what has been last said we have almost crossed the imaginary line by which we were to divide the preparation in external fact from that which was more inward in thought and feeling. To deal with this latter may seem almost ridiculous : since to do so must involve the presumption of summarizing in a few lines the drift of the literature and thought of antiquity. Yet, in the briefest words, it may be possible to suggest a few true outlines of the shape which an account of that drift should take. It would certainly represent the mental history of the classical world in its relation to the Gospel as supplying a double preparation, positive and negative : a positive preparation by evolving ideas which the Gospel could work into its own fabric, or a frame of mind which would make for it a suitable 'nidus' and a receptive soil : a negative preparation by the breakdown of human nature's own constructive and speculative efforts, and by the room thus left for a revelation which would unite the broken and useless fragments of thought and minister to unsatisfied needs. And of these the negative seems the more predominant and the more direct. In so saying we are guided by what appears to be the teaching of the New Testament. It seems as though the main upshot of that time was, and was meant to be, the failure of the world 'by wisdom'[1] to find the truth : though when this has been recognised and acknowledged, then the world might find, as we may find, that all the while in this unattaining and abortive thought God had put impulses from His own wisdom, and prepared materials for His own coming work. It is the typical history of the 'natural man' : and though what is primary and indispensable is that the natural man should learn the poverty and misery of his own state, and be ready to die to his life, yet the natural man too is the true though perverted work of God,

[1] 1 Cor. i. 21.

and in his thoughts and instincts, his emotions and speculations, must be found a witness to which the revelation will appeal, and a response which it will elicit. It is impossible not to follow the track so suggested, and to see in the early stages of Greek life, the lusty youth-time of the natural man. Casting off the bright and truthful simplicity, and the happy story-telling of its childhood, it begins (we speak of the times between 600 and 450 B.C.) to try its young energies upon the problems of the world : it suggests its explanations, quick, ingenious, one-sided, changing, of how the world came to be : 'it came from water,' 'from air,' 'from fire : ' 'it came from the dance of atoms : ' 'nay, but these give us only the *how*, it came from something more than these, it came from mind : ' 'are you sure what *it* is ? fix upon any part of it and you will find it slip through your fingers, for all is change, and change is all we know ; ' these are the quick *premières ébauches* of its young speculation. But already there is a sound of alarm in the air. That challenge asking whether there was an 'it' at all ; and if so, whether by parity of cavil there was any solidity in the other assumptions of thought, in 'good' and 'evil,' 'truth' and 'falsehood,' 'beauty' and 'ugliness ; ' or at least anything beyond such mere relative and convenient meaning as there is in 'big' or 'little,' 'thick' or 'thin,' 'wet' or 'dry'—this sobers men. Thought feels its own dangers. It must try its hand more seriously at some true constructive work : and so there follows that great period in which, steadied by the strong grip and sharp discipline of the great prophet of natural conscience and natural instinct, Socrates, it addresses itself to its great task of wringing her secret from the world. It is done and necessarily done in the sheer self-reliance of the unaided mind, yet of the mind in the fullest sense of the word ; not the mere critical understanding, but the whole spiritual and rational energy of the man, not disowning its dependence on a discipline of character and a severe and painful training of its own powers. The results, so splendid and yet so inadequate, so rich in great intuitions and suggestions, so patient and successful in much of its detail, is preserved to us in the work of Plato and Aristotle. Christian thought can never be interested in disparaging that work : Christian thinkers at different times have done special honour to different aspects of it : and the position of Aristotle in the works of Dante, and of Aquinas, and in the frescoes of the Spanish chapel, is the sign of the ungrudged admiration given by what in our modern way we might regard as among the least appreciative and discriminating of Christian times. But the most ungrudging admiration cannot prevent our seeing, and history compels us to see, what it lacked. It lacked a foundation upon a Rock. It had the certainty, if certainty at all, which belongs to profound intuitions and to a wide interpretation of experience, not that which makes a definite, settled, and above all communicable conviction. All the while narrower, pettier, more captious, or more ordinary minds had been asking 'what is truth' in a very different spirit; had displayed the independence and captiousness of youth, and not its hopeful and trustful creativeness. And more and more this lower element began to prevail. When it became a question not of projecting systems which should impress and absorb the higher minds of a few generations, but of providing that which should pass on with men, the common run of men, into the advancing years, and stand the strain of the world's middle life; then it was found that the human mind unaided was more powerful to destroy than to build or to maintain. The dark horse of Plato's chariot pulled down his fellow: in the unaided human understanding the critical faculty proved stronger than the constructive: without the point of attachment in a central truth to which men's high thoughts could reach and cling, or (to change the figure) without a clearly-disclosed goal of truth towards which they could be seen to tend and converge, they could not maintain or justify themselves: 'the carnal mind' was against them and unworthy of them: as regards any real adoption of them by mankind for fruitful and trustworthy convictions, they passed away, according to that law of which the modern poet speaks:—

> Eternal hopes are man's
> Which when they should maintain themselves aloft
> Want due consistence: like a pillar of smoke
> That with majestic energy from earth
> Rises but, having reached the thinner air,
> Melts and dissolves, and is no longer seen[1].

We shall not be wrong in saying that the course of philosophy after Aristotle displayed increasingly the collapse of the experiment of speculative self-reliance. Scepticism was not confined to the 'Sceptics,' nor even shared only by the Epicureans: it deeply underlay the philosophy of the Stoics. But as with advancing life men baffled in their early sanguineness fall back (both for good and evil) and content themselves with the energies of practical life, so the mind of that day baffled and despairing of the speculative problem did not abandon, but transferred, its self-reliance; men threw themselves with a sort of defiance into the organization of conduct; 'imperturbableness' and 'self-sufficiency' became watchwords of their thought[2]. This is the character of Stoicism: this explains its vogue and wide indirect influence; its curious likeness to its apparently quite alien contemporary, Epicureanism, in a common cultivation of self-sufficingness; and, finally, its ready alliance with the natural tendencies of Roman character when it passed from Greece to Rome.

---

[1] Wordsworth, *Excursion* iv.   [2] Ἀταραξία (Epicurean): αὐτάρκεια.

Here again was a great experiment, which had no mean success. We admire almost with awe its unsparing thoroughness, its austerity, its unworldliness, its courage, its endurance. In its later forms, when some power has touched it with gentleness, we yield it even a warmer and tenderer admiration. Only what we cannot do is to disguise its failure as a great spiritual experiment. We cannot forget how it left the mass of men untouched, how it concentrated strength by what it neglected of human sympathy and effort, how it revealed a disease and palsy of human nature which it could not cure : how at its heart it had no certainty of conviction to give peace and to resist the forces of decay. Humanity will never, perhaps, wind itself higher. But it was a height on which human strength is insufficient to stand. There lacked a sure word of truth : the joy and fruitfulness of an inspiration: a grace which could minister to the weakness, as well as summon the forces, of human nature. We cannot be blind to its failure unless we share it : unless, that is, we are trying to satisfy ourselves by some philosophy of life which misses its secrets, has no key to many of its problems, and at heart despairs of its solution. The experiment of moral self-reliance, then, failed in its turn.

But we spoke of a positive as well as a negative upshot to all this Gentile history : a positive contribution to the preparation for Christ. Where shall we look for this ? Surely alongside of, and in the same plane with, the failures. If one chief result of the history of the ancient world was to exhibit the insufficiency of man's efforts to find truth and righteousness and life, this must be completely shewn in proportion as the efforts were noble, and therefore in proportion as they realized (though, at the moment, only for disappointment) the capacities, the possibilities, the true desires and ideals of man. If man the race, like man the individual, was finally to find salvation by dying to himself, to his own natural man, he could only do this when it had been adequately and magnificently proved both that he could not save himself, and how splendidly worth saving he was. He must do his best, that he may despair of his best. Do we not feel that this is just what was worked out by the histories of Greece and Rome ? They are splendid experiments of human power. Diverse in their method, they combine in this result. In Greece the experiment is by way of spontaneity, of free lively development, conditioned only by its own instincts of taste and beauty. And Rome represents the alternative plan of seeking strength by discipline, by subordination, by distrust of novelty, by sacrifice of individuality to the corporate life, and of sentiment and opinion to the rule of law. Both realize deathless types of matured human life, of its beauty, its brilliant graces, its dignity, its honour, its strength. Perhaps, according to the onesidedness which limits so severely the works and lives of men, it might have been impossible that these possibilities of his nature should have been *first* realized with the same solidity and fulness in presence of those mighty truths, speaking of what was above man, which brooded over the history of the Jews and came forth into the world with the Gospel. Yet they are indispensable to the fulness of the Christian work: they are the human material: and that material must be first-rate in its kind. We owe it perhaps permanently to Greece and Rome that we recognise fully the grace of God's original workmanship in man, the validity of his instincts, his individual value, the sacredness and strength of all his natural social bonds, the wisdom and power possessed by his incorporated life. These are things which we could never have realized if all the world had been brought up in the barbarous societies of ancient Europe or under the great despotisms of Egypt and Asia. The religions of Asia may perhaps shew us by contrast the immense importance to a religion of being able to build with sound and adequate materials on the human side. That Greece and Rome did contribute specially in this way to the work of the true religion may be shewn by the way in which men have again and again turned back to these original sources for fresh impulses of liberty or vigour.

But these things had their day and passed. The age of Pericles and of Demosthenes, the great days of the Roman Republic, are only epochs in the history, long past at the era of our Lord. We look to see whether there is any positive preparation for Him and His Gospel in the whole drift of that history, and especially in tendencies which took a developed form closer to the era of Christianity [1].

General and popular impressions about the character and course of the history will put us on the track of a true answer. It is impossible to look at the history of the classical world without getting a double impression, that it is a history of failure and degeneracy, and yet that it is a history of bettering and progress. If we take the world at the Christian era, the times of political brilliancy and energy are over, and men are sinking into a uniformity of servility and stagnation: morally the ancient severity is lost, and the laws of Augustus are freely coping with the results of a general dissoluteness as to morality and marriage: economically society is disfigured by a vast slave system, by the disappearance of honest and thriving free labour, and by great developments of luxury and pauperism: in literature, though it is the 'golden age,' the signs are not wanting,

---

[1] The words 'era of Christianity' are used intentionally rather than the more precise 'era of Christ,' because anything which (without being influenced unless in the most impalpable way by Chris-tianity) prepared the world through the first and even the second century of the era to receive the Gospel may be fairly included as preparation for the revelation of Christ.

in artificiality and the excessive study of form, of imminent rapid decline into the later rhetorical culture : in philosophy speculation had run itself out into scepticism and self-destruction : and in religion a disbelief in the ancient gods and a doubt of all Divine providence is matter of open profession. And yet there is a bettering. The laws of the Empire become a model of humanity, equitableness, and simplicity. Seneca and Epictetus rise to thoughts of moral purity and sublimity and delicacy which at times seem hardly unworthy of the New Testament : and their humane and comprehensive ideas have cast off the limitations which the narrow life of Greek cities set to those of their greater predecessors.

Here then is a great clearing of the stage, and a great predisposing of thought and sentiment, for a religion which proclaimed a good tidings for all men without distinction of ' Jew or Greek, Barbarian and Scythian, bond or free'; for a religion of compassion ; for a religion wholly spiritual and unpolitical. There are traces distinct and widespread of special tendencies to such a religion, and they are connected with the best side of the life of the time. The enormous diffusion of the ' collegia' or clubs, in which the members were drawn together without distinction of rank, or even of free and slave, in a partly religious bond, shews the instinct of the time feeling for a religion of brotherhood. There is a delicacy of family life as seen in Plutarch, in Pliny, in Fronto, which shews readiness for a religion such as should regenerate the simple instincts and relations of humanity. In the position and function of the philosophers (who sometimes half-remind one of mendicant friars[1], sometimes of the confessor or chaplain in families of rank, in their relation to education and to the vicissitudes of later life) there is implied a concentration of thought and interest upon character and upon the discipline of individual life, a sensibility to spiritual need, which all indicates a ground prepared for Christian influence. And, finally, whether it be from the stealing in of Eastern influences, or from a reaction against the cold scepticism of Ciceronian times, or from a half-political half-genuine sense of the necessity of religion to society, or from a sort of awed impression created by the marvellous fortune of Rome, or from the steady impact of the clear strong deep religious faith of the Jews scattered everywhere, and everywhere, as we know, to an extraordinary extent leavening society, or, as time went on, from a subtle influence of Christianity not yet accepted or even consciously known,—there was, it is notorious, a return towards religion in the mind of men. The temples were again thronged : priests became philosophers. In Neo-Platonism thought again looks upward, and the last phase of Greek philosophy was in the phrase of the dry and dispassionate

[1] Capes, *Age of Antonines.*

Zeller[1] 'a philosophy of Revelation' which sought knowledge partly in the inner revelation of the Deity and partly in religious tradition. This movement was indeed a rival of Christianity; it came to put out some of its strength in conscious rivalry, or it tried in Gnostic heresies to rearrange Christianity on its own lines; but it was the result and witness of a disposition of men's hearts which made way for the Gospel.

It was not, then, merely true that the failures of the heathen world left it empty, hungering, distrustful of itself; not merely that the world of that particular epoch gave extraordinary facilities of an outward kind for the diffusion of a world-religion: but also that in some of its most characteristic and deepest workings, in thoughts and dispositions which it had purchased at a great cost of ancient glories and liberties and of all that was proud and distinctive in Greek and Roman religion, there was that which would make men ready for Christianity and cause it to be to them, as it could not have been to their ancestors, intelligible, possible, and congenial.

II. Dr. Westcott has drawn, in a useful phrase, the invaluable distinction between a *tendency towards*, and a *tendency to produce*, the truth of Christianity[2].

If we have been able to trace a real shaping of the lines inward and outward of the world's order disposing it for a true religion, the impression which this makes on us must be enormously increased if (1) we can see that that religion, when it comes, is most obviously a thing which *comes to* the Gentile world, and does not *grow out of* it either by blending of tendencies, or by constructive individual genius: and if (2) we are able to indicate another and perfectly distinct course of shaping and preparation which at the required moment yielded the material and equipment for the religion which was to go out upon the world.

That this was so is in a sense upon the face of history. The Christian Church, it has been said, appeared at first as a Jewish sect. 'The salvation' Christ declared was 'of the Jews.' He came ('not to destroy but) to fulfil' the system amidst which He arose. Such sayings put us upon the track of a special preparation for the Gospel.

---

[1] *Philosophy of the Greeks : Eclectics,* p. 20 (tr. Alleyne).

[2] *Gospel of the Resurrection* (3rd ed.), p. 72. It is interesting to notice that according to so dispassionate an observer as M. Gaston Boissier (*La Religion Romaine d'Auguste aux Antonins*), who has done so much to trace the better tendencies of the Imperial period, the evidence suggests some such distinction, even as regards some of the main practical results of Christianity.

For example, there was a tendency to ameliorate slavery on principles of general humanity, but there was no hint of a possibility of an end to slavery. There were some signs of mutual interest between classes, but no progress towards the effective appearance of a true philanthropy such as the Christian. In such cases, however, the validity of the distinctions must be debateable and fluctuating. It is absolute as regards the Incarnation.

Let us follow it. And (as the phrase is chosen to imply) we look here for something kindred indeed in many of its methods to that general preparation which we have hitherto traced, but yet more coherent, positive, and concentrated. For we pass in a sense at this point (to use language of the day), from the preparation of an environment suitable to the Gospel, to a preparation of the organism itself. Such language is obviously open to criticisms and misconceptions of more kinds than one. But it is sufficiently defensible historically and theologically to justify us in gaining the clearness which it gives.

I shall attempt to present the signs of this preparation by considering successively these three points.

(1) The relations between Israel and the world at the Christian era.

(2) The fitness of Israel to be the seed-plot of a world-religion, and of the world-religion given by Christ.

(3) The character of the process by which the Israel, so fitted, and so placed, had come to be.

(1) Many a reader of Mommsen's *History of Rome* will have been surprised by finding that the ideal political construction which the writer's knowledge and imagination have ascribed to Caesar was to consist of three elements—the Roman, the Hellenic, and the Jewish[1]. Yet striking as the paradox is, it is chiefly in the facts themselves. Whether we look at the ethnological character of the Jews amidst a system whose strength is from the West; or at their historical position, as a nation in some sense in decadence, with a history of independence and glories long lost; or at the minuteness of their original seat, and its insignificance at that time as (ordinarily) a subordinate district under the Roman province of Syria, it is alike surprising that it should be possible to speak of them as the third factor of the Roman Empire. Yet, in the main, the same surprise is created by any acquaintance with the circumstances of the Jewish Dispersion, as it may be learnt from easily accessible books, such as Edersheim's or Schürer's[2]. There is first the ubiquity of the race: testified alike by Josephus, Strabo, and Philo, and by the witness of inscriptions. They are everywhere, and everywhere in force, throughout the Roman world. Outside the Roman world their great colonies in Babylon and Mesopotamia are another headquarters of the race. They are an eighth part (one million) of the population of Egypt: they yield 10,000 at the least to one massacre in Antioch. To numbers and ubiquity they add privilege in the shape of rights and immunities, begun by the policy of the successors of Alexander,

---

[1] Bk. V. c. xi. *The New Monarchy.*
[2] Edersheim's *Life and Times of Jesus the Messiah:* Schürer, *History of* the *Jewish People in the time of Jesus Christ.*

but vigorously taken up and pushed by Rome as early as 139 B.C., greatly developed by Caesar round whose pyre at Rome they wept, and maintained by the almost consistent policy of the earlier Empire : rights of equal citizenship in the towns where they lived, and equal enjoyment of the boons granted to citizens : rights of self-government and internal administration : and rights or immunities guarding their distinctive customs, such as their observance of the Sabbath or their transmission of tribute to Jerusalem. The opportunities thus secured from without were vigorously turned to account by their trading instinct, their tenacity, their power of living at a low cost, and above all by their admirable freemasonry among themselves, which bound Jews throughout the world into a society of self-help, and must have greatly assisted the enterprises which depend on facility of information, communication, and movement. So far we merely get an impression of their importance. But there are other points which, while they greatly heighten this impression, add to it that of remarkable peculiarity. To ask what was their influence plunges us into a tumult of paradoxes. They had, for example, everywhere the double character of citizens and strangers, speaking the language of the countries where they dwelt, ' being Antiochenes,' as Josephus says, ' at Antioch, Ephesians at Ephesus,' and so forth : possessing and using the rights and franchises of citizens, and yet every one of them counting the Holy Land his country and Jerusalem his capital : respecting the Sanhedrin of Jerusalem as the supreme authority of the race : sending up their tribute annually, flocking thither themselves in vast numbers to keep the feasts, or again not seldom returning there to die. They possessed in fact the combined advantages of the most elastic diffusion, and the strongest national concentration. Such a position could hardly make their relations to their neighbours entirely simple or harmonious. It ' involved an internal contradiction[1].' It could not but be felt that while enjoying all the advantages of citizenship, their hearts were really elsewhere. From all the religious and social side of the common life, which in the ancient world was far less separable from the political than it is now, they were sensibly aliens. They were visibly making the best of two inconsistent positions. And accordingly the irritation against them in the towns (we have a glimpse of it in Acts xix. 34) and the ensuing encroachments and riots, form as chronic a feature of the position, as does their protection by the Empire. But the causes of irritation went wider and deeper. It has been said that ' the feelings cherished towards the Jews throughout the entire Graeco-Roman world were not so much those of hatred as of pure contempt[2].' Their exterior was doubtless unlovely : a Jewry, as M. Renan reminds us, was perhaps not more attractive in ancient than in modern times.

[1] Schürer, II. ii. 273.   [2] Schürer, II. ii. 297.

But what was even more offensive, especially to that cosmopolitan age, and what struck it as altogether the dominant characteristic of the Jews, was their stubborn and inhuman perversity. They would be unlike all the rest of the world. Tacitus has even formulated this for them as the principle guiding their whole action, reduced to practice in details which were singularly well fitted to exhibit its offensiveness [1]. His picture should be read by any one who wishes to realize how cultivated opinion thought of them: and, even if evidence were lacking, we can see that this was just the kind of dislike to be shared by all classes, cultivated and uncultivated alike. Yet it is against the background of this intense prejudice, ever more scornful and irritated as it was exasperated by the incidents of daily contact at close quarters, that we have to paint the phenomena, as striking and as abundantly testified, of the vast and penetrating influence of the Jews over their neighbours. These also lie upon the surface. In very various degrees multitudes (of whom women doubtless formed a considerable majority) adopted the customs and brought themselves into connection with the religion of the Jews. The boasts or claims of Josephus, who refers any sceptical contemporary to 'his own country or his own family,' are confirmed by the admissions of classical writers, by the indignant sarcasms directed against the converts, and by the vivid touches in the Acts of the Apostles [2]. 'Victi victoribus leges dederunt' is the strong phrase of Seneca, and it was a very persuasive influence which could cause it to be said that in Damascus 'nearly the whole female population was devoted to Judaism': which could give S. Paul's Jewish opponents in the towns of Greece and Asia Minor the power at one time of raising the mob, at another of working upon the 'chief' and 'honourable women,' the ladies of the upper classes: or which could bring 'almost the whole city' together in a provincial town because a new teacher appears in the Jews' synagogue [3]. This influence had its results in a considerable number of actual proselytes who through circumcision received admission, somewhat grudging indeed and guarded, within the Jewish pale, but still more in a much larger number of adherents (the 'devout persons,' 'devout Greeks,' &c., of the Acts [4]) attracted by the doctrines, and acquainted with the Scriptures of Israel, who formed a fringe of partly leavened Gentile life round every synagogue.

We hardly need evidence to shew us that to this picture of the influence of Jew over Gentile, there need to be added another which will shew how the subtle, persuasive, and powerful culture of the Graeco-Roman world made itself felt upon the Jews of the Dispersion. The contrast between the Jews of Palestine and those of the Disper-

[1] Tac. *Hist.* v. 4.
[2] Schürer, II. ii. 308.
[3] Acts xvii. 5, xiv. 5, xiii. 50, 44.
[4] Acts xiii. 43, &c.

sion, the translation of the Scriptures into Greek, the rise of a literature which in different ways tried to recommend what was Jewish to
the heathen or to fuse what was Jewish with what was Greek, the
single figure of Philo at Alexandria, are all evidences of an influence,
which must have told continually with penetrating power on all that
was ablest and most thoughtful in the Jewish mind. It was not the
least considerable result of this that all the great thoughts and beliefs
of Israel learned to talk the language of the civilized world, and
so acquired before the time of Christ an adequate and congenial
vehicle.

Such was the position of Israel at the Christian era. It was one
which had been gradually brought about during the last three centuries B. C.; but it only came to its full growth in the last few decades
(the Jewish settlement in Rome may date from Pompey's time) under
favour of the imperial policy and the peace of the times : and it was
soon to change ; indeed the fall of Jerusalem A. D. 70 altered it within
and without. Thus it stood complete during the half-century in which
the work of founding the Christian Church throughout the Empire
was accomplished, and then passed away. We remark upon it how
admirable an organization it offered for the dissemination of a world-
religion, originated upon Jewish soil. The significance of this, occurring at the time when such a religion actually appeared, is heightened
when we observe that the position had continued long enough fully to
try the experiment of what by its own forces Judaism could accomplish
for the world. As S. James argued [1] 'Moses had,' now for a long
time, ' in every city them that preach him, being read in the synagogues every Sabbath day'—and it might have so gone on for ever
without any conversion of the Gentile world. That world could never
have been drawn within a system, which, however zealous to make
proselytes, had nothing better to offer to those whom it made than
that they might come in, if they liked, and sit down in the lowest
place, tolerated rather than welcomed, dependents rather than members
of an intensely national community, leaving father and mother and all
that they had, not for a position of spiritual freedom, but for a change
of earthly nationality.

(2) But we trench upon the second question. What was the nation
that held this position of vantage ? What signs are there about it
which suggest a special preparation for a purposed result ?

It is one answer to this question to say that this wonderfully placed
people had, alone among the nations, a genuine faith, a genuine hope,
and a genuine charity. They at least, says Seneca, when he complains
of their influence, ' knew the reasons of their customs.' There was a
raison d'être to their religion. In a world which still kept up the forms

[1] Acts xv. 21.

I

of worship and respect for gods whose character and existence could not stand the criticism of its own best moral and religious insight, any more than that of its scepticism; or which was framing for itself thoughts of Deity by intellectual abstraction; or which was betraying its real ignorance of the very idea of God by worshipping the two great powers which, as a matter of fact, it knew to be mighty, Nature and the Roman Empire,—the Jew had a *faith*, distinct, colossal, and unfailing, in a Living God, Maker of heaven and earth. This we may be sure was the inner secret of the true attraction which drew the hearts of such men as Cornelius the centurion to the despised and repulsive Jew. This God, they further believed, was their God for ever and ever. 'Let us kneel,' they said, 'before the Lord our Maker, for He is the Lord our God.' And therefore, let them have gained it how they may, they had an indomitable *hope*, or rather, confidence, which all unpropitiousness of outer appearances had only served to stimulate, that He would bring them through, that He had a purpose for them, and that He would bring it to pass: that the world was no mechanical system of meaningless vicissitudes, but an order, of which indeed they little realized the scope, moving under the hand of a Ruler for a purpose of glory and beneficence. That the confidence of the extraordinary destiny which, under this order, was reserved for Israel, as well as the present possession of the Divine law and covenant, should have produced an intense sense of unity and fellowship was a matter of course. The Roman is obliged to recognise their mutual *charity*, however deformed, as he thinks, by their antipathy to all who were not of their kindred and faith.

But such an answer to our question, though it brings before us a sign, and a sign of the very highest, that is of the moral and spiritual order, does not perhaps set us at the point from which the whole meaning of the position opens to us most naturally. It may do this more effectually to ask whether there was any material in Judaism for a world-religion, and for that world-religion which grew out of it?

Perhaps if we performed the futile task of trying to imagine a world-religion, we should, with some generality of consent, define as its essentials three or four points which it is striking to find were fundamentals of the religion of Israel, and at that time of no other. We should require a doctrine of God, lofty, spiritual, moral: a doctrine of man which should affirm and secure his spiritual being and his immortality: and a doctrine of the relations between God and man which should give reality to prayer and to the belief in providence, and root man's sense of responsibility in the fact of his obligation to a righteousness outside and above himself, a doctrine in short of judgment. It needs no words to shew how the religion of Israel in its full development not only taught these truths, but gave them the dignity and importance which belong to the cornerstones of a religion.

But then along with these that religion taught other beliefs as clearly conceived, which seemed to be of the most opposite character : just as distinctive and exclusive as the former were universal. It taught the obligation in every detail of a very stringent written law, and of a ceremonial and sacrificial system, centred at Jerusalem, and forming the recognised communication between God and man. It taught a special election of Israel and covenant of God with Israel, a special purpose and future for Israel. Nor was the conception of the participation by other nations in the blessings of Messiah's rule, (to which we, reading for example the prophecies of Isaiah in the light of the sequel, cannot but give a dominant place,) more to an Israelite than a striking incident in a distinctively Israelite glory.

It would seem then, combining these two sides, that there was in Israel the foundation on which a religion for the world could be laid, but that it could only be made available under stringent and, as it might appear, impossible conditions. An attempt to make a religion by extracting the universal truths in Judaism would have been simply to desert at once the vantage-ground which it was proposed to occupy, because it would have conflicted directly with every Jewish instinct, belief, tradition, and hope. If the thing was to be done, it must be done by some power and teaching which, while extricating into clearness all that was truest in the theology and morality of Israel, was also able to shew to the judgment of plain men and earnest seekers, that it constituted a true climax of Israel's history, a true fulfilment of the promises and prophecies which Jews had now made matters of notoriety everywhere, a true final cause of all the peculiar and distinctive system of Israel. It must be able to take Israel to witness, and therefore it must be able to convince men not only that it had a high theology and a refined morality, but that God had 'visited His people' : and that 'what He had spoken unto the fathers He had so fulfilled.' It must produce accordingly not only doctrine, but fact. It must carry on, what was implied in the whole discipline of Israel, the assertion that truth was not a matter of speculation, but a word from God; or the knowledge of a dealing of God with man clothing itself with reality, embodying itself in fact, making a home for itself in history. It is true that the Judaism of the synagogue in its idolatry of the law, had assumed the appearance of a paper system, but in that form it had no promise or power of expansion : and on the side where the religion of Israel admitted of development into some higher and wider state, it was distinctly a religion not of theory or teaching only, but of Divine action revealing itself in history.

It will not escape any observer of the beginnings of Christianity that it was precisely this attempt which the Gospel of Jesus made. If we watch S. Paul speaking to his Gentile audiences at Lystra or Athens, he brings to bear upon the instincts of his hearers the strong magnet of a clear and definite Theism. But these addresses themselves implicitly contain another element : and we must now look to them for examples of the process, the careful earnest process, by which the Gospel did its rapid and yet most gradual work of conversion. Unquestionably, as S. Paul himself affirms, and as the Acts and the early apologetic writers shew us, it was done by asserting, and making good the assertion with careful proof and reasoning, that in the historical appearance and character of Jesus Christ, in His treatment while on earth, in His resurrection and heavenly exaltation, was to be found the true, natural, and legitimate fulfilment of that to which the Scriptures in various ways, direct and indirect, pointed, and of that which the hope of Israel, slowly fashioned by the Scriptures under the discipline of experience, had learnt to expect. This could be pressed home most directly on Jews, but it was available also for the large prepared class among Gentiles, to whom the pre-existence of these prophecies and anticipations was known matter of fact, and to some of whom the Jewish Scriptures had been a personal discipline : the truth of the Gospel was one 'now made manifest and by the Scriptures of the prophets, according to the commandment of the everlasting God, made known to all nations for the obedience of faith.' The double requirement was fulfilled, and a religion, intrinsically universal and eternal, was seen by spiritually clear-sighted eyes to be in a most real and organic sense the flower of Israel's stalk.

(3) If it has appeared that in the placing of the nation at the era, and in its character and belief, there was something much to be 'wondered at,' and, more definitely, something marvellously suited, not indeed to generate such a religion as that of the Gospel, but to foster and assist its growth when the seed of Divine fact should be sown on the prepared soil ; then we shall ask, finally, whether there is anything of like striking significance in the way in which this state of things had come about ? Let us pass by the causes by which the people of Israel obtained their external position. These, even including a thing so remarkable as the spontaneous restoration by an Oriental Empire of a deported people, are not in themselves different from the ordinary workings of history ; though in combination they may contribute to deepen the impression of a hand fashioning out of many elements, and in many ways, a single great result. But how had the Jews come to be what they were ? how had they gained the religious treasure which they possessed, and the tenacity of religious and national life which played guardian to it ? The whole course of

Israel's history must, in one sense, give the answer to this question: and there are no controversies more difficult or more unsolved than those which are now raging round the problem of that course, its origin, stages, and order. But it may be possible to make some reflections on it without entangling ourselves very much in those controversies.

(a) At the outset it is impossible not to be struck by the interest which the Jews themselves felt in the process of their history. That interest belongs to the very centre of their life and thought. It is not an offshoot of national vainglory, for (as has been so often remarked) it resulted in a record full-charged with the incidents of national failure and defection: it is not the result of a self-conscious people analysing its own moral and other development, for though the moral judgment is indeed always at work in the narratives and the poems, it is more occupied in drawing out the teaching of recurring sequences of sin and punishment than in framing a picture of the whole. The result is to lay a picture of development before us, but the aim is to treasure and record every detail of God's dealings with the nation of His choice. This is what gives continuity and unity to the whole: this is what lends to it its intense and characteristic uniqueness. And when we look steadily at this, we perceive afresh, what familiarity almost conceals from us, the distinctive quality of Israel's religion; that it is not a system of teaching, nor a tradition of worship, nor a personal discipline, though it may include all these; but that it is in itself a belief in the working of God, Who is the God of all the earth, but specially the God of Israel, and Who works indeed everywhere, but in an altogether special sense in Israel. In reflecting on their history they contemplate the object of their faith. Hence truth is to them not a philosophic acquisition, but lies in the words which had come from God faithfully treasured and received: it is *revealed* in word and act: goodness, in man or nation, is the faithful adherence to those conditions, under which the good purpose of God can work itself out and take effect: it is a correspondence to a purpose of *grace*: and the centre and depositary of their hope is neither the human race, nor any association for moral and religious effort, but an organism raised by Him who raises all the organisms of nature from a chosen seed, and drawn onwards through the stages by which family passes into nation and kingdom, and then through that higher discipline by which the natural commonwealth changes into the spiritual community of the faithful 'remnant.' If any one will try to realize the impression which Christianity made upon the heathen world, he will not fail to see how the new truth was able to impress men because it found these conceptions of revelation, grace, and an organic society of God's choice and shaping, all so strange and so impressive to the heathen world, ingrained as the natural elements of religion in the men whom it made its instruments.

But why did the Jews so regard their history? For the answer we may revert to the other question, What made them what they were at the Christian era? For they had gone through a crisis calculated to destroy both their existence and their religion. It has been in fashion with some writers to emphasize the resemblances, and minimize the differences, between the religion of Israel and that of its neighbours. In view of this it becomes important to note the specific peril of ancient religions. That peril was that the close association of the nation with its god caused the failure of the one to appear a failure of the other, and to endanger or destroy the respect paid to him. The religion of a subdued or ruined people was, as we may say, a demonstrated failure. Sennacherib's defiance of Hezekiah urges this with a conqueror's irony [1]. The case of the Ten Tribes had, probably, given an illustration of it within the circle of Israel itself. And in Judah, upon any shewing, there was enough of the feeling that Jehovah was responsible for His people, of the conviction that He would certainly protect His own, of the confidence resting on prosperity and liable to be shaken by its loss, to make the downfall of the state, carrying with it that of the Temple and the outer order of religion, an enormous peril to the religion itself and with it to the very existence of Israel. It is not difficult to discern the agency by which the peril was averted. That agency was Prophecy. Modern criticism, though it may quarrel with the inspiration or predictive power of the prophets, has given fresh and unbiassed witness to their importance as an historical phenomenon. Kuenen [2], for example, points out how at every turning-point in Israel's later history there stands a man who claims to bring a word of God to the people. Prof. Huxley [3], in a recent article, has told us that 'a vigorous minority of Babylonian Jews,' that is, the Jews upon whom the full forces of prophecy bore, 'created the first consistent, remorseless, naked Monotheism, which, so far as history records, appeared in the world . . . and they inseparably united therewith an ethical code, which, for its purity and its efficiency as a bond of social life, was, and is, unsurpassed.' Of whatever fact may underlie this description, the prophets are at once evidence and authors.

Now prophecy confronted the impending peril in the name of Jehovah: on the one side it displayed the enemy (whether as by Isaiah it prescribed a bound to his advance, or as by Jeremiah announced the catastrophe to be wrought by him) as himself utterly in Jehovah's hands, His axe or saw for discipline upon the trees of the forest; on the other side it shewed that Jehovah's obligation to Israel

[1] Isaiah xxxvi. 18.   [2] *Hibbert Lectures,* 1882, p. 231.
[3] *Nineteenth Century,* April, 1886.

was conditioned by His essential righteousness; that national disaster might be Jehovah's necessary vengeance, and that His purpose for Israel—which it re-asserted with fullest emphasis—might need to be realized for an Israel purified by such discipline, a shoot from the stock of the felled tree, the remnant of an 'afflicted and poor people[1].' And prophecy was beforehand with all this : it was not an afterthought to explain away a calamity : and so it fashioned in Israel at least a core of spiritual faith, to which outward disaster of polity and religion, however destructive, was not confounding, and which had stamina enough in it to draw wholesome though bitter nourishment from the hard Captivity discipline. This, when the flood came, was an ark for Israel's religion, and, in its religion, for the national life, which re-organized itself under new conditions round the nucleus of the religion.

Thus, at the crisis and hinge of the historical development which issued in the wonderfully placed and constituted Israel of Christ's time, and which was crowned by the New Religion, we find this agency, which in itself would arrest our wonder. The more we look at it, the more wonderful it is. Every suggestion of comparison with heathen oracles, divination and the rest, can only bring out with more vivid effect the contrast and difference between it and all such things. It claims by the mouth of men transparently earnest and honest, to speak from God. It brings with it the highest credentials, moral, spiritual, historical: *moral,* for it spends what at first sight seems all its strength in the intrepid and scathing rebuke of the evils immediately round it, especially in the high places of society, against the lust, cruelty, avarice, frivolity, insolence, foul worships, which it found so rankly abundant: *spiritual,* for it speaks the language of an absolutely unworldly faith, and accomplishes a great spiritual work, such as we can hardly over-estimate, unless indeed with Prof. Huxley we distort its proportions so as to prejudice the earlier religion from which it sprang or the Christianity to which it contributed : *historical,* because occurring at the very crisis of Israel's history (750–550), it gained credence and authority from the witness of events, and dealt with an emergency of the most perilous and bewildering kind, as not the most skilful opportunist could have dealt with it, by a use, as sublime as simple, of the principles of righteousness and faith. If we compare what the prophets did for their contemporaries and what they did for the future of Israel and the world, and see that this was done, not by two sets of utterances working two different ways, but by a single blended strain of prophecy, we gain a double impression, of which the twofold force is astonishing indeed. It is gained without pressing their claim to predictive power, at least beyond the horizons

[1] Isaiah x. 15; xi. 1; Zeph. iii. 12.

of their own period. But it is impossible for any careful and candid reader of the words of the prophets to stop there, and not to feel that there is another element in them, not contained in a passage here and there but for ever reappearing, interwoven with the rest, and evidently felt by the prophets themselves to be in some sense necessary for the vindication and completion of their whole teaching. It is an element of anticipation and foresight. We see that this is so, and we see in part the method of it. It is bound up with, it springs out of, all that is spiritually and morally greatest in the prophets. Their marvellous, clear-sighted, steady certainty that the Lord who sitteth above rules all, that He is holy, and that unrighteousness in man or nations cannot prevail; their insight piercing through the surface of history to under-lying laws of providential order; the strange conviction or conscious-ness, felt throughout the nation but centering in the prophets, that this God had a purpose for Israel :—these deep things, which, however they came and whatever we think of them, make Israel's distinctive and peculiar glory, were accompanied by, and issued in, anticipations of a future which would vindicate and respond to them. Just as the belief in a future life for God's children was not taught as a set doctrine to the Jews, but grew with the growth of their knowledge of the Living and Holy God, and of man's relation as a spiritual being to Him, so with the predictions of which we speak. As it was given to the prophets to realize the great spiritual truths of present because eternal moment which they taught, it was given to them also to discern that these truths pointed to a future which should bring them vindica-tion. The cloudy time of trial and confusion would one day come to a close; the Sun whose rays they caught would one day shine out; the partial and passing deliverances in which they taught men to see God's hand must one day issue in a deliverance of deeper moment, of lasting and adequate significance; there would be an unbaring of God's arm, a manifesting of His power to decide, to justify, to condemn, and it would be seen in some final form why and how Israel was, in a distinctive sense, the people of the God of the whole earth; that union between God and His people, of which the prophets were themselves mediators and which was so miserably imperfect and so constantly broken, would one day be complete; and, finally, even the very instruments which He was using in the present, the Anointed King, the chosen Royal House, the Prophet-Servant of God, the holy hill of Zion, were charged with a meaning of which the significance was only in the future to become clear. Thus, in this free, deep, spiritual—let us say it out, inspired—manner the predictions of prophecy emerge and gather shape. Thus among the people which was most conserva-tive and jealous of its own religious privilege, the promise most deeply cherished was one in which all nations of the earth should be blessed, and there is heard the strange announcement of a 'new covenant.' Thus it comes about that the most satisfying and satisfied of all religions becomes the one which, in its deepest meaning, in the minds of its most faithful followers, strains forward most completely beyond itself. Thus, as it has been said, 'Prophecy takes off its crown and lays it at the feet of One who is to be.' Thus a people who have become intensely and inexorably monotheistic and to whom the Deity becomes more and more remote in awful majesty so that they do not dare to name His Name, carry down with them Scriptures which discover the strange vision of a human King with Divine attributes and strain towards some manifestation of God in present nearness. Thus amidst the pictures in which, with every varying detail, using the scenery, the personages, the nations, the ideas of its own day, the instinct of prophetic anticipation finds expression, there emerges, with gradually gathering strength, a definite Hope, and some clear lineaments of that which is to be.

For, be it observed, at this point interpretation, declaring what the prophets seem to us to-day to mean, passes into and gives way to historical fact. The most sceptical cannot deny either that the words in which the prophets spoke of the future, did as a matter of fact crystallize into a hope, a hope such as has no parallel in history, and of which distorted rumours were able to stir and interest the heathen world : or that they were, long before the time of Jesus, interpreted as sketching features, some general and shadowy, some curiously distinct and particular, of Messiah's work and kingdom.

And then, face to face with this, stands another fact as confessedly historical. For, 'in the fulness of the time,' it did appear to men of many kinds who had the books in their hands, men with every reason for judging seriously and critically, and in most cases with the strongest prejudice in favour of an adverse judgment, that these prophecies were fulfilled in a King and a Kingdom such as they never dreamt of till they saw them. It would be a strange chapter in the history of delusion, if there were no more to add. But there is to add, first, that the King and the Kingdom whereto, (in no small part upon the seeming perilous ground of this correspondence with prophecy,) these men gave their faith, have proved to win such a spiritual empire as they claimed : and, further, that men like ourselves, judging at the cool distance of two thousand years, are unable to deny that in the truest sense of 'fulfilment,' as it would be judged by a religious mind, Jesus and His Kingdom do 'fulfil the prophets,' fulfil their assertion of a unique religious destiny for Israel by which the nations were to profit, of a time when the righteousness of God should be revealed for the discomfiture of pride and sin and for the help of the meek, of a nearer dwelling of God with

His people, of a new covenant, and of the lasting reign of a perfect Ruler.

To some minds it may weaken, but to others it will certainly intensify, the impression thus created, if they are asked to observe that now and again there occur in the Jewish Scriptures words, passages, events, in which with startling distinctness, independence, and minuteness there stand forth features of what was to be. It is as if the anticipation which fills the air with glow focussed itself here and there in sparkling points of light which form and flash and fade away again. We may confidently assert that in the case of such passages as the 22nd and 110th Psalms or the 9th and 53rd Chapters of Isaiah the harder task is for him who will deny, than for him who will assert, a direct correspondence between prediction and fulfilment. If they stood alone, general scientific considerations might make it necessary to undertake the harder task. Standing out as they do from such a context and background as has been here indicated, the interpretation which sees in them the work of a Divine providence shaping out a 'sign' for the purpose which in each Christian age, and especially in the first, it has actually subserved, is the interpretation which is truest to all the facts. They are the special self-betrayal of a power which is at work throughout, of which the spiritual ear hears the sound, though we are often unable distinctly to see the footprints.

It seems then impossible, upon such a view of the phenomena of prophecy as has been here roughly and insufficiently indicated, to deny that whatever appearance of preparation we may discern in the condition outward and inward of the Jews in the time of Christ, is strongly corroborated by a like appearance of preparation in the process by which they had become what they were.

(*b*) We have selected out of all the foregoing history the epoch and the influence of the prophets for several reasons. They preside over the most critical period of Israel's history. They seem to bring to most pronounced expression the spirit and character which pervades the whole of that history. They are known to us through their own writings : and we are therefore on ground where (comparatively speaking) the premises are uncontroverted. And as it is the fashion perhaps to discredit the argument of prophecy—partly, no doubt, on account of the technical form in which it was ordinarily presented— it is important to re-assert that in all its main strength that argument holds its ground, reinforced indeed, as we think, by the increased power to apprehend its breadth and solidity which our more histori- cally trained modern minds should have gained. But selection of what is most salient should imply no neglect of the rest ; and the argument, or view of the facts,—which has here for clearness sake been abbreviated, and mainly centralized upon the work and implications of prophecy,—can be deepened as the drift of the great lines of Israel's discipline is more deeply realized. Thus, for example, little or nothing has been here said of the Law. Yet, without foreclosing any discussion as to its sources and development, we can see that the law of God was a factor in every stage of Israel's history, and that in the making of the prepared Israel of Christ's time, the law in its fullest and most developed shape was, and had been for ages, a paramount influence. No influence more concentrated and potent can be found in history. And to see the deepest drift of it we have no need to speculate on what might have been, or was sure to be. Historical documents point us to what was. The Epistles to the Romans and the Galatians, and the Epistle to the Hebrews, lay open respectively two ways of its working. On the one side it appears as a great witness for righteousness. Men were schooled to live under a sense of peremptory obligation; to comply scrupulously, exactly, submissively with an unquestioned authority. This sense and temper is liable to great abuse: it lends itself when abused to a mechanical morality, to a morbid casuistry, to the complacency of an external perfectness. It was so abused very widely among the Jews. But it is nevertheless an indispensable factor in a true morality, to which it lends the special power of command: and in Israel it conferred this power because it connected obligation with the will of a righteous God. This is expressed in the repeated sanction 'I am the Lord your God,' following precept after precept of the law, and in the summary claim 'Be ye holy, for I am holy.' Evidently here there is that which transcends all mechanical schemes of obedience; there is an infinite standard. As such it pointed and impelled onwards towards the true religion in which faith and holiness should be entirely at one. As such meanwhile it stimulated and dismayed the deeper spirits: stimulating them by the loftiness of its demand, dismaying them by the proved impossibility of that perfect compliance which alone was compliance at all. Thus the foundations were laid of a temper at once robust and humble, confident and diffident; though they were laid upon a contradiction which the law had in itself no power to resolve. There was indeed (here we take up the guidance of the Epistle to the Hebrews) one part of the law which acknowledged that contradiction, which half promised to resolve it, but having no real power to do so, could only shape and deepen the demand for some solution. This was, of course, the sacrificial system. The sacrificial system opens up quite other thoughts from those of strict demand and strict obedience. It points to quite another side of religious and moral development. Yet it starts from the same truth of a Holy God Who requires, and inasmuch as He is holy must require, a perfect obedience. Only it acknowledges the inevitable fact of disobedience. It embodies the sense of need. It appeals to, and as part of the Divine law it reveals, a quality in the Supreme Goodness which can go beyond commanding and condemning, to forgive and reconcile. It creates in a word the spirit of humility, and it feels, at the least, after a God of love.

What a profound preparation there is in this for the life which Christ blessed in the Beatitudes and inaugurated by all that He was and did, and for the truth of the Divine being and character which was set forth in Him. Yet the law only prepared for this, and made the demand which this met. It made no answer to its own demand. It could not reconcile its own severity, and its own hopes of mercy: its apparatus of sacrifice was in itself absolutely and obviously insufficient for any solution of the contradiction. It was a marvellous discipline which, while it trained its people so far, demanded the more urgently something which all its training could never give nor reach.

(*c*) The work of prophecy and the work of the law was also (if we can distinguish causes which were so much affected by one another) the work of history. To the work of the prophets, indeed, the history of both the past and the succeeding times was essential, the former to supply their work with a standing ground, the latter to engrain its teaching into the life of the nation. We look back, and we ask, What gave the prophets their advantage, what was the fulcrum of their lever? Trained to observe the processes of religious evolution, we must refuse to believe with Professor Huxley that a lofty monotheism and a noble morality sprang out of the ground among a 'minority of Babylonian Jews.' But we shall be prepared to find that the rudimentary stages differ much from the mature. The beginnings of life, as we know them, are laid in darkness : they emerge crude and childish : the physical and outward almost conceals the germ of spiritual and rational being which nevertheless is the self, and which will increasingly assert itself and rule. It may be so with that organism which God was to make the shrine of His Incarnation. We may have to learn that the beginnings of Israel are more obscure, more elementary, less distinctive from surrounding religions, than we had supposed. We need not fear to be as bold as Amos in recognising that what was in one aspect the unique calling of God's Son out of Egypt [2], was in another but one among the Divinely ruled processes of history, such as brought up the Philistines from Caphtor and the Syrians from Kir [2]. We need not be more afraid than Ezekiel to say that the peculiar people were an offshoot (if so it should be) of natural stocks, with the Amorite for father and the

---

[1] Hosea xi. 1. [2] Amos ix. 7.

Hittite for mother [1]. But all this will hardly take from us that sense of continuous shaping of a thing towards a Divine event which has always been among the supports of faith. We shall see that the prophetic appeals imply a past, and that their whole force lies in what they assume, and only recal to their hearers; the special possession of Israel by Jehovah, His selection of them for His own, His deliverances of them from Egypt and onwards, giving the earnest of a future purpose for which they were preserved, and for which His definite promises were committed to them, to the seed of Abraham, the house of Israel, the line of David. These things the prophets imply, standing upon these they speak with all the force of those who need only bid the people to realize and to remember, or at most to receive from God some fresh confirmation and enlargement of their hopes [2].

Or again, from the work of the prophets we look forward, and when we have recovered from our surprise at seeing that a dreary interval of five centuries separates the Evangelical prophecy, which seemed so ready for the flower of the Gospel, from the time of its blooming, we discern how the processes of that interval were utilized in realizing, ingraining, diffusing the great truths of prophetic teaching. The return without a monarchy and under an ecclesiastical governor, and the dispersion through many lands, necessitated in act that transformation of the political into the spiritual polity, almost of the nation into the Church, of which Isaiah's work was the germ. The institution of the synagogues, which belongs to this time and in which public worship was detached from all local associations and from the ancient forms of material sacrifice, was, as it were, the spiritual organ of the new ubiquitous cosmopolitan Jewish life. Yet contemporaneously the centralizing influences gained strength. The conservative work of Ezra and of the Scribes and Rabbis at whose head he stands, gathered up and preserved the treasures which gave a consciously spiritual character to Israel's national loyalty; and guarded with the hedge of a scrupulous literalism, what needed some such defence to secure it against the perils implied in being carried wide over the world. By the resistance in Palestine under Syrian

---

[1] Ezekiel xvi. 3.

[2] It is interesting to note that, according to the record preserved by Israel of their own history, that which Kuenen says of later times,—that 'at each turning-point of the history stands a man who claims to bring a word from God,' —is exactly true of the older history too; Abraham, Moses, Samuel, David, are all in this sense prophets. Yet there is no appearance of a later age forming a past in its own likeness. The prophets do not imagine an earlier row of prophets like themselves, put in like the portraits of the early Scottish kings at Holyrood, to fill the blanks of history. The early figures are not cut to prophetic pattern; they have each their distinct individuality of character and office, only they have a unity of Divine commission and service.

rule to Hellenizing insolence, and in the Dispersion to the fascinations and pleasures of Hellenizing culture, and by the great Maccabean struggle, the nation was identified with religious earnestness and zeal in a way of which we only see the caricature and distortion in the Pharisaism which our Lord denounced.

Thus, if we compare our Lord's time with the great age of prophecy, we see how much has been acquired. Time has been given for the prophetic influences to work. There has been loss, but there has also been gain. That conscious, explicit, and magnificently uncompromising Monotheism, which in the mouth of the Evangelical prophet was quivering with the glow and passion of freshly inspired realization, has by 'the end of the age' had time to bring everything in the sphere of religion under its influence. It had discovered its points of contact with the highest aspirations of the Greek thought which on intellectual lines felt its way towards God. And it had unfolded its own corollaries: it had drawn along with it the great spiritual truths which cohere with the belief in one Living and True God: and Israel in the Pharisee epoch had passed, we hardly know how, into secure if not undisputed possession of the belief in a future life, in a world of spirits, and in the spiritual character of prayer.

But there was another and more direct manner, in which the work of history interlaced with what we have indicated as the work of the law. In the formation of the temper of chastened confidence which is so characteristic of later Israel, a part must evidently be given to the discipline of national experience saddened by departed glory, and with the shadows thickening over it. Just as we can see that the populations of the Empire were in a sense more ready to learn of Christ than the young self-reliant Greeks of Sparta or Athens could have been, so we can see in such language as that of the 119th Psalm or of the 9th chapter of Daniel a temper to which the meek and lowly Christ would make an appeal which might have been lost upon the rough times of the judges or the prosperous age of the monarchy. Old age has come and with it the wisdom of a chastened spirit. This is not difficult to see, and it is important to take it into account. It means that the comparatively normal discipline of life has brought with it (as doubtless it is meant to do alike in personal and national life) a spiritual gain. But it is important to see how much of the process and the effect remains unexplained. The chastening is obvious, but whence the confidence?

It is in some far less normal cause, in something which seems distinctive of Israel, that we have to find the adequate explanation of the whole result. We have to ask (as Pascal so keenly felt [1]) why a nation records its failures and misfortunes as being chastisements of

[1] *Pensées,* ii. 7 § 2.

wilful, repeated, and disgraceful fault, and then jealously guards the record as its most cherished possession. It would be easy to suggest that there is in this an egotism clothing itself in humility: and to point out that this egotism would explain the confidence which still looked forward to the future, which anticipated greatness for an 'afflicted and poor people,' and a blessing to all the nations of the earth from its own history. Only this is just to slur the difficulty, and under the invidious word 'egotism' to disguise that wonderful instinct of a destiny and a mission which is so strangely unlike egotism, and which allowed, or even produced, in so profound a form the self-condemnation which egotism refuses.

Doubtless the effects of these preparing forces were felt, and their meanings discerned, only by a few. Not only were they 'not all Israel that were of Israel,' but the bulk of the nation and its representative and official leaders were blind. They were off the way, down the false tracks of literalist Rabbinism, or of one-sided Essene asceticism, or of earthly visions of a restored kingdom, or (as in Alexandria) of a philosophized Judaism. The issues were the crucifixion of the Lord, and all which Judaism, without and within the Church, did to extinguish the Gospel and persecute its followers in its first age. It is right to refer to this, but there are probably few to whom it would cause any difficulty. To the observer of the world's history it is a common sight that the true issues and the distinctive work of a people is worked out not by the many or by the prominent, but by the few, and often the obscure. To the student of Jewish history that which has made Israel what it is in world-significance appears throughout the course of its history as a gold thread running through a web of very different texture. It can be no surprise that the end should be of a piece with the rest. There, in a climax of sharpest contrast, we see the antithesis which marks the history throughout. The training issues in a S. Mary, a Simeon, in those who 'waited for the consolation of Israel' on the one side, and in the 'Scribes and Pharisees, hypocrites,' on the other. The natural issue of Israel's life and tendencies is seen in the cold and sterile impotence which, because it is the 'corruption of the best,' is the most irreversible spiritual ruin; while beside and amidst this there was fashioned by a grace and power above nature, though in a perfectly natural way, the true Israel which realize all that 'Israel according to the flesh' professed yet betrayed, guarded yet obscured. And if we have at all rightly discerned as a principle of Divine preparation that it should be negative as well as positive, and should demonstrate to the world before Christ was given, how little the world's own wisdom or effort could supply His place: we shall not wonder that time was thus given for Israel to try out as it were its second experiment, and to shew that by its selfishness and arrogance, by its 'carnalness,' it could warp and distort its later spiritual constitution, even more than its former temporal one, out of all likeness of what God would have it be. 'The last state of the man' was 'worse than the first[1].'

But the observation of these predominant currents and forms of Jewish life and thought and religion has this further value, that it shews the variety, the energy, and the unlikeness to one another of the tendencies present in Israel. They emphasize the fact that the history of Israel was in no sense working itself out towards the *production* by its own forces of the true religion which went forth from the midst of it. They remind us how intractable the problem of finding by human ingenuity the solution which could harmonize in one issue elements so powerful and so alien from each other; which with a perfect spiritual liberty could combine an assertion of the permanent value of the law; which with no withdrawal from and despair of the world could secure all that was sought by Essene purity and self-denial; which, itself utterly unworldly, could satisfy the idea of a restored monarchy and a glory for Israel; which while bringing no philosophy could achieve what Jewish philosophizing had desired, in a capture of the world's reason by Jewish truth.

III. In the last words we touch that with which this essay may perhaps fitly end. If its drift has been in any sense true, there stands before us, as perhaps the most striking feature of the whole situation, the co-existence of the two preparations, the one general, indirect, contributory, and consisting only in an impressive convergence and centering of the lines of ordinary historical sequences; the other special, directly introductory, and characterized by the presence of a distinctive power, call it what we may, a genius for religion, or more truly and adequately a special grace of the Spirit of God, which is new and above ordinary experience, even as life is when it enters the rest of nature, and reason is when it appears in the world of life. The two preparations pursue their course unconscious of one another, almost exclusive of one another. Greek wisdom and Roman power have no dream of coming to receive from the narrow national cult of humbled and subject Israel. And Israel, even taught by the great prophets, could hardly find a place in her vision of the future for any destiny of the nations of the world. To this antagonism, or more strictly this ignoring of one another, there are exceptions, exceptions of the kind which emphasize the character of the situation which they hardly modify. Two streams of such force and volume as those of

---

[1] S. Matt. xii. 45. It should be observed that the words were spoken of 'this wicked generation.'

Jewish religion and classical life or culture could not touch and leave one another altogether uninfluenced, though the influence was characteristically different. On the side of the world the spiritual needs of individuals caused numbers, not inconsiderable, to receive influences which made them ready to act as seeding ground and ferment for the Gospel. On the side of Israel, the strong sense of mission and of truth made the contact with Greek culture suggest the ambition to use it as a great instrument, to teach it to acknowledge and witness to the God of Israel, who was God of the whole earth: and the results, in the Greek of the Septuagint and in the Helleno-Judaic writings of Alexandria and elsewhere, were invaluable in fashioning language and thought for Christ's service. But all the more distinctly, in the first case, does the antagonism, the gulf fixed, the mutual aversion, the impossibility humanly speaking of fusion between Jew and Gentile come out before our eyes. And, in the second case, the unreal romancings of the Sibylline works, the apparently isolated work of Philo, and the opportunism of a politician like Josephus, have all the character of hybrids, and shew no sign of the vital fusion by which out of a great wedlock a new thing comes to be.

The two preparations stand apart: they go their own way. There is indeed in them a strange parallelism of common human experience and human need. Both have tried their experiments, made their ventures, won their successes, gone through their disciplines of disenchantment and failure. Both are conscious of the dying of life: in Israel there is 'no prophet more'; outside it philosophy has not the creativeness and energy of youth but the quiet acquiescence and mild prudence of age, and life, public and private, is without adequate scope or aim. In both the 'tendencies towards' a Gospel are as far as possible from making a 'tendency to produce' one. In both there is the same desire for which the Jew alone can find conscious expression: it is 'Quicken me!' Both need life. Both have no help in themselves. But in the lines which they follow and the hopes which they frame there is neither likeness nor compatibility. 'The Greeks seek after wisdom[1].' The intellect, and those who are distinctively men of the intellect, can hardly imagine human advance otherwise than in terms of the intellect. Philosophy conceives of it as a conquest of philosophical result, or even as an increase of philosophical material. It is the pain of an advanced and critical time, like that of which we speak, to feel this, and yet to feel that the experiments of speculation have gone far enough to shew that by none of their alternative ways can there be any way out to the peace of certain truth. And yet it seems that, without abdication of reason, there is no possibility of going any other way: the Greeks (and in this sense all the

[1] 1 Cor. i. 22.

world was Greek) could only look for what they wanted in the form of a new philosophy.

But 'the Jews require a sign.' Totally different, but equally exclusive, were the conditions under which the Jew could conceive of a new epoch. The dread of exhausted resources did not haunt him, for he looked not to human capacity but to Divine gift and interposition. But he thought that he knew the form in which such interposition would come ; it was not to be primarily a teaching, (it is the Samaritan and not the Jew who is recorded as expecting in Messiah one who, 'when He is come, will tell us all things [1]') ; it must appear in action, ' with observation [2],' with pomp and scenic display, with signs, and signs which, in a very visible and tangible sense, should seem to be from heaven [3], in particular with circumstances of triumph and conquest, and with an exaltation of Israel to the glories of her monarchy many times enlarged.

Such are the demands ; the things sought and needed ; the conditions prescribed ; definite, severally uncompromising, mutually unlike, and even conflicting. And then from out of Israel, without moral or political earthquake, without overwhelming display of supernatural force, nay even, to a superficial eye, with all the appearance of weakness and failure, without any rescue for Israel, with no attempt to present itself in philosophical form, with none of the strain and elaboration of a conscious effort to combine many in one, but rather with a paradoxical and offending 'simplicity' and 'foolishness' of mere assertion :—there comes forth a Thing in which on the one side Jews—whom we all recognise to be the best Jews, Jews in the truest and deepest sense—find the whole spirit and meaning, even down to its detail, of the life and the hope of Israel summed up and fulfilled ; which left them no sense of disappointment, but rather a consciousness of having had hopes only too narrow and low ; which gave them the exulting sense of 'reigning as kings,' with a ' King of Israel' : while on the other side this same Thing was felt by ' Greeks ' as a ' wisdom' flooding their reasons with a light of truth and wisdom (*sophia*), which met the search of philosophy (*philo-sophia*) [4], but also in simple and wise alike drew forth and ministered to needs which philosophy had but half seen and wholly failed to satisfy, enabling conscience to be candid and yet at peace, building up a new cosmopolitan fellowship, and restoring to human life dignity and value, not only in phrase and theory, but in truth. 'There came forth a

---

[1] S. John iv. 25.
[2] S. Luke xvii. 20.
[3] S. Matt. xii. 38 ; S. John vi. 30, 31, in each case following some of our Lord's own signs.

[4] This comes before us vividly in Justin Martyr's account of his own conversion. *Dial. c. Tryph.* 3 ff. 'Thus and for this reason I am a philosopher.'

Thing,' or rather there came forth One, in Whom all this was done. The question rises, 'Whom say we that He is?' And though the answer must be reached in different ways by different men, and the witness to Him in Whom is the sum of all, must needs be of many kinds ; yet the convergence of many lines (as we have been permitted to trace it) to One in whom they are all combined and yet transcended, to One whom they can usher in but were powerless to produce, may be no slight corroboration of the answer which was accepted, as we have to remember, by the lowly Jesus with significant solemnity : 'Thou art the Christ,' the Fulfiller of all high and inspired Jewish hope ; 'the Son of the Living God [1],' His Son,—as the Son of Man, in whom all that is human reaches fulness ; and as the Son of God, who brings down to man what he has been allowed to prove to himself that he cannot discover or create.

[1] S. Matt. xvi. 16.

V.

THE INCARNATION AND DEVELOPMENT.

I. THE last few years have witnessed the gradual acceptance by Christian thinkers of the great scientific generalization of our age, which is briefly, if somewhat vaguely, described as the Theory of Evolution. History has repeated itself, and another of the 'oppositions of science' to theology has proved upon inquiry to be no opposition at all. Such oppositions and reconciliations are older than Christianity, and are part of what is often called the dialectical movement; the movement, that is to say, by question and answer, out of which all progress comes. But the result of such a process is something more than the mere repetition of a twice-told tale. It is an advance in our theological thinking; a definite increase of insight; a fresh and fuller appreciation of those 'many ways' in which 'God fulfils Himself.' For great scientific discoveries, like the heliocentric astronomy, are not merely new facts to be assimilated; they involve new ways of looking at things. And this has been pre-eminently the case with the law of evolution; which, once observed, has rapidly extended to every department of thought and history, and altered our attitude towards all knowledge. Organisms, nations, languages, institutions, customs, creeds, have all come to be regarded in the light of their development, and we feel that to understand what a thing really is, we must examine how it came to be. Evolution is in the air. It is the category of the age; a 'partus temporis'; a necessary consequence of our wider field of comparison. We cannot place ourselves outside it, or limit the scope of its operation. And our religious opinions, like all things else that have come down on the current of development, must justify their existence by an appeal to the past.

It is the object of the following pages to consider what popular misconceptions of the central doctrine of our religion, the Incarnation, have been remedied; what more or less forgotten aspects of it have been restored to their due place; what new lights have been thrown upon the fulness of its meaning, in the course of our discussion of the various views of evolution.

In face of the historical spirit of the age, the study of past theology can never again be regarded as merely a piece of religious antiquarianism. And there are two classes of mind to which it should be of especial service. Many an earnest worker in the Christian cause, conscious how little the refinements of philosophy can influence for good or evil the majority of men, and generously impatient of all labour wasted, when the labourers are so few, is apt to under-estimate what he considers the less practical departments of theology ; forgetful that there are souls, and those among the noblest, to whom the primary avenue of access is the intellect, and who can only be led homeward by the illuminative way. The Christian of this type may be materially helped towards welcoming wider views, by being convinced that what he has been too easily apt to regard as metaphysical subtleties, or as dangerous innovations, or as questionable accommodations of the Gospel to the exigencies of passing controversy, are after all an integral part of the great Catholic tradition. On the other hand, many plausible attacks upon the Christian creed are due to the inadequate methods of its professed interpreters. Fragments of doctrine, torn from their context and deprived of their due proportions, are brandished in the eyes of men by well-meaning but ignorant apologists as containing the sum total of the Christian faith, with the lamentable consequence that even earnest seekers after truth, and much more its unearnest and merely factious adversaries, mislead themselves and others into thinking Christianity discredited, when in reality they have all along been only criticising its caricature. Such men need reminding that Christianity is greater than its isolated interpreters or misinterpreters in any age ; that in the course of its long history it has accumulated answers to many an objection which they in their ignorance think new ; and that, in the confidence of its universal mission and the memory of its many victories, it still claims to be sympathetic, adequate, adaptable to the problems and perplexities of each successive age.

The general tendency of thought since the Reformation has been in the direction of these partial presentations of Christianity. The Reformers, from various causes, were so occupied with what is now called Soteriology, or the scheme of salvation, that they paid but scant attention to the other aspects of the Gospel. And the consequence was that a whole side of the great Christian tradition, and one on which many of its greatest thinkers had lavished the labours of a lifetime, was allowed almost unconsciously to lapse into comparative oblivion ; and the religion of the Incarnation was narrowed into the religion of the Atonement. Men's views of the faith dwindled and became subjective and self-regarding, while the gulf was daily widened between things sacred and things secular ; among which latter, art and science, and the whole political and social order, gradually came to be classed.

Far otherwise was it with the great thinkers of the early Church; and that not from an under-estimate of the saving power of the Cross, which was bearing daily fruit around them, of penitence, and sanctity, and martyrdom; but from their regarding Christian salvation in its context. They realized that redemption was a means to an end, and that end the reconsecration of the whole universe to God. And so the very completeness of their grasp on the Atonement led them to dwell upon the cosmical significance of the Incarnation, its purpose to 'gather together all things in one.' For it was an age in which the problems of the universe were keenly felt. Philosophical thinking, if less mature, was not less exuberant than now, and had already a great past behind it. And the natural world, though its structural secrets were little understood, fascinated the imagination and strained the heart with its appealing beauty. Spiritualism, superstition, scepticism, were tried in turn but could not satisfy. The questionings of the intellect still pressed for a solution. And the souls of Christians were stirred to proclaim that the new power which they felt within them, restoring, quickening, harmonizing the whole of their inner life, would also prove the key to all these mysteries of matter and of mind.

So it was that the theology of the Incarnation was gradually drawn out, from the teaching of S. Paul and of S. John. The identity of Him Who was made man and dwelt among us, with Him by Whom all things were made and by Whom all things consist; His eternal pre-existence as the reason and the word of God, the Logos; His indwelling presence in the universe as the source and condition of all its life, and in man as the light of his intellectual being; His Resurrection, His Ascension,—all these thoughts were woven into one magnificent picture, wherein creation was viewed as the embodiment of the Divine ideas, and therefore the revelation of the Divine character; manifesting its Maker with increasing clearness at each successive stage in the great scale of being, till in the fulness of time He Himself became man, and thereby lifted human nature, and with it the material universe to which man is so intimately linked; and triumphing over the sin and death under which creation groaned and travailed, opened by His Resurrection and then by His Ascension vistas of the glorious destiny purposed for His creatures before the world was. 'Factus est quod sumus nos, uti nos perficeret esse quod est ipse [1].'

Such is the view of the Incarnation in what may be called its intellectual aspect, which we find gradually expressed with increasing clearness by the Fathers, from Justin to Athanasius. And with all its deep suggestiveness, it is still a severely simple picture, drawn in but

[1] Irenaeus.

few outlines, and those strictly scriptural. It was born of no abstract love of metaphysic, and stands in striking contrast to the wild speculations of the time. Its motive and its method were both intensely practical; its motive being to present Christianity to the mind as well as to the heart; and its method no more than to connect and interpret and explain the definite statements of S. Paul and S. John. Passing over the dark ages, when thought was in comparative abeyance, and the energies of the Church absorbed in the work of conversion and organization, we come, in the twelfth and following centuries, to a second period of intellectual ferment, less brilliant than that which characterized the decadence of the old civilization, but instinct with all the fire and restlessness of youth. Unsobered as yet by experience, and unsupplied with adequate material from without, thought preyed upon itself and revelled in its new-found powers of speculation. Fragments of the various heresies which the Fathers had answered and outlived reappeared with all the halo of novelty around them. Religions were crudely compared and sceptical inferences drawn. Popular unbelief, checked in a measure by authority, avenged itself by ridicule of all things sacred. It was a period of intense intellectual unrest, too many-sided and inconsequent to be easily described. But as far as the anti-Christian influences of the time can be summarized they were mainly two :—the Arabic pantheism, and the materialism which was fostered in the medical schools ; kindred errors, both concerned with an undue estimate of matter. And how did Christian theology meet them ? Not by laying stress, like the later Deists, upon God's infinite distance from the world, but upon the closeness of His intimacy with it : by reviving, that is, with increased emphasis the Patristic doctrine of the Incarnation, as the climax and the keystone of the whole visible creation. There is a greater divergence of opinion, perhaps, among the Schoolmen than among the Fathers ; and a far greater amount of that unprofitable subtlety for which they are apt to be somewhat too unintelligently ridiculed. But on the point before us, as on all others of primary importance, they are substantially unanimous, and never fail in dignity.

'As the thought of the Divine mind is called the Word, Who is the Son, so the unfolding of that thought in external action (per opera exteriora) is named the word of the Word [1].'

'The whole world is a kind of bodily and visible Gospel of that Word by which it was created [2].'

'Every creature is a theophany [3].'

'Every creature is a Divine word, for it tells of God [4].'

---

[1] S. Thom. Aq. *c. Gent.* iv. 13.
[2] H. de Boseham (Migne) v. 190. p. 1353.
[3] Scot. Er. (Migne) v. 122. p. 302.
[4] S. Bonav. *In Eccles.* ci. t. ix.

'The wisdom of God, when first it issued in creation, came not to us naked, but clothed in the apparel of created things. And then when the same wisdom would manifest Himself to us as the Son of God, He took upon Him a garment of flesh and so was seen of men [1].'

'The Incarnation is the exaltation of human nature and consummation of the Universe [2].'

Such quotations might be multiplied indefinitely from the pages of the Schoolmen and scholastic theologians. And the line of thought which they indicate seems to lead us by a natural sequence to view the Incarnation as being the pre-destined climax of creation, independently of human sin. The thought is of course a mere speculation, 'beyond that which is written,' but from its first appearance in the twelfth century it has been regarded with increasing favour; for it is full of rich suggestiveness, and seems to throw a deeper meaning into all our investigations of the world's gradual development.

Again, from the relation of the Word to the universe follows His relation to the human mind. For 'that life was the light of men.'

'The created intellect is the imparted likeness of God,' says S. Thomas; and again, 'Every intellectual process has its origin in the Word of God Who is the Divine Reason.' 'The light of intellect is imprinted upon us by God Himself (immediate a Deo).' 'God continually works in the mind, as being both the cause and the guide of its natural light.' 'In every object of sensitive or rational experience God Himself lies hid [3].' 'All intelligences know God implicitly, in every object of their knowledge [4].' 'Christ is our internal teacher, and no truth of any kind is known but through Him; though He speaks not in language as we do, but by interior illumination [5].' 'The philosophers have taught us the sciences, for God revealed them to them [6].'

II. The point to be noticed in the teaching of which such passages are scattered samples, is that the Schoolmen and orthodox mystics of the middle age, with Pantheism, materialism, rationalism surging all around them, and perfectly conscious of the fact, met these errors, not by denying the reality of matter, or the capacity of reason, as later apologists have often done, but by claiming for both a place in the Theology of the Word. And this Theology of the Word was, in reality, quite independent of, and unaffected by, the subtleties and fallacies and false opinions of the age, cobwebs of the unfurnished intellect which time has swept away. It was a magnificent framework, outside and above the limited knowledge of the day and the peculiarities of individual thinkers; an inheritance from the Patristic tradition,

---

[1] H. de S. Victor. (Migne) v. 177. p. 580.
[2] S. Thom. Aquinas.
[3] S. Bonav. *de Reduct.* sub fin.
[4] S. Thom. Aq. *de Verit.* 22. 2. 1.
[5] S. Bonav. *Lum. Eccles.* S. 12.
[6] Id. *Lum. Eccles.* S. 5.

which the Fathers, in their turn, had not invented, but received as Apostolic doctrine from Apostolic men, and only made more explicit by gradual definition, during centuries when, it has been fairly said, 'the highest reason, as independently exercised by the wise of the world, was entirely coincident with the highest reason as inspiring the Church [1].' We have now to consider whether this view of the Incarnation, which, though in the countries most influenced by the Reformation it has dropped too much out of sight, has yet never really died out of the Church at large, is in any way incompatible with the results of modern science; or whether, on the contrary, it does not provide an outline to which science is slowly but surely giving reality and content.

And at the outset we must bear in mind one truth which is now recognised on all sides as final—viz. that the finite intellect cannot transcend the conditions of finitude, and cannot therefore reach, or even conceive itself as reaching, an absolute, or, in Kantian phraseology, a speculative knowledge of the beginning of things. Whatever strides science may make in time to come towards decomposing atoms and forces into simpler and yet simpler elements, those elements will still have issued from a secret laboratory into which science cannot enter, and the human mind will be as far as ever from knowing what they really are. Further, this initial limitation must of necessity qualify our knowledge in its every stage. If we cannot know the secret of the elements in their simplicity, neither can we know the secret of their successive combinations. Before the beginning of our present system, and behind the whole course of its continuous development, there is a vast region of possibility, which lies wholly and for ever beyond the power of science to affirm or to deny. It is in this region that Christian theology claims to have its roots, and of this region that it professes to give its adherents certitude, under conditions and by methods of its own. And of those conditions and methods it fearlessly asserts that they are nowise inconsistent with any ascertained or ascertainable result of secular philosophy.

As regards the origin of things, this is obvious. Science may resolve the complicated life of the material universe into a few elementary forces, light and heat and electricity, and these perhaps into modifications of some still simpler energy; but of the origin of energy ($\tau\grave{o}$ $\pi\rho\hat{\omega}\tau o\nu$ $\kappa\iota\nu o\hat{\nu}\nu$) it knows no more than did the Greeks of old. Theology asserts that in the beginning was the Word, and in Him was life, the life of all things created : in other words, that He is the source of all that energy, whose persistent, irresistible versatility of action is for ever at work moulding and clothing and peopling worlds. The two conceptions are complementary, and cannot contradict each other.

But to pass from the origin to the development of things : the new

[1] Mark Pattison.

way of looking at nature was thought at first both by its adherents and opponents alike to be inimical to the doctrine of final causes. And here was a direct issue joined with Theology at once : for the presence of final causes or design in the universe has not only been in all ages one of the strongest supports for natural religion ; it is contained in the very notion of a rational creation, a creation by an Eternal Reason. And this was supposed to be directly negatived by the doctrine of the survival of the fittest through natural selection : for if of a thousand forms, which came by chance into existence, the one which happened to correspond best with its environment survived, while the remainder disappeared, the adaptation of the survivor to its circumstances would have all the appearance of design, while in reality due to accident. If, therefore, this principle acted exclusively throughout the universe, the result would be a semblance of design without any of its reality, from which no theological inference could be drawn. But this consequence of natural selection obviously depends upon the exclusiveness of its action. If it is only one factor among many in the world's development ; while there are instances of adaptation in nature, and those the more numerous, for which it fails to account, what has been called its dysteleological significance is at an end. Now its own author soon saw and admitted the inadequacy of the theory of natural selection, even in biology, the field of its first observation, to account for all the facts : while countless phenomena in other regions, such as the mechanical principles involved in the structure of the universe, the laws of crystallography and chemical combination, the beauty of nature taken in connection with its effect upon the mind, irresistibly suggest design, and render the alternative hypothesis, from its mere mathematical improbability, almost inconceivable. And there is now, therefore, a general disposition to admit that the force of this particular attack upon the doctrine of final causes has been considerably overstated.

But in the course of its discussion an important difference has been brought to light between external and internal purposes or ends. The kind of design in nature which first arrested early thinkers was its usefulness to man. Even in scenery, it has been suggested, they saw the utility before the beauty. And so they came to look upon all natural phenomena as having for their final cause the good of man ; and the world as a machine, a contrivance of which the parts have no value except as contributing to the work of the whole, and the whole exists only to produce a result outside and independent of itself, an external end, as if corn should exist solely to provide food for man. This was not an untrue conception ; a shallow thing to say of the reason for which Socrates believed in God ; but it was partial and inadequate, as Bacon and Spinoza shewed. And we have now come to regard the world not as a machine, but as an organism, a system in which, while the parts contribute to the growth of the whole, the whole also reacts upon the development of the parts ; and whose primary purpose is its own perfection, something that is contained within and not outside itself, an internal end : while in their turn the myriad parts of this universal organism are also lesser organisms, ends in and for themselves, pursuing each its lonely ideal of individual completeness. Now when we look at nature in this way, and watch the complex and subtle processes by which a crystal, a leaf, a lily, a moth, a bird, a star realize their respective ideals with undisturbed, unfailing accuracy, we cannot help attributing them to an intelligent Creator. But when we further find that in the very course of pursuing their primary ends, and becoming perfect after their kind, the various parts of the universe do in fact also become means, and with infinite ingenuity of correspondence and adaptation, subserve not only one but a thousand secondary ends, linking and weaving themselves together by their mutual ministration into an orderly, harmonious, complicated whole, the signs of intelligence grow clearer still. And when, beyond all this, we discover the quality of beauty in every moment and situation of this complex life ; the drop of water that circulates from sea to cloud, and cloud to earth, and earth to plant, and plant to life-blood, shining the while with strange spiritual significance in the sunset and the rainbow and the dewdrop and the tear ; the universal presence of this attribute, so unessential to the course of nature, but so infinitely powerful in its appeal to the human mind, is reasonably urged as a crowning proof of purposeful design.

The treatment which these various aspects of teleology have received, during the last few years, may be fairly called exhaustive : and the result of all the sifting controversy has been to place the evidence for design in nature on a stronger base than ever : partly because we feel that we have faced the utmost that can be urged against it ; partly because, under scientific guidance, we have acquired a more real, as distinct from a merely notional apprehension of the manifold adaptations of structure to function, which the universe presents ; and these adaptations and correspondences, when grasped in their infinite multiplicity, furnish us with a far worthier and grander view of teleology than the mechanical theory of earlier days.

All this is in perfect harmony with our Christian creed, that all things were made by the Eternal Reason ; but more than this, it illustrates and is illustrated by the further doctrine of His indwelling presence in the things of His creation ; rendering each of them at once a revelation and a prophecy, a thing of beauty and finished workmanship, worthy to exist for its own sake, and yet a step to higher purposes, an instrument for grander work.

> God tastes an infinite joy
> In infinite ways—one everlasting bliss,
> From whom all being emanates, all power
> Proceeds : in whom is life for evermore,
> Yet whom existence in its lowest form
> Includes ; where dwells enjoyment, there is He :
> With still a flying point of bliss remote,
> A happiness in store afar, a sphere
> Of distant glory in full view.

And science has done us good service in recalling this doctrine to mind. For it has a religious as well as a theological importance, constituting, as it does, the element of truth in that higher Pantheism which is so common in the present day. Whether the term higher Pantheism is happily chosen or not, the thing which it denotes is quite distinct from Pantheism proper, with its logical denial of human personality and freedom. It is the name of an emotion rather than a creed ; that indescribable mystic emotion which the poet, the artist, the man of science, and all their kindred feel in contemplating the beauty or the wonder of the world. Vague as it is, and indefinite, this sentiment is still one of the strongest of which our nature is susceptible, and should be recognised as an integral element in all true religion. Yet for want of such recognition on the part of Christians it is often allowed to gravitate nearer and nearer to pure Pantheism, with which it has, in reality, no essential affinity. We cannot therefore overestimate the importance of restoring to its due place in theology the doctrine of the Divine immanence in nature, to which this sentiment is the instinctive witness. Fathers, schoolmen, mystics, who were quite as alive to any danger of Pantheism as ourselves, yet astonish us by the boldness of their language upon this point ; and we need not fear to transgress the limits of the Christian tradition in saying that the physical immanence of God the Word in His creation can hardly be overstated, as long as His moral transcendence of it is also kept in view.

'God dwelleth within all things, and without all things, above all things and beneath all things [1],' says S. Gregory the Great.

'The immediate operation of the Creator is closer to everything than the operation of any secondary cause,' says S. Thomas [2].

And Cornelius a Lapide, after comparing our dependence upon God to that of a ray on the sun, an embryo on the womb, a bird on the air, concludes with the words, 'Seeing then that we *are* thus united to God physically, we *ought* also to be united to Him morally [3].'

Here are three typical theologians, in three different ages, not one of them a mystic even, using as the language of sober theology words every whit as strong as any of the famous Pantheistic passages in our

---

[1] *Mag. Mor.* ii. 12.　　　[2] S. Thom. Aq. ii. *Sent.* i. 1.
[3] *In Act. Apost.* c. 17. v. 28.

modern literature ; and yet when met with in that literature they are commonly regarded as pleasing expressions of poetic dreams, very far away from, if not even inconsistent with what is thought to be dogmatic Christianity.

To sum up then, the reopening of the teleological question has not only led to its fuller and more final answer, but has incidentally contributed to revive among us an important aspect of the Theology of the Word.

The next point upon which the theory of evolution came in contact with received opinion, was its account of the origin of man. Man, it was maintained, in certain quarters, was only the latest and most complex product of a purely material process of development. His reason, with all its functions of imagination, conscience, will, was only a result of his sensibility, and that of his nervous tissue, and that again of matter less and less finely organized, till at last a primitive protoplasm was reached ; while what had been called his fall was in reality his rise, being due to the fact that with the birth of reason came self-consciousness ; or the feeling of a distinction between self and the outer world, ripening into a sense, and strictly speaking an illusory sense of discord between the two.

Theologians first thought it necessary to contest every detail of this development, beginning with the antiquity of man ; and some are still inclined to intrench themselves in one or two positions which they think impregnable, such as the essential difference in kind between organized and inorganic matter, or again between animal instinct and the self-conscious reason of man : while others are content to assume a sceptical attitude and point to the disagreement between the men of science themselves, as sufficient evidence of their untruth. But none of these views are theologically needed. The first is certainly, the second possibly unsound, and the third, to say the least of it, unkind. It is quite true that the evolution of man is at present nothing more than an hypothesis, and an hypothesis open to very grave scientific objections. The attempts to analyse reason and conscience back into unconscious and unmoral elements, for all their unquestioned ingenuity, are still far from being conclusive ; and then there is the geological admissibility of the time which it would require, and that is still a matter of hopeless controversy between scientific experts. And even if these and numerous kindred difficulties were to be removed in time to come, the hypothesis would still be no nearer demonstration ; for the only evidence we can possibly obtain of pre-historic man is his handiwork of one kind or another, his implements or pictures, things implying the use of reason. In other words, we can only prove his existence through his rationality; through his having been, on the point in question, identical in kind with what now he is. And suspense of judgment therefore upon the whole controversy is, at present, the only scientific state of mind.

But there are facts upon the other side; the undoubted antiquity of the human race; the gradual growth which can be scientifically traced, in our thought and language and morality, and therefore, to the extent that functions react upon their faculties, even in our conscience and our reason too ; and then the immense presumption from the gathering proofs of all other development, that man will be no exception to the universal law. All these positive indications at least suggest the possibility that the difficulties of the theory may one day vanish, and its widest chasms close. And we cannot therefore be too emphatic in asserting that theology would have nothing whatever to fear from such a result. When we see energy and atoms building up an harmonious order, we feel there is an inner secret in the energy and atoms, which we cannot hope to penetrate by merely watching them at work. And so, when we see human minds and wills weaving a veil over the universe, of thought and love and holiness, and are told that all these things are but higher modes of material nature, we only feel that the inner secret of material nature must be yet more wonderful than we supposed. But though our wonder may increase, our difficulties will not. If we believe, as we have seen that Christian Theology has always believed, in a Divine Creator not only present behind the beginning of matter but immanent in its every phase, and co-operating with its every phenomenon, the method of His working, though full of speculative interest, will be of no controversial importance. Time was when the different kinds of created things were thought to be severed by impassable barriers. But many of these barriers have already given way before science, and species are seen to be no more independent than the individuals that compose them. If the remaining barriers between unreason and reason, or between lifelessness and life should in like manner one day vanish, we shall need to readjust the focus of our spiritual eye to the enlarged vision, but nothing more. Our Creator will be known to have worked otherwise indeed than we had thought, but in a way quite as conceivable, and to the imagination more magnificent. And all is alike covered by the words ' without Him was not anything made that was made : and in Him was life.' In fact the evolutionary origin of man is a far less serious question than the attack upon final causes. Its biblical aspect has grown insignificant in proportion as we have learned to regard the Hebrew cosmology in a true light. And the popular outcry which it raised was largely due to sentiment, and sentiment not altogether untinged by human pride.

We may pass on therefore from the evolution of man and his mind in general, to his various modes of mental activity in science and philosophy and art. Here the Christian doctrine is twofold: first, that all the objects of our thought, mathematical relations, scientific laws, social systems, ideals of art, are ideas of the Divine Wisdom, the Logos, written upon the pages of the world; and secondly, that our power of reading them, our thinking faculty acts and only can act rightly by Divine assistance; that the same 'motion and power that impels' 'all objects of all thought' impels also 'all thinking things.' And both these statements are met by objection. In the first place, it is urged, there is no fixity in the universe, and it cannot therefore be the embodiment of Divine ideas. All things live and move under our eyes. Species bear no evidence of having been created in their completeness; on the contrary they are perpetually undergoing transmutation, and cannot therefore represent ideas, cannot have been created on a plan. For ideas, in proportion to their perfection, must be definite, clean-cut, clear. The answer to this objection is contained in what has been already said upon the subject of organic teleology. But an analogy drawn from human thinking may illustrate it further. It is in reality the ideas which our mind has done with, its dead ideas which are clean-cut and definite and fixed. The ideas which at any moment go to form our mental life are quick and active and full of movement, and melt into each other and are ever developing anew. A book is no sooner finished and done with, than it strikes its author as inadequate. It becomes antiquated as soon as its ideas have been assimilated by the public mind. And that because the thought of author and public alike is alive, and ever moving onward; incapable of being chained to any one mode of expression; incapable of being stereotyped. The highest notion we can frame therefore of a mind greater than our own is of one that has no dead ideas, no abstract or antiquated formulae, but whose whole content is entirely, essentially alive. And the perpetual development which we are learning to trace throughout the universe around us would be the natural expression therefore of that Logos Who is the Life.

But when we turn from the objective to the subjective side of knowledge, we are met with a second objection. The doctrine that the Divine Logos co-operates with the human reason, is supposed to be inconsistent with the undoubted fact that many earnest and successful thinkers have been if not atheistic, at least agnostic; unable, that is, to attain to the very knowledge to which, as it would seem on the Christian hypothesis, all intellectual effort should inevitably lead. But this difficulty is only superficial. When we say that the Divine reason assists, we do not mean that it supersedes the human. An initiative still lies with man; and he must choose of his own accord the particular field of his intellectual pursuit. When he has chosen his line of study, and followed it with the requisite devotion, he will arrive at the kind of truth to which that particular study leads, the physicist at laws of nature, the philosopher at laws of thought, the artist at ideal beauty, the moralist at ethical truth; and in each case, as we believe, by Divine assistance, his discoveries being in fact revelations. But the method, the education, the experience involved in different studies are so distinct, that few in a lifetime can reach the eminence that teaches with authority, or even the intelligence that thoroughly appreciates, more than one department of the complex world of thought. And if a man wanders from his own province into unfamiliar regions, he naturally meets with failure in proportion to his hardihood. In the case of the special sciences this is universally recognised. No astronomer would think of dogmatizing on a question of geology, nor a biologist on the details of chemistry or physics. But when it is a question between science and philosophy, the rule is often forgotten; and the spectacle of scientific specialists blundering about in metaphysics is painfully common in the present day: while strange to say, in the case of theology this forgetfulness reaches a climax, and men claim casually to have an opinion upon transcendent mysteries, without any of the preparation which they would be the first to declare needful for success in the smallest subsection of any one of the branches of science.

Nor is preparation all that is wanted. Science is impossible without experiment, and experiment is the lower analogue of what in religion is called experience. As experiment alone gives certainty in the one case, so does experience alone in the other. And it is only the man who has undergone such experience, with all its imperative demands upon his whole character and life, that can justly expect satisfaction of his religious doubts and needs; while only those who, like S. Paul or S. Augustine, have experienced it in an exceptional degree, are entitled to speak with authority upon the things to which it leads. Here again a human analogy may help us. For in studying a human character there are different planes upon which we may approach it. There are the external aspects of the man, the fashion of his garments, the routine of his life, the regulation of his time, his official habits; all which, it may be noted in passing, in the case of a great character, are uniform, not because they were not once the free creation of his will, but because he knows the practical value of uniformity in all such things; and all these externals are open to the observation even of a stranger. Then there are the man's thoughts, which may be withheld or revealed at his pleasure; and these can only be understood by kindred minds, who have been trained to understand them. Lastly, there are his will and affections, the region of his motives, the secret chamber in which his real personality resides; and these are only known to those intimate friends and associates whose intuition is quickened by the sympathy of love. Now all these stages are gone through in the formation of a friendship. First we are struck by a man's appearance, and so led to listen to his conversation, and thence to make his acquaintance, and at last to become his friend. And so with the knowledge of God. The man of science, as such, can discover the uniformities of His action in external nature. The moral philosopher will further see that these actions 'make for righteousness' and that there is a moral law. But it is only to the spiritual yearning of our whole personality that He reveals Himself as a person. This analogy will make the Christian position intelligible ; but for Christians it is more than an analogy. It is simply a statement of facts. For, to Christians, the Incarnation is the final sanction of 'anthropomorphism,' revealing the Eternal Word as strictly a Person, in the ordinary sense and with all the attributes which we commonly attach to the name[1].

Consequently, upon all this we are quite consistent in maintaining that all great teachers of whatever kind are vehicles of revelation, each in his proper sphere, and in accepting their verified conclusions as Divinely true ; while we reject them the moment they transgress their limits, as thereby convicted of unsound thinking, and therefore deprived of the Divine assistance which was the secret of their previous success. And though such transgression may in many cases involve a minimum of moral error, there are abundant instances in the history of thought that it is not always so. Francis Bacon, and the penitent, pardoned Abelard are typical, in different degrees, of a countless multitude of lesser men.

'For our knowledge of first principles,' says S. Augustine, 'we have recourse to that inner truth that presides over the mind. And that indwelling teacher of the mind is Christ, the changeless virtue and eternal wisdom of God, to which every rational soul has recourse. But so much only is revealed to each as his own good or evil will enables him to receive[2].'

'Nor is it the fault of the Word,' adds S. Thomas, 'that all men do not attain to the knowledge of the truth, but some remain in darkness. It is the fault of men who do not turn to the Word and so cannot fully receive Him. Whence there is still more or less darkness remaining among men, in proportion to the lesser or greater degree in which they turn to the Word and receive Him. And so John, to preclude any thought of deficiency in the illuminating power of the Word, after saying "that life was the light of men," adds "the light shineth in darkness, and the darkness comprehended it not." The darkness is not because the Word does not shine, but because some do not receive the light of the Word; as while the light of the material sun

[1] Cp. p. 46.   [2] S. Aug. *de Magist.* 38. t. i. p. 916.

is shining over the world, it is only dark to those whose eyes are closed or feeble [1].'

It has been necessary to dwell upon this doctrine because it has an important bearing upon two further questions, which the philosophy of evolution has brought into new prominence, the relation of Christianity to previous philosophy and other religions. It was the fashion, not long ago, to give an undue value to the part played by environment or surrounding circumstances in the creation of characters and institutions and creeds, to the exclusion of all elements of native originality. And the attempt was made accordingly, in various ways, to represent Christianity as the natural product of the different religions and philosophies which were current in the world at the time of its appearing. But the further study of evolution has qualified this whole mode of thought by the way in which, as we have seen above, it has led us to look at things as organisms rather than machines. A machine has no internal principle of unity. Its unity is impressed upon it from without. And it may be granted therefore, for the sake of argument, that we might conceive a machine or number of machines as formed like the patterns in a caleidoscope by a happy coincidence of atoms; and man, if he were only a machine, as strictly the creature of circumstance. But an organism is a different thing. Dependent as it is upon its environment in an hundred various ways, it is yet more dependent upon its own selective and assimilative capacity, in other words upon its own individuality, its self. And so the notions of individuality, originality, personal identity have been restored to their place in the world of thought. The old error lingers on, and is sometimes crudely re-asserted, especially in its anti-Christian bearing; but it has been discredited by science, and is in fact a thing of the past. And in consequence of this, the attempt can no longer be plausibly made to account for Christianity apart from the personality of Jesus Christ. The mythical theories have had their day. And it is recognised on all hands that mere aspiration can no more create a religion than appetite can create food. A foundation needs a founder.

But the attack thus diverted from our religion glances off on our theology. The Christian religion, it is granted, was founded by Jesus Christ; but its theological interpretation is viewed as a misinterpretation, a malign legacy from the dying philosophies of Greece. This objection is as old as the second century, and has been revived at intervals in various forms, and with varying degrees of success. Modern historical criticism has only fortified it with fresh instances. But it has no force whatever if we believe that the Divine Word was for ever working in the world in co-operation with human reason;

[1] S. Thom. Aq. *cont. Gent.* iv. 13.

inspiring the higher minds among the Jews with their thirst for holiness, and so making ready for the coming of the Holy One in Jewish flesh : but inspiring the Greeks also with their intellectual eagerness, and preparing them to recognise Him as the Eternal Reason, the Word, the Truth; and to define and defend, and demonstrate that Truth to the outer world. The fact that Greek philosophy had passed its zenith and was declining did not make its influence upon Christianity an evil one, a corruption of the living by the dead. It was only dying to be incorporated in a larger life. The food that supports our existence owes its power of nutrition to the fact, that it too once lived with an inferior life of its own. And so the Greek philosophy was capable of assimilation by the Christian organism, from the fact that it too had once been vitally inspired by the life that is the light of men. And the true successors of Plato and Aristotle were the men of progress who realized this fact; not Celsus, Lucian, Porphyry, but the Fathers of the Church.

Clement and Origen, Athanasius and Augustine, the Gregories and Basil understood Greek philosophy as clearly as S. Paul understood Judaism, and recognised its completion as plainly in the Incarnation of the Word. Nor was this view of the Incarnation in the one case, any more than in the other, assumed for a merely apologetic purpose. These men were essentially philosophers, among the foremost of their age. They knew and have testified what philosophy had done for their souls, and what it could not do; how far it had led them forward; and of what longings it had left them full. True, philosophy had as little expected Wisdom to become incarnate, and that amongst the barbarians, the outcast and the poor, as Judaism had expected Messiah to suffer, and to suffer at the hand of Jews. But no sooner was the Incarnation accomplished, than it flooded the whole past of Greece no less than Judaea with a new light. This was what it all meant; this was what it unwittingly aimed at; the long process of dialectic and prophecy were here united in their goal.

'Those who lived under the guidance of the Eternal Reason (μετὰ λόγου βιώσαντες) as Socrates, Heraclitus, and such-like men, are Christians,' run the well-known words of Justin Martyr, 'even though they were reckoned to be atheists in their day.' (Ap. i. 46.) Different minds have always differed, and will continue to differ widely as to the degree in which Greek thought contributed to the doctrines of the Trinity and the Incarnation. It is a difficult and delicate question for historical criticism to decide. But the essential thing to bear in mind is that the Christian doctrine of the Logos amply covers any possible view which criticism may establish upon the point. For, in the light of that doctrine, it is merely a question of the degree in which the Eternal Word chose to reveal Himself through one agency rather than another.

Any attack, therefore, upon our theology for its connection with Greek thought, is powerless to disturb us; since we accept the fact but give it another, a deeper interpretation : while we rejoice in every fresh proof that the great thoughts of the Greek mind were guided by a higher power, and consecrated to a nobler end than ever their authors dreamed of; and that the true classic culture is no alien element but a legitimate ingredient in Catholic, complete Christianity.

And the same line of thought gives us a clue to the history of religious development, the latest field to which the philosophy of evolution has been extended. For though a superficial comparison of religions, with a more or less sceptical result, has often been attempted before, as for instance in the thirteenth century with its well-known story of the three impostors; anything like a scientific study of them has been impossible till now. For now for the first time we are beginning to have the facts before us; the facts consisting in the original documents of the various historic creeds, and accumulated observations on the religious ideas of uncivilized races. In both these fields very much remains to be done; but still there is enough done already to justify a few generalizations. But the subject is intensely complex, and there has been far too great a tendency, as in all new sciences, to rush to premature conclusions. For example, there is the shallow scepticism which seizes upon facts, like the many parallelisms between the moral precepts of earlier religions and the sermon on the Mount, as a convincing proof that Christianity contains nothing that is new. No serious student of comparative religions would justify such an inference; but it is a very common and mischievous fallacy in the half-culture of the day. Then there is the rash orthodoxy, that is over eager to accept any result that tallies with its own preconceived opinions as, for instance, the belief in a primitive monotheism. No doubt several very competent authorities think that the present evidence points in that direction. But a majority of critics equally competent think otherwise. And meanwhile, there is a mass of evidence still waiting collection and interpretation, which may one day throw further light upon the point. Under such circumstances, therefore, it is as impolitic as it is unscientific to identify Christian apology with a position which may one day prove untenable. Attention has already been called to a similar imprudence in connection with Biogenesis, and the history of past apology is full of warnings against such conduct. Then, again, there is the converse view which is often as glibly stated as if it were already a scientific truism; the view that religion was evolved out of non-religious elements, such as the appearance of dead ancestors in dreams. This rests, to begin with, on the supposition that the opinions of uncivilized man, as we now find him, are the nearest to those of man in his primitive condition ; which, considering that degradation is a recognised factor in history, and that degradation acts more powerfully in religion than in any other region, is a very considerable assumption. But even granting this, the psychological possibility of the process in question, as well as the lapse of time sufficient for its operation, are both as yet unproved. It is an hypothetical process, happening in an hypothetical period ; but, logically considered, nothing more.

All this should make us cautious in approaching the comparative study of religions. Still, even in its present stage, it has reached some general results. In the first place, the universality of religion is established as an empirical fact. Man, with a few insignificant exceptions which may fairly be put down to degradation, within the limits of our observation, is everywhere religious. The notion that religion was an invention of interested priestcraft has vanished, like many other eighteenth century fictions, before nineteenth century science. Even in the savage races, where priestcraft is most conspicuous, the priest has never created the religion, but always the religion the priest. Beyond this fact it is unsafe to dogmatize. There is abundant evidence of early nature-worship in very various forms, but whether this was the degraded offspring of purer conceptions, or as is more generally supposed the primitive parent from which those conceptions sprang, is still an open question. The universality of the fact is all that is certain.

Again, there is a progressive tendency observable in the religions of the world ; but the progress is of a particular kind, and largely counteracted by degeneracy. Individuals elevate, masses degrade religion. There is no progress by insensible modifications ; no improvement of a religion in committee. Councils like those of Asoka or Chosroes can only sift and popularise and publish what it needed a Buddha or Zarathustra to create. And so religion is handed on, from one great teacher to another, never rising above the level of its founder or last reformer, till another founder or reformer comes ; while in the interval it is materialized, vulgarized, degraded.

And from the nature of this progress, as the work of great individuals, another consequence has historically followed ; viz. that all the pre-Christian religions have been partial, have emphasized, that is to say, unduly if not exclusively one requirement or another of the religious consciousness, but never its complex whole. For the individual teacher, however great, cannot proclaim with prophetic intensity more than one aspect of a truth ; and his followers invariably tend to isolate and exaggerate this aspect, while any who attempt to supply its complement are regarded with suspicion. Hence the parties and sects and heresies of which religious history is full. The simplest illustration of this is the fundamental distinction between Theism and Pantheism, or the transcendence and immanence of God; the one often said to be a Semitic, the other an Aryan tendency of thought. But however this may be, both these principles must be represented in any system which would really satisfy the whole of our religious instincts; while, as a matter of fact, they were separated by all the pre-Christian religions, and are separated by Mahometanism and Buddhism, the only two religious systems which compete with Christianity to-day.

These, then, are a few broad results of our comparative survey of religions. That religion, however humble the mode of its first appearing, is yet universal to man. That it progresses through the agency of the great individual, the unique personality, the spiritual genius; while popular influence is a counter-agent and makes for its decay. That its various developments have all been partial, and therefore needed completion, if the cravings of the human spirit were ever to be set at rest.

And all this is in perfect harmony with our Christian belief in a God Who, from the day of man's first appearance in the dim twilight of the world, left not Himself without witness in sun and moon, and rain and storm-cloud, and the courses of the stars, and the promptings of conscience, and the love of kin: and Who the while was lighting every man that cometh into the world, the primaeval hunter, the shepherd chieftain, the poets of the Vedas and the Gathas, the Chaldaean astronomer, the Egyptian priest, each, at least in a measure, to spell that witness out aright; ever and anon when a heart was ready revealing Himself with greater clearness, to one or another chosen spirit, and by their means to other men; till at length, in the fulness of time, when Jews were yearning for one in whom righteousness should triumph visibly; and Greeks sighing over the divorce between truth and power, and wondering whether the wise man ever would indeed be king; and artists and ascetics wandering equally astray, in vain attempt to solve the problem of the spirit and the flesh; 'the Word was made Flesh and dwelt among us, full of grace and truth.' The pre-Christian religions were the age-long prayer. The Incarnation was the answer. Nor are we tied to any particular view of the pre-historic stages of this development. We only postulate that whenever and however man became truly man, he was from that moment religious, or capable of religion; and this postulate deals with the region that lies beyond the reach of science, though all scientific observation is, as we have seen, directly in its favour.

In short, the history of the pre-Christian religion is like that of pre-Christian philosophy, a long preparation for the Gospel. We are familiar enough with this thought in its Jewish application from the teaching of the Epistle to the Hebrews. But it seems to be often forgotten that the principles laid down in that Epistle admit of no limitation to any single race of men. They are naturally illustrated from Hebrew history in a writing addressed to Hebrews. But their scope is universal. They compel their own application to every religious history, which the growth of our knowledge brings to light. And from this point of view the many pagan adumbrations of Christian doctrine, similarities of practice, coincidences of ritual, analogies of phrase and symbol, fall naturally into place. The fathers and early missionaries were often perplexed by these phenomena, and did not scruple to attribute them to diabolic imitation. And even in the present day they are capable of disturbing timid minds, when unexpectedly presented before them. But all this is unphilosophical, for in the light of evolution the occurrence of such analogies is a thing to be expected; while to the eye of faith they do but emphasize the claim of Christianity to be universal, by shewing that it contains in spiritual summary the religious thoughts and practices and ways of prayer and worship, not of one people only, but of all the races of men.

'In the whole of our Christian faith,' says Thomassin, 'there is nothing which does not in the highest degree harmonize with that natural philosophy which Wisdom, who made all things, infused into every created mind, and wrote upon the very marrow of the reason ; so that, however obscured by the foul pleasures of the senses, it never can be wholly done away. It was this hidden and intimate love of the human mind, however marred, for the incorruptible truth, which won the whole world over to the gospel of Christ, when once that Gospel was proclaimed [1].'

But when all this has been said, there is a lingering suspicion in many minds, that even if the details of the doctrine of development are not inconsistent with Christianity, its whole drift is incompatible with any system of opinion which claims to possess finality. And if Christianity were only a system of opinion, the objection might be plausible enough. But its claim to possess finality rests upon its further claim to be much more than a system of opinion. The doctrine of development or evolution, we must remember, is not a doctrine of limitless change, like the old Greek notion of perpetual flux. Species once developed are seen to be persistent, in proportion to their versatility, their power, i.e. of adapting themselves to the changes of the world around them. And because man, through his mental capacity, possesses this power to an almost unlimited extent, the human species is virtually permanent. Now in scientific language, the Incarnation may be said to have introduced a new species into the world—a

[1] Thomassin, *Incarn.* i. 15.

Divine man transcending past humanity, as humanity transcended the rest of the animal creation, and communicating His vital energy by a spiritual process to subsequent generations of men. And thus viewed, there is nothing unreasonable in the claim of Christianity to be at least as permanent as the race which it has raised to a higher power, and endued with a novel strength.

III. But in saying this we touch new ground. As long as we confine ourselves to speaking of the Eternal Word as operating in the mysterious region which lies behind phenomena, we are safe it may be said from refutation, because we are dealing with the unknown. But when we go on to assert that He has flashed through our atmosphere, and been seen of men, scintillating signs and wonders in His path, we are at once open to critical attack. And this brings us to the real point at issue between Christianity and its modern opponents. It is not the substantive body of our knowledge, but the critical faculty which has been sharpened in its acquisition that really comes in conflict with our creed. Assuming Christianity to be true, there is, as we have seen, nothing in it inconsistent with any ascertained scientific fact. But what is called the negative criticism assumes that it cannot be true, because the miraculous element in it contradicts experience. Still criticism is a very different thing from science, a subjective thing into which imagination and personal idiosyncrasy enter largely, and which needs therefore in its turn to be rigorously criticised. And the statement that Christianity contradicts experience suggests two reflections, *in limine.*

In the first place the origin of all things is mysterious, the origin of matter, the origin of energy, the origin of life, the origin of thought. And present experience is no criterion of any of these things. What were their birth throes, what were their accompanying signs and wonders, when the morning stars sang together in the dawn of their appearing, we do not and cannot know. If therefore the Incarnation was, as Christians believe, another instance of a new beginning, present experience will neither enable us to assert or deny, what its attendant circumstances may or may not have been. The logical impossibility of proving a negative is proverbial. And on a subject, whose conditions are unknown to us, the very attempt becomes ridiculous. And secondly, it is a mistake to suppose that as a matter of strict evidence, the Christian Church has ever rested its claims upon its miracles. A confirmatory factor indeed, in a complication of converging arguments, they have been, and still are to many minds. But to others, who in the present day are probably the larger class, it is not so easy to believe Christianity on account of miracles, as miracles on account of Christianity. For now, as ever, the real burden of the proof of Christianity is to be sought in our present experience.

There is a fact of experience as old as history, as widely spread as is the human race, and more intensely, irresistibly, importunately real than all the gathered experience of art and policy and science,—the fact which philosophers call moral evil, and Christians sin. It rests upon questionable interpretation of an Eastern allegory. We breathe it, we feel it, we commit it, we see its havoc all around us. It is no dogma, but a sad, solemn, inevitable fact. The animal creation has a law of its being, a condition of its perfection, which it instinctively and invariably pursues. Man has a law of his being, a condition of his perfection, which he instinctively tends to disobey. And what he does to-day, he has been doing from the first record of his existence.

> Video meliora proboque,
> Deteriora sequor.

Philosophers have from time to time attempted to explain this dark experience away, and here and there men of happy temperament, living among calm surroundings, have been comparatively unconscious of the evil in the world. But the common conscience is alike unaffected by the ingenuity of the one class, or the apathy of the other; while it thrills to the voices of men like S. Paul or S. Augustine, Dante or John Bunyan, Loyola or Luther; recognising in their sighs and tears and lamentations, the echo of its own unutterable sorrow made articulate. Nor is sin confined to one department of our being. It poisons the very springs of life, and taints its every action. It corrupts art; it hampers science; it paralyses the efforts of the politician and the patriot; and diseased bodies, and broken hearts, and mental and spiritual agony, are amongst its daily, its hourly results. It would seem indeed superfluous to insist upon these things, if their importance were not so often ignored in the course of anti-Christian argument. But when we are met by an appeal to experience, it is necessary to insist that no element of experience be left out.

And moral evil, independently of any theory of its nature or its origin, is a plain palpable fact, and a fact of such stupendous magnitude as to constitute by far the most serious problem of our life.

Now it is also a fact of present experience that there are scattered throughout Christendom, men of every age, temperament, character, and antecedents, for whom this problem is practically solved : men who have a personal conviction that their own past sins are done away with, and the whole grasp of evil upon them loosened, and who in consequence rise to heights of character and conduct, which they know that they would never have otherwise attained. And all this they agree to attribute, in however varying phrases, to the personal influence upon them of Jesus Christ. Further, these men had a spiritual ancestry. Others in the last generation believed and felt, and acted as they now act and feel and believe. And so their lineage can be traced backward, age by age, swelling into a great multitude whom no man can number, till we come to the historic records of Him whom they all look back to, and find that He claimed the power on earth to forgive sins. And there the phenomenon ceases. Pre-Christian antiquity contains nothing analogous to it. Consciousness of sin, and prayers for pardon, and purgatorial penances, and sacrifices, and incantations, and magic formulae are there in abundance ; and hopes, among certain races, of the coming of a great deliverer. But never the same sense of sin forgiven, nor the consequent rebound of the enfranchised soul. Yet neither a code of morality which was not essentially new, nor the example of a life receding with every age into a dimmer past, would have been adequate to produce this result. It has all the appearance of being, what it historically has claimed to be. the entrance of an essentially new life into the world, quickening its palsied energies, as with an electric touch. And the more we realize in the bitterness of our own experience, or that of others, the essential malignity of moral evil, the more strictly supernatural does this energy appear. When, therefore, we are told that miracles contradict experience, we point to the daily occurrence of this spiritual miracle and ask 'whether is it easier to say thy sins be forgiven thee, or to say arise and walk ? ' We meet experience with experience, the negative experience that miracles have not happened with the positive experience that they are happening now : an old argument, which so far from weakening, modern science has immensely strengthened, by its insistence on the intimate union between material and spiritual things. For spirit and matter, as we call them, are now known to intermingle, and blend, and fringe off, and fade into each other, in a way that daily justifies us more in our belief that the possessor of the key to one must be the possessor of the key to both, and that He who can save the soul can raise the dead.

Here then is our answer to the negative criticism, or rather to the negative hypothesis, by which many critics are misled. Of course we do not expect for it unanimous assent. It is founded on a specific experience ; and strangers to that experience are naturally unable to appreciate its force. But neither should they claim to judge it. For the critic of an experience must be its expert. And the accumulated verdict of the spiritual experts of all ages, should at least meet with grave respect from the very men who are most familiar with the importance of the maxim, ' Cuique in sua arte credendum.' Christianity distinctly declines to be proved first, and practised afterwards. Its practice and its proof go hand in hand. And its real evidence is its power.

We now see why the Atonement has often assumed such exclusive

ominence in the minds of Christian men. They have felt that it was
e secret of their own regenerate life, their best intellectual apology,
eir most attractive missionary appeal; and so have come to think
at the other aspects of the Incarnation might be banished from the
ulpit and the market-place, to the seclusion of the schools. But this
as proved to be a fatal mistake. Truth cannot be mutilated with
npunity. And this gradual substitution of a detached doctrine for a
atholic creed, has led directly to the charge which is now so common,
at Christianity is inadequate to life; with no message to ordinary
en, in their ordinary moments, no bearing upon the aims, occupa-
ons, interests, enthusiasms, amusements, which are human nature's
aily food.

But we have already seen what a misconception this implies of the
ncarnation. The Incarnation opened heaven, for it was the revelation
f the Word; but it also reconsecrated earth, for the Word was made
lesh and dwelt among us. And it is impossible to read history with-
ut feeling how profoundly the religion of the Incarnation has been a
eligion of humanity. The human body itself, which heathendom had
o degraded, that noble minds could only view it as the enemy and
rison of the soul, acquired a new meaning, exhibited new graces,
hone with a new lustre in the light of the Word made Flesh; and
hence, in widening circles, the family, society, the state, felt in their
urn the impulse of the Christian spirit, with its

> touches of things common,
> Till they rose to touch the spheres.

Literature revived; art flamed into fuller life; even science in its
arly days owed more than men often think, to the Christian temper
nd the Christian reverence for things once called common or unclean.
While the optimism, the belief in the future, the atmosphere of hope-
ulness, which has made our progress and achievements possible, and
vhich, when all counter currents have been allowed for, so deeply
differentiates the modern from the ancient world, dates, as a fact of
istory, from those buoyant days of the early church, when the creed
f suicide was vanquished before the creed of martyrdom, Seneca
efore S. Paul. It is true that secular civilization has co-operated with
Christianity to produce the modern world. But secular civilization is,
s we have seen, in the Christian view, nothing less than the providen-
ial correlative and counterpart of the Incarnation. For the Word
did not desert the rest of His creation to become Incarnate. Natural
eligion, and natural morality, and the natural play of intellect have
heir function in the Christian as they had in the pre-Christian ages;
and are still kindled by the light that lighteth every man coming into
he world. And hence it is that secular thought has so often corrected

and counteracted the evil of a Christianity grown professional, ar false, and foul.

Still, when all allowance for other influence has been made ; and a the ill done in its name admitted to the full ; Christianity remains, th only power which has regenerated personal life, and that beyond th circle even of its professed adherents, the light of it far outshining th lamp which has held its flame. And personal life is after all the battl ground, on which the progress of the race must be decided. Nor ev indeed should this be more apparent than in the present day. Fe materialism, that old enemy alike of the Christian and the huma cause, has passed from the study to the street. No one indeed ma regret this more than the high-souled scientific thinker, whose li belies the inevitable consequences of his creed. But the ruthless log of human passion is drawing those consequences fiercely ; and th luxury of the rich, and the communistic cry of the poor, and the des cration of marriage, and the disintegration of society, and selfishness policy, and earthliness in art, are plausibly pleading science in the favour. And with all this Christianity claims, as of old, to cop because it is the religion of the Incarnation. For the real strength materialism lies in the justice which it does to the material side nature—the loveliness of earth and sea and sky and sun and star ; th wonder of the mechanism which controls alike the rushing comet an the falling leaf ; the human body crowning both, at once earth's faire flower and most marvellous machine. And Christianity is the on religion which does equal justice to this truth, while precluding i illegitimate perversion. It includes the truth, by the essential impor ance which it assigns to the human body, and therefore to the who material order, with which that body is so intimately one ; while excludes its perversion, by shewing the cause of that importance to li in its connection, communion, union with the spirit, and conseque capacity for endless degrees of glory.

And though its own first vocation is to seek and save souls one b one, it consecrates in passing every field of thought and action, where the quickened energies of souls may find their scope. It welcomes th discoveries of science, as ultimately due to Divine revelation, and pa of the providential education of the world. It recalls to art the day when, in catacomb and cloister, she learned her noblest mission to b the service of the Word made Flesh. It appeals to democracy as th religion of the fishermen who gathered round the carpenter's Son. points the social reformer to the pattern of a perfect man, laying dow His life alike for enemy and friend. While it crowns all earthly aims wit a hope full of immortality, as prophetic of eternal occupations othe where. And however many a new meaning may yet be found in th Incarnation, however many a misconception of it fade before fulle ght; we can conceive no phase of progress which has not the Incarnation for its guiding star; no age which cannot make the prayer of the fifth century its own—

'O God of unchangeable power and eternal light, look favourably on Thy whole Church, that wonderful and sacred mystery; and by the tranquil operation of Thy perpetual Providence, carry out the work of man's salvation; and let the whole world feel and see that things which were cast down are being raised up, and things which had grown old are being made new, and all things are returning to perfection through Him, from whom they took their origin, even through our Lord Jesus Christ [1].'

[1] Gelasian, quoted by Bright, *Ancient Collects*, p. 98.

VI.

THE INCARNATION AS THE BASIS OF DOGMA.

I. MANY years ago, in undergraduate days, I was speaking once to a friend of my hope of beginning some little acquaintance with Theology. I well remember the air of nicely mingled civility and contemptuousness, with which my friend, wishing to sympathize, at once drew a distinction for me between speculative and dogmatic Theology and assumed that I could not mean that the mere study of dogmatic Theology could have any sort of attractiveness. I do not think that I accepted his kindly overture; but it certainly made me consider more than once afterwards, whether the ' mere study of dogmatic Theology could after all be so slavish and profitless an employment as had been implied. On the whole, however, I settled with myself that his condemnation, however obviously candid and even impressive, must nevertheless remain, so far as I was concerned, a surprise and an enigma. For what, after all, did the study of dogmatic Theology mean but the study of those truths which the mind of Christ's Church upon earth has believed to be at once the most certain and the most important truths of man's history, nature and destiny, in this world and for ever ?

It is impossible, however, not to feel that my friend, in his objection represented what was, and is, a very widespread instinct against the study of dogma. Some think, for instance, that to practical men exactnesses of doctrinal statement, even if true, are immaterial. Others think that any exactness of doctrinal statement is convicted, by its mere exactness, of untruth ; for that knowledge about things unseen can only be indefinite in character. If, indeed, religious knowledge is a process of evolution simply, if it means only a gradual development towards ever-increasing definiteness of religious supposition, then no doubt its exactness may be the condemnation of dogma. But then, no doubt, to make room for such a view, the whole fact of historical Christianity must be first displaced.

Is it put as an impossibility, that there *cannot* be any definite or certain Theology ? Can there, then, be a Revelation ? Can there be an Incarnation? Those only are consistent, who assert that all three are impossible, and who understand that in so doing they are limiting the possibilities, and therefore *pro tanto* questioning the reality of a Personal God. But if there be a Personal God, what are the adequate grounds on which it is nevertheless laid down that he *cannot* directly reveal Himself? Or, if He can reveal Himself, on what ground can the *à priori* assertion rest, that theological truth must be uncertain or indefinite? The Christian Church claims to have both definite and certain knowledge. These claims can never be met by any *à priori* judgment that such knowledge is impossible. Such a judgment is too slenderly based to bear the weight of argument. To argue from it would be to commit the very fault so often imputed to the dogmatist. It would be a flagrant instance of dogmatic assertion (and that for the most important of argumentative purposes) of what we could not possibly know.

The claim of the Church to knowledge through the Incarnation can only be rationally met, and only really answered, when the claim itself, and its evidence, are seriously examined. Herein lies, and will always lie, the heart of the struggle for or against the dogmatic character of the Church. Anything else is only the fringe of the matter. Any rebutting of *à priori* presumptions against dogma is a mere clearing of the way for battle. Thus it is said, perhaps, that the objection is to the degree of definiteness, or to the tone of authority. It is fancied that dogma in its very nature, quite apart from its contents, is a curtailment of the rights, and a limitation of the powers, of mind. Is dogma, the most definite and authoritative, fettering to the freedom of intellect? We can see in a moment the entire unreality of the objection, by simply substituting for it another question. Is truth fettering to intellect? Does the utmost certitude of truth limit freedom of mind? Because, if not, dogma, so far as it coincides with truth, cannot fetter either. If perfect knowledge of truth could paralyse the intellect, what (is it worth while to ask) do we mean by intellect? Do we mean something which must for ever be struggling with difficulties which it cannot overcome? Is it necessary for the idea of mind that it should be baffled? Is it a creature only of the tangle and the fog? And if ever the day should come, when after struggling, more or less ineffectually, with the tangle and the fog, man should emerge at last in clear sunshine upon the mountain top, will mind cease to have any faculty or place, because the knowledge of truth has come? At least, it we understand this to be the conception of mind, it need not frighten us quite so much as it did, to be told that dogma interferes with mind. But if, however different from our experience the employment of mind would be in the presence of perfect knowledge, we cannot so conceive of mind as to admit that truth could possibly be its enemy or its destruction, then we may certainly insist that no amount of dogma, so far as it is true, can limit or fetter the freedom of intellect. But then we are at once thrown back upon the question ; is the dogmatic teaching of the Church true ? No statement which absolutely coincides with truth can hurt the freedom of mind. But mistaken presumption of truth can, and does, limit it ; and so does authority, if it prevents the examination of truth. Dogma, then, is, as dogma, a wrong to mind just so far as it can be convicted of either of these things ; so far as it forbids examination, or so far as it asserts what is not strictly true.

As to the first of these two suggestions against dogma, it is quite enough simply to deny it. The Church, as a teacher of dogmatic truth, does not forbid the freest and completest inquiry into the truths which she enunciates. The question is not whether dogmatic theologians have ever dreaded inquiry into truth ; but whether the dogmatic Church, as such, precludes or forbids it. True, she enunciates some truths as true ; and holds those, in different measures, unwise and wrong, who contradict her truths. But she does not, therefore, forbid the fullest exercise of intellect upon them; nor tremble lest intellect, rightly wielded, should contradict them. Indeed for eighteen centuries she has been engaged, and will be engaged to the end, in examining with a power and discipline of intellect, which she alone ever has, or could have, evoked, into the meaning and exactness of her own knowledge. But she does warn inquirers that successful inquiry into her truths is no work of merely ingenious disputation, but needs the exactest discipline and balance of all the faculties of our human nature.

We return, then, to the second suggestion ; and I repeat that the question has for us become, not whether dogma in the abstract is desirable or undesirable, but whether the dogmas of the Christian Church are true or not true. Dogma that is true can only be undesirable in so far as truth is undesirable.

Whether the dogmas of the Church are true or not true, is itself a question of evidence.

Before, however, making any remark upon the nature of this evidence in the case of religion, we may remember that the possession of dogma is in no way peculiar to religion. There is no region of research or knowledge which does not present to the student its own ' dogmata,' or truths ascertained and agreed upon ; nor does any one, in the name of freedom of intellect, persist in treating these always as open questions.

But perhaps if we venture thus to claim the ascertained truths of any science as dogmas, the scientific answer will be ready. They differ, it will be felt, from the nature of religious dogmas, in two important respects. The first difference is, that they are offered for acceptance with their full proofs, from the first moment that they are offered at all.

The student could not, it may be, have discovered for himself the law of gravitation, or the circulation of the blood ; but he can, when these discoveries are once set before him by another, see forthwith not only the coherency of the principles, but the cogency of their proof. The second difference is, that when they have been accepted by the student, proof and all, they still claim no allegiance beyond what his intelligence cannot but freely give; he is still free to supersede or upset them, if he can. He accepts them indeed provisionally, as identical with the truth so far as the truth on the subject is yet known ; yet not necessarily as final truth. He accepts them as truths which all his further study will comment upon ; presumably indeed in the way of continual illustration and corroboration,—so that what he accepts for study will be more and more certainly proved by the study—but also, if you please, in the way of correction ; for if his study can supersede, or even in any measure correct or alter them,—why, so much the better both for science and for him ! Why should not this be equally true of Theology? Why should religious dogmas be received without these conditions, as certainly and finally true?

To begin with, then, some exception may be taken to the statement that the student who accepts a scientific doctrine, has the full evidence before him from the beginning. That it is not altogether so is evident from the simple consideration, just mentioned, that his work is a progressive one; and that the whole course of his experience tends, and will tend, to deepen the certainty of his first principles. But in so far as the proof of any leading principle is being deepened and strengthened by the student's daily work, so far it is clear that the amount of certainty about his principles with which at first he began, must be less than that with which he ends at last ; and therefore that the proof presented to him at the beginning, however much it may have been adequate to the purpose, (even though it may have been the completest proof capable of being presented in the way of exposition from the lip to the ear) was nevertheless most incomplete in comparison with the fulness of attainable proof. And further, it may certainly be said also, that in the convincingness of this evidence as at first presented, authority, whether more or less, had an undoubted part. At the very least it had a negative place, as a guarantee to the young mind rejoicing in the ingenuity of the apparent demonstration, that the apparent demonstration was not vitiated by some unseen fallacy, or that there was not a series of other considerations behind, which would rob the lesson just learnt of its practical usefulness. Often, indeed, the degree of authority in the first scientific convictions would be very much higher. Often, however helpful the arguments or illustrations of a principle may seem, the really overruling consideration will at first be this, that the whole scientific world has absolutely accepted the principle as truth.

M

So much is this the case, that if an average student should find himself unable in any point to receive the ascertained truths of his science with intelligent agreement, he would not hesitate to assume that the whole fault lay with himself; he would really be convinced in his soul that the dicta of his scientific teachers were right, and that he himself would see the certainty of them by and by.

Now in both these two respects the acceptance of religious dogma is not essentially in contrast, but rather is parallel, with that of scientific principles. For religious truth is neither in its first acceptance a mere matter of blind submission to authority, nor is it stagnant and unprogressive after it is accepted. However different in other ways the leading truths of the Creed may be from scientific principles; in this respect at least they are not different,—that not one of them is ever brought for the acceptance of men without some really intelligent evidence and ground for acceptance. If any man is asked to accept them, without any intelligent ground for the acceptance, we may be bold perhaps to assert that it would be his duty to refuse. Of course however, authority will itself be a large part of his intelligent ground a larger part or a smaller according to circumstances. But then there is no proper antithesis between believing in deference to authority and believing in deference to reason, unless it is understood that the authority believed in was accepted at first as authority *without reason* or maintained in spite of the subsequent refusal of reason to give confirmatory witness to its assertions. Even in the cases in which there seems to be least use of reason, the case of a young child learning at his mother's knee, or of a man whose spirit has suffered and been broken, and who gives himself up at last to the mere guidance of a friend or a teacher, the authority, when accepted at all, is accepted on grounds essentially reasonable. The child's reasoning may differ in quality from the prodigal's; but the child trusts father or mother on grounds which are wholly, if unconsciously, a product of the strictest reason; and the prodigal has felt in his inmost soul alike the deadness of his own spiritual being, and the power and the beauty which are in the life of the teacher upon whom he throws himself. And this is not the only point; for the reasonable mind in one is not a thing different in nature from the reasonable mind in another, or from the eternal reason which is in God. The truths, therefore, which we are taught about God, and man, and Christ, about sin, and redemption from sin and the heaven of holiness, and which seem to be accepted as a mere act of not unreasonable dutifulness, do reasonably withal commend themselves, in some shape or measure, even to the callow mind from its earliest immaturity. There is that in the very consciousness of child or of criminal, with which they are in essential harmony. That in him with which they are in essential correspondence bears witness of them

Nor is anyone, in his acceptance of them, wholly insensible of this witness to their truth, which is, in fact, engraven upon his own conscious being.

To 'take religion on trust,' then, as it is sometimes derisively called, is not really to act in defiance of, or apart from, reason. It is an exercise of reason up to a certain point,—just so, and so far as, the experience of the person warrants. He sees what to trust, and why. He sees where understanding and experience which transcend his own would point. And he seeks for the rational test of further experience in the only way in which it can be had. He defers to the voice of experience, in faith that his own experience will by and by prove its truthfulness. On a medical question, men would not dispute, they would loudly proclaim, the reasonableness and wisdom of such a course. Yet there are those who suppose that the truths of religion are to admit of a complete preliminary intellectual verification, a verification apart from special training and experience, such as they might more reasonably expect in any other subject-matter than religion, but such as, in fact, they hardly expect elsewhere.

The doctrines of the Church, then, accepted at first on reasonable evidence, which in a greater or less degree, but perhaps never wholly, consists in authority reasonably accepted as authority, are then in all the experience of spiritual life receiving continual comment, explanation, corroboration. The whole experience of Christian life must be a growth in the apprehension and certainty of Christian truth. A Christian neophyte may believe every word of his Creed, and believe neither ignorantly nor unintelligently. But the veteran Christian of four-score will transcend the child at least as much in the degree of certainty, with which the doctrines of the Church are to his entire faculties mental, moral, and spiritual, proved and known to be true, as he can possibly do in his merely intellectual apprehension of the history or meaning of the words. We may say, indeed, that the life of a professing Christian which is not a life of growth in the apprehension of doctrinal truth, must necessarily be a retrogression; just as the life of so-called scientific study, which is not continually illuminating afresh, and deepening the certainty of its own scientific principles, must gradually come to hold even its own scientific principles less and less certainly, and to mean by them less and less.

But even if it may be shewn that there is not quite so essential a contrast as there seemed to be, between the character of theological and scientific dogmas, by reason of the proofs which are offered, along with his principles, to the student of any science; yet still it will be felt that they differ essentially in the tone and manner with which they respectively speak to intellect. The truths of the one claim at once to possess an intellectual finality, and to command a moral allegiance, which the truths of the other do not.

It may be worth while to say in reply, first of all, that there cannot be a real contrast of finality between them, so far as they are both really true. What is really true is really true. Neither 'absolutely,' 'finally,' nor any other adverb in the language will make the statement a stronger one. What we call scientific truths are not in fact liable to correction, except in so far as they may perhaps, after all, not be quite scientific truths, except (that is) in respect of such admixture of erroneous supposition, as still has clung to them after general acceptance. And on the other hand, so far as any mistaken assumptions are mixed up with our apprehension of religious truths, so far these too *are* liable to receive, and in the history of Church doctrine are continually receiving, correction. It is, after all, a truism. In either sphere the truths, so far as they really are truths, are true absolutely : but are corrigible in so far as our statement of them still contains anything that is other than truth. We may put it, perhaps, in another way still. If, to assume an impossible hypothesis, any one could really prove, not merely that there were some exaggerations or misconceptions in the traditional mode of statement of some doctrinal truths, but that our really essential Faith was wrong, we may grant hypothetically (seeing that truth is supreme) that he would do us all a mighty service, at however tremendous a cost. Similarly of course it must be owned, that if any one could prove the earth to be flat and stationary, and the law of gravitation to be the precise contradictory of truth, he would do immense service to science. But none the less, the scientific certainty on these points is so complete, that if anyone seriously assailed them, it would be felt that he could only be dealing with the evidence in a way which tended to compromise the credit of his own reason ; and he would therefore be reasonably held to be, as it is roughly phrased, a fool or a madman. And we must claim that for us the certainty of some theological propositions is so complete, that when anyone assails them, we are no less reasonable in regarding him with concern, rather for his own truth's sake than for the truth of our religion ; and that, if miracles or 'an angel from heaven' should seem to bear witness for him, it would still be no bigotry, but in the strictest sense our reasonable course, to refuse the witness, and to treat it as merely an attempt to ensnare us into falsehood to the real requirements of our reason and conscience.

Is the conclusion, then, that there is after all no difference at all between the truths of Theology and of Science, in respect of their claim to authority ? On the contrary, there remains a perfectly real contrast of authority between them ; only it is to be looked for elsewhere than among the conditions upon which our belief in them respectively is based.

There are two distinct senses in which the doctrines of the Creed may be said to be authoritative. It may be meant that the authoritativeness is in the manner in which they are presented to us; that is to say, that (whatever their content may be) they are statements which we believe, and are to believe, on the sole ground that we are told to do so, without any appeal to reason of our own; or it may be meant that they are statements whose content is of such nature and inherent importance, that we cannot, in fact, believe them, without thereby necessarily being involved in a train of consequential obligations of thought and life. In this latter case the authoritativeness lies not in the manner of their presentation to us or our acceptance of them, but in that which is involved in the nature of the truths themselves, *if and when* they are believed.

Is it true to say of the Creeds that they are 'authoritative' in the former sense? that is to say that they challenge our allegiance, and we are bound to believe them, because we are told that they are true, without examination on our part, and without reason? It has indeed been stated already that, as between pupils and teachers, there is in religious learning, as there is in all human learning whatever, scientific or otherwise, a certain legitimate and important field for authority reasonably accepted as authority, that is, the authority of men more learned and experienced than ourselves. Even this, of course, means that the pupil believes the things taught to be strictly rational to the teacher, though they be not so, as yet, to himself. But is it true, in speaking of religion, to carry this one step further; and to say that in this sphere our *whole* belief, and duty of belief, rests upon authority as its ultimate foundation, the authority not of man's experience, but of God's command? It must, no doubt, be freely owned on all sides, that if there be a creed commanded of God, we certainly are bound to believe it. But is there? or when, or how, was it commanded? Does anyone answer, through our Lord Jesus Christ? or through His Church? or through the Bible? But who is He? or what is the Bible? or how do we know? To accept doctrines, which we otherwise should not accept, because we are told to do so, without knowing first who told us, or why we should believe him, is simply not a reasonable possibility. But to ask these questions and to have answers to them, and believe because we are satisfied in some way as to the answers to them, is certainly not to rest the act of believing on a foundation of mere authority: essentially rather it is, to go over part of the ground of the Creed first, and be satisfied as to the correctness of its main substance, and *therefore* to believe it. A Christian will not deny that the doctrines of the Creed are entitled in fact to be held as authoritative, in both of the senses distinguished above. But we cannot believe them on God's authority till we have first believed in the authority of God. And, therefore, their authoritativeness in what we have called the first sense is not really the ultimate ground of our accepting them : for it is not itself accepted and apprehended by us, except as a consequence of our first believing that which is the main substance of the Creed.   It may be the warrant to us of this or that detail considered apart : but it is not, and cannot ever be, the original and sufficient cause of our believing the whole.   *Credo ut intelligam* may be the most true and most reasonable motto of the large part of Christian faith and life : but it is not inconsistent with—it is founded upon—an ultimate under-lying *intellexi ut crederem.*

There is, then, a real and abiding difference between theological and scientific dogmas, in respect of the authority with which they speak to us.   But the difference is one which does not affect at all the method or grounds of our original belief in them respectively : it is to be found exclusively in the different subject-matter of the two when believed.

And herein, also, it is that we find the real answer to the other form of question, viz., why should Theology claim to be so much more final than science ?   Much as science has conquered of the realm of truth, it does not profess to have conquered more than a little.   Of the vast residuum it says nothing.   It has no idea how small a proportion its present knowledge may bear to that which will one day be known. Nay, the further it advances in knowledge of truth, so much the smaller a proportion does its realized truth seem to it to bear to that which remains unexplored.   Why should the theologian be less patient of additions to theological knowledge, such as may some day throw all his present creeds into comparative obscurity ?   Why should the Christian Creed be fixed and inexpansive ?   The question is formidable only in an abstract form.   The reasonable answer to it confronts us the moment we consider what is the subject-matter of the Creed. Scientific principles are in their very nature fragments of a truth which is practically infinite.   But the Christian Creed, if true at all, cannot possibly be a fragment of truth.   For the Christian Creed does not simply enunciate so many abstract principles of natural or supernatural life or governance.   It introduces us straight to a supreme Person, Himself the beginning and end, the author and upholder of all.   Such a doctrine may be false ; but it cannot be a fragment.   The child who believes in God, believes in everything, though he knows hardly any-thing.   He has infinitely more yet to learn, as to what his own belief means.   But he has nothing to add to it.   The perfect knowledge of the universe would not add to it, but would only explain it.   Is it, then, by virtue of his personal relation to a Personality which is Itself supreme and all inclusive, that he is guilty of no presumption, even though in the face of the modest disavowals of scientific men, he must maintain that his own creed is, in its proper nature, even when all admissions have been made, rather a complete and conclusive, than a partial or a tentative, statement of truth. But this difference between him and them is the result neither of any arrogance in his temper, nor any lack in his logic, but it follows necessarily from the nature of the subject-matter of his creed, if and when it is believed.

But still this fact that, if true, they are truths which by the obvious necessity of their subject-matter speak to our intellects and consciences with a tone of such Divinely commanding authority, ought not to make me or anyone accept them as true, unless the evidence for them is adequate. The question is not how authoritative they would be, if true; nor how important or inclusive they would be, if true; nor is any amount of contingent importance or authority adequate evidence for their truth, but only a motive for enquiring into its evidence. The question is, are they true? or are they not true? and the question is a question of evidence.

II. And now, in recurring once more to the subject of the evidence by which the dogmas of religion are proved, from which we diverged just now, we find, in respect of it, a second reality of contrast between theological truths and the truths of material science. For whilst in both cases equally we depend upon evidence, and evidence that is adequate; it does not follow that the evidence for both is in all points similar in kind. In great part indeed it is so; but it is certainly not so altogether. For when we speak of the evidence of religious truths, it is to be remembered that the full evidence by which our consciences are wholly convinced of them, is not of one kind only, but of all kinds. The facts of religion address themselves to the whole nature of man ; and it is only by the whole nature of man that they can ever be fully apprehended. Man is not a being of intellectual conceptions or faculties only. And because he is not so, therefore no set of principles which could be apprehended by the intellect alone (as the theorems of Euclid may appear to be), and which make for their acceptance no demand at all upon the qualities of his moral or spiritual being, could really present, as religion professes to present, a system of truth and life which would be adequate to the scope of his whole nature. It is undoubtedly the case that just as the truths of religion account for, and appeal to, his whole being, so the evidence for them appeals to his whole being also. For its complete appreciation there are requirements other than intellectual. There must be not only certain endowments of mind, but the life of a moral being. There must be moral affections, moral perceptions, spiritual affinities and satisfactions. Even if the primary conviction of his reason may be apart from these, yet of the fully developed evidence, which is the real possession of the Christian believer, these are a most important and necessary part. Without these, his certainty, adequate though it might be, would be far less profound than it is. These are to him essential ingredients in the richness and the fulness of the evidence which to him is everywhere. Now for this necessary width of the full confirmatory evidence of religion, it is impossible for the religious man, with the utmost desire to make every allowance and apology that is possible, to offer any apology at all. So far from being a mark of inconsistency or feebleness, it is a necessary note of the completeness of religion. Religion professes to have for its subject-matter, and in a measure incomplete, but relatively adequate, to include, to account for, and to direct, the whole range of all man's history, all man's capacities, explored or unexplored, all man's destiny now and for ever. If its truths and their evidence were found to address themselves exclusively to the intellect, in isolation from the other qualities and experiences of man's nature, it would be self-convicted of inadequacy. If men full of worldliness of heart and self-indulgence could be capable of understanding the revelation of religious truth as accurately, of embracing it as completely, of apprehending the depth and the width of the evidence for it (with which all human nature really is saturated) as thoroughly as the prayerful and the penitent, this would not mean that religion or religious evidence had been lifted up, on to a higher and more properly scientific level, but rather that it had shrunk down into correspondence merely with a part, and not the noblest part, of man's present nature.

It would be far beyond the scope of this paper to discuss kinds of evidence, or argue in defence of the position that there is real evidence for religious truth, which is none the less properly evidence, because it is different in kind from the evidence for the propositions of material science : but it may be permissible, at least, in passing to record the claim, and to insist that religious men, in confining themselves to strictly historical or logical arguments, are necessarily omitting much which is nevertheless, to them, real ground. There are evidences which can speak to the heart, the imagination, the conscience, as well as the intelligence. Or, perhaps, we shall come nearer to an exact expression of the truth, by saying that the intelligence, which can apprehend and pronounce upon the evidence of truths of spiritual consciousness, is an intelligence identical in name, but not identical in nature, with that which can well weigh and judge purely logical—or even that which can pronounce upon moral—problems. The intelligence of a moral character, or of a spiritual personality, differs not in range only, but in quality, from that of a merely 'rational animal.' If the moral and the spiritual intelligence did not contain quite other elements, drawn from quite other experiences and possibilities, they could not work upon their higher subject-matter at all. To the religious man, therefore, it must seem strictly unreasonable, in the examination of truths which professedly correspond to man's whole nature, and need his whole nature and experience for the interpretation of them, to begin by shutting out, as irrelevant, what we will modestly call the half of man's nature; and to demand that the truths shall be so stated and so proved, as that the statements and proofs shall correspond exclusively with the other half, and find in that other half their whole interpretation, and their whole evidence.

It may, indeed, be desirable to guard against a misconception, by the express admission that there is some necessary ambiguity in the terms employed. We may seem to have unduly extended both the verbal meaning, and the sphere of importance, of 'evidence' and 'proof.' Undoubtedly there is a sense in which it would be, not merely true to admit, but important to insist, that in the acceptance of religious truth, Faith neither is, nor ever can be, displaced, in order that Demonstration may be enthroned in her place. But then Demonstration is a word which belongs to strictly logical nomenclature. And the very point here insisted on is that the strictly logical presentment of religion is, in reference to the real presentment of religion, most inadequate. Undoubtedly, if everything else is shorn away, and religion remains solely and only in the form of strict logic, without sentiment, without imagination, without experience of duty, or sin, or right, or aspiration, or anything else which belongs to the spiritual consciousness of human personalities, the logic of it is, and must be, imperfectly conclusive.

Now words such as 'evidence,' 'proof,' 'intelligence,' are no doubt often used in connection with processes of the intellect taken apart— the intellect of a being merely rational. In insisting, therefore, that the word evidence, when used in reference to religious subject-matter, must include data which, to the observer of physical phenomena, would seem vague and impalpable; and that intelligence, as adequately trained to apprehend and give judgment upon religious evidence, is in some respects other, and more, than that intelligence which can deal with evidence into which no element of spiritual consciousness enters; we differ, perhaps, at the most, more in form than reality, from those who simply deprecate the appeal to 'evidence' or 'proof' in matters of faith.

To the religious man, then, the fulness of Christian evidence is as many-sided as human life. There is historical evidence—itself of at least a dozen different kinds,—literary evidence, metaphysical evidence, moral evidence, evidence of sorrow and joy, of goodness and of evil, of sin and of pardon, of despair and of hope, of life and of death; evidence which defies enumerating; into this the whole gradual life of the Christian grows; and there is no part nor element of life which does not to him perpetually elucidate and confirm the knowledge which has been given him. Everything that is or has been, every consciousness, every possibility, even every doubt or wavering, becomes to the Christian a part of the certainty—an element in the absorbing reality —of his Creed.

But this is rather the end than the beginning. Certainly it is not thus that the Creed of the Church can present itself to those whose life is still independent of the Creed.

Let us consider, then, how the truths of the Creed did first, in fact, introduce themselves to human consciousness. There are three several stages of its presentment in history, of which the central one is so overmastering in importance, that it alone gives their character to the other two. They are, first, the leading up, in the world's history and consciousness, to the life of Jesus Christ; secondly, the life and death of Jesus Christ; thirdly, the results, in history and consciousness, of the life and death of Jesus Christ. We may say, perhaps, that of the first of these the main outcome was belief in God; and such a God, that belief in Him carried with it the two corollaries of aspiration after righteousness, and conviction of sin. We may say that the third of these means the establishment of the Church upon earth, and the articulating of her consciousness according to the Creeds. But in any case all the three are plainly historical, matters of historical inquiry, of historical evidence; and all plainly depend entirely upon the intermediate one, the history of a certain human life which purports to be—which either is, or is not—the hinge-point of all history whatever.

All turns, then, upon a certain passage of history. Is the history, as believed by Christians, true or false? The Christian record of that history is the New Testament. Indeed, of that history, the New Testament is the only record. Is, then, the history of the teaching and the work, the life and the death, of Jesus Christ, presented to us in the New Testament as a chapter of historical fact,—is it historical fact, or is it not? The Incarnation is either a fact, or a fiction. The Incarnation means also for Christians the Atonement. For our present purpose, the Incarnation may be taken as necessarily including the Atonement. But still of this complex fact the dilemma stands. If it is not true, it is false. There is no middle term. If it is not true, then, whether dogma in itself is, or is not, desirable, at least all the dogma of the Christian Church is false.

The Incarnation and the Atonement together are not presented in the New Testament as, by their own mere statement, guaranteeing themselves. On the contrary, there is one single, definite, historical fact, which is represented there as the central heart and core of the evidence upon which the conviction of their truth depends. This fact is the resurrection of Jesus Christ from the dead. Though this is not the whole of the Christian Creed, yet this, according to S. Paul, is, to the whole of the Christian Creed, crucial. 'If there be no resurrection from the dead, then is Christ not risen ; and if Christ be not risen, then is our preaching vain, and your faith is also vain. Yea, and we are found false witnesses of God ; because we have testified of God, that He raised up Christ ; whom He raised not up, if so be that the dead rise not. For if the dead rise not, then is not Christ raised ; and if Christ be not raised, your faith is vain, ye are yet in your sins.' To be direct personal evidence of a certain fact, and that fact the resurrection ;—this was, in the view of S. Peter and the Apostles, the first qualification, and the central meaning, of Apostleship : 'must one be ordained *to be a witness with us of His resurrection* ;' 'this Jesus hath God raised up, *whereof we are all witnesses.*' Upon the historical truth or falsehood, then, of the resurrection, hangs the whole question of the nature and work of Jesus Christ, the whole doctrine of Incarnation and Atonement.

But in saying this, it is necessary to guard our proper meaning. If we admit the fact of the Resurrection to be cardinal, what is the fact of the Resurrection which is in question? It is as far as possible from being simply a question whether 'a man' could or could not, did or did not, reappear, after death, in life. When we speak of the historical fact, we must mean at least the whole fact with all that it was and meant, complex as it was and many-sided ; not with its meaning or its proof isolated upon a single page of the book of history, but having far-reaching affinities, parts essentially of its interpretation and of its evidence, entwined in the depths of the whole constitution of our nature, and the whole drama of history from the first moment to the last. However much Christians may have at times to argue about the simple evidence for the 'yes' or 'no' of the Resurrection of Jesus, as if it were the alleged resurrection of any other man that was in question, neither the question itself, nor the evidence about it, can possibly be, in fact, of the same nature or upon the same level, as the evidence about another. No amount of conviction of the reappearance in life of any other man, would have any similar meaning, or carry any similar consequences. The inherent character of Him who rose, and the necessary connection between what He was, and had said and claimed for Himself, on the one hand, and on the other His rising out of death ; this is an essential part of that fact of the resurrection, which comes up for proof or disproof. The fact that Jesus Christ, *being what He was*, the climax and fulfilment of a thousand converging lines— nay, of all the antecedent history of mankind—rose from the dead, and by that fact of resurrection (solemnly fore-announced, yet none the less totally unlooked for) illuminated and explained for the first time all that before had seemed enigmatical or contradictory in what He was,—and indeed in all humanity; this is the real fact of the resurrection which confronts us. It is this vast fact which is either true or false. The resurrection of the crucified Jesus cannot possibly be a bare or simple fact. When viewed as a material manifestation of the moment only, it is at least misunderstood; it may be unintelligible. It is, no doubt, an event in history; and yet it confronts us, even there in its place and witness in history, not simply as a finite historical event, but as an eternal counsel and infinite act of God.

Yet there are times when we must consent to leave much of all this for the moment, on one side. Whatever else the event in history may carry with it, of course it must stand its ground as a mere historical event. The mere fact may be but a part of it; yet all will be overthrown if the fact be not fact. And so, though the truths of the Christian religion, and the evidence for them, be at least as wide as was represented above, yet they present themselves to our minds still as they presented themselves at first to the minds of men, within the sphere and the rules of ordinary human history and historical evidence. Here are events written on the page of history. Examine them. Are they historically false or true? If they be not false, what do they mean and involve? This is the modest way in which they present themselves.

No one will now dispute that Jesus died upon the Cross. If He did not, on the third day, rise again from that death to life;—cadit quaestio —all Christian dogma, all Christian faith, is at an end. Something might still be true which might be of interest; something, even, which for sheer want of a better, might be still the most interesting fact in the world's long history; but something which, from the first line to the last, would be essentially different from the Catholic faith. But, on the other hand, if He did so rise again, then the fact of His resurrection necessarily raises further questions as to His nature and being,—necessarily requires the understanding of further truths for its own intelligent explanation. Now the present paper is not an evidential treatise. It is no part of our task to attempt to prove the historical reality of the resurrection. What it does concern us to notice is the way in which the determination of all Christian truth hinges upon it. If it falls, all the rest will drift away, anchorless and unsubstantial, into the region of a merely beautiful dreamland. As dreamland, indeed, it may still captivate and inspire; but anchor of sure fact there will be none. It will only be a beautiful imagination,—a false mirage reflected from, based upon, falsehood. No doubt imagination is sovereign in the lives of men. But then imagination means the vivifying of truth, not the spectral embodiment of a lie.

On the other hand, if the fact of the resurrection stands, then it cannot stand alone. If Jesus Christ so lived and taught as even the most indefinite believers concede that He lived and taught, if He then died on the Cross, *and rose again the third day from the dead,* you have indeed already the foundation dogma of the Creed ; and having that, you cannot possibly rest in it : that foundation fact will absolutely compel you to ask and to answer certain further necessary questions ; and whatever intelligible answer you may choose to give to them will be essentially a dogmatic definition. Who or what was this man who thus lived, thus spoke, thus died, and thus rose from the dead ? As a matter of fact, the whole Church of Christ in history (including the men who had been His own companions, trained and inspired by Himself,) taught and believed, without shadow of hesitation, that He was very God. Very gradually, indeed, had they advanced to this ; step by step, through their growing intimacy with a character whose very excellences were only enigmatical and confounding, so long as the master-truth, which lay behind them, was ignored. And very tentative, on His side, was the method of His self-revelation ; through qualities, through inherent powers, through explicit teachings, slowly felt, slowly recognised, as transcendent, as impossible, except in relation to a truth which, after long misconceptions and perplexities, is seen by them at last not only to be true, but to be the essential truth which He Himself requires of them. For, be the method as gradual and as tentative as you please, these witnesses, who are, in fact, the only witnesses the world ever has had, or can have, of His inner life and teaching, testify unhesitatingly not only that all true acceptance of Him was, in their judgment, acceptance of Him as God, but that His life and death were penetrated by the consciousness of His own Godhead ; and by the deliberate purpose (through whatever unexpected patience of method) of convincing the whole world in the end of His Godhead, and receiving universal belief, and universal worship, as God.

Now no one to-day disputes that He was truly man. Is it true that He was very God ? It is either true or false. As to the fact there are only the two alternatives. And between the two the gulf is impassable. If it is not false, it is true. If it is not absolutely true, it is absolutely false. According to the faith of the Catholic Church it is absolutely true. According to the highest form of Arianism, not less than according to the barest Socinianism, it is (however you may try to gloss it over) absolutely false.

Once more, it is quite beyond our province to marshal or press argumentatively the proofs that He was indeed God. But it is necessary to see with perfect clearness, how the question must have been raised, and being raised must have been answered. The very life of the Church was belief in Him; and she could not remain fundamentally uncertain as to who or what He was in whom she believed. This was the one thing which had never been allowed to those who drew near Christ. All through His ministry those who came near Him, and felt the spell of His presence, His holiness, His power, were undergoing a training and a sifting. Moment by moment, step by step, the accumulating evidence of His transcendently perfect humanity kept forcing more and more upon them all the question which He would never let them escape, the question by which they were to be tested and judged; 'What think ye of Christ?' 'If ye believe not that I am He, ye shall die in your sins.'

If there is a true historical sense in which the clear definition of the doctrine of the Divinity of Jesus Christ must be assigned to the Councils of the fourth and fifth centuries, yet it would be a great historical blunder to state or imagine, as inference, that till then the doctrine was only held partially or with imperfect consciousness in the Catholic Church. The Church did not, as a result of those controversies, develop the consciousness of any new doctrine : the development of her consciousness was rather in respect of the shallow but tempting logic which would deform, or the delusions which might counterfeit, her doctrine, and of the perils to which these must lead. It may be a question, indeed, how far the words implicit and explicit do, or do not, represent the distinction between the dogmatic consciousness of the Apostolic and the Conciliar ages. The difficulty in determining depends solely on this, that the words themselves are used with different meanings. Thus, sometimes men are said to hold implicitly what they never perhaps suspected themselves of holding, if it can be shewn to be a more or less legitimate outcome, or logical development, of their belief. If such men advance inferentially from point to point, their explicit belief at a later time may be, in many particulars, materially different from what it had been at an earlier ; even though it might be logically shewn that the earlier thought was, more or less directly, the parent of the later. Now in any such sense as this we shall stoutly maintain that, from the beginning, the Church held dogmatic truths not implicitly, but explicitly and positively. They who baptized into the threefold Name of the Father, and of the Son, and of the Holy Ghost ; whose blessing was 'The grace of the Lord Jesus Christ, and the love of God, and the communion of the Holy Ghost' ; who, living in the Spirit, lived in Christ; whose highest worship was the Communion of the Body and the Blood of Christ, and whose perfectness of life was Christ ; they, so living and worshipping, did not hold the Godhead of Jesus Christ implicitly ; they did not hold something out of which the doctrine of the Trinity might come to be unfolded. On the other hand, you may use the same contrast of words, meaning merely that you have, through cross-questioning or otherwise, obtained a power which you did not possess, of defining, in thought and in words, the limits of your belief, and distinguishing it precisely from whatever does not belong to it. You hold still what you always meant to hold. You say still what you always meant to say. But it is your intellectual mastery over your own meaning which is altered. Like a person fresh from the encounter of a keen cross-examination, you are furnished now, as you were not before, with distinctions and comparisons, with definitions and measurements,—in a word, with all that intellectual equipment, that furniture of alert perception and exact language, by which you are able to realize for yourself, as well as to define to others, what that meaning exactly is, and what it is not, which itself was before, as truly as it is now, the very thing that you meant.

In this sense, no doubt, the definitions of councils did make Christian consciousness more explicit in relation to positive truth. They acquired, indeed, no new truth. Primarily they were rather, on this side or on that, a blocking off of such false forms of thought or avenues of unbalanced inference, as forced themselves forward, one by one, amidst the intellectual efforts of the time, to challenge the acceptance of Christian people. Primarily they are not the Church saying 'yes' to fresh truths, or developments, or forms of consciousness; but rather saying 'no' to untrue and misleading modes of shaping and stating her truth. Only indirectly, in that effort, the Church acquires through them a new definiteness of mastery for the intellect in reference to the exactness of her own meaning.

It is comparatively easy for those who are convinced of a truth to struggle against its open contradiction. But false modes of stating their truth, and unbalanced inferences from their truth, are often staggering to minds which would be unperplexed by any less insidious form of error. It may be that, in all ages of the Church, even those who are born and bred in undoubting faith in the Person of Jesus, have to pass, more or less explicitly, through their own experience of hesitation and exaggeration, of reaction and counter-reaction, before they are quite in a position to define, or maintain by argument in the face of insidious alternatives, the exact proportion of their own Catholic belief.

Not unsuggestively, indeed, nor indirectly, do the oscillations of the public consciousness in the era of the councils, as to the due expression of Catholic belief, reproduce on a larger scale, and therefore with more magnified clumsiness, the alternating exaggerations of such a single struggling mind. The natural thought begins, as a matter of course, as Apostles had begun of old, with the perfect and obvious certainty that Jesus was a man. Then comes the mighty crisis to natural thought. With infinite heavings and strugglings, and every conceivable expedient of evasion, it strains to avoid the immense conclusion which challenges it, catching eagerly at every refinement, if so be it may be possible to stop short of full acceptance of a truth so staggering (when it comes to be measured intellectually) as that the Man Jesus was Himself the Eternal God. Now however grossly unjust it might be to think of Arianism as if it ever meant, or held, Jesus Christ to be merely a man; yet it is true that in respect of the one great question which is at the root of Christian faith,—is He God, or is He not?—it stands as offering alternatives and expedients, by which the plain answer 'yes' may be avoided; by which therefore the answer 'no' is in effect maintained; for between 'God' and 'not God' the distinction cannot be bridged. This, then, is the real hinge-point of the Catholic faith. But when this, the greatest of all battles of belief, is won at last, in spite of every variety of Arian and semi-Arian refining; forthwith the undisciplined mind, always ready to exaggerate, always difficult of balance, begins so to run into ardour of expression of its truth, as in effect to make unreal the other half of the doctrine of the Incarnation. The first great wonder once grasped, it is so natural, in fervour of insistance on the very Godhead, to forget or deny the simple completeness of the very Manhood! It seems so hard,—almost wanting in reverence,—still to conceive of Him then as perfectly human, —human body and human soul! What more obvious reaction in the mind of any pupil not yet perfectly steadied and balanced? Yet these few short sentences represent not untruly the real process of education, painfully accomplished by those intellectual struggles which culminated in the councils of Nicaea and Constantinople, in 325 and 381 respectively. And when the pupil is steadied from this second excess, and the Godhead and the Manhood are both grasped, each severally, each completely, there follows again a perfectly natural result in a new uncertainty about the union of the two in Jesus. Again it seems an instinct of reverence which shrinks from the truth. For the Manhood, it is urged, though complete, body, soul, and spirit, must yet remain, in Him, a thing separable and separate from His own original Divine personality. But if the human nature was not verily His own nature, if it was animated by any consciousness which was not absolutely His own consciousness, the consciousness of His one undivided personality, —what or whence in Him was this other than His own individual consciousness? Is it so, then, the mind begins necessarily to ask itself, that the mystery of the Incarnate Life was the mystery of a double consciousness, a double personality? two distinguishable existences, two selves, two identities, side by side, harmonious, allied, yet nowhere really meeting in any one underlying principle of unity? It was necessary that the doubt should be raised, that its meaning and results might be measured. But it is this which becomes the Nestorianism against which the council of Ephesus in 431 set the seal of Catholic belief. Once more, the natural reaction from Nestorianism, when the believer is keenly alert against its danger, is so to insist upon the indivisible Personal unity, as to shrink from the admission of any distinguishableness in Him, actual or possible, between the two natures or characters which He united, between the human and the Divine elements in His one consciousness. But this is either once more to curtail the true completeness of the human nature, or to fuse it with the Divine into some new thing not truly identical with either. And this is the Monophysitism of 451, the subject-matter of the fourth great general council at Chalcedon.

It is said, indeed, that the ages of councils were uncritical ages ; and that their decisions are therefore not to be accepted as authoritative on questions of minute theological criticism, for which their uncritical spirit made them specially unfit. The assertion is perhaps a little beside the mark. You have not to plead that they were likely to be uncritical, but to shew that they were in fact wrong. It is clear that they were not specially unfit either to arrive at a definiteness of meaning, or to express what they meant. They were sure what they meant ; and have expressed it with perfect clearness. The question is not how critical they were likely to be, but whether their meaning—which is clear—is right or wrong. Whatever antecedent probability there may be either in the minds of nineteenth century critics against their correctness, or in the minds of Churchmen accustomed to defer to them in favour of it ; it is certain that no one who is really doubtful about the truth of Christianity, will be called upon to accept it in deference to the mere authority of the Councils. However much more they may be to ourselves, to such an one as this they must stand at least as witnesses of what the consciousness of the Christian community set its seal to, in the way of interpretation of its own original deposit of belief. We do not much care to argue whether they belonged to an age of criticism or not. Yet we must needs be ready to listen to anyone who can prove that their determinations were wrong. Councils, we admit, and Creeds, cannot go behind, but must wholly rest upon the history of our Lord Jesus Christ. If anyone could seriously convict the Creeds of being unscriptural, we must listen to him and bow,—as scientific men would have to bow to anyone who really could prove the fundamental propositions of their science to be wrong. But meanwhile, so complete is the historical acceptance of the Creeds, and their consecration in the consciousness of the Church ; that there is at least as clear a presumption that we are uncatholic in differing from them, as there would be that we were unscientific if we dissented from the most universally accepted faiths of science.

Now even this, the most commonplace statement of the growth of

N

Christian definitions, will serve to mark what the nature of dogma is. So far from faith without it being a thing more spiritual or pure, faith without it is a thing irrational. Faith in what? I cannot have faith without an object. Faith in Jesus Christ? But who is Jesus Christ? Is He a dead man? Is He, as a dead man, no longer in any existence? Or am I, at least, necessarily ignorant as to whether He and other dead men have any existence, actual or probable? Or is He a man indeed,—no more; and dead indeed; but, as other good men, alive after death somehow in the blessedness of God? And what then did His life mean? or His strange deliberate dying? or what connection have they of meaning or power with me? And this God that you speak of; do I know anything of Him? or what? or how? Or again, is Jesus Himself the living God? And are the things true which are handed down to me in the Church as taught by Himself about the relations of God? Is He my living Master; my very Redeemer by the Cross; my eternal Judge? and where and how have I contact in life or soul with the benefits of His Cross, or the power of His help? If indeed I have nothing to do with Him, and no interest in His history, it is possible for me to go on without caring to answer such questions. But faith in Him can have no meaning while these are ignored. The question whether He is or is not God, is one which cannot but be asked and answered.

And either answer to the question is alike dogmatic. The Arian is no less dogmatic than the Catholic. A dogmatic faith is only a definite faith; and that upon questions upon which it has become irrational to remain indefinite, after I have once been brought to a certain point of acquaintance with them. The question between the Catholic and the Arian is, not whose doctrine evades definiteness of determination, but whose dogma is in accord with the truth and its evidence. The negative answer to the question proposed would only be unjudicial, not undogmatic. Meanwhile, the affirmative answer would be so complete a concession of the whole position, that if it has once been made, as much has really been admitted, so far as any battle about dogma goes, as if the whole formal statement of the Athanasian Creed had been expressly, as it will have been implicitly, included. There is nothing, then, really to fight against in these words, ' The right faith is, that we believe and confess that our Lord Jesus Christ, the Son of God, is God and Man; God, of the substance of the Father, begotten before the worlds : and Man, of the substance of His mother, born in the world; perfect God, and perfect Man : of a reasonable soul and human flesh subsisting ; equal to the Father, as touching His Godhead ; and inferior to the Father, as touching His Manhood. Who although He be God and Man : yet He is not two, but one Christ ; One ; not by conversion of the Godhead into flesh ; but by taking of the Manhood into God ; One altogether ; not by confusion of substance, but by unity of Person.'

Another thing which perhaps the same commonplace statement may illustrate as to the character of Christian dogma, is its largeness and equity. It is harmony ; it is proportion ; it is the protest of balanced completeness against all that partiality, which, by exaggerating something that is true, distorts the proportion and simplicity of truth. Every several form of error,—we admit it willingly,—grew out of, and represented, a truth. Catholic doctrine alone preserves the proportion of truth. To work and to think within the lines of dogmatic faith, is to work and to think upon the true and harmonious conception of the Person of Jesus Christ—' Quem nosse vivere, Cui servire regnare.' In this knowledge certainly there is no limitedness, and in this subordination no slavery.

The meaning of Christian dogma, then, so far as we have at present had anything to do with it, is simply this. It is the self-realizing of the consciousness of the Christian community in respect of the answer to be given to that one great question, fundamental and inevitable, with which all in all times who would approach Christ must be met,— ' Whom say ye that I am ? '

But, it will be felt, it is all very well to insist so much upon this one point, which it is comparatively easy to represent as the necessary answer of a truthful conscience to a question which is forced upon it by the plainest evidence ;—but are there not a great many Christian doctrines besides ? What of the rest of them,—' all the articles of the Christian faith,' as the Catechism says ? I have ventured to speak at length upon this one, not because it is easier to handle conveniently than the others, but because it directly carries, if it does not contain, everything. It is not only that this is in itself so tremendous a dogma, that no one who affirms this can possibly quarrel any longer with the principle of dogmatic definition, but that this so inevitably involves all the other propositions of the Creed, that no one, whose conscience has accepted this, will find it easy to separate between it and the whole Christian faith.

The Christian Creed consists of three parts only ; and all three are, 'Belief in God.' ' I believe in God, the Father, the Son, and the Holy Ghost' is, in brief, the whole Christian Creed. Its shortest expression is in three words (which three words are but one), ' Holy, Holy, Holy.' The definitions of the Apostles', of the Nicene, and of the Athanasian Creeds, none of them really travel outside of this. Take, for example, the doctrine of the Holy Trinity. Intellectually it is, of course, antecedent to the doctrine of the Incarnation and the Atonement. But it will be observed that it is made known to us not antecedently, but as a consequence of our previous conviction of the

Incarnation. Moreover, when it is made known, it is made known rather incidentally than directly. Even though it is, when revealed and apprehended, the inclusive sum of our faith, yet there is, in the revelation, no formal unfolding of it, as of a mysterious truth set to challenge our express contemplation and worship. There is nothing here to be found in the least corresponding with the explicit challenge, 'Whom say ye that I am?' or 'On this rock will I build My Church;' but rather indirectly, so far as our contemplation of the Incarnation, and its abiding consequences, requires for its own necessary interpretation to our understanding, that we should have some insight into the mystery of the distinction of Persons in the Godhead, so far, and in reference to that purpose, the mystery of the Holy Trinity grows gradually into clearness of revelation to our consciousness. It is clear that any distinctness of conception whatever as to the meaning of Incarnation would be impossible, without some revelation of mutual relations between the Sender and the Sent, the Immutable and the Incarnate, the Father and the Son. If it is less clear from the first, it is surely not less certain, that any conception we may have of the relation so revealed between the Father and the Son, would be fainter by far, and less intelligible than it is, if it were not for that which our Lord Jesus Christ has told us as to the office and nature of the Holy Spirit; if with our growing conception of distinctness and relation as between the Sender and the Sent, we had not also some added conception of that Blessed Spirit of Holiness, Who, emanating from both, is the Spirit of both alike, and is thereby also the very bond of perfectness of Love whereby both are united in One; and whereby, further, all spirits in whom God's presence dwells, are united, so far, in a real oneness of spirit with one another and with God. And it is quite certain, that whether we seem to anyone to be right or no in treating this revelation of the Holy Ghost as a necessary, if incidental, part of what we had need to be taught of the revelation of the Father and the Son, in order to make Incarnation properly intelligible; it is altogether essential for that other purpose, in connection with which the revelation is more immediately made, that is, for any understanding on our part of the abiding work of God in His Church, after the Resurrection and Ascension. ' The holy Catholic Church, the Communion of Saints, the Forgiveness of sins, the Resurrection of the body, and the life everlasting;' these are not miscellaneous items thrown in at the end of the Creed after the doctrine of the Holy Trinity is finished, but they are essential parts of the understanding of the doctrine of the Holy Ghost: and on the other hand, without the revelation of the Person and work of the Holy Ghost, those doctrines, practical though they be, and vital for practice,—no less indeed than the very essence and meaning of the work of the Incarnation from the day of Ascension forwards, that is to say the whole historical effect and fruit of the Incarnation,—would be evacuated of all living meaning, and would become for us only the empty phrases of a far-away baseless yearning, which even now (apart from the life of the Holy Spirit informing us) they are ever too ready to become.

It is hoped that even such brief statements may at least serve to indicate how it is true that the whole of our Christian creed, even those parts which seem most separable from it, or antecedent to it, are for us really contained in the one crucial doctrine of the Incarnation, that is, of the eternal Godhead of the Man Christ Jesus. And this will compel us once more to recognise the simplicity of Christian dogma. It does not mean a complicated system of arbitrary definitions upon a great variety of subjects of religious speculation, formulated one after another by human ingenuity, and imposed by human despotism upon the consciences of the unthinking or the submissive; it means rather the simple expression (guarded according to experience of misconception) of the fundamental fact of the Incarnation, together with such revelation as to the relations of the Divine Being, and the wonder of His work amongst men, as is clearly lit up by the event of the Incarnation itself, and is required for such apprehension of the meaning and effects of the Incarnation, as Jesus Christ held to be meet and necessary for us.

And so it is with all parts of Christian doctrine. If they would be found to be necessarily contained in a full unfolding of the great truth which the Creed so briefly and simply declares, then they really are parts of our faith, because they are really involved in the understanding of the threefold revelation to man of the Name of God, which is the sum total of our faith. But if the Name of our God does not contain them, they are not in our creed or our faith. Is there, for example, a visible Church? Is there an Apostolic Ministry? The answer depends on the inquiry as to what is revealed, first in Scripture, and then in history, as to the method of the working of the Spirit of Christ in the world. Did the Old Testament prefigure, in action and in utterance, did the Incarnation require, did the Gospels interpret or comment upon, did the Apostles organize or govern, any definitely articulated society, with ceremonies or officers, rules or discipline, of its own? Was this, the method of association and membership, or was some other, the mode of the working of the Spirit of the Christ among men? Is the work of Christ, in redeeming and reconciling to God, is His present relation to the world, properly intelligible, or not,—apart from the Church? Is the ministry of the Church, or are the sacraments of the Church, to those who thoughtfully read Scripture and history, a demonstrable part, or normal condition, of the working of the Holy Ghost in the Church? If so, belief in them is contained in my words, not only when

I say, 'I believe in the holy Catholic Church,' but also, though less plainly, when I say, 'I believe in the Holy Ghost.' But if not, it is not contained. If they are really separable from the Catholic Church, truly understood, or from the understanding of the Holy Spirit and His work, then they are no part of what any Christian need believe. But so far as the holy Catholic Church,—so far as the orderly, covenanted work of the Holy Spirit in the world,—involves and contains the idea of the ministry or the sacraments, so far every Christian will know, just in proportion as he knows the true meaning of his creed, that he is bound to them. It is no part of my business to pursue the question of the sacraments or the ministry further here.

It may be observed, perhaps, that the Creed contains no proposition expressly about ourselves,—about the fall, for instance, or about sin. Yet in and from the first word of the Creed, I of course am present there : and as to formal propositions about myself, it may be that they are not so much articles of belief, as, rather, conditions of mind antecedent to belief, conditions of self-consciousness to which belief fits and responds, and without which the Creed itself would be unintelligible. But what is thus necessarily implied and involved in the terms of the Creed, is after all substantially contained in that Creed to which it is a condition of intelligibleness. Of course my creed necessarily presupposes myself. I cannot believe at all, except I am, and have a certain history and faculties. I cannot believe in God as Father, as Almighty, as Creator, without implying and including within that belief the fundamental facts of my nature and relation to Him. I cannot believe in the Incarnation and the Redemption, their meaning or their consequences, I cannot believe in the Holy Spirit, or have any intelligent apprehension of His working, except there be implied, as conditions of my consciousness necessary to that intelligence, some apprehension of that which is meant by the fall, some inalienable sense of evil, of sin, of the banishment from God which is the fruit of sin, of the inherent contradiction to my nature, the unnatural penalty and horror, which the banishment of sin involves. So probation, judgment, heaven, hell, are beliefs which grow by inevitable consequence out of the apprehension, once grasped, of the nature and distinction of good and evil ; they are necessary corollaries from the full perception of the eternal rightness of right, the eternal wrongness of wrong, the eternal separation and contrast between right and wrong ; in a word, from belief in God on the part of man.

Perhaps this illustration may serve to shew how much, that is not obvious in the letter, may nevertheless be really contained in man's utterance of the Name of God.

III. But while the doctrines of the Church which her Creeds express are thus as simple as they are profound, it is no doubt true that there has grown up round about them a considerable body of theological teaching, more or less complicated, which is really of the nature of comment upon them, or explication of their nature and meaning. When we speak of the dogmas of Christianity, it is right to distinguish, with the clearest possible line of demarcation, between all this mass of explanatory teaching (more or less authoritative as it may from time to time appear to be) and the central truths themselves, which are our real certainties. The doctrine itself is one thing : the theories explicative of the doctrine are another. They may be of the highest value in their own time and place ; but they are not the immutable principles of Church truth. To say this is not really to depreciate the work of theological writers and teachers of different ages ; but it is to assign to their work its true position. The current mode of explaining a doctrine in one age, and bringing it home by illustrations to the imagination of men, may be discredited and superseded in another. When the current mode of statement or illustration begins to be more or less discredited, the minds of quiet people are apt to be distressed. This is because very few of us can distinguish between the truths themselves which we hold, and the (often mistaken) modes of expression by which we seem to explain our truths to ourselves. Even when our explanation is substantially true, the doctrine is still a different thing from our explanation of it ; and if any imperfection is detected in our explanation of it, it is not truth which suffers ; it is only that truth is being distinguished from our imperfect and unconscious glosses ; and thereby in the end the truth can only be served. Perhaps no illustration of this can be more convincing than that which the history of the doctrine of Atonement supplies. That Christ died upon the cross for us, that He offered Himself as a sacrifice, and that we are redeemed through His blood, this is a belief fundamental to Christianity ; nor has the Church ever wavered for an instant in her strong faith in this. But when we go further, and come to the different illustrations that have been given to make the precise nature of Atonement clear to human logic, when in fact we enter upon the domain of explicative theories, we have not only left the sure ground of the Creeds, and embarked upon views which may or may not be correct, but we find, as a fact, that the modes of thought which seemed adequately to explain the doctrine to the conscience of some ages, have not only failed to satisfy, but have actually shocked and offended, others. The teaching that God was angry, but that Jesus, as a result of gentler mercy, and through His innocent blood, appeased, by satisfying, the wrath of the Father, and so reconciled God to us ; the teaching that Satan had obtained a right over man, but that Jesus, by giving up Himself, paid a splendid ransom into the hands of Satan ; the teaching that a debt was due from humanity to God, and that Jesus, clothed as man, alone could deliver man by discharging God's debt : these—be they popular blunderings, or genuine efforts of Theology—may, in their times, have both helped and wounded consciences ; but whether they be to us as helps or hindrances, it is of the utmost importance that we should discriminate them, or others which may have succeeded to them as theories explanatory of the Atonement, from our cardinal belief in the Atonement itself. We may have rightly seen what is vicious in these statements, and we may have greatly improved upon them, but however much more helpful our modes of exposition may prove themselves to our own minds or those of our hearers, we may only be repeating the old error, and leading the way to fresh distresses in the future, if we confound our mode of explanatory comment with the truth of the doctrine itself, and claim that the mysterious fact of the Atonement means exactly that which is our own best approach to a statement, in illustrative words, of what it expresses to us.

But it may be asked, Are you not saying too much? Does not this seem to mean that the doctrines themselves are little better than unintelligible symbols, which need not indeed be changed for the simple reason that they can be made to mean whatever is necessary to suit the times? No, the truth of them does not change ; and even the changeful modes of presenting them are less changeful, after all, than they seem. They cannot indefinitely vary ; there is one thing which unites them all, and that is the truth itself which lies behind them all. The Atonement is a fact, whether I can adequately expound it or no. The Atonement is a fact, which my attempted expositions do indeed represent, more or less correctly, more or less clumsily, even when I seem most to have failed. Much as they may seem to differ, and inconsistent as they may appear with each other, yet not one of them really represents untruth but truth. Imperfect images they may be, and in respect of their imperfections, diverse and distorting ; yet there is not one of the theories of Atonement referred to above—not even such as are now seen to contain most error— which did not, as seriously held, represent and convey some real image of the truth. It may be that the truth which they represented was conveyed in an inexact way ; and that afterwards, when attention was concentrated on the points of inexactness, the statement became, and would have become, more and more misleading ; it was no longer then a possible vehicle of truth ; but what it had really conveyed to those to whom it was living, was a real soul-enlightening image of the truth of the Atonement. It was an imperfect image ; it was even in part a distorted image,—as everything that I see through my window is in part distorted. But it was a real image of the real truth none the less.

Local and popular modes of exposition then are often as the medium through which dogmatic truth is seen and apprehended,—not always, certainly, without distortion. But the more catholic the truth, the more it retains its identity of form, however remote from each other, in place or time, the diverse types of mind which view and teach it, so much the purer must it be from accidental or temporary conditionings ; so much the nearer, in rank, to a fundamental doctrine of the Catholic Church.

We do not, of course, distinguish Catholic dogma from theological literature, as though the one were bare facts, and the other all explanations of the facts. But we may rightly confine the use of the word 'dogma' to the fundamental facts, together with such explanation of them as the Church has agreed, by universal instinct, or by dogmatic decree endorsed through ecumenical acceptance, to be essential to a reasonable apprehension of the facts.

It is the more important to guard with unfaltering clearness this distinction between dogma on the one hand, and theological literature on the other, because it is, no doubt, in the sphere of explanatory theories and expressions, that most of those controversies find their place, which distress quiet minds, and rouse hot battles of orthodoxy between sincere Christian combatants. If it could be recognised at the time how far the apparent innovators of successive generations were really questioning not the doctrines themselves, but certain traditional modes of thought and teaching which have wrongly adhered to the doctrines, there would be fewer accusations of heterodoxy, and less distress and perplexity amongst the orthodox. But it is natural enough that this should not be perceived by the defenders, when the innovators themselves are so often both blind and indifferent to it. And it is just herein that the different innovators are apt to make themselves indefensible. Too often they think that they are making real advance upon the doctrines of the Church and her Creeds, and they are elated, instead of being ashamed, at the thought. They make light of loyalty, they despise the birthright of their Churchmanship, and find their own self-exaltation in the very consciousness of offending their brethren. This, whether done under provocation or no, is to depart from the spirit of the Church of Christ, in temper and meaning at least,—even though their work in the long run should prove (as it must so far as there is truth in it) only to serve the interest and work of the Church.

It is easier to see this in retrospect than in struggle. But perhaps those who look back upon the struggles of the last generation within the Church, will recognise that the orthodox thought of the present day has been not a little cleared and served, not merely by the work of orthodox defence, but in no small part by the work of the 'liberalizers' also. To say this, is by no means necessarily to acquit the liberalizers, or to cast a slur upon those who fought against them. Such condemnations or acquittals depend upon other considerations, which do not concern us here. But putting wholly aside as irrelevant all condemnation or acquittal of individuals, we may yet acknowledge that the work done has in the end served the cause of the truth and the Church. This is said, of course, of its real intellectual outcome; certainly not of the unsettling of souls by the way. And it is also to be noted that even when the fruit of their work has been in a real sense, after all, accepted and incorporated, it is hardly ever in the sense, and never quite with the results, which they, so far as they had allowed themselves to be malcontents, had supposed. But if whatever is good and true in their work becomes, after all, an element in the consciousness of the Church, might not the work itself have been done, all along, in perfect Church loyalty? In so far as different earnest writers of a generation ago, or of to-day, are really, whether consciously or not, making a contribution to one of the great theological tasks of our time, in so far (that is) as they are helping towards the correction of erroneous fancies of popular theology,—helping, for instance, to modify that superstitious over-statement about 'justification' which would really leave no meaning in 'righteousness;' or to limit the grossness of the theory often represented by the word 'imputation;' or to rebuke the nervous selfishness of religionists whose one idea of the meaning of religion was 'to be saved;' or to qualify the materialism or superstition of ignorant sacramentalists; or to banish dogmatic realisms about hell, or explications of atonement which malign God's Fatherhood; or the freezing chill and paralysis of all life supposed before now to be necessarily involved in the Apostolic words 'predestination' and 'election;' so far they are really, though it may be from the outside and very indirectly, doing the work of the Church. But the pity of it is that the men who do this kind of service are so apt to spoil it, by overvaluing themselves and forgetting the loveliness and the power of perfect subordination to the Church. We may own that Church people and Church rulers have too often been the stumbling-block. It is they who again and again have seemed to fight against everything, and by intellectual apathy, and stern moral proscription of every form of mental difficulty (wherein oftentimes are the birth-throes of enlightenment) to drive living and growing intelligence out of the Church. It is true that the greatest of Churchmen would, if the badge of their work were submissiveness, have sometimes to wait awhile, and bear delay, and wrong from inferior minds, with the patience of humility. Yes; but that work of theirs, if it once were stamped with this seal of patient submissiveness, would be a glory to the Church for ever, like the work of her quiet confessors, the work of a Scupoli, a Ken, or a Fénelon; instead of being, as it more often seems to be, a great offending and perplexing of thousands of the very consciences which deserve to be treated most tenderly, and therefore also a wrong and a loss to the conscience and character of the writer.

Are statements like these a concession to the antidogmatist? If so, they are one to which, in the name of truth, he is heartily welcome. And perhaps, under the same high sanction we may add what will look, to some minds, like another. We claimed some time since that the Creed must be, to Christians, rather a complete and conclusive than a partial or a tentative statement of truth. Yet there is one sense in which we may own that even the definitions of the Creeds may themselves be called relative and temporary. For we must not claim for phrases of earthly coinage a more than earthly and relative completeness. The Creeds are temporary, in that they are a complete and sufficient statement of truth only for time. And therefore they are only quite perfectly adequate to express those truths which have their place in time. But we, in respect of truths which transcend time, if we cannot as yet be freed from the trammels and limits of earthly thought and expression, yet can recognise at least the fact, that we are, even in our Creeds, still labouring within those trammels. We may have ground for believing the Creeds of the Church to be the most perfectly balanced and harmonious expression of the truth whereof our earthly knowledge is, or will be, capable. Yet when we struggle, as in the language of the Athanasian Creed, to express the relations which have been exhibited to us in the eternal Godhead through the use of the words 'Person' and 'Substance,' or ὑπόστασις and οὐσία; or when we thus profess our belief in the Person of the Holy Ghost, 'The Holy Ghost is of the Father and of the Son: neither made, nor created, nor begotten, but proceeding,' need we fear to own that the instruments which, perforce, we make use of upon earth, even in the Creeds of the Church, are necessarily imperfect instruments; the power of conception imperfect; the power of phrase and imagery imperfect also; and that their sufficiency of truth (though not their correctness meanwhile) is so far temporary that it is limited to earth and to time; and that, in the perfect light and knowledge of the presence of God, the perfectest knowledge represented by them will be superseded and absorbed, while the glosses and materialisms with which, in various ways, we may have been unconsciously clothing them to our own imaginations, will be—not superseded only but corrected, and, it may be, reproved? Moreover, if the truths represented in the Creeds are wider and deeper than our conceptions of them, we can admit that there may possibly be particulars in which, even now, the experience of spiritual life may deepen and enlarge the meaning, to us, of our Creeds ; as, for instance, the words heaven and hell may present to us ideas differing, in the direction of more correctness, from those which they presented to some of our forefathers. It is not that the Creeds will be some day corrected. It is not that we shall see hereafter how false they were, but how far the best conceptions which they opened to us,—the best, that is, that our earthly faculties were capable of, lagged in their clumsiness behind the perfect apprehension of the truths which they had, nevertheless, not untruly represented ; but which we then shall have power to see and know as they are. The truth which is dimly imaged for us in the Creeds, will never belie, but will infinitely transcend, what their words represented on earth.

But it will very naturally be asked by what right we speak thus of the Creeds. In the very moment of admitting, in one sense, their incompleteness and want of finality, by what right do we lay down still that they are final and complete to the end of time ; that is, perhaps, through ages of human advance, of which we may have now no conception at all? Such a question does not apply to the strictly historical statements which constitute the foundation of our creed, but to those interpretations of historical fact, and to those assertions about the Divine Being and its relations, which necessarily transcend time and experience. And after all, perhaps, the answer is not difficult. We have to consider, first, that for the very reason that these beliefs do absolutely transcend time and experience, therefore no human development which belongs merely to time and experience, can, in itself, displace or improve upon them ; and secondly, that our knowledge of these truths is really derived from a Divine revelation, which took place, as we believe, within time and experience. We may say, indeed, that the statements of this Divine revelation are corroborated to us, by such elements of thought as our reason (which we believe to be also in its reality Divine) is able to supply. It remains, however, that they can only really be proved or disproved, by arguments which go to prove or disprove the truth of the historical Incarnation, and of the revelations which it contains.

It follows from hence that we have a valid right to hold them not only true, but final in their statement of truth for this present world exactly so far as we have a right to believe that our historical revelation is, for time, a final one. Should there, indeed, be a wholly fresh revelation, the amount of truth hitherto revealed might be superseded ; but nothing short of a revelation can supersede it. The idea that any advance of human reason could be inconsistent with it, involves for the Christian who believes human reason to be divinely reflected and divinely implanted, nothing less than an unthinkable contradiction. We may therefore believe it in any case to be final, till the coming of further revelation: and so far as there is anything in the truth already revealed to us, which may warrant us in feeling confident that there is no fresh revelation in store, within the limits of time, by which the revelation of Jesus Christ will be superseded, just so far and no further are we justified in claiming for those clauses in the Creed, whose subject-matter transcends time and experience, that they are the completest expressions of their truths which can be reached in time.

IV. It may, perhaps, be a matter of prudence to refer for a moment to what are called the 'damnatory clauses' of the Athanasian Creed; though it would not be necessary to do so for the purpose of any positive statement or explanation of Christian doctrine. These clauses, however, to the positive statement add a negative. It is easy to misunderstand them, and even, by misrepresenting, to make them appear grotesque. But if the question be as to what they really mean, they are, after all, to the Christian, an obvious and necessary corollary of the Creed which is his life. There is but One God, and One Heaven, and One Salvation; not a choice of alternative salvations, or heavens, or gods. There is One Incarnation, One Cross, One Divine restoring and exalting of humanity. There is One Spirit of God, One Church—the fabric and the method of the working of the Spirit,—One Spiritual Covenant with man. Man must have part in this One, or he has part in none; for there is no other. Man must have knowledge of this One, belief in this One; or there is none for him to believe in or to know. God's covenant is with His Church on earth; and the statements of the Creed are the representation in words of that knowledge of the truth which the Church possesses, the possession of which is her life. The Athanasian Creed is not addressed to outsiders, but to those who are within the Church. For encouragement, or (if necessary) for warning, it insists to them on the uniqueness of their faith. To have hold on God is to have hold on Life. To revolt from God is to revolt from Life. This is so, to those who have or ought to have learnt that it is so, both in fact and in thought. Thus, in fact, to drop out of communion with the Incarnation of Christ, is to drop out of communion with the inner realities and possibilities of humanity. But the mind, and its convictions and meanings, cannot wholly be separated from the facts of the life. There comes, at least in most lives, a time when the man's own allegiance to the facts is a necessary condition of his identification with them. 'If ye believe not that I am He, ye shall die in your sins.' There comes a point at which the mind's refusal of the doctrines of religion is the man's revolt from the facts; and *such* a revolt is repudiation of the One revelation of God, the One Incarnation, the One Salvation, the One Church or Covenant. This must be broadly true, true in the abstract, as principle, unless truth and falsehood right and wrong, are fundamentally false distinctions, and every man is to be equally good, and equally compelled to heaven. At what point any individual person, or class of persons, does, or does not, in the sight of the Judge who knows the whole inward history, and tries the most secret motive, fall within the scope of this principle, and incur the final condemnation of rebellion against the one light and hope of all humanity, is another question altogether. Any such application of the principle to the case of individuals belongs only to God the Judge, and would be an arrogant impiety in any man. Even when such a question may have to be determined ecclesiastically, the ecclesiastical condemnation and sentence, though expressly representing in shadow the eternal sentence, is none the less quite distinct and indeed in its ultimate motive even contrasted with it. But however unchristian it may be to say that A or B will perish everlastingly, the principle nevertheless is true, that the truth which the Creed embodies, the truth of which Christ's Incarnation is the pivot and centre, is *the only* deliverance from everlasting perishing; and that whole-hearted union and communion with this truth, is that true state of Church life which alone has the certain seal of the covenant of God. This broad truth it is, the necessary complement of any holding of the Christian creed as true, which these clauses affirm. If it be said, 'your Athanasian Creed is simple and trenchant; it has no qualifications such as you admit'; our reply would be threefold. First, the Creed is part of our heritage from the past, and its phraseology is not our handiwork; but we know that the necessary qualifications with which we understand its phraseology have been generally recognised by the Church from which we inherit it. Secondly, the *Quicunque vult* is, strictly, not so much a creed as a canticle; it has never been used as a test of Church communion; and it speaks on a point like this, as the *Te Deum* would speak, in the language not of judicial award but of devotional loyalty. Thirdly, the qualifications with which we say that any generalisation about man's responsibility for belief, whether in this 'canticle' or in scripture, must necessarily be understood, are only such as all men apply to any similar generalisation about responsibility for conduct. 'If ye believe not that I am He, ye shall die in your sins,' is paralleled by 'They which do such things shall not inherit the kingdom of God.' We claim only to interpret the one as rationally as all men understand the other.

It has seemed to be desirable, while insisting upon the claims of dogma, not indeed in the name of allegiance to imposed authority, but in the name of truth, and on the ground of its simple identity with truth, to try to state, with the utmost possible plainness, whatever could be truly admitted in the way of apparent qualification of those claims. Truth is supreme, and eternal; and dogma, so far as it coincides with truth, is, of course, all that truth is. For the dogmatic position of the Church and her Creeds, we claim that it is the true and simple expression upon earth of the highest truth that is, or can be, known. But dogmatic theologians are not infallible, and so far as the name of dogma has been claimed for mistaken presumption or misleading statement of truth, so far may dogma have seemed to fight against truth. The words, indeed, 'dogmatic' and 'dogmatism' have acquired a bad reputation. But this is not the fault of dogma. A dogmatist, in the invidious sense of the word, does not mean one who studies dogma, but rather one who foolishly utters what are not dogmas as if they were. The dogmatic temper is the temper of one who is imperiously confident that he is right when he is not. That is to say, the words dogma, dogmatic, dogmatize, &c., are commonly used of something which is the mere abuse and travesty of their proper meaning. It is hard that dogma itself should be prejudiced by this caricaturing misuse of its name.

Meanwhile, if real charges be brought against any part of our dogmatic creed, we are willing most honestly to examine into them. In so far as they are made against current suppositions, which are separable from our essential belief,—separable as, for example, we now see various details of traditional belief about the first chapter of Genesis to be separable—we join our critics in the examination with a mind as open as they could desire. And it must, in simple candour, be admitted further, that upon the appearance of any new form of thought, Churchmen have not generally been quick of mind to discriminate the essential from the non-essential, so as to receive at first, with any openness of mind, what they had afterwards to admit that they might have received from the first. But not even this admission must prevent us from claiming, that when that to which exception is taken does really belong to the essential truths of our creed, which to us are more absolutely established certainties than anything in heaven and earth besides, they must pardon us if, while we are still willing to give the most candid hearing possible to everything that they have to urge, we yet cannot, if we would, divest ourselves of the deepest certainties of our existence;—cannot therefore pretend to argue with more openness of mind than would scientific professors— say with a champion who undertook to prove that the globe was flat, or that the sun went round the earth. We are ready to listen to everything. We are fully prepared to find that the champion may produce in evidence some phenomena which we shall be unable to account for. We have found it before; we are not unaccustomed to finding it (though, in good time, the perplexity always unravels itself); and we shall be in no way disconcerted if we find it again. But we cannot pretend meanwhile to hold all the truth which our consciences have known in suspense.

V. What was said just now about the Creeds will not, it is hoped, appear to any minds to fail in the entire respect which is due to them. Yet it makes it, perhaps, the more incumbent upon us to take notice of another form of attack upon dogma, which connects itself with an attitude about the Creeds, such as may seem at first sight to be not wholly dissimilar; though presently all the foundations of dogma are dissolved by it. But in point of fact, if we admit that what the Creeds mean on earth, is less than what the same truths will mean in heaven, or that there may be, even here, a clumsier, and a completer, understanding of them; this is a position essentially different from maintaining that what the Creeds both say and mean, is not only less than, but (if strictly taken) inconsistent with, the real truth; and that not in any transcendent sense, as celestial beings, with wholly other faculties, may conceivably have power of apprehending it in heaven, but as the more intelligent among us may, and do, see it now. This is not only to admit that the Creeds are built up, perforce, of materials which belong to this earth; but to treat them as mere serviceable fictions for the teaching of the uncivilized or the young. The deliberate unbeliever, indeed, assumes that the Creeds mean what they say, and that the Church understands the Creeds. Assuming this, he parts company with the Church, because he holds that the statements of her Creeds are, in fact, fictitious. But it may surprise us to find that there is another form of this view of the fictitiousness of Creeds, and that here the critic speaks, not at all in the character of an unbeliever, but rather in that of an enlightened Churchman. All Christian truth, he says, is true. Even the Creeds in a real sense represent the truth. But the Church's understanding and expression of Christian truth in the Creeds, is, none the less, strictly, a misrepresentation of the truth. Though the truth of Christ lies behind the Church's Creeds, yet they have so overlaid, and thereby, in strict speech, misstated it, that it is only the patience of criticism, which cutting bravely adrift from the authority of traditional interpretation, has succeeded in discriminating between the Creeds and the meaning of the Creeds, and behind what are practically the fictions of dogmatic Christianity, has re-discovered the germs of Christian truth. Neither the facts of the life of Jesus Christ, nor His teaching, nor His consciousness in regard of Himself, were as we have been taught, but were something different. He never thought nor taught of Himself as personally God, nor did He perform any miracles, nor did He rise on the third day from the dead. Whatever scriptures state these things explicitly, are proved by that very fact to be glosses or errors. And yet, all the while, everything is true spiritually. The record of the Incarnate Life is true literally, it may be, at comparatively few points; certainly not the story of the Birth; certainly not the story of the Resurrection; certainly not any incident which involves, or any expression which implies, miracle. But the Birth, the Resurrection, the miracles, every one of them, represent, in the most splendid of imaginative language and portraiture, essential spiritual truths. They are fictions, but vivid representations, in fiction, of fact; splendid truths, therefore, so long as they are understood to be literally fictitious, but perversions of truth, if taken for truth of fact.

It is this conception which was set forth not long ago with a singular power and persuasiveness by the author of *The Kernel and the Husk.* The lofty level of thought, the restraint and felicity of language, above all the deeply religious spirit of the author, invest his arguments with a charm of unusual attractiveness. The arguments are not such as it is wholly pleasant to see thus recommended. He deals in detail, in the course of the volume, with much of the narrative of Scripture, with the purpose of shewing how one by one the various records, including of course the Birth and Resurrection, have grown to their present form out of realities which contained no miracle, and which therefore differed essentially from the historical scriptures and faith of the Church.

It is no part of our task to enter upon such details. Nor is it necessary. The struggle against such a theory of Christianity will not be fought out on details. It may be conceded that many of the miracles, taken singly, can easily be made to fall in with conjectural theories as to a mythical origin, *if only the antecedent conviction* against their reality as miracles *be cogent enough* really to require that the necessary force should be put upon the evidence. Some indeed may lend themselves to the process with a facility which fairly surprises us. Others seem still to be very obstinate, and force the rationalizer into strange hypotheses. But after all, the real question, through one and all, is not how easily this or that miracle can be made, by squeezing of evidence, to square with a rationalizing hypothesis; but what is the strength of the argument for the rationalizing hypothesis itself, which is the warrant for squeezing the evidence at all.

The Evangelists say that Jesus taught in the synagogue at Capernaum. Our author takes for granted that He did so. The Evangelists say that Jesus miraculously multiplied loaves and fishes in the wilderness. Our author takes for granted that He did not so. Now why this contrast? Incidentally, indeed, it may be remarked that on the author's own general method, this multiplication of loaves ought to be one of the most certain facts in the life of Christ, as it is emphasized in every Gospel. But this is by the way. The real ground of the contrast in the treatment of the same evidence is a certain prior conviction with which the evidence is approached. Now we are not

O

contending that any such sifting of evidence in the light of prior tests is inadmissible. On the contrary, there is hardly anyone who does not, on a similar principle, explain the differences (for example) in the accounts of the title upon the Cross, or the difficulty as to whether Jesus healed one blind man or two, on the way into, or out from, Jericho ; but we do say that the admissibleness of such a method of interpreting absolutely depends upon the certainty of the correctness of the prior conviction itself.

The various details of ingenuity, then, with which he explains away particular incidents, are to us of quite subordinate interest. Everything depends upon the cogency of the grounds for explaining away at all. A large part of the book is occupied in explaining away the facts of Christianity, as the Christian Church has hitherto understood them ; an explaining away which may be more or less necessary, more or less satisfactory, if the premisses which require it are once admitted ; but which certainly is wholly unnecessary, and wholly unsatisfactory, if those premisses are denied.

The prior conviction in the book in question is that miracles neither do, nor did, happen in fact, and therefore that any narrative which involves them is incredible. All the ingenuities of conjecture on individual points become relevant subsequently to, and in reliance upon, this underlying principle. Admit this, and they are forthwith interesting and valuable. Deny this, and they lose their importance at once. It is the pressure of this prior conviction which seems to give life and force to a number of suggestions, about other stories, and particularly about that of the Resurrection, which, apart from this animating conviction, would be felt to be very lifeless ; and to a total experiment of subjective reconstruction, which, but for the strength of the antecedent conviction, would have been impossible to men of reverent thought and modest utterance. The teaching of the book will therefore really be accepted or the reverse, precisely according as the minds of its readers do, or do not, incline to admit the hypothesis upon which it depends.

It is probable, indeed, that the author would demur to this statement, at least when put so simply ; on the ground that, though he avows the conviction, yet he has reached the conviction itself by no *à priori* road, but as the result of wide observation and unprejudiced scrutiny of evidence. Now it is not at all meant to be asserted that the conviction against miracle is itself reached merely by an *à priori* method. No doubt it has, in fact, been arrived at, in those minds which have fully arrived at it, not *à priori*, but as the result of a great induction from experience ; practically indeed, as it seems to them, from experience as good as universal. The weight of the evidence in this direction is neither denied nor forgotten. Yet even when it most impresses us, of course it is obvious still to reply to ourselves that however powerful this array of experience may appear so long as there are no instances to the contrary, yet any one contrary instance will break at once the cogency of the induction. The case of Jesus Christ is put forward as being unique. Its uniqueness is not really qualified by the fact that some others, among those nearest to Himself, were by Him enabled—avowedly in *His* power, not their own,—to do acts which were impossible to other men. This is only a wider extension of His unique power, not a qualification of it. Against such a case, put forward on evidence definite and multiform, and put forward as essentially unique, an argument from induction is no argument at all. It is a misnomer to call the induction an argument. The induction, in fact, is merely an observation that other persons did not perform similar miracles; and that, if Jesus Christ did so, He was unique. But this is no answer to the Christian position. It is part of the position itself.

And so the matter must be referred for settlement to the evidence that is actually forthcoming about Jesus Christ. But it is plain that the inductive presumption against miracle, derived from experience of other men, must not come in to warp or rule this evidence. It may be present indeed as a sort of cross-examining counsel, as a consideration requiring that the evidence should be most minutely scrutinized, and suggesting all sorts of questions with a view to this. But into the evidence itself, it cannot be permitted to intrude.

Now, it is part of our complaint against such writers as the author of *The Kernel and the Husk*, that however much their general presumption against miracle may have been inductively and patiently reached; yet when they come to deal with the evidence about Jesus Christ, this conviction (which ought to stand on one side inquiringly) becomes to them an underlying postulate; it is settled beforehand; it is present with them in their exegesis, not simply as a motive for sifting the evidence carefully, but as a touchstone of truth by which it may all be tried. Probably the author would believe that he has reached his conviction against the miracles of Jesus of Nazareth, not merely from a general induction as to the absence of miracle in the lives of others, but also from an unprejudiced scrutiny of the evidence of the life of Jesus Christ Himself. But this is just what we are not at all prepared to concede. On the contrary, we maintain that his scrutiny is wholly prejudiced. Examine the evidence with a bias sufficiently powerful against belief in miracle; and you may end in the result which this author reaches. Examine it without such a bias; and you will find yourself at every turn protesting against his mode of treating the evidence. It is a scrutiny of the evidence *on the basis of the inadmissibleness of miracles*, which gives him that coherent theory about the growth of the Christian tradition, and those consequent principles of interpretation of the text of the Gospels, which he appears to regard as the simple result of the evidence itself.

We shall very likely be surprised to find that, after all, the abstract impossibility of miracle is not laid down,—nay, is expressly disclaimed, —by him. Miracle (if we rightly understand) is not impossible absolutely,—not even, he adds, *à priori* improbable; yet it is *equivalent* to an impossibility, because the will of the Father indwelt wholly in Jesus, and because the perfect uniformity of natural processes as we have experienced them, is, *in fact*, and with no exceptions, the will of the Father[1]. No general reflections upon our dependence, in ordinary life, on the good faith of an uniform nature, ought to blind us to the fact that this last position neither has, nor can have, any adequate ground at all. It is surprising that with so weak a statement of the impossibility of miracle, the principle of the impossibility of miracle should have to bear the extraordinary weight that is put upon it. Nothing short of a demonstration of this impossibility would fully justify the critical position that is adopted. For it is, in fact, upon this impossibility that the whole re-reading of the history is based.

It is probably true that if once the hypothesis of the impossibility of miracle be accepted as practically certain, an earnest mind, penetrated with this as its overruling principle, and dwelling upon the Gospels always and only in the light of this, will be compelled gradually to re-read in one place and re-interpret in another, until the whole has been, by steps that upon the hypothesis were irresistible, metamorphosed into a form as unlike as possible, indeed, to what it wore at first, but still one which can be felt to be precious and beautiful. But we are entitled to point out how absolutely this re-reading of the evidence depends upon the truth of the principle which underlies it. For the sake of this, all sorts of violence has to be done to what would otherwise be, in one incident after another, the obvious meaning of words, the obvious outcome of evidence. Without the certainty of this, the new method of reading must be critically condemned as baseless and arbitrary. This alone makes it rationally possible. Without the strong cogency of this it falls instantly to pieces.

Now orthodox Christians are sometimes accused of reading their historical evidence in the light of a preconception. They begin with the doctrine of the Creed, and read all records of fact with the conviction of that doctrine in their hearts and consciences. We need not be altogether concerned to combat this statement. Perhaps few records are read, or would ever be read intelligently, except in the light of the reader's preconceptions. But our point is to see clearly that at all events the new reading of the Gospel history is itself so entirely the

---

[1] See especially the concluding paragraphs of letter xix.

outcome and creature of its antecedent principle, that it cannot without that hold together for an instant.

Let us be content, for the moment, to view the orthodox Christian and the new rationalist as both alike really reading the Gospel narrative in the light of a preconceived principle; the one viewing everything on the basis of the perfect Divinity of the historical Jesus Christ (with the corollary that it is impossible for us to determine *à priori* what power His perfect Humanity—for which we have no precedent—would, or would not, naturally and necessarily exhibit); the other viewing everything on the basis of the absolute impossibility, or at least the incredibleness, of miracle. We might point out that the former in his hypothesis has a principle which absolutely fits and perfectly accounts for every part of the evidence which confronts him; while the latter is compelled, by the cogency of his principle, to reconstruct for himself almost every chapter of the evidence. And if we go one step further back, and ask, what is the antecedent reasonableness of the one hypothesis, or of the other? from what source is each derived? We must claim it as simple fact, that the former hypothesis is itself the direct outcome of the evidence,—the inevitable outcome, indeed, so long as the evidence stands: while the other is, at bottom, an assumption, held absolutely in the teeth of the evidence actually existing in respect of the life and consciousness of Jesus of Nazareth, and itself on other grounds not merely unproved, but essentially incapable of proof[1].

But if our hypothesis is itself the outcome of the evidence, and fits with perfect exactness into all its intricacies, then we yield far too much if we treat it as on the level of a mere preconception. To persist in reading the New Testament by the light of the preconception of the dogma of Christ's Godhead (with the corollary that no miracle is incredible as miracle), is to be prejudiced only in the same sense in which the scientist is prejudiced who persists in studying the records of astronomy in the light of certain preconceptions as to the parabola or the law of gravitation.

But what is the case with the other hypothesis? By it the historical Jesus Christ is swept away; and another personality, which does not exist in the history at all, but which the history has suggested to certain earnest-minded critics of our own day, is substituted in His place. All those who witnessed of His words and deeds to the Church, all those whose witness the Church has accepted and sealed, are thoroughly mistaken, mistaken in the very points which to them were funda-

---

[1] 'The question of miracles seems now to be admitted on all hands to be simply a question of evidence.' These are the words as much of Professor Huxley as of the Duke of Argyll. *Nineteenth Century,* April 1887, p. 483: cp. Feb. 1887, pp. 201, etc.

mental. However honest they may have been in their superstitious ignorance, they certainly bore to the world what was, in fact, false testimony. It is impressive, with a strange impressiveness, to follow this hypothesis through the story of Christ's life ; and see with what ingenuity, often plausible, often pathetic, the old facts are refashioned to meet the new principle.

Cardinal, of course, in difficulty as in importance, is the narrative of the Resurrection ; that plain statement of fact, to testify whereto was the primary qualification, and primary function, of Apostleship ; and which, from S. Peter and S. Paul downwards, has always been recognised as cardinal to the faith of the Church.

Now given ; first, the certain conviction that no miracle occurred ; and secondly, a working hypothesis as to the growth of the Christian Scriptures, which not only enables, but requires, you to set aside, on grounds of subjective criticism, all such evidence as seems to you to be improbable ; and it follows that, if you are still of a very religious mind, you will probably have to take refuge in what may yet be to you the beautiful story of a Resurrection exclusively spiritual.

You must, of course, deal very violently with the direct evidence. But that is already covered by the general theory you have reached as to the historical genesis and value (or lack of value) of the books of the New Testament. And, of course, in adopting such a view of the books of the New Testament, you are reducing to a phantasm the reality of your belief in the Holy Catholic Church, which has enshrined and consecrated, as perfectest truth, what are really at best only fables,— capable, indeed, of clumsily representing the truth to the childish or the stupid, but beginning to be absolutely pernicious to minds which have reached a certain point of intelligent education.

Tolerating these things, however, you may admit the truth of the Resurrection (as you may admit every proposition of the Creed) in words ; only in a sense so refined, so exclusively spiritual, that no bodily reality of resurrection is left. There is no resurrection in your creed correlative to the dying. There is no resurrection more, or more demonstrable, than what we believe to be true of men in general. There is no resurrection which enters within the ordinary sphere of human history, or admits any direct contact with the normal methods of human evidence or human proof. The question raised is not whether current imaginations of the Resurrection may possibly be more or less exaggerated in the way of materialism, but whether there was any corporeal reality of resurrection at all. And the question is settled in the negative. The foundation fact of the Creed is etherealized away ; and all the rest, with it, becomes together impalpable and subjective.

We do not say that there is not a large element which is true, in the thought of such a writer as we have been considering. Where the mind is so devoutly in earnest, it is no hard task to believe that it too must be animated originally by truth. We need not say, therefore, that the work of this earnestness may not serve us all, and contribute to the thought of us all. It may well be true that in our bald understanding of the doctrine of the Resurrection,—or indeed of the whole Incarnation, from beginning to end,—we have, many of us, too little imagined the scope and depth of its spiritual import. If our orthodoxy has been so well content with insisting mechanically upon the literal fact, as not only to forget, but to disdain or disown in any measure, the vast spiritual realities which it ought to express to us; then our stupidity, or narrowness, in orthodoxy, is in part to blame, for the distaste which they have created towards orthodoxy in some natures more sensitive than our own. In so far as they can, in this respect, return good for evil, we will not be slow to acknowledge our debt to them. We will be grateful for any new suggestion they can discover, as to the moral beauty or import of the Resurrection, or of the Incarnation, or of any or every other miracle, considered upon its moral side as allegory. Some ways at least there may be, in which their insistance may tend to deepen for us our understanding of truths, whose more spiritual aspects we had dwelt upon perhaps, in some cases,—perhaps had even imagined,—far too little. But doubtless that true element of their work, which the mind of the Catholic Church will assimilate, will be greatly modified from the form in which it now presents itself—to them as to others. It will, to say the least, be positive rather than negative; stimulating spiritual sensibilities, but not by explaining away the facts of the body; widening (it may be) our insight into the divineness of history, and the depth of the meaning of certain events which happened in it,—but not shattering both it and them, by dissolving their historical truth.

Meanwhile of the one-sided aspect we can but say that no doubt transcendental spiritualism has a great attractiveness. The Magian aspiration always was fascinating. Individuals, indeed, of enthusiastic sympathies, trained themselves in dogmatic truth, and indulging their freest speculations always on a background of inveterate dogmatic instinct, may fancy the 'spiritualized Christianity' to be in itself a stable and a living completeness; but as a system, it will neither produce life nor perpetuate it. It is an attempt to improve upon the Church of Christ, upon the conditions of human nature, upon the facts of history. The Church of Christ is not so. The Church of Christ does not ignore the fundamental conditions of human experience. The Church of Christ is balanced, harmonious, all-embracing, all-adjusting. The Incarnation was the sanctifying of both parts of human nature, not the abolition of either. The Church, the Sacraments, human nature, Jesus Christ Himself, all are twofold; all are earthly objective, as well as transcendental spiritual. And so long as this world is real as well as the next; so long as man is body as well as soul; so long all attempts to evaporate the body and its realities are foredoomed to a necessary and a salutary failure. The religion, which attempts to be rid of the bodily side of things spiritual, sooner or later loses hold of all reality. Pure spiritualism, however noble the aspiration, however living the energy with which it starts, always has ended at last, and will always end, in evanescence.

VII.

THE ATONEMENT.

I. THEOLOGICAL doctrine, describing, as it professes to do, the dealings of an all-wise Person with the human race, must be a consistent
whole, each part of which reflects the oneness of the will on which it is
based. What we call particular doctrines are in reality only various
applications to various human conditions of one great uniform method
of Divine government, which is the expression in human affairs of one
Divine will. The theological statement of any part of this method
ought to bear on its face the marks of the whole from which it is
temporarily separated ; for though it may be necessary to make now
this, now that doctrine prominent, to isolate it and lay stress on it, this
should be done in such a way that in each special truth the whole
should, in a manner, be contained. We must be able to trace out in
each the lines of the Divine action which is only fully displayed in the
whole. Neglect of this not only makes our faith as a whole weak and
incoherent, but deprives the doctrines themselves of the illumination
and strength which are afforded by the discovery in them of mutual
likeness and harmony. They become first unintelligible and then
inconceivable, and the revelation of the character of God, which should
be perceived in every part of His dealings with men, becomes confused
and dim to us. This has been especially the case with the Atonement.
In the course of religious controversy this doctrine has become separated from the rest, at one time neglected, at another over emphasized,
till in its isolation it has been so stated as to be almost incredible.
Men could not indeed be brought to disbelieve in forgiveness, however
attained, and the conviction of remission of sins through and in the
Blood of Christ has survived all the theories which have been framed
to account for it ; but nevertheless, the unreality of these theories has
been a disaster to the Christian faith. Some of them have strained
our belief in the moral attributes of God, others have given men easy
thoughts of sin and its consequences. This has been so because they
have treated the Atonement apart from the whole body of facts which
make up the Christian conception of God and His dealings with men.
In this essay the attempt will be made to present the doctrine in its
relation to the other great Christian truths : to the doctrines, that is,
of God, of the Incarnation, of sin.

(1) On the human side the fact with which we have to deal is the fact of sin. Of this conception the Bible, the most complete record of the religious history of man, is full from the first page to the last. Throughout the whole course of Jewish development, the idea that man has offended the justice of God was one of the abiding elements in the religious consciousness of the race. But it was by no means confined to the Jews. They have been truly called the conservators of the idea of sin; but it has never been permanently absent, in some form or other, from the human mind, although we learn most about it, and can see it in its clearest, most intense form, in the Hebrew religion. Now this conception of sin in its effect on the human soul is of a twofold character. Sin is felt to be alienation from God, Who is the source of life, and strength, and peace, and in consequence of that alienation the whole nature is weakened and corrupted. In this aspect sin is a state in which the will is separated from the Divine will, the life is cut off from the life of God which He designed us to share. When men come to realize what is meant by union with God, and to feel the awful consequences of separation, there arises at once the longing for a return, a reconciliation; but this longing has by itself no power to effect so great a change. To pass from alienation to union is to pass from darkness to light, from evil to good, and can only be accomplished by that very power, the power of a life united to God, which has been forfeited by sin. Only in union with God can man accomplish anything that is good; and, therefore, so long as he is alienated from God, he can only long for, he cannot obtain, his reunion with the Divine life. Sin therefore, thus considered, is not only wickedness; it is also misery and hopelessness. Sinners are 'without God in the world,' and for that reason they 'have no hope.'

This is the aspect of sin as a state of the sinful soul, and as affecting the present relation between man and God. It has destroyed the union, has broken down even the sacrificial bridge, for it has made all acceptable offerings impossible. Man's will is weakened, therefore he has not strength to offer himself completely and unreservedly to God; his nature is corrupted and stained, therefore his offering, could he make it, could not be accepted. Sin is a hopeless state of weakness and uncleanness. But there is another, in one sense an earlier, more fundamental aspect of sin. The sins of the past have produced not merely weakness and corruption, but also guilt. The sinner feels himself guilty before God. If we examine the idea of guilt, as realized by the conscience, it will be seen to contain the belief in an external power, or law, or person against whom the offence has been committed, and also an internal feeling, the acknowledgment of ill-desert, a sense of being under sentence, and that justly. Whether the punishment which is felt to be the due reward of the offence has been borne or not, the conception of punishment, when the offence has been committed, cannot be avoided, and it brings with it a conviction of its justice. These two elements, the external and the internal element, seem to be necessary to the full conception of guilt. The common fallacy that a self-indulgent sinner is no one's enemy but his own would, were it true, involve the further inference that such a sinner would not feel himself guilty. But it is precisely because the consciousness of sin does not and cannot stop here that, over and above any injury to self, any weakness or even corruption produced by sin, we speak of its guilt. 'Against Thee, Thee only, have I sinned, and done that which is evil in Thy sight.' This belief in an external power, whose condemnation has been incurred by sin, may take various forms; for the power may be represented as impersonal or as personal, as law or as God. For our present purposes, however, the distinction is immaterial: the essential point is that it is something external to ourselves, not merely the echo of the sinner's own self-inflicted pain and injury. We cannot, however, limit it to this. For it is not merely an external power, it is also a just power that is presented to the sense of guilt. Before bare power, unrighteous or non-moral, an offender may be compelled to submit, but he will not feel guilt. The state of mind expressed by Mill's well-known defiance is his who has offended a superior power which he cannot believe to be just, and it is very far removed from the feeling of guiltiness [1]. The sense of guilt implies the righteousness as well as the power of that against which we have offended ; it is a moral conviction. Guiltiness, then, regarded in one aspect is the sense of sin, in another it is the recognition of the law of righteousness, or, if we may now assume the religious point of view, it is the conviction of the wrath of God against sin.

It is plain, if we will only scrutinise closely and candidly the conception of sin and guilt, that no merely 'subjective' explanation will account for the facts revealed by our consciousness. Even if we had no scriptural evidence to guide us, the evidence, that is, to take it at the lowest, of a series of specially qualified witnesses to religious phenomena, our own hearts would tell us of the wrath of God against sin. It is irresistibly felt that there is a Power hostile to sin, and that this Power has decreed a righteous punishment for the offences which are the external signs and results of the sinful state. Whatever the punishment may be, a question we need not now discuss, the sinner's con-

---

[1] Mill, *Examination of Sir W. Hamilton's Philosophy*, p. 103. 'I will call no being good, who is not what I mean when I apply that epithet to my fellow-creatures ; and if such a being can sentence me to hell for not so calling him, to hell I will go.'

science warns him of it. He may apparently, or for a time, escape it; but it is none the less felt to be the fitting expression of Divine wrath, the righteous manifestation of the hostility of God's nature to sin and all its consequences. Guilt, then, like sin, has its twofold character. It is the belief in an external hostility to sin expressing itself in punishment, and also the conviction that such punishment is righteous and just. Thus, when once God is recognised as the offended Person, the acknowledgment of the righteousness of His judgment follows. 'Against Thee, Thee only, have I sinned, and done that which is evil in Thy sight; that Thou mightest be justified when Thou speakest, and be clear when Thou judgest.'

(2) Corresponding to the sense of sin in its twofold aspect we find, not only in the Mosaic system or in the scriptural history, but almost universally established, the system of sacrifice. It is not necessary to maintain that sacrifice, in its essential idea, was intended to express the consciousness of sin. Rather, it seems to be, essentially, the expression of the very opposite of sin, of that relation of man to God which sin destroyed[1]. It is sometimes said that sacrifice is the recognition of God's sovereignty, the tribute paid by His subjects. This is, of course, a necessary element in the conception of sacrifice, for God is our King; but it does not satisfy the whole consciousness which man has of his original relation to God. That is a relation, not of subjection only, but of union at least as close as that of sons to a Father, a union whereby we derive life from His life, and render back absolute unquestioning love to Him. Sacrifice is, in its highest, original meaning, the outward expression of this love. As human love naturally takes outward form in gifts, and the closer, the more fervent it is, makes those gifts more and more personal, till at last it wholly gives itself; so sacrifice should be the recognition of our union with God, an expression of our love for Him, giving Him all that we have and all that we are. Submission, reverence, love are the original feelings which sacrifice was intended to represent; and it may be called, therefore, the expression of man's relations to God in their purest form, unmarred and unbroken by sin. But this is only the original, ideal meaning, for with the intrusion of sin another element appears in sacrifice; and men attempt, by their offerings, to expiate their offences, to cover their sins, to wipe out their guilt, to propitiate Divine wrath. But though this new element is introduced, the original intention is not altogether lost. The union has been destroyed by sin, but even in the sin-offerings under the Law there was expressed the endeavour to regain it, to enter once more into living relations with God: while the normal sacrifices of the congregation went beyond this, and represented the exercise of a right based on union with God,

---

[1] Cf. Holland, *Logic and Life*, pp. 107, 108.

the presentation of the people before Him. Thus we must recognise in the Mosaic sacrifices—the most complete and typical form of the sacrificial idea—the twofold aspect which corresponds to the twofold effect of sin on the human race. There is the offering, sometimes the bloodless offering, by which was typified simply man's dependence on God, his submission to Him, his life derived from Him and therefore rendered back to Him. From this point of view the sacrifice culminated, not in the slaying and offering of the victim, but in the sprinkling of the blood, the 'principle of life,' upon the altar. The priestly mediators brought the blood, which 'maketh atonement by reason of the life,' before God, and sprinkled it upon the altar, in order that the lost union with God in the covenant might be restored, and life once more derived from God as it had been offered to Him. The whole system was indeed only partial, temporary, external. The Mosaic sacrifices 'sanctified unto the cleanness of the flesh,' they did not 'cleanse the conscience from dead works to serve the living God.' So the restoration which the special sin-offerings accomplished was merely external and temporary, the reunion of the offender with the congregation of Israel from which his fault had separated him. But as this excommunication symbolised the loss, brought about by sin, of life with God, so the reunion with the congregation typified the reunion of the sinner with God. As a system, then, the Mosaic sacrifices both corresponded to a deep desire of the human heart, the desire to recover the lost relation to the Divine life, and also by their imperfection pointed forward to a time when, by means of a more perfect offering, that restoration should be complete, accomplished once for all, and eternal. This is one aspect of the sacrificial system. But before this typical restoration of life, there came the mysterious act which corresponded to the sense of guilt. Leaving aside the lesser offerings of the shew-bread and the incense, it may be said generally that in every sacrifice the slaying of a victim was a necessary element. And there is deep significance in the manner in which the slaying was performed. The hands of the offerer laid upon the victim's head denoted, according to the unvarying use of the Old Testament, the representative character of the animal offered, and thus the victim was, so to speak, laden with the guilt of him who sought for pardon and reconciliation. The victim was then slain by the offerer himself, and the death thus became an acknowledgment of the justice of God's punishments for sin : it was as if the offerer declared, 'This representative of my guilt I here, by my own act, doom to death, in satisfaction of the righteous law of vengeance against sin, for "the soul that sinneth it shall die."' It was not, therefore, till the sense of personal guilt had been expressed by the act which constituted the victim a representative of the offerer, and by the slaying which typified the need of expiation by suffering for sin, that the sacrifice was fit to be presented before God by the mediation of the priest, and the blood, 'the life which had willingly passed through death [1],' could be sprinkled as a token of restored life in God. A careful study of the Mosaic sacrifices will shew the twofold character impressed upon them. Both aspects are necessary, they may even be described as two sides of the same fact. Before God can be approached by a sinner he must expiate his sin by suffering, must perfectly satisfy the demands of the law, must atone for the past which has loaded him with guilt : and then, as part of the same series of acts, the life so sacrificed, so purified by the expiatory death, is accepted by God, and being restored from Him, becomes the symbol and the means of union with Him. Forgiveness for the past, cleansing in the present, hope for the future, are thus united in one great symbolic ceremony.

The Mosaic system was only external, 'sanctifying unto the cleanness of the flesh'; partial, for it provided no expiation for the graver moral transgressions ; temporary, for the sacrifices had to be repeated 'day by day'; provisional, for 'if there was perfection through the Levitical priesthood . . . what further need was there that another priest should arise after the order of Melchizedek ?' In spite, however, of these obvious defects and limitations in the Mosaic system, there was a constant tendency among the Jews to rest content with it, to rely upon the efficacy of these external sacrifices and ceremonies for their whole religion, to believe that 'the blood of bulls and goats' could 'put away sin,' and that no inner spiritual repentance or renovation was required. And the highest minds of the nation, represented by the prophets, were keenly alive to this danger : their rebukes and remonstrances shew how strongly they felt the imperfection of the sacrificial system, how it failed to satisfy the really religious cravings of spiritual minds. Yet there it was, divinely ordained, clearly necessary as the expression of the national religious life, profoundly significant. It could not be dispensed with, yet it could not satisfy : in its incompleteness, as well as in its symbolism, it pointed forward, and foreshadowed a perfect expiation.

(3) This examination of the sacrificial system of the Old Testament is necessary in a discussion of the doctrine of the Atonement, for several reasons. The institutions of the Law were, in the first place, ordained by God, and therefore intended to reveal in some degree His purposes, His mind towards man. We thus find in them traces of the fuller revelation which came afterwards, and the two dispensations throw light on each other. Then again, it was from the Law that the Jews derived their religious language : their conceptions of sacrifice, of atonement, of the effects of sin, were moulded by the influence of

---

[1] Milligan, *The Resurrection*, p. 278.

the Mosaic ceremonies. For this reason the apostolic doctrine of the Atonement must be looked at in connection with the ideas inspired by the Law, although, of course, the life and work of our Lord so enlarged the religious conceptions of the Apostles as to constitute a fresh revelation. But it was a revelation on the lines, so to speak, of the old; it took up and continued the ideas implanted by the Mosaic religion, and displayed the fulfilment of the earlier promises and forecasts. It is, therefore, from the Old Testament that we have to learn the vocabulary of the apostolic writings. As the Messianic hopes and phraseology throw light upon the apostolic conception of the Kingdom of Christ, so the sacrificial ceremonies and language of the Law throw light upon the apostolic conception of the Sacrifice, the Atonement of Christ. But this is not all. The Mosaic institutions, in their general outlines, were no arbitrary and artificial symbols, but corresponded to religious feelings, needs, aspirations that may truly be called natural and universal. This conception of sin in its twofold aspect of alienation and of guilt, and this idea of sacrifice as effecting man's restoration to union with God, and also as expiating his guilt by suffering, correspond to what the human conscience, when deeply and sincerely investigated, declares to be its inmost secret. Every man who has once realized sin, can also realize the feelings of the Jew who longed to make an expiation for the guilt of the past, to suffer some loss, some penalty that would cover his sin, and who therefore brought his offering before God, made the unconscious victim his representative, the bearer of his guilt, and by slaying it strove to make atonement. We feel the same need, the same longing. This load of guilt has to be laid down somehow : this past sinfulness must meet with a punishment which will make expiation for it : before this lost union with God can be restored we must be assured of pardon, must know that the wrath of God no longer abides on us, but has been turned away, and finds no longer in us the sin which is the one obstacle to the free course of Divine love. And then we know further that bitter truth which came to the loftiest minds among the Jews, that no sacrifice of ours can have atoning value, for God demands the offering of ourselves, and we are so weakened by sin that we cannot give ourselves up to Him, so polluted by sin that we cannot be well-pleasing in His eyes. In order to atone, sacrifice must be no outward ceremony, the offering of this or that possession, the fulfilment of this or that externally-imposed ordinance, but the entire surrender of self to God, and to His law, a surrender dictated from within by the free impulse of the will. Therefore, just as the spiritually-minded Jew felt the continual discrepancy between the external ceremonies which he was bound to fulfil, and the complete submission to the will of God which they could not effect, and without which they were wholly inadequate, so every awakened conscience must feel the fruitlessness of any outward expression of devotion and obedience so long as there is no complete sacrifice of self.

These, then, seem to be the conditions which must be satisfied before an atonement can meet the needs of the human heart and conscience, whether these are inferred from an examination of the Hebrew religious institutions or are gathered from our own knowledge of ourselves and of others. There is, first of all, the consciousness of guilt, of an offended God, of a law transgressed, of punishment impending, to expiate which some sacrifice is necessary, but no sacrifice adequate to which can be offered by us as we are. Propitiation is the first demand of the law, and we cannot, of ourselves, propitiate Him whose anger we have righteously incurred. Secondly, we long for an abiding union with Him, and for the full bestowal of the Divine life which results from that union alone. Propitiation is not enough by itself, though propitiation is the necessary first step in the process of reconciliation. Aliens, by our own sinful acts, and by the sin of our forefathers, from the life of God, we yet long to return and to live once more in Him. But this is equally impossible for us to accomplish of ourselves. By sin we have exiled ourselves, but we cannot return by mere force of will. Both as propitiation, therefore, and as reunion, the Atonement must come from without and cannot be accomplished by those who themselves have need of it. But there is a third condition, apparently irreconcileable with the other two. This same consciousness of guilt which demands an expiation demands that it shall be personal, the satisfaction of the sense of personal responsibility, and of the unconquerable conviction of our own freedom. The propitiatory sacrifice which is to effect our reunion must, for we are powerless to offer it, come from without: but at the same time we cannot but feel that it must come into contact with the will, it must be the inward sacrifice, the freewill offering of the whole nature that has sinned.

II. If the redemptive work of Christ satisfies these conditions it is evident that it is not a simple, but a very complex fact. The fault of many of the theories of the Atonement has been that, though none of them failed to be partially true, they were limited to one or other of the various aspects which that mysterious fact presents. It is certain, again, that of this complex fact no adequate explanation can be given. At every stage in the process which is generally summed up in the one word Atonement we are in presence of forces which issue from infinity and pass out of our sight even while we are contemplating their effects. And even if the Atonement could be altogether reduced, so to speak, to terms of human experience, it will be shewn that man's forgiveness, the nearest analogy of which we have any knowledge, is an experience of which no logical explanation can be given, which seems to share, indeed, something of the mystery of its Divine anti-type. But though it is almost blasphemous to pretend to fathom the depth of the Atonement, to lay out the whole truth so as to satisfy the formulae of human reason, it is necessary so to understand it as to discern its response to the imperative demands of the sense of sin and the desire for forgiveness. Whatever the ultimate mysteries of the death of Christ may be, it is certain that it has had power to convince men of forgiveness and to give them a new life. It must therefore in some way satisfy the conditions which, as we have seen, are laid down by human consciousness and experience. It is under the threefold aspect required by those conditions that the doctrine of the Atonement will be here presented.

1. The death of Christ is, in the first place, to be regarded as propitiatory. On the one hand there is man's desire, natural and almost instinctive, to make expiation for his guilt : on the other there is the tremendous fact of the wrath of God against sin. The death of Christ is the expiation for those past sins which have laid the burden of guilt upon the human soul, and it is also the propitiation of the wrath of God. As we have seen, over against the sense of sin and of liability to the Divine wrath there has always ex-isted the idea of sacrifice by which that wrath might be averted. Man could not offer an acceptable sacrifice : it has been offered for him by Christ. That is the simplest, and it would seem the most scriptural way of stating the central truth, which is also the deepest mystery, of the Atonement, and it seems to sum up and include the various other metaphors and descriptions of the redemptive work of Christ. But its mere statement at once suggests questions, the consider-ation of which will lead to a fuller understanding of the doctrine. Thus we have to ask, What is it which is propitiated by Christ's death? In other words, What is meant by the wrath of God against sin?

(*a*) It should be remembered that though there is great danger in anthropomorphism, and though most of the superstition which has ever been the shadow cast by religion on the world has arisen from an exaggerated conception of the likeness of God to ourselves, yet there is, after all, no other way of knowing God than by representing Him under conceptions formed by our own consciousness and experience, and this method is pre-eminently incumbent upon us who believe that man is made 'in the image of God.' We are certain, for instance, that love, pity, justice, are affections which, however imperfectly they may be found in us, do make for goodness, and if we may not ascribe these same affections, infinitely raised and purified, to God, we have no means of conceiving His character, of knowing 'with whom we have to deal.'

P

Our knowledge, even of ourselves, is after all fragmentary[1], and thus truths of whose certainty we are convinced may seem irreconcileably opposed to each other. Our conception of love, for example, is a fragment, and we cannot trace it up to the meeting-point at which it is reconciled with justice, so that in our moral judgments we are continually oscillating, as it were, between the two. But this fact should not hinder us from ascribing to God in their fullest degree both love and justice, confident that in Him they are harmonized because we are confident from the verdict of our own consciences that both are good, and because even in such imperfect reflections of His image as, for instance, parental love, we see at least a partial harmony of them. When then a doubt arises as to the literal explanation of the phrase 'the wrath of God,' the difficulty must not be met by the simple assertion that we cannot reconcile the idea of wrath with that of the love of God : we must ask whether wrath, as it exists in us, is a good and righteous affection, or whether it is always and entirely evil. To this question there can be but one answer. We are conscious of a righteous anger, of an affection of displeasure that a good man ought to feel against sin and evil, and this is amply justified by the scriptural references to righteous anger, and by the accounts of our Lord's displays of indignation against evil. But though we are thus compelled to find room, so to speak, for anger in our conception of God's character, it is not therefore necessary to ascribe to Him that disturbance of the spiritual nature, or that change in the direction of the will, which are almost invariable accompaniments of human anger. These are the defects of the human affection, from which arises the sinful tendency in our anger, and which cannot be thought of in connection with the all-holy and all-wise God. On the other hand, it is not possible to limit the conception of the 'wrath of God' to the acts whereby sin is or will be punished, which was the explanation of some of the Fathers, or to think of it as in the future only, to come into existence only on the day of judgment, as has been attempted by some modern theologians. The scriptural expressions, including as we must the passages which speak of our Lord's anger, cannot be so weakened. 'The wrath of God' seems to denote no changeful impulse or passing feeling, but the fixed and necessary hostility of the Divine Nature to sin ; and the idea must further include the manifestation of that hostility, whenever sin comes before God, in external acts of vengeance, punishment and destruction. God's anger is not only the

[1] Cf. Mozley, *University Sermons*, p. 177 (2nd ed.) : 'Justice is a fragment, mercy is a fragment, mediation is a fragment ; justice, mercy, mediation as a reason of mercy—all three ; what indeed are they but great vistas and openings into an invisible world in which is the point of view which brings them all together ?'

displeasure of an offended Person : it is possible that this is altogether a wrong conception of it : it must be further the expression of justice, which not only hates but punishes. The relation of the Divine Nature to sin is thus twofold : it is the personal hostility, if we may call it so, of holiness to sin, and it is also the righteousness which punishes sin because it is lawless. The two ideas are intimately connected, and not unfrequently, when we should have expected to find in the Bible the wrath of God spoken of, the language of judgment and righteousness is substituted for it. Sin is necessarily hateful to the holiness of God, but also, because sin is lawlessness, it is judged, condemned, and punished by Him in accordance with the immutable law of righteousness, which is the law of His own Nature. Therefore, to turn from God's wrath against sin to the mode in which that wrath may be averted, it results that the sacrifice offered for sin must be both a propitiation and a satisfaction. Anger, so we think, is but a feeling, and may be ousted by another feeling ; love can strive against wrath and overcome it ; the Divine hatred of sin need raise no obstacle to the free forgiveness of the sinner. So we might think ; but a true ethical insight shews us that this affection of anger, of hatred, is in reality the expression of justice, and derives from the law of righteousness, which is not above God, nor is it dependent on His Will, for it is Himself. 'He cannot deny Himself'; He cannot put away His wrath, until the demands of Law have been satisfied, until the sacrifice has been offered to expiate, to cover, to atone for the sins of the world. The reconciliation to be effected is not merely the reconciliation of man to God by the change wrought in man's rebellious nature, but it is also the propitiation of God Himself, whose wrath unappeased and whose justice unsatisfied are the barriers thrown across the sinner's path to restoration.

(*b*) But how, we ask further, was this propitiation made by the Sacrifice on the Cross? Or, to put the question rather differently, what was it that gave to the death of Christ its propitiatory value? In attempting to suggest an answer to this question, it is necessary to bear in mind the distinction between the actual event, or series of events, which constituted the Propitiatory Sacrifice, and that inner element which was thereby manifested, and which gave to the actual event its worth. S. Bernard expressed the distinction in the well-known words 'Not His death, but His willing acceptance of death, was pleasing to God,' and there can be no doubt that throughout the New Testament special stress is laid upon the perfect obedience manifested in the life and death of Christ, upon the accomplishment of His Father's will which He ever kept in view, and upon the contrast thus marked between the Mosaic sacrifices and the one atoning offering. ' Sacrifices and offerings and whole burnt offerings and sacrifices for sin Thou wouldest not, neither hadst pleasure therein ... then hath He said, Lo, I am come to do Thy will.'

That the perfect obedience displayed in the passion and death of our Lord was the element which gave to the sacrifice its propitiatory value will be more readily understood when it is remembered that the essence of man's sin was from the first disobedience, the rebellion of the human will against the commands of God. The perfect sacrifice was offered by One Who, being man with all man's liability to temptation, that is with all the instruments of sin at His disposal[1], and exposed to every suggestion to set up His will against that of the Father, yet throughout His life continued unswervingly bent on doing 'not His own will, but the will of the Father Who sent Him,' and Who thus displayed the original perfection of human nature, the unbroken union with the life of God. On the cross the final struggle, the supreme temptation took place. The obedience shewn throughout His life was there manifested in death. ' He became obedient unto death, even the death of the cross.' At any moment of the passion a single acquiescence in evil, a single submission to the law of unrighteousness, a single swerving of His will from its choice of absolute obedience, would, we may believe, have ended all the shame and torture. And therefore there was needed at every moment a real effort of His human will to keep itself in union with the will of God[2]; it was not a mere submission at the outset once for all, but a continuous series of voluntary acts of resignation and obedience. Here then is the spirit of sacrifice which God demands, and which could not be found in the sacrifices of the Mosaic law, or in any offering of sinful man. The essence of the Atonement was the mind of Christ therein displayed, the obedience gradually learnt and therein perfected, the will of Christ therein proved to be one with the Father's will.

But we may discern a further element of propitiation in the death of our Lord. The law of righteousness, the justice of God, demands not only obedience in the present, but retribution for the past. 'The sins done aforetime' had been 'passed over in the forbearance of God' for His own purposes, which are not revealed to us: this 'passing over' had obscured the true nature of sin and of the Divine justice. Men had come to have easy thoughts of sin and its consequences; the

---

[1] Cf. *Ch. Quarterly Review*, xvi. p. 289 on ' Our Lord's Human Example.' ' Christ, of course, had every faculty of human nature, everything that man sins with, and therefore every instrument or faculty of sin.'

[2] In the last two sentences a slight change has been made in consequence of a criticism which showed that it was possible to misunderstand the language

originally employed, which however was intended to convey precisely the same meaning, and which could be amply justified by such a passage as e.g. S. Anselm, *Cur Deus Homo*, ii. 10, ' Possumus igitur dicere de Christo quia potuit mentiri, si subaudiatur, si vellet.' Cf. also [Boetius] *c. Eutychen et Nestorium*, c. viii. (*Opuscula Sacra*, ed. Peifer, pp. 214 ff.)

heathen felt but vaguely the burden of guilt, the Jew trusted in the mere external works of the law. In the death of Christ a manifestation was made of the righteousness of God, of His wrath, the absolute hostility of His nature to sin. 'God set Him forth to be a propitiation, through faith, by His blood, to shew His righteousness, because of the passing over of the sins done aforetime, in the forbearance of God.' But this manifestation of Divine justice might have been made by mere punishment: it became a propitiation, in that He, the self-chosen victim, by His acceptance of it, recognised the righteousness of the law which was vindicated on the cross. Men had refused to acknowledge God's justice in the consequences of sin; nothing but the willing acceptance of suffering, as the due portion of the human nature in which the sin was wrought, could have so declared the justice of God's law as to be a propitiation of Divine wrath. The cross was, on the one hand, the proclamation of God's ordinance against sin, on the other it was the response of man at length acknowledging the righteousness of the condemnation [1].

But on looking more closely into the matter, it is obvious that these explanations are not by themselves enough to account for the scriptural facts which we call the Atonement. We cannot ignore that, whether we consider the Old Testament anticipations, or the New Testament narrative of our Lord's work, His death, apart from the obedience manifested in it, occupies a unique place, and that stress is laid on it which would be unaccountable were it *only* the extreme trial of His obedience. The frequent declaration that it was necessary, that 'it behoved Christ to die,' seems to point to something exceptional in it, something more than the mere close of His spotless life. So again the mysterious dread and horror with which He looked forward to it testify to something in it which goes far beyond any human experience of death [2]. And what we gather from the New Testament must be combined with the Old Testament premonitions of Christ's death, as typified by the Mosaic sacrifices. There can be no question that death was, speaking generally, an integral part of the idea of sacrifice for sin, and that the distinguishing ceremonial of the slaying of the victim points to a special significance in death as connected with expiation and propitiation. Therefore, although we may still recognise that it was the spirit of obedience and voluntary sub-

[1] Cf. McLeod Campbell, *The Nature of the Atonement*, pp. 117, 118, 119, 127, 347: 'That oneness of mind with the Father, which towards man took the form of condemnation of sin, would in the Son's dealing with the Father in relation to our sins, take the form of a perfect confession of our sins. This confession, as to its own nature, must have been *a perfect Amen in humanity to the judgment of God on the sin of man.*' 'In Christ tasting death [as] the wages of sin ... was a perfecting of the Divine response in humanity to the Divine condemnation of sin.'

[2] See Dale, *Atonement*, pp. 49 ff.; Schmidt in Herzog's *Real. Encykl.* xvi. 403.

mission which gave atoning value to the death of Christ, we cannot ignore the necessity of death as the appointed form which the obedience took. Had He not obeyed, He would not have atoned; but had He not died, the obedience would have lacked just that element which made it an atonement for sin. The obedience was intended to issue in death. S. Bernard's saying, though true as he meant it, is, if taken quite literally, too sharp an antithesis. There is nothing well-pleasing to God in death alone, it is true; but there is, so He has revealed it, something well-pleasing to His righteousness, something propitiatory in death, if as a further condition the perfect obedience of the victim is thereby displayed.

We are driven to the same conclusion by the second explanation of our Lord's sacrifice given above. It is not enough to say that He died in order to manifest God's righteous judgment against sin, for the question remains, Why is death the requisite manifestation of judgment? If He endured it because it is the only fitting punishment, why is it in such a signal manner the penalty of sin? We can point indeed to the Divine principle, 'The soul that sinneth, it shall die,' as we can point to God's declared will that expiation shall be made by means of death, but in neither case, whether death be looked upon as the punishment or as the expiation of sin, is there any explanation of its unique position. It may well be that here we are confronted by the final mystery, and that the propitiatory virtue of Christ's death, typified by the slaying of animal victims under the law, foreshadowed by the almost universal belief in the expiation of blood, acknowledged with wondering gratitude by the human heart, depends upon the un-searchable will and hidden purposes of God, except in so far as we can see in it the manifestation at once of Christ's perfect obedience and of the righteousness of Divine judgment. If an attempt is made to penetrate further into the mystery of Redemption, it can be but a speculation, but it will be saved from overboldness if it follows the general lines of God's action as revealed in His Word.

Some light may be thrown upon the mystery of Christ's death by considering the scriptural view of death in general as the penalty of sin. It is not the mere physical act of dying, for that, as S. Athanasius says, is natural to man [1], and can be traced in the animal world in the ages before man existed. Besides, our Lord is said to have delivered us from death, and this clearly cannot mean physical death, since to this all men are still subject, but rather spiritual death; and the death which is spoken of as the penalty of sin must therefore also be spiritual.

---

[1] *De Incarn. Verbi* 4, 'Man is by nature mortal.' S. Athanasius held, however, that this 'natural corruption' would have been suspended, but for the Fall, by the help of the Logos empowering man to live the Divine life. See on the whole subject, *The Christian Doctrine of Sin*, App. ii. p. 536.

In this sense death can be no other than the final removal from us of God's presence, the completion of the alienation from the Divine life which sin began. But, considering the close connection, throughout the Bible, of physical and spiritual death, may it not be that the former is more than the symbol and type of the latter, that it is actually its consummation? If, again, death be truly represented by the Christian consciousness as the close of man's probation, does not this also point to its being the moment when the light of God's presence, the strength of His life, is finally withdrawn from the impenitent sinner, and the spiritual death, which is the one essential punishment of sin, falls upon him? The sentence of death, then, under which the whole world lay apart from the Atonement [1], was the declaration that every man who by inheritance and by his own act shared in Adam's sin, should at the moment of physical death experience also the full measure of spiritual death. The common lot of death thus involved the consciousness of separation from the life of God, and when we so regard it, we can understand something of the horror which its anticipation brought upon the soul of the Son of God [2]. He must pass through this last and most awful human experience ; not only because it was human, but because by the victorious endurance of it alone could the propitiation be accomplished. The thought throws light upon the prominence given to the death of Christ, upon His dread of it, upon His mysterious cry of dereliction upon the cross. It shews us how, though the experience was common to man, yet in Him it was in a twofold manner unique. The withdrawal of God's presence, awful as it is to the sin-hardened nature of man, must have been immeasurably more bitter to Him Who was One with the Father, whose 'meat was to do the will of His Father.' Just as we may believe the tortures of the cross to have been specially grievous to the perfect body which was unstained by sin, though other men have endured them, so, though all have to pass through death with its accompanying terror of the loss of God's presence, none can realize what that experience was to Him, because He was the Son of God. The death of Christ was therefore unique because of the nature of Him Who underwent it. But it was also unique in its results. No other death had been a propitiation for sin, for in no other death had this overwhelming consciousness of dereliction been endured victoriously, with no failure of perfect obedience, no shrinking of the will from the ordained task. In this final experience the offering was complete, the essence of the propitiation was secured, for the actual result of all human sin was herein made

---

[1] It should be remembered that the Church has always regarded the Atonement as having a *retrospective* effect, extending back to the first representa-

tives of the human race.

[2] Cf. Schmidt in Herzog's *Real. Encykl.*, Art. Versönung, vol. xvi. p. 403.

the very revelation of holiness itself, the means whereby the union with the will of God, so far from being finally broken, was finally perfected. The propitiatory value, therefore, of the sacrifice of Christ lay in His absolute obedience, in His willing acceptance of suffering which was thereby acknowledged as the due reward of sin, and in the death which was the essential form of both, for death is the culminating point of the alienation from God, which is both sin and its punishment. He alone endured it victoriously and without sin ; He alone, therefore, transformed it from the sign and occasion of God's wrath into a well-pleasing offering ; He took the punishment and made it a propitiation. 'The chastisement of our peace was upon Him ; and with His stripes we are healed.'

(c) So far we have considered the sacrifice of Christ in its aspect Godwards : we have tried to find an answer to the question, How did the death of Christ propitiate the wrath of God ? There remains the further question, How was it a sacrifice for us ? It was, we can see, a perfect offering acceptable to God : but how has it availed 'for us men' ? The mind shrinks from a purely external Atonement, and part of the imperfection of the Mosaic sacrifices consisted in the merely artificial relation between the offender and the victim. In the perfect sacrifice this relation must be real ; and we are thus led to the truth, so often overlooked, but impressed on every page of the New Testament, that He who died for our sins was our true representative in that He was truly man. Without for the present going into the more mystical doctrine of Christ as the second Adam, the spiritual head of our race, what is here emphasized is the reality and perfection of His human nature, which gave Him the right to offer a representative sacrifice [1]. 'For verily not of angels doth He take hold, but He taketh hold of the seed of Abraham. Wherefore it behoved Him in all things to be made like unto His brethren, that He might be a merciful and faithful High Priest in things pertaining to God, to make propitiation for the sins of the people.' Being thus 'taken from among men,' He was 'appointed for—or, on behalf of—men,' and the justification of His Priesthood is the complete reality of His humanity, which, if we may so speak, overlay and hid His Divinity, so that 'though He was a Son,' unchangeably 'in the form of God,' 'yet learnt He obedience by the things which He suffered,' and thus became for us a perfect Priest. The sinless perfection of Christ, far from removing Him out of the sphere of our sinful lives, made Him perfectly repre-

---

[1] Irenaeus is full of this thought, though it is not disentangled from other explanations of the death of Christ. Cf. especially V. xxiii. 2 : 'Recapitulans enim universum hominem in se ab initio usque ad finem, recapitulatus et mortem ejus.' Cf. also Athanasius, *de Incarn. Verbi* 9, in which he suggests that it was the Divine power of the Logos in the bodily nature of Christ that made His sacrifice representative, as well as His death victorious over death.

sentative; for He not only possessed in their greatest perfection all the powers and capacities which are the instruments of sin, but in the strength of His sinlessness and of His love He could feel for all men and accept them as His brethren, though they were sinners. Our High Priest 'hath been in all points like as we are, yet without sin.' The holiest man has some part of his nature stunted and repressed by sin, and is so far incomplete, unrepresentative: but He, unweakened and unmarred in any point by sin, can without holding anything back represent human nature in its perfection and entirety.

The representative character of Christ is manifested in a different aspect, according as He is regarded as the victim or as the priest offering the sacrifice. As the victim He must be the sin-bearer, for the transfer of guilt—which under the Mosaic system was merely symbolised by the act of laying hands on the victim's head—must for a true propitiatory sacrifice be more than external and artificial. That is to say, there must be a real meaning in S. Paul's tremendous words, 'Him Who knew no sin He made to be sin on our behalf,' in the passages in which He is described as bearing our sins [1], in the great prophecy which told that 'the Lord hath laid on Him the iniquity of us all.' How can we find an explanation of the paradox so boldly stated by S. Paul, that He who knew no sin was yet made sin? We may not surely take all these plain phrases to mean that He bore the *punishment* of our sins: it would have been easy to say that had it been meant. No, the relation typified by the Mosaic offerings must be real, and yet the expression 'He made Him to be sin' cannot without blasphemy be understood to mean that God the Father actually made His Son to sin. The solution of the difficulty can only be found in the truth of the Incarnation. In order that the sacrifice might be representative, He took upon Him the whole of our human nature, and became flesh, conditioned though that fleshly nature was throughout by sin [2]. It was not only in His death that we contemplate Him as the sin-bearer, but throughout His life He was, as it were, conditioned by the sinfulness of those with whom His human nature brought Him into close and manifold relations. The Crucifixion does not come as the unexpectedly shameful end of a glorious and untroubled life, though it was undoubtedly in a special sense the manifestation of the 'curse' under which He laid Himself. We cannot say that at a given moment in His life, as when the sinner's hands were laid upon the victim's head and his guilt was transferred, He

---

[1] See especially Heb. ix. 28, which is an echo of the LXX. of Is. liii. 12.

[2] Athan. *c. Ar.* i. 43: 'He put on the flesh which was enslaved to sin.' Cf. also Augustine, *de Musica* VI. iv:

'Hominem sine peccato, non sine peccatoris conditione suscepit. Nam et nasci humanitus, et pati et mori voluit.' I owe this reference to Norris, *Rudiments of Theology*, p. 61 *n.*

began to bear our iniquity, for the very nature which He took, freed though it was in Him from hereditary guilt, was in itself, by its necessary human relations, sin-bearing. Nor did His personal sinlessness make this impossible or unreal; rather it intensified it. As S. Matthew tells us, even in relation to bodily sickness and infirmity, that He bore what He took away—'Himself took our infirmities, and bare our diseases'—so it was with our redemption from sin. In taking it away, He had to bear its weight, intensified by reason of that very self-sacrificing love which made Him realize with more than human keenness the sinfulness of the human nature into which He had come. There is thus nothing artificial or external in His sin-bearing, for His human nature was so real and so perfect that He was involved, so to speak, in all the consequences of the sin which is so tremendous a factor in human life, even to the enduring of the very sufferings and death which in us are the penal results and final outcome of sin, but in Him were the means of His free self-sacrifice.

Once more He was our representative as the Priest who offered the sacrifice. The requisite conditions of such an office are stated, in the Epistle to the Hebrews, to be complete human sympathy, and yet such separateness from sin, and from all limitations of incompleteness, as can only be Divine. 'It behoved Him in all things to be made like unto His brethren, that He might be a merciful and faithful high priest;' 'but He, because He abideth for ever, hath His priesthood unchangeable . . . for such a high priest became us, holy, harmless, undefiled, separated from sinners, and made higher than the heavens;' 'for the law appointeth men high priests, having infirmity; but the word of the oath, which was after the law, appointeth a Son, perfected for evermore[1].' In these and similar passages the doctrine of the Priesthood of Christ is developed, and it is obvious that quite as much stress is laid on His unlikeness, as on His likeness to us[2]. He is our representative as Priest, because He is both man and more than man, and can therefore perform for us what we could not and cannot perform for ourselves, in offering the perfect propitiatory sacrifice. Here is the true vicariousness of the Atonement, which consisted, not, as we shall see later, in the substitution of His punishment for ours, but in His offering the sacrifice which man had neither purity nor power to offer. From out of the very heart and centre of the human nature which was so enslaved and corrupted by sin that no human offering was acceptable to God there is raised the sinless sacrifice of perfect humanity by the God-Man, our great High Priest : human in

---

[1] Heb. ii. 17 ; vii. 24, 26, 28 : cf. ix. 13, 14, 24, 25, 26 ; x. 11, 12, 13, 14.

[2] Cf. Athan. *c. Ar.* ii. 69 : 'He sends His own Son, and He becomes Son of Man, by taking created flesh ; that, since all were under sentence of death, He, *being other than them all*, might Himself for all offer to death His own body.'

the completeness of His sympathy, Divine in the unique power of His Priesthood. So is the condition of the law of righteousness fulfilled, and the sacrifice of obedience unto death is offered by His submission to all that constitutes in sinners the consummation and the punishment of their sin, which He transformed into the occasion and the manifestation of His perfect holiness. And it is a representative sacrifice, for unique though it is, it consists of no unheard-of experience, of no merely symbolical ceremony, unrelated and unmeaning to us; but of just those universal incidents of suffering which, though He must have felt them with a bitterness unknown to us, are intensely human—poverty, misunderstanding, failure, treachery, rejection, bodily anguish, spiritual desolation, death. 'Surely He hath borne our griefs, and carried our sorrows ... The chastisement of our peace was upon Him,' and therefore 'by His stripes we are healed.'

2. It is not enough to consider the death of Christ only as propitiatory, or as standing alone in relation to our redemption. We have seen how it secured our propitiation, and in what sense it has a unique place in relation both to our Lord Himself and to man. There remains the further aspect of His redemptive work, in which it is regarded as effecting our reunion with God by delivering us from the power of sin, and by filling us with the Divine gift of life. This, it should be noticed, is the conception of our Lord's work which was chiefly in the minds of the early Christian writers, though in almost all it was combined with the acknowledgment of His deliverance of man from guilt and from the wrath of God by His representative propitiation[1]. But to their consciousness the power of sin and of the spiritual forces with which man is surrounded was so continually present, that they were naturally inclined to look mainly at that side of the Atonement which represents it as the victory over sin and Satan and the restoration of man to the life of God. And this view, though by no means to the exclusion of the propitiatory aspect, is amply justified by the Bible. Considered as restoration, there seem to be three grades or stages of redemption indicated in the New Testament. First, there is the unanimous declaration that the object of our Lord's life and death was to free us from sin. In the most sacrificial descriptions of His work this further result of the Atonement is implied. The 'Lamb of God' is to 'take away the *sin* of the world'; His Blood was to be 'shed for the remission of *sins*'; by 'the precious Blood of Jesus Christ as of a Lamb without blemish' men were 'redeemed from their

---

[1] The two aspects of the Atonement are frequently presented by S. Athanasius, *de Incarn. Verbi.* Thus (ch. 10) 'By the sacrifice of His own Body He *both* put an end to the law which was against us, and gave us a fresh beginning of life, in that He bestowed on us the hope of resurrection.' Cf. also chs. 8 and 9. Again (ch. 25), 'As He offered His Body unto death for all; so by it He again threw open the way to heaven.'

vain conversation'; He 'gave Himself for us, that He might redeem us from all *iniquity*.' In the next place, this deliverance from sin is identified with the gift of life, which is repeatedly connected with our Lord's life and death. 'I am come that they might have life'; for 'I will give My flesh for the life of the world.' 'He died for all, that they which live should not henceforth live unto themselves, but unto Him who died for them and rose again.' He 'bare our sins in His own body on the tree, that we being dead to sins might live unto righteousness.' Lastly, this new life is to issue in union with the life of God in Christ. 'Christ suffered for sins, the just for the unjust, that He might bring us to God.' 'In Christ Jesus ye that once were far off are made nigh in the Blood of Christ.' In such passages the Apostles are only drawing out the meaning of our Lord's own declaration, 'I, if I be lifted up, will draw all men unto Me.'

Our Lord's death is thus intimately connected by the New Testament writers with the restoration of man to union with God by means of the gift of life; but it should be noticed that, unique and necessary as His death was, it is continually spoken of in close connection with the Resurrection or the Ascension, for in these, as was foreshadowed by the typical ceremonies of the Law, the sacrifice culminated by the presentation of the 'life which had willingly passed through death' before the altar of God's presence. The reason is clear. Pardon for the past, deliverance from guilt, propitiation of the just wrath of God, are necessary and all-important; but they cannot stand alone. They must, for man is helpless and weak, be succeeded by the gift of life, and for this we must look to those mighty acts in which the One Sacrifice reached its full consummation. Thus our Lord Himself declares that He died in order to rise again; 'I lay down My life that [in order that] I may take it again.' So to S. Paul the Resurrection is the necessary completion of the process which was begun by the death. 'He was delivered for our offences, and was raised again for our justification.' 'If while we were enemies, we were reconciled to God through the death of His Son, much more being reconciled, shall we be saved through [in] His life.' 'We were buried with Him through baptism unto death; that [in order that] like as Christ was raised from the dead through the glory of the Father, so we also might walk in newness of life.' Even the passages which speak of our salvation as effected by virtue of Christ's Blood, refer, according to the Jewish conception of the 'blood which is the life,' not only, or even chiefly, to the bloodshedding in death, but to the heavenly 'sprinkling' of the principle of life, its presentation in heaven by means of the Resurrection and Ascension. The whole process is described in what may be called the central core of S. Paul's theology, the eighth chapter of the Epistle to the Romans. 'It is Christ Jesus that died, yea rather, that was raised from the dead, who is at the Right Hand of God, who also maketh intercession for us.' It has been the fault of much popular theology to think only of our deliverance from wrath by the sacrificial death of Christ, and to neglect the infinitely important continuation of the process thus begun. The Gospel is a religion of life, the call to a life of union with God by means of the grace which flows from the mediation of the risen and ascended Saviour. We need not discuss the comparative importance of the two aspects of the work of Atonement, for propitiation and reunion, pardon and life are alike necessary elements in salvation, and by the love of God in Christ are united in the sacrifice which was begun on Calvary, and is for ever presented for our redemption before the throne of God in heaven.

3. So far we have been considering the Atonement as our Lord's work on behalf of men : we have now to consider it as meeting the inevitable demand of the human conscience that this vicarious sacrifice shall in some way satisfy man's sense of personal responsibility ; that by means of the Atonement man shall, so far as he can, make amends for his own sin. The charge of injustice, as it is generally urged against the doctrine of the Atonement, rests, as will be shewn, upon a fundamental misconception as to the nature of Christ's work for us ; but it is also commonly assumed that by the death of Christ all was done for man, and nothing in man, so that we are thereby relieved of all responsibility for our own wilful acts. It is this notion that we have now to investigate. First, however, we must acknowledge the truth contained in it. The Atonement is, after all, God's forgiveness of us in Christ, and no forgiveness is conceivable which does not in some degree relieve the offender of the consequences of his offence. Human forgiveness, though it may in some cases, perhaps, remit no part of the external penalty due to wrong-doing, must, in the very act of forgiving, put away and abolish the anger of the offended person, the alienation which the offence has caused, and which is certainly part, sometimes the greatest part, of the penal consequences of an offence. Human forgiveness, therefore, necessarily transgresses the strict law of retribution : yet no one can seriously contend that forgiveness is either impossible or immoral. And more than this, there is even in our imperfect forgiveness a power to blot out guilt, and to restore the offender to new life. Inexplicable though the fact may be, experience tells us that forgiveness avails to lift the load of guilt that presses upon an offender. A change passes over him that can only be described as regenerative, life-giving ; and thus the assurance of pardon, however conveyed, may be said to obliterate in some degree the consequences of the past [1]. It is true that this result of forgiveness cannot be explained logically so as to satisfy the reason, but the possibility and

[1] Cf. Westcott, *Historic Faith*, p. 133.

the power of pardon are nevertheless facts of human experience. The Atonement is undoubtedly a mystery, but all forgiveness is a mystery. The Atonement undoubtedly transgresses the strict law of exact retribution, but all forgiveness transgresses it. And we may believe that human forgiveness is, in spite of all its imperfection, like that of God, for this is surely the lesson of the Lord's Prayer, 'Forgive us our trespasses, as we forgive them that trespass against us.' Experience and conscience, therefore, lead us to expect that the Divine method of forgiveness will both disprove the exaggerated idea of personal responsibility, which is based on a false estimate of man's power, and will also transcend reason by rising into a region of mystery and of miracle[1]. We have to deal in this sphere of pardon with a God Who 'declares His almighty power most chiefly in showing mercy and pity.'

One aspect of this mystery is to be found in the truth, stamped on every page of the New Testament, of the mystical union between Christ and His people. By virtue of this union His acts are ascribed to us; and thus, according to S. Paul, we died in Him, we are raised in Him, and the sacrifice which He offered, we have also offered, as in Him. The doctrine of the Second Adam, of the spiritual headship of Christ, would not indeed if it stood alone satisfy the demands of the conscience; but when taken in connection with the practical sacramental teaching which is based upon it, it points to the solution of the problem. By the Incarnation we are taken up into Him, and therefore the acts that in His human nature He performed are our acts, by virtue of that union which is described by Him as the union of a vine with its branches, by S. Paul as that of the head with the members of a body. But in considering the results of this union, the reciprocal communication of the weakness of our bodily nature to Him, of His victorious deeds in the body to us, a distinction must be drawn between that part of His work which can, and that which cannot be shared by us. Of one part of His work, of the sacrifice which He offered for man's guilt, the essence was its vicariousness. Man could not and never can offer a sacrifice which can avail to propitiate for the sins of the past. It is only in virtue of that one final and perfect propitiation that we can draw nigh to God, can accomplish anything good, can recognise that we are delivered from wrath. The sins of the past are cancelled, the guilt is wiped out: in this respect all was accomplished by Him for us who are in Him, and nothing remains for us to do. He as

[1] Cf. Magee, *The Gospel and the Age*, pp. 270 ff. Bishop Magee, however, seems to exaggerate the certainty and relentlessness of the temporal punishment of sin (cf. against this Dale, *The Atonement*, Lect. viii) and to overlook the force of the analogy from human experience of forgiveness.

our Representative, because He shares our nature, can offer for us a prevailing sacrifice ; only as His brethren, because He has united us to Him, are we enabled to plead the sacrifice which He offered. It is indeed offered for us, for it was utterly impossible that we could offer it for ourselves ; it was the necessary initial step, which man could not take, towards union with the righteous Father. As our spiritual head, the second Adam, the captain of our salvation, He had the right of offering on our behalf ; as in Him by virtue of the Incarnation we are empowered to claim the infinite blessings of the redemption so obtained [1]. If this is mysterious, irrational, transcendental, so is all morality ; for at the root of all morality lies the power of self-sacrifice, which is nothing but the impulse of love to make a vicarious offering for its fellows, and the virtue of such an offering to restore and to quicken [2]. The righteousness of God required from the human nature which had sinned the sacrifice of a perfect obedience manifested in and through death : that is the unique and unapproachable mystery of the Atonement ; but that the sacrifice should be offered by a sinless Man, and that we should be accepted by God in virtue of His propitiation and because of our union with Him, that, though mysterious enough, as human reason counts mystery, is prefigured and illustrated and explained by all the deepest experiences of the race, by all that is most human, though it most evades logical analysis, in our moral consciousness [3].

There is then no additional propitiation demanded from us. The Atonement, in this aspect, requires nothing from us, for the forgiveness is there, bestowed upon us by God in consequence of the sacrifice of Jesus Christ. But like the gifts of grace which come after forgiveness, the forgiveness itself has to be personally accepted by us ; it must be brought into contact with each man's will. So regarded, the Atonement, though the great gift of reconciliation is absolutely free, the product of the spontaneous love of God, does lay upon us an obligation. On our part faith is demanded that we may realize, and appropriate, and associate ourselves with the pardon which is ours in Christ. This is not the place for a full discussion of justifying faith : it is enough to indicate what seems to be its relation to the Atonement, as being man's share in the propitiatory work of Christ. It is often said that the faith which justifies is simply trust [4], but it must surely be a more complex moral act than this.

---

[1] Cf. Ath. *c. Ar.* iii. 34. 'As the Lord in putting on the body, became Man, so we men are made gods by the Word, being taken into Him through His Flesh, and from henceforth inherit life eternal.'

[2] For this thought fully drawn out, see Holland, *Creed and Character*, pp. 212 ff.

[3] On the truth of the solidarity of all men in Christ, see Westcott, *The Victory of the Cross*, pp. 6–53.

[4] See e.g. Moule, *Outlines of Christian Doctrine*, p. 185.

If faith is the acceptance of Christ's propitiation, it must contain, in the first place, that longing for reconciliation which springs from the personal consciousness of sin as alienation from God, and from horror of its guilt and power. There must then ensue the recognition of man's complete powerlessness to free himself from sin, and a deeply humble sense of dependence on God's mercy; but this mere trust in His mercy is not enough, for it would not satisfy the sense of sin. The sinner has to own that God is not merely benevolent, and that sin must be punished. Therefore faith must contain the recognition of the justice of the Divine law against sin, manifested in the death of Christ. Faith, in short, starts from the longing for a representative to atone for us, and it ends with the recognition of Christ as our representative, of His Atonement as sufficient, and of His death as displaying the due reward of sin. For the Atonement cannot be a mere external act. If Christ is our representative, He must be acknowledged by those whom He represents : otherwise His endurance of suffering would avail nothing for them, for God will not be satisfied with the mere infliction of punishment. But if the result of His death is that men are brought, one by one, age after age, to acknowledge the righteousness of the law for which He suffered, to recognise the result of sin to which sin has blinded them, then there has been made on their part the first step towards the great reconciliation. Faith identifies the individual with the sacrifice which has been offered for him, and therefore with Christ's attitude towards God and towards sin, and though it is but the first step, yet it is emphatically that by reason of which we are justified. For since we are thus identified with the sacrifice, God accepts the first step for the whole course, of which it is the pledge and anticipation. We are justified because we believe in God, but also because God believes in us[1]. Faith, being what it is, a complex moral act whereby Christ's propitiation is accepted by man, implies an attitude of mind towards sin so right that, though it is but the first movement of the soul in Christ, God takes it for the whole, sees us as wholly in Him, reckons it to us as righteousness. But only because it is as a matter of fact the first, the hardest, perhaps, and the most necessary, but still only the first step towards complete sanctification. And, if we now ask what is the further course of sanctification, the answer will shew the full relation of the sacrifice of Christ to man's will and conscience. For the life of sanctification is nothing else but the 'imitation of Christ' in that task of 'learning obedience' to which His life was devoted, and which His death completed. In us, too, as in Him, that task has

[1] Cf. Aug. *de Trin.* i. 10: 'Tales nos amat Deus, quales futuri sumus, non quales sumus.'

to be accomplished by suffering. 'He learnt obedience by the things which He suffered.' 'It became Him ... in bringing many sons unto glory, to make the Captain of their salvation perfect through sufferings.' That same path towards perfection lies before all who are justified by faith in His atoning sacrifice. For justification is a spiritual act answering to the spiritual act of faith. The spiritual germ of vitality thus implanted in us has to be developed in the sphere in which the consequences of sin naturally and inevitably work themselves out, in the bodily nature of man. 'Even we,' says S. Paul, 'which have the firstfruits of the Spirit,' even we are waiting for the further process, for 'the adoption, to wit, the redemption of our body.' And the process consists in so following 'the Captain of our salvation' that, like Him, we accept every one of those sufferings which are the consequences of sin, but accept them not as punishment imposed from without upon unwilling offenders, but as the material of our freewill sacrifice. From no one pang or trial of our nature has He delivered us, indeed, He has rather laid them upon us more unsparingly, more inevitably. But the sufferings from which He would not deliver us He has transformed for us. They are no longer penal, but remedial and penitential. Pain has become the chastisement of a Father who loves us, and death the passage into His very presence. And this He has done for us by the bestowal upon us of spiritual vitality. The germ is implanted by the act of forgiveness which removes the wrath and the impending death, and this germ of life, cherished and developed by the gifts which flow from His mediation and intercession, by the Holy Spirit Whom He sends to dwell in us, works on all the penalties of sin, and makes them the sacrifice which we offer in Him. This is the 'law of the Spirit of life.' 'If Christ be in you, the body is dead because of sin ; but the Spirit is life because of righteousness. But if the Spirit of Him that raised up Jesus from the dead dwell in you, He that raised up Christ from the dead shall also quicken your mortal bodies by His Spirit that dwelleth in you.'

Our personal share then in the Atonement is not mere passivity. It consists, first, in the acceptance of God's forgiveness in Christ, our self-identification with Christ's atoning attitude, and then in working out, by the power of the life bestowed upon us, all the consequences of forgiveness, the transformation of punishment into sacrifice, the imitation of Christ in His perfect obedience to the law of righteousness, the gradual sanctification of body, soul and spirit by the grace which enables us to ' suffer with Him.'

III. The doctrine of Atonement, more than any of the great truths of Christianity, has been misconceived and misrepresented, and has therefore not only been rejected itself, but has sometimes been the cause of the rejection of the whole Christian system. The truth of the vicarious sacrifice has been isolated till it has almost become untrue, and, mysterious as it undoubtedly is, it has been so stated as to be not only mysterious, but contrary to reason and even to conscience. One most terrible misconception it is hardly necessary to do more than mention. The truth of the wrath of God against sin and of the love of Christ by which that wrath was removed, has been perverted into a belief in a divergence of will between God the Father and God the Son, as if it was the Father's will that sinners should perish, the Son's will that they should be saved; as if the Atonement consisted in the propitiation of the wrathful God by the substituted punishment of the innocent for the guilty. It will be seen that while this statement seems to represent the Catholic doctrine, in reality it introduces a most vital difference. There can be no divergence of will between the Persons of the Blessed Trinity ; and, in regard to this special dealing with man, we have the clearest testimony of Revelation that the whole Godhead shared in the work. Here, as always, God the Father is revealed as the source and origin of all good. 'God so loved the world that He gave His only begotten Son, that whosoever believeth in Him should not perish, but have everlasting life.' 'God was in Christ reconciling the world to Himself.' The beginning and the end of the Atonement is the love of God : the death of Christ was not the cause, but the revelation of that love[1]. That it was the second Person of the Trinity who was actually the means of our redemption may be ascribed to that original relation of the Logos to the human race, by which He was both its Creator and its perfect exemplar[2]. But nothing can be further from the truth than to imagine that His was all the love which saved us, the Father's all the wrath which condemned us. If the death of Christ was necessary to propitiate the wrath of the Father, it was necessary to propitiate His own wrath also; if it manifested His love, it manifested the Father's love also. The absolute, unbroken, unity of will between the Father and the Son is the secret of the atoning sacrifice.

Again, the isolation of the truth of the Atonement from other parts of Christian doctrine has led to a mode of stating it which deprives us of all motive to action, of all responsibility for our own salvation. Just as the misconception noticed above arose from a failure to grasp the whole truth of our Lord's Divinity, so this error springs from ignoring His perfect Humanity. Christ is regarded as having no vital or real relation to us, and His work is therefore wholly external, a

---

[1] This is well stated by McLeod Campbell, l. c. p. 16.
[2] Cf. Athan. *de Inc. passim*, esp. chs. 20 and 42. Hooker, *Eccles. Pol.* V. li.

3, ' It seemeth a thing unconsonant that the world should honour any other as the Saviour but Him Whom it honoureth as the Creator of the world.'

mere gift from above. But what has already been said will shew
that from the first the Atonement has been taught as the offering of
our spiritual Head, in Whom we are redeemed, and whose example we
are able to follow as having Him in us. Salvation is thus given to us
indeed, but it is given to us because we are in Christ, and we have
to work out our share in it because of the responsibility, the call to
sacrifice which that union with Him lays upon us. 'Work out your
own salvation with fear and trembling, for it is God which worketh
in you both to will and to do.' It is all from God and of God; but
God has come into our life, and taken us up into Him, and called
upon us to follow Him in the way of the cross.

And this leads us to consider another error, or rather another form
of the same error. Nothing is more common than to hear the doctrine
of Atonement stated as if the work of Christ consisted in His endurance
of our punishment in order that we might not endure it. This view of
the doctrine leads to the objections—perhaps the commonest of all the
difficulties found in what men take for Christianity—that the punishment of the innocent instead of the guilty is unjust, and that punishment
cannot be borne by anyone but the sinner. We have seen that the
real vicariousness of our Lord's work lay in the offering of the perfect
sacrifice: the theory we are now considering holds, on the contrary,
that it lay in the substitution of His punishment for ours. A partial
truth is contained in this theory; for our Lord did endure sufferings,
and, as has been already said, they were the very sufferings which are,
in sinners, the penalties of sin. But as a simple matter of fact and
experience, the sufferings and the pains of death which He endured
have not been remitted to us; and that which is remitted, the eternal
penalty of alienation from God, was not, could not be endured by Him.
For alienation from God is, essentially, a state of sin; it is sin, regarded
both in its origin and in its necessary result. It could not, therefore,
be borne by Christ, 'in Whom was no sin,' between Whom and the
Father was no alienation. Attempts have been made to establish a
quantitative relation between our Lord's sufferings and the punishment
which is thereby remitted to us, to prove that the eternal nature of the
Sufferer made His death equivalent to eternal punishment. But even
if such attempts, in so mysterious a region, could succeed, it would be
vain to establish a quantitative equivalence where there is no qualitative
relation. Eternal punishment is 'eternal sin[1],' and as such could
never be endured by the sinless Son of God.

But we have to face the question which naturally follows. What,
then, did His sufferings and death mean? Why did He endure what
are to us the temporal penalties, the diverse consequences of sin?
And if He endured them, why are they not remitted to us? It is true,

---

[1] Cf. the true reading of S. Mark iii. 29, R. V.

as has been shewn, that He bore just those sufferings which are the results and penalties of sin, even to that tremendous final experience in which man loses sight of God as he enters the valley of the shadow of death ; but He bore them, not that we might be freed from them, for we have deserved them, but that we might be enabled to bear them, as He did, victoriously and in unbroken union with God. He, the Innocent, suffered, but the guilty do not 'go free ;' for the very end and object of all the obedience that He learnt was, that He might lead man along the same path of suffering, not 'free,' but gladly submissive to the pains, which, but for Him, would be the overwhelming penalties of our sins. It may be true that 'punishment cannot be borne by anyone but the sinner[1],' and therefore it may be right not to call Christ's sufferings punishment, especially as the expression is significantly avoided in the New Testament. But it is certainly not true that the sufferings which result from sin cannot be borne by anyone but the sinner: every day demonstrates the falsity of such an assertion. Sufferings borne in the wrong spirit, unsubmissively or without recognition of their justice, are penal ; but the spirit of humility and obedience makes them remedial and purgatorial. Christ, by so bearing the pains which sin brought upon human nature, and which the special sin of His enemies heaped upon Him, has not only offered the one perfect sacrifice, but has also given us strength to make the same submission, to learn the same obedience and to share the same sacrifice.

IV. There are many topics connected with the Atonement which it is impossible here to discuss, but which seem to fall into their right place and proportion if those aspects of Christ's redeeming work which have been dwelt upon are kept firmly in mind. The central mystery of the cross, the forgiveness, the removal of wrath, thereby freely bestowed upon us, remains a mystery, and must always be an insuperable difficulty to those who depend wholly on reason, or who trust wholly in man's power to extricate himself from the destruction wrought by his sin, as it was an offence to the Jew, and foolishness to the Greek. But mystery though it is to the intellect, there is a moral fitness[2] in the bestowal of forgiveness because of the obedience of Christ shewn in His sacrificial death, which appeals irresistibly to the moral consciousness of mankind. The witness of this is the trustful gratitude with which the doctrine of Christ crucified has been accepted by Christians, learned and unlearned, from the age of its first preaching. The human heart accepts it, and by the cross is assured of forgiveness :

[1] W. R. Greg.

[2] It should be noticed that the Greek Fathers and the English divines for the most part confine themselves to shewing this moral fitness and consonance with God's moral nature in the Atonement, and do not attempt to prove its absolute necessity. Cf. Athanasius, *de Incarn. Verbi*, ch. 6 ; Hooker, *Eccles. Pol.* V. li. 3 ; Butler, *Analogy*, pt. ii. c. 5.

'to them which are called' it is 'Christ the power of God, and the wisdom of God.'

But if we may appeal to experience in support of this mysterious truth, much more may we claim the same support for the plainer, more human aspect of the Atonement. As S. Athanasius in his day[1], so we in ours may appeal for the practical and visible proof of the Atonement, to the complete change in man's relation to sorrow and suffering, and in the Christian view of death[2]. This is no small matter. When we realize what suffering is in human life, the vast place which it has in our experience, its power of absorbing the mind, its culmination in the final pangs of death, and when we see the transformation, however gradual and imperfect it may be, of all this into the means and material of the sacrifice which the follower of Christ is gladly willing to offer to the Father of our Lord Jesus Christ, we realize the full force of the great words telling of the destruction 'through death of him that *had the power of death*, that is the devil,' and of the deliverance of 'them who through fear of death were all their lifetime subject to bondage.' And the transformation, the destruction, the deliverance, consist in this that from these sufferings His sacrifice has removed the element of rebellion, the hopelessness of alienation, the sting of sin. They are ours, because they were His ; but they are ours *as* they were His, purified and perfected by obedience, by the offering of a holy Will ; 'by the which Will we are sanctified through the offering of the body of Jesus Christ once for all.'

[1] Cf. *De Incarn. Verbi*, chs. 27, 28, 29.

[2] Cf. Carlyle's apostrophe to Marie Antoinette on her way to the scaffold : 'Think of *Him* Whom thou worshippest, the Crucified,—Who also treading the winepress *alone*, fronted sorrow still deeper ; and triumphed over it, and made it Holy, and built of it a "Sanctuary of Sorrow" for thee and all the wretched.' *Miscellaneous Essays*, vol. v. p. 165 (ed. 1872).

THE HOLY SPIRIT AND INSPIRATION.

I. THE appeal to 'experience' in religion, whether personal or general, brings before the mind so many associations of ungoverned enthusiasm and untrustworthy fanaticism, that it does not easily commend itself to those of us who are most concerned to be reasonable. And yet, in one form or another, it is an essential part of the appeal which Christianity makes on its own behalf since the day when Jesus Christ met the question 'Art thou He that should come, or do we look for another?' by pointing to the transforming effect of His work; 'The blind receive their sight, and the lame walk; the lepers are cleansed, and the deaf hear; the dead are raised up, and the poor have the Gospel preached to them.'

The fact is that in current appeals to experience the fault, where there is a fault, lies not in the appeal but in the nature of the experience appealed to. What is meant by the term is often an excited state of feeling, rather than a permanent transformation of the whole moral, intellectual, and physical being of man. Or it is something which seems individual and eccentric, or something confined to a particular class of persons under special conditions of education or of ignorance, or something which other religions besides Christianity have been conspicuous for producing. When a meaning broad and full, and at the same time exact enough, has been given to experience the appeal is essential to Christianity, because Christianity professes to be not a mere record of the past, but a present life, and there is no life where there is no experience.

It will be worth while, then, to bear in mind how freely the original defenders of the Christian Church appealed, like their Master, to facts of experience. Thus we find an individual, like S. Cyprian, recalling the time of his baptism, and the personal experience of illumination and power which it brought with it:—

'Such were my frequent musings: for whereas I was encumbered with the many sins of my past life, which it seemed impossible to be rid of, so I had used myself to give way to my clinging infirmities, and, from despair of better things, to humour the evils of my heart, as slaves born in my house, and my proper offspring. But after that life-giving water succoured me, washing away the stain of former years, and pouring into my cleansed and hallowed breast the light which comes from heaven, after that I drank in the Heavenly Spirit, and was created into a new man by a second birth,—then marvellously what before was doubtful became plain to me, what was hidden was revealed, what was dark began to shine, what was before difficult, now had a way and a means, what had seemed impossible, now could be achieved, what was in me of the guilty flesh, now confessed that it was earthy, what was quickened in me by the Holy Ghost, now had a growth according to God [1].'

Again, we find an apologist like S. Athanasius, resting the stress of his argument on behalf of Christ upon what He has done in the world, and specially on the spiritual force He exercises on masses of men, 'drawing them to religion, persuading them to virtue, teaching them immortality, leading them to the desire of heavenly things, revealing the knowledge of the Father, inspiring power over death, shewing each man to himself, abolishing the godlessness of idolatry [2].'

The Fathers of the Christian Church appealed in this way to experience, because Christianity as they knew, is essentially not a past event, but a present life, a life first manifested in Christ and then perpetuated in His Church. Christianity is a manifested life,—a thing, therefore, like all other forms of life, known not in itself but in its effects, its fruits, its results. Christianity is a manifested life, and it is this because it is the sphere in which the Spirit, the Life-giver, finds His freeest and most unhindered activity. The Christian Church is the scene of the intensest, the most vigorous, the richest, the most 'abundant' life that the universe knows, because in a preeminent sense it is the 'Spirit-bearing body.' The Spirit is life; that is His chief characteristic. We may indeed elucidate the idea of spirit by negations; by negation of materiality, of circumscription, of limitation; but the positive conception we are to attach to spirit is the conception of life; and where life is most penetrating, profound, invincible, rational, conscious of God, there in fullest freedom of operation is the Holy Spirit [3].

Thus, obviously enough, the doctrine of the Spirit is no remote or esoteric thing; it is no mere ultimate object of the rapt contemplation of the mystic; it is the doctrine of that wherein God touches man most nearly, most familiarly, in common life. Last in the eternal order of the Divine Being, ' proceeding from the Father and the Son,' the Holy Spirit is the first point of contact with God in the order of human experience [4].

---

[1] Cyprian, *ad Donatum* 3. Trans. in *Library of the Fathers*, iii. p. 3.

[2] Athanasius, *de Incarnatione*, 31, 48-52.

[3] See S. Basil's fine definition of the term in his treatise *on the Holy Spirit*, ix. 22. This treatise has been translated by the Rev. G. Lewis for the 'Religious Tract Society.'

[4] See Basil, as above, xvi. 37 : ' We

'I believe in the Holy Ghost, the giver of life.' All life is His operation. 'Wherever the Holy Spirit is, there is also life ; and wherever
life is, there is also the Holy Spirit [1].' Thus if creation takes its rise
in the will of the Father, if it finds its law in the being of the Word or
Son, yet the effective instrument of creation, the 'finger of God,' the
moving principle of vitalization is the Holy Spirit, 'the divider and
distributor of the gifts of life [2].'

Nature is one great body, and there is breath in the body ; but this
breath is not self-originated life, it is the influence of the Divine Spirit.
'By the word of the Lord were the heavens made, and all the host of
them by the breath of His mouth.' The Spirit, the breath of God,
was brooding upon the face of the waters of chaos ere life and order
were. It is the sending forth of the breath of God, which is the giving
to things of the gift of life ; it is the withdrawal of that breath which
is their annihilation [3]. So keenly indeed were the Christians of the
early period conscious of the one life of nature as the universal evidence of the one Spirit, that it was a point of the charge against Origen
that his language seemed to involve an exclusion of the Holy Spirit
from nature, and a limitation of His activity to the Church [4]. The
whole of life is certainly His. And yet, because His special attribute
is holiness, it is in rational natures, which alone are capable of holiness,
that He exerts His special influence. A special in-breathing of the
Divine Spirit gave to man his proper being [5]. In humanity, made after
the Divine Image, it was the original intention of God that the Spirit
should find His chiefest joy, building the edifice of a social life in which
nature was to find its crown and justification : a life of conscious and
free sonship, in which the gifts of God should be not only received, but
recognised as His, and consciously used in willing and glad homage to
the Divine Giver, in reverent execution of the law of development impressed by the Divine Reason, in the realized fellowship of the Blessed
Spirit of knowledge and love. The history of humanity has in fact
been a development, but a development the continuity of which is most

---

must not suppose because the Apostle
(1 Cor. xii. 4) mentions the Spirit first,
and the Son second, and God the Father
third, that the order at the present day
has been quite reversed. For he made
his beginning from our end of the relation : for it is by receiving the gifts, that
we come in contact with the Distributor ;
then we come to consider the Sender ;
then we carry back our thought to the
Fount and Cause of the good things.' Cf.
xviii. 47 : 'The way of the knowledge
of God is from one Spirit, by the one
Son, to the one Father : and reversely,
the natural goodness of God, His holiness of nature, His royal rank taking
their rise from the Father, reach the
Spirit though the Only-begotten.'

[1] Ambrose, *de Spiritu Sancto*, i. 15,
172.

[2] So Irenaeus, Cyril of Jerusalem,
Athanasius, Basil, Didymus, Victorinus,
express the relation of the Divine Persons in Creation.

[3] Ps. xxxiii. 6; Gen. i. 2 ; Ps. civ.
29, 30.

[4] Huet. *Origeniana*, *L.* ii. *Qu.* 2. c.
xxvii. Cf. Athan. *Epp. ad Serapion.* i,
23–31 ; iv. 9–12.

[5] Gen. ii. 7.

apparent in that department in which man appears simply as the child of nature, the most perfect and interesting of her products, consciously adapting himself to his environment and moulded by it. This indeed has been so much the case that the facts of the history of civilization have been used, at least plausibly, as an argument against our race really possessing moral freedom at all. Such a use of the facts is, we recognise, not justifiable. It leaves out of consideration some of the most striking elements in human history, and some of the most certain facts in human consciousness. But the very plausibleness of the argument is suggestive. It means that comparatively very few men have been at pains to realize their true freedom ; that men in masses have been dominated by the mere forces of nature ; or, in other words, that human history presents broadly the record of a one-sided, a distorted development. For man was not meant for merely natural evolution, mere self-adaptation to the 'things that are seen.' The consciousness that he was meant for something higher has tinged his most brilliant physical successes, his greatest triumphs of civilization and art, with the bitterness of remorse, the misery of conscious lawlessness.

Our race was created for conscious fellowship with God, for sonship, for the life of spirit. And it is just in this department that its failure has been most conspicuous. It is here that the Divine Spirit has found His chiefest disappointment. Everywhere He has found rebellion— not everywhere without exception, for 'in every age entering into holy souls, He has made them sons of God and prophets': but everywhere in such a general sense that sin in fact and in its consequences covers the whole region of humanity. In the highest department of created life, where alone lawlessness was possible, because what was asked for was the co-operation of free service to carry out a freely accepted ideal[1],—there alone is the record of lawlessness, the record of the Spirit striving with man, but resisted, rejected, ignored, quenched. Thus the word, which in fact most forcibly characterizes man's spiritual history, so far as it has been according to the mind of God, is not progress, but recovery, or redemption. It is not natural but supernatural—supernatural, that is, in view of the false nature which man made for himself by excluding God. Otherwise the work of redemption is only the reconstitution of the nature which God designed. It is the recovery within the limits of a chosen race and by a deliberate process of limitation, of a state of things which had been intended to be universal[2]. The 'elect' represent not the special purpose of God for a few, but the universal purpose which under the circumstances can only be realized through a few. The hedging in of the few, the drawing of the lines so close, the method of exclusion again and again renewed all down the history of redemption, represents the love of the Divine

---

[1] Athan. *de Incarn.* xliii. 3.   [2] Athan. *l.c.* xii. 5, xliii. 4.

Spirit ever baffled in the mass, preserving the truth of God in a 'remnant,' an elect body; who themselves escaping the corruption which is in the world, become in their turn a fresh centre from which the restorative influence can flow out upon mankind. Rejected in the world, He secures for Himself a sphere of operations in the Jews, isolating Abraham, giving the law for a hedge, keeping alive in the nation the sense of its vocation by the inspiration of prophets. Again and again baffled in the body of the Jewish nation, He falls back upon the faithful remnant, and keeps alive in *them* that prospective sonship which was meant to be the vocation of the whole nation: sometimes in narrower, sometimes in broader channels, the purpose of love moves on till the Spirit finds in the Son of Man, the Anointed One, the perfect realization of the destiny of man, the manhood in which He can freely and fully work: 'He came down upon the Son of God, made son of man, accustoming Himself in His case to dwell in the human race, and to repose in man, and to dwell in God's creatures, working out in them the will of the Father, and recovering them from their old nature into the newness of Christ[1].' In Christ humanity is perfect, because in Him it retains no part of that false independence which, in all its manifold forms, is the secret of sin. In Christ humanity is perfect and complete, in ungrudging and unimpaired obedience to the movement of the Divine Spirit, Whose creation it was, Whose organ it gave itself to be. The Spirit anoints Him; the Spirit drives Him into the wilderness; the Spirit gives Him the law of His mission; in the power of the Spirit He works His miracles; in the Holy Spirit He lifts up the voice of human thankfulness to the Divine Father; in the Spirit He offers Himself without spot to God; in the power of the Spirit He is raised from the dead[2]. All that perfect human life had been a life of obedience, of progressive obedience, a gradual learning in each stage of experience what obedience meant[3]; it had been a life of obedience which became propitiatory as it bore loyally, submissively, lovingly, all the heritage of pain and misery in which sin in its long history had involved our manhood, all the agony of that insult and rejection in which sin revealed itself by antagonism to Him—bore it, and by bearing it turned it into the material of His accepted sacrifice. He was obedient unto death. And because He thus made our human nature the organ of a life of perfect obedience, therefore He can go on to make that same humanity, freed from all the limitations of this lower world and glorified in the Spirit at the right hand of God, at once the organ of

---

[1] Iren. *c. Hær.* iii. 17, 1.
[2] S. Mark i. 10, 12. S. Luke iv. 1, 18; x. 21. S. Matt. xii. 28. Heb. ix. 14. Rom. viii. 11. (These two last passages at least imply the action of the Holy Spirit in the Sacrifice and Resurrection of Christ.
[3] Heb. v. 7-10. Phil. ii. 8.

Divine supremacy over the universe of created things, and (itself become quickening Spirit[1]) the fount to all the sons of obedience and faith of its own life. Christ is the second Adam, who having 'recapitulated the long development of humanity into Himself[2],' taken up into Himself, that is, and healed its wounds and fructified its barrenness, gives it a fresh start by a new birth from Him. The Spirit coming forth at Pentecost out of His uplifted manhood, as from a glorious fountain of new life[3], perpetuates all its richness, its power, its fulness in the organized society which He prepared and built for the Spirit's habitation. The Church, His Spirit-bearing body, comes forth into the world, not as the exclusive sphere of the Spirit's operations, for 'that breath bloweth where it listeth[4];' but as the special and covenanted sphere of His regular and uniform operation, the place where He is pledged to dwell and to work; the centre marked out and hedged in, whence ever and again proceeds forth anew the work of human recovery; the home where, in spite of sin and imperfection, is ever kept alive the picture of what the Christian life is, that is, of what common human life is meant to be and can become.

Of the work of the Holy Spirit in the Church we may note four characteristics.

1. It is *social*. It treats man as a 'social being,' who cannot realize himself in isolation. For no other reason than because grace is the restoration of nature[5], the true, the redeemed humanity, is presented to us as a society or Church. This is apparent with reference to either of the gifts which summarize the essence of the Church's life, grace, or truth. Sacraments are the ordained instruments of grace, and sacraments are in one of their aspects *social* ceremonies—of incorporation, or restoration, or bestowal of authority, or fraternal sharing of the bread of life. They presuppose a social organization. Those who have attempted to explain why there should be in the Church an apostolic succession of ministers, have seen the grounds of such appointment in the necessity for preserving in a catholic society, which lacks the natural links of race or language or common habitation, a visible and obligatory bond of association[6].

The same fact appears in reference to the truth, the knowledge of God and of the true nature and needs of man, which constitutes one main part of the Christian life. That too is no mere individual

[1] 1 Cor. xv. 45, 'The last Adam became a life-giving Spirit.' S. John vi. 63, 'Spirit and Life.'
[2] Iren. iii. 18, 1, and frequently elsewhere.
[3] Iren. iii. 24, 1. Cf. H. C. G. Moule's *Veni Creator*, pp. 39-40.
[4] S. John iii. 4. The intention of this passage is to express not that the Spirit is lawless in His operations, but that He is beyond our control.
[5] Aug. *de Spiritu et Littera*, xxvii. 47, 'Grace is not the negation of nature, but its restoration.'
[6] Raymund of Sabunde, *Theol. Nat.* tit. 303.

illumination. It is 'a rule of faith,' an 'apostolic tradition,' 'a pattern of sound words,' embodied in Holy Scripture and perpetuated in a teaching Church, within the scope of which each individual is to be brought to have his mind and conscience fashioned by it, normally from earliest years. It would be going beyond the province of this essay to stop to prove that from the beginnings of the Christian life, a man was understood to become a Christian and receive the benefits of redemption, by no other means than incorporation into the Christian society.

2. But none the less on account of this social method *the Spirit nourishes individuality.* The very idea of the Spirit's gift is that of an intenser life. Intenser life is more individualized life, for our life becomes richer and fuller only by the intensification of personality and character. Thus Christianity has always trusted to strongly marked character as the means by which religion is propagated. It does not advance as an abstract doctrine, but by the subtle, penetrating influences of personality. It is the illuminated man who becomes a centre of illumination. 'As clear transparent bodies if a ray of light fall on them become radiant themselves and diffuse their splendour all around, so souls illuminated by the indwelling Spirit are rendered spiritual themselves and impart their grace to others [1].' Thus, from the first, Christianity has tended to intensify individual life in a thousand ways, and has gloried in the varieties of disposition and character which the full life of the Spirit develops. The Church expects to see the same variety of life in herself as she witnesses in Nature.

'One and the same rain,' says S. Cyril of Jerusalem to his cate-chumens, 'comes down upon all the world, yet it becomes white in the lily, and red in the rose, and purple in the violets and pansies, and different and various in all the several kinds; it is one thing in the palm tree and another in the vine, and all in all things. In itself, indeed, it is uniform and changes not, but by adapting itself to the nature of each thing that receives it, it becomes what is appropriate to each. Thus also the Holy Ghost, one and uniform and undivided in Himself, distributes His grace to every man as He wills. He employs the tongue of one man for wisdom; the soul of another He enlightens by prophecy; to another He gives power to drive away devils; to another He gives to interpret the Divine Scriptures; He invigorates one man's self-command; He teaches another the way to give alms; another He teaches to fast and train himself; another He trains for martyrdom; diverse to different men, yet not diverse from Himself [2].'

---

[1] Basil, *de Spiritu Sancto* ix. 23 (Lewis' translation). Cf. Newman's *Univ. Sermons*, 'Personal Influence the means of propagating the truth.'

[2] Cyril, *Catech.* xvi. 12. The attention to the differences of individual

Nor was this belief in the differences of the Spirit's work a mere abstract theory. In fact the Church life of the early centuries did present an aspect of great variety: not only in the dispositions of individuals, for that will always be observable where human nature is allowed to subsist, but in the types of life and thought cultivated in different parts of the Church. Early in the life of Christianity did something like the Roman type of Catholicism shew itself, but it shewed itself as one among several types of ecclesiasticism, easily distinguishable from what Alexandria or Africa or Antioch nourished and produced.

And what is true in the life of religion as a whole is true in the department of the intellect. Here again the authority of the collective society, the 'rule of faith,' is meant to nourish and quicken, not to crush, individuality. Each individual Christian owes the profoundest deference to the common tradition. Thus to 'keep the traditions' is at all times, and not least in Scripture, a common Christian exhortation. But this common tradition is not meant to be a merely external law. It is meant to pass by the ordinary processes of education into the individual consciousness, and there, because it represents truth, to impart freedom. Thus S. Paul speaks of the developed Christian, 'the man who is spiritual,' as 'judging all things and himself judged of none.' And S. John makes the ground of Christian certainty to lie not in an external authority, but in a personal gift: 'ye have an unction from the Holy One and ye know all things;' 'ye need not that any one teach you[1].' There is then an individual 'inspiration[2],' as well as an inspiration of the whole body, only this inspiration is not barely individual or separatist. As it proceeds out of the society, so it ends in it. It ends by making each person more individualized, more developed in personal characteristics, but for that very reason more conscious of his own incompleteness, more ready to recognise himself as only one member of the perfect Manhood.

The idea of authority is in fact a perfectly simple one. It never received better expression than by Plato when he describes it as the function of the society by a carefully regulated education to implant right instincts, right affections and antipathies, in the growing mind of the child, at a time when he cannot know the reason of things: in order that as the mind develops it may recognise the right reason of things by a certain inner kinship, and welcome truth as a friend[3]. Authority, according to such a view of it, is a necessary schooling of

---

character is very noticeable in S. Basil's monastic rule: see the *Regulae fusius tractatae,* resp. 19, and the *Constit. Monast.* 4. Also in the writings of Gregory of Nazianzus, Chrysostom, and Gregory the Great *on the Pastoral Office.*

[1] 1 Cor. ii. 15. 1 S. John ii. 20–27.
[2] Clement Alex. *Strom.* v. 13. 88.
[3] *Republic,* 401 D, 402 A.

the individual temperament. Thus, we are told that in the judgment of the philosopher Hegel, 'The basis of sound education was . . the submission of the mind to an external lesson, which must be learnt by every one, and even learnt by rote, with utter disregard of individual tastes and desires ; only out of this self-abnegation, and submission to be guided and taught, could any originality spring which was worth preserving[1].' In fact, we all recognise the necessity for such external discipline in all departments. Few people like good art, for instance, at first. Probably they are attracted by what is weak but arrests attention by obvious and superficial merits. The standards which artistic authority has erected, the accepted canons of good taste and judgment, do not commend themselves at first as right or natural. But modest and well-disposed people take it for granted at starting that the orthodox judgment will turn out to be right ; and they set themselves to school to learn why the artists and poets of great name are great, till their own judgment becomes enlightened, and they understand what at first they took on trust. It was the instinctive perception of this function of authority which made the Church insist so much on the principle 'credo ut intelligam.' The Creed represents the catholic judgment, the highest knowledge of God and the spiritual life granted to man by the Divine Revelation. Let a man put himself to school in the Church with reverence and godly fear, and his own judgment will become enlightened. He will come to say with S. Anselm, 'I give thee thanks, good Lord ; because what first I believed by Thy gift, I now understand by Thy illumination[2].'

Such an idea of authority leaves much for the individual to do. It is the reaction of the individual on the society which is to keep the common tradition pure and unnarrowed. The Church has in Holy Scripture the highest expression of the mind of Christ. The familiarity of all its members with this flawless and catholic image is to ward off in each generation that tendency to deteriorate and to become materialised which belongs to all 'traditions.' The individual illumination is thus to react as a purifying force upon the common mind of the Christian society. The individual Christian is to pay the debt of his education, by himself 'testing all things and holding fast that which is good.' Specially gifted individuals from time to time will be needed to effect more or less sudden 'reversions to type,' to the undying type of apostolic teaching[3]. But such a true reformer is quite distinct in

[1] Caird's *Hegel* (Blackwood's Philosophical Classics), p. 72.

[2] Anselm, *Proslog.* 4 ; he adds, 'So that even if I were unwilling to *believe* that Thou art, I could not cease to understand it.' But the whole relation of authority and reason is most completely grasped and stated by S. Augustine : see Cunningham, *S. Austin* (Cambridge Univ. Press, 1886), pp. 9, 157 ff.

[3] Dr. Salmon, *Infallibility*, p. 115, has a clever comparison of the authority

idea from the heretic. He reforms; he does not innovate. His note is to restore; not to reject. And the absence of necessity for fundamental rejection comes from this simple fact, that the Christian Creed is rational and true. If any man comes to us and says that he has studied and assimilated the Christian Creed with all the care and reverence in his ability, and has rejected it because he finds it irrational and false, we cannot complain of him[1]. We cannot ask him to accept it though he thinks it false. We do not at all complain of his having inquired and thought freely—only we venture to assure him, with a confidence which can hardly fail to be irritating, because it is confident, that he is mistaken, that he has thought not only freely, but erroneously. When Christianity adopts, as in the modern Romanist system, a different tone, proscribing free inquiry as 'rationalistic,' and making the appeal to antiquity, in order to test the present teaching of the Church, a 'treason and a heresy[2],' it is abjuring its own rational heritage, and adopting a method which Charles Kingsley had good reason to call Manichaean. It is the test of the Church's legitimate tenure that she can encourage free inquiry into her title-deeds.

3. Thirdly, the Spirit claims for His own, and *consecrates the whole of nature.* One Spirit was the original author of all that is; and all that exists is in its essence very good. It is only sin which has produced the appearance of antagonism between the Divine operation and human freedom, or between the spiritual and the material. Thus the humanity of Christ, which is the Spirit's perfect work, exhibits in its perfection how every faculty of human nature, spiritual and physical, is enriched and vitalized, not annihilated, by the closest conceivable interaction of the Divine Energy. This principle, as carried out in the Church, occupies a prominent place in the earliest theology; in part because Montanism, with its pagan idea of inspiration, as an ecstasy which deprived its subject of reason, gave the Church an opportunity of emphasizing that the fullest action of the Spirit, in the case of her inspired men, intensified and did not supersede their own thought, judgment, and individuality; still more because Gnostic dualism, turning every antithesis of nature and grace, of spirit and flesh, of natural and supernatural, into an antagonism, forced upon the Church the assertion of her own true and comprehensive Creed. That every-

---

of the Church to that of the town clock. The value we assign to having such an authoritative standard of the right time does not prevent our recognising the importance of having it regulated. 'And if we desired to remove an error which had accumulated during a long season of neglect, it would be very unfair to represent us as wishing to silence the clock, or else as wishing to allow every townsman to get up and push the hands backwards and forwards as he pleased.'

[1] But cf. pp. 143–5, 167–9, 189–190.

[2] Manning, *Temporal Mission of the Holy Ghost,* third edit. pp. 9, 29, 238–240.

thing in Christianity is realized 'in flesh as in spirit' is the constantly reiterated cry of S. Ignatius, who of all men was most 'spiritual.' That the spiritual is not the immaterial, that we become spiritual not by any change or curtailment of nature, not by any depreciation or ignoring of the body, is the constantly asserted principle of S. Irenaeus[1]. And the earliest writers in general emphasize the visible organization of the Church, and the institution of external sacraments, as negations of the false principle which would sunder nature from God, and repudiate the unity of the material and the spiritual which the Word had been made Flesh in order to reveal and to perpetuate.

4. But the unity of the spirit and the flesh, of faith and experience, of God and the world, is certainly not an accomplished fact. On the contrary, dualism is always making appeals which strike home to our present experience. Thus if the Church was to maintain the unity of all things, it could only be by laying great stress upon the ravages which sin had wrought, and upon *the gradualness of the Spirit's method* in recovery. The Old Testament, for example, presented a most unspiritual appearance. Its material sacrifices, its low standard of morals, its worldliness, were constantly being objected to by the Gnostic and Manichaean sects, who could not tolerate the Old Testament canon. 'But you are ignoring,' the Church replied, 'the gradualness of the Spirit's method.' He lifts man by little and little, He condescends to man's infirmity : He puts up with him as he is, if only He can at the last bring him back to God.

It is of the essence of the New Testament, as the religion of the Incarnation, to be final and catholic : on the other hand, it is of the essence of the Old Testament to be imperfect because it represents a gradual process of education by which man was lifted out of depths of sin and ignorance. That this is the case, and that in consequence the justification of the Old Testament method lies not in itself at any particular stage, but in its result taken as a whole, is a thought very familiar to modern Christians[2]. But it is important to make plain that it was a thought equally familiar to the Fathers of the Christian

---

[1] See, for instance, *c. Haer.* v. 10, 2. 'The wild olive does not change its substance [when it is grafted in, see Rom. xi. 17], but only the quality of its fruit, and takes a new name, no longer being called an oleaster but an olive ; so also man when he is by faith grafted in, and receives the Spirit of God, does not lose his fleshly substance, but changes the quality of the works which are his fruits, and takes another name indicating his improved condition, and is no longer described as flesh and blood, but as a spiritual man.' So also v. 6, 1, 'whom the apostle calls "spiritual" because they have the Spirit, not because they have been robbed of the flesh and become bare spirit.' It is the recognition of this principle that makes most of the language of the Fathers on fasting so healthy and sensible. The end of fasting is not to destroy the flesh, but to free the spirit.

[2] See especially Mozley's *Lectures on the Old Testament*, x. : 'The end the test of progressive revelation.'

Church. Thus S. Gregory of Nazianzus, speaking of God's dealings with the Jews of old, describes how, in order to gain the co-operation of man's good will in working for his recovery, He dealt 'after the manner of a schoolmaster or a physician, and while curtailing part of their ancestral customs, tolerated the rest, making some concession to their tastes, just as physicians make their medicines palatable that they may be taken by their patients. For men do not easily abandon what long custom has consecrated. Thus the first law, while it abolished their idols, tolerated their sacrifices; the second, while it abolished their sacrifices, allowed them to be circumcised : then when once they had accepted the removal of what was taken from them, they went further and gave up what had been conceded to them—in the first case their sacrifices, in the second their practice of circumcision—and they became instead of heathens, Jews, instead of Jews, Christians, being betrayed as it were by gradual changes into acceptance of the Gospel[1].' Again, S. Chrysostom explains how it is the very merit of the Old Testament that it has taught us to think things intolerable, which under it were tolerated. 'Do not ask,' he says, 'how these (Old Testament precepts) can be good, now when the need for them is past : ask how they were good when the period required them. Or rather, if you wish, do inquire into their merit even now. It is still conspicuous, and lies in nothing so much as what now enables us to find fault with them. Their highest praise is that we now see them to be defective. If they had not trained us well, so that we became susceptible of higher things, we should not have now seen their deficiency.' Then he shews how under the old law swearing by the true God was allowed to avoid swearing by idols, the worse ill. 'But is not swearing at all of the evil one?' he asks. 'Undoubtedly, now, after this long course of training, but then not. And how can the same thing be good at one time and bad at another? I ask rather, how should it not be so, when we have regard to the plain teaching of the fact of growth in all things, fruits of the earth or acquirements of man ? Look at man's own nature ; the food, the occupations which suit his infancy, are repulsive to his manhood. Or consider facts of history. All agree that murder is an invention of Satan, yet this very act at a suitable time made Phineas to be honoured with the high priesthood. Phineas' murder "was reckoned to him for righteousness." Just in the same way Abraham obtained an even higher

---

[1] Greg. Naz. *Orat.* xxxi. 25. Many of the greatest of the ancient Christian writers depreciate the sacrificial law as a mere concession, made to avoid worse things, when the incident of the calf shewed that the first legislation of the Ten Commandments was too spiritual : so Jerome *in Isai.* i, 12, *In Jer.* vii. 21. Cf. Justin, *Trypho* 19. Chrys. *adv. Jud.* iv. 6. Epiphan. *Haer.* lxvi. 71. *Constt. ap.* i. 6 ; vi. 20. This method of interpretation is perhaps derived from the Epistle of Barnabas, 2-4.

honour for being not a murderer only but what was much worse, a child-murderer. We must not then look at the facts in themselves only, but investigate with attention the period also, the cause, the motive, the difference of persons, and all the attendant circumstances : so only can one get at the truth[1].'

Once more S. Basil : ' Surely it is absolutely infantile and worthy of a child who must be really fed on milk, to be ignorant of the great mystery of our salvation—that just as we received our earliest instruction, so, in exercising unto godliness and going on unto perfection, we were first trained by lessons easy to apprehend and suited to our intelligence. He Who regulates our lives deals with us as those who have been reared in darkness, and gradually accustoms our eyes to the light of truth. For He spares our weakness, and in the depth of the riches of His wisdom and the unsearchable judgments of His understanding adopts this gentle treatment, so well adapted to our needs, accustoming us first to see the shadow of objects, and to look at the sun's reflection in water, so that we may not be suddenly blinded by the exposure to the pure light. By parity of reasoning, the law being a shadow of things to come, and the typical teaching of the prophets, which is the truth darkly, have been devised as exercises for the eyes of the heart, inasmuch as it will be easy for us to pass from these to wisdom hidden in mystery[2].'

In the same spirit was the Church's answer to the difficulties which facts of personal experience were constantly putting in the way of her claims. Churchmen were frequently seen to be vulgar, ignorant, imperfect, sinful. If, in spite of manifold evils existing within her, the Church could still appeal to her fruits, it must be by comparison with what was to be found elsewhere, or by taking in a large area for comparison, or by appealing to her special grounds of hope. In fact, what she represented was a hope, not a realization ; a tendency, not a result ; a life in process, not a ripened fruit. But then she claimed that this was God's way. ' He loves us not as we are, but as we are becoming[3].' Let but a man once lay hold of the life-giving principle of faith, and God sets a value on him, life has a promise for him, altogether out of proportion to present attainments. For God estimates him, in view of all the forces of a new life which are set loose to work upon him, and he can assure himself that the movement of recovery which he has begun to feel stirring within him will carry him on through eternal ages, beyond what he can ask or think.

---

[1] Chrys. *in Matth. Homil.* xvii. 5-6 (slightly abbreviated). Cf. *Libell. Faustin. et Marcellin.* in *Bibl. Vet. Patrum.* tom. v. 657 d.

[2] *On the Holy Spirit,* xiv. 33 (Lewis' trans.).

[3] Aug. *de Trin.* i. 10, 21. This principle alone gives a basis for the doctrine of ' imputation' so far as it is true. God deals with us, e.g. in absolution, by anticipation of what is to come about in us, in Christ.

It is because of this gradualness of the Spirit's method that it lays so great a strain on human patience. The spiritually-minded of all ages have tended to find the visible Church a very troubled and imperfect home. Most startling disclosures of the actual state of ecclesiastical disorder and moral collapse, may be gathered out of the Christian Fathers. Thus to found a 'pure Church' has been the instinct of impatient zeal since Tertullian's day. But the instinct has to be restrained, the visible Church has to be borne with, because it is the Spirit's purpose to provide a home for the training and improvement of the imperfect. 'Let both grow together unto the harvest.' 'A bruised reed will He not break, and smoking flax will He not quench.' The Church must have her terms of communion, moral and intellectual: this is essential to keep her fundamental principles intact, and to prevent her betraying her secret springs of strength and recovery. But short of this necessity she is tolerant. It is her note to be tolerant, morally and theologically. She is the mother, not the magistrate. No doubt her balanced duty is one difficult to fulfil. At times she has been puritanical, at others morally lax; at times doctrinally lax, at others rigid. But however well or ill she has fulfilled the obligations laid on her, this is her ideal. She is the guardian, the depository of a great gift, a mighty presence, which in its essence is unchanging and perfect, but is realized very imperfectly in her experience and manifested life. This is what S. Thomas Aquinas means when he says 'that to believe *in* the Church is only possible if we mean by it to believe in the Spirit vivifying the Church[1].' The true self of the Church is the Holy Spirit, but a great deal in the Church at any date does not belong to her true self, and is obscuring the Spirit's mind. Thus the treasure is in earthen vessels, it is sometimes a light hid under a bushel; and the Church is the probation of faith, as well as its encouragement.

It will not be out of place to conclude this review of the Spirit's method in the Church by calling attention to the emphasis which, from the first, Christians laid upon the fact that the animating principle both of their individual lives and of their society as a whole, was nothing less than the Holy Spirit Himself. To know Him was (as against all the philosophical schools, and in a sense in which the same could not be said even of the Divine Word) their peculiar privilege, to possess Him their summary characteristic. Under the old covenant, and in all the various avenues of approach to the Church, men could be the subjects of the Spirit's guidance and could be receiving gifts from Him; but the 'initiated' Christian, baptized and confirmed, possessed not merely His gifts but Himself. He is in the Church, as the 'Vicar of Christ,' in Whose presence Christ Himself is with them.

[1] Thom. Aq. *Summa Theol.* pars sec. sec. Qu. 1. Art. ix.

He is the consecrator of every sacrament, and the substance of His own sacramental gifts. The services of ordained men indeed are required for the administration of sacraments, but as ministers simply of a Power higher than themselves, of a Personal Spirit Who indeed is invoked by their ministry, and pledges Himself to respond to their invocations, but never subjects Himself to their power. Therefore the unworthiness of the minister diminishes in no way the efficacy of the sacrament, or the reality of the gift given, because the ministry of men neither creates the gift nor adds to or diminishes its force. He is the giver of the gift, and the gift He gives is the same to all. Only the meagreness of human faith and love restrains the largeness of His bounty and conditions the Thing received by the narrowness and variability of the faculty which receives it. According to our faith is it done to us, and where there is no faith and no love there the grace is equally, in S. Augustine's phrase, present and profitless [1].

II. In something of this way the early Christian writers—and it has seemed better to let them speak for us—teach the doctrine of the Holy Spirit. What they teach is grounded in part on actual experience, in part on the revelation of the being and action of God made once for all in the Person of Jesus Christ and recorded in the New Testament. On this mingled basis of experience and Holy Scripture they passed back from the doctrine of the Holy Spirit as He is operative in the world, to the Theology of His Person. They passed back but slowly, with great hesitation, even unwillingness. Nothing, we may say, was further removed from the Fathers than the easy-going assumption that because we are the subjects of a revelation, therefore we are able to speculate with tolerably complete information about the mysteries which lie beyond experience. The truth that 'we know in part,' we see 'in a glass darkly,' was profoundly impressed upon their minds. God manifested Himself, S. Gregory of Nazianzus tells, in such a way as to escape the nets of our syllogisms, and to shew Himself superior to our logical distinctions. If we expect to find our logic equal to express Him, we shew only our mad presumption, 'we who are not able even to know what lies at our feet, or to count the waves of the

---

[1] The above paragraph is a summary of expressions constantly met with in the Fathers. It is S. Ambrose who protests against the idea that the priest can be spoken of as having power over the Divine Things which he ministers, see *De Spiritu Sancto*, praef. 18, lib. i. 11, 118 : 'nostra sunt servitia sed tua sacramenta. Neque enim humanae opis est divina conferre.' S. Augustine, among others, draws the distinction between gifts from the Spirit and the gift of Himself. *Ep.* cxciv. : 'aliter adiuvat nondum inhabitans, aliter inhabitans : nam nondum inhabitans adiuvat ut sint fideles, inhabitans adiuvat iam fideles.' Didymus, *de Spiritu Sancto* 15, calls attention to the distinction in the New Testament between πνεῦμα (without the article) i.e. 'a spiritual gift,' and τὸ πνεῦμα, i.e. the Spirit Himself : cf. Westcott on S. John vii. 39.

sea, or the drops of rain, or the days of the world, much less to fathom the depths of God, and give account of His nature which transcends alike our reason and our power of expression [1].' Besides this, the early theologians realized the obligation of keeping to Holy Scripture —of not being wise 'above that which is written'—and they were conscious of the danger of building on isolated texts of Scripture or of treating its 'simple and untechnical' language as if it was the language of a formal treatise [2].

For these reasons they were cautious in theological speculation. Yet the facts and relationships introduced into the world of experience by the revelation of the Son represent eternal realities, if under great limitations yet still truly, and thus make possible a real security up to a certain point on what lies beyond the unassisted human knowledge. Thus, first, when the Arian movement passed from the denial of the true Godhead of Christ to a similar position with reference to the Holy Spirit, the Christian Church felt itself fully justified alike by its past traditions [3], and by its Scriptures, in emphasizing the personal distinctness and the true Godhead of the Holy Spirit. Unless all Christ's language was an illusion, the Holy Spirit was really personal and really distinct from Himself and the Father; nor could One who was associated with the Father and the Son in all the essentially Divine operations of nature and grace, be less than truly and really God, an essential element in the Eternal Being. The Arian controversy in its earlier stages had disposed of the notion that Christian theology could at any cost admit the conception of a created personality, clothed with Divine attributes and exercising Divine functions.

Secondly, the consideration that the relations manifested in the Incarnation in terms of our experience between the Father, the Son, and the Holy Ghost, express transcendent and eternal relations, led the Church to speak of the Holy Ghost as proceeding from the Father, as the unique fount of Godhead, through the Son: or in somewhat less nicely discriminated language 'from the Father and the Son [4].' In the fifth century there is a tendency to use in the East the former, in the West the latter mode of expression, but without any essential difference. Nor can it be said that the causes which were at work later to divide the Eastern and the Western Churches on the subject of the procession of the Holy Ghost, were so much really theological as ecclesiastical and political.

Thirdly, the accurate consideration of the language in which is

---

[1] Greg. Naz. *Orat.* xxxi. 8.
[2] See Athan. *Epp. ad Serapion.* i. 17. Cyril Hieros. *Cat.* xvi. 24. Iren. v. 13, 2. Basil, *de Spiritu Sancto*, iii. 5.

[3] The *Dict. of Chr. Biog.*, Art. HOLY GHOST (by Dr. Swete), has an admirable summary of the theology of the subject.
[4] See Godet on S. John xv. 26, 27.

expressed the relation of Christ to the Holy Spirit, helped the Church to guard the doctrine of the Trinity from the associations of Tritheism. For the coming of the Holy Spirit is clearly spoken of in Holy Scripture as coincident with and involving the coming of Christ. 'While we are illuminated by the Holy Spirit, it is Christ who illuminates us : when we drink in the Spirit, it is Christ we drink.' The Spirit is distinct from Christ—'another Paraclete'—yet in His coming, Christ comes : in His indwelling is the indwelling of the Father and the Son [1]. How can this be ? Because the 'Persons' of the Holy Trinity are not to be thought of as distinct individuals, as three Gods. No doubt in our ordinary language, persons are understood to be separate, and mutually exclusive beings. Even in regard to ourselves deeper reflection shews us that our personalities are very far from being as separate as they appear to be on the surface : and with regard to God, it was only with an expressed apology for the imperfection of human language that the Church spoke of the Divine Three, as Three *Persons* at all. But 'we have no celestial language,' and the word is the only one which will express what Christ's language implies about Himself, the Father, and the Spirit. Only while we use it, it must be understood to express mutual inclusion, not mutual exclusion.

Wherever the Father works, He works essentially and inevitably through the Son and the Spirit ; whenever the Son acts, He acts from the Father by the Holy Spirit ; whenever the Holy Spirit comes, He brings with Him in His coming the Son and the Father. Thus when an image was necessary to interpret in part the Divine relationships, the Fathers sought it nowhere so much as in the three distinct yet inseparable elements of man's spiritual nature ; the triune character of which Plato had already brought into notice, and which is in fact an earthly image, however inadequate, of the Triune God [2].

---

[1] Athan. *Epp. ad Serap.* i. 19. S. John xiv. 16, 18, 23.

[2] Plato's human trinity is made up of reason, spirit [θυμός], and desire : S. Augustine's of memory (i. e. personal identity), reason, and will ; or mind, knowledge, and love. Nothing has been said in the text of Patristic and more recent attempts to express the function of the Holy Spirit in the inner relations of the Trinity. Some of the Fathers speak of the Holy Spirit as completing the circle of the Divine Life, or as 'the return of God upon Himself,' 'the bond of the Father and the Son.' This eternal function would interpret His temporal mission to bring all creatures back into union with God. Not very differently S. Augustine speaks of Him as the Love of the Father and the Son : 'Vides Trini-tatem si caritatem vides. Ecce tria sunt ; amans et quod amatur et amor.' And this Love is itself personal and co-ordinate : 'commune aliquid est Patris et Filii ; at ipsa communio consubstantialis et coaeterna.' But in such speculation they allow themselves with much reserve and expression of unwillingness.

In fact it is easy to see that an eternally living God, knowing and loving, must be a God Whose Being involves eternal relationships. Knowledge involves a relation of subject and object : to make love possible there must be a lover and a loved. It is more difficult to see how a perfect relationship must be threefold ; but there are true lines of thought which lead up to this, such, for instance, as make us see first in the family, the type of complete life. Love

III. Hitherto nothing has been said about that part of the Holy Spirit's work which is called the inspiration of Scripture. It has been kept to the last because of the great importance of putting it in context with less familiar truths. The Scriptures have, it is a commonplace to say, suffered greatly from being isolated. This is as true whether we are considering them as a source of evidence or as the sphere of inspiration.

As a source of evidence they contain the record of historical facts with some of which at any rate the Creed of Christendom is inseparably interwoven. Thus it is impossible for Christians who know what they are about, to depreciate the importance of the historical evidence for those facts at least of which the Creed contains a summary. But the tendency with books of historical evidence has been, at least till recently, to exaggerate the extent to which the mere evidence of remote facts can compel belief. What we should make of the New Testament record, what estimate we should be able to form of the Person of Jesus Christ and the meaning of His life and work, if it was contained simply in some old manuscripts, or unearthed in some way by antiquaries out of the Syrian sand, it is impossible to say. In order to have grounds for believing the facts, in order to be susceptible of their evidence, we require an antecedent state of conception and expectation. A whole set of presuppositions about God, about the slavery of sin, about the reasonableness of redemption, must be present with us. So only can the facts presented to us in the Gospel come to us as credible things, or as parts of an intelligible universe, correlated elements in a rational whole. Now the work of the Spirit in the Church has been to keep alive and real these presuppositions, this frame of mind. He convinces of sin, of righteousness, of judgment. He does this not merely in isolated individuals however numerous, but in an organized continuous society. The spiritual life of the Church assures me that in desiring union with God, in feeling the burden of sin, in hungering for redemption, I am not doing an eccentric, abnormal thing. I am doing only what belongs to the best and richest movement of humanity. More than this, it assures me that assent to the claims and promises of Jesus Christ satisfies these spiritual needs in such a way as to produce the strongest, the most lasting, the most catholic sort of human character. The historical life of the Church thus in every age 'setting to its seal' that God's

which is only a relation of two, is selfish or unsatisfied: it demands an object and a product of mutual love. See especially Richard of S. Victor, *de Trin.* Pars i. lib. iii. cc. 14, 15 : ' Communio amoris non potest esse omnino minus quam in tribus personis. Nihil autem (ut dictum est) gloriosius, nihil magnificentius, quam quicquid habes utile et dulce *in com-* *mune deducere* : . . . . hujusmodi dulcedinis delicias solus non possidet qui in exhibita sibi dilectione socium *et condilectum* non habet ; quamdiu *condilectum* non habet, praecipui gaudii communione caret.' See also Sartorius, *Doctrine of Divine Love* (Clark's Foreign Theol. Libr.), p. 16.

offer in Christ is true, reproduces the original 'witness,' commends it to conscience and reason, spans the gulf of the ages, and brings down remote and alien incidents into close and intelligible familiarity. Lotze speaks of revelation as 'either contained in some divine act of historic occurrence, or continually repeated in men's hearts [1].' But in fact the antithesis is not an alternative. The strength of the Christian Creed is that it is both. It is a revelation continuously renewed in men's hearts by an organized and systematic operation of the Spirit in the Church, while at the same time it finds its guarantee and security in certain Divine acts of historic occurrence.

Once more, the belief in the Holy Scriptures as inspired requires to be held in context by the belief in the general action of the Holy Spirit upon the Christian society and the individual soul. It is, we may perhaps say, becoming more and more difficult to believe in the Bible without believing in the Church. The Apostles, indeed,—and the New Testament canon consists largely of the words of Apostles—have an authority which, reasonably considered, is unique, and stands by itself as that of the accredited witnesses of Christ; but when we find them appealing to members of the Church, they appeal not as the possessors of an absolute authority or of a Spirit in which others do not share. They are the ministers of a 'tradition' to which they themselves are subject, a tradition 'once for all delivered [2]:' they appeal to those who hear them as men 'who have an unction from the Holy One and know all things.' The tone in fact of the apostolic writers forces us to regard the spirit in which the Church lives, as co-operating with, and in a real sense limiting, the spirit in which they themselves speak and write. Thus in fact the apostolic writings were written as occasion required, within the Church, and for the Church. They presuppose membership in it and familiarity with its tradition. They are secondary, not primary, instructors; for edification, not for initiation. Nor, in fact, can a hard and fast line be drawn between what lies within and what lies without the canon. For example, Protestantism of an unecclesiastical sort has built upon the Epistle to the Hebrews as much as upon any book of the New Testament. This book is of unknown authorship. If 'Pauline' it is pretty certainly not S. Paul's. In large part it is the judgment of the Church which enables us to draw a line between it and S. Clement's 'scripture.' The line indeed our own judgment approves. The Epistle to the Hebrews and S. Clement's letter are closely linked together, but the latter depends on the former: it is secondary and the other is primary. Yet how narrow is the historical interval between them. How impossible to tear the one from the other. How seemingly irrational to attribute absolute authority to the anonymous

[1] *Microcosmus*, B. ix. C. iv. (E. T. vol. ii. p. 660.)
[2] See especially Gal. i. 8, 9.

Epistle to the Hebrews which represents apostolic teaching at second hand[1], and then to interpret it in a sense hostile to the Epistle of Clement, which represents exactly the same stream of apostolic teaching only one short stage lower down. For Clement interprets the high priesthood of Christ in a sense which, instead of excluding, makes it the basis of, the ministerial hierarchy of the Church. Or to put the matter more broadly, how irrational it is, considering the intimate links by which the New Testament canon is bound up with the historic Church, not to accept the mind of the Church, especially when we have its consent down independent lines of tradition, as interpreting the mind of the apostolic writers. Most rational surely is the attitude of the early Church towards Scripture. The Scripture was regarded as the highest utterance of the Spirit, the unique and constant test of the Church's life and teaching. But the Spirit in the Church interpreted the meaning of Scripture. Thus the Church taught and the Scripture tested and verified or corrected her teaching : and this because all was of one piece, the life of the Church including the Scriptures, the inspired writers themselves appealing to the Spirit in the Churches[2].

And now, what is to be said about this, at present, much controverted subject of the inspiration of Holy Scripture? What does the doctrine imply, and what attitude does belief in it involve towards the modern critical treatment of the inspired literature?

1. Let us bear carefully in mind the place which the doctrine holds in the building up of a Christian faith. It is in fact an important part of the superstructure, but it is not among the *bases* of the Christian belief. The Christian creed asserts the reality of certain historical facts. To these facts, in the Church's name, we claim assent : but we do so on grounds which, so far, are quite independent of the *inspiration* of the evangelic records. All that we claim to shew at this stage is that they are historical : not historical so as to be absolutely without error, but historical in the general sense, so as to be trustworthy. All that is necessary for faith in Christ is to be found in the moral dispositions which predispose to belief, and make intelligible and credible the thing to be believed : coupled with such acceptance of the generally historical character of the Gospels, and of the trustworthiness of the other apostolic documents, as justifies belief that our Lord was actually born of the Virgin Mary, manifested as the Son of God 'with power according to a spirit of holiness,' crucified, raised again the third day from the dead, exalted to the right hand of the Father, the founder of the Church and the source to it of the informing Spirit.

---

[1] Heb. ii. 3.
[2] See further on the fatal results of separating the Spirit's work in Scripture, from His work in the Church, Coleridge, *Remains* iii. 93, iv. 118 ; or quoted by Hare, *Mission of the Comforter*, Note H. vol. ii. pp. 468, 474.

In all this no claim is made for any special belief as to the method of the Spirit's work in the Scripture or in the Church. Logically such belief follows, does not precede, belief in Christ. Indeed, in the past, Christian apologists have made a great mistake in allowing opponents to advance as objections against the historical character of the Gospel narrative, what are really objections not against its historical character —not such as could tell against the substantially historical character of secular documents—but against a certain view of the meaning of inspiration. Let it be laid down then that Christianity brings with it indeed a doctrine of the inspiration of Holy Scriptures, but is not based upon it [1].

2. But such a doctrine it does bring with it. Our Lord and His Apostles are clearly found to believe and to teach that the Scriptures of the Old Testament were given by inspiration of God ; and the Christian Church from the earliest days postulated the same belief about the Scriptures of the New Testament. To disbelieve that 'the Scriptures were spoken by the Holy Ghost,' was equivalent to being 'an unbeliever [2].'

Thus, when once a man finds himself a believer in Christ, he will find himself in a position where alike the authority of his Master and the 'communis sensus' of the society he belongs to, give into his hand certain documents and declare them inspired.

3. What in its general idea does this mean?

S. Athanasius expresses the function of the Jews in the world in a luminous phrase, when he describes them as having been the 'sacred school for all the world of the knowledge of God and of the spiritual life [3].' Every race has its special vocation, and we recognise in the great writers of each race the interpreters of that vocation. They are specially gifted individuals, but not merely individuals. The race speaks in them : Rome is interpreted by Virgil, and Greece by Aeschylus or Plato. Now every believer in God must see in these special missions of races, a Divine inspiration. If we can once get down to the bottom of human life, below its pride, its wilfulness, its pretentiousness, down to its essence, we get to God and to a movement of His Spirit [4]. Thus every race has its inspiration and its prophets.

But the inspiration of the Jews was supernatural. What does this mean? That the Jews were selected—not to be the school for humanity in any of the arts and sciences which involve the thought of God only indirectly, and can therefore be carried on without a fundamental restora-

---

[1] This distinction was drawn by Bishop Clifford, *Fortnightly Review*, Jan. 1887, p. 145.
[2] Cf. the quotation in Eusebius, *H.E.* v. 28.

[3] Athan. *de Incarn.* 12. Cf. Ewald's preface to his *History of Israel*.
[4] See Gratry, *Henri Perreyve*, pp. 162, 163.

tion of man into that relation to God which sin had clouded or broken, —but to be the school of that fundamental restoration itself. Therefore, in the case of the Jews the inspiration is both in itself more direct and more intense, and also involves a direct consciousness on the part of its subjects. In the race, indeed, the consciousness might be dim ; but the consciousness, as the prophets all assure us, did belong to the race, and not merely to its individual interpreters. They speak as recalling the people to something which they know, or ought to know, not as preachers of a new religion. They were ' the conscience of the state[1].' But special men, prophets, psalmists, moralists, historians, were thus the inspired interpreters of the Divine message to and in the race : and their inspiration lies in this, that they were the subjects of a movement of the Holy Ghost, so shaping, controlling, quickening their minds and thoughts and aspirations, as to make them the instruments through which was imparted ' the knowledge of God and of the spiritual life.'

Various are the degrees of this inspiration : the inspiration of the prophet is direct, continuous, absorbing. The inspiration of the writer of Ecclesiastes, on the other hand, is such as to lead him to ponder on all the phases of a worldly experience, passing through many a false conclusion, and cynical denial, till at the last his thought is led to unite itself to the great stream of Divine movement by finding the only possible solution of the problems of life in the recognition of God, and in obedience to Him.

Various also are the sorts of literature inspired : for the supernatural fertilizes and does not annihilate the natural. The Church repudiated the Montanist conception of inspiration, according to which the inspired man speaks in ecstasy, as the passive unconscious instrument of the Spirit ; and the metaphors which would describe the Holy Spirit as acting upon a man ' like a flute player breathing into his flute,' or ' a plectrum striking a lyre,' have always a suspicion of heresy attaching to their use[2]. As the humanity of Christ is none the less a true humanity for being conditioned by absolute oneness with God, so the human activity is none the less free, conscious, rational, because the Spirit inspires it. The poet is a poet, the philosopher a philosopher, the historian an historian, each with his own idiosyncrasies, ways, and methods, to be interpreted each by the laws of his own literature. And just as truly as physiology, in telling us more and more about the human body, is telling us about the body which the Son of God assumed, so with the growth of our knowledge about the kinds and

---

[1] Delitzsch, *O. T. History of Redemption*, p. 106. Cf. Prof. Robertson Smith, *Prophets of Israel*, p. 108.
[2] See Epiphan. *Haer.* xlviii. 4. West-

cott, *Introd. to the Study of the Gospels*, App. B, sect. ii. 4, sect. iv. 4. Mason, *Faith of the Gospel*, p. 255.

sequences of human literature, shall we know more and more about the literature of the Jews which the Holy Spirit inspired.

What then is meant by the inspiration of Holy Scripture? If we begin our inquiry with the account of creation with which the Bible opens, we may take note of its affinities in general substance with the Babylonian and Phoenician cosmogonies; but we are much more struck with its differences, and it is in these we shall look for its inspiration. We observe that it has for its motive and impulse not the satisfaction of a fantastic curiosity, nor the later interest of scientific discovery, but to reveal certain fundamental religious principles: that everything as we see it was made by God: that it has no being in itself but at God's will: on the other hand, that everything is in its essence good, as the product of the good God: that man, besides sharing the physical nature of all creation, has a special relation to God, as made in God's image, to be God's vice-gerent: that sin, and all that sin brings with it of misery and death, came not of man's nature but of his disobedience to God and rejection of the limitations under which He put him: that in spite of all that sin brought about, God has not left man to himself, that there is a hope and a promise. These are the fundamental principles of true religion and progressive morality, and in these lies the supernatural inspiration of the Bible account of creation [1].

As we pass on down the record of Genesis, we do not find ourselves in any doubt as to the primary and certain meaning of its inspiration. The first traditions of the race are all given there *from a special point of view*. In that point of view lies the inspiration. It is that everything is presented to us as illustrating God's dealings with man—God's judgment on sin: His call of a single man to work out a universal mission: His gradual delimitation of a chosen race: His care for the race: His over-ruling of evil to work out His purpose. The narrative of Genesis has all the fullest wealth of human interest, but it is in the unveiling of the hand of God that its special characteristic lies. As we go on into the history, we find the recorders acting like the recorders of other nations, collecting, sorting, adapting, combining their materials, but in this inspired—that the animating motive of their work is not to bring out the national glory or to flatter the national vanity, nor, like the motive of a modern historian, the mere interest in fact, but to keep before the chosen people the record of how God has dealt with them. This, as we perceive, gives them a special sense of the value of fact [2]. They record what God has done,

[1] See Professor Driver's admirable article on 'the cosmogony of Genesis.' *Expositor*, Jan. 1886.

[2] Professor Cheyne, speaking of such narratives of Scriptures as the record of Elijah, protests against the supposition that they are 'true to fact.' 'True to fact! Who goes to the artist for hard

how God did in such and such ways take action on behalf of His peculiar people, delivering them, punishing them, teaching them, keeping them, disciplining them for higher ends. And none who have eyes to see God's spiritual purposes can doubt that those historians read aright the chronicles of the kings of Israel. The spiritual significance which they see is the true significance. God's special purpose was on Israel.

It is not necessary to emphasize in what consists the special inspiration of psalmists or of prophets. The psalmists take some of the highest places among the poets of all nations, but the poetic faculty is directed to one great end, to reveal the soul in its relation to God, in its exultations and in its self-abasements. 'Where . . . did they come from, those piercing lightning-like gleams of strange spiritual truth, those magnificent out-looks upon the kingdom of God, those raptures at His presence and His glory, those wonderful disclosures of self-knowledge, those pure out-pourings of the love of God? Surely here is something more than the mere working of the mind of man, Surely . . . they repeat the whispers of the Spirit of God, they reflect the very light of the Eternal Wisdom[1].'

In the case of prophets once more we get the most obvious and typical instances of inspiration[2]. The prophets make a direct claim to be the instruments of the Divine Spirit. Not that the Divine Spirit supersedes their human faculties, but He intensifies them. They see deeper under the surface of life what God is doing, and therefore further into the future what He will do. No doubt their predictive knowledge is general, it is of the issue to which things tend. It is not at least usually a knowledge 'of times and of seasons which the Father hath put in His own power.' Thus at times they foreshorten the distance, and place the great deliverance and the 'day of Jehovah'

[1] Church, *Discipline of the Christian Character*, p. 57. This work seems to me the best existing answer to the question, in what does the inspiration of the Old Testament consist.

dry facts? Why even the historians of antiquity thought it no part of their duty to give the mere prose of life. How much less can the unconscious artists of the imaginative East have described their heroes with relentless photographic accuracy!' (*The Hallowing of Criticism*, p. 5.) But it seems to me that such a passage, by treating the recorders of the Old Testament as 'artists,' ignores their obvious intention to lay stress on what God has actually done, the deliverances He has actually wrought. They, at least, like the Greek historical 'artist' of the defeat of Persia, would have laid great stress on the facts having happened.

[2] Cf. pp. 118-122. In view of criticisms it may be explained that in the account of the prophet given above only that view of his inspiration is taken into consideration which appeals first to the enquirer (cf. the words in the next paragraph 'in this general sense at least'). When once this primary assurance of inspiration is gained the evidence of detailed prophecies will be found cogent. As we compare the anticipations of the Messiah or of the 'Righteous Servant' in such passages as Ps. xxii., Is. liii., vii. 14, or ix. 6, 7, with their fulfilment in Jesus Christ, we recognise a special action of the Holy Ghost, marking even in details the continuity of His method. Cf. p. 122 referred to above.

in the too immediate foreground [1]. The prophetic inspiration is thus consistent with erroneous anticipations as to the circumstances and the opportunity of God's self-revelation, just as the apostolic inspiration admitted of S. Paul expecting the second coming of Christ within his own life-time. But the prophets claim to be directly and really inspired to teach and interpret what God is doing and commanding in their own age, and to forecast what in judgment and redemptive mercy God means to do and must do in the Divine event. The figure of the king Messiah dawns upon their horizon with increasing definiteness of outline and characteristic, and we, with the experience of history between us and them, are sure that the correspondence of prophecy and fulfilment can be due to no other cause than that they spoke in fact the 'word of the Lord.'

Thus there is built up for us in the literature of a nation, marked by an unparalleled unity of purpose and character, a spiritual fabric, which in its result we cannot but recognise as the action of the Divine Spirit. A knowledge of God and of the spiritual life gradually appears, not as the product of human ingenuity, but as the result of Divine communication : and the outcome of this communication is to produce an organic whole which postulates a climax not yet reached, a redemption not yet given, a hope not yet satisfied. In this general sense at least no Christian ought to feel a difficulty in believing, and believing with joy, in the inspiration of the Old Testament : nor can he feel that he is left without a standard by which to judge what it means. Christ, the goal of Old Testament development, stands forth as the test and measure of its inspiration.

The New Testament consists of writings of Apostles or of men of sub-apostolic rank, like S. Luke and probably the author of the Epistle to the Hebrews. There is not, except perhaps in the case of the Apocalypse, any sign of an inspiration to write, other than the inspiration which gave power to teach. What then is, whether for writing or for teaching, the inspiration of an Apostle?

If Jesus Christ both was, and knew Himself to be, the Revealer of the Father, it almost stands to reason that He must have secured that His revelation should be, without material alloy, communicated to the Church which was to enshrine and perpetuate it. Thus, in fact, we find that He spent His chief pains on the training of His apostolic witnesses. And all the training which He gave them while He was present among them was only to prepare them to receive the Holy Ghost Who, after He was gone, was to be poured out upon them to qualify them to bear His witness among men.

---

[1] See for instance Micah v. 2–6. On the subject of the limitations of prophetic foresight, as on the whole subject of prophecy, let me refer to Dr. Ed. Riehm, *Messianic Prophecy* (Clark's trans.), pp. 79, 86 ff., 114, 157–162.

'Ye shall receive power, when the Holy Ghost is come upon you, and ye shall be My witnesses:' 'These things have I spoken unto you while yet abiding with you. And the Comforter, even the Holy Ghost, Whom the Father will send in My name, He shall teach you all things, and bring to your remembrance all that I said unto you.' 'I have yet many things to say unto you, but ye cannot bear them now. Howbeit when He, the Spirit of truth, is come, He will guide you into all the truth [1].'

Thus the Church sees in the Apostles men specially and deliberately qualified to interpret Christ to the world. It understands by their inspiration an endowment which enables men of all ages to take their teaching as representing, and not misrepresenting, His teaching and Himself. In S. John's Gospel, for example, we have an account of our Lord which has obviously passed through the medium of a most remarkable personality. We have the outcome of the meditation, as well as the recollection, of the Apostle. But, as the evidence assures us that the Gospel is really S. John's, so the Church unhesitatingly accepts S. John's strong and repeated asseveration that he is interpreting and not distorting the record, the personality, the claims of Jesus Christ. ' He bears record, and his record is true [2].'

This assurance is indeed not without verification : it is verified by the unity of testimony which, under all differences of character and circumstance, we find among the apostolic witnesses. The accepted doctrine of the Church when S. Paul wrote his ' undoubted Epistles,'— the points of agreement amidst all differences between him and the Judaizers—gives us substantially the same conception of the Person of the Incarnate Son of God as we find in S. John [3]. The same conception of what He was, is required to interpret the record of what He did and said in the Synoptic Gospels. Further, the witness of the Apostles, though it receives its final guarantee through the belief in their inspiration, has its natural basis in the prolonged training by which—'companying with them all the time that He went in and out among them, beginning from the baptism of John, until the day that He was received up,'—they were prepared to be His witnesses. Thus if an act of faith is asked of us in the apostolic inspiration, it is a reasonable act of faith.

If we pass from the writings properly apostolic to those like S. Luke's records, which represent apostolic teaching at second hand, we do not find that the inspiration of their writers was of such sort as enabled them to dispense with the ordinary means or guarantees of accuracy.

[1] Acts i. 8. S. John xiv. 25, 26 ; xvi. 12, 13.
[2] S. John xix. 35 ; xxi. 24. 1 S. John i. 1-3.
[3] See Prof. Sanday's *What the first Christians thought about Christ*. (Oxford House Papers : Rivington.)

The simple claim of S. Luke's preface to have had the best means of information and to have taken the greatest care in the use of them, is on this score most instructive. We should suppose that their inspiration was part of the whole spiritual endowment of their life which made them the trusted friends of the Apostles, and qualified them to be the chosen instruments to record their teaching, in the midst of a Church whose quick and eager memory of 'the tradition' would have acted as a check to prevent any material error creeping into the record.

4. It will be remembered that when inspiration is spoken of by S. Paul, he mentions it as a positive endowment which qualifies the writings of those who were its subjects, to be permanent sources of spiritual instruction. 'Every Scripture inspired of God is also profitable for teaching, for reproof, for correction, for instruction which is in righteousness[1].' Following out this idea of Holy Scripture then, we are led to think of the belief in inspiration as having this primary practical result : that we submit ourselves to the teaching of every book which is given to us as inspired. We are to put ourselves to school with each in turn of the inspired writers ; with S. James, for example, in the New Testament, as well as with S. John and S. Paul ; with S. Luke as well as with S. Matthew ; with the Pastoral Epistles as well as with the Epistle to the Galatians[2]. At starting each of us, according to his predisposition, is conscious of liking some books of Scripture better than others. This, however, should lead us to recognise that in some way we specially need the teaching which is less attractive to us. We should set ourselves to study what we like less, till that too has had its proper effect in moulding our conscience and character. It is hardly possible to estimate how much division would have been avoided in the Church if those, for example, who were most ecclesiastically disposed had been at pains to assimilate the teaching of the Epistle to the Romans, and those who most valued 'the freedom of the Gospel' had recognised a special obligation to deepen their hold on the Epistles to the Corinthians and the Pastoral Epistles and the Epistle of S. James.

To believe in the inspiration of Holy Scripture is to put ourselves to school with every part of the Old Testament, as of the New. True, the Old Testament is imperfect, but for that very reason has a special value. 'The real use of the earlier record is not to add something to the things revealed in Christ, but to give us that clear and all-sided insight into the meaning and practical worth of the perfect scheme of Divine grace which can only be attained by tracing its growth[3].'

---

[1] 2 Tim. iii. 16.
[2] Mr. Horton's book on *Inspiration and the Bible* is almost naively lacking in this quality of impartial regard to inspired books.
[3] Prof. Robertson Smith, *Prophets of Israel*, p. 6.

We see in the Old Testament the elements, each in separation, which went to make up the perfect whole, and which must still lie at the basis of all rightly formed life of individuals and societies.

Thus to believe, for instance, in the inspiration of the Old Testament forces us to recognise a real element of the Divine education in the imprecatory Psalms. They are not the utterances of selfish spite [1]: they are the claim which righteous Israel makes upon God that He should vindicate Himself, and let their eyes see how 'righteousness turns again unto judgment.' The claim is made in a form which belongs to an early stage of spiritual education; to a time when *this life* was regarded as the scene in which God must finally vindicate Himself, and when the large powers and possibilities of the Divine compassion were very imperfectly recognised. But behind these limitations, which characterize the greater part of the Old Testament, the claim of these Psalms still remains a necessary part of the claim of the Christian soul. We must not only recognise the reality of Divine judgments in time and eternity, bodily and spiritual; we must not only acquiesce in them because they are God's; we must go on to claim of God the manifestation of His just judgment, so that holiness and joy, sin and failure, shall be seen to coincide.

To recognise then the inspiration of the Bible is to put ourselves to school in every part of it, and everywhere to bear in mind the admonition of the *De Imitatione* 'that every Scripture must be read in the same spirit in which it was written.' So far it will not be a point in dispute among Christians what inspiration means, or what its purpose is. ' The Councils of Trent and the Vatican,' writes Cardinal Newman, ' tell us distinctly the object and the promise of Scriptural inspiration. They specify "faith and moral conduct" as the drift of that teaching which has the guarantee of inspiration [2].' Nor can it be denied that the more Holy Scripture is read from this point of view, the more confidently it is treated as the inspired guide of faith and conduct, no less in the types of character which it sets before us than in its direct instruction, the more the experience and appreciation of its inspiration grows upon us, so that to deny or to doubt it comes to mean to deny or to doubt a matter plain to the senses. Indeed what has been said under this head will probably appear to those practised in the spiritual use of Holy Scripture as an understatement, perhaps not easy to justify, of the sense in which the Scripture is the Word of God, and the spiritual food of the soul [3].

[1] Cf. Prof. Robertson Smith, *The Old Testament in the Jewish Church*, Lect. vii. p. 207 : 'Another point in which criticism removes a serious difficulty is the interpretation of the imprecatory psalms.'

[2] See *Nineteenth Century*, Feb. 1884,

p. 189.

[3] 'When from time to time,' says S. Bernard to his monks, 'anything that was hidden or obscure in the Scriptures has come out into the light to any one of you, at once the voice of exultation and thankfulness for the

5. But here certain important questions arise. (*a*) The revelation of God was made in a historical process. Its record is in large part the record of a national life : it is historical. Now the inspiration of the recorder lies, as we have seen, primarily in this, that he sees the hand of God in the history and interprets His purpose. Further, we must add, his sense of the working of God in history, increases his realization of the importance of historical fact. Thus there is a profound air of historical truthfulness pervading the Old Testament record from Abraham downward. The weaknesses, the sins, of Israel's heroes are not spared. Their sin and its punishment is always before us. There is no flattering of national pride, no giving the reins to boastfulness. In all this the Old Testament appears to be in marked contrast, as to contemporary Assyrian monuments, so also to a good deal of much later ecclesiastical history. But does the inspiration of the recorder guarantee the exact historical truth of what he records? And in matter of fact can the record, with due regard to legitimate historical criticism, be pronounced true? Now, to the latter of these two questions (and they are quite distinct questions), we may reply that there is nothing to prevent our believing, as our faith certainly strongly disposes us to believe, that the record from Abraham downward is in substance in the strict sense historical. Of course the battle of historical truth cannot be fought on the field of the Old Testament, as it can on that of the New, because it is so vast and indecisive, and because (however certainly ancient is such a narrative as that contained in Genesis xiv.) very little of the early record can be securely traced to a period near the events. Thus the Church cannot *insist upon* the historical character of the earliest records of the ancient Church in detail, as she can on the historical character of the Gospels or the Acts of the Apostles. On the other hand, as it seems the more probable opinion that the Hebrews must have been acquainted with the art of writing in some form long before the Exodus, there is no reason to doubt the existence of some written records among them from very early days[1]. Internal evidence again certainly commends to our acceptance the history of the patriarchs, of the Egyptian bondage, of the great redemption, of the wanderings, as well as of the later period

nourishment of spiritual food that has been received, must rise as from a banquet to delight the ears of God.'

[1] See the Annual Address (1889) delivered at the Victoria Institute by Prof. Sayce, on the cuneiform tablets of Tel el-amarna, pp. 4, 14 f. : 'We learn that in the fifteenth century before our era—a century before the Exodus— active literary intercourse was going on throughout the civilized world of Western Asia, between Babylonia and Egypt and the smaller states of Palestine . . . This intercourse was carried on by means of the Babylonian language and the complicated Babylonian script. How educated the old world was, we are but just beginning to learn. But we have already learnt enough to discover how important a bearing it has on the criticism of the Old Testament.'

as to which there would be less dispute. In a word we are, we believe, not wrong in anticipating that the Church will continue to believe and to teach that the Old Testament from Abraham downwards is really historical, and that there will be nothing to make such belief and teaching unreasonable or wilful. But within the limits of what is substantially historical, there is still room for an admixture of what, though marked by spiritual purpose, is yet not strictly historical —for instance, for a feature which characterizes all early history, the attribution to first founders of what is really the remoter result of their institutions. Now historical criticism[1] assures us that this process has been largely at work in the Pentateuch. By an analysis, for instance, the force of which is very great, it distinguishes distinct stages in the growth of the law of worship : at least an early stage such as is represented in 'the Book of the Covenant[2],' a second stage in the Book of Deuteronomy, a last stage in 'the Priestly Code.' What we may suppose to have happened is that Moses himself established a certain germ of ceremonial enactment in connection with the ark and its sacred tent, and with the 'ten words '; and that this developed always as 'the law of Moses,' the whole result being constantly attributed, probably unconsciously and certainly not from any intention to deceive, to the original founder. This view would certainly imply that the recorders of Israel's history were subject to the ordinary laws in the estimate of evidence, that their inspiration did not consist in a miraculous communication to them of facts as they originally happened : but if we believe that the law, as it grew, really did represent the Divine intention for the Jews, gradually worked out upon the basis of a Mosaic institution, there is nothing materially untruthful, though there is something uncritical, in attributing the whole legislation to Moses acting under the Divine command. It would be only of a piece with the attribution of the collection of Psalms to David and of Proverbs to Solomon. Nor does the supposition that the law was of gradual growth interfere in any way with the symbolical and typical value of its various ordinances.

Once again, the same school of criticism would assure us that the Books of Chronicles represent a later and less historical version of Israel's history than that given in Samuel and Kings[3] : they represent, according to this view, the version of that history which had become current in the priestly schools. What we are asked to admit is not conscious perversion, but unconscious idealizing of history, the reading back into past records of a ritual development which was really later. Now inspiration excludes conscious deception or pious fraud, but it

[1] See Driver, *Crit. notes on Sunday-School lessons* (Scribner : New York).
[2] Ex. xx. xxii–xxiii. xxxiii.

[3] The Books of Kings seem to be compiled from the point of view of the Deuteronomist.

appears to be quite consistent with this sort of idealizing; always supposing that the result read back into the earlier history does represent the real purpose of God and only anticipates its realization.

Here then is one great question. Inspiration certainly means the illumination of the judgment of the recorder. 'By the contact of the Holy Spirit,' says Origen, 'they became clearer in their mental perceptions, and their souls were filled with a brighter light[1].' But have we any reason to believe that it means, over and above this, the miraculous communication of facts not otherwise to be known, a miraculous communication such as would make the recorder independent of the ordinary processes of historical tradition? Certainly neither S. Luke's preface to his Gospel, nor the evidence of any inspired record, justifies us in this assumption. Nor would it appear that spiritual illumination, even in the highest degree, has any tendency to lift men out of the natural conditions of knowledge which belong to their time. Certainly in the similar case of exegesis, it would appear that S. Paul is left to the method of his time, though he uses it with inspired insight into the function and meaning of law and of prophecy as a whole. Thus, without pronouncing an opinion, where we have no right to do so, on the critical questions at present under discussion, we may maintain with considerable assurance that there is nothing in the doctrine of inspiration to prevent our recognising a considerable idealizing element in the Old Testament history. The reason is of course obvious enough why what can be admitted in the Old Testament, could not without results disastrous to the Christian Creed, be admitted in the New. It is because the Old Testament is the record of how God produced a need, or anticipation, or ideal, while the New Testament records how in fact He satisfied it. The absolute coincidence of idea and fact is vital in the realization, not in the preparation for it. It is equally obvious, too, that where fact is of supreme importance, as in the New Testament, the evidence has none of the ambiguity or remoteness which belongs to much of the record of the preparation.

(*b*) But once again; we find all sorts of literature in the inspired volume: men can be inspired to think and to write for God under all the forms of natural genius. Now one form of genius is the dramatic: its essence is to make characters, real or imaginary, the vehicles for an ideal presentation. It presents embodied ideas. Now the Song of Solomon is of the nature of a drama. The Book of Job, although it works on an historical basis, is, it can hardly be denied, mainly dramatic. The Book of Wisdom, which with us is among the books of the Bible, though in the second rank outside the canon, and which is inside the canon of the Roman Church, professes to be written by

---

[1] Origen, *c. Cels.* vii. 4.

Solomon[1], but is certainly written not by him, but in his person by another author. We may then conceive the same to be true of Ecclesiastes, and of Deuteronomy; i. e. we may suppose Deuteronomy to be a republication of the law 'in the spirit and power' of Moses put dramatically into his mouth. Criticism goes further, and asks us to regard Jonah and Daniel, among the prophetic books, as dramatic compositions worked up on a basis of history. The discussion of these books has often been approached from a point of view from which the miraculous is necessarily unhistorical. With such a point of view we are not concerned. The possibility and reality of miracles has to be vindicated first of all in the field of the New Testament; and one who admits them there, cannot reasonably exclude their possibility in the earlier history. The question must be treated simply on literary and evidential grounds[2]. But we would contend that if criticism should shew these books to be probably dramatic, that would be no hindrance to their performing 'an important canonical function,' or to their being inspired. Dramatic composition has played an immense part in training the human mind. It is as far removed as possible from a violation of truth, though in an uncritical age its results may very soon pass for history. It admits of being inspired as much as poetry, or history, and indeed there are few who could feel a difficulty in recognising as inspired the teaching of the books of Jonah and Daniel[3]. It is maintained then that the Church leaves open to literary criticism the question whether several of the writings of the Old Testament are or are not dramatic. Certainly the fact that they have not commonly been taken to be so in the past will be no evidence to the contrary, unless it can be denied that a literary criticism is being developed, which is as really new an intellectual product as the scientific development, and as such, certain to reverse a good many of the literary judgments of previous ages. We are being asked to make considerable changes in our literary conception of the Scriptures, but not greater changes than were involved in the acceptance of the heliocentric astronomy.

[1] E. g. chs. vii. ix. The Roman Church admits that it is, to use Newman's phrase, 'a prosopopeia'; 'our Bibles say, "it is written in the person of Solomon" and "it is uncertain who was the writer,"' l. c. p. 197. It is important to bear in mind that the Western Church in general has, since S. Augustine's day, admitted into the canon a book the literary method of which is thus confessedly dramatic. Newman makes this the ground for saying that the same may be true of Ecclesiastes.

[2] On the evidence of O. T. miracles I may refer to Mr. Samuel Cox's Essay: *Miracles, an Argument and a Challenge.* (Kegan Paul, 1884.)

[3] Of course the distinction must be maintained in the case of the book of Daniel between a 'pious fraud' which cannot be inspired, and an idealizing personification which, as a normal type of literature, can. Further study will probably solve the special difficulty which on the critical hypothesis attaches to the book of Daniel from this point of view: see Stanton, *Jewish and Christian Messiah*, p. 109, note 1.

(*c*) Once again : an enlarged study of comparative history has led to our perceiving that the various sorts of mental or literary activity develop in their different lines out of an earlier condition in which they lie fused and undifferentiated. This we can vaguely call the mythical stage of mental evolution. A myth is not a falsehood ; it is a product of mental activity, as instructive and rich as any later product, but its characteristic is that it is not yet distinguished into history, and poetry, and philosophy. It is all of these in the germ, as dream and imagination, and thought and experience, are fused in the mental furniture of a child's mind. 'These myths or current stories,' says Grote writing of Greek history, 'the spontaneous and earliest growth of the Greek mind, constituted at the same time the entire intellectual stock of the age to which they belonged. They are the common root of all those different ramifications into which the mental activity of the Greeks subsequently diverged ; containing as it were the preface and germ of the positive history and philosophy, the dogmatic theology and the professed romance, which we shall hereafter trace, each in its separate development.' Now has the Jewish history such earlier stage : does it pass back out of history into myth ? In particular, are not its earlier narratives, before the call of Abraham, of the nature of myth, in which we cannot distinguish the historical germ, though we do not at all deny that it exists ? The inspiration of these narratives is as conspicuous as that of any part of Scripture, but is there anything to prevent our regarding these great inspirations about the origin of all things,—the nature of sin, the judgment of God on sin, and the alienation among men which follows their alienation from God,—as conveyed to us in that form of myth or allegorical picture, which is the earliest mode in which the mind of man apprehended truth ?

6. In spite of the arbitrariness and the irreligion which have often been associated with the modern development of historical criticism in its application to the Old Testament, the present writer believes that it represents none the less a real advance in literary analysis, and is reaching results as sure, where it is fairly used, as scientific inquiry, though the results in the one case as in the other are often hard to disentangle from their less permanent accompaniments. Believing this, and feeling in consequence that the warning which the name of Galileo must ever bring before the memory of churchmen, is not unneeded now, he believes also that the Church is in no way restrained from admitting the modifications just hinted at, in what has latterly been the current idea of inspiration.

The Church is not restrained, in the first place, by having committed herself to any dogmatic definitions of the meaning of inspiration [1]. It

[1] This is certainly true of the Church as a whole. For the most that can be said in the same sense of the Roman Church, see Newman in the article above cited.

is remarkable indeed that Origen's almost reckless mysticism, and his accompanying repudiation of the historical character of large parts of the narrative of the Old Testament, and of some parts of the New [1], though it did not gain acceptance, and indeed had no right to it (for it had no sound basis), on the other hand never roused the Church to contrary definitions. Nor is it only Origen who disputed the historical character of parts of the narrative of Holy Scripture. Clement before him in Alexandria, and the mediaeval Anselm in the West, treat the seven days' creation as allegory and not history. Athanasius speaks of paradise as a ' figure.' A mediaeval Greek writer, who had more of Irenaeus than remains to us, declared that ' he did not know how those who kept to the letter and took the account of the temptation historically rather than allegorically, could meet the arguments of Irenaeus against them.' Further than this, it cannot be denied that the mystical method, as a whole, tended to the depreciation of the historical sense, in comparison with the spiritual teaching which it conveyed [2]. In a different line, Chrysostom, of the literal school of interpreters, explains quite in the tone of a modern apologist, how the discrepancies in detail between the different Gospels, assure us of the independence of the witnesses, and do not touch the facts of importance, in which all agree.

The Church is not tied then by any existing definitions. We cannot make any exact claim upon any one's belief in regard to inspiration, simply because we have no authoritative definition to bring to bear upon him. Those of us who believe most in the inspiration of the Church, will see a Divine Providence in this absence of dogma, because we shall perceive that only now is the state of knowledge such as admits of the question being legitimately raised.

Nor does it seem that the use which our Lord made of the Old Testament is an argument against the proposed concessions. Our Lord, in His use of the Old Testament, does indeed endorse with the utmost emphasis the Jewish view of their own history. He does thus imply, on the one hand, the real inspiration of their canon in its completeness, and, on the other hand, that He Himself was the goal of that inspired leading and the standard of that inspiration. ' Your father Abraham rejoiced to see My day : ' ' I am not come to destroy, but to fulfil.' This, and it is the important matter for all that concerns our

---

[1] *De Principiis*, iv. 15, 16, 17. His point is that incidents which could not have occurred in fact, or at least did not occur, are inserted in the narrative of the Old and New Testaments, that their very historical impossibility or improbability may drive us to the consideration of their spiritual significance. ' The at-tentive reader may notice . . . innumerable other passages, like these, so that he will be convinced that in the histories that are literally recorded, circumstances are inserted that did not occur.' Cf. Bigg, *Christian Platonists*, pp. 137-8.

[2] Cf. Jerome, *ad Nepotian. ep.* lii. 2.

spiritual education, is not in dispute. What is questioned is that our Lord's words foreclose certain critical positions as to the character of Old Testament literature. For example, does His use of Jonah's resurrection, as a *type* of His own, depend in any real degree upon whether it is historical fact or allegory [1]? It is of the essence of a type to *suggest* an idea, as of the antitype to *realize* it. The narrative of Jonah suggested certainly the idea of resurrection after three days, of triumph over death, and by suggesting this gave our Lord what His discourse required. Once more, our Lord uses the time before the flood [2] to illustrate the carelessness of men before His own coming. He is using the flood here as a typical judgment, as elsewhere He uses other contemporary visitations for a like purpose. In referring to the flood He certainly suggests that He is treating it as typical, for He introduces circumstances—'eating and drinking, marrying and giving in marriage '— which have no counterpart in the original narrative. Nothing in His use of it depends on its being more than a typical instance. Once more, He argues with the Pharisees on the assumption of the Davidic authorship of Psalm cx [3]. But it must be noticed that He is asking a question rather than making a statement—a question, moreover, which does not admit of being turned into a statement without suggesting the conclusion, of which rationalistic critics have not hesitated to avail themselves, that David's Lord could not be David's son. There are, we notice, other occasions when our Lord asked questions which cannot be made the basis of positive propositions [4]. It was in fact part of His method to lead men to examine their own principles without at the time suggesting any positive conclusion at all.

It may also fairly be represented, on a review of our Lord's teaching as a whole, that if He had intended to convey instruction to us on critical and literary questions, He would have made His purpose plainer. It is contrary to His whole method to reveal His Godhead by any anticipations of natural knowledge. The Incarnation was a self-emptying of God to reveal Himself under conditions of human nature and from the human point of view. We are able to draw a distinction between what He revealed and what He used. He revealed God, His mind, His character, His claim, within certain limits His Threefold Being : He revealed man, his sinfulness, his need, his capacity : He revealed His purpose of redemption, and founded His Church as a home in which man was to be through all the ages reconciled to God in knowledge and love. All this He revealed, but through, and under

---

[1] S. Matt. xii. 40.
[2] S. Matt. xxiv. 37-39.
[3] S. Matt. xxii. 41-46.
[4] See especially S. Mark x. 17-18 (and parallel passages), where our Lord's question, if converted into a positive proposition, suggests a repudiation of personal goodness. Cf. also the question in S. John x. 34-36 where, though the argument is *a fortiori*, still the true character of our Lord's sonship is hardly suggested.

conditions of, a true human nature. Thus He *used* human nature, its relation to God, its conditions of experience, its growth in knowledge, its limitation of knowledge [1]. He feels as we men ought to feel: He sees as we ought to see. We can thus distinguish more or less between the Divine truth which He reveals, and the human nature which He uses. Now when He speaks of the ' sun rising' He is using ordinary human knowledge. He willed so to restrain the beams of Deity as to observe the limits of the science of His age, and He puts Himself in the same relation to its historical knowledge. Thus He does not reveal His eternity by statements as to what had happened in the past, or was to happen in the future, outside the ken of existing history [2]. He made His Godhead gradually manifest by His attitude towards men and things about Him, by His moral and spiritual claims, by His expressed relation to His Father, not by any miraculous exemptions of Himself from the conditions of natural knowledge in its own proper province. Thus the utterances of Christ about the Old Testament do not seem to be nearly definite or clear enough to allow of our supposing that in this case He is departing from the general method of the Incarnation, by bringing to bear the unveiled omniscience of the Godhead, to anticipate or foreclose a development of natural knowledge.

But if we thus plead that theology may leave the field open for free discussion of these questions which Biblical criticism has recently been raising, we shall probably be bidden to 'remember Tübingen,' and not be over-trustful of a criticism which at least exhibits in some of its most prominent representatives a great deal of arbitrariness, of love of 'new views' for their own sake, and a great lack of that reverence and spiritual insight which is at least as much needed for understanding the books of the Bible, as accurate knowledge and fair investigation. To this the present writer would be disposed to reply that, if the Christian Church has been enabled to defeat the critical attack, so far as it threatened destruction to the historical basis of the New Testament, it has not been by foreclosing the question with an appeal to dogma, but by facing in fair and frank discussion the

[1] This limitation of knowledge must not be confused with fallibility or liability to human delusion, because it was doubtless guarded by the Divine purpose which led Jesus Christ to take it upon Himself.

[2] Of course He gave prophetic indications of the coming judgment, but on the analogy of inspired prophecy. He did not reveal ' times and seasons,' and declared that it was not within the scope of His mission to do so. See esp. S. Mark xiii. 32. He exhibits supernatural insight into men's characters and lives.

But He never exhibits the omniscience of bare Godhead in the realm of natural knowledge ; such as would be required to anticipate the results of modern science or criticism. This ' self-emptying' of God in the Incarnation is, we must always remember, no failure of power, but a continuous act of Self-sacrifice : cf. 2 Cor. viii. 9 and Phil. ii. 7. Indeed God ' declares His almighty power most chiefly' in this condescension, whereby He 'beggared Himself' of Divine prerogatives, to put Himself in our place.

problems raised. A similar treatment of Old Testament problems will enable us to distinguish between what is reasonable and reverent, and what is high-handed and irreligious in contemporary criticism whether German, French, or English. Even in regard to what makes *prima facie* a reasonable claim, we do not prejudice the decision by declaring the field open : in all probability there will always remain more than one school of legitimate opinion on the subject : indeed the purpose of the latter part of this essay has not been to inquire how much we can without irrationality believe inspiration to involve ; but rather, how much may legitimately and without real loss be conceded. For, without doubt, if consistently with entire loyalty to our Lord and His Church, we can regard as open the questions specified above, we are removing great obstacles from the path to belief of many who certainly wish to believe, and do not exhibit any undue scepticism. Nor does there appear to be any real danger that the criticism of the Old Testament will ultimately diminish our reverence for it. In the case of the New Testament certainly we are justified in feeling that modern investigation has resulted in immensely augmenting our understanding of the different books, and has distinctly fortified and enriched our sense of their inspiration. Why then should we hesitate to believe that the similar investigation of the Old Testament will in its result similarly enrich our sense that 'God in divers portions and divers manners spake of old times unto the fathers,' and that the Inspiration of Holy Scriptures will always be recognised as the most conspicuous of the modes in which the Holy Spirit has mercifully wrought for the illumination and encouragement of our race?

'For whatsoever things were written aforetime were written for our learning, that we through patience and comfort of the Scriptures might have hope.'

IX.

THE CHURCH.

CHRISTIANITY claims to be at once a life, a truth, and a worship; and, on all these accounts, it needs must find expression in a church. For, in the first place, the life of an individual remains dwarfed and stunted as long as it is lived in isolation; it is in its origin the outcome of other lives; it is at every moment of its existence dependent upon others; it reaches perfection only when it arrives at a conscious sense of its own deficiencies and limitations, and, therefore, of its dependence, and through such a sense realizes with thankfulness its true relation to the rest of life around it. Again, the knowledge of truth comes to the individual first through the mediation of others, of his parents and teachers; as he grows, and his own intellect works more freely, yet its results only gain consistency, security, width, when tested by the results of other workers; and directly we wish to propagate these results, they must be embodied in the lives of others, in societies, in organizations. Without these, ideas remain in the air, abstract, intangible, appealing perhaps to the philosophic few, but high above the reach of the many, the simple. 'All human society is the receptacle, nursery, and dwelling-place of ideas, shaped and limited according to the nature of the society—ideas which live and act on it and in it; which are preserved, passed on, and transmitted from one portion of it to another, from one generation to another; which would be merely abstractions or individual opinions if they were not endowed with the common life which their reception in a society gives them [1].'

These two principles are, obviously, not confined to religious questions. They apply to morality, to society, to politics. They are assumed in all ethical and political treatises. The need of co-operation for common life underlies the whole structure of the Republic of Plato; it is implied in Aristotle's definition of man as a social animal, and in his close association of Ethics with Politics: is has created the family, the tribe, the state; each fresh assertion of the principle, each breaking down of the barriers which separate family from family, tribe from tribe, nation from nation, has been a step forward in civilization.

[1] The Dean of S. Paul's on *The Christian Church*. Oxford House Papers, No. xvii. where this truth is excellently worked out and applied to the Church.

The strength of co-operation for the propagation of ideas is seen in the persistence with which certain nations retain hold on political theories or peculiar features of character ; it is seen in the recurring formation of philosophic schools or religious sects or guilds, as soon as any new truth, intellectual or religious, has been discovered, or any moral quality, such as temperance or purity, has needed to be emphasized. The most individualistic of Christian sects have found themselves forced to be ecclesiastical, to define their creeds and to perfect their organization, as soon as they have begun to be missionary.

These principles are as wide as society ; but religion takes them up and applies them on the highest level. Religion is, almost universally, the link which binds man to man, no less than that which binds man to a Power above him. So in the Christian Church—if we may anticipate, for a moment, our special application of the principle—the new-born child is taken at once and incorporated into a body of believers ; from the first it draws its life from God through the body ; it is taught that throughout life it must keep in touch with the body ; it must be in a right relation to the other members ; it must draw life from them ; it must contribute life to them. And, further, this body has existed always and exists still as the home of certain *ideas*, ideas about God and about human life, which were revealed in Jesus Christ, and which it has to attest in its teaching and embody in its life. It is to be a body of visible persons, themselves the light of the world, expressing so that others can see the manifold wisdom of God, winning others to belief in the unity of God, by the sight of their own one-ness. The first principle might be expressed in the words of Festus to Paracelsus, when the latter had claimed to be God's special instrument in the world ;

> Were I elect like you,
> I would encircle me with love, and raise
> A rampart of my fellows : it should seem
> Impossible for me to fail, so watched
> By gentle friends who made their cause my own.
> They should ward off fate's envy :—the great gift,
> Extravagant when claimed by me alone,
> Being so a gift to them as well as me[1]:

the second principle by lines applied originally to the Incarnation, but which we may legitimately transfer to the Church, which continues the work of the Incarnation,

> And so the Word had breath, and wrought
> With human hands the Creed of Creeds
> In loveliness of perfect deeds,
> More strong than all poetic thought[2].

[1] Browning, *Paracelsus*, ii. p. 30, ed. 1888.   [2] Tennyson, *In Memoriam*, xxxvi.

But, further, religion adds a third application of its own to this principle of co-operation : for a church grows also out of the necessities of worship. The ritual needed for the offering of sacrifice almost necessitates of itself a number of persons for its performance. No doubt, an individual can worship God in private, but so his worship tends to be self-centred and narrow : for the full expression of his religious relation to others, for expiating a wrong done by him to his neighbours or to the whole community, for expressing gratitude for mercies which have come to him through others, there must be the common meeting : and the community as a whole has its great victories for which to thank God, its national dangers for which to pray, its national sins for which to offer expiation ; and hence, common religious acts have been the universal accompaniment of national life, and have in their turn reacted upon it.

The idea of a Church, then, as conceived in its most general form, and without especial reference to the Christian Church, is this, that it widens life by deepening the sense of brotherhood ; that it teaches, strengthens, and propagates ideas by enshrining truth in living witnesses, by checking the results of isolated thinkers by contact with other thinkers, and by securing permanency for the ideas ; and that it expands and deepens worship by eliminating all that is selfish and narrow, and giving expression to common aims and feelings.

We pass from such *à priori* ideas to the evidence of the Bible. There we find that these principles were embodied first in Judaism. There the whole nation was the Church. The Jew entered into the religious privileges of his life, not by any conscious act of his own, but by being born of Jewish parents ; he retained his true life by remaining in contact with his nation. The union of the different members of the nation with each other is so intimate that the whole nation is spoken of as a personal unit. It is called ' God's Son,' His ' first-born Son,' ' Jehovah's servant.' The ideal of prophecy is essentially that of a restored nation rejoicing in the rule of national righteousness. Again, the nation was chosen out specially to bear witness to truth, truth about the nature of God, the Almighty, the Eternal, the Holy ; truth embodied in the facts of history, and deepened in the revelations of prophecy ; truths which the fathers teach their children, ' that they should not hide them from the children of the generations to come [1].' In the striking phrase of S. Athanasius, the law and the prophets were ' a sacred school of the knowledge of God and of spiritual life for the whole world [2].' Their worship, too, was essentially social and national. From the first it centred round great national events, the fortunes of the harvest, or the crises of national history : the individual was purified from sin that he might be worthy to take part in the national service ;

---

[1] Ps. lxxviii. 3, 4. [2] *De Inc.* 12.

the events of the nation's history were celebrated in religious hymns; the capital of the nation became the one and only recognised centre for the highest worship.

But Judaism adds to these principles a further principle of its own. It claims that such privileges as were granted to it, were not granted to it for its own sake, but that it might be a source of blessing to all nations : it assumes that they are on a lower religious level than itself; that instead of each nation progressing equally along the line of religious life, truth, and worship, other nations have fallen backward and the Jew has been chosen out for a special privilege. It is the principle that God works by 'limitation,' by apparent 'exclusiveness,' by that which is in its essence 'sacerdotalism'; the principle that God does not give His gifts equally to all, but specially to a few, that they may use them for the good of the whole. This principle seems at first sight to offend some modern abstract ideas of justice and equality; but the moment we examine the facts of life, we find it prevailing universally. Each nation has its peculiar gift : the Greek makes his parallel claim to be specially gifted with the love of knowledge and the power of artistic expression ; the Roman with the power of rule and the belief in law. Or, again, within a single nation, it is the artist who enables us to see the beauty of a face or a landscape which had escaped us before :

> Art was given for that,
> God uses us to help each other so,
> Lending our minds out.

It is the poet who interprets our inner nature or the magic of the external world, and becomes

> A priest to us all
> Of the wonder and bloom of the world,
> Which we see with his eyes and are glad :

he sings

> Till the world is wrought
> To sympathy with hopes and fears *it heeded not*[1].

And this principle does not stop short of religious influences. Conscience is itself a witness to it, as it implies that all parts of our nature are not sufficient guides to themselves, but that God has gifted one special faculty with power to control the rest. 'Men of character,' it has been said, 'are the conscience of the society to which they belong.' In the Jewish nation itself, the prophets were the circle of Jehovah's friends; they knew His secrets, they kept alive the ideal of the nation. 'What the soul is in the body, that are Christians in the world' was the parallel claim of an early apologist[2]. Analogies crowd in, then, on every side, to shew how rational is this claim on the part of Judaism.

---

[1] Browning, *Fra Lippo Lippi* : M. Arnold, *The Youth of Nature* : Shelley, *The Skylark.*
[2] *Ep. ad Diogn.* vi.

Revelation only accepts this fact, and adds to it the assertion that it is no accident but a part of the Divine Purpose. It is the result of God's election. The Jewish nation, and subsequently the Christian Church, is not only a blessing to the rest of the world, but it is conscious that it is a blessing. This truth has been revealed to it partly to keep it ever mindful of its sense of dependence upon the Giver of all good gifts, partly to give it tenacity and courage to cling to a gift which it knows to be of inestimable value for all mankind. 'The election was simply a method of procedure adopted by God in His wisdom by which He designed to fit the few for blessing the many, one for blessing all [1].'

It must be from considerations such as these that we approach the foundation of the Christian Church and the Incarnation of our Lord Jesus Christ on which it rests. We approach it with the expectation that we shall find these principles embodied in it, for Christianity sprang directly out of Judaism, and so would naturally inherit its principles: and to go deeper still, the very essence of the Incarnation lies in the consecration of human life and human means. He who before had been acting invisibly upon the world as the Word, implanting life and light in man, now entered visibly into human flesh. All tendencies which made for the fulness of life and truth before His coming, all that tended to enlighten, elevate, combine men, had been His unknown working: now they are known to be His. The Infinite appears in finite form; the spiritual takes the material in which to express itself; human media are consecrated to deeper ends, and charged with a fuller meaning than before: so that, in Hooker's words, 'We cannot now conceive how God should, without man, exercise Divine power or receive the glory of Divine praise [2].' 'What you do now even after the flesh, that is spiritual' is the bold paradox of S. Ignatius; and he adds the reason, 'for you do all in Christ Jesus [3].' Thus—

> In this twofold sphere, the twofold man
> Holds firmly to the natural, to reach
> The spiritual beyond it . . . . .
> The whole temporal show related royally
> And built up to eterne significance
> Through the open arms of God [4].

The Incarnation, then, takes up all the three principles of which we have spoken: but, from the very finality which it claims for itself, it puts a mark of finality upon each of them, and so, in this respect, marks

---

[1] Bruce, *The Chief End of Revelation*, p. 116.

[2] *Eccl. Pol.* v. 54. Cf. Iren. *adv. Haer.* iii. 20: 'Gloria enim hominis Deus; operationis vero Dei et omnis sapien-

tiae Ejus et virtutis receptaculum homo.'

[3] Ign. *ad Eph.* viii. ἃ δὲ καὶ κατὰ σάρκα πράσσετε, ταῦτα πνευματικά ἐστιν· ἐν Ἰησοῦ γὰρ Χριστῷ πάντα πράσσετε.

[4] *Aurora Leigh*, vii. p. 302.

off the application of them in the Christian Church from all other applications of the same principles. The principle of co-operation for spiritual life is taken up; the Jewish nation is expanded into an universal brotherhood; this includes all men, without any distinction of race; it includes the quick and the dead; it aims at the highest spiritual perfection. It is final in this sense, that nothing can be wider in extent or deeper in aim; but it is final also in the sense that the life *has been* manifested. Christians do not combine to work up to some unsuspected ideal: they combine to draw out and express in their common life the perfection that was in Christ. The principle of association for the propagation of ideas is taken up, but they are truths about God and His relation to human nature: they are truths which have been revealed, which have been once for all delivered to the saints. Finally, the principle of association for worship is taken up; the worship is made as wide as humanity; it is to be as spiritual as God; but it, too, rests on final facts, on the facts of creation and redemption: it centres round the one complete sacrifice for sin.

Let us consider each of these points more in detail.

I. The Church is an organization for the purpose of spiritual life; an universal brotherhood knit together to build up each of its members into holiness; 'the only great school of virtue existing.' But if this is so, if it is universal, is the principle of 'limitation,' of 'exclusiveness,' gone? Certainly not. It is there, and it is most instructive to notice how it arises [1]. Christ chose a small body of disciples to be in close contact with Himself, to share His work, and to receive His deeper teaching. This will not surprise us after the analogies of the prophets, the poets, the artists of the world. The saints too may be few, and God may lend their spirits out for the good of others. But, moreover, in the first formation of the Church we are able to watch the process of limitation, as historically worked out; and we see that it arises not from any narrowness, any grudging of His blessings, on the part of Christ, but from the narrowness, the limitations in man. Man is 'straitened' not in God, not in Christ, but in his own affections. God willed all men to be saved: Christ went about doing good and calling all to a change of heart, to a share in the kingdom of Heaven: but such a call made demands upon His hearers; it required that they should give up old prejudices about the Messianic kingdom, that they should be willing to leave father and mother and houses and lands for the truth's sake, that they should lay aside all the things that defile a man, that they should aim at being perfect, that they should not only hear but understand the word, that they should trust Him even when His sayings were hard. And these demands produced the limitations.

[1] Cp. H. S. Holland, *Creed and Character*, Sermons III—VIII.

The Pharisees preferred the glory of men to the glory which came from God; the masses in Galilee cared only for the bread that perisheth; many of the disciples turned back; and so He could not commit Himself unto them, because He knew what was in man. Not to them, not to any chance person, but to the Twelve, to those who had stood these tests, to those who had, in spite of all perplexity, seen in Him the Son of the Living God, to them He could commit Himself, they could share His secrets; they could be taught clearly the certainty and the meaning of His coming death, for they had begun to learn what self-sacrifice meant; they could do His work and organize His Church; they could bind and loose in His Name; they could represent Him when He was gone. These are the elect; they who had the will to listen to the call [1]; they who were 'magnanimous to correspond with heaven'; to them He gave at Pentecost the full conscious gift of the Holy Spirit, and so at last formed them into the Church, the Church which was to continue His work, which was to convey His grace, which was to go into the whole world, holding this life as a treasure for the sake of the whole world, praying and giving thanks for all men, because the unity of God and the unity of the mediation of Christ inspires them with hope that all may be one in Him [2].

The day of Pentecost was thus the birthday of the Church. Before there were followers of the Lord; now there was the Church: and this as the result of a new act, for which all that preceded had been but preparation: now the Church was born in becoming the possessor of a common corporate life. The Spirit was given to the whole body of Christians together: it was not given to an individual here and there in such a way that such Spirit-bearing individuals could then come together and form a Church. It was given corporately, so that they who received the Spirit realized at once a unity which preceded any individual action of their own. So the Church has gone forth offering its message freely to all; in Christ Jesus there is neither Jew nor Gentile; the message is given openly, 'without any veil,' to all; all are accepted who will submit themselves to Baptism, i. e. all who recognise the element of evil and of weakness in their own life, who are willing to die to it and receive fresh life and strength from the Risen Lord, and to submit their life to His discipline. That is the Church as presented to us in the New Testament. Metaphor after metaphor is lavished upon it by our Lord and by S. Paul in order to make clear the conception of it. He is the Vine, His disciples are the branches; they draw all their life from Him: apart from Him they can do nothing; if in union with Him, they bear fruit. The Church is a household,

---

[1] Πάντων τοίνυν ἀνθρώπων κεκλημένων, οἱ ὑπακοῦσαι βουληθέντες, κλητοὶ ὠνομάσθησαν, Clem. Alex. *Strom.* I. xviii. 89.

[2] Cp. 1 Tim. ii. 1-6.

T

a scene of active work, of 'skilled and trained activity': each member with his own work, some as mere members of the household, others as rulers set over the household to give them meat in due season, each with talents to be used faithfully for the Master. It is a family, in which 'all ye are brethren,' laying obligations of love between brother and brother, calling out self-sacrifice for the good of others, deepening in each the sense of the value of the lives of others. It is the Body of Christ, that which grows stronger and stronger, that which draws its life from the Head and must hold to Him, that in which Christian is linked to Christian in sympathy and complete interdependence, that without which the Head would be incomplete, the necessary organ for completing Christ's work on earth, that which the Spirit takes as its channel for manifesting to the world the very 'life of God.' It is God's Temple; visible, made up of parts, which are fitted in to one another in symmetry; beautiful with a spiritual beauty; for there a living God is present; there He speaks to His own; there they offer to Him a rational service[1]. It is the Bride of Christ, the dearest object of Christ's love, which gives herself to Him for His service, which for His sake keeps herself pure in life and doctrine; which receives from Him all the treasures of His love, so that as He had received the fulness of God, 'the aggregate of the Divine attributes, virtues, and energies' from the Father, the Church receives all this from Him and manifests it forth to the world of men and of angels.

But this picture, it will be urged, is only a prophecy of the future; the evidence of S. Paul's Epistles will also shew us a very different scene in real life, a body with tendencies to divisions, to selfishness, to sin. This is quite true, but the ideal is never thought of as something different from the real; the ideal is not simply in heaven nor the real simply on earth; the real is the ideal, though not yet completely developed; the ideal is the actual basis of the real as much as the goal to which the real is tending. The members of the Church have been consecrated; they are holy; they are 'unleavened'; they have put on Christ; they have by their self-committal to Him received a righteousness which they can work out into perfection. Again, they are brothers; they have been made children of God by adoption: as they have realized the sense of sonship, they realize also the closeness of the tie between themselves and the other sons, their common sympathies, hopes and aims. True, they are not yet perfect either in holiness or in love: the very purpose of the Church is to make them perfect. It takes the individual at his birth, it incorporates him into its own life, it watches over him from beginning to end, it feeds him with spiritual food, it disciplines him by spiritual laws, it blesses him at all the

[1] For the whole of this last paragraph cf. H. S. Holland, *On behalf of Belief,* Sermons VI and VII.

chief moments of life, it takes him away from his own isolation, trains him in social aims and social duties by social sacraments, finally, gives him back to God with its benediction.

Such a conception of the Church as a nursery, a school, a home, implies of necessity that it should be visible, and that it should be one. It is a visible body, because it has in some sense to represent the Incarnate Lord. In the Incarnation spirit took material form and expressed itself thereby; in the risen Lord—and it is the risen Lord who gives the Spirit to the Church—there was still a spiritual body. This is not to deny the invisible reality of spiritual unity which under-lies the external visible unity. It is only to say that completeness means both. In the language of S. Ignatius, as Christ Jesus was at once material and spiritual, so, the unity of the Church should be at once material and spiritual[1].

The idea of an invisible Church to express the body of true be-lievers, who alone are the Church, to whatever community they belong, so that the visible Church becomes an unimportant thing, is an idea entirely at variance with Scripture and all pre-reformation teaching. The phrase is first found in almost contemporary writings of Luther and of Zwingli; it is akin to the teaching of Hus and of Wiclif; and, no doubt, there are thoughts and phrases in earlier writers that are more or less akin to it. From the first there was obviously a distinc-tion between the true and untrue Christian, between the spiritual and the fleshly, between the vessels to honour and the vessels to dishonour, and the first of these classes, those who persevere to the end, whom man cannot know and God only knows, those who, if thought of in the light of God's eternal purposes, are the predestined, these were treated and spoken of as 'the Church properly so called,' 'the true body of Christ.' Christians 'who do the will of the Father will belong to the first Church, the spiritual Church founded before the sun and moon.' Those who have lived in perfect righteousness according to the Gospel 'will rest in the holy hill of God, in the highest Church, in which are gathered the philosophers of God[2].'

Again, the Church on earth is regarded as 'a copy of the Church in heaven in which God's will is done': but in each case there is no contrast between the visible and the invisible Church. The invisible Church is in these cases either the ideal of the visible; or that part of the visible organized Church which has remained true to its aims. So too with regard to those who are not conscious believers; the possi-

---

[1] S. Ignatius, *ad Eph.* vii. εἶς ἰατρός ἐστι, σαρκικὸς, καὶ πνευματικὸς, as com-pared with *ad Magn.* xiii. ἵνα ἕνωσις ᾖ σαρκικὴ τε καὶ πνευματική.

[2] Pseudo-Clem. Rom. *Ep.* ii. 14;

Clem. Alex. *Str.* vi. 14; iv. 8. For these and other illustrations cf. Seeberg, *Der Begriff der Christlichen Kirche* (Er-langen, 1885), cap. i; and Gore, *Church and the Ministry,* ed. i. pp. 19, 28, 136.

bility of their salvation, in a qualified way, is heartily recognised, but the confusion is not made of calling them members of the Church.

The fatal danger is when the belief in the invisible Church is used to discredit the visible Church and the importance of belonging to it. It is scarcely too much to say, that all stress laid upon the invisible Church tends to lower the demands of holiness and brotherhood. It is a visible Church, and such a Church as can attract outsiders, which calls out the fruits of faith into active energy; it is a visible Church such as can combine Christians in active work, which tests brotherhood, which rubs away idiosyncrasy, which destroys vanity and jealousy, which restrains personal ambition, which trains in the power of common work, which, as our own powers fail, or are proved inadequate, for some task on which our heart had been set, still fills us with hope that God will work through others that which it is clear He will not work through us. It is a visible Church alone which is 'the home of the lonely.' Encompassed as we are now from our birth by Christian friends and associations, we tend to forget how much we depend on the spiritual help and sympathy of others. The greatness of our blessings blinds us to their presence, and we seem to stand in our own strength while we are leaning upon others. The relation of the soul to God is a tender thing; personal religion, which seems so strong, while in a Christian atmosphere, tends to grow weak, to totter, to fall, as we stand alone in some distant country, amid low moral standards and heathen faiths. Such solitude does indeed often, in those who are strong, deepen, in a marvellous way, the invisible communion with God and the ties that knit us with the absent; but the result is often fatal to the weak. It throws both strong and weak alike into closer sympathy with those who share a common faith. It is a visible Church which supplies this sympathy, which gives the assurance that each soul, as it is drawn to God, shall not stand alone; but that it shall find around it strengthening hands and sympathetic hearts, which shall train it till, as in the quiet confidence of a home, it shall blossom into the full Christian life.

The principle of the unity of the Church is very similar. That, again, is primarily and essentially a spiritual unity. The ultimate source is, according to the Lord's own teaching, the unity of the Godhead : 'that they may be one, even as we are one.' The effect of the outpouring of the Spirit is to make the multitude of them that believed 'of one heart and one soul.' Baptism becomes the source of unity, 'In one Spirit were we all baptized into one body :' the 'one bread' becomes the security of union. 'We who are many are one bread, one body, for we all partake of the one bread.' More fully still is the unity drawn out in the Epistle to the Ephesians. 'There is one body and one Spirit, even as ye are called in one hope of our calling, one Lord, one faith, one baptism, one God and Father of all.' The unity starts with being spiritual; it is the power of the One God drawing men together by His action upon their spirits; uniting them in the service of one Lord who has redeemed them, but it issues in 'one body.' Nothing can be stronger than the assertion of such unity. But in what does this unity lie, and what is to be the safeguard of it? No one answer is possible to this question. Clearly, one part of the answer is, a unity of spiritual aim, 'one hope of your calling:' another answer is, a common basis of belief, common trust in the same Lord, 'one faith;' a further answer is, common social sacraments, 'one baptism,' 'one bread.' All these lie on the face of these passages of S. Paul. Are we to add to them 'a common government,' 'an apostolical succession?' Was this of the essence or a late addition, a result of subsequent confederation intended to guarantee the permanence of dogma? No doubt, the circumstances of subsequent history moulded the exact form of the ministry, and emphasized the importance of external organization under particular circumstances; but this is no less true of the other points of unity; the unity of spiritual life was worked out in one way in the times of public discipline and penance, in another way when these fell into disuse: the unity of faith was brought into prominence in the times of the formulating of the Creeds. So the unity of external organization was emphasized when it was threatened by the Gnostic, Novatian, and Donatist controversies. But the germ of it is there from the first, and it was no later addition. The spiritual unity derived from the Lord is imparted through Sacraments; but this at once links the inward life and spiritual unity with some form of external organization. And so the writer of the Epistle to the Ephesians after his great description of Christian unity, goes on at once to speak of the ministry. The apostles, prophets, evangelists, pastors, teachers, these are special gifts of the ascended Lord to the Church; and they are given for the very purpose of securing unity, 'for the perfecting of the saints unto the work of ministering, unto the building up of the body of Christ, till we all attain unto the unity of the faith.' No less significantly, when S. Paul is applying to the Church the metaphor of the body and its members in order to emphasize the unity of the whole, does he rank apostles, prophets, teachers, as the most important members of the body [1].

The history of the early Church, so far as it can be traced, points the same way. The Lord appointed His body of twelve: He gave them the power to bind and to loose, the power to exercise discipline over offending members of the Church. At first, the Christian Church is a purely Jewish body; it continues in the Apostles' fellowship as well as doctrine; they distribute its alms; they punish unworthy

[1] 1 Cor. xii. 28.

members; they arrange its differences; they appoint subordinate officers; they ratify their actions, and sanction the admission of Samaritans and proselytes to the Church; but the various members throughout Judea, Galilee, and Samaria, are embraced in the single conception of one Church[1]. Then under the guidance of Paul and Barnabas, the Gentiles are brought in and formed into churches; the danger to unity becomes acute. According to the Acts of the Apostles, it is surmounted by reference to the Church at Jerusalem; the Apostles and Elders there decide the question, and the Gentile Churches are thus kept in communion with it. S. Paul's letters, with all the difficulty there is of reconciling every detail with the historian's account, present us with essentially the same picture. In dealing with his own Churches, he claims absolute right, as apostle, to hand on and lay down traditions, to punish, to forgive, to govern: he leaves some class of ministers in every Church under his guidance; each Church is to administer discipline over unworthy members. But the Churches cannot act independently: the Church at Corinth is not to act as though it were the fountain head of Christianity, or the only Gentile Church; it is to remember the customs in other Churches. Further than this, above 'all the Churches,' appears already as one body ' the Church,' in which God has set apostles[2]; within it there are separate spheres of work, Paul and Barnabas are to go to the Gentiles, the leading Jewish apostles to the Jews; S. Paul will not intrude beyond the province assigned to him; he makes his Gentile Churches to contribute to the needs of the Jewish Church, and realize the debt which they owe to them. Any divisions in a local Church cannot be tolerated, as being inconsistent with the unity of Christ, with His cross, and with the significance of baptism. Peter stands condemned when he wishes to separate himself and so causes division between Jew and Gentile.

The importance attached to external organization is surely implied in all of this, and the circumstances of the second century forced out into clearness what was so implied. Gnosticism, Montanism, Novatianism all tended to found new bodies, which claimed to be the true Church. How was the individual Christian to test their claims? It was in the face of this question that Church writers, notably S. Cyprian and S. Irenaeus, emphasized the importance of historical continuity in the Church as secured by the apostolical succession of the episcopate. The unity of the Church came primarily, they urged, from God, from heaven, from the Father; it was secured by the foundation of the Church upon the Apostles; the bishops have succeeded to the Apostles and so become the guardians of the unity of the Church. As soon

---

[1] Cp. Acts ix. 31 ἡ ἐκκλησία καθ' ὅλης τῆς Ἰουδαίας καὶ Γαλιλαίας καὶ Σαμαρείας.

[2] I Cor. xii. 28, xv. 9; Gal. i. 13; Phil. iii. 6; Eph. i. 22, iii. 10, 21; Col. i. 18, 24; I Tim. iii. 15.

then as we find the Christian episcopate universally organized, we find it treated as an institution received from the Apostles and as carrying with it the principle of historic continuity. So it has remained ever since, side by side with the other safeguards of unity, the sacraments and the common faith. The Roman Church has added to it what seemed a further safeguard of unity, the test of communion with itself; but this was a later claim, a claim which was persistently resented, and which was urged with disastrous results. The Reformed Churches of the Continent, in their protest against that additional test, have rejected the whole principle of historic continuity; they have remained satisfied with the bond of a common faith and of common sacraments: but the result can scarcely be said to be as yet a securer unity. Even an Unitarian historian recognises heartily that the characteristic of the Church in England is this continuity. 'There is no point,' urges Mr. Beard[1], 'at which it can be said, here the old Church ends, here the new begins. . . . The retention of the Episcopate by the English Reformers at once helped to preserve this continuity and marked it in the distinctest way. . . . It is an obvious historical fact that Parker was the successor of Augustine, just as clearly as Lanfranc and Becket.'

This, then, is what the Church claims to be as the home of grace, the channel of spiritual life. It claims to be a body of living persons who have given themselves up to the call of Christ to carry on His work in the world; a body which was organized by Himself thus far that the Apostles were put in sole authority over it; a body which received the Spirit to dwell within it at Pentecost; a body which propagated itself by spiritual birth; a body in which the ministerial power was handed on by the Apostles to their successors, which has remained so organized till the present day, and has moved on through the world, sometimes allied with, sometimes in separation from the State, always independent of it; a body which lays on each of its members the duty of holiness, and the obligation of love, and trains them in both.

But two objections arise here, which must be dealt with shortly. It is urged first, this is an unworthy limitation: we ought to love all men; to treat all men as brothers; why limit this love, this feeling of brotherhood to the baptized, to the Church? True, we ought to love and honour all men, to do good to all men. The love of the Christian, like the love of Christ, knows no limits; but the limitations are in man himself. All human nature is not lovable: all men are not love-worthy. Love must, at least, mean a different thing; it must weaken its connotation if applied to all men; there may be pity, there may be faith, there may be a prophetic anticipating love for the sinner and the criminal, as we recall their origin and forecast the possibilities of their future; but love in the highest sense, love that delights in and admires its object, love

[1] *Hibbert Lectures,* 1883, p. 311.

that is sure of a response, the sense of brotherhood which knows that it can trust a brother—these are not possible with the wanton, the selfish, the hypocrite. Though man has social instincts which draw him into co-operation with others; he has also tendencies to selfishness and impurity which work against the spirit of brotherhood and make it impossible. Not till we have some security that the man's real self is on the side of unselfishness, can we trust him; and baptism with its gifts of grace, baptism with its death to the selfish nature, baptism with its profession of allegiance to the leadership of Christ, this, at least, gives us some security. Even Comte, with his longing for brotherhood, tells us that in forming our conception of humanity we must not take in all men, but those only who are really assimilable, in virtue of a real co-operation towards the common existence, and Mr. Cotter Morison would eliminate and suppress those who have no altruistic affection. We limit, then, only so far as seems necessary to gain reality; we train men in the narrower circle of brotherhood, that they may become enthusiasts for it, and go forth as missionaries to raise others to their own level. As for those who lie outside Christianity, the Church, like our Lord Himself in the parable of the sheep and the goats, like S. Paul in his anticipation of the judgment day, recognises all the good there is in them; like Justin Martyr and many of the early Fathers, it traces in them the work of the Divine Word; and yet none the less did these writers claim and does the Church still claim for itself the conscious gift of spiritual life, in a sense higher than anything that lies outside itself.

But many, who would follow thus far, would draw another line, and would include within the Church all the baptized, whether professing churchmen or not. Once more, so far as we draw any distinction within the limits of the baptized, it is for the sake of reality. We recognise that every atom of their faith is genuine, that so far as they have one Lord, one faith, one baptism, they are true members of the Church; that so far as they have banded themselves together into a society, they have something akin to the reality of the Church, and gain some of its social blessings. But then it is they who have banded themselves together into a society: and that means they have done it at their own risk. We rest upon the validity of our sacraments, because they were founded by the Lord Himself, because they have His special promises, because they have been handed down in regular and valid channels to us. Have they equal security that their sacraments are valid? Again, we must hold that schism means something of evil: that it causes weakness: that it thus prevents the full work of brotherhood, of knitting Christian with Christian in common worship: that so it prevents the complete witness of the Church in the world; that in so far as such Christians are schismatic, they are untrue and harmful members of the Church. The full complete claim of the Church is that it is a body visibly meeting together in a common life, and forming by historical continuity a part of the actual body founded by our Lord Himself. It would be unreal to apply this conception of a complete historic brotherhood to those who have separated themselves from the Church's worship, and whose boast is that they were founded by Wesley, or Luther, or Calvin. A Church so founded is not historically founded by Christ. It may have been founded to carry on the work of Christ, it may have been founded in imitation of Him, and with the sincerest loyalty to His person, but it cannot be said to have been founded by Him. Even if circumstances have justified it, it is at any rate not the ideal; and whatever confessions the historic Church may have to make of its own shortcomings, it still must witness to the ideal of a visible unity and historical continuity. Amid the divisions of Christendom, and in face of her own shortcomings, the Church of England does not claim to be the full complete representation of the Church of Christ. She is only one national expression of the Catholic Church : she feels that 'it is safer for us to widen the pale of the kingdom of God, than to deny the fruits of the Spirit [1];' she has ever on her lips the prayer, 'Remember not, Lord, our offences, nor the offences of our forefathers, neither take vengeance of our sins,' and yet she must make her claim boldly and fearlessly to have retained the true ideal of the Church ; to be loyal to the essential principle that her life comes historically from Christ and not from man.

II. But the Church is the school of truth as well as the school of virtue. Its ministers form a priesthood of truth as well as a priesthood of sacrifice. Its priests' lips have 'to keep knowledge.' Christianity is, as the School of Alexandria loved to represent it, a Divine philosophy, and the Church its school.

This conception of the Church starts from our Lord's own words. His Apostles are to be as scribes instructed unto the kingdom of Heaven ; they are to have the scribes' power to decide what is and what is not binding in the kingdom ; the Spirit is to lead them into all truth ; they are to make disciples of all the nations, 'teaching them to observe all things whatsoever I commanded you.' The function of the Church then with regard to truth is primarily to bear witness to that which has been revealed. It does not primarily reveal, it tells of the truths which have been embodied in the historic life of Jesus Christ or explained in His teaching. 'One is its teacher ; One is its master, even the Christ.' It holds a 'faith once delivered to the saints.' Hence, from the first, there grew up some quasi-authoritative formula, in which we can see the germ of the later Creeds, which each Christian

---

[1] Bp. Forbes, *Explanation of the Nicene Creed*, p. 290.

Missionary would teach to his converts. S. Paul himself received from others and handed on to the Corinthians, as his first message to them, some such half-stereotyped Creed, narrating the central facts of the Death and Resurrection of the Lord; his teaching was as a mould which shaped the lives of the converts as they were poured, like so much molten metal, into it. It was authoritative, not even an angel from heaven could preach another gospel. As time went on and false teaching spread, this side of the Church's work is emphasized more and more. The Church is to be the pillar and ground-work of the truth. Timothy and Titus are to hold fast the deposit, to prevent false teaching, to secure wholesomeness of doctrine no less than sobriety of life.

The contests of the next centuries bring out this idea of witness into clearer prominence, and the Episcopate, as it had been the guarantee of unity, becomes now the guarantee of truth. Thus, S. Ignatius is face to face with Docetic and Gnostic teaching; with him the bishops are 'in the mind of Jesus Christ;' they are to be treated 'as the Lord;' to avoid heresy, it is necessary to avoid 'separation from the God of Jesus Christ, from the Bishop and the ordinances of the Apostles;' the one bishop is ranked with the one Eucharist, the one flesh of Jesus Christ, the one cup, the one altar, as the source of unity; submission to the Bishop and the Presbyters is a means towards holiness, towards spiritual strength and spiritual joy[1]. These are incidental expressions in letters written at a moment of spiritual excitement: but the same appeal reappears in calmer controversial treatises. S. Irenaeus argues against Gnosticism on exactly the same grounds. Truth is essentially a thing *received*; it was received by the Apostles from Christ. He was the truth Himself; He revealed it to His Apostles; they embodied it in their writings and handed it on to the Bishops and Presbyters who succeeded them; hence the test of truth is to be sought in Holy Scripture and in the teaching of those Churches which were founded directly by the Apostles[2]. With equal strength Tertullian urges that the truth was received by the churches from the Apostles, by the Apostles from Christ, by Christ from God; it is therefore independent of individuals; it must be sought for in Holy Scripture, but as the canon of that is not fixed, and its interpretation is at times doubtful, it must be supplemented by the evidence of the apostolic Churches; and he challenges the heretics to produce the origin of their churches and shew that the series of bishops runs back to some Apostle or apostolic man[3].

The Church is thus primarily a witness: the strength of its authority

---

[1] *ad Eph.* ii. iii. vi. xx ; *ad Trall.* vii. xiii ; *ad Phil.* iv. vii ; *ad Smyrn.* viii. ix.

[2] Irenaeus, *adv. Haer.*, cp. esp. I.

10, II. 9, III. 1, 2, 3, 4, 5, 12, 24.

[3] *Praescript. adv. Haereticos* ; cp. esp. 3, 6, 15-21.

lies in the many sides from which the witness comes; but the exigencies of controversy, and indeed of thought even apart from controversy, rendered necessary another function in respect to truth. The Church was compelled to formulate, to express its witness in relation to the intellectual difficulties of the time. Christianity is indeed essentially a matter not of the intellect, but of the will, a personal relation of trust in a personal God. Its first instinct is, as the first instinct of friendship would be, to resent intellectual analysis and dogmatic definition. But as the need of telling others about a friend, or defending him against slander, would compel us to analyse his qualities and define his attractiveness; so it was with the Church's relation to the Lord. It bore witness to the impression which His life had made upon His followers that He was Divine; it bore witness to the facts of the life that attested it and to His own statements. But the claim was denied; it needed justifying; it needed to be shewn to be consistent with other truths, such as the unity of God, and the reality of His own human nature, and so definition was forced upon the Church. The germ of such definitions is found in the New Testament; the deeper Christological teaching of the Epistles to the Ephesians and to the Colossians, and of the prologue of S. John are instances of such intellectual analysis and formulation, and were evidently written in the face of controversy. The technical decisions of the great councils of the fourth and fifth centuries and their expression in the Nicene and 'Athanasian' Creeds are the outcome of the same tendency. Yet even in them, the Church acts, in a sense, as a witness; the Scriptures are appealed to as the ultimate authority; the Creed is the summary of its chief doctrines: the one aim is to secure and express the truth witnessed to by churches throughout the world, to eliminate novelty and caprice; the new definitions are accepted, because they alone are felt to express the instinct of the Church's worship. By this time the canon of Holy Scripture was fixed. It becomes thenceforth an undying fountain of life from which the water of pure doctrine can be drawn. Tradition and development can always be checked by that.

In the truths then which the Church teaches we may distinguish two classes. First, there are the central truths to which it bears absolute witness; such as the Fatherhood of God, the Person and work of Jesus Christ, the Redemption of all mankind, the origin and purpose of human life. These it teaches authoritatively. Its conduct is exactly analogous to that of a parent teaching the moral law to his children; teaching the commandments authoritatively at first, till the child can be educated to understand the reason of them. So the Church says to her children, or to those who are seeking after truth 'there is an absolute truth in religion as well as in morality: we have tested it; generations of the saints have found it true. It is a truth independent of individual teachers; independent of the shifting moods of opinion at any particular period; and you must accept it on our authority first. Further, these are truths which affect life, therefore they cannot be apprehended merely by the intellect. You must commit yourself to them; act upon them; there is a time when the seeker after truth sees where it lies; then it must cease to be an open question. "You must seek till you find, but when you have once found truth, you must commit yourself to it[1]." You must believe that you may understand; but it is *that* you may understand.' The dogma is authoritatively taught, that the individual may be kept safe from mere individual caprice and fancifulness, but also that he himself may come to a rational understanding of his belief. No doubt the truth is so wide that to the end of our lives we shall still feel the need of guidance and of teaching. 'As long as we live,' said Calvin, 'our weakness will not allow us to be discharged from school.' Like S. Ignatius on his way to martyrdom, the Christian may feel at his dying day, 'Now I begin to be a disciple;' but the aim of the Church is to make each member have a rational hold upon his faith. When we are young we accept a doctrine because the Church teaches it to us; when we are grown up, we love the Church because it taught us the doctrine. 'The Churchman never surrenders his individual responsibility. But he may and must surrender some portion at least of his independence, and he benefits greatly by the surrender[2].' Submission to the authority of the Church is the merging of our mere individualism in the whole historic life of the great Christian brotherhood; it is making ourselves at one with the one religion in its most permanent and least merely local form. It is surrendering our individuality only to empty it of its narrowness[3].'

Secondly, there are other truths, which are rather deductions from these central points or statements of them in accordance with the needs of the age; such as the mode of the relation of the Divine and human natures in Christ, of free-will to predestination, or the method of the Atonement, or the nature of the Inspiration of Holy Scripture. If, in any case, a point of this kind has consciously come before the whole Church and been reasoned out and been decided upon, such a decision raises it into the higher class of truths, which are taught authoritatively; but if this is not so, the matter remains an open question. It remains a question for the theologians; it is not imposed on individual Christians; though it may at any time become ripe for decision. The very fixity of the great central doctrines allows the Church to give a remarkable freedom to individual opinion on all

[1] Tertullian. *Praescr.* 9: 'Quaerendum est donec invenias, et credendum ubi inveneris.'

[2] Hawkins' *Sermons on the Church*,

p. 77.

[3] Rev. C. Gore, *Roman Catholic Claims.* p. 51.

other points. Practically, how much wider is the summary of the rule of faith as given in Irenaeus (III. 4), or Tertullian (*Praescr.* 13), or Origen (*De Principiis*), or in the Apostles' or Nicene Creed, than the tests of orthodoxy that would be imposed in a modern religious, or scientific circle! S. Vincent of Lerins is the great champion of antiquity as the test of truth; yet he who lays it down that 'to declare any new truth to Catholic Christians over and above that which they have received never was allowed, nowhere is allowed, and never will be allowed,' also insists on the duty of development, of growth, within the true lines of the central truths. 'Is there,' he assumes an objector to urge, 'to be no growth within the Church? Nay, let there be growth to the greatest extent; who would be so grudging to man, such an enemy to God, as to attempt to prevent it; but yet let it be such that it be growth, not change of the faith. . . . As time goes on, it is right that the old truths should be elaborated, polished, filed down; it is wrong that they should be changed, maimed or mutilated. They should be made clear, have light thrown on them, be marked off from each other; but they must not lose their fulness, their entirety, their essential character[1].' So it has happened in the course of the Christian history; doctrines like that of the Atonement have been restated afresh to meet the needs of the age. So it is happening still; doctrines like that of the method of creation or of the limits of inspiration are still before the Church. The Church is slow to decide, to formulate: it stands aside, it reiterates its central truths, it says that whatever claims to be discovered must ultimately fit in with the central truths; creation must remain God's work; the Bible must remain God's revelation of Himself; but for a time it is content to wait, loyal to fact from whatever side it comes; confident alike in the many-sidedness and in the unity of truth. While he accepts and while he searches, the Churchman can enjoy alike the inquiry of truth which is the love-making or wooing of it, the knowledge of truth which is the presence of it, and the belief of truth which is the enjoying of it, and all these together, says Lord Bacon, are the sovereign good of human nature[2].

Thus far we have in this part considered the Church's function with regard to truth from the point of view of those whom it has to teach. Its function is no less important from the point of view of the truth itself. As spiritual life is a tender plant that needs care and training; so spiritual truth is a precious gem, that may easily be lost and therefore needs careful guarding. 'The gem requires a casket, the casket a keeper.' Truth is indeed great and will prevail, but not apart from the action of men: not unless there are those who believe in it, take pains about it and propagate it. This is the case even with scientific truths; *à fortiori* therefore, with moral and religious truths which

---

[1] *Commonitorium* ix. and xxiii.   [2] Bacon, Essay on *Truth.*

affect life and need to be translated into life before they can be really understood. The comparative study of religions is shewing us more and more how much of deep spiritual truth there is in heathen religions, but it is shewing us equally how little power this truth had to hold its own, how it was overlaid, crushed out, stifled. The truth of the unity of God underlies much of the polytheism of India, Greece, and Rome; but it is only the philosopher and the scholar that can find it there. It is only in the Jewish Church, the nation which stood alone from other nations as a witness to the truth, that it retained its hold as a permanent force. The Fatherhood of God is implied in the very names and titles of most of the chief heathen gods; but what a difference in its meaning and force since the time of Jesus Christ! It is not only that He expanded and deepened its meaning, so that it implied the fatherhood of all men alike, and a communication of a spiritual nature to all; it is also, and much more, that He committed the truth as a sacred deposit to a Church, each member of which aimed at shewing himself as the son of a perfect Father, and which witnessed to the universal Fatherhood by the fact of an universal brotherhood.

The very truths of natural religion, which heathenism tended to degrade, found a safe home within the Church; the knowledge of the Creator, His eternal power and Godhead, which the nations had known but lost, because they glorified Him not as God, neither were thankful, has been kept alive in the Eucharistic services of the Church, repeating through the ages its praise of the Creator: 'We praise Thee, we bless Thee, we worship Thee, we give thanks to Thee, for Thy great glory, O Lord God, heavenly King, God the Father Almighty.'

III. We pass naturally to the third point: the Church is the home of worship. It is the Temple of the Lord. As a teaching body, it had carried on and spiritualized the work of the Jewish Synagogue: it also took up and spiritualized the conceptions of prayer and praise and sacrifice which clustered round the Jewish Temple. The Body of Christ was to take the place of the Temple when the Jews destroyed it[1]. And here, as in all other respects, the body is the organ and representative of the risen Lord. He, when on earth, had been a priest in the deepest sense of the word: He, as the representative of the Father, had mediated the Father's blessings to man: He, as one with man, had become a merciful and faithful high-priest for man; He had offered His whole life to God for the service of man; He had by the offering of His pure will made purification of sins: He lives still, a priest for ever, pleading, interceding for mankind.

[1] S. John ii. 19–21.

And so the Church, His body, carries on this priestly work on earth. 'Sacerdotalism, priestliness, is the prime element of her being[1].' She is the source of blessing to mankind; she pleads and intercedes and gives herself for all mankind. Christians, as a body, are 'a royal priesthood.' Christ made them 'priests unto His God and Father,' they can 'enter in into the holy place,' like priests, 'with hearts sprinkled from an evil conscience and bodies washed with pure water.' They are 'the genuine high-priestly race of God:' 'every righteous man ranks as a priest :' 'to the whole Church is a priesthood given[2].' This priesthood is exercised throughout life, as each Christian gives his life to God's service, and the whole Church devotes itself for the good of the whole world. But it finds its expression in worship, for worship is the Godward aspect of life. It expresses, it emphasizes, it helps to make permanent the feelings that mould life. It is the recognition that our life comes from God: that it has been redeemed by God ; it is the quiet joyous resting upon the facts of His love; it is the conscious spiritual offering of our life to God; it is the adoration of His majesty. This worship the Church leads and organizes. 'In the Church and in Christ Jesus' is to be given 'the glory to God unto all generations for ever and ever.' In the Apocalypse, it is pictured as praising God alike for His work in Creation and in Redemption. In the Eucharist the Church shews forth the Lord's Death till He come[3]. Hence this act of Eucharistic worship, above all others, has become the centre of unity. In it the Church has offered its best to God : all the more external gifts of art, such as architecture, painting, and music, have been consecrated in worship : but deeper still, in it each Christian has taken up his own life, his body and soul, and offered it as a holy, lively, and reasonable sacrifice unto God, a service in spirit and in truth : and deeper still, he recognises that his life does not stand alone ; through the common ties of humanity in Christ he is linked on by a strange solidarity with all mankind ; his life depends on theirs and theirs on his, and so he offers it not for himself only but for all; in the power of Christ he intercedes for all mankind : and deeper still, he feels in the presence of the Holiness of God how unworthy his own offering and his own prayers are, and he pleads, he recalls before the Father, as the source of his own hope and his own power of self-sacrifice, the one complete offering made for all mankind.

So the Church performs its universal priesthood[4]; so it leads a

---

[1] From a striking and bold article by Prof. Milligan, in the *Expositor*, March, 1889.

[2] 1 S. Peter ii. 9 ; Rev. i. 6 ; Heb. x. 19. Justin Martyr, *Dialog. c. Tryph.* 116 ; Irenaeus iv. 8 ; Origen, *Hom. vi. in Lev.* 5. For other instances cp.

Seeberg, *ubi supra*, or Gore, *Church and the Ministry*, pp. 87–90.

[3] Eph. iii. 21 (R.V.) ; Rev. iv. 11, v. 11–14 ; 1 Cor. xi. 26.

[4] Cf. the striking account of the true Christian sacrifice in S. Aug. *De Civ. Dei*, x. 6 : 'Profecto efficitur ut tota

worship, bright, joyous, amidst all the trials and perplexities of the world, for it tells of suffering vanquished; simple in its essence, so that poor as well as rich can rally round it; yet deep and profound in its mysteries, so that the most intellectual cannot fathom it. It is an universal priesthood, for it needs the consecration of every life : and yet this function too of the Church naturally has its organs, whose task it is to make its offerings and to stand before it as the types of self-consecration. The Church has from the first special persons who perform its liturgy, its public ministering to the Lord[1]. It is in connection with worship, and the meetings of the Church that S. Paul emphasizes the need of unity and subordination, and dwells upon God's special setting of Apostles, Prophets and Teachers in the Church[2]. The Epistle of Clement to the Corinthians may be open to difficult questions of interpretation in its language about the ministry, but this at least is clear that order and subordination are treated as the necessary outcome of love, which is of the essence of the Church; that this order and subordination is specially needed in all details of worship; that it had been so in Judaism, and must be so, *à fortiori*, in the Christian Church ; that as Christ came from God, so the Apostles from Christ, and their successors from them; and therefore it must be wrong to throw off subordination to those who were so appointed and who have blamelessly offered the gifts[3]. 'The Church,' said S. Augustine, 'from the time of the Apostles, through most undoubted succession of the bishops, perseveres till the present moment, and offers to God in the Body of Christ the sacrifice of praise[4].' As the teaching function of the whole Church does not militate against the special order of teachers, so the priestly function of the whole does not militate against a special order of priests. We cannot speak of those who are ordained as ' going into the Church '—and it is hard to estimate the harm done by that fatal phrase—for that implies that the laity are not of the Church, but we can call them priests in a special sense; for they give themselves up in a deeper way to the service of God ; they are specially trained and purified for His service ; they are put as representatives of the whole Church in a way in which no other is, able to know and to sympathize with its wants, its joys, its failings ; able therefore to intercede for it with God and to bring His blessings to it. As the Church stands in relation to the world, so they stand to the Church ; they fill up that which is lacking of the afflictions

ipsa redempta civitas, hoc est congregatio societasque sanctorum universale sacrificium offeratur Deo per sacerdotem magnum, qui etiam se ipsum obtulit in passione pro nobis, ut tanti capitis corpus essemus . . . Hoc est sacrificium Christianorum, *multi unum corpus in Christo.* Quod etiam sacramento altaris

fidelibus noto frequentat ecclesia, ut ei demonstretur, quod in ea re, quam offert, ipsa offeratur.'

[1] Acts xiii. 1.

[2] 1 Cor. xi–xiv.; cp. 1 Tim. ii.

[3] Clem. *ad Cor.* 1. esp. 40–45.

[4] *Contra Adv. Leg. et Proph.* xx. 39.

of Christ in their flesh for His body's sake which is the Church, whereof they are made ministers; they convey spiritual gifts and benediction to the Church.

To complete the conception of the Church, it would be necessary to add the thought of the Church expectant and triumphant, the presence of the blessed dead. For they too strengthen and complete each aspect of the Church's work. The great cloud of witnesses, the heroes of faith, who watch their brethren on earth, they, by their example, aid the spiritual life and strengthen us to lay aside every weight and the sin that doth so easily beset us: their virtues reflect parts of the manifold glory of the Son of Man. With their heirs *noblesse oblige*; each Christian born of such ancestry is able to be like the Athenian Lycurgus, independent of the world, bold and outspoken, because of his noble birth[1]. The record of their writings strengthens the witness to the faith once delivered to the saints, and binds us to loyalty to that which has stood the test of ages. They, 'the general assembly and church of the firstborn enrolled in heaven,' themselves, we believe, worship God with a purer worship than ours; the thought of their presence in worship, as we join with angels and archangels and all the company of heaven, lifts our hearts to a wider, more spiritual adoration.

But for our present purpose it is with the Church militant we have to deal: the Church on earth, the visible organ of the risen Lord, the organ of redemption, of revelation, of worship; the chief instrument designed by the Lord for the establishment of the kingdom of Heaven upon earth. That is our ideal of it. But what of the reality? of the historical facts? Has not the Church crushed out individual life and freedom? has it not thrown its shield over laxity? has it not repressed zeal and so driven piety into nonconformity? has it not tried to check scientific truth and condemned a Galileo? has it not made worship a matter of form and reduced it to externalism? So its opponents ask, and its defenders admit that there is much of truth in these charges. They admit that it has looked very different from its ideal. 'It has looked like an obscure and unpopular sect; it has looked like a wonderful human institution vying with the greatest in age and power; it has looked like a great usurpation; it has looked like an overgrown and worn-out system; it has been obscured by the outward accidents of splendour or disaster; it has been enriched, it has been plundered; at one time throned above emperors, at another under the heel of the vilest; it has been dishonoured by the crimes of its governors, by truckling to the world, by the idolatry of power, by greed and selfishness, by their unbelief in their own mission, by the deep stain of

---

[1] Παῤῥησιαστὴς διὰ τὴν εὐγένειαν, Plutarch. *Vitae x Orat.* 7.

U

profligacy, by the deep stain of blood[1].' The Church has, indeed, many confessions to make, of its failure to be true to its ideal. But there are several considerations which must be borne in mind when we pass judgment upon it.

In the first place, it was committed to human hands, 'the treasure is in earthen vessels;' and while it gains thus in reality, in human sympathy, in touching the facts of every-day life, it is exposed to all the risks of imperfection, mistake, perversion. But further, as S. Augustine said, we still can say, 'Non adhuc regnat hoc regnum.' The Church has never had free play; it has never been in a position to carry out its ideal. At first, a persecuted sect, it had not the power; then, when it became established and gained the power, there burst into it an influx of half-Christianized converts who lowered its moral level or misunderstood its doctrines; then, with the break up of the Roman Empire, it had to tame and civilize the new races of Europe; and finally, the divisions of the Reformation have weakened its witness in the world. But, more important still, the very greatness of the ideal has caused the difficulty of its realization, and has exposed itself to caricature and to one-sidedness. The richer, the more many-sided, the more complete an ideal is, the less possible is it for any one generation to express it completely, the more likely is it that one side of truth will be pressed to the exclusion of some, if not of all the rest.

This may be tested in each of the points which we have considered. The Church is an organization for spiritual life, for holiness. It makes the bold claim to be the society of saints; but at once there arises the conflict between the ideal and the actual state of men. Press the ideal, and you will narrow the Church to those who are externally leading good lives or who are conscious of conversion to Christ. This was the line taken by the Novatians, by the Donatists, by the Puritans, by the Baptists, and the Church was thereby narrowed. On the other hand, dwell only on the actual state, the weakness, the failures of human nature, and you acquiesce in a low level of morality. The Church aims at being true to both; it will not exclude any from its embrace who are willing to submit to its laws; it takes children and trains them; it takes the imperfect and disciplines them; it rejects none, save such as rejoice in their iniquity and deliberately refuse to submit to discipline.

But again, this suggests another class of difficulties, all those which are associated with the relation of the individual to the society, difficulties which are parallel to the difficulties in politics, which are not yet solved there, and which are always needing re-adjustment. Here again it is possible to overpress either side: the

[1] The Dean of S. Paul's, *Advent Sermons*, p. 73.

claims of the society may be urged to the detriment of the individual, the central organization may crush out national life and give no scope for individual development, and so there arises the imperial absolutism of the mediaeval Church. On the other hand, it is equally possible to exaggerate the claims of individualism, of independence, of freedom, and the result is division and disaster to the whole society; the individual is only anxious to save his own soul, and religion is claimed to be only a thing between a man and his God; common Church life becomes impossible, and the witness of the Church to the world, and thereby its power for missionary work, becomes weakened. As before, the Church ideal strives to combine both sides of the truth. It values, it insists on, the rights of each individual soul; its mission is to convey the Spirit to it, that is to say, to waken it up to a consciousness of its own individual relation to God, its own personal responsibility in God's sight; it does bid each individual save his own soul. But it keeps also before him the claims of the society; it says to him that in saving his soul he must lose it in service for others; when his soul is saved, it must be used for active service with others in joint work. It does say that the society is more important for the world than any one individual member of it, and that each individual gets real strength when he speaks and acts not for himself but as representing the society behind him. It is possible to think of the Church as an organization existing for the spiritual good of the individual; but it is possible also, and it is a deeper view, to think of the individual as existing for the good of the Church, like a singer training himself not to display his own voice but to strengthen the general effect of the whole choir. That is the ideal of the Church, a body which quickens the individual into full conscious life, that the individual may devote his life to the service of the whole. Its life is like that of a great moving flight of birds, each with its own life, yet swaying and rising and turning as by a common impulse,

> Their jubilant activity evolves
> Hundreds of curves and circlets, to and fro,
> Upwards and downwards; progress intricate
> Yet unperplexed, as if one spirit swayed
> Their indefatigable flight[1].

The Church, again, is the teacher of truth; but in the acquisition of truth there are always two elements. There are the fixed facts of life, with which theory deals, and the accumulation of past thought upon the facts; there is also the creative spirit which plays upon these, which re-adapts, combines, discovers. The teacher of any science has to convey to his pupil the accumulated theories of the past and to quicken in him fresh power of thinking: he speaks first with

---

[1] Wordsworth, *The Recluse.*

authority, though of course with assurance that his authority is rational, and that the pupil will understand it ultimately. The teacher of morality, the parent, teaches even more strongly with authority, though he too trusts that the child will ultimately accept the law on rational grounds. The pupil needs at once a receptive and a critical faculty. The absence or exaggeration of either is equally fatal. Here again the Church ideal tries to combine both sides and to insist upon the real unity of all truth, and this makes its task so difficult. At times the whole stress has been laid on the permanent elements in the faith, and the result has been, as often in the Oriental Church, a tendency to intellectual stagnation : at other times the present speaking voice of the Church has been emphasized, and any theory has been hastily adopted as absolutely true, without due consideration of its relation to other truths. At times authority has been over-emphasized, and the acceptance of dogma has seemed to be made the equivalent of a living trust in a personal God : at others the duty of individual search after truth, of individual conviction has been pressed ; the traditions of the past have been ignored ; nothing has been of value except that which has commended itself to the individual reason, and the result has been confusion, uncertainty, the denial of the greatness and the mystery and the width of truth, and too often a moral and spiritual paralysis. Meanwhile the Church has tried to hold to both sides : it has insisted on the ultimate unity of all knowledge : starting from the axiom that One is our teacher, even Christ, and believing that all truth comes from His inspiration as the Word of God, it has refused to acquiesce in intellectual contradiction ; it has ever held, with King Lear, 'that "ay" and "no" too is no good divinity.' The truths of philosophy and religion must be one : the truths of science and religion must be one[1]. In the desire to see this, the Church has been hasty, it has rejected scientific truth, because it did not fall in with its interpretation of the Bible. It has made its mistakes, but it has done so out of a noble principle. It would be easy to gain consistency by sacrificing either side ; it is hard to combine the two : and this is what the Church has tried to do : it has upheld the belief of the ultimate synthesis of all knowledge. In exactly the same way, the sects have often gained force, popularity, effectiveness for the moment by the emphasis laid on some one truth ; the Church has gained strength, solidity, permanence, by its witness to the whole body of truth.

The same tendency may be shortly illustrated with regard to the function of worship. That too is a complex act ; in that there should

---

[1] Cp. Socrates iii. 16 Τὸ γὰρ καλόν, ἔνθα ἂν ᾖ ἴδιον τῆς ἀληθείας ἐστίν. S. Aug. *de doctr. Chr.* ii. 18 : 'quisquis bonus verusque Christianus est, Domini sui esse intellegat ubique invenerit veritatem.'

be the free conscious act of the individual, worshipping in spirit and in truth a God whom he knows as a personal God; but clearly this is not all; the whole society must express its corporate life in corporate worship. Its influence is something over and above the influence of its individual members, and that influence must be exercised on the side of God; it must be recognised as coming from God; it must be solemnly consecrated to God's service. The society has a right then to call upon its individual members to join in this corporate action. On the one hand lies the danger of the overpressure of the society, where the service of the individual is unwilling or apathetic: on the other hand the danger of individualism and sectarianism, in which the whole conception of public worship is lowered and the individual is never trained in religious matters to feel the kindling power of a common enthusiasm, to be lifted above himself in the wave of a common joy. The Church has aimed at combining both; by the insistance on confession and absolution it has tried to train the individual to a sense of personal penitence and personal gratitude: but these have only prepared him to share in the common worship of the society.

But the Church has had to do even more than this. Not only has it aimed at keeping in due proportion the conflicting elements in life, in truth, and in worship; it has also had to keep alive the three sides at once, and to keep them in their true relation to each other. To be at one and the same time the home of life and truth and worship, this belongs to its ideal and this adds new difficulties. Sometimes one element has preponderated, sometimes another: but its aim is always to preserve the three. It has historically preserved the synthesis of the three more than any other Christian body. It has moved through the ages doing its work, however imperfectly. It has kept historic continuity with the past: it has disciplined life and raised the standard of morality and united the nations of the world. It has been a witness to a spiritual world, to the fact that men have interests above material things, and that these deeper spiritual interests can combine them with the strongest links. It has gone out as a *Catholic* Church, knowing that it contains in its message truths that can win their way to every nation; and therefore it has never ceased to be a *Missionary* Church, as it needs that each nation should draw out into prominence some aspect of its truth, and reveal in life some side of its virtue. It has enshrined, protected, witnessed to the truth; both as an 'authoritative republication of natural religion,' keeping alive the knowledge of God, and of His moral government of the world[1], and as a revelation of redemption. It has drawn up the canon of Holy Scripture and formulated its Creeds: it still witnesses to the unity of knowledge: it has held up before the world an ideal of worship, at once social and indi-

---

[1] Butler's *Analogy*, Pt. ii. ch. I.

vidual. Its truths have indeed spread beyond itself, so that men find them now in bodies opposed to it; and therefore are perplexed and do not know where their allegiance is really due. It has indeed been itself often untrue to its mission; but ever and again it has re-asserted itself with a strange recuperative power, for, as the fountain of its life, there is ever the power of the Holy Spirit, sent by the risen Lord; to check temporary failures or accretions of teachings, there has been the perpetual re-appeal to Holy Scripture and the Creeds; to control idiosyncrasies of worship, there has been the permanent element of its Liturgies. Its very failures have come from its inherent greatness; they are the proof of great capacities, the omen of a greater future. Like S. Paul, it holds on its way ' by glory and dishonour, by evil report and good report, as deceiving and yet true, as unknown and yet well-known; as dying and behold it lives; as chastened and not killed; as sorrowful yet always rejoicing; as poor and yet making many rich; as having nothing and yet possessing all things.'

Does the world need the witness of the Church's life less now than in past ages? Less? nay, for many reasons more. The widening opportunities of intercourse are opening up new nations, whose existence had only been suspected before; they are bringing the various parts of human kind into a closer touch with each other. The problems of civilization are more complex; and the more complicated a piece of machinery is, the more difficult it is to keep it in order; so small a defect may throw the whole out of gear. The wider our knowledge of humanity, the greater need of a Catholic Church, which shall raise its voice above the din of conquest and the bustle of commerce, and insist that all races shall be treated with justice and tenderness as made of one blood; which shall welcome all men freely into its own brotherhood, and conveying to them the gifts of the Spirit, shall help them to shew forth in their lives fresh beauties of the richly-variegated wisdom of God. The growth of our huge towns, 'where numbers overwhelm humanity,' and the accumulation of wealth bring the danger nearer home: amidst social upheavings and the striving of class with class, there is need of a Church to rise above rich and poor alike, which shall embrace both; which shall teach both a real visible brotherhood amid all external inequalities; which shall teach the poor the dignity of labour wrought for the good of the whole society, and teach the rich the duty and the blessing of the consecration of their wealth. With the wider use of machinery and the restless rush of money-getting, it is important that there should be the appeal of the Church that no man or woman shall be degraded into being a mere machine; because each is a living soul, capable of personal responsibility, capable of a pure life, capable of a knowledge of God.

Amid the increasing specialization of studies, amid all the new discoveries of science and historical criticism, with all the perplexities that arise as to the interpretation and inspiration of the Bible, now, if ever, there is need of a Church, which conscious of its own spiritual life, knowing that its spiritual truths have stood the test of centuries, has patience and courage to face all these new facts and see their bearing and take their measure ; which all the while shall go on teaching to its children with an absolute but rational authority the central facts of the spiritual life, and shall never doubt the ultimate unity of all truth.

Amid the uncertainties of individualism, the fantastic services of those who tend to reduce worship to a mere matter of emotion, amid the sorrows and perplexities of modern life, the world needs the witness of a rational and corporate worship, which recognises the deepest sufferings of human nature enshrined in its very heart, yet recognises also the way in which suffering when accepted freely, is blessed of God ; which worships at once a crucified and a risen Lord. Over against the divisions of race and continent the Church raises still its witness to the possibility of an universal brotherhood : over against despair and dispersion it speaks of faith and the unity of knowledge : over against pessimism it lifts up a perpetual Eucharist.

X.

SACRAMENTS.

IT is the characteristic distinction of some men's work that they are resolute to take into just account all the elements and conditions of the matter with which they deal. They will not purchase simplicity at the expense of facts ; they will not, by any act of arbitrary exclusion or unreal abstraction, give up even the most distant hope of some real attainment for the sake of securing a present appearance of completeness. They recognise and insist upon all the complexity of that at which they look ; they may see many traits in it to which they can assign no definite place or meaning, but they will not ignore or disparage these ; they will not forget them, even though for a while they may have to defer the closer study of them ; they will dutifully bear them in mind, and carry them along through all their work ; they will let them tell with full weight in qualifying, deferring, or precluding the formation of any theory about that of which these traits, trivial or important, explained or unexplained, are a genuine part. It is difficult to find a name for this rare and distinctive excellence. But it is that which more than any other quality gives permanence and fruitfulness to work : for even the fragmentary and loosely ordered outcome of such thought is wont to prove germinant and quickening as time goes on. Patience, honesty, reverence, and unselfishness, are virtues which appear congenial with such a character of mind ; and the high, undaunted faith which is the secret of its strength and the assurance of its great reward has been told by Mr. Browning in *A Grammarian's Funeral* :—

> Was it not great? did not he throw on God
> (He loves the burthen)—
> God's task to make the heavenly period
> Perfect the earthen [1]?

---

[1] In *Rabbi Ben Ezra* the true measure of such work's beneficence is shewn :—

> Not on the vulgar mass
> Called 'work,' must sentence pass,
> Things done, that took the eye and had the price ;
> O'er which, from level stand,
> The low world laid its hand,
> Found straightway to its mind, could value in a trice :

It will be the chief aim of this essay to shew that in the embodiment and presentation of Christianity by the Church of Christ there may be seen an excellence analogous, at least, to this distinctive characteristic of the work that all approve as best and truest upon earth ; that in contrast with many religious systems, attaining a high degree of moral beauty and spiritual fervour, the historic Church meets human life in full front; that it has been taught and enabled, in its ministry of Sacraments, to deal with the entirety of man's nature, not slighting, or excluding, or despairing of any true part of his being. But it is necessary at the outset to define, in general and provisional terms, the nature and the principle of that element in the Church's faith and life which is here under consideration, and in which especially this amplitude and catholicity of dealing with human nature is to be sought. By the Sacramental system, then, is meant the regular use of sensible objects, agents, and acts as being the means or instruments of Divine energies, 'the vehicles of saving and sanctifying power [1].' The under-lying belief, the basal and characteristic principle of this system, may be thus stated. As the inmost being of man rises to the realization of its true life, to the knowledge and apprehension of God and of itself, in the act of faith, and as He whose Spirit quickened it for that act, greets its venture with fresh gifts of light and strength, it is His will that these gifts should be conveyed by means or organs taken from this world, and addressed to human senses. His Holy Spirit bears into the faithful soul the communication of its risen Lord's renewing manhood ; and for the conveyance of that unseen gift He takes things and acts that can be seen, and words that can be heard ; His way is viewless as the wind; but He comes and works by means of which the senses are aware ; and His hidden energy accepts a visible order and outward implements for the achievement of its purpose.

The limits of this essay preclude the discussion of the larger questions which beset the terms of these definitions. Previous essays have dealt with those truths which are necessarily involved in any declaration of belief about the Christian Sacraments. The Being of God, the Incarnation of the Eternal Word, the Atonement, the Resurrection and Ascension of Christ, the Person and Mission of the Holy Ghost, these are indeed implied in the Sacramental system of the Church, not simply as component and essential parts of the same building, nor as mere logical data, but rather as the activities of the bodily life are

> But all the world's coarse thumb
> And finger failed to plumb,
> So passed in making up the main account ;
> All instincts immature,
> All purposes unsure,
> That weighed not as his work, yet swelled the man's amount.

[1] Cf. A. Knox, *Remains*, ii. 138.

pre-supposed in the exertion of the body's strength. But these cannot here be spoken of : it is from preceding pages of this book that thoughts and convictions must be gathered, without which much that is here said will seem either unsubstantial, or merely technical. It must be owned that the severance of any subject from its context entails not only incompleteness, but also a certain disproportion and obscurity in its treatment; since the lines of thought which run out into the context are lines down which light comes, light that is lost if they are closed. Indeed anything like a full presentation or a formal defence of a detached part of Christian teaching and practice seems intrinsically very difficult, and within the limits of an essay impossible. There are, however, two questions which must be asked concerning each several part of the whole structure, and in regard to which something may here be said. The first is : Does this part match with its surroundings in Christianity; is it a harmonious and congenial element in the whole order, in the great body of doctrine to which it claims to belong? The second is : Does it match with the surroundings on which it claims to act, with its environment in human life; is it apt for the purpose to which it is addressed and the conditions among which it comes? It is here proposed, as has been said, to consider in regard to the Sacramental system the second especially of these two questions : but its consideration will involve some thoughts which may perhaps be a sufficient answer to the first. And thus something may also be gained beyond the range of the present inquiry ; for it seems fair to hold that any part of Christian teaching in regard to which both these questions can be answered in the affirmative, has a strong tendency at all events to commend the claim of the whole scheme with which it is inwoven and essentially continuous. For the perfection of inner coherence in a structure whose main lines, at least, were projected in the world under circumstances which preclude the thought of scientific or artificial elaboration, and the perfection of adaptation, not to the wishes and tastes of men, nor to the arrangements of society, but to the deepest, fullest, surest truth of humanity; these are characteristics which we should expect to find in a revelation from God to man, and be surprised to find elsewhere.

I. Probably there come to most men who have got beyond the happy confidence of youth, and the unhappy confidence of self-satisfaction, times at which they seem to themselves to be living in a somewhat perplexed and dimly lighted world, with tasks for which their strength is insufficient, among problems which they cannot solve. And Christianity is held out to them, or has been received by them, as a way of life under these circumstances, as a method and a means of living rightly ; a system which does not indeed take all the perplexity out of the world, or all the difficulties out of their course, but which will give them light and strength enough to keep in the right track, to use their time well, to take their proper place, and do their proper work, and so to move towards the realization of all the many parts and possibilities of their nature ; a goal which may seem to grow both larger and more distant the more one thinks about it. Christianity professes to be that Divine word, which was faintly surmised of old [1], and in due time was sent forth to bear men wisely and surely through this world. Plainly one of the first and fairest questions which may be asked in regard to it is, whether it shews a perfect understanding of the nature with which it claims to deal, and the life which it claims to guide.

Now when we set ourselves to think what we are for whom a possible and satisfactory way of life is sought, what that nature is, whose right principles and conditions of development are to be determined, one of the first things which we discern is an apparently invincible complexity. The life we have to order is a twofold life, it moves through a twofold course of experience : the facts, the activities in which we are conscious of it, are of two kinds ; and men ordinarily distinguish them as bodily and spiritual. Some such distinction is recognised and understood by the simplest of us : it is imbedded beyond possibility of expulsion in all language : stubbornly and successfully it resists all efforts to abolish it. We know for ourselves that either of the two groups of facts may stand out in clearer light, in keener consciousness, at certain times : we may even for a while, a little while, lose sight of either of them and seem to be wholly occupied with the other : but presently the neglected facts will re-assert their rights : neither the one group nor the other may long be set aside without risk of the Nemesis which avenges slighted truths :—the Nemesis of disproportion and disease. We may confuse our sense of the distinction ; we may shift or blur or bend whatever line had seemed to mark it : we may insist on the qualifying phenomena which forbid us to think of any barrier as impenetrable ; but we cannot so exalt or push forward either realm as utterly to extrude, absorb, or annihilate the other : we cannot, with consistency or sanity, live as though our life were merely spiritual or merely bodily. It is as impossible steadily to regard the spirit as a mere function or product of the body, as it is to treat the body with entire indifference, as a casually adjacent fragment of the external world. But further, as the distinction of the two elements in our being seems insuperable, so does their union seem essential to the integrity of our life. Any abstraction of one element, as though it could detach itself from the other and live on its own resources, is felt to be unreal and destructive of our proper nature. So it has been finely said, ' Materialism itself has here done valuable service in correcting the exaggeration of a one-sided spiritualism. It is

[1] Cf. Plato, *Phaedo*, 85 C, D.

common, but erroneous, to speak of man's body as being related to his spirit only as is the casket to the jewel which it contains. But, as a matter of fact, the personal spirit of man strikes its roots far and deep into the encompassing frame of sense, with which, from the first moment of its existence, it has been so intimately associated .... The spirit can indeed exist independently of the body, but this independent existence is not its emancipation from a prison-house of matter and sense; it is a temporary and abnormal divorce from the companion whose presence is needed to complete its life [1].' If we try to imagine our life in abstraction from the body we can only think of it as incomplete and isolated; as impoverished, deficient, and expectant. And certainly in our present state, in the interval between what we call birth and death, the severance of the two elements is inconceivable: they are knit together in incessant and indissoluble communion. In no activity, no experience of either, can the other be utterly discarded: 'for each action and reaction passing between them is a fibre of that which forms their mutual bond [2].' Even into those energies of which men speak as purely spiritual, the bodily life will find its way, will send its help or hindrance: sickness, hunger, weariness, and desire: these are but some of its messengers to the spirit, messengers who will not always be denied. And in every conscious action of the bodily life the presence of the spirit is to be discerned. The merely animal fulfilment of merely animal demands, devoid of moral quality, is only possible within that dark tract of instinct which lies below the range of our consciousness. When once desire is consciously directed to its object, (wherever the desire has originated and whatever be the nature of the object,) a moral quality appears, a moral issue is determined: and the act of the body becomes an event in the life of the spirit [3]. The blind life of brute creatures is as far out of our reach as is the pure energy of angels: we can never let the body simply go its own way; for in the essential complexity of our being, another sense is ever waiting upon the conscious exercise of those five senses that we share with lower animals:—the sense of duty and of sin.

Thus complex are we,—we who crave more light and strength, who want to find the conditions of our health and growth, who lift up our eyes unto the hills from whence cometh our help. It would be interesting to consider from how many different points of view the complexity has been recognised, resented, slandered, or ignored; and how steadily it has held its own. It may need some exercise of faith (that

[1] H. P. Liddon, *Some Elements of Religion*, pp. 116, 117. Cf. the wonderful venture towards a conception of the disembodied soul and of its manner of life, in the *Dream of Gerontius*: and also in *Battle and After*, by R. St. John Tyrwhitt, p. 7.

[2] Lotze, *Microcosmus*, Bk. III. c. i. § 2.

[3] Cf. T. H. Green, *Prolegomena to Ethics*, Bk. II. ch. ii. §§ 125, 126.

is to say, of reasonable patience amidst half-lights and fragments) to keep the truth before one, and to allow it its just bearing upon thought and conduct, without exaggeration, or self-deception, or one-sidedness; but there is neither health of body nor peace of mind in trifling with it.

To us, then, being thus complex, Christianity presents a plan, a principle, a rule of life. And that primary and inevitable question which has been already indicated may therefore take this definite form:—Does the scheme proposed to us acknowledge this our complexity? does it provide for us in the entirety of our nature, with all that we feel to be essential to our completeness? or must a part of our being be huddled out of sight as we enter the precinct of the Church?

II. (1) Certainly the whole history and character of the Christian Revelation would encourage us to hope that its bearing upon life would be as broad as the whole of human nature; and that no true part of our being would be excluded from its light, refused its welcome, or driven from its feast. When we consider how Christianity came into the world, it would seem strange and disappointing if its hold on human life were partial and not inclusive: if, for instance, the body found no place prepared, no help or hope provided for it. This was excellently said by Alexander Knox: 'The gospel commenced in an accommodation to man's animal exigencies which was as admirable as it was gracious; and which the hosts of heaven contemplated with delight and wonder. The Incarnation of the co-eternal Son, through which S. John was enabled to declare what he and his fellow Apostles "had seen with their eyes, what they had looked upon, and their hands had handled, of the Word of Life," was in the first instance, so to consult human nature in its animal and sensitive capacity, as to give the strongest pledge that a dispensation thus introduced would, in every subordinate provision, manifest the same spirit and operate on the same principle. For could it be thought that the first wonderful accommodation of Godhead to the sensitive apprehensions of man should be wholly temporary? and that though that mystery of godliness was ever to be regarded as the vital source of all spiritual benefits and blessings, no continuance of this wise and gracious condescension should be manifested in the means, whereby its results were to be perpetuated, and made effectual[1]?' It would be possible to follow this mode of thought to a remoter point, and to mark in the revealed relation of the Eternal Word to the whole creation a sure ground for believing that whensoever, in the fulness of time, God should be pleased to bring the world, through its highest type, into union with Himself, the access to that union would be as wide as the fulness of

[1] A. Knox, *Remains*, vol. ii. pp. 228, 229. The writer of this essay desires to acknowledge with gratitude the help he has found in the remarkable treatise here referred to.

the nature in which He made man at the beginning : that the attractive and uplifting bands of love would hold and draw to Him every true element of that nature. But it is enough for our present purpose to look steadily at the Advent and the Life of Christ : to see how carefully and tenderly every fragment of the form He takes is disentangled from the deforming evil which He could not take : how perfect are the lineaments of the humanity He wears, how freely and clearly all that is characteristic of our nature is displayed in His most holy life ; where ' the hiding of His power,' the restraining of the beams of Deity [1] leaves room for the disclosure in Him of whatever weakness and limitation properly belongs to us. Surely it would be strange if the grace and truth which came among us thus, proved partial or restricted in their later dealing with our manhood : if any tract of our life were unvisited by their light and blessing : if anything which He took were slighted in His kingdom, forgotten in His ministry, precluded from His worship. The Incarnation was indeed in itself a great earnest of the recognition which would be accorded in the Christian life to the whole of our complex nature. But there are, more particularly, two points in the coming and work of our Lord which seem peculiarly intended to foreshow some abiding elevation of the material and visible to share the honour of the spiritual element in our life. They are so familiar to us that it may not be easy to do full justice to their significance.

(2) For it does seem deeply significant that when the Word was made flesh and dwelt among us, He took up the lines of a history replete with forecasts of the consecration of material things : He met the truest aspirations of a people trained to unhesitating exultation in a visible worship, encouraged by manifold experience to look for the blessings of Divine goodness through sensible means, accustomed and commanded to seek for God's especial presence in an appointed place and amidst sights on which their eyes would rest with thankful confidence. That Church and nation ' of whom as concerning the flesh Christ came,' must have seemed indeed irrevocably and essentially committed to the principle that when man is brought near to God it is with the entirety of his manhood : that God is to be glorified alike in the body and in the spirit : and that His mercy really is over all His works. Doubtless barriers were to be broken down, when the time of prophecy and training passed on into the freedom of realization : limitations were to be taken away, distinctions abrogated by Him in Whom is neither Jew nor Greek, neither bond nor free, neither male nor female : but religion would surely have grown in reality *narrower* and not wider, if the body had been dismissed from its duty and gladness in the light of God's countenance, if the spirit alone had been bidden

[1] Cf. Hooker, V. liv. 6.

to draw near, to worship, to taste and see how gracious the Lord is. Through all the amplitude of the Christian dispensation, there would have been a sense of loss, of impoverishment, of expectation encouraged and unsatisfied, had this been so; for in the preparatory system of Judaism, whatever had been lacking, still the whole nature of man had felt the Hand of God and heard His Voice. It would have seemed strange if with the wider extension of God's light to all the world there had been a narrowing of its range in the life of each several man[1].

(3) And then, again, it is to be marked that our Lord Himself by repeated acts sustained and emphasized this acceptance of the visible as the organ or vehicle of the Divine. His blessing was given by the visible laying on of hands, and His miracles were wrought not by the bare silent energy of His Almighty will, not even in many cases by the mere utterance of His word, but through the employment of acts or objects, impressive to the bodily element in man, and declaring the consecration of the material for the work of God. Alike in the blessings bestowed and in the manner of their bestowal men must have felt that there was with Him no disparagement of the body, no forgetfulness of its need, no lack of care for its welfare, its honour, or its hope. Perhaps it may even be that had we watched the scene in the Galilean town as the sun was setting, and in the cool of the evening they that had any sick with divers diseases brought them unto Him; as He moved about among those wasted, suffering forms, and on one after another laid His hands and healed them; it may even be that what would have struck us first of all would have been the bringing in of a better hope for the bodily life of man and the replenishing of a familiar act, a common gesture, with a grace and power that it had but vaguely hinted at before.

We have, then, (1) in the Incarnation of the Son of God, (2) in the essential character of the history ordered as an especial preparation for His coming, and (3) in certain conspicuous features of His ministry on earth, a strong encouragement to expect that in the life thus brought into the world, in the way thus opened out, there would be evinced a large-hearted care for the whole nature of men : that no unreal abstraction would be demanded, and no part of humanity be disinherited : that in the choice of its means, in the scope of its beneficence, and in the delineation of its aim, Christianity would deal with us as we are, and prove that God has not made us thus for nought. An endeavour will be made to show how this great hope is greeted in the Sacramental system, and uplifted and led on towards the end of all true hope. But it seems necessary first to adduce the grounds for

---

[1] Cf. A. Knox, ii. 210.

saying that that system has been from the beginning an integral part of Christianity.

III. When we turn to look at the presentation of the Sacramental principle in the Gospels, our first impression may be that the place it holds there is less than that which is given to it in the teaching and practice of the Church: that it is by a disproportionate growth that the doctrine of Sacraments has gained so much space and so great prominence in Catholic theology. But the impression certainly ought not to be lasting. For it is due to our forgetfulness of the conditions under which Christianity came into the world: the characteristics and habits of religious thought with which it had to deal. We can draw no reasonable inference from the brevity or length with which a truth is enunciated in the Gospels until we have inquired what were the previous convictions of those to whom our Lord spoke: what preparation had in that particular regard been made for His teaching. We ought to look for some difference in the manner of revelation corresponding to the difference of need when a wholly new principle of thought has to be borne into unready minds, and when a fresh direction has to be given to an expectation already alert and confident, a new light to be thrown on the true worth and meaning of an existing belief about God's ways towards men. Amplitude and iteration would indeed have been necessary for any teaching which was to dislodge the Sacramental principle out of the minds of those among whom our Lord came—to preclude them from seeking the mercy of God through visible means. But if the Divine purpose was not to destroy but to fulfil; not to discredit as mere misapprehensions the convictions men had received, but to raise and purify them by disclosing the response which God had prepared for them: to disengage them from that which had been partial, preparatory, transient, and to fasten them on their true satisfaction: then we might reverently expect that the method of this teaching would probably be such as in the New Testament is shewn to us in regard to the doctrine of Sacraments.

(1) For, in the first place, we find abundant and pervading signs that the general principle is taken up into Christianity and carried on as a characteristic note of its plan and work. The regular communication of its prerogative and characteristic gift through outward means: the embodiment of grace in ordinances: the designation of visible agents, acts, and substances, to be the instruments and vehicles of Divine virtue:—this principle is so intimately and essentially woven into the texture of Christianity that it cannot be got out without destroying the whole fabric. As our Saviour gradually sets forth the outlines of His design for the redemption of the world, at point after point the Sacramental principle is affirmed, and material instruments

are designated for the achievement of His work. 'He proclaims Himself the Founder of a world-wide and imperishable Society,' 'the Kingdom of Heaven' or 'the Kingdom of God[1];' and while the claims and energies of this kingdom penetrate the hidden depths of life, so that it is indeed 'a moral empire,' and 'a realm of souls,' yet none the less is it openly to take its place in human history. It is not an unsubstantial haze of vague spirituality, precarious and indistinct, hovering or said to hover half way between earth and sky, with no precise attachment to either. At once, it is the kingdom of Heaven, and it is to have all the apparel of a visible society : it touches this earth with a definite and inclusive hold ; it ennobles material conditions by a frank acceptance. As in the Incarnation, so also in the preparation of the Church to be the ever-present witness to Christ, the guardian of His truth, and the home of His people, the principle was sustained that, in the redemption of the world, God would be pleased to take the instruments of His work out of that world which He was renewing : that the quickening Spirit would not repel or destroy the material order, but would assume, pervade, and use it.

(2) And, in the second place, the particular expressions of the general principle thus reaffirmed were authoritatively appointed : the approved anticipation of men was left in no uncertainty as to its response and sanction : men were told plainly what were the outward and visible signs which God had chosen in this world to be the means whereby His inward and spiritual grace should be received. It is difficult indeed to imagine any way in which more weight and incisiveness could have been given to the appointment of the two great Sacraments than in the way which Christ was pleased to use :—any way in which Baptism and the Eucharist could have been more firmly and impressively designated as the vital and distinctive acts of the Christian Church. We can hardly wonder at their pre-eminence in Christian thought and life when we remember how they were fastened upon the consciousness of the Church. Their antecedents lay in that long mysterious course of history which Almighty God had led on through the strange discipline of the changeful centuries to the coming of Christ. And then, there had been in Christ's teaching certain utterances which seemed to have a peculiar character : which were plainly of essential importance, concerning things necessary for all His disciples, bearing on the primary conditions of their life : and yet utterances which were left unexplained, however men might be troubled, offended, overstrained, discouraged by them : left as though their explanation was impossible, until the occurrence of events which could not be forestalled[2].

[1] H. P. Liddon, *Bampton Lectures*, pp. 101-105.
[2] Cf. S. John iii. 3-13 ; vi. 51-67.

But such utterances, if they could not be understood, could still less be forgotten : they lived in the memory, they haunted the imagination, they sustained expectancy : they were as a prophetic conviction in the mind, strong, deep, fragmentary, and unsatisfied. Who can measure the consilient force with which, in moments of intensest thought and feeling, moments when all the besetting conditions seemed quick with some imminent disclosure, the Divine commands, meeting, illuminating, establishing those former utterances, would be riveted upon the hearts of men and clenched for ever into the faith and practice of the Church, with a dominance never to be forgotten or infringed, as a very primal law of life ? In the unique, controlling awe of His impending agony and crucifixion :—in the heralded majesty of His appearance to the disciples upon the mountain where He had appointed them, and with the proclamation of the absolute authority given to Him in heaven and in earth : so did our Lord enact the ordinances to which His earlier words had pointed, and in which at length their meaning was made clear : so did He institute His two great Sacraments : so did He disentangle the Sacramental principle from all that had been temporary, accidental, disciplinary, accommodated, in its past embodiment, and determine what should be the form of its two main expressions, for all ages and for all men in His Church 'until His coming again,' ' even unto the end of the world.'

It may be in place here briefly to suggest a few thoughts with regard to that which was secured by this authoritative designation of the outward sign in each great Sacrament, beyond all that could have been attained by the general enunciation of the Sacramental principle.

Much might be said—and much more, doubtless, be still left unsaid—about the especial fitness of the very elements thus chosen from the material world to be the vehicles of saving grace :—for the water and the bread and wine are called to their place in the Divine work with deep and far-reaching associations already belonging to them. Again, the very simplicity and commonness of the elements taken into God's nearest service may have been a part of the reason why they were appointed : for in no other way could the minds of men have been more surely and permanently hindered from many of the mistakes to which in the past they had been prone : in no other way could the Sacramental principle have been more perfectly disengaged from the misconceptions which had confused its purity: in no other way could men have been more plainly taught that in no expense of this world's goods, in no labour of their own hands, in no virtue of the material elements, but only in the sustained energy of His will, who took and penetrated and employed them, lay the efficacy of the Sacrament. The very plainness of the element hallowed in the Sacrament was to urge up men's thoughts from it to Him. But, above all, the decisive appointment of particular signs and acts may seem to have been necessary in order that the Sacraments might take their places as acts emanating from, upheld by, and characteristic of the Church's corporate life, and not merely concerned with the spiritual welfare of the individual. So S. Paul appeals to Baptism and to the Eucharist as both effecting and involving the communion of saints[1]. By Sacraments men are to be taken out of the narrowness and isolation of their own lives, out of all engrossing preoccupation with their own state, into the ample air, the generous gladness, the unselfish hope of the City of God : they are to escape from all daily pettiness, all morbid self-interest, all preposterous conviction of their own importance, into a fellowship which spans all ages and all lands. By Baptism and the Eucharist the communion of saints is extended and sustained : they are the distinctive acts of the Body of Christ : and as such He designated their essential form, to abide unaltered through all that changed around them. And even those who stand aloof from them and from the faith on which they rest, may feel the unmatched greatness of an act that has held its place in human life through all the revolutions of more than 1800 years : an act that in its essential characteristics is to-day what it was when imperial Rome was venerated as eternal : an act that is every day renewed, with some measure, at least, of the same faith and hope and love, in every land where Christ is owned.

(3) The Sacramental principle had been most plainly adopted by our Lord : the spiritual forces with which He would renew the face of the earth were to be exerted through material instruments : and He Himself had secured the principle from uncertainty or vagueness or individualism in its expression by appointing, with the utmost weight and penetration of His authority, the definite form of two great ordinances, which were to begin and to advance the supernatural life of His members, to extend the range of His Church, and to maintain its unity. In the acts and letters of His apostles we see how His teaching and bidding had been understood : how promptly and decisively His Church declared its life, its work, its mission, to be Sacramental. The meaning and emphasis of His commandment appear in the obedience of those to whom it was given : in the first words of authoritative counsel uttered by an apostle : in the first act of the Spirit-bearing Body: and thenceforward in the characteristic habits of the Christian life[2].

From the first the prominence of Sacraments and Sacramental rites is constant. In the teaching of later ages their prominence may have been relatively greater, in contrast with the poverty of faith and life in

[1] 1 Cor. x. 17 ; Gal. iii. 27, 28 ; Eph. iv. 5.
[2] Acts ii. 38, 41, 42.

those who insisted on their power while they forgot their meaning; but absolutely it would be hard to devise a higher place for them than that which they hold in S. Paul's Epistles. To be living a life received, nourished, and characterised by Baptism and by the Eucharist—this is the distinctive note of a Christian—thus does he differ from other men. The Sacrament by which he became a member of Christ's body must determine throughout the two distinctive qualities of his inner life : its severance from all forms of worldliness, all dependence on natural advantages, or natural strength, all confidence in the satisfaction of external rules ; and its unfailing newness, as issuing from Him who, being raised from the dead, dieth no more, and as carrying through all its activities the air and light of heaven [1]. And the Sacrament which continually renews in him the presence of his Lord, meeting with unstinted wealth the demands of work and growth, assuring and advancing the dominance of the new manhood in him : this in like manner must determine the sustained simplicity of his bearing towards those who with him are members of the one Body, quickened and informed by the one Life [2]. That men may receive eternal life through Jesus Christ : that is the end of all labours in His name : to this all else is tributary and conducive : and there is no hesitation as to the visible means by which God will effect this end in all those who have ' faith to be healed.' And in this sense it may perhaps be said that in Christianity even doctrine holds not indeed a subordinate but (that which involves nothing but dignity) a subservient place ; since it is the strength and glory of Christian doctrine that it essentially ' leads on to something higher—to the sacramental participation in the atoning sacrifice of Christ [3].'

IV. Thus then there appears at the beginning the dominance of that note which has sounded on through all succeeding ages ; thus may we trace from the first days the dispensation of Divine energy through agents and acts and efficacious symbols gathered out of this visible world. It remains to be shewn with what reason it can be alleged that herein the Church evinces its recognition of the complexity of human nature, and guards the truth, that in the entirety of his being man has to do with God, the Creator, Redeemer, Sanctifier of his soul and body. Along three lines of thought this may in some degree appear ; and if the evidence that can be indicated is recognised as in any measure real, it would be unphilosophic to set it aside because it may be fragmentary and inconclusive : since fragments are all that in such a matter we are likely as yet to see.

(1) First, then, there is a profound far-reaching import in the bare

---

[1] Cf. Rom. vi. 3, 4; Gal. iii. 27, 28 ; Col. ii. 12, 20-23.

[2] Cf. 1 Cor. x. 17, xii. 25, 26.

[3] W. Shirley, *The Church in the Apostolic Age*, p. 103.

fact that material and visible means are thus hallowed to effect the work of God, to bear His unseen grace. For it must not be thought that in this Sacramental union of the visible and the invisible we have only an interesting parallel to the twofold nature of man, a neat and curious symmetry, a striking bit of symbolism or accommodation. Nor is the deepest significance of the Sacramental principle brought out when it is said quite truly that ' it has pleased God to bind His invisible operations to outward and visible methods,' 'lest that which is thus invisible should for that reason be disbelieved or counterfeited or in any of the various ways in which human incredulity or human enthusiasm might do it wrong, abused to the injury of man [1].' We may see in this aspect of the system that it has indeed secondary advantages of the highest worth ; but its surpassing glory is in its primary and essential character, as the regular employment of visible means for the achievement of Divine mysteries. For thus our whole estimate of this world is affected. Its simplest objects have their kindred, as it were, in the court, in the very presence chamber of the Most High ; and actions such as we see in it day after day have been advanced to a supreme distinction.

And so through Sacramental elements and acts Christianity maintains its strong inclusive hold upon the whole of life. The consecration of material elements to be the vehicles of Divine grace keeps up on earth that vindication and defence of the material against the insults of sham spiritualism which was achieved for ever by the Incarnation and Ascension of Jesus Christ. We seem to see the material world rising from height to height ; pierced, indeed, and, as it were, surprised at every stage by strange hints of a destiny beyond all likelihood; yet only gradually laying aside the inertness of its lower forms, gradually seeming to yield itself, not merely to the external fashioning of spirit, but also to its inner and transforming occupation : till in humanity it comes within sight of that which God has been preparing for it, even the reception of His own image and likeness. And yet this is but the beginning : and though sin delays the end, and holds back the crown of all, it is but for a time ; in due season there is made known that absolutely highest honour to which God has been leading on the work of His hands, even that in its highest type it should be taken into God ; that the Eternal Word should be made man, and from a human mother receive our nature, so that a material body should be His body ; His in birth, and growth, and death ; His in all its relations with the visible world ; His for suffering, for weariness, for tears, for hunger ; His upon the cross and in the tomb ; His to rise with ; and, at length, His at the right hand of God. Thus was the visible received up into glory ; thus was the forecast of spiritual capacity in the material perfectly realized ;

[1] Moberly's *Bampton Lectures*, pp. 29, 30.

and by the body of the ascended Saviour, an entrance for the whole being of man into the realm of spirit is assured. 'There is a spiritual body[1]:' no part of the material order can be quite untouched by the light that issues from those astounding words, and from the triumph they record. And that truth, that triumph, that possibility of un-hindered interpenetration between the spiritual and the material is pre-eminently attested upon earth by the two great Sacraments of the Christian Church. In those mysteries where water is sanctified to the washing away of sin, and where material substances are made spiritual food, there is a continual witness of the victory that has been won, a real earnest of that which shall hereafter be achieved, a vivid declara-tion that the barrier between the spiritual and the material is not absolute or eternal.

Nor is this deep truth without practical and far-reaching consequences in human life. For immediately it thus appears that the unreal spiritu-ality which consists in a barren and boastful disparagement of ritual observance or of outward acts[2], of earthly relationships or of secular life, of natural feelings or of bodily health, clashes with Christian teaching as sharply as it does with human nature and with common sense. And then, in perfect accordance with this principle, the spiritual energy of the Church is sacramentally conveyed for the hallowing of stage after stage in the due order of a human life, as body, soul, and spirit are advanced towards the end for which they were created. Not only in the initial act whereby all are bidden to enter into the kingdom of God, and, at the dawn of consciousness, the onset of evil is fore-stalled by the cleansing and regenerating work of God the Holy Ghost— not only in the ever-needed, ever-ready mystery of glory whereby, amidst the stains and sorrows of the world, all may again and again be 'filled with the very essence of restoration and of life[3];' but at other moments too, when the soul of man rises up towards God in the divinely-quickened venture of faith, the strength of the Most High is perfected in human weakness, and in Sacramental acts the things that are not seen enter into the history of the things that are seen. It is most unfortunate that the associations of controversy should hinder men from frankly and thankfully recognising the wide range of Sacra-mental action in Christian life. The dispute as to the number of the Sacraments is indeed 'a question of a name[4]:' and it ought to have been acknowledged all along that the name was being used with different and shifting meanings. That men knew that it did not desig-nate an essentially distinct class of exactly equivalent units is shewn on all sides; S. Thomas Aquinas seems to doubt, at least, whether there

---

[1] 1 Cor. xv. 44.
[2] Cf. Professor Milligan, *The Resur-rection of Our Lord*, Lect. vi. Pt. i. § c.

[3] Bright's *Ancient Collects*, p. 152.
[4] C. Gore, *Roman Catholic Claims*, p. 170.

are not more than seven Sacraments, divides the seven into groups
with very important notes of difference, and decides that the Eucharist
is 'Sacramentorum omnium potissimum [1] :' Calvin was not unwilling
that the laying on of hands should be called a Sacrament, though he
would not reckon it 'inter ordinaria Sacramenta [2] ;' the Council of
Trent has an anathema for anyone who says that the seven Sacraments
are so equal that none is more worthy than another [3] : Richard Baxter
distinguishes between 'three sorts of Sacraments;' in the second
sense of the name, in which it is taken to mean 'any solemn *Investiture*
of a person by ministerial delivery, in a state of Church-privileges, or
some special gospel-mercy,' he grants 'that there are five Sacraments—
Baptism, Confirmation, Absolution, the Lord's Supper and Ordination;' and elsewhere he declares that 'they that peremptorily say
without distinguishing that there are but two Sacraments in all, do but
harden them (the Papists) by the unwarrantable narrowing of the
word [4].' There is indeed no reason why anyone should hesitate to
mark the Love of God meeting in Sacramental ordinances the need of
man at point after point in the course of his probation. Differences in
the manner of appointment or in the range of application may involve
no difference at all in the reality of the power exercised and the grace
conveyed. And so we may see the Spirit-bearing Church, with whole-
hearted recognition of all the elements and wants of human life, proffer-
ing to men through visible means the manifold gifts of grace needed for
their progress and welfare in the way until they reach the Country. As
temptation grows more complex and severe, and the soul begins to
realize the warfare that it has to wage, the Personal indwelling of the
Holy Ghost, vouchsafed by the laying on of hands, completes the preparation of Christ's soldier : as the desolating sense of failure threatens
to unnerve the will and to take such hold upon the soul that it is not
able to look up, the authoritative message of forgiveness brings again
the strength of purity and the light of hope, and recalls the scattered
forces of the inner life to expel the encroaching evil and to regain
whatever had been lost. For special vocations there are special means
of grace ; by ordination God vouchsafes to guilty men the glory of the
priesthood : and in Christian marriage He confers the grace that
hallows human love to be the brightness and the safeguard of an
earthly home, and the earnest of the home in Heaven. And thus in
the manifold employment of the Sacramental principle there again
appears that characteristic excellence of Christianity which is secured
in the very nature of Sacraments : namely, its recognition of the whole
problem with which it claims to deal. It speaks to us as we are : there

---

[1] S. Th. iii. Qu. LXV. Art. 1, 4, 3.

[2] Calv. *Inst.* IV. xiv. 20.

[3] Conc. Trident. Sess. VII. Can. iii.

[4] Richard Baxter, *Confirmation and*
Restauration, pp. 88, 89 ; *Ecclesiastical*
Cases of Conscience, Qu. 99. Cf. J. S.
Pollock, *Richard Baxter on the Sacra-*
ments, § 58.

is no true need of which it will not take account : it will lead us without loss to the realization of our entire being.

(2) Secondly, Sacraments are a constant witness against our readiness to forget, to ignore, or to explain away the claim of Christianity to penetrate the bodily life, and to affect the body itself, replenishing it here with powers which are strange to it, lifting it out of the reach or mastery of passions which falsely boast that they are congenial with it, leading it on towards its everlasting rest, beyond all weakness and dishonour, in the glory of God. This claim, with the deeply mysterious but wholly reasonable hope which it engenders, has been set forth by Hooker, with his unfaltering strength of thought and words : ' Doth any man doubt that even from the flesh of Christ our very bodies do receive that life which shall make them glorious at the latter day, and for which they are already accounted parts of His blessed body ? Our corruptible bodies could never live the life they shall live, were it not that here they are joined with His body, which is incorruptible, and that His is in ours as a cause of immortality, a cause by removing, through the death and merit of His own flesh, that which hindered the life of ours. Christ is therefore, both as God and as man, that true Vine whereof we both spiritually and corporally are branches. The mixture of His bodily substance with ours is a thing which the ancient Fathers disclaim. Yet the mixture of His flesh with ours they speak of, to signify what our very bodies through mystical conjunction receive from that vital efficacy which we know to be in His : and from bodily mixtures they borrow divers similitudes rather to declare the truth, than the manner of coherence between His sacred and the sanctified bodies of saints [1].' The body, as well as the spirit, is accessible to the Divine life : there are avenues by which the energy of Christ's perfect and glorified manhood can penetrate, inform, affect, transfigure our whole being, bodily and spiritual. His prevalence in the life of the body and the change He works in it, may be very gradual, discerned in incoherent fragments, interrupted by surprising disappointments, hampered by limitations which it would be unlike Him now to overbear : but the change is real. The body is not left inert and brutish and uncheered, while the spirit is being carried

---

[1] Hooker V. lvi. 9 : cf. E. B. Pusey, *University Sermons*, p. 11, ' This is (if we may reverently so speak) the order of the mystery of the Incarnation, that the Eternal Word so took our flesh into Himself, as to impart to it His own inherent life ; so then we partaking of it, that life is transmitted on to us also, and not to our souls only, but our bodies also, since we become flesh of His flesh, and bone of His bone, and

He who is wholly life, is imparted to us wholly. The Life which He is, spreads around, first giving its own vitality to that sinless flesh which He united indissolubly with Himself, and in it encircling and vivifying our whole nature, and then, through that bread which is His flesh, finding an entrance to us individually, penetrating us, soul and body and spirit, and irradiating and transforming us into His own light and life.'

on from strength to strength, with growing light and freedom and majesty: it also rises at its Saviour's touch, and finds from Him the earnest of its liberation and advancement.

The work of grace upon the bodily nature of man may indeed be a matter of which we ought not to think save very humbly and tentatively: it is easy and perilous to overstate or to mis-read the evidence: but there is peril also in ignoring it. The language of our Blessed Lord; the clear conviction of His apostles; the intrepid quietude of His martyrs; the patience of the saints; their splendid and unrivalled endurance in His service; the change that may be marked in the looks and voices and instinctive acts of some who seem to be most nearly His :—here is such guidance for thought and hope as we ought not to dismiss because we cannot make up a theory about it. There are real facts—though they may be fragmentary, and require very careful handling—to warrant us in praying that our sinful bodies may be made clean by His body, as well as that our souls may be washed by His most precious blood.

It is this truth, with the higher aspirations, the more venturous hopes and efforts which it suggests, that the Sacramental system of the Church keeps in its due prominence. It is at all events not incongruous to think that the spiritual grace which is conveyed by visible means may pass through our spiritual nature to tell upon that which is visible. He who comes spiritually under a visible form may well be believed to work spiritually upon a visible nature. It is not, of course, to be thought for a moment that our bodies can at all after their own manner receive that Food which is wholly spiritual : nor that the visible element in a Sacrament gives to our bodies any hold upon the invisible grace, any power to appropriate to themselves by their own proper energies that which is incorporeal and supra-sensuous. 'Only the soul or spirit of man can take in and feed upon a spiritual nutriment [1] :' it is only (so far as our thoughts can go) through the avenue, by the medium of the faithful soul that the spiritual force of the Sacrament can penetrate to the body. But the fact that the spiritual virtue comes to us under a form of which our bodily senses take cognizance is at least a pledge that the body is not forgotten in the work of sanctification. And it is something more than this :—it is an assurance of that invasion and penetration of the material by the spiritual which is the very ground of all our hope for the redemption of the body. There is in the very nature of a Sacrament the forecast of some such hope as this :—that He who said of the material bread 'This is My Body,' may, in His own time, through changes which we cannot imagine, take to Himself and lift into the transfiguring realm of spirit our material bodies as well as our souls ; seizing, disclosing,

---

[1] J. B. Mozley, *Lectures and other Theological Papers*, p. 204.

perfecting capacities which under their present conditions we hardly suspect in them. And, perhaps, yet more than this may be said: for there would seem to be warrant for trusting that, in spite of all hindrance and delay, His word of power even now goes forth towards this work, and in the holy Eucharist has its efficacy throughout our whole nature. It is the thought to which Hooker points in words of endless import: 'there ensueth a kind of transubstantiation in us, a true change both of soul and body, an alteration from death to life;' words which rest on those of S. Irenaeus: 'As bread from the earth receiving the invocation of God is no longer common bread but the Eucharist, consisting of two things, an earthly and a heavenly; so our bodies also receiving the Eucharist are no longer corruptible, having the hope of the Resurrection [1].' Alike in us and in the Sacrament the powers of the world to come invade the present, and already move towards the victory which shall be hereafter.

(3) And thus, in the third place, the ministry of Sacraments is a perpetual prophecy of the glory that shall be revealed in us; the glory that shall pervade and transfigure our whole being. 'Till He come;' 'until His coming again;' that note of expectancy, of looking towards the east and watching for the return of a great light, discloses a deep truth about the Christian Sacraments. They sanction and confirm, as ever-present witnesses of a Divine assent, certain thoughts which will not let men rest in any low contentment with the things of time—with the approval, the success, the gratification, or the systems of this world. They declare with a perpetual insistance the mysteriousness of our present being: they have a certain fellowship with those strange flashes and pulsations we have felt of a life which seems astray and alien here, which yet somehow suggests the thought that could we commit ourselves wholly to its guidance, could we be replenished with its power, we should not walk in darkness, but rather, even in this world, be as the children of light:—and so they take the side of faith and patience against the attractions of completeness and security and achievement and repose. For they offer to guide into the way of peace, to welcome into an ordered, hallowed, course of loving service and of steady growth, those passing thrills of an intenser life, which if they be forgotten, denied, misunderstood, or surrendered to the abuse of wilfulness and vanity, may so subtly and terribly be unto us an occasion of falling.

It is given sometimes to a poet to sink a shaft, as it were, into the very depths of the inner life: to penetrate its secret treasuries, and to return, Prometheus-like, with a gift of fire and of light to men. The venturesome words that record such a moment of penetration and insight never lose their power: they seem to have caught something

---

[1] Hooker V. lxvii. 11; S. Irenaeus iv. 18.

of the everlasting freshness of that world of which they speak : and
one man after another may find in them, at some time of need or
gladness or awakening, the utterance of thoughts which else he might
have been too shy or too faint-hearted to acknowledge even to himself.
There is such a splendid venture of courage for the truth's sake in
those lines of Wordsworth which surely no familiarity can deprive of
their claim to reverence and gratitude ; the lines in which he tells his
thankfulness,

> For those obstinate questionings
> Of sense and outward things,
> Fallings from us, vanishings ;
> Blank misgivings of a creature
> Moving about in worlds not realized,
> High instincts before which our mortal nature
> Did tremble like a guilty thing surprized :
> . . . . . Those first affections,
> Those shadowy recollections,
> Which, be they what they may,
> Are yet the fountain-light of all our day,
> Are yet a master-light of all our seeing ;
> Uphold us, cherish, and have power to make
> Our noisy years seem moments in the being
> Of the eternal Silence.

It may be doubted whether any life is left wholly unvisited by some
misgiving, some dim, faltering instinct, some pulse of hope or sorrow,
which is akin to that which these words disclose; and the moments of
such visitation are the supreme opportunities of a human soul, the
crises of its tragedy. Then the things that belong to its peace are
being proffered to it; then the Sibyl stands before it with the treasures
of unimagined wisdom. We rise, and we live and grow and see by
the right understanding and employment of such moments ; by the
fresh acts of self-committal which they render possible : and in all the
infinite pathos of this world there is no misery comparable with this—
that they should cease to trouble us. Whatever a man may believe or
disbelieve, he will do well to trust these moments when they come :
and, perhaps, if he has grace to know and use them, he may be nearer
to the kingdom of God than he at all suspects. But Christianity does
not leave such 'shoots of everlastingness' wholly unexplained or un-
provided for.

They are in truth the fountain light of all our seeing, for they are
the disclosure, the assertion, the stepping forward of His presence who
alone sustains our life, our thought, our love. And, being this, they
are therefore also the tokens, the emerging witness of a work that has
begun in us, a life that is astir, a process of change that may be
carried forward to an issue which, even faintly surmised, might make
all other desire die away in us.

That we should be perfectly set free from sin; that God should so dwell in us and pervade our whole being that no part should lag behind the other; that whatsoever weakness or reluctance or coarseness may have clung about the body here should utterly pass away, being driven back by the victorious onset of the Spirit of God, claiming us wholly, body, soul, and spirit for His own; that whatsoever pure and true delight has here engaged us should be found, faultless and unwearied, in that energy which shall be at once our work and our rest for ever;—this is how Christianity represents to us the end of our development: and if indeed the powers which are to achieve so vast a change are already setting about their work in us, it is not strange that we should be disturbed now and then with some suspicion of it. We may understand alike the severity of external discipline, and the sharp disturbance and upheaval of anything like complacency, in a nature that is being here led on towards so splendid and inconceivable a transfiguration.

But Christianity does not merely declare to us the origin and meaning of these strange invasions of our ordinary life; these emergings, as it were, of that which is behind our normal activity, when the light, the strength, the love in which alone we live seems to push aside the curtain on which the background of our daily life is painted, and to appear unveiled among the things of time. He who telleth the number of the stars and calleth them all by their names, He who sendeth the springs into the valleys, and sweetly and mightily ordereth all things; He would not have these moments of intenser life, of keener consciousness, of quicker and more excellent growth, to be precarious and unaccountable, to be abrupt and arbitrary as the rush of the meteor which is gone before the eye has clearly seen it, or could use its light. They come from Him; they are the moments in which He makes His power to be known; in which His hand is felt, and His voice pervades the soul; the moments when His presence advances, as it were, and bends over us, and we know that it is He, Himself. And must we merely wait in blank and idle helplessness for that which we so greatly need; for that which is our only source of strength and growth? Must we wait, flagging and fruitless, with just a vague hope that the quickening presence may chance to visit us again, lighting on us with arbitrary beneficence, as the insect lights upon the plant, that it may bring forth fruit in due season? Must we wonder through days and months, yes, and through years perhaps of dim and desolate bewilderment, whether it was a real presence that came to us; with nothing but the fading memory of an individual and unconfirmed impression to sustain our hope, to keep the door against the gathering forces of doubt and worldliness and despair? Must we find our way as best we can, by guidance given long ago, imperfectly realized even then, and more and more hazily remembered, more drearily inadequate as time goes on, and the path grows rougher and less clear? Is the greatest effort to be demanded of us just when our strength is least and our light lowest [1]? Surely it is not His way to be thus arbitrary in compassion, thus desultory and precarious in shewing mercy. Surely He would not have us stray and faint and suffer thus. No, His compassions fail not; and, with the orderliness of a father's love, He has made us sure of all we need; and the historic Church and the triumphs of His saints declare that He is true. He has, with the certainty of His own unchanging word, promised that the unseen gift, which is the power of saintliness in sinful man, shall be given to all faithful, humble souls by ordered means through appointed acts. We need not vaguely hope that we may somehow receive His grace; for He has told us where and how we are to find it, and what are the conditions of its unhindered entrance into our souls. We need not be always going back to wonder whether our sins have been forgiven, or laboriously stirring up the glow of a past conviction; for there is a ministry which He has empowered to convey to us that cleansing glory which is ever ready to transfigure penitence into peace and thanksgiving. We need not live an utterly unequal life, stumbling to and fro between our ideal and our caricature [2]; for He has prepared for us a way which leads from strength to strength; and we know where He is ready to meet us and to replenish us with life and light. There is a glory that shall be revealed in us; and here on earth we may so draw near and take it to ourselves that its quiet incoming tide may more and more pervade our being; with radiance ever steadier and more transforming; till, in this world and beyond it, He has made a perfect work: till we are wholly ruled and gladdened by His presence, and wholly wrought into His image. For not by vague waves of feeling or by moments of experience which admit no certain measure, no unvarying test, no objective verification, but by an actual change, a cleansing and renewal of our manhood, a transformation which we can mark in human lives and human faces, or trace in that strange trait of saintliness which Christianity has wrought into the rough fabric of human history, may the reality of Sacramental grace be known on earth; known clearly enough, at all events, to make us hopeful about its perfect work in those who shall hereafter be presented faultless in body, soul and spirit before the throne of God.

[1] Cf. A. Knox, ii. 234-6.
[2] Cf. Martensen, *Christian Dogmatics*, p. 182.

XI.

CHRISTIANITY AND POLITICS.

THE aim of this essay is to investigate some of the relations of Christianity to human society, and to point out some of the main lines of influence which the Christian Church brings to bear on the organized centres of social life.

We are met at the outset by two widely-differing conceptions of the mode and direction in which Christianity acts as a regenerating influence on the life of mankind. On the one side, Christianity is identified with civilization, and the function of the Church is regarded as simply the gathering up, from age to age, of the higher aspirations of mankind : her call is to enter into, to sympathize with, and to perpetuate whatever is pure, noble, and of good report, in laws and institutions, in art, music, and poetry, in industry and commerce, as well as in the moral and religious usages and beliefs of mankind. Christianity is thus not a higher order, standing over against and correcting a lower, but is itself the product or rather the natural outgrowth of the progressive moral consciousness of mankind. The value of this mode of thought is in emphasizing the sacredness of secular interests and duties, and in its protest against dividing the field of conscience, and assigning to the one part a greater sanctity than to the other. 'As our salvation depends as certainly upon our behaviour in things relating to civil life, as in things relating to the service of God, it follows that they are both equally matters of conscience and salvation [1].' Its weakness lies in its not sufficiently recognising one decisive fact of human nature, the fact of sin. No one, as it seems to us, looking at human nature, in himself or others, with clear, open, unprejudiced eyes, can doubt the existence of sin, its corrupting influence on the whole nature, and yet its fundamental unnaturalness. But if states and societies are as the individuals who compose them, then any theory of society must rest on a theory of man ; and the theory of man is imperfect unless it recognises the fact of sin.

On the other hand, the recoil from secularism, or the overwhelming sense of the power and destructiveness of sin in the lives of men and of

[1] Law, *Third letter to the Bishop of Bangor,* second edition, 1762, p. 66.

societies, leads others to draw sharp the distinction between things sacred and things secular. The order of things, it is said, of which the Incarnation is the starting-point, is admittedly higher than that secular order which existed before it, and which even now surrounds it as darkness encompasses light. Let us put on one side political life, local and national interests, all that sphere of mixed social relations, which is so imperfect, so full of fierce passions, of strife, envy, and ambition, so productive of distractions and entanglements. Let us concentrate our own thoughts on sin, and devote our own lives to its remedy. Let us at least keep our own hands clean, and use for our own discipline that narrower sphere which is sufficient. No doubt individuals will find their vocation in some such attitude as this : and for some it may be wise to abstain from political and social interests, in order thus to strengthen their influence in other directions. But we are not now considering the call of individual Christians, but the attitude of the Christian Church as a whole : and it would be easy to accumulate references to shew that the leading minds of Christendom have declined to recognise, except in cases of special vocation, as the duty of Christians, the abdication of responsibility for the problems, the entanglements, the more or less secular issues of the ordinary social life of mankind. Christianity, in the words of a modern writer, has both to deliver humanity from its limitations, and to bring it to a true knowledge of itself [1].

These two conceptions of the relation of the Christian society to the issues and interests of the life amid which it moves, correspond to two aspects of the Incarnation, which the deepest Christian thought holds in solution. On the one side, the human life of the Word of God may be regarded as a fulfilment, the restoration of an order, marred, indeed, and broken, but never completely lost, the binding together of all truth, all goodness, all beauty, into one perfect life ; on the other, it is a reversal, the beginning of a new order, the undoing of a great wrong which has eaten deep into human nature, the lifting up of mankind out of the helpless slavery of sin into the freedom of righteousness. These two aspects of the Incarnation are not contradictory but complementary. However difficult it may be for us to find their unity in thought, they had their unity in a life.

In the same way, the problem with which Christianity has to deal in its relations to human society has two sides. It cannot hold itself aloof from the great currents and movements of that ever-flowing and ebbing human life, in which it shares, which it has to redeem, to purify, and to quicken. ' In the great sea of human society, part of it, yet distinguishable from it, is the stream of the existence of the Church [2].' And

---

[1] Martensen, *Christian Ethics*, special part, second division, Eng. Transl. p. 98.

[2] Church, Oxford House Papers, No. xvii, *The Christian Church*, p. 10.

yet it has to maintain, as a debt it owes to future generations as well as the present, the purity of its own moral standard, the independence of its own deepest life.

To spiritualize life without ceasing to be spiritual, to maintain a high morality while at the same time interpenetrating a non-Christian or very imperfectly Christianized society with its own moral habits and manners, is a task which presupposes great cohesion and tenacity on the part of the Christian Church. And it is for that reason that in speaking of the Church we shall have mainly in view that solid, highly articulated, permanent core of Christendom [1], which, however broken into fragments, and weakened by its own divisions, maintains a clearly-marked type, on the side of doctrine in its creeds and sacred writings, on the side of worship in its sacraments and traditional liturgies, on the side of organization in its ministry, as well as holding the life of Christ its standard of perfect living. Those Christian bodies which float, more or less closely knit together, around the central core of the Church, have often rendered great services in advancing on special points the standard of social and personal morality, and they are more flexible, and able rapidly to throw themselves into new crusades ; but it may well be doubted if their work could have been done at all without the more rigid and stable body behind them, with its slow movements, but greater Catholicity of aim and sympathy; and certainly it would in the long run have been better done, if, like the great monastic bodies, they had remained as distinct organizations within the Church.

What, then, is the attitude of the Church towards human society, and especially towards human society as gathered up and concentrated in States ? What duties does it recognise towards nations, towards human society as a whole ?

I. There is a certain order of debated questions, on which it cannot be said that the Christian Church is pledged to one side or the other—she leaves them open. Individual Christians take one side or the other. The Christian society recognises that the differences are due to diversities of temperament and national character, and to the varying conditions under which human societies live, and therefore that they may be best left to human experience to solve.

In this class of questions would come the problem debated since the time of Herodotus, but to which no general answer is really possible, What is the best form of government ? On this problem the Church is, so to speak, frankly opportunist. Here we may quote the view of S. Augustine, as stated in the *De Civitate Dei* [2] : ' The Heavenly City, in its wanderings on earth, summons its citizens from among all nations .... being itself indifferent to whatever differences there may be in

---

[1] Holland, *Creed and Character*, first edition, 1887, p. 156.   [2] xix. 17.

the customs, laws, and institutions by which earthly peace is sought after or preserved, not rescinding or destroying any of them, but rather keeping and following after them as different means adopted by different races for obtaining the one common end of earthly peace, provided only they are no obstacle to the religion by which men are taught the worship of the one supreme and true God.' In the same spirit, in his dialogue *De libero Arbitrio*[1], he dwells on the mutable character of human law. That law is temporal, which, 'though just, may yet be justly changed from time to time,' i.e. as the conditions change. Thus, a Democracy is best adapted to a grave and temperate people, public-spirited and willing to make sacrifices for the common good; while it is better for a more corrupt, more easily flattered people, greedy of private gain, to be under an Aristocracy or a Monarchy. Or if we wish for a more modern statement of the traditional view of the Christian Church, we shall find it in an encyclical letter[2] of Leo XIII : 'The right of sovereignty in itself is not necessarily united with any particular form of government : it can rightly assume, now one form, now another, provided only that each of these forms does in very deed secure useful results and the common good.' It will be noticed that two qualifications are introduced, the one by S. Augustine, the other by Pope Leo, limiting their acceptance of all forms of government. It is possible for Christian citizens to take an active part in every *de facto* government which (1) does not hinder the free and peaceable practice of the Christian religion, and (2) whose real aim is the common good, and which does, in fact, work for the advantage of its subjects. Not all governments, even in the nineteenth century, satisfy these tests.

In the same way, there have been the widest differences between Christian thinkers on the most important questions, in which auto-cratic and democratic leanings shew themselves, such, for instance, as that of the origin of sovereignty, i.e. of that rule of man over man, which is the foundation of civil society. The view indicated, though not worked out by S. Augustine[3], that the rule of man over man had its origin in the Fall, and was therefore part of the secondary, not the primary condition of mankind, is used by Gregory VII as a weapon of assault on the temporal power, by Bossuet as a safe ground on which to rest the duty of obedience to an absolute Monarchy. The other side is taken by S. Thomas Aquinas. He finds the origin of temporal rule in the social nature of man, accepting and making his own the Aristotelian account of man as by nature a being fitted for a common life. Thus, in a state of innocence, there would have been no slavery indeed, but government, with its recognition of the differences in ability and know-ledge among men, and of the consequent duty incumbent on the wise and experienced of using their faculties for the common good. Political

---

[1] i. 6.   [2] *Immortale Dei.*   [3] Aug. *De Civ. Dei,* xix. 14, 15.

Y

rule would thus be, not a consequence of sin, but a result of man's inherently social nature.

Differences such as these among those who equally start from fundamentally Christian presuppositions can only be taken to shew that we are wrong in supposing that the Christian Church is bound up with either of the two great political leanings which have appeared in civil communities in all ages of the world, and which have their ground in human nature itself. ' In every country of civilized man, acknowledging the rights of property, and by means of determined boundaries and common laws, united into one people or nation, the two antagonist powers or opposite interests of the State . . . are those of permanence and of progression[1].' The Church recognises these diverse powers or interests as natural, and therefore accepts the fact of their existence, without identifying herself with either of them.

II. But it would surely be a mistake to suppose that because the Church is neutral on certain questions of Politics, that therefore she has no direct teaching to give on the vital questions which arise with regard to the organized common life of mankind. In the rebound from the minimizing views of the function of the State, which were associated in England with the Ricardian School of Economics and the philosophic Radicalism of J. S. Mill, men are ready to go all lengths in exalting the position of the State as the moral guide of social life. The tendency is to assign the whole sphere of public morals to the State, and 'private' morals to the individual, acting, if he pleases, under the guidance of one or other of the Christian bodies. However much we may welcome the freer recognition of corporate responsibility, and the nobler conception of the State as having a moral end ; yet we cannot help perceiving that certain limitations are, as by a self-acting law, imposed on its moral influence.

(1) The State has been called the 'armed conscience of the community[2].' Looked at on the moral side, as a guide of the conscience of individuals, its arms are its defect. But that defect is not remediable : it is inevitable. For the State has to deal with various grades of character, responding to a vast complexity of motives, which may be roughly classified under three heads, those of duty, self-interest, fear of punishment. To some 'you ought' is a sufficient appeal, to others 'you had better,' while to a third class the only effective appeal is 'you must.' Now the State in order to perform its most elementary business, that of securing the conditions of an ordered and civilized life, has to deal first of all with those who are only susceptible of the lowest motive, the dread of punishment. And in dealing with them, it must

---

[1] S. T. Coleridge, *Church and State,* edited by H. N. Coleridge, 1839, p. 24.

[2] A. C. Bradley, 'Aristotle's Conception of the State,' in *Hellenica,* 1880, p. 243.

of necessity use coercive force[1]. But the force-associations which thus grow up around all State-action weaken and enervate its appeal to the higher motives, those of duty and rational self-interest. The very suspicion of compulsion taints the act done from duty.

Again, there can be little doubt of the vast influence exercised on morals by human law and institutions. It is well known to those who are at all acquainted with the life of the poor in large towns, that in many cases conscience is mainly informed by positive law. But all that human law can do is to secure a minimum of morality[2]. No doubt it is true that indirectly positive law can do something more than this, because good citizens will abstain from all actions which, in however remote a degree, are likely to bring them into collision with the law. But in the main it is true to say that what law can secure is the observance on pain of punishment of a minimum moral standard, which itself shifts with the public opinion of society, rising as it rises, falling as it falls.

Certainly the State is sacred: it is 'of God': it is no necessary evil: but a noble organ of good living. But yet there are these natural limitations to the effective exercise of its functions, as a moral guide. Firstly, it has to use force, and, therefore, its appeal to the higher motive is weakened. Secondly, it can only secure a minimum of morality, shifting with the general morality of the community.

Now it is exactly at these points that the Church steps in to supplement the moral action of the State, not as one part supplements another part of a single whole, but rather as a higher supplements a lower order.

It is in its appeal to the higher motives that the State is weak: it is in its appeal to the higher motives that the Church is strong. If there have been times when the Church has allowed herself to claim or to assume temporal power, or without assuming it, to be so closely implicated with the secular authority that Church and State appeared to men as one body interested in and maintaining the existing order, if she has used the weapons of persecution, or handed men over to the secular arm, then has she so far weakened and loosened her own hold on the higher motives which move men to action. She may have become apparently more powerful, but it has always been at the cost, perhaps unperceived at the time, of some sacrifice of her own spirituality, and of the loftiness of that moral appeal in which her true strength lies. 'There is something in the very spirit of the Christian Church which revolts from the application of coercive force[3].'

[1] 'Metu coercet,' Aug. *De lib. Arb.* i. 15.
[2] Compare Aug. *De lib. Arb.* i. 5.
[3] Art. on 'Future Retribution,' *Church Quarterly*, July, 1888.

And so, alongside of the moral minima of the secular law, the Christian Church maintains moral maxima, moral ideals, or rather a moral ideal, ' Be ye therefore perfect, even as your Father which is in heaven is perfect [1].' ' Till we all come unto a perfect man, unto the measure of the stature of the fulness of Christ [2].' It is not that the law is undervalued, or contemned, but that Christians are urged to bring their conduct under principles which will carry them far beyond the mere obedience to law. It is sufficient to quote from the Sermon on the Mount, 'Blessed are the meek . . . Blessed are ye, when men shall revile you, and persecute you, and say all manner of evil against you falsely, for my sake . . . I say unto you, that ye resist not evil : but whosoever shall smite thee on thy right cheek, turn to him the other also. And if any man will sue thee at the law, and take away thy coat, let him have thy cloke also [3].'

The law and institutions of a people rest upon and give expression to a group of moral principles and ideals : they are not the only realization of those principles and ideals, but one ; art and literature would be others ; further, they realize them mainly on the negative side, in the mode of prohibition. As that group of principles and ideals changes, they change, sometimes for the better, sometimes for the worse. At first sight it seems as if there was no essential difference in this respect between the laws and institutions of a nation, and the manners and institutions of the Christian Church, except that the one gives a more positive and constructive expression to the moral standard of the time than the other. But there is this difference, that the Christian Church has its moral standard in the past, in the life of the Son of Man; it too recognises change, as age succeeds age, but the new duties are regarded not as new, but as newly brought forth out of an already existing treasure, as the completer manifestation under new conditions of the meaning of the life of Christ. On the threshold of Christian morality there lies that by which all its subsequent stages may be tested, and which is the measure of advance or retrogression. It is this permanent element, preceding the element of change and of development, in Christian morality, which gives it its authority as against the moral product of one nation or one age.

It is exactly this authority which has enabled the Church to appeal with such force to duty as precedent to right, and to love as higher than justice. We can best illustrate this steady appeal to higher motives by tracing the steps by which Christian teachers have brought out, one by one, the different aspects of the relations of governors and governed looked at in the light of Christian anthropology and Christian sociology. The first principles governing the attitude of indi-

[1] S. Matt. v. 48.   [2] Eph. iv. 13.   [3] S. Matt. v. 5, 11, 39, 40.

vidual Christians towards the various organizations of human society are laid down in the words of Christ, ' Render unto Caesar the things which are Caesar's, and unto God the things that are God's[1].' The command, taken in connection with its context, involves two principles, first, the recognition of the claims of civil society, and, secondly, their limitation by a higher order of claims, where they come into conflict with the first. The passage in the Epistle to the Romans[2], in which S. Paul deals with the duties of Christians towards 'the powers that be,' is a commentary on his Master's teaching. It shews the connection of the first of these principles with the second, by tracing it back to its ground in the will of God. It brings it into relation to love, the central motive of the Christian character. Briefly summarized, the stages of S. Paul's argument are as follows: (1) he shews that all power is of Divine origin: 'there is no power but of God.' Thus those who wield secular power are ministers of God. (2) The administration of earthly rewards and punishments by the secular power makes for good, and for this reason God uses it in His governance of the world. Therefore temporal authority is to be obeyed 'not only for wrath, but also for conscience sake,' i. e. not merely to avoid earthly punishment, but as a duty. (3) This duty may be regarded as one application of the general maxim of justice, 'Render to all their dues.' But (4) all these scattered dues are to a Christian summed up under one vast debt, always in process of payment, but never completely paid. 'Owe no man anything, but to love one another.' 'Love is the fulfilling of the law.' These passages of the New Testament put in the clearest light the duty of obedience to civil authority. They lay down its theological ground in the derivation of all power from God; and its moral ground by shewing that such obedience is one form of justice, and justice itself one aspect of love. They thus give to the commands of those wielding authority in human society the firmest sanctions. If on the one side Christianity seems to set up conscience, as the guardian of the things of God, against positive law, it gives on the other a Divine sanction and consecration to the whole order of things connected with the State by shewing its ministerial relation to, its defined place and function in, God's ordering of the world.

This was the side of our Lord's saying which needed enforcing on the Christians of S. Paul's time. The civil authority was the Roman Empire with its overwhelming force and its almost entire externality to Christianity. The danger, then, was the spirit of passionate revolt against the secular power. Men who were filled with the new wine of the Spirit, who were turning the world upside down, found it hard to submit to the decrees of an alien power, wielded by heathen: they

[1] S. Matt. xxii. 21.
[2] Rom. xiii. 1-10. Compare S. Peter's teaching in 1 S. Pet. ii. 13-17.

pleaded their Christian liberty; they could not understand that such a power was 'ordained of God.' The early Christian Fathers found it sufficient, even when the Roman Empire was gradually becoming Christian, to bring home to consciences the teaching of S. Paul. There was no need then to emphasize in words the other side of our Lord's saying. There was little danger of undue subservience to the civil power being regarded with anything but disapproval: the danger was of men not giving it the obedience which was its due. 'We honour the Emperor,' says Tertullian[1], 'so far as we may, and so far as honour is due to him, as the first after God . . . . as one who has only God for his superior.' 'If the Emperor demands tribute,' says Ambrose[2], 'we do not refuse it: the lands of the Church pay tribute; if the Emperor wishes for our lands, he has the power to take them—none of us will resist him . . . . we render to Caesar what is Caesar's.' S. Augustine, with his Stoical leaning and his Roman sense of order, was little inclined to encourage men to resist, in any case, established powers. 'What matters it under whose rule a man lives who is to die, provided only his rulers do not force him to do impious and unjust things[3]?' Only in one passage of S. Chrysostom[4], among the writers of the first four centuries, is a gloss given to S. Paul's words, 'There is no power but of God,' which distinguishes the delegation of power in general from God, and the delegation of power by God to any particular ruler, and so suggests the possibility of a *de facto* ruler to whom obedience was not due.

But this attitude of the early Christian teachers was a very different thing from that attitude of the English Caroline divines, which gave so fatal a bent to the teaching of the English Church of the seventeenth century in the sphere which lies on the borderland of Theology and Politics. What the early Fathers taught their Christian followers was that it was their duty to obey in secular matters the powers lawfully set over them. What the English divines taught was the Divine right of princes and the subjects' duty of non-resistance. In the great battle which was being fought out in England between arbitrary power and freedom, they threw the whole weight of the English Church on the side of the former. It was a fatal error as a matter of policy, for it was the losing side. But, what is hardly sufficiently realized, it was most untrue to the tradition of the Church, and of the Church in England.

It was contrary to the tradition of the Church. For after the rise of Christianity to the high places of the world, followed by the break-up

---

[1] *Ad Scap.* II.
[2] *Oratio in Auxentium de basilicis tradendis.*
[3] Aug. *De Civ. Dei*, v. 17, but cp. *De bono Conj.* 16, for a recognition of the possibility of the unjust use of legitimate power.
[4] *Hom.* xxiii. on *Rom.* xiii. 1.

of the Roman Empire, and the formation of the mediaeval States, weakly knit together by personal ties, and with uncertain claims on the allegiance of their subjects, two new aspects of the relations of governors and governed had been brought out in Christian teaching. First, stress was laid on the duty of those holding power. Emperors and kings, magistrates and officers, who were Christians, had a claim for guidance and instruction in the exercise of their various functions. The claim was met by shewing them that, whatever the earthly source of authority may be, all just power is of God, and therefore must be regarded, not as a privilege, nor as a personal right, but as a *trust* to be undertaken for the good of others, and as a ministry for God and man. Thus a government which has for its aim anything else than the common good is, properly speaking, not a government at all. Whether its form is monarchical or not, it is simply a tyranny[1]. Secondly, the Middle Age theologians supplemented S. Paul's teaching by shewing the possible right of resistance to an unlawful government, or to one that failed to perform its duties. Such right of resistance might arise in two cases: (1) that of unjust acquisition of power, (2) that of its unjust use. Unjust acquisition might take place in two ways: (*a*) when an unworthy person acquired power, but by legitimate means: in this case it was the duty of subjects to submit, because the form of power came from God; (*b*) when power was acquired by force or fraud: in this case, subjects had the right to depose the ruler, if they had the power, supposing, however, that the illegitimate assumption of power had not been legitimated by subsequent consent. Unjust use might also take place in two ways: (*a*) when the ruler commanded something contrary to virtue, in which case it was a duty to disobey; or (*b*) when he went outside his rights, in which case subjects were not bound to obey, but it was not necessarily their duty to disobey. And so cases might arise in which it was lawful to enfranchise oneself, even from a legitimate power. 'Some who have received power from God, yet if they abuse it, deserve to have it taken from them. Both the one and the other come of God[2].'

Nor was the political teaching of the Caroline divines in agreement with the tradition of the Church in England. It is not necessary to go back to the great Archbishops who led, in earlier days, the struggle for English freedom. It is sufficient to recur to the teaching of the greatest of English post-Reformation theologians, at once soaked through and

[1] Tyrannicide was defended by some of the more extreme opponents of the temporal power, like John of Salisbury, the secretary of Thomas Becket (*Policraticus* VIII. 17, 'Tyrannus pravitatis imago; plerumque etiam occidendus'). But it was condemned by the sounder judgment of Aquinas (*De Reg. Princ.* I. 6, 'Hoc apostolicae doctrinae non congruit').

[2] Thomas Aquinas, *Comm. Sent.* XLIV. q. 2 a. 2; q. 1 a. 2. In *Comm. Pol.* v. 1 § 2 he goes so far as to make insurrection in certain cases a duty.

through with the spirit of Catholic antiquity, and in complete agreement with the English Reformation settlement. Richard Hooker had no sympathy with that doctrine of Divine right which his mediaeval masters looked upon as a quasi-heretical doctrine[1]. He found the first origin of government in the consent of the governed, and he anticipates Hobbes and Locke in his account of the 'first original conveyance, when power was derived from the whole into one[2].' Further, he points out that the king's power is strictly limited (except in the case of conquest or of special appointment by God), not only by the original compact, but also by after-agreement made with the king's consent or silent allowance[3]. And men are not bound in conscience to obey such usurpers 'as in the exercise of their power do more than they have been authorized to do[4].' But on the other hand, he maintains strongly, as against those who thought that human laws could in no sort touch the conscience, the duty of civil obedience in agreement with the law of God, and the sacredness, the 'Divine institution,' of duly-constituted authority, whether 'God Himself doth deliver, or men by light of nature find out the kind thereof.'

Thus, the main points which have been brought out by Christian teaching as to the relation of Christian citizens to the civil authority are: (1) first and foremost, the duty of obedience for conscience' sake, a duty which stands on the same level, and is invested with the same sanctions as the most sacred claims; (2) the duty, in case of the civil authority issuing commands contrary to virtue or religion, of disobedience on the same grounds as those which lead to obedience in the former case; (3) the duty of those wielding authority to use it for the common good, and so as not to hinder, if they cannot promote, the Christian religion; (4) the right, which may be said in certain extreme cases to rise almost to a duty, of resistance to the arbitrary or unconstitutional extension of authority to cases outside its province.

The same emphasis on higher motives is characteristic of Christian treatment of the questions connected with property. Christianity is certainly not pledged to uphold any particular form of property as such. Whether property had better be held by individuals, or by small groups, as in the case of the primitive Teutonic villages, or of the modern Russian or Indian village communities, or again by the State, as is the proposal of Socialists, is a matter for experience and common sense to decide. But where Christian ethics steps in is, firstly, to shew that property is secondary not primary, a means and not an end. Thus, in so far as Socialism looks to the moral regeneration of society

---

[1] Janet, *Histoire de la Science politique*, third edition, 1887, vol. i. p. 330.
[2] Hooker, *Eccl. Pol.* VIII. ii. 5, 9. Cp. I. x. 4.

[3] *Eccl. Pol.* VIII. ii. 11.
[4] *Eccl. Pol.* VIII. App. No. I. (ed. Keble). Cp. I. x. 8.

by a merely mechanical alteration of the distribution of the products of industry or of the mode of holding property, it has to be reminded that a change of heart and will is the only true starting-point of moral improvement. On the other hand, it cannot be too often asserted that the accumulation of riches is not in itself a good at all. Neither riches nor poverty make men better in themselves. Their effect on character depends on the use made of them, though no doubt the responsibility of those who have property is greater, because they have one instrument the more for the purposes of life. And so, secondly, Christianity urges that *if* there is private property, its true character as a trust shall be recognised, its rights respected and its attendant duties performed. These truths it keeps steadily before men's eyes by the perpetual object-lesson of the life of the early Church of Jerusalem, in which those who had property sold it, and brought the proceeds and laid them at the Apostles' feet, and distribution was made unto every man according to his needs [1], an object-lesson enforced and renewed by the example of the monastic communities, with their vow of voluntary poverty, and their common purse. So strongly did the early Fathers insist on the duty, almost the debt, of the rich to the poor, that isolated passages may be quoted which read like a condemnation of all private property [2], but this was not their real drift. The obligation which they urged was the obligation of charity.

(2) So far we have considered the way in which Christianity has strengthened and defined on the side of duty, which itself is one form of charity or love, the motives which make men good citizens, good property-holders, and so has supplemented the moral forces of the State, by raising the common standard of opinion and conviction on which ultimately all possibility of State-action rests. But the word charity is used not only in the wider, but also in a narrower sense, of one special form of love, the love of the strong who stoops to help the weak.

It is admitted on all hands that charity in this sense has been a mark of the Christian type of character, but the uniqueness of Christian charity has probably been exaggerated. The better Stoics recognised the active service of mankind, and especially of the poor and miserable, as part of the ideal of a perfect life. Their severity was crossed by pity. As Seneca puts it in one pregnant phrase, they held that 'wherever a man is, there is room for doing good [3].' And so Stoicism had its alimentationes, or homes for orphan children, its distributions of grain, its provisions for the sick and for strangers [4]. Christianity and

---

[1] Acts iv. 34, 35.
[2] Especially in S. Ambrose ; the passages are collected in Dubief, *Essai sur les idées politiques de S. Augustin,* 1859, ch. vi. S. Augustine himself opposed the obligatory Communism, advocated by Pelagianism ; cp. *Ep.* 157 (Ed. Bened.) to Hilary, quoted by Dubief.
[3] Sen. *De vita beata,* 24.
[4] Uhlhorn, *Christian Charity in the*

Stoicism, it may seem, were walking along the same road; but the difference was this, 'what pagan charity was doing tardily, and as it were with the painful calculation of old age, the Church was doing, almost without thinking about it, in the plenary masterfulness of youth, because it was her very being thus to do[1].' She did it with all the ease and grace of perfect naturalness, not as valuing charity without love, for 'if I bestow all my goods to feed the poor, and if I give my body to be burned, but have not love, it profiteth me nothing[2],' but because love forthwith blossomed forth into charity. 'And the disciples were called Christians first in Antioch. And in these days came prophets from Jerusalem unto Antioch. And there stood up one of them named Agabus, and signified by the spirit that there should be great dearth throughout all the world . . . Then the disciples, every man according to his ability, determined to send relief unto the brethren which dwelt in Judæa[3].'

And so it became the recognised and traditional duty of the Church to maintain the cause of the weak against the strong, of the poor against the rich, of the oppressed against the oppressors. The Bishops of the fourth and fifth centuries exercised 'a kind of religious tribunate[4].' In the Middle Ages, the Church urged on those in public and private stations the duties of charity, pity, humanity. The author of the latter part of the *De Regimine Principum*[5] ascribed to S. Thomas Aquinas lays down as one of the chief duties of a king, the care of the weak and the succour of the miserable. Nor did the Church in England in pre-Reformation times fail in her duty in this respect. She pleaded for the manumission or at least the humane usage of the serfs. She undertook through her monasteries the relief of the poor. Her prohibition of usury, however mistaken it may seem to us, was a real protection to debtors against one of the worst forms of tyranny, that of the unscrupulous creditor. Since the Reformation her record has not been so clean. The shock of the Reformation left her weak. The traditional sanctions of her authority were shaken. In the long struggle of the seventeenth century her close association with the Stuart cause left her powerless to touch the stronger half of the nation. She was not independent enough to act as arbiter, and in committing herself without reserve to opposition to the national claim for freedom she was untrue to her earlier and better traditions. At the same time allowance must be made for the licence, the disorder, and the recklessness with which the claims of liberty were associated, and for the identification of the popular party with views of religion, which, what-

---

Ancient Church, Eng. Transl. 1883, Bk. I. ch. i. pp. 18–21, 41, 42.

[1] Pater, *Marius the Epicurean*, Vol. II. ch. xxii. p. 127.

[2] 1 Cor. xiii. 3 (R.V.).

[3] Acts xi. 26–29 ; cp. also Acts iv. 34, 35, quoted above.

[4] Dubief, p. 11.

[5] II. 15.

ever else may be said for them, are not those of the Church. The leading churchmen believed that its triumph meant the disappearance of that historical Church, which they rightly regarded as the only effective safeguard of English Christianity. After the Restoration the Church was stronger, and the increase of strength shews itself on the one side in greater independence of the Crown, and on the other in the outburst of numerous religious and charitable societies and foundations. Queen Anne's Bounty is an instance of the charity, if it be not rather the justice, of one distinguished daughter of the Church. The 'Religious Societies' which in a quiet and unassuming way were a great influence in social life, had among their objects the visiting and relief of the poor, the apprenticing of the young, the maintenance of poor scholars at the University. Charity schools were established throughout the country : hospitals and parochial libraries founded, while societies like the Society for the Propagation of the Gospel in Foreign Parts, and the Society for Promoting Christian Knowledge date back to the last years of the seventeenth and the first of the eighteenth centuries[1]. Then as the Georgian period begins, all this vigorous life seems for a long period to die down, or only to find vent in the great Wesleyan movement which, beginning within the Church, passes out beyond it, and ultimately becomes stereotyped in more or less pronounced separation from her communion. It was the policy of the ruling Whig oligarchy to keep down the Church, and they succeeded—to the grave loss of English morality. If in some degree the Church in England at the present time is speaking with firmer accent on questions of personal and class morality, and giving more effective witness against the luxury and neglect of their work-people, which are the besetting sins of the great English manufacturing classes, it is due partly to the revival in England of the true idea of the Church as a great spiritual society, and partly to the fact that English statesmen, from sheer inability owing to the conditions of political life to do otherwise, have left her more free to manage her own business and to develop her mission to the English people in accordance with the laws and aspirations of her own inner life.

It is especially necessary in a great industrial society such as that of modern England that the Christian law of self-sacrifice, which crosses and modifies the purely competitive tendency leading each individual to seek his own interest and that of his family, should be strongly and effectively presented. No doubt it is true that the increased knowledge of the structure and laws of social life which we possess, have made charity more difficult than in the Middle Ages : they have not made it less necessary, or a less essential feature of the Christian character. And so, in a democratic age, the protection of the weak and the

[1] Overton, *Life in the English Church*, 1660-1714, Ch. v.

oppressed will take a different colour. Whether supreme control is in the hands of one or many, it may be used tyrannically. And the most effective exercise of the tribunate of the Church will lie in guarding the rights of conscience and the great national interest of religion against hasty and unfair pressure. And this brings us to our next point.

(3) The drift of the argument has been to shew the incompleteness and inevitable limitations of the State, considered as a moral guide of the social life of mankind. But that incompleteness rises to its maximum, those limitations press most closely when we pass from morality to religion. If it is the highest duty of the State to maintain true and vital religion [1], it is a duty which of itself it is altogether incompetent to perform. If the experience of the Middle Ages shewed conclusively that the subordination of the State to the Church did not tend either to good government, or to the maintenance, pure and undefiled, of the Christian religion, the experience of English post-Reformation history has as conclusively shewn that the subordination of the Church to the State leads on the one hand to the secularization of the Church, and on the other to a grave danger to national life, through the loss of a spiritual authority strong enough, as well as vigilant and independent enough, to reprove social sins and to call to account large and influential classes. The conditions under which the Tudor idea of a Christian commonwealth was possible have passed away, and there seem to remain two possible conclusions from the premises.

The first is that it is expedient in the interests of both that Church and State should be separate from one another, as e.g. in America, and left free to develop, each on its own lines, their respective missions in the national service—'a free Church in a free State.' The current of opinion in England in favour of disestablishment, undoubtedly a strong, though probably not at the present time an increasing one, is fed from many smaller streams. There are Agnostics who believe that religion is the enemy of progress, and that Christianity especially shackles free thought, and hinders the advance of social reformation, and to whom therefore it seems a clear duty to undermine by every means open to them the hold of Christianity on the centres of social and intellectual life, on schools and universities, families and states. They favour disestablishment as one means to this end. Two principal causes seem to move those who are primarily statesmen in the direction of disestablishment. One is the conception of the State as the great controlling and guiding organization of human life [2], supreme over all

---

[1] Hooker, *Eccl. Pol.* VIII. i. 4. In all commonwealths, things spiritual ought above temporal to be provided for. And of things spiritual, the chiefest is religion. Cp. V. i. 2.

[2] We have already shewn reasons for thinking that though no doubt the State has *a* great co-ordinating and regulative function in regard to human life, it is not fitted for the part of *the* moral guide of mankind.

partial societies and voluntary associations formed to guard parts or sides of life, and the attempt to mould national life by this guiding idea and its logical consequences. This attempt is encouraged by the extreme simplicity of the English Constitution in its actual working, and by the legally unlimited power of Parliament [1]. The other is their practical experience that in view of the divided condition of English Christianity, the most stubborn and intractable difficulties in legislation arise from, or are aggravated by, religious differences. They suppose that these would be lessened if the State took the position of impartial arbiter between rival denominations. Among Nonconformists there are no doubt some who, looking at the Church as the natural rival of their own society, think to weaken her by disestablishment, but there are also many who believe that disestablishment would be a gain to English religion, and that the life of the Church would be more real, more pure, more governed by the highest motives, if she were freed from all direct connection with the State. Lastly, there is no doubt that the idea of the return to the looser relations between Church and State which prevailed in the earliest Christian centuries, has a great attraction for a considerable body of churchmen. They would perhaps have been willing enough to accept the royal supremacy under a religious sovereign in thorough harmony with the beliefs and modes of working of the Church, but the revolution by which the House of Commons has risen to supreme power in England, has given it, not in the theory, but in the actual working of the constitution, the ultimate control over matters ecclesiastical as well as civil, and they hold that by stifling the free utterance of the voice of the Church the House of Commons is doing an injury to religion compared to which disestablishment would be a lesser evil.

On the other hand, if we look beyond our own country, we have the opinion of the venerable Dr. Döllinger, reported by Dr. Liddon, that the disestablishment of the Church in England would be an injury to the cause of religion throughout Europe. And so weighty an opinion may well make us carefully scrutinize those difficulties and tendencies which make for disestablishment. It is no doubt true that from one point of view the *idea* of the Church as a great spiritual society seems to require her entire freedom to control her own development, and therefore the absence of all formal connection with the State. But there is nothing more deeply illogical and irrational, in any sense of logic in which it is near to life and therefore true, than the attempt to solve a

---

[1] Dicey, *Law of the Constitution,* second edition, 1886, lecture ii. p. 36, 'The principle of Parliamentary sovereignty means neither more nor less than this, namely, that Parliament thus defined has, under the English Constitution, the right to make or unmake any law whatever ; and, further, that no person or body is recognised by the law of England as having a right to override or set aside the legislation of Parliament.'

great problem, spiritual, moral, political, social, by neglecting all its factors but one, even if it be the most important one. Nor does it follow that, because we recognise that in a certain condition of things, more harm than good will be done by a particular application of a truth which we accept, therefore we have ceased to hold that truth. It only shews that our ideal is complex.

And so from another point of view the most perfect ordering of things would seem to be one in which Church and State were two parts of one whole, recognising one another's functions and limits, and mutually supporting one another. Thus religion would be put in its true place as at once the foundation and the coping stone of national life. And the State with all its administration would be given a distinctly Christian character. The difficulty in England is to maintain this point of view in connection with the increasingly non-religious (not necessarily anti-religious) colouring of the State, and of the fierce struggles of party government which destroy the reverence which might otherwise attach to the State and its organs. As the State has become increasingly lay, its moral weight has sunk, its hold on consciences become less. But the truth remains that religion is an element in the highest national life. 'A national Church alone can consecrate the whole life of a people [1].' And a national Church can only mean an established Church, and a Church which either has great inherited wealth of its own, or is supported in part by national funds. 'Of all parts of this subject,' says Mr. Gladstone [2], 'probably none have been so thoroughly wrought out as the insufficiency of the voluntary principle.' It is insufficient (i.e. for maintaining national religion), first, because after a certain level of moral deterioration has been reached by individuals or masses of people, the demand for religion is least where the want is greatest ; and secondly, because in consequence of the structure of social life there are always large classes of the community who, while just provided with the bare necessaries of life, have not sufficient means to enable them to sustain the expense of the organs of the higher life in any form. We recognise this in the case of education ; we can hardly refuse to recognise it in the case of religion.

For these reasons we are thrown back on the second possible conclusion from the data, viz. that it is desirable that there should be some definite and permanent connection between Church and State, but not such connection as will either subordinate the State to the Church or the Church to the State. And such a result would seem to be best attainable by some such system of relations as that between the Established Church and the State in Scotland, or the Roman Catholic Church and the State in France. Thus in Scotland, on the critical

[1] Westcott, *Social Aspects of Christianity*, ch. v. p. 76.

[2] *The State in its relations with the Church*, p. 41.

point of jurisdiction, the position is this. The Church Courts are final : there is no appeal to a Civil Court except on the ground of excess of jurisdiction. And the judgment of the Church Courts, so far as it involves civil consequences, may be enforced by application to the Civil Courts[1]. In France we have to distinguish the relations of Church and State as constitutionally defined from those relations in their actual working. No constitutional relations, however admirable, can work when the State constantly encroaches, and where its whole attitude is one of hostility to the Church. In theory, however, the position in France is, except on one point, much the same as in Scotland. There is a complete system of ecclesiastical jurisdiction in the Roman Catholic Church based on the Canon Law and administered by the bishops acting as judges. From their decisions there is no appeal to the Civil Courts except on the ground of abuse (appel d'abus). On the other hand, the Ecclesiastical Courts have no coercive jurisdiction, nor are their sentences carried out by the Civil Courts[2]. They bind, therefore, only *in foro conscientiae* and this is found sufficient. There is one point worthy of special notice in the French system, that while the relations of the State to the Roman Catholic (once the Gallican) Church are regulated by a special Concordat, two leading Protestant bodies, the French Reformed Church, and the Church of the Augsburg Confession, as well as the Jewish body, are also endowed. Alongside of a system by which the Church is established there is a concurrent endowment of other Christian and even non-Christian denominations.

In Scotland the relations of Church and State rest on the Act of

[1] *Report of the Ecclesiastical Courts Commission,* Vol. II. p. 601. Answers to questions,—Scotland, Established Church.

'No appeal lies to a Civil Court in matters of discipline or on the ground of excess of punishment. But if under the form of discipline the Church Courts were to inflict Church censures (involving civil consequences) on a minister for *e. g.* obeying the law of the land, a question . . . . might be brought before the Civil Court on the ground of excess of jurisdiction. It is believed that in no case would the Civil Court entertain an appeal from a judgment of an Ecclesiastical Court on a question of doctrine, or enter on an examination of the soundness of such a judgment before enforcing its civil consequences.

'Any questions which have arisen on points of ritual . . . . have hitherto been decided exclusively by the Church Courts.' (A qualifying sentence follows as to possible extreme cases justifying, on the failure to obtain redress from the General Assembly, an appeal to the Civil Court.)

[2] *Report of Eccl. Courts Commission,* Vol. II. p. 605. Answers to questions, —France.

'The State remains *lay,* and does not interpose, except when the acts of the clergy are offences at Common Law, or when there is a *cas d'abus* in which either the public order or individual interests are injured. In which case the Council of State is summoned at the instance of the Government, or on the complaint of the citizens, to repress abuses and annul the *acts of abuse* (actes d'abus) on the part of the clergy.

'To recapitulate, the minister, as citizen, has to submit to the Common Law ; as priest, he belongs entirely to the jurisdiction of the Church, with which the State *does not interfere,* and with which it has not to interfere, for it is solely in the domain of conscience.'

Union, in France on the Concordat made by Napoleon with the Pope in 1801. In England there is no definite formulated agreement; and any such agreement would be entirely contrary to the English genius. But in a deeper sense, there is a contract, which is the product of 1200 years of history, of which the terms vary from generation to generation, and which is commended by each age to the forbearance and the statesmanship of its successors. The terms of that contract are in the main fixed by the State. In any case, whether the Church remains established or not, the State has ultimate power over her temporal possessions, as over all temporal possessions held within its territory. But, if the Church is to remain connected with the State, perpetual difficulties must arise, unless means are found to leave the Church free, in matters as well of doctrine as of ritual, both to legislate through her own organs, and to exercise an independent spiritual jurisdiction. It is for the interest of the State that the Church should be allowed to make her service for the English nation as fruitful, as powerful, and as little a hindrance to her own spirituality as possible.

III. Lastly we may consider the way in which the Church, quite irrespective of any direct connection with the State, as a natural consequence of its position as a spiritual society and of its teaching as to fundamental moral and spiritual truths, acts as a purifying and elevating agent on the general social life of mankind, on all its manifestations and organs.

If man is 'metaphysical *nolens volens*,' it is equally true that he is metapolitical, to use Martensen's happy word, *nolens volens*. And metapolitic means 'that which precedes the political as its presupposition, that which lies outside and beyond it as its aim and object, and by which the political element is to be pervaded as by its soul, its intellectually vivifying principle [1]. Every statesman, every real leader of men, has consciously or unconsciously, such a metapolitic; he holds, that is, certain views as to man's place in the world, as to the meaning and possibility of progress, as to the aims as distinct from the machinery of government, as to the relations of nations to one another and to humanity, which determine his general attitude towards all kinds of questions with which he has to deal. It is clear, for instance, that the groups of ideas which govern the fatalist, the pessimist, and the humanitarian, are widely different.

Now the Church is the home and dwelling-place of certain great regulative ideas as to man's destiny and function, and his relation to God and other men, the treasure-house to which they were committed, or the soil in which they germinated. These ideas, if accepted and acted on, or so far as accepted and acted on, must transform and

[1] Martensen, *Christian Ethics*, special part, second division, English Translation, p. 100.

remodel, not only the inward life, but also the whole outward life in all its spheres. Thus S. Paul deduces from the Christian conception of man, the duties of husbands, wives, fathers, children, masters, servants, subjects, rich persons, old men, old women, young men, young women. And so, now rapidly, now slowly, according to the vigour and purity at successive periods of the Christian society, now thrown inwards by periods of persecution or by the rising tide of evil, now borne outwards in periods of rapid expansion and missionary enterprise, now brought to bear on new conditions of life and new social groupings, now traced back to their source, and tested by the life and words of the Word of God, the Christian ideas of man, and of his relation to God radiate through the life of mankind, at once sustaining and correcting its aspirations, and its ideals of righteousness.

The root ideas of this Christian anthropology rest on the Christian conception of God as one yet threefold. Thus on the one side, Christianity attaches to the individual personality a supreme and infinite value as the inmost nature of one made in the image of God, redeemed by the self-sacrifice of Christ, and indwelt by the Spirit of God. And thus it develops the sense of separate personal responsibility. It is on this basis that what is true in humanitarianism rests. Behind all class and social differences lies the human personality in virtue of which all men are equal[1]. But on the other side it frankly recognises man's inherently social nature. It is not good for man to be alone. And family, State, and the Church on earth are training places for a perfected common life in the City of God.

The effect of this conception of man and his destiny is to place the State and its associations in their true position as not ultimate but secondary, as means and not ends. Alongside of the earthly kingdom, with its wealth, its honours, its ambitions, its wide and far-reaching influence, it sets another kingdom, the City of God, with its own standards, its own principles, its own glory, its own blessedness, as the end of mankind, the goal of history. 'The nations shall walk amidst the light thereof, and the kings of the earth do bring their glory into it[2]. And, in so doing, it judges and corrects the splendour of earthly States.

In thus contrasting the earthly State with the City of God, Christianity is no doubt exposed to the old accusation, that it makes men bad citizens. And the old answer is still true, 'let those who think that the doctrine of Jesus Christ cannot contribute to the happiness of the State, give us soldiers and officers such as it bids them to be, subjects and citizens as faithful as Jesus Christ commands, husbands, wives,

---

[1] Cp. Aug. *De Civ. Dei*, v. 24, of Christian Emperors, 'we think them happy if they remember themselves to be *men*.'

[2] Rev. xxi. 24 (R.V.).

fathers, mothers, children, masters, servants, kings, judges, living according to the laws of religion, men as punctual in their payment of taxes, as pure in their handling of public funds as are the true Christians : they will be soon forced to admit that the maxims of the Gospel when practised cannot but give a State great happiness and great prosperity [1].' It is not too much but too little Christianity which destroys States ; for passion and wilfulness are the great disintegrating forces of the world, and everything which strengthens individuals to resist them, so far strengthens the bonds of social union. But the service which Christianity renders to States goes far beyond this negative result. If the true meaning of progress be moral, and not material, there can be no greater contribution to the well-being of society than that of maintaining the Christian type of character with its humility, its purity, its sincerity, and again its strong and beneficent activity.

In the present discussion the State has been put first and the Church second. In order of time the State is first. And what has been attempted has been to shew how starting with the State and its institutions, the higher order which was initiated by the historical Incarnation (though not without preparatory and imperfect anticipations in earlier and especially in Jewish history), comes in to mould, to purify, and to supplement. But these words only express partial aspects of the whole process by which a higher order acts on a lower. It interpenetrates far more deeply than can be expressed in any classification of the modes of its operation. The Christian religion has been acting on the group of States which we call Christendom from the first days when stable organization formed themselves after the entrance of the new life of the Germanic races into the remains of the dying Roman Empire. It has been the strongest of all the influences that have moulded them throughout their history. It has pierced and penetrated the life of individuals, the life of families, the life of guilds, as well as the laws and institutions, the writings and works of art in which they have embodied their thoughts and hopes. They are in a sense its children. It is impossible to regard them as S. Augustine regarded pagan Rome. But deep and penetrating as has been her influence and manifold her consequent implications with the existing national and social life of mankind, the Church is essentially Catholic, and only incidentally national. It is their Catholic character so far as it remains, at least their Catholic ideal, which gives to the different fragments of the Church their strength and power. The ' Church of England' is a peculiarly misleading term. The Church of Christ in England is, as Coleridge pointed out, the safer and truer phrase. And this fundamental Catholicism, this correspondence not to one or

[1] Aug. *Ep. ad Marcellinum*, 138, 15.

another nation, but to humanity, rests on the appeal to deeper and more permanent needs than those on which the State rests. It is thus that the true type of the Church is rather in the family than in the State, because the family is the primitive unit of organized social life. Not in the order of time, but in the order of reason, the Church is prior to the State, for man is at once inherently social and inherently religious. And therefore it is only in the Church that he can be all that it is his true nature to be

CHRISTIAN ETHICS.

THE study of early Church History suggests the conclusion that the Christian religion was recognised as a rule, or fashion of life, before it was discovered to be a philosophy and a creed. To be complete, therefore, any account of Christianity must include the presentation of it as a Divine ' way of life '—a coherent system of practical ethics, marked by characteristic conceptions of freedom, duty, the moral standard, the highest end of life, and the conditions of human perfection. Such is the task we are about to attempt. To the necessary limitations of a sketch in outline, the reader may ascribe a general avoidance of controversial, and a preference for positive, statements ; as also the fact that some large and interesting branches of the subject are dismissed with no more than a passing allusion.

It may be admitted, at the outset, that non-religious ethical speculation has in a measure paved the way for a re-statement of the Christian theory, by its inquiries into the source and nature—the rational basis and binding force—of moral obligation. For it may be maintained that in Christianity, rightly understood, is to be found an adequate answer to the question which all schools of thought agree in regarding as fundamental—the question '*Why* must I do right ?'

On the other hand, the Christian Church claims to meet the plain needs of average human nature by her answer to the question, '*How* am I to do right ?' She claims to have at command practical means of solving a problem which is admittedly abandoned as hopeless by the ethics of naturalism. If Jesus Christ gave profound extension to the ideas of duty and obligation, He was also the first who pointed humanity to the unfailing source of moral power. In this respect Christianity presents a favourable contrast to other systems, the tendency of which is to be so concerned with the Ideal as to underrate the importance and pressure of the Actual. Christianity claims to be in contact with facts ; such facts as sin, moral impotence, perverted will, the tyranny of habit. And while she is large-hearted and eagle-spirited in her scope—dealing with all possible relationships in which a human being may stand, whether to God above him, his fellow-men about him, or the sum of physical life below him; the Church is none the less definite and practical in method and aim; witness the importance she attaches to the individual character, the recreation of which is at least a step towards a regeneration of society.

The chief point of distinction, however, between Christian and non-Christian ethics is to be found in a difference of view as to the relation existing between morality and religion. A system which so closely connects the idea of Good with the doctrine of God, must needs at every point present conduct as inseparably related to truth, and character to creed. It has been noticed indeed that Pliny's letter to Trajan—the earliest record we possess of the impression produced on an intelligent Pagan by the new religion—testifies to the intimate connection of morals with dogma and worship. What the Christian consciousness accepted as truth for the intellect, it embraced also as law for the will. Whether then we have regard to the practical purpose, or the wide outlook of the Christian system, we shall feel the difficulty of giving even a fair outline of so vast a subject in so limited a space. If the idea of Good corresponds in any sense to the conception of God, that idea must have an infinite depth of significance, and range of application. If the recreation of human nature be a practicable aim, no department of anthropology or psychology can be without its interest for ethics. It must suffice to indicate, rather than unfold, the points which seem to be of primary importance.

Christian Morals are based on dogmatic postulates. The foundation of our science is laid, not merely in the study of man's nature, his functions and capacities, but in revealed truths as to the nature and character of God, His creative purpose, His requirement of His creatures. We believe that Christ came to liberate human thought from systems of morality having their centre or source in man [1].

> Man is not God, but hath God's end to serve;
> A Master to obey, a course to take,
> Somewhat to cast off, somewhat to become . . .
> How could man have progression otherwise?

The postulates may conveniently be distributed under three main heads : the doctrine of God, of Man, of Christ.

For the purpose of ethics, two simple truths as to the Being of God require attention.

God is an Infinite, but *Personal* Being; existing from eternity in the completeness of His own blessedness, yet willing to become the centre of a realm of personalities. To this end He called into exis-

---

[1] 1 S. Pet. i. 21 ὥστε τὴν πίστιν ὑμῶν καὶ ἐλπίδα εἶναι εἰς θεόν.

tence a world of personal beings, in a sense independent of Himself, but destined, in communion and intercourse with Himself, to find and fulfil the law of their creaturely perfection. To these free and rational beings, Almighty God deigns to stand in self-imposed relations.

Again, God is an *Ethical* Being: He is essentially Holy and Loving.

He is Holy; and appoints that for the entire realm of personality, as for Himself, holiness should be the absolute law. He alone can communicate to His creatures the idea of holiness; of a supreme, eternal, ethical Good. The Good exists only in Him; is the essential expression of His Nature, the reflected light of His Personality. The idea of ethical Good is not therefore due to a natural process by which the accumulated social traditions of our race are invested with the name, and sanction, of moral Law. The idea is communicated, derived from the living Source of Good freely acting on the faculties of intelligent creatures who are capable of receiving such communications 'in divers parts and in divers manners [1].'

The apprehension of moral Law thus appears to correspond with a progressive apprehension of God. Along with the idea of the unity and absoluteness of God, heathendom lost the sense of an absolute moral Law [2]; and conversely, in proportion as the Divine Nature manifests Itself more fully to human intelligence, the idea of moral Good gains expansion and depth.

God is also Love: a truth which as it helps our thought to a more profound and consistent view of His mysterious Being, so implies that God must needs will His rational creature to be what He Himself is, 'holy and blameless before Him [3];' to engage itself in activities resembling His own; to be free with His Freedom; enlightened by His Light [4]. Nor can we think that Divine Love is content with a bare revelation of moral *requirement*. We believe that what God requires, He is ready and able to impart; He will empower man to render what His righteousness exacts. Finally, if His purpose for man be interrupted or thwarted, He will 'devise means' for its final and victorious fulfilment. He, the Author of Creation, will in due time provide for a recreation, not less potent and complete in its effects than the evil power which has invaded and marred the first creation [5]. For we can form no idea of Love other than that of an active, energizing principle by which a personal Being reveals Himself; a Being tenacious of His purpose, multiform in His expedients, supremely patient in His beneficent activity. The God pre-supposed in Christian

[1] Heb. i. 1.
[2] See Dorner, *Syst. of Christian Ethics*, § 35.
[3] Eph. i. 4.
[4] Cp. Plato, *Tim.* xxix. E.
[5] Athan. *de Incarn.* x.

Ethics is One who displays holiness combined with power, love controlled by wisdom : in a word, He is the God of redemptive history. Thus morality finds its starting-point in theology[1].

The Christian account of *Man* next engages attention. We confine ourselves to an inquiry into three points: what is man's essential nature, his ideal destiny, his present condition ?

We have already observed that in Christian Ethics man is not the central object of study. The moral universe tends towards a more comprehensive end than the perfection of humanity. Nevertheless Christianity is specially marked by a particular conception of man. Regarding him as a being destined for union with, capable of likeness to God, she offers an account of man's failure to fulfil his true destiny, and witnesses to a Divine remedy for his present condition. The familiar contrast between humanity as it might become, and as it is, gives significance to the peculiarly Christian doctrine of sin. It is the dignity of the sufferer that makes the mischief so ruinous ; it is the greatness of the issue at stake that makes a Divine movement towards man for his recovery at once credible, and worthy of God[2].

First, then, we presuppose a certain view of man's nature. Christianity lays stress on the principle of *personality*, with its determining elements, will and self-consciousness. It is for psychology to accurately define personality. For ethics it is simply an ultimate, all-important fact. It is that element in man which makes him morally akin to God, and capable of holding communion with Him; that which places him in conscious relation to Law; gives him a representative character as God's vice-gerent on earth, and conveys the right to dominion over physical nature. If religion consists in personal relations between man and God, religious ethics must be concerned with the right culture and development of personality.

But in virtue of his creaturely position, man's personality cannot be an end to itself[3]. The tendency of Greek thought was to regard man as a self-centred being ; to look for the springs of moral action, and the power of progress, within human nature itself. Thus Aristotle's ideal is the self-development of the individual under the guidance of reason, and in accordance with the law of his being. The question is, what is this law, and what the ground of its obligation ? Personality, we answer, marked man from the first as a being destined for communion with, and free imitation of God[4]. Personality enables man to be

---

[1] Clem. Alex. *Quis Dives*, etc. vii. ἀρχὴ καὶ κρηπὶς ζωῆς, ἐπιστήμη θεοῦ, τοῦ ὄντως ὄντος . . . ἡ μὲν γὰρ τούτου ἄγνοια θάνατός ἐστιν, ἡ δὲ ἐπίγνωσις αὐτοῦ καὶ οἰκείωσις, καὶ πρὸς αὐτὸν ἀγάπη καὶ ἐξομοίωσις, μόνη ζωή.

[2] Aug. *de moribus Eccl.* xii.
[3] Athan. *cont. Gentes*, iii. describes the aversion of man from God as beginning in ' self-contemplation ' (ἑαυτοὺς κατανοεῖν ἤρξαντο).
[4] Ath. *c. Gent.* ii.

receptive of a message and a call from God. It confers on each possessor of it an absolute dignity and worth. *Personality*—here is our crucial fact; enabling us to take a just measure of man, and of our duty towards him. One of the deepest truths brought to light by the Gospel was the value of the personal life, of the single soul, in God's sight. Man is great, not merely because he thinks, and can recognise moral relationships and obligations; but chiefly because he was created for union with God; and was destined to find blessedness and perfection in Him alone. Christianity therefore rates highly the worth of the individual; and her task is to develop each human personality—to bring each into contact with the Personality of God [1].

For, secondly, man has an ideal destiny [2]—life in union with God, a destiny which, as it cannot be realized under present conditions of existence, postulates the further truth of personal immortality [3]. Man is capable of progressive assimilation to God, of ever deeper spiritual affinity to Him [4]. Such must be the ideal end of a being of whom it is revealed that he was made 'in the image of God.'

But the thought of the 'Divine image' leads us a step further. Whatever be the precise import of the expression, it at least implies that the Good, which is the essence of the *Divine,* is also a vital element in the perfection of *Human* nature. It remains to indicate the way in which man is capable of recognising Good as the law of his being, and embodying it in a character. Christianity, as a moral system, offers an account of *conscience* and of *freedom.*

The Scriptural doctrine of conscience represents it as the faculty which places man in conscious relation to moral Law, as the expression of the Divine nature and requirement. In a brief sketch it is enough to lay stress on two points.

1. Conscience appears to be an original and constant principle in human nature. To assign to it a merely empirical origin—to derive it from social evolution, from the circumstances, prevalent beliefs, traditional customs of a human community, is inadequate, inasmuch as no such supposed origin will satisfactorily account for the authoritativeness, the spontaneity, the 'categorical imperative' of conscience [5]. Further, the functions attributed to this faculty in Scripture, e.g. 'judging,' 'accusing,' 'witnessing,' 'legislating'—all convey the idea that man stands in relation to moral Law as something outside and

---

[1] Wace, *Boyle Lectures,* ser. 1, Lect. vii. Cp. Col. i. 28.

[2] 2 Cor. v. 4, 5 ὁ κατεργασάμενος ἡμᾶς εἰς αὐτὸ τοῦτο θεός.

[3] Lactant. *Div. Inst.* iii. 12, 'Haec vita praesens et corporalis beata esse non potest, quia malis est subjecta per corpus . . . Si cadit *beatitudo,* ergo et *immortalitas* cadit in hominem, quae beata est.'

[4] Eph. v. 1. Ep. *ad Diog.* x.

[5] Bp. Butler's sermons emphasize this side of the doctrine of conscience, esp. the *Preface.* Cp. Flint, *Theism,* lect. vii.

independent of himself, yet laying an unconditional claim on his will. In the Christian system the existence of conscience in some form is regarded as a primary and universal fact. Its permanent character is everywhere the same; its function, that of persistently witnessing to man that he stands in necessary relation to ethical Good.

2. The language of the Bible throughout implies that conscience in its earliest stage is an imperfect organ, capable like other faculties of being cultivated and developed. Our Lord's reference to the inward 'eye' (S. Matt. vi. 22) suggests a fruitful analogy in studying the growth of conscience. In its germ, conscience is like an untrained sense, exercising itself on variable object-matter, and hence not uniform in the quality of its dictates. It is enough to point out that this fact is amply recognised by New Testament writers. S. Paul speaks more than once of progress in knowledge and perception as a feature of the Christian mind, and the faculty of discerning the Good is said to grow by exercising itself on concrete material [1]. So again, the moral faculty is impaired by unfaithfulness to its direction; the moral chaos in which the heathen world was finally plunged resulted from such unfaithfulness on a wide scale. The Gentiles knew God, but did not act on their knowledge. They 'became darkened;' they lost the power of moral perception [2].

To enlarge on this subject forms no part of our present plan. It is fair, however, to cordially acknowledge that Christian thought is indebted to psychological research for deeper and more accurate conceptions of the moral faculty; and the possibility of large variation both in the dictates of conscience, and the certainty of its guidance, may be freely admitted. And yet it has been justly observed that the question of the origin of this faculty is not one with which ethics are primarily concerned. That inquiry is wholly distinct from the question of its capacities and functions *when in a developed state* [3]. The unconditional claim of conscience—this is the constant factor which meets us amid all variations of standard and condition. It is enough that conscience is that organ of the soul by which it apprehends moral truth, and is laid under obligation to fulfil it. A Christian is content to describe it as God's voice; or, in a poet's words,

> God's most intimate presence in the soul
> And His most perfect image in the world.

For Conscience, while making an absolute claim on man's will, appeals to him as a being endowed with a power of choice: and thus we pass to the subject of *freedom*. What is freedom, in the Christian

---

[1] See Phil. i. 9, and Heb. v. 14 (the Greek).
[2] Rom. i. 21. Athan. *cont. Gentes*, iii–xi.
[3] Wace, *Boyle Lect.*, ser. 1, Lect. II.

sense? In the New Testament freedom is connected with truth. 'The truth,' it is said, 'shall make you free.' If man stands in a real relation to the Good, his true freedom can only mean freedom to correspond with, and fulfil the law of his nature[1]. The formal power of choice with which man is born—a power which in fact is seen to be extremely limited[2]—is only the rudimentary stage of freedom. Will is as yet subject to numberless restrictions, such that they seem utterly to preclude an unfettered choice. It is limited, for example, by the influence of heredity to an extent which often appears to determine unconditionally the choice between different courses of action. 'Determinism' has at least liberated our thinking from the crude idea of freedom as man's power 'to do as he likes.' True liberty can only mean freedom from false dependence, emancipation of the will from the undue pressure of external forces, or inherited tendencies. The condition of 'perfect freedom' is that in which man yields an unforced accord to the Good—his correspondence with it as the law of life. And as his formal power of choice becomes by habit more and more determined towards a fixed adherence to the Good, he begins to taste the 'glorious liberty' of a right relation to God and His Law. He becomes free with the liberty which is 'freedom not to sin,' he finds himself 'under the sole rule of God most free[3].'

Lastly, Christianity as a moral system is distinguished by her view of man's present condition. His upward development has been interrupted. In theological language he is a 'fallen' being, and the path of ethical progress is a way of *recovery*[4]. Man's capacity of corresponding with the ideal, of free self-conformity to it, though not destroyed, is at least seriously impaired. His spiritual capacities are not what they were once in a fair way to be ; they are weakened and depraved, and man's advance towards a free power of self-determination is in fact hindered by a radical defect of will—in Christian language by the principle of Sin. The Bible gives an account of sin, its first cause, its consequences in human history. Christian Ethics make allowance for this factor ; systems which overlook it or minimize it inevitably lose contact with the actual problem to be solved, with life as it is. Their tendency at best is to treat moral, as on a level with physical, evil: as an obstruction, a hindrance, but not a vital defect inherent in human nature. Not such is the Christian view of sin. For sin conditions the

---

[1] Anselm, *Cur Deus Homo*, I. xii. 'Libertas non est nisi ad hoc quod expedit aut quod decet.'

[2] See Martineau, *Types of Eth. Theory*, vol. i. 93 ; ii. 39 [Ed. 2]. Holland, *Creed and Character*, Serm. X.

[3] Aug. *de mor. Eccl.* xxi. '[Deo] solo dominante liberrimus.' Observe that as

freedom grows, the choice becomes more restricted by the law πάντα ἔξεστιν, ἀλλ' οὐ πάντα συμφέρει (1 Cor. x. 23). Cp. Pet. Lomb. *Sent.* ii. xxv. 7.

[4] Cyp. *de op. et eleem.* i. 'Pater Filium misit ut *reparare* nos posset.' Such language is usual with the Fathers.

work of the Incarnate Son Himself. Not only does Christ set Himself to re-erect the true standard of character. He devotes Himself also to dealing with the actual ravages of moral evil. He teaches its intrinsic nature, its source in the will, the inviolable law of its retribution; He reveals the destructive potency of its effects; He labours as the Good Physician to remove its temporal penalties; He provides, in His atoning Sacrifice of Himself, the one and only countervailing remedy[1].

Such postulates respecting the Nature of God and of Man find their complement and point of contact in the Catholic doctrine of the Incarnation. As to the Person of Christ, it is enough to premise that the Christian system of ethics is intelligible only on the basis of a complete recognition of all that our Lord claimed to be. He came to reveal among men the nature, the ways, the will of the All-Holy; to present the true pattern of human goodness; to be the perfect representative of man before God[2]. He is the Revealer of God, as being Himself in the fullest sense One with God; He is the pattern of humanity, in virtue of His sinless manhood; the representative, through His organic union with our race. His Resurrection and Ascension together are the condition of His recreative action as a quickening Spirit on the entire nature of man. In a word His Person, His work, His character form the central point of ethical inquiry and contemplation[3]. To arrive at the true *differentiae* of Christian morals we need to study more profoundly the character and purpose of Jesus Christ.

I. *Christ's Revelation of the Highest Good.*

To the Christian moralist the entire universe presents itself in the light of a revealed purpose as capable of receiving a spiritual impress, and as moving towards an ethical consummation. For although man is the crown of the physical creation, he cannot be independent of it in his advance towards the proper perfection of his being. The destiny of nature is bound up with that of humanity, in so far as nature tends towards some form of ethical consciousness, presents the material conditions of moral action, is capable of being appropriated or modified by moral forces—will and personality. Thus an inquiry into the Highest Good for man gives to ethics a natural point of contact with metaphysics[4].

[1] The whole subject of sin, guilt, punishment is germane to our subject, but for present purposes must be left on one side.

[2] Iren. iii. 18. 7 [Stieren] ἔδει γὰρ τὸν μεσίτην θεοῦ τε καὶ ἀνθρώπων διὰ τῆς ἰδίας πρὸς ἑκατέρους οἰκειότητος εἰς φιλίαν καὶ ὁμόνοιαν τοὺς ἀμφοτέρους συναγαγεῖν, καὶ θεῷ μὲν παραστῆσαι τὸν ἄνθρωπον, ἀνθρώποις δὲ γνωρίσαι τὸν θεόν.

[3] Heb. iii. 1. Cyp. *de idol. van.* xi. 'Quod homo est, esse Christus voluit, ut et homo possit esse quod Christus est.'

[4] Bern. *de consid.* v. 1, 'Quid quod et inferioribus eges? . . Nonne praepos-

Christ Himself points our thought to this ideal region by presenting to us as the Highest Good, as the ultimate object of moral effort, *the kingdom of God*[1]. A precise definition of this expression may be left to a formal treatise; but a certain complexity in the idea may be briefly elucidated.

In the first instance the kingdom of God is spoken of by our Lord as a Good to be appropriated by *man*, through conscious and disciplined moral effort. In this sense the kingdom is already 'within' men[2], though not in its nature, or perfected stage. It is an actual state, spiritual and moral; an inward process or movement; a present possession. The attainment of this state involves 'Blessedness'—a word the true meaning of which is open to misconception. 'Blessedness' is not 'a mere future existence of imaginary beatitude[3];' not a bare independence of natural necessities; nor is it identical with, though it may include, 'happiness.' The instinct in human nature to which Christ appealed is more fundamental than the desire of 'happiness.' The word employed by Him to convey His meaning had by ancient usage been connected with supposed conditions and modes of the Divine existence. 'Blessedness' in fact consists in a living relation to God, in a progressive likeness to Him; in its final stage it is nothing less than the possession of God. God is the Highest Good[4].

The kingdom of God is also to be conceived as the goal of the entire movement of the universe : but while nature tends blindly towards some ideal end, the history of mankind is the record of a Divinely-directed movement carried on through free human agency[5]. For an ethical world two factors are required; physical nature, the sphere of force and necessity; rational personality, conscious of freedom and of the claim of authority. The goal of the universe is therefore a kingdom in which each element, physical nature and personality, finds its appropriate sphere, the one subordinate, the other dominant. We discern a prophecy of this result in Bacon's great

---

terum hoc et indignum? Plane superiorum quaedam injuria est inferiorum operam desiderare : a qua injuria nemo hominum perfecte vindicabitur nisi cum quisque evaserit in libertatem filiorum Dei.'

[1] S. Matt. vi. 33.

[2] S. Luke xvii. 21 ; S. Matt. xiii. 45 foll. (Parable of the Pearl). Cp. Rom. xiv. 17 ἡ βασιλεία τοῦ θεοῦ .. ἐστιν .. δικαιοσύνη καὶ εἰρήνη καὶ χαρὰ ἐν πνεύματι ἁλίῳ.

[3] Wace, *ubi sup.* Lect. VIII. Ambr. *de off. min.* ii. 3, 4.

[4] Aug. *de mor. Eccl.* xiii. ' Bonorum

summa Deus nobis est ; Deus est nobis summum bonum.' *Ib.* xviii. 'Secutio Dei, beatitatis appetitus est ; consecutio, ipsa beatitas.'

[5] Thom. Aquin. *Summa,* i. ii^ae. Qu. i. 2, 'Illa quae rationem habent seipsa movent ad finem, quia habent dominium suorum actuum per liberum arbitrium . . . Illa vero quae ratione carent tendunt in finem propter naturalem inclinationem quasi ab alio mota, non autem a seipsis, cum non cognoscant rationem finis ; et ideo nihil in finem ordinare possunt, sed solum in finem ab alio ordinantur.'

conception of a 'regnum hominis' attainable by intelligent obedience to nature. The Bible is full of a greater thought. It foresees a kingdom of intelligent beings whose law is the service of God ; a state in which the inner harmony of man's restored nature will be reflected in a worthy outward environment. This ideal kingdom, however, has its preparatory stage on earth. Though the present condition of it only faintly foreshadows the promised glory of the future, it has nevertheless been in fact set up among men, 'not in word, but in power.' For the main factor that makes such a kingdom ideally possible, already operates—namely, creaturely life realizing its true dependence on God, human will and human character responding to the will and purpose of God [1].

Such is the kingdom for which we look, and its Centre and Head is the living Christ [2]. He is the type after which the new personality is to be fashioned. He who unveils this world of spiritual beings and powers, is Himself the source of its movement, the centre of its attraction, the surety of its final triumph.

There cannot but result from this hope a particular view of the present world. It is characteristic of the Christian spirit frankly to recognise the natural world in its due subordination to personality, in its subserviency to ethical ends. An absolute idealism is not less alien to this standpoint than a crude materialism. The Christian is not blind to the tokens of interdependence between the worlds of matter and spirit ; the fact indeed of such relation gives peculiar colour to the Christian regard for nature. Nature is precious as the sphere in which a Divine Life is manifested, as the object of Divine Love [3]. And yet, in the light of revelation, the universe cannot be contemplated without mingled emotions. The Christian knows something of the pain, and of the satisfaction which in their unchastened form we call Pessimism and Optimism. For there must be sorrow in the recollection of the causal link that unites physical to moral evil. Though pain has value as the condition of nobler phases of life, and heightened spirituality of character, it is nevertheless an evil producing in a healthy nature something more than a transient disturbance. Pain is the sensible, even if remote, outcome of moral perversity, of misdirected desire. It pervades impartially the physical universe, but seems in manifold instances to point beyond itself to its source in human sin.

And yet there is a Christian optimism—a thankful joy even amid present conditions. There is the joy of at least a rudimentary realization of the chief Good ; the joy of setting a seal, as it were, to the truth

[1] See Godet, *Comm. on 1 Corinthians* [Clark], vol. i. p. 236.

[2] S. Matt. xix. 28 ; S. Luke xxii. 30.
[3] S. John iii. 16.

of God[1]. The 'powers of the world to come' are already within reach; they can be set in motion, felt, tested, enjoyed. There is a known end of creation by the light of which all forms and products of human enterprize can be judged. Thus even the growth and organized strength of evil does not dismay the Christian; for he knows that the advance of the kingdom is certain, whatever be the hindrances opposed to it, and that God's invincible will controls and overrules all that seems most lawless, and hostile to His purpose. 'The city of God,' says S. Augustine, 'is a pilgrim sojourning by faith among evil men, abiding patiently the day when righteousness shall turn to judgment, and victory bring peace.' In his assurance that 'all things work together for good to them that love God,' that the end is certain, and human fears are blind, the Christian can be free from illusions or extravagant hopes, yet not cast down, 'sorrowful, yet alway rejoicing,' 'perplexed, but not in despair[2].'

II. *Christ's Revelation of the Moral Law, its authority, sanctions, and content.*

On the place and meaning of freedom in Christian Ethics we have already touched. Our formal freedom is the ground of moral responsibility—that element in us to which Law makes its authoritative appeal. From the thought of freedom in relation to a moral universe we pass naturally to that of Law.

And first, it is convenient to inquire what is the *revealed basis of obligation* in general?

The most conspicuous feature of the Sermon on the Mount—that first great outline of Christian morality—is its authoritative tone. We instinctively turn to it in searching for a fundamental principle of obligation, a ground of authority for Law. Nor are we disappointed, for our question is met by the consideration that this great discourse is primarily a revelation of the personal God in His holy relation to mankind. It is with this personal relationship that the claim of moral Good on man's will is seen to be uniformly connected. The Good in fact presents itself to man in the shape of a *personal appeal :* 'Be ye holy, for I am holy.' Morality appears as God's exhortation to man to embrace and fulfil the true law of his nature. 'Be ye perfect,' it is said, 'even as your Father which is in heaven is perfect[3].' The Good is thus at once the explicit declaration of the Divine will, and the condition of human perfection. Already the coldness of abstract Law

---

[1] S. John iii. 33. See Dorner's *System of Ethics* [Clark], § 47.

[2] 2 Cor. iv. 8; vi. 10. Cp. Rom. viii. 28.

[3] S. Matt. v. 48. Butler, *Serm.* 3

'Your obligation to obey this Law is its being the Law of your nature . . . The correspondence of actions to the nature of the agent renders them natural.'

begins to disappear. Law is seen to be not an abstraction merely, but inseparably connected with the living Personality behind it. It is the self-revelation of a loving Being, appealing to the object of His Love, and seeking its highest welfare. Obligation is transformed, and is seen to be the tie of vital relationship between persons[1].

Further, it must be borne in mind that Christ's teaching as to obligation was accompanied by the promise of a supernatural gift—the gift of a new capacity to fulfil the Law. The Good had hitherto been known, howsoever imperfectly, as requirement. Ethical progress before Christ's coming could only tend to deepen this knowledge. We know indeed what was the object of that long providential discipline of humanity which culminated in the Incarnation : how it ended by driving man to look and long for a condition of things which should no longer be marked by hopeless severance of the actual from the obligatory. With the advent of the Redeemer, a new joy dawned on the world—the possibility of goodness.

We learn then that the ground of obligation is God's will for the perfection of His creatures—His desire that they should be like Himself[2]. The sense of obligation is indeed never absent from the consciousness of Christ Himself. ' We must work,' He says, 'the works of Him that sent Me while it is day.' ' My meat is to do the will of Him that sent Me, and to finish His work[3] : '—in which utterances we discern the principle we need. Only when duty presents itself in the form of personal appeal, only when obedience is kindled and enriched by feeling, can law become a bond, not of constraint, but of love.

It follows that obligation, thus founded on personal relationship to God, is absolute and independent of variation in the specific demands of Law. Human goodness will consist in correspondence to the will of God, and the degree of clearness with which a man apprehends that will is the measure of his obligation. This principle seems to preclude any idea of 'supererogatory works,' and tends to neutralise for the individual conscience the distinction between 'commands' and 'counsels of perfection,' the spirit in which Law is ideally fulfilled being that of sonship, eager, loyal, and generous[4].

The universal obligation of moral Law is by Christ connected for practical purposes with a system of *sanctions*. As to the Christian doctrine of rewards and punishments it is only necessary to observe,

[1] Cp. Bp. Ellicott, *The Being of God*, p. 120.

[2] Rom. ii. 18 (γινώσκεις τὸ θέλημα) implies that when a man knows God's *will*, he knows his *duty*.

[3] S. John ix. 4 ; iv. 34. Cp. vi. 40 ; S. Luke iv. 43. See also Rom. xii. 2 ; Eph. v. 17, etc.

[4] The case of the young man (S. Matt. xix. 21) shews how obligation is extended by contact with Christ, i. e. by closer relation to God. The general principle is that each is bound to follow the law of his personal perfection as it unveils itself to him. See Bengel *in loc.* and cp. S. Luke xvii. 10.

that any ethical system which has regard to the condition of man *as he is*, finds itself constrained, for disciplinary ends, to lay a certain stress on this point. Further, it should be noticed that the nature of these sanctions is seldom clearly understood. They occupy a place in Christ's teaching, because it is His wont to deal with human nature as He finds it : He points, however, not so much to a future state, as to a present spiritual sphere in which conduct is indissolubly linked to consequence, and there operate 'the searching laws of a spiritual kingdom[1].' The sanctions with which Christ enforces His doctrine may thus be regarded as pointing to a reign of Law in the spiritual realm which He reveals to mankind. He seems indeed to recognise the occasional need of appeals to fear, as likely to rouse the conscience and will. He sets before us the prospect of spiritual judgments acting, at least partially, in the sphere of the present life. His more frequent appeal, however, is to what may be called the enlightened self-interest of men. Their true life, He tells them, is to be found or acquired in a consecration, a sacrifice of the natural life to the claims and calls of the Divine kingdom[2]. Such sacrifice, such co-operation with God, is its own ineffable reward.

What then, it may be asked, are the *motives*, the inducements to action, appealed to by Christianity ? how far are imperfect motives recognised ? and in view of the fact that no mere sense of relation to Law is in general likely to move the human will, where does the Gospel find its 'moral dynamic'—its highest motive ?

We have seen that Christianity in a peculiar degree combines the presentation of duty with an appeal to feeling. In the same way by connecting obligation to obey God with a revelation of His Love, Jesus Christ solves the most difficult problem of ethics. The highest motive is *Love to God*, kindled not only by the contemplation of His Perfections, but also by a passionate sense of what He has wrought in order to make possible the fulfilment of His Law. 'We love Him,' says S. John, 'because He first loved us.' We do not, however, expect the motive of actions to be in all cases identical, or uniformly praiseworthy. A practical system must recognise very different stages of maturity in character ; and the possibility of imperfect or mixed motives is frankly allowed by Christian thinkers, and seems to be sanctioned by our Lord Himself[3]. It may be said on the whole that while the Gospel

[1] Wace, Lect. II.

[2] S. Matt. xvi. 25, 26. The discussion of 'Christian consolations,' by Mr. Cotter Morison, *Service of Man*, overlooks the fact that Christ's object was not to 'console' men, but to set before them the truth, and the law of their own perfection. The 'consolations' of Christianity can be won only if they are never made the *object* of life. They are a *reward*, but never, in the higher forms of Christian consciousness, an *aim*. See *Church Quart. Rev.*, Jan. 1888, p. 268.

[3] Witness the discussions on *fear* commonly found in mediaeval theology. Bruce, *Parabolic teaching of Christ*, p. 359 foll., has some good remarks on this

ever appeals to man's desire for his own good, it adapts itself and condescends to widely varying forms and degrees of that desire, by way
of educating it to greater disinterestedness and purity[1]. We may
fittingly speak of 'a hierarchy of motives,' and can view with equan-
imity those attacks on Christianity which represent it as a thinly-
disguised appeal to selfishness. For the reward promised to man is
one which will only appeal to him in so far as he has parted with his
old self, and has made the Divine purpose his own. The reward is joy
—the 'joy of the Lord;' the joy of a worthy cause embraced and
advanced; of a task achieved, of labour crowned by nobler and wider
service. Such joy could only be an inspiring motive to self-forgetful
love, which finds the fulfilment of every aspiration, the satisfaction of
every desire in God and in His work[2].

Christian duty, the content of the Law, demands somewhat larger
treatment. It has been suggested that the conception of morality as a
Divine code, as 'the positive law of a theocratic community,' which
seems characteristic of early Christian writings on morals—is a legacy
from Judaism[3]. Be this as it may—the *distinctive* feature of Christianity is that henceforth the Law is not contemplated apart from the
Personality of God. The Law is 'holy, just, and good,' because it
reflects His character. Obedience to it is acknowledged to be the indispensable condition of true union between God and His creatures.
For Jesus Christ teaches us to discern in the Law the self-unveiling of
a Being whose holiness and love it reflects, as well as His purpose for
man.

The revealed Law is comprised in the Decalogue. It seems needless to vindicate at length the paramount place which this fundamental
code occupies in Christian thought[4]. Suffice it to say that in broad
outline it defines the conditions of a right relation to God, and to all
that He has made. And the Law is 'spiritual[5].' Though for educa-
tive purposes primarily concerned with action, it makes reference to
inward disposition, and thereby anticipates the main characteristic of
Christian goodness. It also recalls the great landmarks of God's

---

point. 'The parabolic form of instruction does not afford scope for the play
of the highest class of motives. It is
essentially popular wisdom, and it is the
way of that which aims at teaching the
million, *to make action spring from
homely motives.*'

[1] Butler, *Analogy*, i. 5.
[2] See H. S. Holland, *Creed and
Character*, Serm. XVIII. Cp. S. Matt.
xxv. 21, Heb. xii. 2. Thom. Aquin.
Summa, ii. ii[ae], xxviii.
[3] Sidgwick, *Outlines of the Hist: of*

Ethics, chap. 3.
[4] Iren. iv. 16, § 3 [Stieren]. God
appears in the decalogue 'praestruens
hominem in suam amicitiam . . . et ideo
[verba] similiter permanent apud nos,
extensionem et augmentum sed non dis-
solutionem accipientia per carnalem
Eius adventum.' Thom. Aquin. *Summa*,
i. ii[ae]. Qu. c. Art. 3, 'Omnia praecepta
[moralia] legis sunt quaedam partes
praeceptorum decalogi.'
[5] Rom. vii. 14.

redemptive action; it sets forth His gracious acts, partly as an incentive to gratitude, partly as a ground of obligation.

In our Lord's teaching we find two truths implied : (1) The absolute priority and permanence of the Decalogue in relation to all other precepts of the Jewish Law. (2) Its essential unity viewed as a Law of love. This latter aspect is anticipated in the book of Deuteronomy, and is explicitly set forth by our Lord. There are, He tells us, two commandments : the first and greatest, love to God; the second 'like unto it,' love to man, with the limitation annexed, ' Thou shalt love thy neighbour as thyself.'

Thus guided by precedent, a Christian, in examining the Law's *content*, may take the Decalogue as a natural basis of division. It may be shortly analysed as embracing a comprehensive outline of man's duty towards (i) God, (ii) his fellow-men, and implicitly towards himself and non-personal creatures.

First stand duties towards God, resulting directly from the personal contact assumed to be possible between God and man. The all-embracing command which involves the fulfilling of the Law is contained in the words, ' Thou shalt love the Lord thy God with all thy heart, and with all thy soul, and with all thy mind[1].' In this ' great commandment' we find the widest point of divergence from Pagan ethics. Man's true centre is God. His perfection is to be sought in creaturely subjection and free conformity to the Divine purpose[2]. The general sphere of God-ward duty is defined in the first four commandments, which are seen to give moral sanction, not only to the outward expression, but to the actual substance of belief ; the distinctive duties enjoined therein have been summarily described as faith, reverence, service[3]. The fourth precept lays down the principle that man is bound to honour God by consecrating a definite portion of time to His worship, and by providing space for the due recreation of that human nature which by creative right is God's, and is destined for union with Him.

The duty of love to our fellow-men follows upon that of love to God. Every man's personality gives him absolute and equal worth in God's sight, and therefore lays us under obligation towards him. Heathen moralists confined the sphere of obligation to a few simple relationships, e. g. family-life, friendship, civic duty. But the revealed law of love to man embraces *every* relationship. ' Every man is neighbour to every man[4].' It is clear that any adequate outline of this precept involves the

---

[1] S. Matt. xxii. 37. Cp. Aug. *de mor. Eccl.* xviii–xx ; *de doc. Christ.* i. 29.
[2] Aug. l.c. ' Maxime Ei propinquat [homo] subjectione ista qua similis fit.'
[3] Thom. Aquin. *Summa*, i. ii[ae]. c. 5,

[4] Principi communitatis tria debet homo, fidelitatem, reverentiam, famulatum.' Cp. Butler, *Analogy*, pt. ii. i.
[4] Aug. *de disc. Christ.* iii. ' Proximus est omni homini omnis homo,' etc.

whole treatment of social duty. Men have their *rights*, i. e. lay us under obligation, both individually and collectively. The individual has his 'duty' to fulfil to the family, the association, the class, the city, the state, the Church which claims him. The immense field of our possible duties towards society, and towards each individual, so far as he comes in contact with us, may be regarded as embraced in the second table of the Decalogue. Thus the fifth commandment lends important sanction not only to the parental claim, but also to the authority of fundamental moral communities—the family, the state, the Church. The following precepts regulate the security of life and personality, of marriage and sexual distinctions, of property, honour, and good name. The tenth commandment anticipates that 'inwardness' which constitutes the special feature of Christian morality. 'It is the commandment,' says an ethical writer, 'which perhaps beyond any of the rest was likely to deepen in the hearts of devout and thoughtful men in the old Jewish times, that sense of their inability to do the will of God, and to fulfil the Divine idea of what human life ought to be, which is indispensable to the surrender of the soul to God[1].'

But according to the Christian theory there are duties to *self*, which seem to follow from the relation in which man stands to God, and form the true measure of his regard for others : ' Thou shalt love thy neighbour as thyself.' There is a right self-love, a right care of the personality as being itself an object of God's love, and so included in the category of things ethically good. What the Christian ought to love, however, is not the old natural self, but the 'new man,' the true image of himself which has absolute worth[2]. A moral complexion is thus given to all that concerns the personal life—the care of health, the culture of faculties, the occasions of self-assertion. Every moment of conscious existence, and every movement of will,—all in fact, that relates to the personality—is brought within the domain of Law. Christianity 'claims to rule the whole man, and leave no part of his life out of the range of its regulating and transforming influence[3].' For in every situation, transaction, or display of feeling, will is required to declare itself : moral activity takes place. Duties to self, as loved by God, are thus implied in the 'great commandment.' For God therein requires of man a consecration of the entire *self*, an inward self-devotion, a reasonable, heartfelt service : He asks for love. From this

[1] R. W. Dale, *The Ten Commandments*, p. 241. Cp. Thom. Aquin. *Summa*, i. ii^{ae}. c. 6 ; Martineau, *Types*, etc., ii. 26.

[2] *Summa*, i. ii^{ae}. c. 5, 'Dilectio sui ipsius includitur in dilectione Dei et proximi ; in hoc enim homo vere se diligit quod se ordinat in Deum.' *Ib.* ii. ii^{ae}. xix. 6, ' Homo se propter Deum,

et in Deo diligit.' Aug. *Serm.*, ccxvi. 8, 'Amate quod eritis : eritis enim filii Dei.' Pascal, *Pensées*, Art. xviii. 15, 'Que l'homme *s'aime*, car il a en lui une nature capable de bien.' Cp. Butler, *Serm.* i. etc.

[3] Sidgwick, *Outlines, etc.*, p. 108. Cp. Dorner, *System, etc.*, p. 459 [Clark].

point of view, sin—the false claim to independence—is simply wrong self-love.

Some would even class all shapes of sin as falling under two main forms of self-assertion, arrogance and sensuality. And S. Augustine suggests a profound view of the development of the true, as compared with the false society, when he says : 'The two cities owe their being to two forms of love ; the earthly, to self-love ; the heavenly, to the love of God [1].'

It remains to extend the principle of love to the non-personal sphere with which man is in contact. We have seen that absolute worth belongs only to personality. But man's relation to the creatures below him in the scale of development, implies a field of duties of which ethics must take cognizance. The non-personal part of nature is ordained for subjugation by man. It is included in his dominion : *terram dedit filiis hominum.* Yet even in the Mosaic Law we find respect enjoined for certain distinctions of nature, which are not to be overridden or confounded. The physical order, like the moral, was to be regarded as sacred [2]. Duties, then, of this kind exist : and they are apparently comprehended in the fourth commandment, which expresses God's creative claim on typical orders of living creatures, ordaining that ' cattle' are to share the benefit of the Sabbath rest. The sixth and eighth commandments again imply the sanctity of physical life, and of personal property. And if we pass behind the decalogue, we find animals included in a sense within God's original and irreversible covenant [3]. The control therefore of human will over nature, animate and inanimate, though comparatively absolute, is yet subject to the restrictions which love suggests. For the natural world also displays the omnipresent control, and watchful providence of a Being ' Whose mercy is over all His works.' Physical life in this sphere may be treated as a means ; but it must also be dealt with ' in harmony with the creative Thought [4].'

In quitting the subject of duty, we do well to mark the infinite extension given to the idea by the treatment of it in connection with the doctrine of an Infinite and Holy God. Our Lord, illustrating His exposition of the ancient Law by a few significant examples, not only opened to His hearers the possibility of a spiritual, transcendent morality, but also laid down a far-reaching principle of obligation. The self-unveiling of the Infinite Being evidently makes an infinite claim on the will and affection of intelligent creatures.

---

[1] Aug. *de Civ. Dei,* xiv. 28.

[2] See Ex. xxi. 33 foll. ; Deut. xxii. 9 foll. ; Levit. xix. etc. *Summa,* i. ii^ae. i. 2, 'Tota irrationalis natura comparatur ad Deum sicut instrumentum ad agens principale.'

[3] Consider Gen. ix. 10. Cp. Gen. viii. 1 ; Prov. xii. 10, etc.

[4] Martensen, *Special Ethics* (*Indiv.*), p. 278 [Clark].

With this extension of morality we might compare a somewhat parallel feature in the aesthetic sphere.

Into the arts also, notably into architecture and music, the Christian spirit introduced the element of mystery, and found expression in them for the idea of infinity—an idea so alien to the Greek genius, which had ever contemplated beauty, and therefore ethical Good, as something essentially limited, measurable, symmetrical, exact[1]. Such a thought might suggest a line of abstract discussion; but practical needs remind us that the true range of obligation is best interpreted to us by a living ideal. As the writer of *Ecce Homo* remarks, 'The law which Christ gave was not only illustrated, but infinitely enlarged, by His deeds. For every deed was itself a precedent to be followed, and therefore to discuss the *legislation* of Christ is to discuss His character; for it may be justly said that *Christ Himself is the Christian Law*[2].'

The transition from the discussion of moral Law to that of Christian character seems at this point natural and simple.

III. *Christ the Pattern of Character.*

The stress which in Christian Ethics is laid upon personality scarcely requires further illustration. The principle of personality underlies our fundamental assumption that man is capable of free communion with, and imitation of, God. We believe that the union between God and man was consummated in and through a Person. Further, the spirit in which fulfilment of the Law is possible—the spirit of filial love—can only exist in personal relations. It corresponds with this general prominence of personality that Christianity presents the ideal standard of human character in a Person.

In passing may be noted the fact that this principle to some extent emerges in ancient systems. Aristotle's definition of virtue naturally occurs to us as admitting the function of an 'expert' (ὁ φρόνιμος, ὁ σπουδαῖος), in the right estimation of moral action. The Stoic again seeks or invents a trustworthy standard in his ideal conception of the 'wise man.' It seems possible that modern non-Christian ethics will ultimately substitute for the cultivated sense of mankind some form of personal ideal[3]. For 'the Law attains its lovable form, its beauty, only when it becomes personal[4];' and it might be said with truth that no idea can be formed of virtues in the harmony of their combination, until they are seen embodied in a person. Just as theology has in the study of Divine truth concentrated her gaze on the Person of Jesus

---

[1] See Trench, *Mediaeval Church History*, Lect. XXVII. Cp. Plato, *Phileb.* 64 E foll.

[2] *Ecce Homo*, c. x. Cp. S. John xxi. 25.

[3] It is significant that Mr. Cotter Morison in his *Service of Man* discusses personal types of Christian saintliness.

[4] Dorner, *System, etc.*, p. 377.

Christ as a *revelation of God*; so ethics, in the effort to formulate the law of moral perfection, must study the same Divine Person as a *type of character*.

It is necessary therefore at the outset to recall some salient features of the great Example.

The character of Jesus Christ has been a subject of study to thinkers of every period in Christian history, and of infinitely varied qualifications for the task. Some have in the supposed interest of morality been tempted to lay disproportionate stress on the fact of our Lord's manhood. They ask how Christ can be an example to humanity, unless he be a Man like other men [1]? From a Christian standpoint, however, it is clear that the efficacy of that Example depends on Christ's being a Man *unlike* other men—unlike them in His relation to the Divine requirement, unlike them in His power of contact with the entire race. Thus we find ourselves in correspondence with dogmatic truth. The mystery of atonement necessitates a sinless Victim ; the Christian conception of human life requires a sinless Example. The perfect pattern of mankind must in one material respect be as far as possible isolated and removed from the race He came to redeem : for sinlessness is a part of the Divine thought concerning human nature.

If again we take into account the scope and significance of His redemptive work, it is vain to compare Christ with ' other great men.' He came not merely as the Example, but as the Redeemer and Saviour of humanity. Were He merely the Example, His departure would have left mankind in even deeper anguish and helplessness than before His coming. Man would have seen the Light, and felt its attraction, only to find himself powerless to follow.

And thus, because Christ is a Man unlike all other men, we need in contemplating His character the caution that 'the Divine Reality is apart from, and even greater than what the greatest have thought of it and said of it [2].' The ideal conception of character presented either in Pagan thought, or even in the volume of Messianic prophecy, has been indefinitely enriched, and illuminated by the LIFE which had before been only dimly foreshadowed, or at the best darkly understood.

Now it may be said, with no violation of the proportion of truth, that the most important part of the Gospel revelation concerned man's true relation to God. In the forefront of Christ's teaching is set the

---

[1] See some remarks on this tendency in Liddon, *Bampton Lectures*, viii ; and an Art. in the *Church Quart. Rev.*, July, 1883, on ' Our Lord's Human Example.' For what follows, cp. Martensen, *Ethics (General)*, pp. 242, 256.

[2] Dean Church, Serm. on *Christ's Example* [*Gifts of Civilization*, Serm. III].

doctrine of the Divine Fatherhood. He impressed this truth on men not more by His express utterances, than by the example of His own habitual attitude towards God. It may be justly allowed that our Lord taught, and displayed among men 'a new type of goodness, the filial and dependent.' In Him we see the activity of 'a perfectly filial will[1].'

It will be useful to expand this suggestive thought somewhat more fully.

First, then, we see in Christ the perfect example of *filial dependence* on God[2]. This dependence is not mere passivity of will—such as the record of the Temptation exhibits ; not simply a confiding trust in the providence and sustaining power of God. We rather see in Christ's spirit of dependence a motive which impels Him to fearless, unfettered activity, and supports Him under the keenest stress of trial and suffering. He speaks and acts ever as One who, in each situation, is aware of the controlling hand of infinite Wisdom and Love. He has that entire security in the certainty of Divine guidance, to which no emergency comes as a surprise, no call for action brings disturbance. He knows that 'the works' which tax His human faculties, and weary His bodily frame, are such as the Father 'has given Him to perfect.' A filial trustfulness is thus the secret at once of His energy and His repose ; His promptness in action and His calmness in awaiting the suitable moment for it ; His unbroken heavenly-mindedness and His self-spending devotion in ministry and works of love. It makes possible the majestic serenity which never deserts Him during the scenes of His Passion. 'I am not alone,' He says, ' because the Father is with Me[3].'

In such a spirit of dependence may be recognised the true law of creaturely life ; and there is nothing in that spirit which degrades or impairs the true dignity of human nature. Nay, there is something in this dependence of a filial heart which seems to chasten and exalt the character, while it quickens the intelligence of man. For in fulfilling his own true law, and responding to the will of his Maker, man finds himself admitted to the secret of the universe ; he is in harmony with the purpose that underlies and guides its entire movement. So also, we venture to say, it is with the Ideal Man. 'Everywhere He sees the Divine unity of thought which permeates, embraces, and binds all

---

[1] R. H. Hutton, Essay on *the Incarnation and Principles of Evidence.* Cp. the remarkable definition of Lactantius, *Div. Inst.* iii. 9, ' Pietas nihil aliud est quam *Dei parentis agnitio.' Ib.* 10, 'Efficitur ut is agnoscat Deum, qui unde ortus sit, quasi recordetur.'

[2] See Trench, *Syn. of the N. T.* § 42

(on ταπεινοφροσύνη). ' In His Human Nature [Christ] must be the pattern of all humility, of all creaturely *dependence* . . . He evermore, as Man, took the place which beseemed the creature in the presence of its Creator.'

[3] S. John xvi. 32.

things together, the spiritual and the material, the visible and the invisible, the earthly and the heavenly, in one vast economy[1].' To Him the promise seems fulfilled, 'Thou shalt be in league with the stones of the field, and the beasts of the field shall be at peace with thee.' To Him the world of humanity, and the world of physical nature disclose their inner law; He knows what is in them; He intuitively reads their secret; He can trace beneath the apparent discords of the universe the outlines of a broken, but recoverable, harmony. And thus the attitude of filial dependence on God is found to be the condition of a right relation to all that He has made; it opens the way to a true understanding of God's ways, and of that living principle of Love which binds all things in one—binds them indeed

> by gold chains about the feet of God.

Next, we may contemplate Christ's character as the type of *filial obedience*[2],—of a complete harmony between human will and the law of holiness. In Christ the ideal of free will is realized[3]. We are not now concerned with the vast issues of that sinless obedience. It is enough to study it as embodying a principle of purely human perfection, enjoined indeed repeatedly in the Old Testament as the one condition of covenantal union with God, but once only in history adequately fulfilled in a human life. Obedience, based on absolute trust in the character and purpose of God; an 'obedience of faith,' yet in its essence the obedience not of a servant, but of a son; an obedience that refuses nothing, shrinks from nothing, questions nothing that presents itself as Divine requirement: such is seen to be the law of Christ's Life, the law to Him of action and of endurance, the rule of prayer, the principle of sacrifice, the motive of service, the well-spring of thanksgiving and joy. If the entire completeness of this obedience becomes One who wears 'the form of a servant;' the willingness of it marks the glad service of a Son. And because the fulfilment by Jesus of the Father's will is spontaneous, free, whole-hearted, sacrificial, it wins acceptance as the offering of One 'well-pleasing' and 'beloved.' Perfected by submission to suffering and death, the obedience of Jesus is stamped with the token of Divine satisfaction by His rising from the dead.

And finally, Christ is the perfect pattern of *filial love*. He taught the human heart that the All-Holy God can be the object of its highest affection, its purest passion, its deepest joy. In Christ we see the filial character consummated; in Him we find the union of serene

---

[1] Martensen, *Ethics* (*General*), p. 255. Cp. Job v. 23.
[2] Christ's earthly life and work are described summarily as ὑπακοή, Rom. v. 19. Cp. Phil. ii. 8.

[3] Aug. *de Praed. Sanct.* xxx. 'An .. in Illo non libera voluntas erat, ac non tanto magis erat, quanto magis peccare non poterat?' Quoted by Liddon, *Bampt. Lect.* [ed. 11], note c.

repose with consuming zeal, unwavering loyalty, and sympathetic self-devotion to the Father's work; in other words we find creaturely perfection, combined with the spirit of sonship. In many and mysterious ways indeed, does this filial love of the true Son display itself: in a hunger and thirst after righteousness ; in a patience which can bide the time, and endure the chastisements, of God; in an overflowing tenderness towards all God-created beings because they are His and in their measure bear witness of Him; in a faith which 'hopeth all things' and labours to make all things perfect. Such is the spirit of the Son : and we 'learn of Him' the loftiness of the height to which a filial love of God may raise human character, the tenacious strength it may impart to human will, the peace it may shed on a human heart. Love is 'the bond of perfectness,' and to wear the image of the Son is to be conformed through Love to the likeness of the Father Himself[1].

The example of virtue is thus seen in a character, of which some aspects have been just considered : and we may pause at this point, in order to form some conclusion as to the factors of virtuous action judged from the Christian standpoint.

To have moral worth, an action must be the outcome of an entire bent, or disposition of the agent. Good fruit is to be expected only from a good tree[2]. In the virtuous act the agent's personality is engaged *as a whole*; his whole nature is directed towards a single object. This inward unity is perhaps what we really mean by 'simplicity.' In such action, the human being most nearly approaches the concentrated and harmonious energy of the Divine Life[3]. The person acts as an undivided whole, each part of his nature is for the time directed aright.

But we are here reminded that man's nature is disordered : it can produce nothing truly good, except in so far as it is restored to harmony by Divine power. God, says Thomas Aquinas, calls us to a supernatural end, which by his natural powers man could not attain. God Himself must therefore impart the supernatural principle necessary to aid man in responding to the call[4]. No act, in short, can be strictly called 'good' which is dissociated from the direct action of God: for 'there is none good but One, that is God:'

> O work thy works in God ; He can rejoice in nought
> Save only in Himself, and what Himself has wrought[5].

---

[1] Aug. *de mor. Eccl.* xxiii. 'Fit ergo per caritatem ut conformemur Deo.'
[2] Dorner, pp. 336, 388. Cp. *Ecce Homo*, p. 136.
[3] Arist. *Eth.* vii. 14. 8 remarks that human nature is not simple (ἁπλῆ), adding ἐπεὶ, εἰ τοῦ ἡ φύσις ἁπλῆ εἴη

ἀεὶ ἡ αὐτὴ πρᾶξις ἡδίστη ἐσται. Διὸ ὁ θεὸς ἀεὶ μίαν καὶ ἁπλῆν χαίρει ἡδονήν, κ.τ.λ. Cp. Bk. x. cc. 4. §9, and 7. § 8.
[4] *Summa*, i. ii[ae]. Qu. lxii. Art. 1. Cp. S. Matt. xix. 17.
[5] Abp. Trench.

We conclude that in a good action there is a true harmony of the different elements in personality—intelligence, affection, will; and further that such harmony presupposes the action of supernatural power on man's nature. It agrees with this that Christian moralists give to the chief principles of virtuous action the name of 'theological virtues,' and regard them as supernaturally imparted.

A good action, then, implies right *intelligence*. There must be an exercise of faith, which is a principle of knowledge—a correspondence between human faculties and an unseen object. Faith accepts the good as the proper element of man's perfection; takes God at His word, and aims at pleasing Him. 'Without faith it is impossible to please Him[1].' Next, *will* asserts itself. Will is directed towards an end desirable and attainable by effort: and thus is inspired by Hope. A study of Christ's example suggests that the highest object of hope for man is the perfection of his nature through the means appointed by God[2]. We see in Christ something of the desire, and the joy of moral achievement. When He said that 'the *workman* is worthy of his reward,' He pointed to the possibility of a true, unselfish pleasure in good work as such: of that thirst for perfection and self-dissatisfaction which distinguishes the true artist from common men.

Lastly, there remains that which is the dominant factor in Christian goodness, Love. There is an element of *passion* in Christlike holiness, which differentiates it from philosophic conceptions of virtue as a tranquil, balanced state[3]. Love gives worth to the fulfilment of duty; embraces, in union with God, the Divine aim of creation; and manifests itself in spontaneity and inventive activity, transforming the fulfilment of obligation into an occasion of joyous and delightful service. Our Lord represents this 'ardent, passionate, devoted state' of heart as the real root of virtue. Without it the most punctilious obedience is nothing; for not to love is not to live[4].

Having thus indicated the place of intelligence, will, and affection in virtuous activity, we are free to study the Christian character, and perhaps ascertain its permanent features—those elements in it which

---

[1] Heb. xi. 6. Cp. 1 S. John iv. 16; Rom. xiv. 23. *Summa*, i. ii^ae. Qu. lxii. art. 3, 'Quantum ad *intellectum* adduntur homini quaedam principia supernaturalia, quae divino lumine capiuntur; et haec sunt credibilia de quibus est fides.' *Ib.* art. 4, 'Per fidem apprehendit intellectus ea quae sperat et amat. Unde opportet quod ordine generationis fides praecedat spem et caritatem.'

[2] S. John iv. 34; v. 36; xvii. 4. Cp. H. S. Holland, *Serm.* on 'The Energy of Unselfishness.' With regard to the relation of *Pleasure* to action, we may observe that pleasure is inseparable from the right and effective exercise of any faculty; and therefore *accompanies* virtuous activity, but can never be the moral *end* of action. Cp. Arist. *Eth.* vii. 12. § 3, etc.

[3] See *Ecce Homo*, c. xiii.

[4] Aug. *de mor. Eccl.* xix. 'Id ipsum quo diligimus Deum mori non potest, nisi dum non diligit Deum: cum mors ipsa sit non diligere Deum.' Cp. Cyp. *de Unit.* xiv.

have survived the test of such wide variety of historical conditions. We have to inquire what is common to the types of Christian life which different ages, states of civilization, and forms of nationality have produced? For character is that which is capable of development in varied situations, of free and spontaneous self-adaptation to every change of environment. Circumstance proves its quality, offers it a field of exercise, and ministers to its growth.

Our task is rather to sketch a *character* than to classify *virtues.* 'The earliest Christians,' says the writer of *Ecce Homo,* 'felt a natural repugnance to describe the goodness at which they aimed by the name of Virtue.' Within limits indeed such a classification is possible : and a principle of division may be applied even to a thing so mysterious, so subtle in its shapes and gradations, so fruitful in surprises, as character. We may, for instance, take as a basis the principle of personality, and consider the Christian personality in its threefold relationship to God, to itself, to its neighbour, and in contact with the hindrances, moral and physical, presented by its environment[1].

I. The Christian personality in relation to God.

The distinctive feature of Christian character consists in consciousness of that filial relation to God which Grace restores ; of the spiritual bond that exists between the human soul and 'Him who is invisible.' Hence the goodness at which the Christian aims is that which will bear the searching light of the Divine eye. 'He chose us out of the world,' says S. Paul, 'that we might be holy and blameless *before Him.*' Thus in its essence Christian character is based on a peculiar sense of relationship to God ; there underlies it a constant desire of union with God, a temper of loyalty, a spirit of thankful dependence, a feeling of nearness to the Divine presence. Were it true, as has been said, that 'the Divine service' had '*become* human service[2],' Christian character as a distinct type would have ceased to be.

From this attitude of mind and will two results follow : first, singleness of aim,—the 'single eye.' The sense of personal relation to God gives directness, truthfulness, simplicity to speech, action, and thought. So far as he is true to his profession a Christian is independent of the current opinions of his age, or community, seeking only to live, 'in all good conscience' towards God. The conviction of an unseen Presence guides his actions ; an unseen Witness penetrates his thought ; an unseen Master holds him accountable. Indeed, S. Paul seems to regard holy living as consisting simply in the endeavour to 'please God[3].'

---

[1] Such classification, corresponding to three cardinal virtues, seems to be implied in S. Paul's words, Tit. ii. 12 ἵνα ... σωφρόνως, καὶ δικαίως καὶ εὐσεβῶς ζήσωμεν.

[2] J. Cotter Morison, *The Service of Man,* p. 194 [ed. 3]. See Eph. i. 4 ; Col. i. 22 ; S. Luke i. 75.

[3] Rom. viii. 8 ; 1 Cor. vii. 32 ; 1 Thess. iv. 1. An instructive contrast

And a second characteristic of the Christian is his view of life in the world, of nature, of humanity itself. He observes, judges, estimates all things from the standpoint of the spiritual mind. He aims at bringing his own thoughts and desires into harmony with the Divine will and purpose. He looks out on the world, with its complex social order, its fascinating interest, its appealing needs, as a sphere in which for a while he is called to move, and to labour. Into the varied tasks and interests of life he can throw himself with large-hearted sympathy, and with the greater fervour because the time is short, and the need of self-forgetful activity urgent. 'Once a real Christian,' writes Lacordaire, 'the world did not vanish before my eyes; it rather assumed nobler proportions as I myself did. I began to see therein a noble sufferer needing help. I could imagine nothing comparable to the happiness of ministering to it under the eye of God, with the help of the Cross, and the Gospel of Christ[1].'

But the world is not the Christian's 'abiding city.' He walks in it, and passes through it in pilgrim fashion, with heart detached from it and all that it can give. He cannot commit himself to the world, nor identify himself with it. He has the internal freedom of a heart that has found its true centre ; he is able to estimate visible things at their real worth, and

> To stand in freedom loosened from this world[2].

Thus to have the 'mind of Christ' is to judge of life and the things of time with His judgment, to see with His eyes, to be inspired by His *Wisdom.* So we find ourselves in natural contact with the division of character by 'cardinal virtues.' 'Prudence' or 'Wisdom' is the outcome of a right relation to God. God only, S. Augustine says, is to be loved ; this world, and all sensible things, are to be used. Prudence is love discerning between the things which bring it nearer to God, and those which hinder it from approaching Him[3].

II. In relation to humanity, and creaturely life in general, the Christian finds scope for 'active morality[4],' for ministering love. The life of union with God inspires and prompts the life of service to mankind. The infinitely varied relationships of life constitute so many forms of moral obligation. Christian *Justice* means nothing less than rendering to *all* their due. The desire to imitate God is at once the

---

might be drawn between the Pagan and Christian use of the word ἀρεσκεία.

[1] *Lacordaire, a biographical sketch,* H. S. Lear, p. 34.

[2] Wordsworth, *The Excursion.* Ep. ad Diog. v. πᾶσα ξένη πατρίς ἐστιν αὐτῶν, καὶ πᾶσα πατρὶς ξένη. This

spirit does not exclude a true *patriotism,* and other civil virtues. Martensen, *Ethics (Social),* § 82.

[3] *De mor. Eccl.* xxxvii and xxv. Cp. Bern. *de Consid.* v. 1.

[4] See the chap. with this title in *Ecce Homo.*

motive and the rule of Christian activity[1]. And this desire finds expression in two distinctively Christian graces : the spirit of *forgiveness* and the spirit of *compassion*.

The inculcation of forgiveness is 'the most striking innovation' in the ethics of the Gospel[2]. Greek thought on the subject presents a remarkable contrast. Aristotle is inclined to regard forgiveness as a form of weakness, but allied to virtue in so far as it involves resistance to passion. The ground of Christian forgiveness is very different. The duty of it follows partly of course from a consideration of the common human nature which the offender shares with the injured ; partly also from a dispassionate view of the injury inflicted. In exercising forgiveness we suppress that false self-love or partiality which magnifies a private injury. The Christian loves himself *not more* than he loves his neighbour. He can put himself in the offender's place, and consider what is for his highest good. He will not allow the sense of injury to interfere with, or override the exercise of good-will even towards enemies. Certainly, the sense of his own moral frailty, and of his indebtedness to Divine mercy, will restrain the Christian from vindictiveness or harshness in regard to the faults of others ; while the fact of the equality of men in relation to their common Father, invests even the anti-social sinner with the dignity of brotherhood[3]. But forgiving love is no mere expression of self-distrust. It is fired by something of the generous hopefulness, the quickness to detect latent capacities of nobleness even in the worst, which is the glory of the Divine forgiveness. It 'rejoiceth not in iniquity, but rejoiceth with the truth;' 'believeth all things, hopeth all things.' The Greek indeed had his idea of forbearance ; to him it meant something less than strict justice ; it was a virtue difficult to place or estimate. Logically, it was scarcely to be praised. At the best it would never have implied the habitual duty of active forgiveness.

Not less distinctive of the Christian character is *compassion*[4], and the active beneficence which results from it. Humanity, by Jesus Christ, was transformed : it was 'changed (to adopt a celebrated phrase) from a restraint to a motive.' Compassion may display itself in readiness both to relieve the physical needs of another, and to edify his character. To love one's fellow-man as one's self implies willing-

---

[1] S. Matt. v. 44 foll. Leo, *Serm. in Quad.* vii. 'Forma conversationis fidelium ab exemplo venit operum divinorum et merito Deus imitationem Sui ab eis exigit, quos ad imaginem et similitudinem suam fecit.' Cp. Iren. iv. 13. 3.
[2] *Ecce Homo*, c. xxii. Cp. Butler, *Serm.* ix. etc.
[3] Leo, *Serm. in Quad.* passim, esp. v,

vi, ix. *Ecce Homo*, c. xxiii. For what follows, see Arist. *Eth.* v. 10. Cp. Eph. iv. 32.
[4] Mozley, *Univ. Serm.* ix. 'Ancient philosophy never opened the mine of happiness which lay in this principle. It was a discovery, like that of a new scientific principle, when it was made ; and Christianity made it.'

ness to benefit him in body and estate by every means; but it is also incompatible with unconcern or apathy as to his spiritual and moral welfare. Love is communicative, and will not withhold its best treasure. Hence compassion prompts missionary activity, and zeal for moral and social reforms. Nor has 'humanity' ceased to be a restraint by becoming a motive. Christian justice contains the principle of '*innocentia*' as well as of '*benevolentia.*' 'Love worketh no ill to his neighbour;' it can inflict no wrong, it can withhold no good; 'therefore love is the fulfilling of the law [1].'

Active morality has many departments. Duty to the 'powers that be'—the order of society, human law, the state, the Church: all this, into which the science of politics inquires, forms part of the obligation involved in love to man. How comprehensive is the reply of an early Apologist to the charge of disloyalty, 'we behave towards Emperors exactly as we do towards our neighbours. To wish, or to do, or to think evil is equally forbidden to us in any case [2].' 'Thou,' cries S. Augustine, apostrophizing the Church,—'Thou bringest within the bond of mutual love every relationship of kindred, every alliance of affinity; Thou unitest citizen to citizen, nation to nation, man to man, not only in society, but in fraternity. Thou teachest kings to seek the welfare of their peoples, and peoples to be subject to kings ... Thou shewest how to all love is due, and injury to none [3]!'

III. In the life of active beneficence, self-sacrifice is no 'occasional heroism,' but an 'habitual mood [4].' And yet from the very nature of Christian love it follows that there is a right self-regard, a zeal for God's kingdom in the soul, a desire for the highest welfare of the personality as an object of worth in itself, and destined to find its perfection in God.

Love to self becomes *Temperance*, that is, the spirit of purifying discipline. Thus, a mark of Christian character is the passion for holiness: i. e. the desire to combine inward purity of thought, desire, and motive, with the external fulfilment of duty.

This process of self-purification is both mental and moral. It includes the culture of imagination not less than the control of appetite;

---

[1] Rom. xiii. 10. Note the following words of S. Aug. (*de doct. Christ.* i. 29): 'Velle debemus, ut *omnes nobiscum diligant Deum*, et totum quod vel eos adjuvamus vel adjuvamur eis, ad unum illum finem referendum est ... Hinc efficitur ut inimicos etiam nostros diligamus. . . *Misereamur*, quia tanto magis nos oderunt, quanto ab illo quem diligimus separati sunt.' Cp. *de disc. Chr.* v. 'Necesse est ut quem diligis tanquam te ipsum, *illuc illum trahas ad quod et tu amas.*' *Ecce Homo*, cc. xvii, xviii.

[2] Tert. *Apol.* 36.
[3] *De mor. Eccl.* lxiii. [Clark] *Obs.* There are duties imposed by our relationship even *to the dead, to posterity*, and of course *to the impersonal creature.* See Martensen, *Ethics (Indiv.*), §§ 116–118. On duties to *posterity*, see a beautiful passage in Ruskin, *Seven Lamps of Architecture*, vi. § 9.
[4] Dean Church, *Disc. of the Christian Character*, p. 101. Cp. *Ecce Homo* [ed. 13], p. 178.

'sobriety' not less in judgment and reflection than in the indulgence of desire ; humility in self-estimate, not less than restraint of passion[1]. The dominant feature of Christian character in this connection is a peculiar self-severity, a deep sense of the ideal as something not yet attained, a strict fidelity to known truth and the claim of moral law, sensitiveness to moral evil, and watchfulness against even its distant approach ; in a word, disciplined rule in the affections, intellect, and will. For as the Hellenist sage says of Wisdom, ' The very true beginning of Her is the desire of discipline, and the beginning of discipline is love[2].' Temperance includes that reverent care of the body which receives so high a sanction in the New Testament ; indeed, respect for the sanctity of the body may be viewed as reverence for the presence of God Himself, and for the place of His abode[3].

IV. Finally, in relation to the hindrances which Virtue encounters— the stress of circumstance, the pressure of misfortune, persecution, loss, temptation, and the like—Love displays itself as *Fortitude*, and finds both a passive and active sphere of exercise.

As a passive virtue fortitude is the 'world-resisting' element in character. The hostility of the world to virtue is only one form of its hostility to God[4]. Fortitude is thus essentially the same in all stages of social development. When the world-principle was embodied in a concrete form, and became in the imperial power of Rome a definite force hostile to the Church[5], fortitude displayed itself for the most part as patience under persecution (S. Augustine in his treatment of this virtue naturally contemplates it under this aspect) ; but the precise form of influence to be resisted will obviously vary from age to age, while the element of *resistance* in Christian character remains constant.

The name of ' fortitude,' however, must not be restricted to passive endurance, prominent as this virtue is in Christ's teaching. Fortitude embraces spheres of action, and will display itself on occasion as *resentment*. Righteous anger has its source in the temper exactly opposed to Stoic apathy respecting sin—that ' loveless view' of mankind which said ' Trouble not thyself ; thy neighbour sins, but he sins for himself[6].' There can be no true love of good without a just abhorrence of evil. Hence it sometimes occurs that love takes the form of indignation and holy zeal—when directed, for example, against oppression, cruelty, ingratitude, deceit, selfishness. Such resentment is a natural and generous emotion, born of sympathy with God Himself.

---

[1] See Rom. xii. 3 ; 2 Cor. x. 5.
[2] Wisdom vi. 17.
[3] 1 Cor. vi. 19.
[4] Ep. *ad Diog.* vi. μισεῖ Χριστιάνους ὁ κόσμος μηδὲν ἀδικούμενος, ὅτι ταῖς ἡδόναις ἀντιτάσσονται.
[5] See Westcott, Essay on *The Church*

and the World [in his ed. of S. John's Epp.].

[6] Trench, *Syn. of N. T.* § xxxvii. On ' Resentment' see *Ecce Homo*, c. xxi ; Butler, *Serm.* viii. Cp. Arist. *Eth.* iv 5. See also Dale, *The Atonement*, Lect. VIII.

Comparing with the Christian conception of resentment Aristotle's discussion of anger, we find that Christian teachers lay stress on the *social end* of resentment. What the good Christian resents is not a personal hurt, but injury and wrong-doing viewed as injurious to his neighbour or the community; such resentment is distinguished by purity of motive; in certain circumstances it is not unwilling to inflict pain.

Moral courage, again, is the form which fortitude assumes under other circumstances, too numerous to be specified. Generally it is displayed on occasions when the Christian is bearing witness to the cause of truth or righteousness before men. No Christian can rid himself of his share in the function of *witness*, committed to His followers by Christ. And fortitude, or manliness, is the virtue of a witness—of the solitary champion of a good cause confronting opposition in any of its forms. The name 'athlete,' which we find applied to martyrs in early times, may remind us that the task which beyond others must needs test a man's power to endure, and to stand alone, is that of witnessing stedfastly for righteousness and truth. Yet the call to bear witness comes in ways unexpected, and difficult to define or classify: it may, for example, be a man's difficult duty to withstand not opponents, but adherents and friends; to hold his own not against 'the sneers and opposition of the bad, but the opinion and authority of the good [1].' With this passing remark we quit the subject.

In the above sketch of Christian character we have confined ourselves to some salient features. We have said nothing of the gracious union it presents of delicacy with strength, of communicativeness with reserve, of energy with restfulness, of passion with tenderness. It is difficult to delineate character without giving a look of formality to what is essentially a mysterious, albeit well-marked, product. In Christian goodness we see the handiwork of the Spirit of God, and where He is, there is liberty.

It is indeed objected that this type of character is too rare, too exalted for the majority of mankind. It is said that a standard of perfection is set before them which it is hopeless to think of attaining; that men are disheartened; that Christian teachers 'ask for the impossible,' and undermine belief in the possibility of virtue. It is further suggested that the rarity of the type proves that the saint 'is born, not made;' and that radical change of character and disposition is impossible [2].

The last point may be noticed in another connection. At present we

---

[1] Dean Church, *Gifts of Civilization*, p. 323. Cp. Martineau, *Types of Eth. Theory*, vol. ii. pp. 200–202.

[2] See *Service of Man*, cc. vii and ix.

These objections have been often met. See Dean Church, *Serm.* on 'Christ's Example.' Liddon, *Bampt. Lect.* [ed. 11] p. 130.

may suggest, in reply to these reflections, one consideration. The objector forgets that Christianity does not merely present a moral standard to men ; it provides them with an entire system of moral education. The Church recognises different degrees of maturity and attainment in her children. It is no part of her method, though possibly an accident of a particular age or set of conditions, that she sets strong meat before babes, and appeals to children as if they were grown men. That very 'individual treatment' of characters on which the writer of the *Service of Man* insists, is a fundamental principle of the Christian system[1].

IV. *Christ the Source of the Recreation of Character.*

The subject which we now approach is, taken as a whole, peculiar to Christian Ethics. For it will be admitted that Christianity alone offers a solution of the practical problem, how is the ideal of virtue to be translated into life and practice ? 'It is the essential weakness,' says a living writer, ' of all mere systems of morality, and of most, if not all, other religions, that they confine themselves to pointing out what the facts of life ought to be, and make no provision whatever for dealing with facts as they are. . . . It is their main defect, not that they conflict with Christianity, but that they fail to touch the problem with which it most directly deals[2].' Of course, in advancing this claim for Christianity, we imply that it is something vastly greater than a system of morals. It is a Divine way of salvation, that is, of deliverance from sin, as well as from its effects ; the process by which the ideal becomes actual in life and character is also, as we have seen, a process of restoration. Christianity, in fact, professes to be a Divinely-provided remedy for disorder and disease ; strictly speaking, therefore, a treatise on ethics must investigate the pathology of sin, regarded as the violation of moral order, and the fatal misdirection of desire. This aspect of the Gospel has been too much disregarded, even by Christian thinkers[3]. It follows, however, from the Scriptural account of man that he has lost something which can only be supernaturally restored : and it is the practical task of ethics to point out the means of renewal, which Divine Wisdom has provided.

The mysterious facts which lie at the root of the recreative process must be briefly noticed. Christian holiness is the reproduction in the individual of the life of the Incarnate Son of God. That this might be

---

[1] Aug. *de mor. Eccl.* lxiii. 'Tu [Ecclesia] pueriliter pueros, fortiter juvenes, quiete senes prout cuiusque non corporis tantum, sed et animi aetas est, exerces ac doces etc.' Cp. Amb. *de Off. Min.* i. 17.

[2] Wace, *Boyle Lect.* (ser. 1) v. Cp.

Ecce Homo, c. ix. We may consider how Christ gives a *practical* turn to speculative inquiries. S. Luke xiii. 23, 24 ; S. John xxi. 21 foll.

[3] E. g. Clem. of Alexandria. See Bigg, *The Christian Platonists of Alexandria,* p. 80.

possible, there took place that series of events which S. John describes as the glorification of Jesus Christ. The life, perfectly well-pleasing to God, and therefore the supreme standard of holiness, passes through the stage of death. The Sacrifice on Calvary removes the barrier raised between the Creator and His creatures by sin. The Resurrection is, on the one hand, the seal of God's acceptance stamped upon His Son's atoning work; on the other, marks the final stage in that process by which Christ's human nature is 'perfected[1].' For by the Resurrection that Nature is spiritualized, is released from earthly limitations, and becomes available as a recreative force. The Ascension is the condition of Christ's manifestation as 'a quickening Spirit,' as the 'power of God.' By sacramental channels He communicates to our entire nature His life-giving humanity, as the means of our recreation after the image of God. Thus the life of the Incarnate is extended in the life of the redeemed, and by a natural and orderly growth, the character of Christ is reproduced in His members through the continuous operation of the Spirit, whose office it is to 'take of the things of Christ and shew them unto' men. He who is outwardly our example thus becomes an inward principle of life.

We now are in a position to estimate the extent to which Christian morality depends on dogmatic truths. Apart from Jesus Christ there can be no true life. The secret of holiness lies in *a permanent relation to a living Christ*. He, by His life and death, 'became unto us Wisdom, Righteousness, Sanctification, Redemption[2].' The example was not upheld in vain; for Christ placed within our reach the spiritual forces by which alone the pattern can be reproduced in human life. 'Sanctification' means the progressive appropriation by man of the life of the Son of God; the formation in him, by successive stages, of the very image of Christ. The objective aspect of sanctification is clearly presented in the Old Testament; holiness there implies consecration, and is thought of chiefly as an objective work of God. In the New Testament, the idea of holiness passes from the sphere of worship to that of morality. But the Old Testament conception is not lost; it is expanded. Holiness, according to the Christian view, results not from the efforts of man, but from the outflow and operation of a Divine Life. Holiness is spoken of as 'the righteousness of God,' as a 'free gift' imparted to man; and in the first instance requires receptivity rather than activity on the part of the human soul.

The ethical significance of baptism is thus intelligible. By baptism the individual is brought into vital contact with the Source of the new

[1] S. Luke xiii. 32; Heb. ii. 10, v. 9. Cp. 1 Cor. xv. 45; and see Gal. ii. 20, iv. 19. Also an Art. in *Ch. Qu. Rev.* No. xxxii, on 'Our Lord's Human Example.'

[2] 1 Cor. i. 30. Cp. Rom. viii. 29. For the thought that follows, see Prof. Bruce on Heb. ii. 11-18 in *Expositor*, No. 50.

life, and enters the sphere within which radiate the spiritual forces that flow from the glorified humanity of Christ ; the germ of *a new personality* is imparted ; the kingdom of God is entered. But in this new birth the work is only begun ; for the ' Grace of God that bringeth salvation' has an abiding home among men. It is misleading to speak of Grace as ' an unknown factor.' Still more so to assert that ' Theology has always been celebrating the power of Grace to the depreciation of Ethics[1].' Grace has its fixed channels and methods, its orderly movement and outflow, its certain conditions, its appointed places and seasons, its definite, though mysterious, laws of operation[2]. Grace is, so to speak, stored and dispensed within the mediatorial kingdom which Christ founded in His Church. From an ethical standpoint the Church of God is before all else *a school of character*[3], the Divinely-appointed sphere in which, normally, the recreation of personality proceeds, in which men are sanctified by being kept in living union and contact with Jesus Christ Himself.

To enumerate the several ' means of grace' committed to the stewardship of the Church is the task of theology, as also to explain the conditions of fruitfully using them. On one point only it may be worth while to make a few remarks.

To Christianity, as we have seen, each individual personality is an end in itself. Each has a right to moral education ; each was called into being that it might embody a particular thought of God, that it might fulfil good works prepared specially for *it*, and correspond with its own separate ideal[4]. Hence, true to the spirit of Him who was a Physician of the sick, Christianity offers her Divine remedies to the worst and most hardened natures. She believes in her power to renew and transfigure them, to achieve in them a moral miracle. Nobler natures, again, she endeavours to train up to the full stature of Christ-like character, sanctifying, consecrating, and elevating the innate capacities of each. Her healing mission extends to all men. She knows nothing of the aristocratic temper of ancient ethics, which would confine the very possibility of a moral life to the few. She rejoices in the infinite variety of typical forms which character may assume. A Christian poet has said—

> There is not on the earth a soul so base
> But may obtain a place,
> In covenanted grace ;
> So that his feeble prayer of faith obtains
> Some loosening of his chains

[1] *Service of Man*, pp. 84, 85.
[2] Chrys. *in Joh. hom.* x. 2 ἅμα δὲ καὶ ἐνδείξασθαι βούλεται ὅτι οὐχ ἁπλῶς οὐδὲ ἡ χάρις ἔπεισιν, ἀλλὰ τοῖς βουλο- μένοις καὶ ἐσπουδακόσι, κ.τ.λ.
[3] See Tit. ii. 11, 12 ἡ χάρις . . . παι-

δεύουσα ἡμᾶς. S. Matt. xxviii. 19, 20. Aug. *de disc. Chr.* i. ' *Disciplinae domus* est Ecclesia Christi.' Butler, *Analogy*, pt. ii. c. 1.
[4] Consider Col. i. 28 ; Eph. ii. 10.

> And earnests of the great release, which rise
> From gift to gift, and reach at length the eternal prize.
>
> All may save self ;—but minds that heavenward tower
>   Aim at a wider power,
>   Gifts on the world to shower.
> And this is not at once ; by fastings gained
>   And trials well sustained ;
> By pureness, righteous deeds, and toils of love,
> Abidance in the truth, and zeal for God above[1].

Now this idea of individual perfection, so characteristic of Christianity, is in the New Testament not dissociated from the idea of a society, family, or household of God, in which alone the *full* development of Christian character can be achieved. Corporate life, with its network of relationships, its mutual services, its common worship, its visible pledges of brotherhood—this is God's great instrument in the edification of character. So far, indeed, as the body is divided or weakened, the pressure it exerts on the individual is hindered, and the free play of its forces diminished[2].

In the Church, then, we have the true school of character, the true 'home of individuality,' and sphere of spiritual edification. The normal course of spiritual growth is one of widely varied experiences : it passes through the stage of repentance with its appropriate works ; it is schooled by the chastening discipline of common life[3] ; it is marked by progressive power of submission to the leadings of grace. This would suggest an interesting line of study, and one suitable for ethical treatment, but must not now detain us. It is advisable, however, in this connection not to overlook the subject of Christian *ascetics* : a word which has often excited unjust suspicion and contempt, and thereby been robbed of the noble associations which rightfully belong to it.

The name 'ascetics' is suitably applied to those Divinely-sanctioned exercises which, by precept and example, Christ commended as aids to holiness—Prayer, Almsgiving, and Fasting. Reflection, indeed, shews that these ordinances occupy a conspicuous place in the Gospel, because they have a natural connection with the three prin-

---

[1] *Lyra Apostolica*, No. xxxvii [signed δ].

[2] Consider Phil. ii. 2, where the description of the Christian example and character is prefaced by an impressive appeal for Unity. The moral guilt of *heresy* partly lies in its being a principle of disunion. Cyp. *de Unit.* xxvi. complains of particular ways in which disunion injures Christian character.

[3] Bruce (*Expositor*, No. 50, p. 84):

'God's paternal discipline, our own self-effort, Christ's example, priestly influence and sympathy, all contribute to the same end, persistency and progress in the Christian life.' It is specially instructive to contrast the Christian with the Pagan estimation of *Labour*, as a factor in the formation of character. See Martensen, *Ethics (Social)*, p. 129.

cipal spheres of Christian duty,—duty towards God, towards man, towards self. They are ways in which devotion to God, love to man, discipline of self, find each an appropriate expression. Reason and experience alike suggest that the Christian character, with its harmonious beauty and delicate strength, can only be the product of continuous spiritual discipline, wise restraint, and regulated effort. A feature, therefore, of Christ's practical teaching is His provision for what is, to average human nature, at least a moral necessity. Presenting Himself as the supreme example of the freedom which can control and use circumstances for a spiritual end, He lays down the threefold rule of Christian ascetics, to guide the wills and affections of those whom He calls to follow His steps.

The end of discipline is, of course, freedom: that is, the perfect dominion of the Spirit in man. Aiming at this liberty the Christian looks on the threefold ordinance of prayer, almsgiving, and fasting as a help to his development; it is to him no mere arbitrary direction imposed by authority, no vexatious restraint on lawful pleasure; but an efficacious aid to Christ-like holiness commended by the practice, and proved by the experience, of holy men in every age, and expressly enjoined by our Lord Himself[1].

It may surprise us somewhat to find *Prayer* included among ascetic exercises. For prayer is the ordinary activity of the human spirit in relation to God : man's natural expression of self-dedication : his effort to embrace God's Will as his choice, God's Law as his rule, God's Perfection as his pattern. Yet because prayer implies regularity, discipline, persevering effort; because it has its different parts, its proper occasions, and methods; because it is the exercise of a distinct faculty; in short, because it is an arduous work, it finds a place among exercises which seem at first sight to be of a more formal character.

This will appear more clearly on consideration of the different parts of prayer. Thus prayer is in part to be viewed as humble acknowledgment of an ideal unattained, and consequent renewal of desire in that direction. As containing, therefore, an element of self-purification, of striving after deeper self-knowledge, prayer includes the practice of self-examination and confession of sin. Regarded, again, as an exercise of affection and intellect, prayer takes the form of *contemplation*, and communion with God, as the supreme object of reverence and love. Thus it is evident that prayer is a real exercise, well fitted to be an education of the soul, and arduous because it implies an intense activity of the entire personality. Even the body has its share in this exercise. It is the appointed instrument of man's spiritual self-oblation; and prayer is the acknowledg-

---

[1] For what follows, see especially the Lenten sermons of S. Leo. Also a very useful book by Canon Furse, *Helps to Holiness.*

ment not only that God is the 'Father of spirits,' but that the body also 'is for the Lord [1].'

Almsgiving is placed by Christ among known and admitted forms of devotion. Viewed simply as an action, it is an obvious outlet of Christian love to man [2]. But almsgiving has another aspect, on which early writers insist with some fullness. It is a means of grace, a purifying element in the spiritual life of the agent. It is not often, perhaps, that this side of the duty is adequately taught. The danger of 'charity' becoming reckless or ill-directed is real, and may cause Christian teachers to be reticent on the subject. Yet this aspect of the truth must not be suppressed. And after all, almsgiving seems to be specially mentioned by our Lord as a type of all works of mercy [3]. Love, in its effort to imitate God, need not be less discriminating than communicative. The Fatherly providence of God is in fact the Christian's inspiration and his model: and we interpret the scope of our Lord's commandment by study of *His* life who 'for our sakes, though rich, became poor,' and 'went about doing good,' and who taught us in one pregnant sentence the mysterious efficacy of almsgiving [4]. It need not be added that true Christian charity is ever controlled by a due sense of the dignity of human nature, and of the moral bond that unites giver and receiver.

Each of the three exercises under consideration is conditioned and aided by the other two. There is a specially close connection, however, between prayer and *fasting*. As a means of self-discipline, fasting has been strangely neglected. Some regard it as a burdensome restraint on the will; others as 'unsuited to a spiritual religion;' others as unduly interfering with Christian liberty. Chiefly, perhaps, the neglect of fasting is due to inexperience of its value as a condition of spiritual power, and forgetfulness of the place assigned to it in the teaching of our Lord and of the early Church. It is thus right to insist, first, on its claim to be a Divine ordinance [5]. There can be nothing superfluous or incongruous in a practice which Christ is so careful to regulate, and which He commends by His own example. But the practice of fasting justifies itself as a point of simple wisdom in the care of the personal life. Christian holiness requires, as we

---

[1] 1 Cor. vi. 13. See Cyp. *de orat. Dom.* iv, on the part of the *body* in prayer.

[2] The particular shape which Almsgiving will assume is obviously to be 'suggested by the special conditions' of the age. See a noble passage in *Ecce Homo* [ed. 13], p. 184, pointing out the way in which the Christian spirit is likely to regard social problems. Cp. Martensen, *Ethics (Social)*, p. 132. This point seems completely overlooked in the *Service of Man*, c. vii.

[3] Aug. *Enchir.* lxxii. 'Multa sunt genera eleemosynarum, quae cum facimus *adjuvamur*.' See also Cyp. *de op. et eleem.* xxv. Leo, *in Quad.* v. 4; *de Res.* i. 1; *de Pent.* i. 6, etc. Bruce, *Parabolic Teaching*, etc., pp. 371-375, has some striking remarks.

[4] S. Luke xi. 41.

[5] Leo, *in Quad.* xii. 2, 'In caelestibus Ecclesiae disciplinis, multum utilitatis adferunt *divinitus instituta* jejunia.' Cp. Hooker, Bk. v. § 72.

have seen, an inward unity of the personality, in which no one element has undue predominance. Bodily instincts and passions, the powers of thought and imagination, the bias of temperament—all have to be brought into subjection to the controlling will. And the result is a character exhibiting a due balance of different elements : a chastened spirit of dependence, spiritualized affections, subdued thoughts, sober judgment, a purified heart, a sensitive conscience, a just fear of un-bridled appetite, a true simplicity. Such is Christ-like holiness ; and one great condition of its attainment is fasting, chiefly in its literal sense of regular abstinence from food[1], though its forms may be as varied as are the avenues of sense-impressions. The motive of fasting may not be always the same : sometimes it is the expression of penitential sorrow for sin, or of the passion for inward purity ; some-times it is used as a special aid to prayer ; sometimes, again, it is the sign of wearisome conflict with the lower nature ; in any case it should be an exercise of love. Thus we regard fasting, not as mere soulless, joyless abstinence ; but as a needful condition of purity, energy, vigour of will, clearness of moral insight, and capacity to impart spiritual gifts to our fellow-men. 'Wise souls,' says S. Leo, 'mortify their bodies and crucify their senses ; and therein set before them-selves God's will, loving themselves the more, in proportion as for the love of God they love not themselves[2].'

Our apology for touching on topics so homely might well be that the practical aim of ethics gives such points importance. There can be no excuse needed, however, in days of wide-spread luxury, and of much needlessly imperfect Christianity, for recalling and re-asserting the necessity of the discipline, as well as of the moral precepts, of the Sermon on the Mount.

V. *Christ's teaching as to the Consummation of God's Kingdom.*

An outline of Christian Ethics would be incomplete without some reference to those eschatological truths which occupy so large a place in theology, and have so direct a bearing on morals. We have already touched on them in connection with the Christian doctrine of the Chief Good. It remains to consider them in relation to the perfection of man's nature.

The word 'perfection' reminds us that there is a goal of the moral process exhibited in history. The visible order of the universe and the history of mankind, are verging towards a consummation, a catastrophe, which relatively to us must be regarded as an end.

---

[1] Ep. *ad Diogn.* vi. κακουργουμένη σιτίοις καὶ πότοις ἡ ψυχὴ βελτιοῦται.

[2] Serm. *de Pass.* xix. 5. Cp. Marten-sen, *Ethics (Indiv.)*, p. 160 ; Martineau, *Types*, etc., vol. ii. 381.

It is no part of our task to discuss the intermediate stage through which the kingdom of God is destined to pass: that stage in which there is to be a supreme manifestation of moral evil, a culmination of those tendencies and an outburst of those forces which already seem to threaten not the framework merely, but the foundations of society. The decay of Christian Churches, the profound corruption of social life, the tyranny of materialistic lawlessness—these seem to be plainly foretold in Scripture, and with a purpose: that of shielding men from a moral despair which might paralyse their efforts, or undermine their patience, as they witness the beginnings of these 'birth-pangs[1]' of a new order. The Christian will ever guard against such a temper of alienation, or self-isolation, from the world, as will lead him to depreciate the national, political, or civil movements of his time. For civilization is appointed to reach, through whatever convulsions, an ethical consummation, the prospect of which must inspire strength to labour, and patience to endure.

The last stage of the kingdom of God is one of glory, to be exhibited in the perfection of the moral community. It is for this that creation waits: to this, as the goal of history, that inspired prophecy points. Two revealed truths are intended to guide our conception of this prospect.

In the first place, the kingdom of God is to be finally *manifested* in its true character[2]: an event which must involve momentous consequences for the physical creation. Scripture sometimes speaks as if beneath the outer semblance of visible nature there lay concealed an inner glory, destined, when the semblance passes, to shine forth in full radiance and splendour[3]. The truth is thus symbolically conveyed that since man is the crown and lord of the physical universe, his final emancipation will carry with it a corresponding change in his outward environment. But this consummation, no less than the progressive movement of mankind towards it, is due to the deliberate working and intervention in history of God Himself. Naturalism points to a precarious prospect of human happiness in the future, as contingent upon 'a perfect adjustment of society[4].' Christianity does not look to any improvement in material conditions, nor to any social process, as likely to bring about an ideal state of humanity. Neither the physical universe, nor man himself, can attain to the goal of their development, or to the perfection of their nature, apart from God[5].

Again, the kingdom of God is to be purified through *judgment*. The exact nature of this judgment it is impossible for thought to

---

[1] S. Matt. xxiv. 8 ἀρχὴ ὠδίνων.
[2] Rom. viii. 19.
[3] 1 Cor. vii. 31 ; 1 S. John ii. 17, etc.

[4] Cp. *The Ethics of Socialism*, by E. Belfort Bax, p. 19.
[5] Cp. Bern. *de consid.* v. 11.

anticipate. But the teaching of revelation is at least so explicit as to discredit any conception of the judgment which would confine its operation to this present scene, or restrict its meaning to any merely natural process. The judgment is, in fact, appointed for a definite hour, and is prefigured in definite historical catastrophes. It will be parallel to, but transcending, those manifestations of Divine power in history which mankind has already experienced. And the effect of this final intervention will be to put an end to that mixed condition of human things which it is our tendency to accept and assume as inevitable and perpetual. Out of God's kingdom will be gathered 'all things that offend;' and the collective mass of humanity will be, with whatever gradations in the stage of perfection attained by each individual, a 'congregation of saints[1].' The principle of Good will so achieve its final triumph.

When we further inquire, as we are impelled to do, what will be the extent of this final triumph, we are met by the fact of our own ignorance, and of Christ's reserve. His simple, severe statements seem intended to discourage fruitless speculation. We are thrown back in this as in other perplexities, on our unfailing assurance of God's character, and on the faint analogies furnished by the present order of things.

The Gospel speaks of a righteous dominion, the sphere of which is to be without limit. We read of a gathering into the kingdom of all that is in true harmony with its purpose. We find warrant for the belief in an intermediate state in which imperfect character may be developed, ignorance enlightened, sin chastened, desire purified. And yet we are assured that the consequences of action and choice abide, and are eternal in their issue; and we know that impenitence must finally, and under awful conditions, separate the soul from God. But we have not enough for a coherent system. All that we can affirm is that the victory of Good seems to demand the preservation of all that has not wilfully set itself in antagonism to Divine Love, Holiness, and Power. We cannot think that helpless ignorance, or inevitable poverty of character will finally sever a human soul from God. Analogy suggests that there will be scope in a future dispensation for the healing ministries, and inventive service of Love. So again, Scripture does not expressly teach that the lost will for ever be in a state of defiance and rebellion. Even in the awful state of final severance from the Divine presence there is room for assent, order, acceptance of penalty; and so far, *evil*, in the sense of the will antagonistic to God's righteous Law—may have ceased to exist. Truth will have prevailed; and all orders of intelligent creatures

---

[1] Ps. cxlix. 1.

will render it homage. The final issue will be seen, and the justice confessed, of all those 'ways' of God which are 'unsearchable and past finding out.' In a word, there will be a complete manifestation of supreme Holiness and Love : of Him, whose 'mercy is over all His works,' and who will continue to stand in direct relation to every soul that He has made, revealing Himself to each either as loving Father or as righteous Judge[1].

It must however be added that what is called 'Universalism' finds no support either in the solemn statements of Jesus Christ, or in the analogy of nature. Man's very power of choice implies the possibility of a sinful state admitting neither of repentance nor of remedy ; not of repentance—for character, growing by separate acts of choice, may become fixed and hardened in its persistent refusal of the good ; not of remedy—for, as even the Greek moralist, with all his belief in the moulding power of law, confesses, there is a degree of moral perversion 'incurable'—that namely which ensues when sin has finally destroyed the faculties to which moral appeal is possible—desire, fear, hope, affection, the sense of shame.

With the end of history corresponds that of the individual man. The ultimate perfection of human character is not only regarded as possible in Scripture—but is suggested by analogy[2] : and of the conditions of perfected human nature, we are enabled to form some idea partly by our knowledge of angelic beings, partly by a study of our Lord's Humanity in its risen state[3].

i. Thus human personality, in its perfected form, implies a state of *harmony*. As each element in human nature will be preserved in its appropriate condition, so each will fulfil its rightful function[4]. The relation between body and spirit will be that which is ethically the highest conceivable. In man will be represented, as in a microcosm, a state of being in which the first creation has been appropriated by, and made the organ of the Divine Spirit[5]. The material body will become one perfectly subservient to, and expressive of, the free movements of a purified spirit[6]. And to this state of personality will belong a final harmony between moral law and freedom. Human

---

[1] See the Bp. of Exeter's *Primary Charge* on this subject. On the principle involved in this 'dual classification' see an impressive passage in Martineau, *Types*, etc., ii. 65–69.

[2] 2 Cor. v. 5 ; Col. i. 28 ; Butler, *Analogy*, i. c. 5.

[3] S. Luke xx. 36 ἰσάγγελοι . . . καὶ υἱοί εἰσιν θεοῦ τῆς ἀναστάσεως υἱοὶ ὄντες. Cp. Leo Magn. *Serm. in Res. Dom.* i. c. 4.

[4] Vinc. Lirin. *Common.* c. xiii. 'Uno-

quoque hominum sine fine victuro, in unoquoque hominum sine fine necessaria utriusque substantiae differentia permanebit.'

[5] Dorner, *System, etc.*, § 2.

[6] Aug. *de Fid. et Symb.* xiii. 'Spirituale corpus intelligitur quod ita spiritui subditum est, ut caelesti habitationi conveniat.' The Resurrection of the flesh is thus seen to have vital relation to the idea of moral perfection. Cp. Thom. Aquin. *Summa*, i. ii^ae. Qu. iv. Art. 6–8.

beings will have become 'partakers of the Divine Nature,' so far as to experience in themselves the union of liberty, holiness, and love:

> Indulging every instinct of the soul
> There where law, life, joy, impulse, are one thing[1].

ii. Perfection further implies a state of *glory*; a word which, whether used of Christ Himself or of His followers, seems in the New Testament to mean the outward manifestation of a holy character. The gradual assimilation to God, which is the law of true human development on earth, is the law of an unending progress. But in the perfect state, character will find due splendour of outward expression. Man's bodily frame will pass through successive stages 'from glory to glory,' to a semblance faithfully reflecting the inward supernatural life[2]. And in the marvellous union of outward with inward recreation consists the 'glory,' of which human nature is capable.

iii. Perfection is consummated by blessedness. The conception of *bliss* as transcending *happiness* (εὐδαιμονία) is peculiar to Christian Ethics. Happiness is a word of earth, and represents a good which may be attained independently of life in God. Bliss is inseparable from a living relation to God. It implies union with God.

But though it is true that 'man possesses the plenitude of his perfection in God,' the analogy of the present dispensation points to a further element in 'blessedness,' namely, that of fellowship in a moral community: the redeemed 'have fellowship one with another,' in an 'indissoluble life[3].' In fact the perfection of the individual, according to God's separate ideal for each, demands that of the moral community. Blessedness thus means that state wherein, by a society of renewed personal beings, 'the Highest Good is loved and enjoyed[4].'

This community of free and perfected beings, with God as its Centre, is the revealed ethical consummation of our race. And as the manifestation of God's kingdom is to Christians the supreme object of aspiration, and the highest matter of prayer, so the effort to advance and extend its sphere is the worthiest task that can be embraced by the will. The conception of such a kingdom, to be made actual through the exertion of human faculties co-operating with the invincible energy of the Divine will, is the greatest thought that ever enriched mankind. In the attempt to further the limits, or

---

[1] Iren. iv. 28. 2, 'Hi semper percipiunt regnum, et proficiunt.' Pet. Lomb. *Sent.* ii. xxv. 7, 'Post confirmationem vero . . . nec vinci poterit nec premi [homo]: et tunc habebit *non posse peccare.*'

[2] S. Matt. xiii. 43; 2 Cor. iii. 18;

[3] I S. John iii. 2.

[3]. I S. John i. 3-7; Heb. vii. 16; Westcott, *Hist. Faith*, p. 147.

[4] Aug. *de mor. Eccl.* iv. ['Beata vita,] cum id quod est hominis optimum, amatur et habetur.'

promote the welfare of this kingdom, man finds his truest happiness, and his noblest field of activity. For he is engaged in the same work as God Himself[1]: he has the same interest in its accomplishment. He has found the absolutely good sphere of effort and desire; all else in which men busy themselves can only be ethically *good* in proportion as it bears on, or hastens the approach of, that 'one far off Divine event.'

VI. *Conclusion.*

It is our Lord's method to present to men an ideal, before He descends to the requirements of practical life. The Sermon on the Mount describes the life of 'blessedness' before it treats of duty; and from duty, passes to the means of holiness. Such an example suggests one or two concluding reflections.

First we may recall the true bearing of a methodical inquiry into Christian Ethics. The kingdom of God stands in contrast with, but in special relation to, all modes and products of social activity. It makes use of all the material which human life offers, or human faculties supply, so far as it is capable of serving a Divine purpose, or revealing any aspect of the Divine Life. For that Life having once for all intervened in history, continues ever to appropriate and hallow all that comes within the wide range of Its outflow; Education, Criticism, Science, Art; Industry, Wealth; Law, Polity—all these are capable of becoming ethical forces, of ministering to man's true end, of contributing something to the highest life. Into the Holy City the kings of the earth bring their glory and honour: and to a Christian Church are addressed the far-reaching words, 'All things are yours[2].'

There is in fact a 'world-appropriating' element in Christianity, as the ethical religion; and it is essential that the significance of this fact should be grasped, if Christian morality is to be rightly apprehended, or fairly presented in systematic form.

Further, in advancing a claim to mould and regenerate human society, the Christian Church can only continue to rely on her traditional instrument,—the recreation of individual character. The social movements which an enlightened Christian judgment approves, are those gradual and irresistible changes which result from the slowly-reached apprehension of some neglected moral truth, as it gradually commends itself to individual consciences. And such movements are to be judged as they display, or bear upon character. If for example a Christian mistrusts the extravagant schemes of some forms of Socialism,—it is not because he is insensible to the wrongs and miseries which suggest a violent remedy, but because all such

---

[1] ἔργα θεοῦ, S. John vi. 28. Cp. S. Matt. vi. 33. [2] Cor. iii. 22.

sweeping proposals would merge the individual life, would repress and mar the fulness of that organized social life which gains elements of richness and diversity from the free play of individuality.

The study of ideals will also have suggested the relation which the Church bears to modern life. The Church, we have seen, is the school of human character; the nurse, therefore, of such civil and social virtues as give stability to human institutions. In her midst, Divine forces are really and manifestly at work, tending to bring about the regeneration of mankind. And in connection with this view of the Church, we need to observe the power of character; the practical 'supremacy of goodness,' or at least its tendency to be supreme; its capacity to control and modify the pressure of circumstance. A condition of all true thinking about the social future will surely be a just estimate of *character* as a social and industrial force; it is a growing sense of this truth that is doing much to revolutionize our economic theories. We are learning perhaps that manfulness, mercy, self-control, pity are among the forces which must be taken into account by social science.

And if the Church is a gift of God to mankind, and there be but one end of all His gifts, namely, the restoration of His image in man, we must believe that the fairest fruits of Christianity, and the many-sided fulness of Christlike character, can appear only in those who live loyal to the moral discipline of the Church, who are ruled by her wisdom, chastened by awe of her beauty, penetrated by her spirit. The kingdom of God is more—infinitely more—than an ideal condition of human society; but we know that the kingdom, even in this limited sense of the word, will be the heritage only of a nation 'bringing forth the fruits thereof.'

APPENDIX I.

ON SOME ASPECTS OF CHRISTIAN DUTY.

THE conception of morality as a system of positive Divine Law, and the 'juridical method' which is said to mark early Christian writers on ethics[1], is perhaps attributable to the growth of an imperial spirit in the Church when she found herself confronted with the task of reducing to order the social chaos into which the fall of the Empire plunged Europe. S. Leo may be said to embody this spirit in a majestic personal form. The mark of Roman authority rests on the ordinances of the Church of this period. It may be that her rules of duty wear something of the aspect of a fixed, unvarying code. The moral problems with which she has to deal are comparatively simple; they admit of clear, concise treatment, in accordance with a fixed system of discipline; sharp distinctions are possible: and the Gospel thus presents to the world the features of an external Law.

Be this as it may, widely different conditions seem now to demand a definite system of Christian duty,—a study of 'special' or 'applied ethics.' The main feature of modern life is not social disorganization, but complexity of relationships; and although in the abstract no such thing is possible as a 'conflict of duties;' yet it is clear that duty is not always simple, or obvious. We need in fact something like a system of casuistry; of ethics applied to novel spheres, and special points of obligation. It is indeed reasonable to expect that as civilization advances, and new realms open up which the Christian spirit must appropriate, the Law of duty will be enriched; there will be expansion of its content: e.g. the development of Industry makes desirable the formulation of the 'Ethics of Labour;' the rise of a special class may raise the question whether 'class virtues' are to be recognised, and how they are to be estimated, by Ethics[2].

In this appendix some purpose may be served by noticing a few pressing moral problems of our time; some spheres of duty as to which guidance or development of principles seems called for.

i. In the sphere of self-regarding duty a point which needs attention is the truth of *personal responsibility*. There are influences at work which threaten the sense of accountability, whether for conduct or belief. There are of course speculative difficulties surrounding the question of freedom; there is wide misconception of its true meaning; but it needs to be clearly taught, that granted all limitations of the power of choice, moral responsibility remains for the use of the character, as of the property, which a man inherits[3]. A

[1] Sidgwick, *Outlines, etc.,* p. 108.
[2] These are perhaps implied in S. Luke iii. 10-14.
[3] Cp. Mr. Cotter Morison, *Service of Man,* p. 214.

man's moral constitution, rigidly defined though it be by heredity, is yet his 'heritage,' his natural endowment, for the right direction of which he is responsible. The weak sense of this plain fact is noticeable in the lax and indulgent tone often used respecting criminals. 'To some of us,' it has been justly said, 'the individual is always innocent and society always guilty [1].' The degree of guilt, however, may be minimized (e. g. by the plea of ignorance), while the fact of it remains.

In this connection statistics of crime have a value which needs to be estimated. Do they point to conditions of society which must be faced as unalterable? or do they not rather usefully indicate the proper channels into which the stream of social energy should be directed?

Again, in the matter of personal *belief*, it is often assumed that there is no responsibility. The question, however, for each individual, if rightly stated, is simply this, 'What has been my attitude towards that which has presented itself to me as truth [2]?'

Another point of importance is the moral culture of *Imagination*, in relation chiefly to aesthetic recreation in its different forms, the Theatre, the pursuit of Art, the reading of Fiction. We are learning by serious experience the enormous power of fancy to kindle passion, and to colour human actions. In view of the spread of depraving literature, energetic assertion of duty towards this department of personality is needed. Such duty seems to be recognised in Phil. iv. 8.

ii. Passing to the sphere of family obligations, it is natural to remark on the break-up of family life which is so common a consequence of highly-developed industry. The employment of women in factories, etc., tends to make them unfit for domestic duties; while that of children encourages a spirit of independence which is not without social danger; thus not only the sense of parental duty, but the respect for parental authority, is impaired. Christians are bound to discountenance, or at least to counteract, this state of things so far as it interferes with the rudiments of moral discipline.

The pressing need of our day, however, would appear to be some clear teaching on the subject of marriage. There are different aspects of the marriage contract recognised in Scripture. But Christianity can make no terms with those theories which have borne fruit in lax legislation on divorce, with all its mischievous results. Marriage, according to the Christian view, is a serious vocation, with its own sacred duties, and special consecration. Improvident marriage is as immoral from a Christian as from an anti-Christian point of view [3]. Ethical considerations ought to guide or restrict the intention to marry; and with regard to the question of population, Christianity condemns any theory which offers a substitute for rational self-restraint. The true end of marriage, again, is something higher than 'happiness'; it is appointed for the mutual enrichment of personality, mutual freedom to fulfil the true ideal of human life. The whole subject has indeed become involved in difficulties which cannot be encountered by any mere statement of principles. There is no doubt, however, of the end which the Christian treatment of this point must keep in view.

---

[1] R. W. Dale, *Cont. Rev.*, May, 1889. Consider S. Luke xxiii. 34.
[2] See Dean Church, *Human Life and its Conditions*, Serm. III. *init.*
[3] See *Service of Man*, pref. xxv. foll.

iii. As to the social sphere generally, we begin by remarking that, from the Christian standpoint, *every transaction* between man and man is to be regarded as *personal*, and therefore *ethical*. The most significant fact perhaps of our time is the process of transition from (so-called) political to ethical economics. To reason rightly on social problems we must ever have regard to *personality*. For ethical purposes the abstract terms Capital, Labour, Production, Wealth, etc., must be replaced by *personal* terms, Employer, Employé, Producer, Man of Wealth, etc. Our problem is how to supersede the technical and legal relation by the personal [1].

This being our fundamental point of view, we find that ethics will treat equally of rights and duties. A Christian theory of *rights* is required. The prevailing view of them is *individualistic*. It is forgotten that the rights of one man have their ground in the obligations of another; they are limited by the claims of other personalities on our own; 'right' is, in fact, a condition making possible the fulfilment of duty. It is thus a matter of Christian concern (to suggest mere examples) that workers should attain to the possibility of free self-development: healthy conditions of work, the enjoyment of domestic life, security of maintenance, perhaps permanence of contract, opportunities of recreation and culture,—everything, in fact, which will give them fair chance of healthful and worthy human life. Christianity can be content with nothing short of this.

On the other hand *duties* call for notice. Modern capitalists form a class whose responsibilities it is difficult adequately to measure. The general principle, however, is easily repeated: that it is the duty of the wealthy, or those who employ workers, to respect the personality of their employés, to treat them not as machines, but as men. Thomas Carlyle well describes the aim that should guide this influential class: 'to be a noble master among noble workers, the first ambition: to be a rich master, only the second.'

Industrial development indeed brings into prominence many questions of duty and right, which can be solved only by deeper apprehension of the Christian standpoint: and of 'morality as an industrial force [2]:' for the ties which bind men in the relation of brotherhood and sonhood are the noblest and strongest.

The duties of a state are matters of controversy, and open a field not lightly to be entered. It is clear, however, that adequate pressure can only be brought to bear on governing classes by an educated public opinion, rather we should say an enlightened moral sense, in the community. It is impossible to foresee the results that might ensue from the growth of moral opinion on such points as the state regulation of vice, the just causes of war, the restriction of the hours of labour, the treatment of semi-civilized dependencies, the true lines to be followed by education. It is this tremendous potency of public opinion that points to the great need of modern democracy: the education, namely, of feeling and character; the cultivation of reverence and the faculty of ad-

---

[1] See Ingram, *Pres. Condition and Prospects of P. l. Economy*, p. 18: 'By habitually regarding labour from the abstract point of view, and overlooking the personality of the labourer, economists are led to leave out of account some of the considerations which most seriously affect the condition of the working man,' etc. Cp. Carlyle, *Past and Present*, the last book.
[2] See the chapter with this title in T. E. Brown, *Studies in Modern Socialism and Labour Problems*, c. xii.

miration, of self-control and sobriety in judgment and thought. How far a merely intellectual training will produce this character can scarcely be a matter of controversy. A vast field of inquiry and study is thus evidently open to economic moralists: and it has been opportunely suggested that the effort to study, 'in the light of the revealed will of God, the intricate problems of society,' might be a common bond between different sections of Christendom, and might promote that unity of God's Church, which is the true condition of effectual social reform [1].

iv. In the Church, or moral community which embraces and leavens the state, special points of duty arise: e.g. respecting the limits of the Church's self-adaptation to the tendencies of the age, and her relation to the anti-Christian principle in society. Hence arise difficult questions as to the true bases of Toleration, and of submission to the civil power. We may be sure that principles of action and thought can be reached only by closer study of Christ's words in relation to modern life [2], as the practical instinct of the Church has interpreted them. A similar problem is raised by the advance of Science and Criticism. Christians are charged with being behind scientific men in their apprehension of 'the morals of assent [3].' Whatever truth there is in such a reproach, it at least utters a note of warning.

v. Once more, if we consider the non-personal realm with which man is brought in contact, we must face the problem of duties towards the lower animals. We have seen that such duties have a ground in reason: but their nature and extent are not well defined. It is important to study our Lord's attitude towards nature, for which He uniformly exhibits, especially in His parables and miracles, such feeling and love. The practice of vivisection, for example, raises a question as to the limits of the *dominium naturae* committed to man; and his right to employ creaturely life as a means. There is of course a practice of vivisection which is utterly immoral: as when it is prompted by mere pleasure in experimenting, or by idle curiosity; or is carried on without strict intention and reasonable prospect of meeting a particular need.

Within the limits of an essay it would be presumptuous to do more than raise such questions as the foregoing; we perhaps best display a sense of their gravity by leaving them as suggestions for systematic discussion. For it has been justly observed with regard to ethical problems that 'the actual solution is itself an art, a gift which cannot be taught.'

[1] See an Article on 'Christian Union,' by Earl Nelson, *Cont. Rev.*, Feb. 1889.
[2] See Martensen, *Ethics (Ind.)*, § 93. Dean Church, *Gifts of Civilization*, Serm. **II.**
[3] Mr. Huxley in *Nineteenth Century* for Nov. 1887.

APPENDIX II.

ON THE CHRISTIAN DOCTRINE OF SIN[1].

'Jesus did not commit Himself unto them, because He knew all men, and needed not that any should testify of man: for He knew what was in man.'—*S. John* ii. 24, 25.

'Sin is lawlessness.'—1 *S. John* iii. 4. [R.V.]

'He knew what was in man.' The words describe our Lord in presence of a fact universally recognized—man's moral unsatisfactoriness. He looks steadily at man's first offer of service, at man's first enthusiasm, when 'many believed in His name,' and He discerns behind it a disqualifying cause; something which prevents Him from trusting man as he is, and from committing to him the great work of His kingdom. He sees sin in man and all that sin involves of moral failure, of refusal to endure, of spiritual blindness, of lawless self-assertion, of passion, of selfishness, of self-will. That there is in human nature this disqualifying taint of sin is, we may say, a fact universally recognized. It is the fact which in slow embittering experience has turned philanthropists into cynics and saddened the wisest. But to our Lord it was a fact present from the first. 'He needed not that any should testify of man.' He reckoned with sin to start with. Therefore He could not use mankind, as it offered itself, for His purposes. It needed a fresh start, a vital re-creation, to fit it for such high ends. 'Except ye be converted and become as little children, ye shall not enter into the kingdom of heaven.' 'Except a man be born again he cannot see the kingdom of God.'

Christ recognizes the fact of sin. All men more or less come to recognize it within them and without. But yet there have been very different ways of explaining it.

For upon the surface it is tempting to interpret the struggle between good and evil, as we know it so sadly well in our narrow experience, as representing a universal conflict between opposite principles. The world is a composite thing, men have supposed, the result of the antagonism of two Principles, two kingdoms, two Gods, one good and the other evil; or they have explained the world as representing the action of a good God upon an intractable material, eternal as Himself, which limits His power and restrains His hand.

---

[1] A sermon preached before the University of Cambridge, at Great St. Mary's Church, on Sunday, March 17, 1889, by the Rev. Charles Gore, and printed in the *Guardian*, March 27. A paragraph of practical exhortation is omitted at the end. Some apology is no doubt needed for the introduction of a Sermon into a volume of Essays. But it was felt (1) that there was under the circumstances an advantage in producing what was not written in view of the criticisms on *Lux Mundi*; (2) that the sermon was not specially homiletic.

On either of these cognate theories[1] the soul of man is naturally represented as a creation of the good Principle or a particle of it, embedded in a vile body of material evil which clogs and hinders and impedes it, which is the seat of lusts and passions, defiling the purity of the spiritual element. The spirit is good and the body is evil. This is the theory upon which so much of Oriental asceticism has proceeded. The object of such asceticism is to liberate the pure spirit from the trammels of the corrupting and imprisoning body. That is most spiritual which is least material. Purification is abstraction from the body. The spirit is akin to God, and will one day win its way up to be re-absorbed in God. The body is material and evil, the seat of sin, and to be dealt with as such. Hence the remorseless persecution of the body which has been exhibited by the devotees of Gnosticism or Brahmanism—the denunciation of marriage, of animal flesh and wine. Hence, on the other hand, the wild rebound into licentiousness which has sometimes characterized Gnostic or Manichaean sects. For, after all, when asceticism has done its utmost we are still in the body. If connection with the body is sin, eating and drinking at all is as sinful as excess; marriage the same as licence. Outward acts become indifferent—indifferently bad. This principle explains the reaction from extreme mortification to extreme licence which characterizes Orientalism.

Once more, in modern times, from a different point of view, materialism has again interpreted sin as an essential part of nature. Ignoring the distinction of what is moral and what is physical, the materialistic Positivism, for instance, of Mr. Cotter Morison represents goodness and badness in men as the simple product of natural forces like goodness and badness in fruits of the earth, each class of good and bad men being essentially and inevitably what it shows itself to be. 'Nothing is gained,' he says, 'by disguising the fact that there is no remedy for a bad heart and no substitute for a good one[2].'

It is common to all the anti-Christian views of sin that at the last resort they make sin natural, a part of nature. It is characteristic of Christ's view of sin—of the Scriptural view of it—that it makes it unnatural. It is characteristic, again, of the non-Christian view that it makes the body, the material, the seat of sin. It is essential to the Christian view to find its seat and only source in the *will*[2].

Take the vilest crime, and Christianity assures you that throughout the transaction, as you may observe it, there is nothing evil in the natural material which is employed, there is only the lawless misuse of material which is in itself good. The worst passions are but the disorderly exercise of feelings and faculties in themselves good and capable of redemption. Lust is only love uncontrolled by the will, and, therefore, lawless. Take the lowest criminal, and Christianity assures you that, however habituated all his nature to run to evil, if you can once get his will—what Scripture calls

---

[1] The first is that of the Manichaeans and some Gnostics. The second that of the Platonists and other Gnostics. But both the theories represent tendencies very commonly at work both among Orientals and in Europe. Recently John Stuart Mill was disposed to embrace the latter theory; see *Three Essays on Religion*, 3rd edition, London, 1874, pp. 58, 243.

[2] *The Service of Man*, London, 1887, p. 295. Cf. p. 293, 'It will perhaps be said that this view does away with moral responsibility . . . . To which the answer is, that the sooner the idea of moral responsibility is got rid of, the better it will be for society and moral education.'

[3] See, for instance, Tertullian, *de paenit.* 3; Anselm, *Cur Deus Homo*, i. 11.

his 'heart'—set right and given to God, that right direction of the will, the heart, will after long battle at last carry with it all the nature; the forces of grace are set free to act when the obstacle of the will's rebellion or apathy is removed, and (though it takes ages beyond this mortal life) at last the whole being will be purified, and what began in the surrender of the will will take effect in the illumination of the intellect and the purifying of the affections. Thus it is that Christianity can represent God as justifying the sinner in virtue of faith. Faith is the first movement of the will and heart by which the sinner, from the far-off country of his exile, seeks his true home, from the depth of his sin, claims Christ as his own. At this first movement God welcomes him. He meets him with His acceptance. He claims him as His true son, because in that first movement of the moral being God sees the pledge of all that is to come. He sees the forces let loose which will bring the final victory. He deals with the sinner by a Divine anticipation, not as he is, but as he is on the way to become[1]. 'His faith is reckoned for righteousness.'

Let us dwell on the Christian view of sin, in its essence, in its appeal, in its practical justification, in its anthropological results.

(1) In its essence. It is expressed by S. John, 'Sin is lawlessness:' ἡ ἁμαρτία ἐστὶν ἡ ἀνομία. The two terms are coincident. For God, and God only, made the world, and there is no other Creator, no other creation. He made it, and pronounced it very good in its completeness. The universe, in all its sum of forces and existences, is good, and of God. The very existence of anything is a pledge of its natural goodness. It exists only because God created it and sustains it and dwells in it. It must cease to exist, S. Augustine tells us, if it were simply evil[2]. Positive existence is always, so far, good.

What then is sin in men or in devils? In one word, *lawlessness*—the violation of nature, the misuse of good by rebellion of the will. Physical decay, death, dissolution, change, these are of nature; sin, on the other hand, is contrary to nature. It is simply misuse, disorder. It has no positive substance. A sinful man is not the man as God made him with something else introduced called sin. He is simply the man as God made him, disordered by ignoring God, by claiming independence of God, by lawlessness. The same act may constitute either the sin of murder or the heroism of a soldier fighting in his country's defence; either the sin of adultery or Christian marriage, because in the one case the act is done in accordance with the God-given law of our being; in the other case in defiance of it. The humanity of Christ and the humanity of the greatest criminal are consubstantial the one with the other. All that the criminal sins with belongs to Christ's nature; He has all the faculties that are used for sin. ' He could sin if He could *will* to sin,' the Fathers tell us, ' but God forbid that we should think of His willing it[3].' What is disordered, ungoverned in the criminal is in Christ perfectly subordinated to a will, itself controlled in loving harmony by the Divine Spirit. If it sounds preposterous to say that the *nature* of the criminal is not of itself sinful, to make the statement reasonable and true we have only

---

[1] Augustine, *de Trin.* i. 10, 21.
[2] Aug. *de mor. Man.* ii. 3, 'Ut ab essentia deficiant et ad non esse tendant? quod malum generale esse clamat verissima ratio.' *Op. imp. c. Jul.* i. 114, 'Non enim potest esse ullum malum nisi in aliquo bono; quia non potest esse nisi in aliqua natura; omnis autem natura, in quantum natura est, bonum est.'

[3] For references, see p. 213, note 1.

to bear in mind the results of sin which have taken slow effect upon his nature in the sequence of generations of bad habit. The body may have become so accustomed to sin, so moulded to sin by forces within and without as to justify S. Paul calling it a 'body of sin [1],' but only in the sense in which our Lord calls money or mammon 'the mammon of unrighteousness [2].' Money, our Lord meant, has become so accustomed, so to speak, to lend itself to the purposes of unrighteousness that it requires attention as alert, wisdom as far-sighted, as that of the unjust steward, in the children of light, to divert it again to its true uses. The body in the same way has been so moulded to sin, accustomed to sin, that it requires the strong hand of an asceticism, rightly motived, to 'keep it under,' to lead it as a slave, to wrest it to good uses. It requires the cutting off of the right hand or the plucking out of the right eye—the disuse for a time, that is, by doing violence to oneself of what has become so misused, so lawless. The bow must be bent violently back, if it is to be made straight. But the end of all this Christian asceticism is the restoration of our whole nature to its true law. We mortify our bodies only to offer them at last a living sacrifice of rational service. At last all the impulses and passions and parts of even the criminal nature shall be subjugated again to the law of the Spirit. Christ shall purify the impure and harmonise the disorderly. Thus down the vista of an endless future Christianity forces us to see the nature of the criminal, if he will but turn Godwards, only reconstituted, not substantially changed, one with Christ in glory. This is the Christian doctrine of sin, the doctrine that Athanasius and Augustine and Anselm, the Christian Fathers as a whole, repeat and reiterate; that sin has no substance; that there is no positively sinful nature; that sin lies not in things, but in our relation to things; that the introduction of sin is simply the privation of order; that moral recovery waits for nothing but the conversion of will [3].

(2) This is the Christian doctrine, and its appeal is to moral experience. Looking at the world from the point of view of physical science, it may appear as if goodness and badness were like good and bad fruit; but to suppose this is to leave out of sight the whole witness of *moral* experience. It was not Christian belief but inextinguishable consciousness that made Byron cry—

> 'Our life is a false nature—'tis not in
> The harmony of things.'

Or Shelley :—

> 'The universe
> In Nature's silent eloquence declares
> That all fulfil the works of love and joy,
> All but the outcast man [4].'

In proportion as the moral consciousness is keen and active, in that proportion men know that sin is not nature, but its violation; that they are not what they are meant to be in sinning; that sin has no analogy in the failures of nature, because it is what they are not, avoidable and morally wrong; that it violates what they fulfil, the law of the world. Natural failure is part of the

---

[1] Rom. v. 6: see Godet's *Commentary* in loc. Clark's *Foreign Theol. Libr.* i. p. 416; and cf. Col. ii. 11, τὸ σῶμα τῆς σαρκός.

[2] S. Luke xvi. 9.

[3] See Origen, *C. Cels.* iv. 65-66; Athan. *C. Gentes*, 6-7; and cf. the index to S. Augustine *s. v.* malum. So far, however, as

each individual identifies himself with sin, it becomes 'his nature': a false nature, obscuring the true, but never annihilating it: cf. Tertullian, *de An.* 41, 'Naturae corruptio alia natura est,' etc. ; and Bernard, *in Cant. Serm.* 82. 2,—admirable passages.

[4] See in Mozley, *Lectures*, etc., x. p. 159.

world's fruitfulness. The seeds that fail supply material for the seeds that grow. Moral failure—sin, that is, as distinguished from mere imperfection—is never fruitful. Sins are always the ' unfruitful works of darkness [1].'

(3) And the justification of this Christian theory lies in its *success*. The moral triumphs of the Church depend upon it. Mr. Herbert Spencer constantly assures us that the fundamental postulates of human experience are assumptions or hypotheses at the bottom, which are continuously verified and justified by the correspondence of the results reached. That is true of the Christian postulate of sin. The hypothesis that sin is not nature, but lack of will, is verified by the victory which follows action upon it. ' According to thy faith be it done to thee '—that is Christ's challenge. Man after man sick of moral paralysis lies at Christ's feet explaining why he cannot get up. ' Take up thy bed and walk,' ' According to thy faith be it unto thee,' is the word of Christ. Claim for your own the morally best. Act on Christ's promise as if it were true and you find it is. This is faith—to act on what transcends experience, to act on what you do not feel possible, to act in faith on a promised strength, and to find it really given only in the using. Faith involves the recognition of our own weakness, the surrender of our own independence into the hands of God ; it gains as its reward the promised help ; it sets free the ' virtue which goes out' of Christ. Reason can only analyse and rationalise what it already experiences. Faith can do what reason, what understanding, at any rate, cannot do—it can yield life up to higher forces than it has yet known. Only when the forces have become in experience thoroughly familiar can they be subjected to the analysis of reason. *Credo ut intelligam.* The justification of the Christian view of sin as something which is not nature, but failure or disorder of will—something therefore which faith, that is the right direction and use of will, can overcome, or put in the way to be overcome—the justification of this view is, I say, to be found in experience. Act against sin, in Christ's name, as if you had strength, and you will find you have. Expect and you receive. It finds its justification not in the recovery of our own lives only, but in that of others. The Christian lifts others by believing in them. He sees in each the subject of redemption. Behind heaps of sin, ingrained habits of sin, he sees a man's true self, true nature, as God made it and intended it to grow, and to this he appeals. ' According to thy faith be it unto thee ' means not only ' You can be saved, if you believe ;' it means also ' You can save others '—save them by believing in them and in God, save them, not according to your own foolish desires, but in accordance with God's intention for them, with the original law of their being. The best modern novel literature is full of this truth. What are the moral recoveries of Jean Valjean in *Les Misérables*, and of Sidney Carton in the *Tale of Two Cities*, and of the selfish old peer in the child story of the *Little Lord Fauntleroy*, but so many instances of the redemptive power of Christian love because it ' believeth all things, hopeth all things,' believes past belief, hopes beyond hope. The justification of the Christian view of sin lies, then, in its success ; partly in the results it actually produces, partly in the larger promise which it opens out beyond the horizon of what we see. ' There is no remedy for a bad character and no substitute for a good one'—that is the only outcome of the physical view of sin. ' According to thy faith, be it unto thee '—that is

[1] Cf. in explanation of this, the Preface, p. xv.

the Christian answer ; there is for thyself no limit to what thou mayest become, on the lines, that is to say, not of thine own ambition, but of God's purpose, except what thou settest by thine own want of faith, thine own failure of moral appetite ; there is in the case of others no limit to what thou mayest help them to become, on the lines, once again, of their fundamental nature—except the limits of their faith and thine.

(4) This Christian view of sin determines in part its whole anthropology. What sin is in us, and now, and in recorded history, sin is also in the whole of humanity. Sin actual is of a piece with sin historical, with sin original. Each man does not start afresh. He inherits the moral conditions from which his life starts. I am aware that a modern school of biologists, headed by Professor Weissmann, is modifying the current doctrine of heredity so far as to deny that acquired character can be transmitted, so far as to deny that the acts or habits of men can physically modify the organisation of their descendants. It is not yet clear that this view, in its extreme form, is at all likely to gain acceptance. But I suppose Christianity can await the result with patience. It may not be in any region to which scientific analysis or investigation can penetrate, but at least in the inner region of man's personality Christianity must maintain that the individual does not start afresh. He starts the subject of sinful tendencies which he did not originate, but which those who went before him did, if not originate, at least let loose from restraint, and so make sinful. Sin is in the race as well as in the individual ; stayed more or less by moral effort and resistance here ; let loose by self-indulgence or luxury there : in varying force and alterable sway therefore, but everywhere more or less present, everywhere making a man conscious not merely of imperfection, but of inward taint, everywhere needing re-creation, recovery, redemption. And everywhere sin is of a piece. My sins are only fresh specimens of what has been going on all along. They work just the same result upon humanity as a whole as the sins of my predecessors, as the first sin : I am driven logically as well as theologically to extend my theory of sin and to generalise it beyond present experience. Sin, not in the individual, as I know him merely, but in the whole of humanity from the first, has been always rebellion, not nature. At the beginning of human life, properly so called, when first a being truly called a man woke up to consciousness of his relation to God, to nature, to himself, he did not find sin part of his being ; he might have obeyed the movement of the Spirit of God and realised his true sonship by keeping his animal nature under the control of the spirit : so he would have fulfilled the law of his destined manhood. Sin at the origin of our human life, as through all its history, was treason to our higher capacity, which made man the slave of the flesh. The 'slave of the flesh,' because he was not meant to be an animal : he was meant to be a spiritual being. And it was the capacity for the higher life which turned to sin his choice of a lower ; which tinged it with the colour of 'remorse,' with the bitterness of 'self-contempt[1].'

---

[1] There is a fundamental mistake in the popular excuse for sensual sin—that it is 'natural.' The mistake lies in the idea that man's animal and spiritual natures are separable, that he can live as pure animal in one part of his life, and pure spirit in another. But as a fact man's life is only lived 'according to nature,' where every part of it is lived 'in flesh and in spirit' : the spiritual motive must control the bodily organ. Only so are his acts really human. If he tries to act as a mere animal he becomes sinful. The

As the essential Christian doctrine of sin finds the guarantee of its permanence in the moral consciousness, so it would not appear to involve any conflict with the disclosures of science. Yet it has been sufficiently distorted in statement for a conflict to have arisen. And the points at issue are briefly three.

(*a*) Broadly, it is said, the Christian religion represents man as starting in a state of perfection and gradually degrading. Science, with all the evidences on its side, represents man as starting in a state of savagery and gradually rising.

This is a most delusive antithesis. It is certainly true that progress has not been uniform. There is such a thing as moral deterioration. A history of the progress of sin from will to intellect, from intellect to heart, till it penetrates the whole nature and plunges it into the lowest depths of denaturalisation represents what has been a fact both in the individual and in society. Such a record of one element in human experience S. Paul gives us in Romans i [1]. Its truth cannot be denied. But so far is this from representing the Christian view of human history as a whole that, on the contrary, the Scriptures stand alone among ancient literatures in presenting the idea of gradual progress, gradual education, movement onwards to a climax. The Bible is the book of development. ' God Who in many parts and many manners spoke of old time . . . . hath in the end of these days spoken by His Son;' and still we move on in the realisation and appropriation of all that is revealed and given in Christ 'till we all come . . . . unto the perfect man.' Nor is it the least true to say that this development is *only* the attempt to regain the platform on which man was first placed. The idea of the first man as a being of developed intellectual and spiritual capacity, perfect in all the range of his faculties—the idea which would admit of our saying with Robert South that ' an Aristotle was but the rubbish of an Adam, and Athens but the rudiments of Paradise '—may be, indeed has been, found in theologians, it may have passed into the imagination of the English nation as part of the debt, theologically very largely a debt of evil, which we owe to the great poem of Milton ; but it is not Scriptural, it is not Christian theology at its best [2]. All the fabric of civilisation the Bible represents as being gradually built up, whether by Jabal, 'who was the father of such as dwell in tents and have cattle,' or by Jubal, 'who was the father of all such as handle the harp and organ,' or by Tubal Cain, ' who was the instructor of every artificer of brass and iron.' There is no impression given us that any of the arts or the knowledge of civilisation existed before. All that we are led to believe is that the historical development of man has not been the development simply as God meant it. It has been tainted through its whole fabric by an element of moral disorder, of human wilfulness. We cannot draw a picture of how human nature was intended

---

evidence of this lies in the fact that while the physical nature of animals contains within itself the check on sensual indulgence, the check in man's case lies in his spiritual faculties. You can have a 'dissipated' man, i. e. a man whose bodily impulses are uncontrolled by will or spirit ; you cannot have a 'dissipated' animal.

[1] It is not intended as a *complete* account,

cf. Rom. ii. 14-15.
[2] In answer to the question whether Adam was formed perfect or imperfect [τέλειος ἢ ἀτελής], Clement replies: 'They shall learn from us that he was not perfect [i. e. complete in development, τέλειος] in respect of his creation, but in a fit condition to receive virtue.' Clem. Alex. *Strom.* vi. 12. 96. Cp. Iren. *c. haer.* iv. 38.

to fight the battle of progress. We cannot relate the state of the savage to the intention of God, any more than we can relate the present state of our great cities to that intention[1]. All we can say is that the state of things as they were in days of savagery, or as they are in days of civilisation, represents a *parody* of the Divine intention for the childhood and manhood of the race. Man was made to grow by gradual effort in range and exercise of every faculty of his being. But all this gradual growth might have been conditioned by a conscious fellowship with God, which would have introduced into it an element of nobility and stability which in fact it has lacked. For the historical development of man has been a development with God only too often left out, the development under conditions of merely physical laws of a being meant to be spiritual[2].

(*b*) 'But no,' the biologist rejoins; 'you will not get off thus easily. Christianity regards even so absolutely natural a fact as death, a fact so inextricably interwoven into the structural growth of the world, as a mere consequence of sin. Christianity is refuted by every evidence of death being a law of physical nature.' So far from this being true, it is the case that the early Christian writers, S. Augustine as well as S. Athanasius, emphasise the truth that death is the law of physical nature; that when man died he was undergoing what belonged to his animal nature. 'Paul,' says Augustine, 'describes man's body as dead, not as mortal, because of sin. Mortal it was by nature, because, as being animal, it was subject to death[3].' In being left to death, Athanasius teaches, man was only left to the law of his physical being[4]. What, in fact, the Christian teachers hold is not that death, but death as it has been known among men, is the penalty of sin, because man's spiritual or supernatural life would have blunted the forces of corruption and lifted him into a higher immortal state. Man would not have died because he would have been spiritual rather than animal. And even here, if we are asked what this means, we must hesitate in our answer. If sin is said to have brought human death, Christ is said to have abolished it. 'This is the bread which cometh down from heaven that a man may eat thereof and not die.' 'If any man eat of this bread he shall live for ever.' 'Whosoever liveth and believeth on Me shall never die.' 'Christ Jesus . . . . abolished death.' Sin, we may suppose, only introduced death in the sense in which Christ abolished it[5]. Christ has not abolished the physical transition, but it ceases to be what death implies:—

> 'Henceforth is death
> But the gate of life immortal.'

---

[1] But we can recognize that before civilisation had developed the checks which society supplies against abrupt deterioration, collapse into savagery would have been much more rapid than it can be in a more developed state.

[2] Cf. Aubrey Moore's *Evolution and Christianity* (Oxford House Papers), pp. 32–3. 'The change which took place at the Fall was a change in the moral region; but it could not be without its effect elsewhere. Even the knowledge of nature becomes confused, without the governing truth of the relation of man to God. The evolution which should have been the harmonious development of the whole man, is checked and impeded in one part, and that the highest part of his nature. And therefore, in spite of all the physical and intellectual advance which man has made, he is always and everywhere the worse for the Fall. However great his development has been, it is still a retarded development, a development slower than it need have been, less regular and less sure than God meant it to be.'

[3] Aug. *De gen. ad litt.* vi. 36. 'Mortalis erat conditione corporis animalis.'

[4] Athan. *de Incarn.* 4.

[5] Cf. Westcott's *Ep. to the Hebrews*, p. 54 (on Hebr. ii. 16).

Death as it has come upon sinful man has been the sad ending of hopes, the rending of his heart-strings, the collapse of his plans, the overshadowing fear, the horrible gulf, the black destruction. In all that makes it death, it has been the result of sin, of the misdirection of his aims and hopes. Had man not sinned there might, indeed, have been a passage from one state to another, a physical dissolution, a moral victory—but it would not have been what men have known as 'death.'

If this be the right way of regarding the matter, as it is certainly permissible, we shall be able to echo in all its breadth Athanasius's teaching, that sin did not directly alter *things*, but only our attitude towards them[1].

(*c*) But, once again, and for the last time, the opponent objects: 'All this theory of original sin is built simply on the supposition that the early chapters of Genesis represent literal history. It falls to the ground if they are myth and not history.' Once again, this is not at all the case. The Christian doctrine of sin finds its chief authorisation in Christ's attitude towards it. Sin (if Christ's witness is true) is not nature; it does not represent God's intention, but something that has baffled for a time God's intention, something that Christ is come to conquer. Moreover, this doctrine of sin is not a mere dogma enunciated on external authority; it finds its verification in experience. The moral experience of Christendom confirms it, and this experience of eighteen centuries reflects itself inevitably on the whole of human life. What interprets sin within this area interprets it through the whole history. With this authority of Christ, verified in the Christian experience, as his firm foundation, the Christian does not hesitate to see in the early chapters of Genesis the action of the inspiring Spirit. It was only the inspiring Spirit Which could assure man that the whole universe was of God's making and very good, that the state in which he found himself represented not his nature, as God meant it to be, but the result of his rebellion, the result, moreover, which God meant to counterwork, nay, which in gradual process He was counter-working. In all the account then of the creation, of the nature of man, of the origin of sin, the Christian sees an action of the inspiring Spirit. He sees it all the more when he compares the record of Genesis with those which are parallel to it in other races. But if an Irenæus, a Clement, an Athanasius, an Anselm could treat the record or part of it as rather allegorical than historical, we can use the same liberty. This is not our present subject. All I want to make clear is that the Christian doctrine of sin rests on a far broader and far surer foundation than the belief that the early chapters of Genesis belong to one form or stage of inspired literature rather than to another. It rests on the strong foundation of the authority of our Lord, accepted and verified by man's moral consciousness.

[1] Athan. *C. Gentes* 7; cf. Aug. on Gen. iii. 18 (*De Gen. ad litt.* iii. 18, 28), where it is said that it is difficult to suppose that 'thorns and thistles' were first produced on the occasion of sin; but we may understand that they then first began to be obstacles to man in the cultivation of the ground: 'spinas et tribulos pariet *tibi.*'

OXFORD: HORACE HART
PRINTER TO THE UNIVERSITY